Global Marketing Strategy

Global Marketing Strategy

Harold Chee

Senior Management Training Consultant,
China–Britain Management Training Centre, Beijing
(formerly of the University of Westminster)

Rod Harris

Head of Department, The School of Business,
Darlington College of Technology

FINANCIAL TIMES
PITMAN PUBLISHING

HF
1416
C44

FINANCIAL TIMES
MANAGEMENT

LONDON · SAN FRANCISCO
KUALA LUMPAR · JOHANNESBURG

*Financial Times Management delivers the knowledge,
skills and understanding that enable students,
managers and organisations to achieve their ambitions,
whatever their needs, wherever they are.*

London Office:
128 Long Acre, London WC2E 9AN
Tel: +44 (0)171 447 2000
Fax: +44 (0)171 240 5771
Website: www.ftmanagement.com

A Division of Financial Times Professional Limited

First published in Great Britain in 1998

© Financial Times Professional Limited 1998

The right of Harold Chee and Rod Harris to be identified as
Authors of this Work has been asserted by them in accordance
with the Copyright, Designs and Patents Act 1988.

ISBN 0 273 62348 6

British Library Cataloguing in Publication Data
A CIP catalogue record for this book can be obtained from the British Library

All rights reserved; no part of this publication may be reproduced, stored
in a retrieval system, or transmitted in any form or by any means, electronic,
mechanical, photocopying, recording, or otherwise without either the prior
written permission of the Publishers or a licence permitting restricted copying
in the United Kingdom issued by the Copyright Licensing Agency Ltd,
90 Tottenham Court Road, London W1P 9HE. This book may not be lent,
resold, hired out or otherwise disposed of by way of trade in any form
of binding or cover other than that in which it is published, without the
prior consent of the Publishers.

10 9 8 7 6 5 4 3 2 1

Typeset by Pantek Arts, Maidstone, Kent
Printed and bound in Great Britain by William Clowes Ltd, Beccles

The Publishers' policy is to use paper manufactured from sustainable forests.

Every effort has been made to trace and acknowledge ownership of copyright.
The Publishers will be glad to make suitable arrangements with any copyright
holder whom it has not been possible to contact.

ABOUT THE AUTHORS

Harold Chee (BA MA MSc MBA DMS PGCE DipEcon. MCIM) is Senior Management Training Consultant at the China–Britain Management Training Centre in Beijing. He was formerly Senior Lecturer in International Business Strategy, Global Marketing & Strategic Management at the University of Westminster Business School in London.

He has been a visiting lecturer at Essex University (UK) and the University of Moscow Institute of Management (Russia), and is currently a visiting Professor at Boston University.

He is subject leader for the International Business & Global Marketing modules, and leader at the International Business Research Group at Westminster Business School. His other research and consultancy interests include Cross-Cultural Management and East Asian Management Systems.

He is engaged as a management and marketing consultant to various organisations and has consulted in Asia-Pacific, Europe and Africa.

Harold is the co-author of *Marketing: A Global Perspective*; *Marketing in the Non-Profit Sector: Trade Unions* and a chapter entitled 'Marketing Strategies to the EU by SouthEast Asian Firms' in *Marketing: A SouthEast Asian Perspective*, as well as various articles and training manuals.

Rod Harris is Head of The School of Business at Darlington College. He has worked extensively in Eastern Europe with universities to upgrade their business education curricula and on joint venture initiatives to help support enterprise development.

He has written books on business and marketing and also produced case material for management programmes and contributed to distance learning modular Masters learning material.

Rod is currently project manager for an on-line management development initiative with large enterprises and SMEs in North-East England.

To Mom and Lucrecia
for their patience, kindness and intelligence.

Harold

BRIEF CONTENTS

CONTENTS

Part 1 CONCEPTUAL OVERVIEW

1 Introduction to global marketing management   3

Introduction · Objectives · The globalisation of world markets · The
motivation for global involvement · The forces determining global market
strategy · The process of internationalisation and marketing: differences
from 'pure' marketing · The need for global thinking · Summary · Review
questions · Discussion questions · Case study: Business opportunities in
China · Further reading · Notes and references

2 Theories of the firm in global markets   26

Introduction · Objectives · Trade and foreign direct investment theories ·
International marketing theories · Research streams · Summary · Review
questions · Discussion questions · Case study: FDI in emerging markets ·
Further reading · Notes and references

3 Strategic marketing planning   48

Introduction · Objectives · The global strategic planning process · The role
of strategic planning · Marketing and corporate strategy · The interaction
between marketing and corporate strategy · General analysis of strategic
options · Summary · Review questions · Discussion questions · Case study:
The marketing/planning framework · Further reading · Notes and references

4 Analysis of global competition   74

Introduction · Objectives · The competitive advantage of nations ·
Dynamics of national advantage · Sources of competitive advantage ·
Leveraging the firm's strength · Avoiding competitive disadvantage · Focus
strategy · Assessing competitors' strategies · The value chain and the
strategic role of global marketing · Summary · Review questions · Discussion
questions · Case study: Reorganisation in the European defence industry ·
Further reading · Notes and references

Part 2 ASSESSING GLOBAL OPPORTUNITIES

Part 3 GLOBAL MARKETING STRATEGIES

LIST OF FIGURES

LIST OF TABLES

LIST OF BOXES

PREFACE

The book has been laid out to provide coherent and hopefully stimulating analysis of the issues related to strategic marketing in an increasingly global economy. Both of the authors have in differing ways extensive experience of work in other countries that we hope shows through in the examples used throughout the book and via the case studies. It is this 'internationalisation' of the text that provides a commentary on current issues relevant to marketing managers drawn from different countries.

Global strategic marketing may be thought to be focusing on a narrow set of issues, but the importance of 'global' lies in the ability to see trends emerging that affect many nations and businesses as well as the development of truly global markets, i.e. ones where common marketing approaches may be adopted. The use of the term 'global' therefore implies that managers, wherever they are based, are aware of trends, developments and future directions, and also of global markets, industries and products that demand changes in how a company is run, how it sees itself and how it presents itself to its chosen market.

The book can be used to move from an awareness of global developments to a more informed understanding of how this applies to businesses now and in the near future. To do this, the structure of each chapter and the grouping together of chapters into six main sections (Parts 1–6) is intended to equip the reader with an awareness of developments and how this applies to all businesses, whether in a truly globalised market or one that is influenced by global trends but is not yet developing similarities with other markets in other countries that require common marketing strategies.

Chapter structure

Using examples drawn from Europe, Asia and North America, the book reveals the common challenges that all marketing managers (and students of marketing) will have to grapple with. The structure of each chapter is straightforward, providing by way of a general introduction the main area and related issues to be reviewed, identifying the chapter objectives which structure the content and then the main text. All chapters contain boxes. These are of two types:

1 *specific examples* that take an issue a stage further, requiring the reader to focus on that particular example;

2 a *technical issue* raised in the text, but which again requires specific attention on the part of the reader to gain a further understanding of its content and nature.

The chapter is completed by a summary followed by review questions, whose main purpose is to act as an *aide-mémoire*. Discussion questions are open-ended for use by students in groups and provide an opportunity to develop analysis and gain further insights. The case study at the end of the chapter takes examples of companies grappling with an international marketing problem or reviewing current research into a specific issue. The case requires review and analysis, focusing attention on the advisability of the solution proposed by the organisation or the direction in which research suggests managers should move.

Lastly, notes and references, and further reading are provided to encourage the reader to go direct to the sources used or to consult books and journals that can provide a further review of a specific aspect. In some chapters, it is recommended that the reader should see themselves in the role of developer of their own 'recommended reading', as the relevant sources can come from a variety of publications and increasingly from the Internet.

Sections of the book

The book is divided into six sections that together form a strategic framework, moving from an overview of global business developments and the role of the firm through to Part 5, which reviews the implementation of strategies.

Each section contains within it chapters that together provide a comprehensive guide, enabling the reader to look at the main theoretical approaches as well as international examples of companies dealing with specific issues and problems relevant to those topics.

Part 6 contains three longer case studies that range over a number of industries and provide the opportunity to tackle a more detailed set of examples, applying techniques and approaches to the resolution of challenges facing each organisation and developing outline (marketing) plans that can take the company forward.

The business world is constantly changing, with new demands made on businesses, pressures brought to bear to be more competitive, to be cost-conscious, more focused on the customer and more aware of natural environmental issues. The approaches used here, with supporting examples, do not suggest that there is one single way to solve a problem, or that a company having developed a successful strategic marketing response will be guaranteed future prosperity. By understanding, applying and then developing further the approaches reviewed in the text, the reader will be better placed to play a more important role in helping their organisation to succeed in the global market place.

ACKNOWLEDGEMENTS

Significant help and assistance in the production of this book has helped us refine our ideas and maintained progress. In particular, staff at our partner East European universities have been helpful in their comments, as have colleagues at the University of Westminster and University College of Ripon and York St John. Jane Powell at Financial Times Pitman Publishing has also helped to keep our sights focused on hitting deadlines, although she despaired on certain occasions at finding out where on the globe she could find us. Needless to say, she usually tracked us down.

We would like to thank Katrine Wahl and Jane Borges, who have worked on part of the manuscript and provided us with advice, support and much-needed inspiration. Our thanks also goes to Pauline Box who typed much of the manuscript and without whose patience this book would not have seen the light of day.

Finally, our partners' understanding of the long hours given over to the preparation of this book, and the help and support they gave us through this ordeal, was a vital part in the success of this project. They are the true heroes, putting up with many inconveniences and difficulties.

PLAN OF THE BOOK

PART 1 – CONCEPTUAL OVERVIEW

Chapter 1 Introduction to global marketing management	Chapter 2 Theories of the firm in global markets	Chapter 3 Strategic marketing planning	Chapter 4 Analysis of global competition

PART 2 – ASSESSING GLOBAL OPPORTUNITIES

Chapter 5 The economic environment	Chapter 6 The social–cultural environment	Chapter 7 The political–legal environment	Chapter 8 Global market research

PART 3 – GLOBAL MARKETING STRATEGIES

Chapter 9 Global competitive market strategies	Chapter 10 Market-entry decisions	Chapter 11 Market-entry strategies	Chapter 12 Export management

PART 4 – THE GLOBAL MARKETING MIX PROGRAMME

Chapter 13 Global product strategies	Chapter 14 Global service strategies	Chapter 15 Global channel strategies
Chapter 16 Global pricing strategies	Chapter 17 Global promotional strategies	Chapter 18 Negotiation strategies

PART 5 – THE IMPLEMENTATION OF GLOBAL MARKETING STRATEGIES

Chapter 19 Organising the global marketing effort	Chapter 20 Controlling global marketing	Chapter 21 The future of global marketing

PART 6 – CASES IN GLOBAL MARKETING

PART 1

Conceptual overview

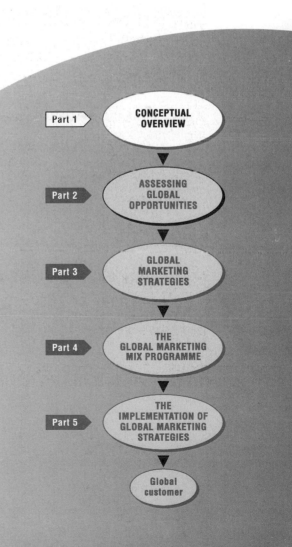

Part 1	CONCEPTUAL OVERVIEW
Part 2	ASSESSING GLOBAL OPPORTUNITIES
Part 3	GLOBAL MARKETING STRATEGIES
Part 4	THE GLOBAL MARKETING MIX PROGRAMME
Part 5	THE IMPLEMENTATION OF GLOBAL MARKETING STRATEGIES
	Global customer

Part 1 of this text is composed of only four chapters, but it covers an immense amount of conceptual material that will provide a useful foundation for the remainder of the text, and introduces the strategic and marketing management framework.

Chapter 1 Introduction to global marketing management

This chapter begins by defining the field and highlights why global marketing is different from domestic operations and what advantages accrue to companies operating internationally. It outlines the need for global marketing activities and goes on to explain why global marketing is imperative for firms and managers in a highly competitive world market.

Chapter 2 Theories of the firm in global markets

A brief but thorough explanation of the major theories of the firm is provided. This chapter not only affords the reader the opportunity to understand the nature of firms operating in international markets, but also explains the factors that have enhanced the development of this situation.

Chapter 3 Strategic marketing planning

This chapter introduces the evolutionary development of strategic marketing planning; the reader is gently introduced to some of the major conceptual frameworks of strategic planning. The relationship between corporate strategy and marketing strategy is emphasised, and the chapter is peppered with examples to illustrate the role and importance of strategic market planning.

Chapter 4 Analysis of global competition

This chapter explores the forces determining the competitive structure both of nations and industries. An understanding of these factors is critical to any firm in analysing the basis of its competitive advantage in international markets. Furthermore, firm-specific competitive advantages can be assessed after an analysis of the competitive nature of the industry is carried out to see whether the firm can levarage these advantages in the global market place.

These four chapters provide the framework for the rest of the text and put global marketing management into context for the reader.

1

Introduction to global marketing management

INTRODUCTION

One of the most talked-about trends in business is the globalisation of markets for goods and services, yet there is often a negative reaction in many countries against the perceived effects of this development. From Germany, the USA and Russia to many developing economies, there are fears that globalisation will result in falling wages, unemployment and increased poverty.

Governments, political parties and trade unions often view this development as at best challenging and at worst sinister. Businesses and their representative organisations, on the other hand, promote the benefits of open trade across political boundaries and the integration of markets to create global opportunities. International markets are critical for companies classified as multinational – Nestlé, Exxon, Philips, Sony, Ford, SmithKline Beecham and many others – who take a global view and structure themselves accordingly.

There are, of course, companies who lack the size of the multinational but who also operate in many countries; these are often referred to as mininationals.[1] The German example of the Mittelstand (medium-sized enterprise), often thought of as the true backbone of that economy, is one that many countries wish to emulate as they focus on exports, undertake important investment, create jobs and can become world leaders in their chosen field.

Companies in downstream activities (production and retailing) as well as those in upstream activities (raw materials and other resources) are involved to some degree in the global market, either in the sale of a finished product or in sourcing raw materials or components. Public sector organisations, with recent changes in public procurement regulations, also see themselves looking beyond their immediate sphere of operation to sourcing from the most competitive bidder.

With the effects of globalisation being felt in the majority of markets, companies would be wise to adopt a global perspective, identifying competitors, new products and opportunities. Major changes in perspective bring restructuring issues to the fore, and the fear of job losses already referred to.

International marketing becomes a vital issue for companies and organisations, taking a broader view of developments that inevitably make the picture more complex, fractured and unfamiliar compared to marketing within a national (home)

3

market. This introductory chapter sets the scene for the book, focusing on the rise of globalisation, the reaction to it and the challenge it provides for businesses. After this introduction, a more detailed analysis is given, looking at the forces shaping globalisation and the way in which organisations need to incorporate this development in their strategic thinking.

Lastly, globalisation brings positive benefits for consumers, helping to increase choice, drive down prices, improve services and create new jobs and opportunities. Globalisation can therefore be seen as a positive force for change that has the potential to raise living standards and drive economies forward.

Objectives

This chapter will examine:

- the globalisation of world markets
- the motivation for global involvement
- the forces determining global market strategy
- the process of internationalisation and marketing and how this differs from 'pure' marketing
- the need for global thinking in strategic marketing.

Box 1.1

IS GLOBALISATION GOOD FOR US?[2]

Early in 1996, Pat Buchanan, a contender for the Republican nomination for the Presidency of the USA, fought what turned out to be an unsuccessful campaign based on protectionist issues. His message found favour with white working- and lower-middle-class voters, who felt that their livelihoods were threatened by imports and massive layoffs. The solution proposed was for the USA to close its borders for five years (to stop immigration from Mexico), to place tariffs on goods from low-wage developing countries and to withdraw from the World Trade Organisation (WTO) and from the North American Free Trade Agreement (NAFTA).[3] This call has some echoes in Russia, where a large number of people are threatened with the loss of their jobs as industry is modernised. Other critical comments have come from groups criticising NAFTA (which covers the USA, Canada and Mexico) from the standpoint of destroying the environment and its threat to civil society.

In Europe, German and French difficulties over the rate of unemployment and threats from non-European imports produced some questioning of the opening up of the European Union (EU) to free trade influences and of what this might mean for the social security provision enjoyed by workers in these countries.

Globalisation is a new phenomenon for the workers, governments and businesses of today, but as an influence it is not new. Relative to world output, cross-border investment flows are only now close to pre-First World War levels. Foreign direct investment (FDI) is estimated to have been nine per cent of world input in 1913, compared to 8.5 per cent in 1991. The argument is that the period 1860–1913 saw changes similar to those that took place in the last two decades, rather than the period of protectionism after the Second World War. Rising globalisation has in both periods been accompanied by a narrowing of

▶ **Box 1.1 continued**

the gap between certain richer and rapidly developing countries. The difference between the two lies in the countries closing the gap. In the first period it was the Scandinavian countries that caught up, whereas now it is the countries based in the Pacific Rim region.

Globalisation would appear to be a healthy development taken from the point of view of South Korea (or in the previous period by Sweden), but unhealthy from those being caught up. Business, of course, cannot take such a parochial view, looking for opportunities to expand trade.

THE GLOBALISATION OF WORLD MARKETS

In the mass media the references to globalisation are too numerous to raise any surprise in the public mind. The world economy has changed from one where national markets are isolated by trade, business and cultural differences which communication difficulties have served to reinforce. The perception now is that with information technology (IT), improved and faster travel links, and the effects of the GATT, plus the move to create a Single Market in Europe, markets can be said to be truly global as well as the firms that serve them. Figure 1.1 supports the view that increasing world trade opportunities are a vital part of economic growth, helping production to increase and ensuring goods are created.

Fig 1.1 GROWTH OF WORLD OUTPUT AND EXPORTS OF MANUFACTURES, 1950–94

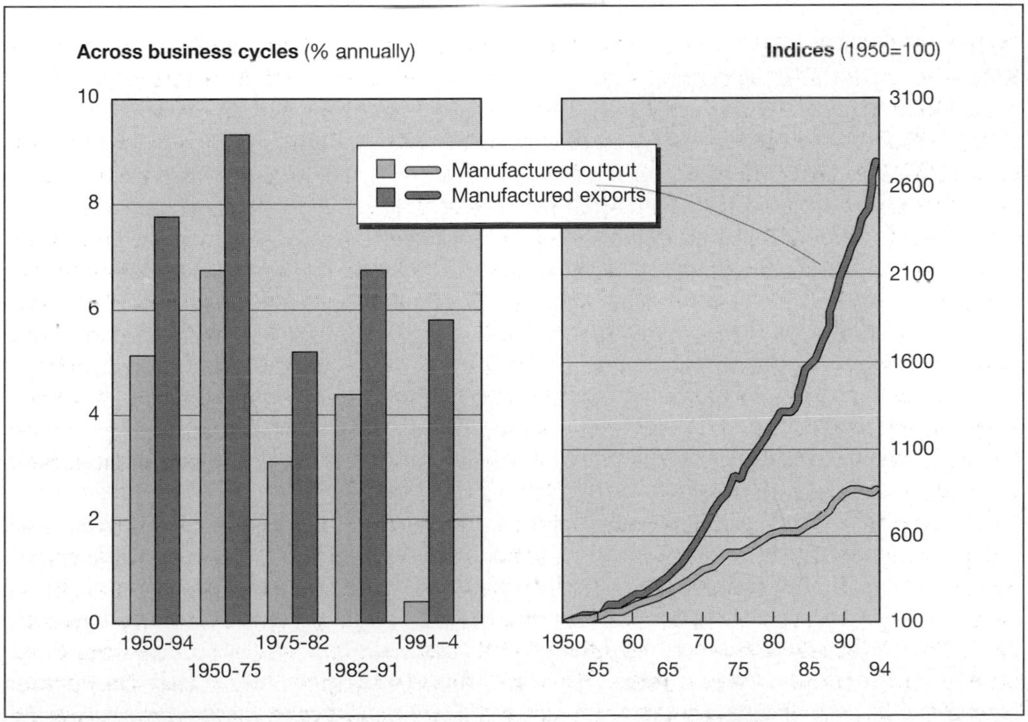

Source: World Trade Organisation.

Box 1.1 casts some doubt on how new this phenomenon actually is, showing that prior to the First World War money and goods flowed as freely as they do now. Differences, of course, exist. Information technology and faster travel have already been mentioned as examples of the way in which companies, their goods and personnel, as well as individuals, can see the world shrinking in terms of time taken to get from one point to another or the ability to communicate face to face via video conferencing with colleagues, fellow students or even friends. The advent of the Internet and more recently the popularity of the Intranet allows firms to improve their performance via teams working on the development of world products along with a slimmed-down organisational structure. Box 1.2 shows how the Ford Motor Company has been able to make use of these developments and to prepare itself to meet the competitive challenge laid down by Japanese and other Pacific Rim car producers. This box also reviews the changes in the radio broadcasting industry and how one firm, GWR, is responding.

Box 1.2

GLOBALISATION AND THE FIRM:[4]
TWO EXAMPLES OF COMPETING ACROSS NATION STATES

For many industries the impact of globalisation has been a feature of the market place for many years, whilst for others it is a relatively new phenomenon. Each industry, and the companies that comprise it, will have their own unique dynamic, by which is meant that the drive towards entering overseas markets will come from different sources. The outcome appears to be the same – i.e. companies move into new (foreign) markets, but the impetus for these moves has to be understood in order to assess the validity of the strategy being pursued.

The car company Ford adopted what it termed 'Ford 2000' an initiative that brought together the European (sales $23bn) and North American (sales $105bn) sides of the company. This is not a straightforward move in that the European and American operations had a separate management structure, products and production facilities. It is a risky strategy in that European customers want cars tailored to their needs in the many countries in which Ford operates; equally difficult are the management challenges of bringing together people who have different perceptions and ways of working.

The main impetus for change has been technology, with the use of computer networks and video links that now permit people around the world to work together on the same project, a factor that should reduce the time it takes to develop a new product from 37 months to under 24, plus a strategy to alter the delivery cycle to less than 15 days. Other changes involve team working, bringing together designers, engineers and production staff, as well as increasing the control over resources that individual managers can wield.

Using today's technology as a device to bring the parts of the company together is done for a purpose, and must face up to the reality of the market place over the longer term. For Ford, which is the market leader in Europe and is catching up with its long-term rival General Motors in the USA, the future is full of uncertainty. Its main strengths lie in the developed markets of Europe and North America, while in the main growth markets of Asia, the Japanese are the significant players. By 2005 the Asian market is projected to be 25 per cent bigger than the American market.

If the competition comes from the Japanese, then Ford has to match their production levels. Toyota, for example, makes 37 cars per worker per year compared to Ford's 20.

▶

> **Box 1.2 continued**

Additionally, the Japanese have global economies of scale, as seen by the very successful Toyota Corolla which sells 1.4m per year. A variety of models for the markets in which Ford is strong cannot deliver the economies of scale that a global model such as the Corolla could provide.

Car production has always considered itself to be global in outlook, with Ford's most recent reorganisation being another change in an industry that is just over 100 years old. Another industry that is just as young (or old) is radio. Commercial radio in the UK is relatively young, but during its lifetime foreign companies have sought to play a part in its development. The UK's second biggest commercial radio group, GWR, has grown rapidly in its home market and is now moving into foreign markets.

The spur to this development has been the restriction on growth in the UK. Ownership rules limit a company to 35 local stations, with GWR already possessing 33, and a 15 per cent share. If growth as an objective is to be pursued, then it can be done only in overseas markets. The company has stations in the USA, Scandanavia, Holland and New Zealand, with more purchases planned. Managing this portfolio is a challenging proposition, particularly as the track record of foreign managers running stations has not been a resounding success.

If the reason for moving into overseas markets is limited opportunities in the home market coupled with deregulation and privatisation in many countries GWR, like Ford, still has to seek opportunities in its home base. In the UK commercial radio advertising revenue grew by 23 per cent in 1995, making it the fastest-growing advertising medium for a third year in a row. This growth can be partly attributed to audience growth: well-managed stations can compete for a larger audience and longer listening hours.

These two companies operate in different markets under different conditions and yet they share the same urge to look at overseas markets and to see a significant benefit to them operating in more than one market. Today's success does not imply a secure future – both companies will be required to review critically their strategies if they are to survive in an increasingly global market.

Box 1.3 provides further examples of exporting opportunities and the benefits gained by companies and countries.

Box 1.3	EXPORT OPPORTUNTIES[5]

Heineken produces its lager in Japan through a joint venture with Kisin, the Japanese brewer. Until 1995, large Japanese retailers were importing cans of Heineken brewed elsewhere in the world, and selling them at a lower price than those produced by the joint venture, a situation that led to competition of Heineken beer against Heineken beer.

The problem of local production retailing at a price greater than the imported products was blamed on the complexity of Japanese distribution, with many people taking a profit between brewer and retailer. The low costs of production of Heineken beer at its Dutch production centres was ample testament to the company's efforts to reduce costs and build a successful export business from this development. '

▶

▶ Box 1.3 continued

This example shows how the company uses brewing partners abroad, its low-cost breweries in Holland and its well-known brand to bolster its position as one of the most international of brewers. So when one problem emerges, such as the clash of local production against imports of its own products, it can switch its emphasis towards solving the problem and ultimately achieve corporate (strategic) objectives.

To many, exporting or doing business in Japan is an exasperating and often fruitless exercise, as various barriers are assumed to exist to make the most determined of company's think again. Of late, however, structural changes within Japan have meant that the economy is now more open to foreign goods than for many years.

One trend that has shown the improved chance of success for exporters is the shrinking of the trade surplus, even though a complete reduction in the surplus is unlikely for some years to come. Japan's taste for foreign goods, from Heineken to German cars such as Audi, has been enhanced by the low cost of imports brought about by the rising yen, but has a momentum of its own as the consumer has been introduced to a wider range of products drawn from many countries.

The success of imports has also coincided with the challenge to the existing retail sector by new and aggressive retailers who have challenged the dominance of the older retailers, and not been afraid to introduce foreign brands to a public that has become more receptive to them. Many believe that the improvement in the fortunes of importers is no mere flash in the pan, as unlike previous periods this one is against a background of low growth and major structural changes in the national economy. Once the economy is open then companies such as Heineken, as they take market share, may find that this is a longer-term phenomenon than has been found in the past. More consumer choice can, therefore, be enhanced by the opening up of an economy that had previously been prey to financial, distribution and technical barriers.

A country such as Argentina, on the other hand, has found that involvement in world trade has paid dividends of a different sort, with exports helping the economy deal with difficult problems. In 1995, Argentina experienced a fall in GDP, accompanied by a fall in fixed investment and a reduction in industrial production. One area, however, stood out. Exports rose by 33 per cent, a move to the export-led growth that the country desired. In many cases, improvements of this type have often come about as a result of devaluation, but in this case the peso–dollar exchange rate was maintained. What, therefore, could explain the move from a trade deficit in 1994 to surplus in 1995? Critics claimed that the improvement was fed by special circumstances which could not be maintained, pointing to a lack of structural adjustment. Others pointed to the subsidy offered to exporters by tax breaks, providing ammunition for the assessment that the currency was overvalued and long-term economic salvation could come from a devaluation.

Special factors have to account for such a dramatic improvement. One factor was the consumer boom in Brazil, a country that is Argentina's main trading partner. Equally, a fall in the value of the US dollar, as happened in 1995, helped the peso, as it was pegged to that currency. Critics, therefore, felt that a devaluation had taken place, but that this was of only temporary benefit.

Structural changes, insofar as productivity gains and low inflation have helped to support longer-term sustainable exports, along with the opening up of once protected industries such as oil and gas, have suggested that structural adjustments are proceeding.

Much of the foreign investment that the country has attracted is export-related, and the reduction of trade barriers agreed as part of the Uruguay Round of GATT in 1994 and membership of Mercosur (a free trade bloc) could help to encourage the export drive.

▶ **Box 1.3 continued**

On their own, exports, which account for only 15 per cent of GDP, could not provide the engine for growth. The government has set a target for exports to account for up to 35 per cent of GDP in the medium term, which would then provide the engine for growth that the country seeks.

These examples reveal that companies and countries can benefit from the enhanced trade opportunities that now exist. Heineken can take advantage of these only if it is flexible and can run its operations successfully. Japan is opening up its markets, providing consumers with more choice and producing the shift in its economy towards the consumer-led focus seen in the USA, France and elsewhere. Argentina, in looking for exports to spur recovery, has taken up the challenge of restructing and maintaining macroeconomic discipline over exchange rates and inflation and to exploit the potential of its industries.

For the marketer, with the focus squarely placed on meeting the needs of the customer, two issues are at the forefront.

Access to markets previously restricted

Access to markets previously restricted, such as India (*see* Box 1.4), creates new opportunities. What is required is to understand the dynamics of the market and the needs of the targeted customer and take advantage of the strengths and competencies of the company to turn this into a profitable activity. This approach still retains the international diversity of the market place and is only partly what globalisation is about.

Box 1.4   DEVELOPING MARKETS AND GLOBALISATION[6]

India is a major developing market that many companies in the developed world are viewing as a long-term investment, particularly as it catches up with the West.

Looking at a developing economy as a place to invest suggests opportunities for the company prepared to take that risk. India, like so many developing economies, however, cannot be seen just as a battleground for companies based in the developed world. Several of its indigenous companies pose a threat to many economies, not because of cheap labour, but because of the skills and expertise they possess.

Globalisation works to help raise living standards and benefits companies in both the developing and the developed world. Two examples from India – cars and software – can reveal this process in operation.

Cars

Car sales in India are growing by 25 per cent a year, for a market estimated to be $2.6bn in 1996. The country's middle class mainly buys two-wheeled vehicles, for a variety of reasons such as coping with traffic jams, the poor road infrastructure and the high price of a new car. The modern car Murati, which is a joint venture between the Indian government and Japan's Suzuki, has 75 per cent of the new car market of 320 000 vehicles.

Since 1993, the once closed car market has been liberalised and new environmental standards introduced. Strong GDP growth, liberalisation and tighter emission controls mean that Birla and Premier, India's two main indigenous producers, have been involved in joint ventures to produce more modern cars – Birla with GM and Premier with Peugeot.

▶

▶ **Box 1.4 continued**

Companies such as Mahindra and Mahindra that make trucks and tractors have also entered the market with a joint venture with Ford to make Escorts and Fiestas. These ventures will double production by 1998, with a difficulty lying in the fact that prices of the new models will be outside the purchasing capacity of the market. Another problem is that models such as the Escort cannot be built to deal with the poor conditions of most of the country's roads. The Murati, as a small-engine model, is affordable and may provide a large share of the growing market.

Joint ventures by car companies such as Mercedes, Daewoo and Honda will inevitably see their investment as long term (some suggest six years) with rising incomes, improved roads and more appropriate models producing the conditions for a more vigorous market.

Investment of this type looks at the Indian economy as containing massive future growth and profitable prospects.

Software

In 1995 Indian software companies had sales of $1.2bn and experienced growth of four per cent per annum. Unlike many developing economies which have focused on export-led manufacturing to fuel economic growth, India has many 'knowledge-based' companies that compete head-on with similar companies from developed economies.

Bangalore, which is the centre of the industry with 300 companies, is the home of Infosys, with clients in America who e-mail their problems to the company at the end of their working day, and have the solutions for the beginning of work the next day. Foreign companies, such as IBM, Motorola and Group Bull, have set up factories in the city and now account for 70 per cent of all investment. Indian workers in this industry are paid well by local standards, but are cheaper than their American and French counterparts, a factor that can partly explain foreign interest. Supplying cheap brainpower would not of itself help secure a viable future; the development of new products in system ideas and software provides the opportunities to earn higher margins and provide an income for future expansion.

The supply of people to this fast-expanding industry is guaranteed by the 20 000 computer science graduates who leave Indian universities every year. However, there are problems: Indian firms expect to lose 20 per cent of their staff every year as they are lured to jobs in the West, and the infrastructure, such as a guaranteed power supply, is not able to keep pace with expanding demand.

Liberalisation of markets, such as the car industry in India, provide a platform for growth for companies taking a long-term view. Traditional industries such as car production can be the main focus of attention for a developing economy, but the software industry in India shows that high-tech as well as low-tech opportunities exist both for India and foreign-owned companies. Taking a broader, and therefore more informed, view can alert many to the opportunities in developing economies.

Foreign direct investment (FDI) has shown that many are seeing the emerging markets as containing huge potential. In 1995 $167bn in private capital was invested in these economies. Asian economies accounted for 60 per cent of private income flow, a move which downgraded the importance given to Latin American countries in the early 1990s. Of the total, $90bn came from FDI, with China as the largest beneficiary with over $38bn.

The increase in FDI compared to, for example, portfolio investment lies in the realisation by firms like IBM, Ford, Daewoo and others that high growth rates, privatisation and

▶

▶ **Box 1.4 continued**

the trend towards the globalisation of production offer new opportunities that require a long-term investment.

Change of this nature is still relatively new in countries like India, where protectionism really only ceased to be accepted government policy in the early 1990s. Membership of the WTO and membership of free trade areas (FTAs) or custom unions (described in Chapter 5) point to a stability in government relations with industry. For the 16 countries outside the WTO, amongst them China, Russia and Vietnam, the chance to bolster their future by teaming up with companies from developed countries would be enhanced if membership of the WTO was secured and they could follow the example of India in the development of a variety of industries to satisfy consumer demand (cars) and to cater for industry needs (software).

Convergence in tastes

Globalisation makes a more dramatic claim than the opening up of trade. Tastes and preferences of customers who live in different nations are thought to be converging. Examples of such convergence would be the desire to purchase a McDonald's meal, to wear Levi jeans or to relax with a Pepsi or Coca-Cola. So whether the purchaser of any of these products lives in Japan, America or Russia they will have the same requirements. This is a more radical interpretation of what it means to be moving to a global economy, with the conclusion that it is an irrelevance to talk of a 'British' or 'Italian' market for these products, as they are essentially the same.

Taking the second interpretation too far can be dangerous; markets still differ in their tastes and preferences for many products. Increasing foreign competition, from wherever it originates, is not the same as the existence of an homogeneous (global) market. With differences, the marketer has to adopt a different approach. With few or no differences the marketer can present a uniform package. (It would be difficult to envisage a marketing approach that did not in some way differ, however similar the market appears to be. McDonald's, often used as an example of a global product, does change the offering to suit local tastes – they offer tea in Russian outlets as the main hot beverage, rather than coffee, a small but significant difference to suit local tastes and expectations.)

The repercussions of the changes outlined above is that global markets require firms of suitable size and financial strength to exploit the opportunities. If a national firm, such as an airline, is not yet perceived to be a global carrier, then the implication is that they should forge alliances and mergers to become one.

Production and its location is a factor in the expansion of the world's economy. Reduction in trade barriers and the intensification of competition can both reduce costs of production (locate in low-cost centres) and provide the same quality as is commonly to be found only in developed economies. (Universal quality standards can now be applied wherever production is located; without this, cheap labour costs would be a barren advantage as firms offering a product to an acceptable standard would generally be preferred.) This is a key issue for the Chinese and Indian economies where they have experienced an increase in such investment as a result of their growth potential and because they offer low-cost labour.

If some markets are no longer seen as national, then the goods that supply them may also be global – i.e. the components of a product are sourced from many countries and may even be supported by services drawn from across the globe. In a review of 29 American cars, such as the Pontiac Le Mann, only 35 per cent of the design, assembly and engineering were directly attributed to American companies. Equally surprising was that a Japanese car, the Nissan Quest, had 75 per cent of its content which could be called American – was this car 'Japanese'?[7]

Companies source products and services from the most competitive supplier, which is an issue for even small and medium-sized enterprises (SMEs), as they can be assisted in their search for the most efficient source. Indeed, the Internet has been blamed by some companies as leading to a loss of market share, as prices can now be compared with other firms who choose to advertise their wares there.

THE MOTIVATION FOR GLOBAL INVOLVEMENT

Global trade is expanding rapidly, with a huge increase in manufactured exports, as Fig. 1.1 on p. 5 shows. In the previous section the two possible reactions to this were outlined. Equally, the scepticism about the degree to which this shows a deeper and broader scope than any previous expansion of world trade was noted. In just four years, 1992–6, the world's regional trade arrangements nearly doubled to over 100, further raising the possibility that these arrangements could be a retreat from free trade. From the point of view of business, this could stifle or enhance company strategies to seek opportunities for investment and growth. If the last global movement could collapse in protectionism, then could the moves now underway to create trading blocs also have a similar fate?

For the individual company, the question is important when looking to invest money and resources in exporting or setting up production in targeted countries. If globalisation is by no means guaranteed, the existing arrangements have to be understood in order to be acted upon. Managers will be facing an increasingly complex political–economic environment. This provides a third issue to globalisation. The first two pointed to increased opportunities for trade plus the emergence of some global (homogeneous) markets, whilst the third aspect focuses on the political and economic arrangements embodied in national trade associations/agreements.

If the term 'globalisation' is interpreted in this way, then what are global opportunities, and what does this mean for marketers?

Global strategies cannot be standard product market strategies that assume the world to be homogeneous and border-free. If a market is homogeneous (still relatively rare) the 100 or so trade agreements subject it to specific and unique rules and regulations. Even here there is no guarantee that the symmetry between a national market and regionalisation will remain intact, or at least subject to the same working assumptions that managers have traditionally used. For example, is it useful to maintain that the national economy of Italy should be treated separately from that of France, or as a member of the EU and a participant in the 'Single Market'? Should it now be accepted that Northern Italy and prosperous areas of France are to be seen as a single entity for marketing purposes?

Global strategies can be pursued by large, medium-sized or even small companies, yet the motivations are diverse and vary from market to market in their significance. With improved travel opportunities and communication, some consumer goods markets have been created as the similarities between the teenage market or business executive, for instance, have become more pronounced. Other spurs are the exploitation of good ideas in a broader market, sourcing from the most efficient supplier wherever they are located or the desire to keep up with competitors who themselves have taken a more global view. This is by no means a complete review of all the reasons why businesses become involved in the global market place, and throughout the book many more will be added, but it highlights the 'push' and 'pull' many firms experience in becoming involved to a greater or lesser extent in business across political borders.

 ## THE FORCES DETERMINING GLOBAL MARKET STRATEGY

Two examples can help to show the forces that are driving change.

1 US investment specialising in lending to firms in the technology and biotechnology field have set up in London. The significance of this lies in their ability to enter the UK financial market, their recognition that firms exist in the UK and Europe who have 'leading-edge' products that require investment, and managers of these firms (often academics) who are eager to exploit the potential of their developments. Taken from any point of view this development shows the forces of globalisation at work, both from the ability of US banks to take a global view and the realisation that UK companies have products the market requires (both in the UK and elsewhere). These developments feed off each other for the benefit of the consumer and the organisations concerned.

2 Bookselling by US and UK retailers has gone on-line, with the US retailers Amazon and Barnes & Noble, and the UK retailers Waterstones and Dillons offering their titles for direct purchase. This provides a catalogue of at least 1 000 000 titles each, plus the possibility of large discounts on a significant number of titles. Here the driving forces can be seen to be technology, industry dynamics and demands of such provision by consumers. (A more detailed review of the forces driving change is provided in Chapters 2–4.)[8]

To benefit in a world of change and discontinuity, as the two examples show, businesses need to prepare themselves and develop responses. The growth of global action offers increased opportunities. All of these require careful examination. All firms, if they intend to become involved directly in the global market, need to understand the implications of these changes for their operations. The job of the marketer is to provide a key role in the process by, amongst other things, researching the market, looking at customer preferences and arriving at a marketing plan that can achieve corporate objectives. In describing these activities various terms are used. These will include 'international', 'multinational', 'multidomestic', 'transnational' and 'global'. Confusingly, these terms are often used interchangeably and in some instances, such as global markets, are used alongside globalisation.

| Box 1.5 | POVERTY AND DEVELOPMENT[9] |

The fast-expanding countries of Asia and the emerging markets of the old Soviet-style economies might suggest that all countries are able to adopt the policies that would open them to the benefits of globalisation. Many countries, in fact, will find that the transition is painful and slow, and that the policies adopted in the past reduce their room for manoeuvre.

The World Bank has established that 41 of the world's poorest countries have high external debts, with the value of these debts to individual donor countries and multilateral institutions being more than 22 per cent of their export earnings. The effects of such high debt can have severe repercussions, with foreign investors deterred and domestic investment held back because companies fear that the proceeds will be taxed to pay back foreign creditors. As the debt is owed to the World Bank or the African Development Bank, it is technically possible to refinance the debt and give these countries a new start. This is a use of scarce resources that can be compared to the next-best use of the money, particularly for those other countries who have high debts, but are deemed to have export growth that will finance the loans.

Many countries require help and assistance from the IMF and the World Bank, particularly in Eastern Europe. The benefits of growth are obvious, but the problem is achieving enough growth to bring jobs and prosperity. South Africa is a country that showed growth in 1995 of 3.5 per cent, but only 12 000 (net) new jobs were created, leaving unemployment at 33 per cent. Growth of 3.5 per cent would be considered good for a developed economy, but is too low for South Africa. The South African Foundation estimates that a six per cent growth figure is required if the country is to absorb the 300 000 new job seekers who appear every year. Growth of this order would have to come, in part, from exports, with the Foundation estimating growth of 10 per cent a year. The problem is that the government deficit and low savings ratio make it difficult to see how internally generated investment could promote growth and provide products for export. Investment has therefore to come from overseas.

The government, in a bid to attract investors, has taken steps towards privatisation and the gradual removal of exchange controls. More specifically, it is also promoting tourism, which accounts for just two per cent of GDP, against an international average of six per cent. The Foundation argues for a more radical solution, with full privatisation, complete abolition of exchange controls, cuts in the budget deficit and a reform of the tax system.

As South Africa participates fully in the world economy after years of boycott, other challenges emerge, particularly with the reduction of tariff barriers to comply with WTO rules. Unless industry is modernised much of it will be lost.

South Africa faces challenges in adapting itself to new circumstances and in boosting GDP growth. Although not heavily indebted, it has been forced to adopt government policies to attract foreign investors and encourage 'home' investment. Those countries with high indebtedness have less room for manoeuvre, having first to seek a solution to the problem of debt and then to boost growth. In all of these examples, the benefits of trading internationally will not be felt for some time to come, and may be held back by a lack of agreement by the international agencies on the best course of action.

Managing in these circumstances will be difficult, with the end of cosy domestic markets and of the safe profits that such situations offer, a problem in South Africa which has an economy dominated by large conglomerates unused to the full effect of competition. Two approaches can be detected. First, to exploit the large established home advantage

> ▶ **Box 1.5 continued**
>
> which companies possess and to move closer to customers by catering to their needs. A difficult balance has also to be struck between profitability and lowering prices to keep foreign competition at bay. Second, to accept that the home advantage has been lost, or soon will be, and to push into overseas markets by creating a global presence and if possible a global brand. This is a more risky approach than the defence of the home market, as competition will have to be met on a world-wide scale.
>
> Business opinion, as represented by the Foundation in South Africa, when calling for the changes outlined above follow the best-practice approach suggested by the IMF and World Bank. Whether all of the local companies are prepared for the challenge of implementing even some of these reforms is doubtful.
>
> Managers, workers and government are seeking to create favourable conditions for growth and have the challenge to take advantage of the opportunities created, so that growth will benefit the majority, rather than those few 'home' and foreign companies that will be best placed to exploit the opportunities of reform.

The multiplicity of environments in international marketing creates a whole new series of operational problems, and the wider the scope of the firm's activities in the international area, the wider the environmental diversities become. The firm operating in the international market will need to address issues that are not so prevalent in domestic markets such as the following:

- *International risks*: these include political, financial and regulatory risks. Political risks arise from possible expropriation of assets, coups, warfare and uncertainty over government policy. The financial risks involve differing inflation rates in various markets and exchange rate and interest rate fluctuations. Regulatory risks arise from the regulation of business practices, discrimination against foreign goods and barriers to trade.

- *Multiple environmental risks*: the diversity of international settings, such as financial markets, labour and business practices, cultural differences, etc., will increase the difficulties of managing foreign operations and the risk of failure.

- *Business conflicts*: conflicts may arise because of differences between the business goals of foreign enterprises and the interests of the host government. These conflicts may arise in a number of areas: for example, the transfer of funds out of the country may conflict with the host government's desire to have the funds reinvested in the economy. International marketers are major agents of change in a market – this could cause considerable difficulties with local habits and customs. For example, the introduction of blue jeans, video products, beauty products, etc. in some markets may cause changes in people's attitudes towards leisure, materialism, and so on, which may or may not be deemed desirable by those in authority.

Firms, therefore, require purpose, knowledge and distinctive competencies different from those relating to domestic marketing. These differences may be ones of degree rather than kind. It could be said that competence in domestic marketing is a necessary but not a sufficient condition for success in international markets.

In addition to having the requisite knowledge, skills and competencies, success in international markets is also a function of the firm's foreign market philosophy, and whether its management has the appropriate attitude and commitment to international business. It could be argued that the lack of these characteristics may partly explain why the majority of UK and European companies have rarely ventured outside their home markets.

A practical effect of the differences between international and domestic marketing is that managers operating in the international sphere will require a broader competence level. This is reflected in a number of ways. First, the future manager of a global firm will need to have 'cultural empathy'. This means being able to recognise cultural differences and understand foreign clients so as to be able to communicate effectively. This empathy can be achieved by developing linguistic skills to a high level, where the person will not only think but also experience emotions in the foreign language. In fact, the future international manager must be both internationally experienced and linguistically competent. Managers with this profile are still a rarity today, although some multinational companies do have management teams with these attributes.

THE PROCESS OF INTERNATIONALISATION AND MARKETING: DIFFERENCES FROM 'PURE' MARKETING

Some firms are very involved with international marketing whilst others show very little interest or motivation. These different attitudes towards international marketing activities can be called international marketing orientations, and we can now distinguish three types.

Ethnocentrism (home-country orientation)

The ethnocentric firm views the marketing operation in a foreign country as secondary. The distinctive features of this approach are:

- the foreign market is seen as a place to dispose of excess output
- the foreign environment and its opportunities are seen as no different from those of the domestic market
- marketing strategies are similar if not identical to those applied to the domestic markets.

This orientation reflects two management views:

- that the rest of the world is similar to the domestic market
- that the programmes implemented for the domestic consumers represent 'best practice' and should appeal to foreign buyers.

The advantage of this approach for any firm is that it is relatively simple, rapid and economical to implement for overseas markets. However, certain facilitating factors are required before this approach can be successfully adopted. The firm would need either technological leadership, high product quality or low production costs, or would need to focus on those overseas markets where consumer needs and conditions for use are similar to those in the domestic market.

However, there are limits to the long-term success of this approach to international marketing as it does not involve any sort of comparative analysis, the identification of similarities and differences in two or more markets, which in turn can help a firm to adapt its marketing strategy for those markets.

Polycentrism (host-country orientation)

The polycentric firm identifies only the differences in each market. The major features of this approach are:

- each market where it operates is treated as if it were unique
- every market will have its own marketing strategy and objectives based on the firm's knowledge of local needs
- the product is modified to suit the local market
- price and promotion are established by each subsidiary
- local nationals make up the salesforce.

In the long term this multidomestic approach is unlikely to be profitable since duplication of effort and strategies may occur as a result of seeing each market as being different and unique. Clusters of markets may exhibit similar market characteristics and hence duplication can be avoided.

According to Majaro,[10] the cluster approach is based on the need to achieve optimum penetration of a group of markets, without the need for the company to spread itself too thinly. These clusters of countries will have highly standardised marketing mixes which can be managed economically. For example, Argentina and Brazil are different markets but there are enough common factors between them (i.e. consumption factors) for a company to adopt a cluster approach. A cluster approach then involves channelling a firm's resources into one or more market segment, and, by concentrating its resources and efforts in these markets, it hopes to capture large market shares.

Geocentrism (world orientation)

The geocentric firm views the world as a single market and tends to see both similarities and differences in various markets. The major features of this approach are:

- the firm will attempt to develop uniform global marketing strategies, i.e. have a high degree of international uniformity in product presentations or promotions
- the firm identifies homogeneous international demand segments that can be targeted with a standard product.

This approach is capable of achieving rapid world-wide distribution of a product, as well as attaining low production costs partly due to economies of scale. The difficulties of this approach are that its success depends on careful and continuous global market research which is expensive and time-consuming. Furthermore, there are important differences between markets which may necessitate the firm having to drop many markets or, alternatively, abandon its global standardisation programmes. However, many large firms, e.g. Coca-Cola, McDonald's and Sony, are trying to develop both global strategies and global products.

It seems that this approach would be the ideal orientation for any firm interested in international marketing if it is to survive and be competitive in the dynamic and tough world environment outlined earlier.

THE NEED FOR GLOBAL THINKING

There are strategic implications for the organisation in moving into a new market. What this means for the firm in the international context is the subject of some debate. Yip[11] focuses on the benefits companies are seeking to obtain by integrating their world-wide strategy (i.e. globalising). This approach contrasts with the common multinational approach where companies have set up country subsidiaries that design, produce and market products tailored to local needs.

To develop a global strategy, three steps are required:

1 develop the core strategy, which is the basis of sustainable competitive advantage;

2 internationalise the core strategy through the expansion of activities;

3 globalise the strategy by integrating it across countries.

Multinationals are familiar with the first two steps but not with the third as this runs counter to the strategy of product adaptation to suit local market requirements.

Yip supports the drive for a global strategy, particularly as trends in many industries are towards such an approach. The industry globalisation drivers that create the potential for a global strategy have to be suited to the company's strategy levels. A few examples can help to show what benefits may come from such an approach.

1 *Market participation*: countries would be selected for their potential contribution to globalisation benefits, rather than on an individual country profit potential.

2 *Product offering*: a global strategy implies that a standardised core product is developed that requires little in the way of adaptation to suit local needs. This reduces costs and provides for more flexibility.

3 *Marketing*: because of a standardised product serving similar needs, the marketing strategy can become more uniform, although some adaptation may be required.

4 *Competitive moves*: with this type of strategy competitive moves are integrated and synchronised across countries. So an attack in a competitor's home market drains their resources and strengthens the hand of the aggressor; a multidomestic strategy would be unable to co-ordinate activities in this way.

So what are the benefits of such an approach? Cost reduction and an improvement of the product, thus providing a better service to customers, built around a core product springs from this approach. Clearly, though, there are drawbacks. Management co-ordination issues, communication problems and a uniform marketing approach could leave the company vulnerable. To decide whether the global strategy is viable would require the company to come to a decision on the global potential of the industry itself. According to this approach, strategies of this type are possibilities that companies should take seriously, and as has been seen, will have a significant impact on marketing.

Is the global market and global strategy that goes with it a distinct possibility? Millington and Bayliss[12] look at the effect of the Single Market in Europe, which had as its main thrust the opening up of national markets, in order to create a large domestic market in which companies could, perhaps for the first time, gain economies of scale and compete successfully around the world. In researching whether integration had occurred that would achieve the required economics of scale, Millington and Bayliss concluded that it had yet to be proved that a single market had been created and that companies were best advised to maintain a national approach as the market showed very real differences. Some of the problems associated with integration are explored further in Box 1.6.

Box 1.6

TAKING ADVANTAGE OF EUROPEAN INTEGRATION[13]

Costs in the EU were, and are, high for a number of reasons:

1 high labour costs and benefits packages;
2 restrictive practices, such as restriction on the hours part-time workers can work;
3 high exchange rates, often the outcome of following the tight monetary policies of the Bundesbank;
4 protection of national markets.

The Single Market plus the reduction of tariffs and barriers to trade agreed under the GATT, and taken forward by the WTO, requires a reduction in costs. Due to many decades of focusing on national markets, over-capacity can be found in many industries and the number of firms competing in particular markets is too many to support efficient production.

Many firms now think of themselves as pan-European, with a product-based strategy whereby products are made in different factories and shipped over a broad geographic area. This often involves narrowing the product range and increasing the markets served by the remaining products.

The pan-European strategy provides economies of scale, one of the benefits said to apply to US companies who can serve a large market. As seen with the example of Ford, approaches of this type provide a focus on improvements in manufacturing and design, and can use state-of-the-art approaches. With such a focus, the organisation of a company changes, with the removal of layers from the old-style bureaucratic structure to the emphasis on teamwork.

Customers benefit from this in obvious ways, such as cost reduction leading to price advantages, but also in other less clear-cut examples, such as the reduction in time between ordering and receiving their purchase.

Table 1.1 STANDARDISATION OF COMPANY PRODUCTS AND OPERATIONS

Item	Non-Pan-European firms			Pan-European firms		
	Much more standard %	More standard %	Not or less standard %	Much more standard %	More standard %	Not or less standard %
Product formulations/ engineering	18	52	31	45	41	14
Packaging	27	37	37	37	47	17
Pricing	21	34	44	37	27	37
Product numbering	17	34	49	44	26	30
Components/parts numbering	16	25	59	46	21	33
Quality assurance standards	50	27	23	80	20	0
Computer systems (such as MRP)	24	40	26	41	38	21

Source: Reprinted from *European Management Journal*, Vol. 13, No. 3, September, Collins, R. and Schmenner, R., 'Taking advantage of Europe's single market' © 1995. With kind permission from Elsevier Science Ltd.

►

> **Box 1.6 continued**

Table 1.1 summarises the main differences between pan-European firms and others. Despite the advantages of this approach there are many obstacles to the creation of such a company. Research shows that obstacles range from the predictable, such as continued problems with different government regulations from country to country, to the more intangible and therefore more threatening negative attitudes of managers. Objections stem from moving personnel from one country to another, through to the problem of managing in different cultural climates. The least difficult area was the resistance of customers to such changes.

Well-managed companies who wish to take the route to pan-Europeanisation should recognise the barriers to the implementation of such a strategy and seek to take their managers and workers along with them. Managers require new skills and approaches to the management of such an operation, particularly as the very nature of team building and an emphasis on project management places an emphasis on co-operation and ways of working that may well be alien to managers drawn from bureaucratic organisations.

Barriers to the creation of more pan-national brands may not be the result of consumer resistance, or of any other external environmental issues, but of the internal resistance to such moves. Threats of redundancy, loss of status as a post is abolished or working alongside others who now treat each other as team members can lead to the maintenance of a national strategy, or (for a multidomestic approach) treating each country to a separate offering of products to suit what is thought to be differing cultural requirements. As other firms take the approach outlined here, this maintenance of the company's status quo may see market share reduced as costs remain high and profits fall due to competition. A pan-European approach is easy to support but more difficult to implement.

How far can the differing approaches of Yip, and Millington and Bayliss be reconciled? The area of agreement is on appraising the market to see what potential exists for a global, multidomestic or national strategy. In the EU, however, the creation of a true Single Market has been held back by cultural, political and economic differences, an issue that casts doubt on the efficiency gains to be made from the creation of a pan-European strategy. Yip, however, is looking at a broader issue – the potential that exists for the development of a global strategy that suits the development of the industry itself. Clearly limiting the horizon to Europe might be too narrow a field in which to develop such a view.

External factors along with internal considerations can create favourable circumstances for a global response. Czinkota and Ronkainen[14] divide these globalisation drivers into market, cost, environmental and competitive factors.

1 *Market factors.* Factors such as the life-styles of consumers in Europe, Japan and elsewhere have already been referred to. To match this development, infrastructure and distribution channels have been developed that make possible the transference of market elements across borders.

   The influence of consumers on globalisation should not be underestimated. This can be seen in the converging life-styles of many groups across the globe, for example the teenage market, but it also contains the dynamic interface of consumers determining where developments take place. Environmental concerns and ethical behaviour are some of the areas where demands for changes transcend national boundaries. Global markets are the creation of both consumers and firms supplying products to serve them.

2 *Cost factors*. Duplication of effort is costly and can produce inefficient conditions for companies, so a global preference, such as the one described for Ford on pp. 6–7, can provide savings that can benefit product development.

3 *Environmental factors*. The general move to the liberalisation of trade along with technological improvement have produced a climate that encourages many companies to take the first step into exporting and then to consider a more committed move into the global market.

4 *Competitive factors*. Many markets are well on the way to being dominated by global companies, so in order to compete effectively companies have to match the skills and tactics of the larger players who can switch resources to a market to build market share or defend themselves against new threats.

To deal with these four factors will require decisions based on market participation, product offering, marketing strategy, location of value-added activities and competitive moves. What is critical is that thought and consideration is given to these issues so that a clear strategy emerges.

Marketing in the domestic, international or global sense follows the strategic approach of the company, with the actual process consisting of four elements: analysis, planning, implementation and control. This approach applies regardless of the type of market being considered, so that the marketing manager can focus attention on the collection of data, the development of the marketing plan and, as importantly, the implementation and control aspects which help to achieve the stated aims and objectives of the company. As noted earlier, the difference lies not in the approach, but in the complexity of the activities entered into when looking at a global approach, compared to the domestic marketing effort.

Whatever the area of focus, marketing is judged on its contribution to the success of the businesses, so the skills and ability of the international marketers, although greater in scope, will still be judged against the objectives set for them. Working alongside other managers who bring with them different perceptions and skills offers further challenges as technology helps to bring down the barriers that exist within the organisation. Responding to a rapidly changing market presents new challenges for the marketer, as well as the need to find new more effective organisational approaches to changing requirements.

SUMMARY

Reductions in trade barriers and economic integration, along with transport and technological developments, have encouraged the increase in world trade that is benefiting many nations. Companies seek to take advantage of these trends by entering new markets or looking to participate in global markets, i.e. markets where a uniformity of needs can produce a similar marketing approach whatever the political and geographical barriers happen to be.

Consumer pressures sometimes expressed through the election of consumer-friendly governments or via the market place have broken out of national confines, creating pan-European and global preferences that can be met by organisations that see themselves as offering what consumers want regardless of location.

Companies, whether multinational in scale or SMEs, can exploit the opportunities on offer. What is required is a considered approach that can make sense of a complex picture, with the company finding competitive advantages in its chosen markets.

The marketing challenge is to see how, with either an export, multidomestic or global strategy, the most appropriate mix can be offered to the customer to achieve corporate objectives. The challenge is also to understand that in many circumstances a global approach can be more effective than attempting to pursue a multidomestic approach.

Globalisation is not a new phenomenon, having been seen prior to the First World War. What is new is the way in which it manifests itself. However, globalisation is challenged by new regional agreements that could role back the move to freer markets, just as happened in the 1920 and 1930s. The impetus to reduce trade barriers is such that this threat is reduced, providing opportunities for companies and for the welfare of the citizens of the fast-growing economies.

If a business is to succeed, then a market orientation is essential with the commitment to global markets and the creation of organisational capabilities and the accumulation of international experience that can focus on the best way to achieve success.

REVIEW QUESTIONS

1 What are the conditions necessary to understand the term 'globalisation'?

2 How far is globalisation a new phenomenon?

3 What is the difference between a global strategy and a multidomestic one?

4 What is a global market, and how far can this development be seen within the European Single Market?

5 Outline the reasons why regional trading agreements pose threats to globalisation.

6 List the main challenges for the marketer that globalisation presents.

DISCUSSION QUESTIONS

1 If the majority of companies serve the domestic market, of what relevance is globalisation?

2 Critics of the Maastricht Treaty argue that the implementation of the Single Market approach is more important than the single currency issue. Outline arguments for and against this standpoint.

3 Emerging markets in developing countries present opportunities to companies. How difficult is it to understand the business environment of such a country and to produce effective marketing plans?

4 What might be the significance of a marketing orientation for companies competing in the global market?

5 What is the challenge that marketing managers face in a world of discontinuous change?

Case study

BUSINESS OPPORTUNITIES IN CHINA[15]

In 1994 the Chinese economy generated exports of $124bn, whilst purchasing $119bn of imports. These figures had grown substantially over the previous decade and were one symptom of the transformation taking place within the country.

A population of 1.2bn (25 per cent of the world's population) and average annual growth of 8.7 per cent provided the background for the World Bank's forecast that the Chinese Economic Area (China, Hong Kong and Taiwan) would become the world's largest absolute economy by 2005. The change in living standards has been pronounced, as Table 1.2 shows.

Table 1.2 CONSUMER DURABLES PER 100 URBAN HOUSEHOLDS, 1981–94

	Colour TV	Washing Machine	Refrigerator
1981	0.59	6.34	0.22
1991	68.41	80.52	48.70
1994	86.21	87.29	62.10

Although the growth figures and other economic and business data are to be treated with some caution (errors and omissions are higher in China than in developed economies), there is no doubt that the economy has started on the road to rapid growth and is catching up with developed countries.

A comparison of China with other centrally-planned economies can be misleading. Unlike the former Soviet Union (FSU) and other East European countries, China introduced reforms much earlier, with major policy changes starting in 1978. State-owned enterprises (SOEs) experience low growth, whilst TVEs (Township, Village Enterprises) and private companies provide the engine for growth. About 10 per cent of SOEs are unofficially bankrupt, kept afloat by subsidies or taken over by other SOEs. Provinces have been provided with increased autonomy, which has resulted in an increase in the discrepancies that exist between the poor and the rich regions of China. Government income has declined, with a high dependency on VAT and with only two per cent of households liable to pay income tax, a situation that means that a safety net to cope with possible increases in unemployment caused by failing SOEs and increases in poverty in some regions has proved difficult to put in place.

A strong economic performance, with increasing consumer affluence, is matched by a rise in inequality. What foreign companies react to is the large market potential and rising affluence and expectations that China offers.

Fedders, an American manufacturer of air-conditioning units, identified China as a target market, particularly as its climate suggests that demand could be high for a compact version that the company specialised in. Fedders had constraints in its own domestic market, particularly the seasonal nature of demand and the perception that the market has reached maturity.

Selecting a market in Asia meant narrowing options down, with the final choice resting between China, India and Indonesia. China was chosen as the best option, as sales had grown from 500 000 units in 1990 to 4m in 1995, making it a market that equalled that of America and with huge growth potential.

Identifying market potential is the first step, and a relatively painless one, on the road to market entry. China, with its unique administrative and business structures, is a difficult market to enter, a fact that may account for the relatively low level of US FDI ($2.5bn in 1994, compared to Hong Kong's $20bn). Fedders's strategy can be summarised as follows.

- Recruitment of 20 speakers of Mandarin (the official language), many of whom were American citizens born and educated in China. The recruits were to be employed in all of the functional areas of the company.

- A local partner, Ningbo General Air-Conditioning Factory, was selected. (It was also looking for a partner to help expand output.) Ningbo had moved to a Special Economic Zone (SEZ), and had opened sales offices in the main cities, established a repair and service centre network and created a brand name – Xinte. The company had few debts and a workforce of 500, a great benefit given problems of overmanning in many Chinese companies.

- Agreement was reached on a joint venture with the goal to boost Ningbo's production to 500 000 within three years, half of which would be exported, a key factor given Fedders's aim to exploit the growth centres in Asia.

The joint venture would be responsible for sales outside China, whilst Fedders would handle all the exports.

Establishing the joint venture was an important event, but then both sides had to understand the other's operation, systems and philosophy. Visits were made by all the senior managers of Fedders to China (accompanied by the original Mandarin-speaking recruits), while Ningbo employees visited the American operation.

Gaining the support of the political authorities is important in many emerging markets, and in this case the regional government gave its support, an important factor in finalising a bank loan, dealing with legal issues and building a network of contacts. Fedders had to take responsibility for all existing employees in China and provide them with housing if required, a major advantage for central and regional government given the problems of providing a safety net mentioned earlier.

Market potential and sorting out joint venture arrangements do not solve the marketing problem. Could the same product be sold in China as in America? Would it flatter the market to be given the most up-to-date model on the American market? The answer to these questions was 'no'. Unlike America, where an air-conditioner is a minor item of purchase, in China it is seen as a major purchase. Therefore, only the most up-to-date model would be required, and it would be subject to a great deal of scrutiny as a major housing item.

The product specification for the Chinese market would be of a split-type, with the fan inside the room and the heat exchanger mounted on the outside wall. This is not a product favoured in America and was not produced by Fedders. A new product for the new market was required.

From the summer to November of 1995 – the initial contact through to the signing of the agreement to create the joint venture, now known as Fedders Xinte (60 per cent owned by Fedders) – was a record for setting up a new organisation.

Suppliers to the company are being encouraged to supply to quality standards, a possible benefit to Fedders in America, as these companies could supply parts more cheaply than their American counterparts, and a benefit to the regional Chinese economy.

Questions

1 *Emerging markets such as China present business opportunities. What difficulties arise if these markets are assumed to operate in similar ways?*

2 *What factors could impede the growth potential of countries such as China?*

3 *Could the strategy adopted by Fedders be copied by other companies?*

4 *Many companies enter markets with existing products. What danger exists with this approach?*

FURTHER READING

Brookes, M., *Measuring World GDP* (London: Goldman Sachs, 1994).

Calori, R. and Lawrence, P., *The Business of Europe* (New York: Sage, 1992).

Daniels, D. and Radebaugh, D., *International Business*, 6th edition (Reading, MA: Addison-Wesley, 1994).

Daniels, J.L. and Daniels, N.C., *Global Vision* (New York: McGraw-Hill, 1993).

Dicken, P., *Global Shift: Industrial Change in a Turbulent World* (New York: Harper & Row, 1986).

Halliburton, C. and Hunerberg, R., 'Pan-European marketing – myth or reality?' in Halliburton, C. and Hunderberg, R. (eds), *European Marketing: Reading and Cases* (Addison-Wesley, 1993).

Hamel, G. and Prahalad, C., *Competing for the Future* (Cambridge, MA: Harvard Business School Press, 1994).

Levitt T., 'The globalization of markets', *Harvard Business Review* (May–June 1983), 92–102.

Ohmae, K., *Borderless World* (London: Collins, 1990).

NOTES AND REFERENCES

1   Douglas, S.P. and Craig, C.S., *Global Marketing Strategy* (New York: McGraw-Hill, 1995).

2   Ogden, C., 'Second thoughts on globalisation', *Time* (February 1996); Flanders, S., 'Mr Buchanan's history lessons', *Financial Times* (19 February 1996).

3   For a fuller review of NAFTA, refer to Chapter 5 on the Economic environment.

4   Douglas, T., 'GWR must be wary of the traps waiting for foreign adventurers', *Marketing Week* (19 February 1996); 'The world that changed the machine', *The Economist* (30 March 1996).

5   'Heineken finds their true global brew', *Financial Times* (7 February 1996); 'Barriers fall to import invaders', *Financial Times* (19 March 1996).

6   'Murati's wager', *The Economist* (2 March 1996); 'Shaken but not stirred', *The Economist* (16 March 1996); 'Bangalore bytes', *The Economist* (23 March 1996).

7   Hill, C.W.L., *International Business: Competing in the Global Marketplace*, international student edition (Homewood, IL: Irwin, 1994).

8   'American banks muscle in on the British technology market', *The Times* (30 July 1997); 'Large UK bookstores to compete on-line with US sites', *Financial Times* (30 July 1997).

9   'Reducing the debt burden', *Financial Times* (4 March 1996); 'No more cosy backyards', *Financial Times* (7 March 1996); 'Investing in South Africa', *Financial Times* (28 March 1996).

10 Majaro, S., *International Marketing* (London: George Allen & Unwin, 1982).

11 Yip, G.S., 'Global strategy . . . in a world of nations' in Mintzberg, H., Quinn, J.B. and Ghoshal, S., *The Strategy Process*, European edition (Englewood Cliffs, NJ: Prentice-Hall, 1995), 716–26.

12 Millington, A. and Bayliss, B., 'Corporate integration and market liberalisation in the EU', *European Management Journal*, 14(2) (April 1996), 139–50.

13 Collins, R. and Schmenner, R., 'Taking advantage of Europe's single market', *European Management Journal*, 13(3) (September 1995), 257–68.

14 Czinkota, M.R. and Ronkainen, I.A., *International Marketing,* 3rd edition (Orlando: The Dryden Press, 1993).

15 Management Brief: 'Keeping cool in China', *The Economist* (16 April 1997); Goodhard, C. and Xu, C., 'The rising power of China', *National Institute Economy Review* (February 1996), 155; 'Doing business in China', Ernst & Young (1994).

2

Theories of the firm in global markets

INTRODUCTION

What gains can come to a nation from international trade? At a time when many nations are seeking to band together in economic and political groupings, most notably in the EU, and when writers such as Ohmae[1] have raised questions on the relevance of the nation-state in an integrated global market place, this would appear to be a problem to be relegated to the pages of history. Of seemingly greater importance would be what makes for a successful firm or region, and what strategies and supporting mechanisms need to be in place to assist the firm in its endeavours?

However, the nation-state is far from dead. Areas such as the Basque region in Spain may wish to become independent, and there are calls for complete independence in Scotland, but these are historic battles between a people who feel themselves to be culturally different from the rest of those who comprise the nation-state, and this tends to reinforce the perception that the nation-state matters. Whatever its long-term future, the political and economic influence will be felt for some time to come, so that reviewing the benefits that accrue to a nation from international trade is a meaningful question, and likewise how far the macroeconomic, microeconomic and business policies of a particular government can assist in creating a favourable environment for such trade to take place.

This chapter provides a review of the benefits to be gained from trade, along with an examination of the competitive position of the firm that brings into focus international marketing as a key factor, looking as it does at socioeconomic change, and the risk and environmental influences that tend to be overlooked or downgraded in many of the theories on international trade.

Objectives

This chapter will examine:

- trade and foreign direct investment theories
- global marketing theories.

TRADE AND FOREIGN DIRECT INVESTMENT THEORIES

Pattern of trade

Looking at the pattern of trade in the world economy it is easy to explain why countries such as Russia export gas and oil, as these are part of their natural resources. However, the majority of trade is not so easy to explain. Why has, for example, the Swiss economy built up exports of chemicals, pharmaceuticals and confectionery, whilst South Korea has exported cars, ships and semiconductors?[2] It is certainly clear that these countries benefit from these exports and many countries turn to them as the main suppliers of these products, but what factors account for their advantages in these industries? A number of theories have been constructed to explain these different patterns of trade and generally they all agree that open or free trade is beneficial for all countries. What they fail to agree on is the significance of these theories for government policy.[3]

Absolute advantage

In *The Wealth of Nations*, Adam Smith argued that the wealth of a country consists of the goods and services available to its citizens. Smith developed the theory of *absolute advantage*, which holds that different countries can produce some goods more efficiently than others. Based on this theory, the question can be posed as to why the citizens of a country should have to purchase domestically produced goods when they could be obtained more cheaply from a country that was more efficient in their production. If trade was unrestricted, each country would operate in those areas where it held absolute advantage, with resources moving to those industries where this applied. Absolute advantage may arise because of differences in factors such as climate, quality of land, natural resources, labour, capital, technology or entrepreneurship. The extent of the benefits of specialisation and trade will depend on the prices at which this takes place. (These issues are taken further in Box 2.1.)

The problem arises when a country has absolute advantage in, say, two products which means that trade will fail to take place in these products.

Comparative advantage

An alternative explanation to absolute advantage is *comparative advantage*; this seeks to deal with the problem of what happens when a country has absolute advantage so that no trade need take place. David Ricardo argued that there are global efficiency gains from trade if a country specialises in those products that it can produce more efficiently than other products, without regard to absolute advantage.

| Box 2.1 | THEORY OF ABSOLUTE AND COMPARATIVE ADVANTAGE |

Absolute advantage

Absolute advantage exists when a country has a cost advantage over another in the production of a product, i.e. fewer resources are used in its production. Equally, a second country has a cost advantage compared to the first in a second product. Using this two-country with two-product example, it is clear that trade and the consequent specialisation by the two

▶ **Box 2.1 continued**

countries will bring benefits when one country has an absolute advantage over another in the production of one product. If both countries focus on the production of the product for which they possess absolute advantage, then output will rise and trade will commence.

The absolute advantage theme also looks at the issue as to why costs differ between nations. According to this theory, costs differ because productivity of factor inputs, especially labour, represents the major determinant of production costs in different countries. Productivity is based on both natural and acquired advantages, with the former being obtained from the benefits of climate, soil and minerals, and the latter looking at the skills and knowledge of the workforce. With both natural and acquired advantages, a nation would produce an item at lower costs than its actual (or potential) trading partners who did not possess the same advantages.

Comparative advantage

The theory of comparative advantage was developed by David Ricardo in the nineteenth century, springing from the theory of absolute advantage as developed by Adam Smith. The theory states that nations should produce those goods for which they have the greatest relative or comparative advantage.

To see how this works, an example using just two nations producing two products will reveal the benefits of specialisation. (The theory can apply to more than just two nations and two products.)

Countries A and B are capable of producing clothing and wheat. In this example, country A has an absolute advantage in the production of both clothing and wheat, as seen from Table 2.1.

Table 2.1 LABOUR COSTS OF PRODUCTION OF ONE UNIT, HOURS

	Clothing	Wheat
Country A	50	100
Country B	200	200

From this it would seem that trade for Country A would be unprofitable, as it is apparently much more efficient in all aspects of production. However, according to the theory of comparative advantage it is still advantageous for trade to take place between the two countries, as long as the relative costs of production differ.

In Country A, 1 unit of clothing costs (50/100) hours of wheat, so 1 unit of clothing can be exchanged for 0.5 unit of wheat. In Country A, the price of clothing is therefore half the price of wheat. In Country B, on the other hand, 1 unit of clothing costs (200/200) hours of wheat or 1 wheat unit. In other words, the price of clothing equals the price of wheat. If Country A engages in trade and imports more than 0.5 unit of wheat for 1 unit of clothing, it will gain from this exchange. Likewise, if Country B imports 1 unit of clothing for less than 1 unit of wheat, it will also be a beneficiary of such trade.

The relative price ratio determines the parameters of trade, so that trade is profitable between price ratios (price of clothing to price of wheat) of 0.5 and 1. Thus, at a price ratio of two-thirds, Country A gains as it can import 1 unit of wheat in return for exporting 1.5 units of clothing. This is the case as it costs Country A 50 hours of labour to produce the

▶

▶ **Box 2.1 continued**

clothing, its effective cost with trade for 1 unit of imported wheat is 75 labour hours. Before trade, it costs Country *A* 100 hours to produce the wheat.

For Country *B*, it would import 1 unit of clothing in exchange for two-thirds of grain; prior to this, Country *B* would have spent 200 hours to produce clothing. Through trade its effective cost of one unit of cloth is 133 hours, i.e. two-thirds of 200, which is cheaper than was possible prior to trade.

From this example, Country *A* will specialise in clothing, while Country *B* will specialise in wheat.

The assumptions made by the theory of comparative advantage are reviewed in the main text, but the most critical feature is that free trade is possible between the two nations, thereby promoting the abolition of trade barriers to the benefit of all countries. With this scenario it makes little sense for countries to erect barriers to trade as this saddles them with industries that are inefficient and hinders those that could take advantage of the opportunity that trade offers.

It would seem from the longevity of this theory and the support it receives from free-market economists, plus research that suggests that the basic proposition is supported by data, that the case for unlimited free trade is unanswerable.

However, once the assumptions are dropped then problems start to emerge that make the theory rather harder to support in practice. For example, the problem of just what is a restriction to free trade is less than clear. Are, for example, environmental controls, imposed by a developed country that stops the import of timber from countries failing to provide sustainable forests, a valid restriction or not? Likewise, is the insistence by developed countries that fridges and air-conditioning units that use refrigerent with CFCs that destroy the ozone layer, but that happen to be used in the production of fridges by the developing countries, a justifiable restriction, or one that protects the developed countries' interests? The theory of comparative advantage supports free international trade, but in no way identifies how it can be achieved.

Box 2.1 gives an example of how comparative advantage provides benefits to both countries and through them to the global economy. The comparative advantage theory is based on a set of assumptions that can be listed as follows.

1 *Full employment.* Both theories of absolute and comparative advantage assume that all resources are fully employed. When countries fail to find themselves in this position, i.e. they suffer from unemployment of the factors of production, then the pressure is on to restrict imports in order to deal with the problem.

2 *Economic efficiency.* Countries may wish to pursue objectives other than those based on pure economic efficiency. Comparative advantage may make countries vulnerable in times of conflict, so some industries may be protected as they are counted as too important for the welfare/survival of the country, despite the fact that other countries possess clear advantages.

3 *Transport costs.* Both the theories of absolute and relative advantage fail to take into account the cost of moving commodities or products from one country to another. In fact, this problem does not invalidate the theory, as a high cost for a low-value, high-volume product would necessitate local production, i.e. the benefits of trade are made redundant.

4 *Mobility of the factors of production*. The theories assume that the factors of land, labour and capital are free to move to the next best use. However, in reality, this is difficult as structural unemployment, for example, shows workers moving out of one job with certain skills, but then failing to find employment as their skills are inappropriate to the new circumstances. Equally, movement of labour between regions is not as fluid as certain economic models would suggest, leaving pockets of high employment.

5 *Marketing*. A key development of the twentieth century has been the attempt by firms to differentiate their products in the market place, which means that products are not standard and therefore not transferable between one country and another. This means that trade theories, such as the theory of comparative advantage, fail to take account of the role of the firm in determining the production of goods and services within a country.

Heckscher–Ohlin theory of factor proportions

One of the areas of weakness of the Smith and Ricardo theories lies in the difficulty of the identification of the types of products that would provide a country with an advantage. The theory, as reviewed in Box 2.1, considers the issues by looking at two countries and two products. Although this explanation is justified on the grounds of clarity, the real world provides a much more complex picture of trade, involving many countries and businesses.

In the 1930s Heckscher and Ohlin developed the factor–proportions or factor endowment theory which stated that differences in countries' endowment of labour relative to their endowment of land and capital could explain differences in factor costs. The Heckscher–Ohlin theory predicts that countries will export those goods that make intensive use of the factors that are available, while they import goods that make intensive use of factors that they find scarce. In a similar way to Ricardo's theory, this theory supports the idea of free trade, but unlike Ricardo it focuses on factor endowments rather than production.

Many international economists prefer the Heckscher–Ohlin theory as it makes fewer simplifying assumptions. Despite this, however, empirical tests undertaken in the 1950s by Wassily Leontief cast some doubts on its validity. According to the theory, the USA, as a country with abundant capital compared to other nations, should have been an exporter of capital-intensive goods and an importer of labour-intensive goods. In fact the USA was found to export fewer capital-intensive goods than it imported. This presented a paradox, which became known as the Leontief Paradox. Various explanations for this exist, but it has not been successfully resolved. One such explanation is that the USA had advantages in the production of new products or goods produced with innovative technologies. Products of this nature could well be less capital-intensive than products whose technology has had time to mature and become part of a 'mass-production' approach. So the USA could be exporting goods that contain a large amount of skilled labour, while importing goods that use large amounts of capital. This leads back to the Ricardo theory that looks at trade from a productivity angle and seems to be able to predict trade flows better than the factor endowment theory.

Foreign direct investment theories

Trade occurs according to some trade theories because of differences in factor endowments between and amongst countries. However, production factors can also move from one country to another, so making factor movement an alternative to trade.

From the point of view of the firm, it often starts with a home base, limiting itself to its local or national market. As firms grow and mature they look for new opportunities and as part of this process look at the benefits to be gained from international trade. Many influences can come to bear on the firm to spur on this search, from the interest of key managers through to major transformation of the external environment such as the emerging markets of Eastern Europe.

What matters here is not the opportunities that present themselves, but how the firm responds to them. This leads to an analysis of the advantages that firms possess compared to competitors in other countries, so that the competitive advantage gained from product differentiation, brand names and trade marks, marketing skills as well as production economies are all exploitable advantages.

The choice is then open to the firm as to how this can be done. Figure 2.1 shows the possibilities open to the firm in its decision on what options to take. It is clear that this provides opportunities greater than just investment in production opportunities abroad and, as Box 2.2 outlines, the management of a company will try to retain flexibility in its decision whatever the method of entry to a new (foreign) market.

Fig 2.1 THE FIRM'S OPTIONS

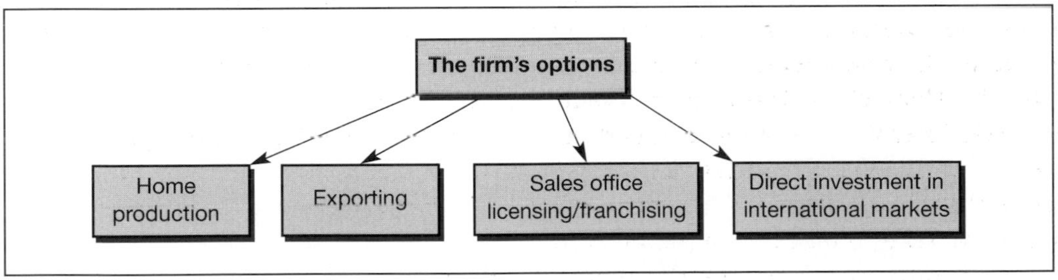

Source: Adapted from Buckley, A. and Tse, K., 'Real operating options and foreign direct investment: a synthetic approach', *European Management Journal*, 14(3) (1996).

Box 2.2

FOREIGN EXPANSION BY FDI[4]

Countries compete with each other to attract foreign direct investment. Indeed, all of the world's 209 countries will attempt to sell themselves to companies who wish to expand their activities. Whether the benefits outweigh the potential drawbacks of this type of investment is the subject of much debate, but this has not stopped the race to attract investment. Whether the country is prosperous such as Canada, or one of the emerging markets such as Romania, the desire is there to attract funds.

In Canada, IKEA, which first started operating in 1976, has annual sales exceeding $300m, and as with many companies approaching the North American market for the first time, chose Canada as a stepping stone into the US market. A similar tactic was used by the company in Europe, with entry into the Swiss market being the forerunner to entry to the much larger German market.

▶

▶ **Box 2.2 continued**

This tactic of entry to a market that in the Canadian case had as high a standard of living as the Scandinavian market, but which gave opportunities to establish a presence in North America whilst learning how the market operated in both that country and the USA, helped the managers of IKEA adapt, where necessary, to the new circumstances and helped reduce the risk associated with such investment. This is an example of good management, as policies were pursued that maintained flexibility whilst reducing risk.

When it comes to investment decisions, this means keeping open the opportunities to make decisions contingent on information becoming available over a period of time. International investment often begins with a small commitment which can be scaled up if circumstances warrant it or curtailed if the market presents a less attractive option than the next best use of investment monies.

Many FDI approaches follow a sequential model that moves from exporting, to a foreign sales subsidiary (or licensing agreement), then moving eventually to investment in production facilities.

The sequential (and incremental) approach has a number of shortcomings. Progress from one stage to another is not fully understood, whilst the approach itself is uni-directional and cannot explain the many examples of divestment or reorientation. Many companies also leap-frog stages. What is certain is that any one stage, say exporting, brings with it risks and uncertainties, and managers will seek to retain flexibility.

According to Buckley and Tse the ability to change tactical direction in response to new information can contribute significantly to value, and such flexibility has to be given due weight at the quantitative appraisal stage. Using pure discounted cash flow (DCF) techniques often takes a static approach to investment appraisal, with the result that single outturn, non-option-oriented DCF analysis is unable to accommodate the tactical flexibility which good managers try to keep open.

Work has been undertaken to try to account for the options that FDI has associated with it. In other words, the decision-making organisation should endeavour to choose a mode of entry and develop an internationalisation strategy which maximises the firm's net present value (NPV) inclusive of real operating options.

The sequential model might imply that all firms would seek to start with exporting, but this on further analysis would not apply to multinationals, who may already possess enough experience of international operations to go directly to FDI. Others may find exporting inappropriate given the nature of their business. IKEA, for example, would have to consider the mode of entry so that its presence was immediately known in a market, rather than simply exporting its merchandise.

FDI can always be reversed, and in many circumstances this has been forced on companies, such as was seen for UK retail bankers in the US market, or part of a reappraisal of operations that involves pulling out of all or certain national markets.

Host countries could pursue a policy of seeking to get multinationals to turn operating options into actual investments by lowering risk factors, such as political risk, that reduces the uncertainty factor. On its own, this would not bring forward investment, as market decisions will be based on the potential profitability of such a move.

For the firm new to international markets, the sequential route would be the preferred approach, on the grounds of risk aversion, having a reversible position and learning how a market operates. For the multinational, with an approach based on NPV maximixation, the sequential approach will not make much business sense. Such a firm may prefer FDI as it may obtain the greatest benefit after this has taken place.

> ▶ **Box 2.2 continued**
>
> Understanding the external constraints on action, such as legal requirements, as well as internal constraints, such as risk aversion, experience, information quality and so on, assists with the appreciation of what unlocks FDI. As has been outlined here, for many firms this approach is not an option, but for firms experienced in the international sphere, or whose very business operations promote FDI, then the appeal of certain countries for establishing operations becomes part of the flow of information that will help to influence the outcome.
>
> In a similar vein, the reversibility of an internationalisation strategy is a situation that many firms will keep open. Here again, understanding the reasons why this happens could also help to explain the flow of global FDI. IKEA's experience both in Western Europe and then Canada is a useful case study in appreciating how managers make decisions of this nature.

Market imperfections, therefore, even assuming that a firm constantly surveys the possibilities open to it, do determine the outcome.

One aspect of investment theory focuses on the firm's desire or incentive to create its own internal markets whenever transactions can be undertaken at a lower cost within it. So the firm may extend direct operations to include all those activities carried out to link the firm to its customers. Location of production in foreign markets can provide transaction advantages, thereby retaining in-house the benefits built up over many years. For example, the use of a firm's R&D by others who may license the product dilutes the benefit to the originator, bringing with it a loss of direct contact.

This approach can explain a motive for direct investment in international markets, but reduces the complexity of the decision process and offers little insight into why firms may disinvest.

FDI theories can help to explain which firms can go international, either because of comparative advantage or to retain the benefits in-house. The theory of international production looks at the issue of where foreign production takes place by looking at location theory and theories of international production. For example, Bradley[5] outlines an eclectic theory that looks at the propensity of a firm to participate in foreign production, being (partially) dependent on locational attractions of its home country's endowment compared to those offered by other locations. Resources here would involve technology, management and entrepreneurial skills as well as the factors of land, capital and labour. Three groups of factors – resource differentials, governmental actions and the characteristics of the business – determine the way in which a firm plays a part in the international exchange of resources. Here we see a major role allocated to governments in influencing, but not determining, business patterns via resource differential and entry conditions, an issue followed up in Boxes 2.3 and 2.4.

Box 2.3   FOREIGN DIRECT INVESTMENT[6]

The globalisation of financial markets has meant that capital can move to those countries that offer the highest returns. Capital crosses borders more easily than labour, so the impact of domestic policy in attracting capital will have a major impact on labour.

In the *World Development Report* of 1995, the World Bank put forward three questions related to capital movement and its effect on labour. First, how can developing and transitional economies (i.e. those moving from a command-style economy to a market-based one) attract more private capital? Second, what can policy makers do to maximise the benefits for workers and minimise the risks? Third, could private capital flowing out of rich countries hurt workers there?

Although the *World Development Report* looks at capital flows in total, which includes both bank lending and FDI, as noted in Chapter 5 the trend has been towards FDI as markets open up due to the effect of the GATT agreements and the move from state control and planning. This has been followed by portfolio investment and bond insurance.

According to the World Bank, capital holders, when assessing the risk of an investment, look for certain favourable conditions. These are good infrastructure, a reliable and skilled workforce, guarantees of the right to repatriate income and capital, and social and political stability. Of course, these conditions are met in different ways and can themselves beg many questions. For example, a reliable and skilled workforce needs to be reviewed carefully, looking at strike records, trade union attitudes, absenteeism, basic literacy, advanced technical skills or access to training. Additionally, the World Bank also includes as key issues for the inward investor, government fiscal policy over a period of time and links with global markets that the country has built up. If the country and its workers are to benefit from this investment, then it is the economic fundamentals that count more than the protection of a market place.

If the above answers the first question on attracting capital, what about the second and third questions on the maximisation of the benefits to workers of such investment and the effect of capital outflows on workers in rich countries? Answering the first of these, the World Bank proposes that although capital outflows are always possible, there are a number of actions that can assist with reducing the risk. The first of these is assuring that governments keep publicly owned external debt as low as possible, putting the burden on private borrowers, rather than taxpayers. This, therefore, implies that financial markets need to be at a stage of development where they are efficient in their operations. Lastly, governments should also look to the exchange rate, interest rates and foreign currency reserves that can deter sudden outflows – or, if they happen, manage the effect.

Will the flow of funds from developed to developing countries harm workers in the former? The picture is complex, especially so when looking at a country such as the UK.

In the 10 years to 1995, the UK had obtained £150bn ($232bn) of direct investment, three times the level of a decade earlier. In 1995, £10bn of total investment found its way to the UK, but £15bn was invested abroad by UK citizens. (A situation typical of the country for the last decade, making it one of the major creditor nations.)

Taking the UK as an example reveals that it is not only flows of capital from rich to poor that count. All countries are in the game of attracting investment to boost employment, bring in new skills and even revive or establish new industries. The reasons why investors choose to invest are comparatively low labour rates, flexible employment conditions, and membership of the EU and hence access to the Single Market (not all of these factors play an equal role and each investment decision is reached after the appraisal of

▶ **Box 2.3 continued**

many factors). According to government statistics, 800 000 jobs have been created or safe-guarded since 1979, with around half of the output of overseas-owned manufacturers being exported, producing a contribution of over £700m a year to UK trade. Figures 2.2 and 2.3 provide overviews of the countries investing and the sectors and approaches used.

Fig 2.2 WHERE THE INVESTMENT IS COMING FROM (1995)

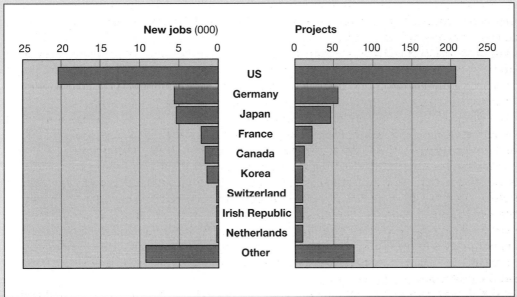

Source: 'Inward investment into the UK', *Financial Times* (18 July 1996), IBB Data.

Fig 2.3 THE FAVOURED SECTORS AND APPROACHES (1995)

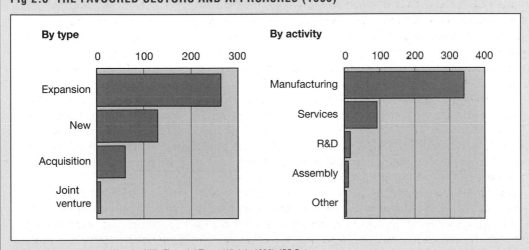

Source: 'Inward investment into the UK', *Financial Times* (18 July 1996), IBB Data.

> ▶ **Box 2.3 continued**

Have workers benefited from this? Arguments against the investment revolve round the following points:

- cheap labour costs attract foreign investment, revealing the UK to be a low-pay economy
- international capital is taking advantage of the reduction in employee protection
- FDI is the government's only solution to a persistently high level of unemployment
- many investments concern themselves with assembling and basic manufacturing techniques, making the UK a 'sweatshop' economy
- tax breaks and financial incentives attract FDI and mean that other 'local' investors are discriminated against.

Countering these accusations, the agencies involved in attracting investors, such as the Invest in Britain Bureau, provide counter-arguments or stress other factors. Again, these can be summarised as follows:

- many of the investments of the 1990s are capital-intensive, with wage rates making up no more than 5–10 per cent of costs, focusing attention on the flexibility of labour; this has also been assisted by non-union agreements
- low corporate tax, at 33 per cent compared to Germany's 45 per cent, attracts investors
- many aspects of activity requiring high skill levels have been attracted, such as design and R&D
- advanced transport and telecommunications links, as well as the significance of the advanced nature of financial markets, help to interest investors
- firms who invest, such as Japan's Fujitsu, are often inclined to increase their investment by further expansion
- many foreign-owned firms pay wages at a higher level than the norm for a region; they also provide a platform for suppliers to match standards of the world's best.

The picture is even more mixed when consideration is given to the net outflow of capital from the UK that has been seen for the last two decades. What is a complex picture for the UK is perhaps simpler for developing countries who wish to attract investment. Capital outflows that occur because a country has failed to get the balance right are always a possibility. A failure of this sort could take a country out of the economic mainstream altogether, with disastrous consequences.

Global integration can be felt in the movement of funds to those locations that offer benefits to the investor. The potential for gains, particularly for developing countries, is enormous. Countries such as South Korea, and now Malaysia and Indonesia, have begun to catch up with the developed countries. But divergence has been the role for most developing countries, and continues to be so. However, those that have sought to increase the international competitiveness of their economies rather than protect them, along with investment in training and education, infrastructure, etc., have boosted their chances of catching up with the rich.

All countries face the same challenge laid down by global integration. Whether rich or poor, the effort to create the right conditions affects them all.

| Box 2.4 | INTERNATIONAL COMPETITIVENESS[7] |

Looking at a country's competitiveness in selected industries is often undertaken on the basis of a trade-based measure, such as revealed competitive advantage. However, this may be too limited a view given that many companies license or franchise production to other firms in other countries, as well as participating in joint ventures or setting up production in other (international) markets. International production is often greater than exporting for many products in developed countries – so, for example, foreign production by US firms in the food industry is estimated to be four times higher than exports, while UK estimates suggest that exports and foreign products are of equal value.

Research undertaken in six EU countries reveals that between 1978 and 1991 exports of manufactured food products from these countries grew by 177 per cent while FDI grew by 320 per cent.

Looking at competitiveness at the industrial sector level rather than focusing on national competitiveness helps to provide insight into what policies may be enacted by government to promote that sector, by help on R&D, regulatory regimes and the most appropriate institutional structures. Governments and the business community tend to take a trade-based approach to sector competitiveness, so that if a sector has a trade deficit, i.e. it imports more than it exports, then it is deemed uncompetitive. However, this approach fails to take account of the activities of Multinational Enterprises (MNEs) and how their activities affect a country's welfare. Researchers in this area have tried to incorporate the work of MNEs – Dunning (1977) has defined a country's competitiveness as '... the ability to supply its own and other country's markets through its own firms, wherever they are located'. Ownership is the defining feature, and location given no significance. This gives rise to foreign production of a country's MNEs being of equal value to imports. Traill and da Silva (1996) argue that competitiveness is a dynamic concept, and if firms gain dynamic advantages from overseas production this may translate into growth in profits returned to domestic shareholders. This in turn produces other advantages associated with innovation and improving efficiency.

This approach is paradoxical for governments who wish to see both foreign MNEs located in the country and see their own 'home' MNEs pursue a successful strategy for growth in international markets. This paradox could be reconciled by the benefits of foreign MNEs in bringing improved management techniques, raising efficiency and diffusing technology to the host country – a benefit recognised by the World Bank. Success for home MNEs overseas means accepting their need to expand foreign production at the expense of domestic production.

When reviewing the trade balance and foreign production of food products for European countries, Traill and da Silva provide the following assessment.

● *France*. Since 1980, trade-based measures have remained stable, while foreign production measures are growing. Since 1986, the first year of the Single Market programme in Europe, there has been rapid growth, indicating that French-owned firms are competing well internationally.

● *Germany*. Here, the country is stronger in trade than in foreign production. However, since the early 1990s the country has experienced a decline in both areas, indicating that it is losing exports and internal production competitiveness relative to other sectors of the economy.

▶

> ▶ **Box 2.4 continued**

● *Italy*. The level of indices that take foreign production into account are generally higher than the trade indices, but recently the trend has been downwards. Italy appears, though, to be a good location for foreign firms as they have located there in some number.

● *UK*. The country has a negative trade balance in food products, with little improvement in export performance noted since the Single European Market programme commenced. However, the inclusion of foreign production shows that British firms are strong performers relative to firms in other countries. Nevertheless, they are holding their position, not improving it.

Analysing the outcomes of this assessment raises many questions for decision makers in the four countries. For the UK, the trade deficit in food products which has been further worsened by the 'mad cow disease' scare has not been closed, which begs questions such as why imports have been able to gain market share and why exporters or potential exporters have seemingly made little headway. Furthermore, although UK firms have done well in terms of foreign production, why has this position remained static? Likewise for Italy and Germany, the erosion of their positions raises issues that policy makers can review. France, although the most successful of the four, is also required to appraise its performance in order to guarantee success.

International competitiveness in the global economy, with increasing integration, can be seen in the traditional sense of export (import) performance or can view MNEs as key players in that they bring with them benefit for their home base.

Likewise, the return to foreign factors of production obtained when foreign MNEs locate in a political territory should not be overlooked, particularly when the subsidiaries of such MNEs are not looked at as subservient but as equal partners within the company.

Where the sources of competitive advantage spring from or how competitiveness can be improved is a major area of investigation. Using trade as well as foreign production information provides a more dynamic overview of the situation facing a particular country.

Product cycles

The theory of product life cycle put forward by Vernon and Wells[8] argues that some products move through the stages of introduction, growth, maturity and decline. This is a familiar explanation of the cycle of events that will happen eventually to all products, but here it is used to explain how production will move location as each stage is reached. The theory assists in explaining why a product that starts out as an export can quite often end up being imported at some later stage.

Before reviewing each stage in the cycle, it is worth keeping in mind the two parts of the theory that Rugman and Hodgetts emphasise:[9]

1 that technology is a crucial factor in creating and developing new products;

2 that market size and structure are important elements that determine trade patterns.

Introduction phase

New products develop as new needs are identified in the home market. This in itself would not suggest the geographic location of production, but as the majority of products are developed for the 'home' market, the location is determined initially by transport costs and the needs of the market for speed of response. This stage is dominated by the industrialised countries and despite the impressive economic performance of Pacific Rim economies, their success is often built on efficient production of existing products. To be ahead of the field, industrialised countries need to develop innovative products and take them successfully through the introductory phase.

Growth

After a successful launch of a product, sales grow and competitors see their chance to enter the market and gain advantages for themselves. It is at this stage that opportunities for exporting are identified. From preceding discussions on the decisions facing managers at this stage, it is not clear that the exporting route is the necessarily preferred option, but by far the majority of companies will take this route. This could be for a number of complex reasons, such as high start-up costs, lack of economies of scale and the further development of process technology that can greatly increase efficiency in the home production base. These internal production issues can also be joined by adaptations or innovations to the product to suit local market needs.

Maturity

As with the traditional product life cycle, this stage is governed by cost considerations as total sales may grow only slowly, although there will be variations on a world-wide basis. As other competitors have also tended to successfully mimic production techniques and also understand the characteristics of the market, profitable opportunities are reduced. At this stage some producers leave the market as profitable opportunities become harder to find, leaving the market more standardised with product types.

Longer production runs for foreign-located plants become possible, especially as maintaining a location in a developed country loses its allure as production advantages have been eaten away. The advantage of location in a developing country increases at this stage.

Decline

At this stage, markets decline in the developed countries as new products take the place of old. For the remaining demand, the source of production will now come from abroad, bringing in cheap imports of the original product.

The product life cycle theory is, therefore, an attempt to explain the phenomenon of a country losing the advantages of production and export opportunities and seemingly suffering from a reversal in fortunes as imports of the product become a reality.

Limitations of the product life cycle theory

For all its plausibility, the theory has some notable limitations. It can explain how certain consumer durables and electronic goods come to be produced in developing economies and exported to developed economies, but it is a simplification of a very complex picture and has difficulty in taking account of the shortened product life cycle's seen in many industries. This can be observed in many electronic products, where constant improvements and innovations mean that improved models are introduced every six months.

Other limitations apply, for example for luxury products, where cost (price) is of little consequence to the consumer. Also for many goods transportation costs may prohibit export whatever the stage reached; marketing can increase product differentiation that reduces the importance of price; technical knowledge possessed by the workforce can enable a company to move from present production of a product to the introduction of the next generation of products.

Further challenges to the product life cycle theory can be envisaged. Production could be moved abroad due to the concerns felt about the exclusion from a key market. Many in the USA and Japan felt that the EU would turn into a protected trade area,[10] thereby excluding firms from one of the richest markets. As a consequence of this firms from both countries decided to locate in Europe. The role of South Korean and Taiwanese companies in locating in the UK market suggests that instead of just an export phase for developing economies there is a further stage as these economies mature and they look to establish a presence in developed markets, as Samsung and others have done in the UK and elsewhere.

Lastly, the development of global products, where the product is launched in the home and foreign markets at the same time, suggests that global rather than multi-domestic strategies are being pursued. The rise of trading blocs such as NAFTA, providing locational advantages for US companies in Mexico, shows that a location may be chosen purely for production purposes rather than for its growing market (although both could apply in the case of Mexico).

The product life cycle does not deal with the key strategy issue of why firms invest abroad, rather than take other options such as licensing or franchising.

New trade theory

This theory, which was first put forward in the 1970s, looks at the benefits of economies of scale and the increasing returns to scale obtained by specialisation, rather than focusing on diminishing returns to scale identified by trade theory and used as an explanation for investment in lower-cost locations.

With the emphasis on economies of scale the new trade theorists argue that only a few firms will be able to prosper in any one industry, a factor that is supported by a superficial glance at the dominance of world trade by the world's largest firms. Countries will have a trade pattern influenced by the profile of large firms that they possess, influenced still further by whether the country has firms that were first into an industry, a benefit known as 'first-mover advantage'. Those who entered the industry in its early phase – say, the manufacturing of computers or the production of cars – can build up market share and obtain economies of scale that set up barriers to entry, as new entrants cannot obtain the same (low) levels of costs.

This theory runs counter to, for instance, the Heckscher–Ohlin theory which argues that countries will export products for which they possess factor endowment advantages. The law of comparative advantage suggests that exports will occur when countries possess comparative advantages in certain industries. New trade theory supports this, in that a country's exports will be determined to a large extent by the number of firms who entered an industry first, and who obtained economies of scale and therefore improved resource utilisation.

Can this theory explain trade patterns? Research has been carried out, but not in sufficient depth to come to any conclusion. What is of note, however, is that it raises the importance of the firm in influencing exports and thereby trade patterns. It is also unique in raising the possibility that government intervention can have an influence on the performance of firms in export markets. New trade theorists look at the benefits of luck, entrepreneurial skill and innovation in providing favourable conditions for first-mover advantages to be obtained. So, was Boeing's dominance[11] of the commercial aircraft market explained only by luck and innovation? Along with Airbus Industrie of Europe, new trade theorists have pointed to the benefits of US government support, particularly for R&D to support the military effort, as key advantages. (Airbus Industrie used this fact to counter US accusations that production of aircraft by Airbus were heavily subsidised and that this accounted for their increase in worldwide sales.) Is it then possible to support government intervention to create first-mover advantages for some firms?

'Picking winners' or even identifying new industries/markets for governments to encourage firms to enter has had a mixed history, being discredited in countries such as the UK, but finding favour in countries such as France where there is a long history of state control and support for business. In the newly emerging economies of Eastern Europe and Russia, governments tend to lean towards the benefits of state help for key sectors, to which new trade theory would lend credibility.

From the marketing management viewpoint, the key issue is the raised profile of individual firms in influencing at least the pattern of trade, focusing on the role of innovation and entrepreneurialship that has hitherto been absent from the economic trade theories reviewed earlier.

INTERNATIONAL MARKETING THEORIES

International marketing is seen by both practitioners and scholars as complex and broad-based. Why should this matter? If the discipline is too broad, containing many different theories and perspectives, then it may be impossible to attempt to define it. This situation would produce difficulties for managers and researchers alike. Too narrow a definition could reduce it to an adjunct of marketing, thereby reducing its relevance and the requirement to carry out research. One answer to the question then is that an acceptable definition can establish a framework and promote research, with the consequent dissemination of results to practitioners, thereby stimulating dialogue.

From the view of trade theories there is an absence of the importance of firms in international trade. New trade theory raised the profile of the firm in as far as it could influence the export performance of a country due to first-mover advantage.

Bradley provides a working definition of international marketing as follows:[12]

> International marketing processes and decisions require the firm to identify needs and wants of customers, to produce assets to give a differential marketing advantage, to communicate information about these assets and to distribute and exchange them internationally through one or a combination of exchange transactions modalities.

This runs, as Bradley acknowledges, very close to definitions of marketing, but contains within it the recognition that international marketing is not a single theory but a number, so it is important to understand what the discipline studies, what problems can be posed and what rules should be applied in integrating the outcome of research.

RESEARCH STREAMS

To bring the focus down to a more practical and applied level, the review of current research streams undertaken by Li and Cavusgil[13] highlights the increasing sophistication and development of a rich body of knowledge found in international marketing, which can be contrasted with other perspectives found for example in trade theories.

Li and Cavusgil identified eight streams contained in international marketing.

1 *Environmental studies.* This was one of the earliest to be established, focusing on the impact of economic, cultural, political and legal variables on international marketing activities.

2 *Comparative studies of market systems.* Involves work on the similarities and differences among market systems and practices in different countries.

3 *International marketing management.* Looks at management issues of export and entry strategies, investment decisions, market segmentation, product and pricing policies, and distribution and service.

4 *Internationalisation process perspective.* Explores the behavioural and attitudinal changes experienced by firms in the process of internationalisation.

5 *International marketing research.* Research comprising contributions on the methodology of conducting research in the international context.

6 *Buyer behaviour.* Examines buyer behaviour in international markets and foreign countries.

7 *Interaction approach.* Examines relationships of networks, co-operative ventures and alliances among international companies.

8 *Market globalisation perspective.* Views world market and customer tastes as converging and looks at the impact of such change on company strategy.

Following on from their review of research in these eight streams, Li and Cavusgil have concluded that rather than International Marketing being a fragmented potpourri discipline, it had evolved over the past 20 years into an integrated and systematic field of study. As importantly, they also conclude that the existence of eight research streams has provided a framework for research that goes some way to supporting the assertion that international marketing has achieved a certain degree of scientific status, as shown by the large amount of empirical work undertaken.

However, despite this progress the two views on the discipline remain:

1 that it still lacks a theoretical base that can provide for a unified theory, partly explained by the number of theoretical perspectives found within it. This view looks at difficulties associated with the differentiation of international marketing from domestic marketing and international business; and

2 that international marketing is enriched with theories that can be adapted and applied to the benefit of all.

What matters here perhaps more than these two views of international marketing is the understanding of the importance of the firm in international markets. Trade theories and FDI have a tendency to downgrade the decisions open to the managers of firms and also reduce the choice of options to an either/or problem. This then highlights the importance of understanding decisions and implementation issues, rather than a description of activities. The task is for the firm to undertake, in the most efficient and effective way, the transfer of assets internationally (either when they transfer tangible assets such as products, often achieved via exporting, or when they transfer intangible assets such as technical know-how or marketing know-how where the transfer can be undertaken via franchising or licensing).

International marketing can bring into focus the challenge facing firms and managers in evaluating opportunities, understanding the position of the firm in terms of its competitive advantage and then finding the most appropriate way to exploit that in international markets. Without the focus on the firm, understanding the flow of FDI or the development of world trade will be reduced. International marketing theory and research provides the required insight into these issues.

SUMMARY

This chapter has reviewed the theories that seek to explain and account for international trade. Trade theories focusing on absolute or comparative advantage seek to identify the benefits gained by countries and their citizens in engaging in trade, usually via specialisation in an industry for which they have unique advantages. Following from this, more recent insights looking at factor endowment and the product life cycle seek to provide explanations of trade and FDI activity.

FDI theories present options to the firm in its decision to go into international markets, but recognition has to be made that the choices open to firms and their desire for flexible responses is an equally important strategic decision as that of entering a market with attention focused on the choice of strategy and its implementation.

Lastly, the significance of international marketing as a discrete discipline was introduced, looking at the two issues of what areas it comprises and whether it can be seen as a unified or diverse discipline. What emerged from the brief review was the importance attached to the role of the firm in international business and, following Bradley's definition, to incorporate good marketing practice with issues about the transfer of assets to gain marketing advantage via a number of exchange transactions possibilities. In a real sense the review undertaken in this chapter has come down from the broad-based question of whether trade brings benefits to the more narrow-focus question of how firms will deal with the complexity of the situation and choices open to them when looking to engage in international trade.

For international marketing management, therefore, the emphasis is on looking at opportunities and choosing those that can be successfully pursued. Chapter 3 reviews corporate strategy and the role of marketing planning within it, and how international strategy can play a key role in corporate success.

REVIEW QUESTIONS

1 Outline the theory of absolute advantage.

2 How does the theory of comparative advantage differ from the ideas of absolute advantage?

3 Outline foreign direct investment (FDI) theories.

4 How is international competitiveness judged?

5 Outline the product life cycle theory of international trade and FDI.

7 What advantages are claimed for pursuing international marketing as a separate academic discipline?

DISCUSSION QUESTIONS

1 Are the theories reviewed in this chapter of use to policy makers in helping provide the right environment for a country's firms?

2 FDI in the UK has been judged a success by the British government. How far can this claim be substantiated?

3 Firms that are successful at marketing in their own country often fail in foreign markets. Why?

4 If the marketing system is a function of environmental variables, is there the possibility of transferring successful marketing knowledge and approaches?

5 Why do trade theories tend to reduce the importance of firms in determining world trade patterns?

Case study

FDI IN EMERGING MARKETS[14]

Vietnam and China are among the few states still governed by Communist Party rule; nevertheless, both countries have instituted wide-ranging economic reforms, with a shift away (however partially) from command-economy principles towards market forces, in a move to improve the economic situation. A key feature in the reform process has been the attempt to attract FDI by opening the way for foreign multinationals to invest, so as to gain advanced technology, access to Western markets, management skills and other benefits.

High expectation of FDI is evident in all the emerging economies of Eastern Europe and Asia, with the entry of MNEs expected to contribute to a change of economic system that would begin to foster the emergence of the private sector.

Research on the trends and benefits of FDI have come to the following conclusions:

1 there is no evidence of a common trend in FDI – every country appears to follow its own path, determined in part by the domestic economy and its institutional environment;

2 advanced emerging economies such as Hungary, Poland and the Czech Republic have built the potential to attract FDI, but those countries most in need receive little in the way of such investment.

China, for example, encourages FDI that promotes the development of its economy and increases foreign exchange. In particular, a project or enterprise should be export oriented or should utilise advanced technology. China allows equity joint ventures and wholly foreign-owned enterprises, plus foreign investment incentives such as the following:

1 Special Economic Zones (SEZs);

2 open economic zones, free trade zones and high-technology industry development zones.

Investing in these zones enables a company to gain the following advantages:

1 reduced enterprise income tax;

2 flexible labour arrangements.

China's experience of FDI has been below its high expectations, with a reluctance amongst foreign firms to transfer or share technology. Sectorally, FDI has been focused on the service sector, labour-intensive manufacturing and oil exploration production.

The FDI environment of China is still a highly challenging one; even with reform, improved legislation and other measures, markets are not fully open and bureaucracy remains a barrier, with officials still likely to seek to interfere in or determine development.

Market regulations still govern much activity, with strict exchange controls governing the inflow and outflow of goods, services and capital owned or generated by foreign investment enterprises. Wages and price controls are gradually being relaxed, and the prices of many items are set by market forces. Ultimately, the aim is that state subsidies will be eliminated altogether and that the labour, projects and financial markets will all be liberalised. However, as part of its attempt to slow inflationary pressures in the economy the government is cautiously implementing a programme of planned price liberalisation.

To help to control inflation, the State Planning Commission submitted plans in 1995 to the State Council to ban 'excessive' profits. The regulations define excess profit making as listing prices that surpass a 'reasonable' percentage of the average price for the same kind of goods in the same area at the same time.

Traditionally, Chinese employees could expect a job for life. As state-run business units, of which there were approximately 99 000 in 1996, come under market pressure, people are being forced to seek employment outside of the state sector. Redundancy, bonuses and overtime payments which used to be totally prohibited are now tolerated, permitting foreign companies to recruit labour direct, some layoffs are possible and incentive schemes have been permitted.

Although different in substance, Vietnam has followed a similar path of reform, but in Vietnam's case the changes have been introduced with more vigour as it seeks to catch up with other developing economies, a problem that was caused by the isolation of the country in the 1970s and 1980s. Vietnam is also conscious that it is only one of a number of medium-sized economies in the region that is vying for FDI, whereas China, with its immense size and potential, is always going to be high on multinationals' list of possible FDI sites.

The competition between China and Vietnam for investment has caused problems for other countries, notably those belonging to ASEAN, which have seen investment directed away from them towards the two socialist states.

China and Vietnam's policy on investment is, as for emerging economies in Europe, a major determinant in the volume and pattern of incoming FDI. This includes the legal framework on the privatisation policy of the country. To appreciate that the approaches are not the same is to understand the environmental constraints that will be faced by the firm which operates in that area. This can be both advantageous and threatening, as when Belarus announced in the summer of 1996 that 75 per cent of all goods sold in the country's shops had to originate from that country.

The market potential of China and, indeed, of Vietnam is enormous, but as with any country the regulatory environment is complex and needs to be understood.

Questions

1 *China attracted a large amount of FDI in the early to mid-1990s. What persuaded firms that now was the time to invest in the country?*

2 *Why are the expectations of developing countries towards FDI so high, and why are they so often disappointed?*

3 *If China sticks to its policy on excessive profits as outlined in the case study, what problems could this present for the marketing manager?*

4 *Are emerging economies any more naïve about FDI than developed economies?*

5 *Land ownership and intellectual property rights are also important parts of the policy environment – what is China's and Vietnam's position on these?*

FURTHER READING

Bartels, R., 'Are domestic markets and international markets dissimilar?', *Journal of Marketing*, 32 (1968), 56–61.

Cateora, P.R., *International Marketing*, 8th edition (New York: Irwin, 1993).

Keegan, W.J., *Global Marketing Management*, 4th edition (Englewood Cliffs, NJ: Prentice-Hall, 1989).

Terpstra, V., *International Marketing*, 3rd edition (Orlando: The Dryden Press, 1983).

Wind, Y. and Robertson, T.S., 'Marketing strategy: new directions for theory and research', *Journal of Marketing*, 47(2) (1983), 12–25.

NOTES AND REFERENCES

1 Ohmae, K., *Putting Global Logic First in the Evolving Global Economy: Making Sense of the New World Order* (Cambridge, MA: Harvard Business School Press, 1995).

2 Porter, M., *The Competitive Advantage of Nations* (London: Macmillan, 1990), Chapter 2.

3 Daniels, J.D. and Radebaugh, L.H., *Business Environment and Operations* (Reading, MA: Addison-Wesley, 1992).

4 Beamish, P., 'European foreign investment: why go to Canada', *European Management Journal* 14(2) (1996); Buckley, A. and Tse, K., 'Real operating options and foreign direct investment: a synthetic approach', *European Management Journal*, 14(3) (1996).

5 Bradley, F., *International Marketing Strategy* (Englewood Cliffs, NJ: Prentice-Hall, 1995), 35.

6 Financial Times Survey – 'Inward investment into the UK', *Financial Times* (18 July 1996); World Bank, *World Development Report 1995* (Oxford University Press, 1995).

7 Traill, B. and da Silva, J.G., 'Measuring international competitiveness: the case of the European food industry', *International Business Review*, 5(2) (1996).

8   Vernon, R. and Wells, L.T., *The Economic Environment of International Business*, 4th edition (Englewood Cliffs, NJ: Prentice-Hall, 1986).

9   Rugman, A.M. and Hodgetts, R.M., *International Business: A Strategic Management Approach* (New York: McGraw-Hill, 1995), 156.

10 Hufbauer, G.C. (ed.), *Europe 1992: An American Perspective* (Washington, DC: The Brookings Insitute, 1990).

11 Whitford, D., 'The sale of the century', *Fortune* (17 February 1997).

12 Bradley, op. cit., 41.

13 Li, T. and Cavusgil, S.T., 'A classification and assessment of research streams in international marketing', *International Business Review*, 4(3) (1995).

14 Krugman, P., 'A country is not a company', *Harvard Business Review* (January–February 1996); 'Doing business in Russia', Ernst & Young (1996); Freeman, N.J., 'Vietnam and China: FDI parallels', *Communist Economies and Economic Transformation*, 6(1) (1994); Meyer, K., 'FDI in the early years of economic transition', *The Economics of Transition*, 3(3) (1995).

Strategic marketing planning

INTRODUCTION

What factors promote the success of some organisations, whilst others which seemingly have just as many advantages struggle to survive? Organisations in the public and private sectors have adopted strategic planning, using approaches that promote an awareness of the broad competitive environment, while taking a critical look at their internal skills and competencies; when taken with an external review, this can suggest a strategy that can be followed and will hopefully be successful. Yet there are many examples of organisations who follow good practice but who get it wrong. Liberty, a UK retail and textile company, pursued a strategy of setting up over 20 regional stores in the UK, whilst establishing three outlets at Heathrow Airport (the world's largest international airport) and entering into a joint venture with Japan's Saison group to establish a small chain of Maji shops, yet saw profits decline. Steps had to be taken to stop the decline, so in the spring of 1996 the decision was taken to close all of the regional stores, whilst keeping the world-famous London store and the Maji and Heathrow outlets. The aim is to exploit the Liberty brand, particularly its ties, scarves and fabrics, whilst setting up new outlets overseas, where it is particularly strong in countries such as France, Spain, Italy and in areas such as East Asia.[1]

Strategy cannot guarantee success, and the strategic process is influenced by those inside and outside the organisation who have vested interests and who can determine its direction. What is important is that an organisation can admit its mistakes, take effective action and prosper. The Liberty example suggests that only by reviewing the options available and knowing where their strengths were and by seeking out the best opportunities, could they take a course of action that was at once painful and expensive (restructuring costs), and contained risks as new overseas markets were entered.

This chapter reviews the strategy process and focuses on the importance marketing plays in this, both in its influence on strategy and from the market planning perspective.

Objectives

This chapter will examine:

- the global strategic planning process
- the role of strategic planning
- the interaction between marketing and corporate strategy.

THE GLOBAL STRATEGIC PLANNING PROCESS

Many researchers[2] on international marketing have focused on the lack of influence of an international or global perspective in marketing thinking and strategic planning. International marketers[3] have also found that their work has been a bolt-on to mainstream marketing activities, usually confined to a specialist section of marketing texts. This can produce problems when looking at all the strategic options facing the firm. To understand the benefits of this, it is necessary to review the importance of strategy and business planning and the role of international marketing.

It is useful at this stage to understand the perspectives taken concerning business strategy that many writers adopt. The first of these focuses on the external environment facing the organisation, suggesting that an understanding of market dynamics should be appreciated in order to align the firm correctly to changing circumstances. From this point of view, superior strategies are ones that create advantageous situations in the present circumstances.

This approach (important though it is, and one that will be given its due place in this chapter and others) tends to overlook the importance of internal factors.

The second approach looks at the creation of competitive advantage through the acquiring and exploitation of specific resources and capabilities (competencies). Strategic positioning, and ultimately success, is dependent on the use of resources to exploit (external) opportunities. However, it is not always clear (as shown in the examples used in this chapter) that an appreciation of external factors and the presence of the best resources and capabilities will ultimately lead to success.

The final approach looks at the process of change and the organisational context in which it takes place. This tends to be more complex to appreciate than the other two approaches, as it looks at the interaction between external and internal factors that can enable or constrain effective strategic responses.

While due credit will be given to all three, the process approach tends to be more difficult to use as it offers few prescriptions on how to achieve superior business performance. While it is possible to be selective in the approach to explaining strategy – i.e. to take the common-sense view that taking the best from each of them will produce an enhanced/superior approach – it is not so easy to merge what might be regarded as three different schools of thought. (*See* Box 3.1 for a more detailed review of this.)

Following Ellis and Williams,[4] it is helpful to draw up a number of informing principles that can guide the review of global business strategy. These principles can be listed as follows:

1 internal or external issues cannot be seen in isolation from one another. It would be difficult to find organisations that were pulled solely by external factors or pushed purely by internal ones;

2 there is no perfect management solution to the strategy problem, each firm is unique and solutions have to be found to the challenge that it faces;

3 time and space must be taken into account when looking at strategy. For example, how does the past influence the present and what factors are currently making their presence felt – perhaps from a point hitherto considered unimportant.

What is strategy?

Planning is an important aspect of most management definitions of strategy, with a focus on rational planning. Hill and Jones[5] outline this approach as the organisation choosing its goals, identifying the strategies open to it, choosing the most appropriate and then allocating resources to its pursuit. Finally, it will be necessary for the organisation to review periodically the success, or otherwise, of the route taken, with changes being identified and new action taken.

This approach has attracted criticism, making the point that many explanations are a rewriting of past events. Mintzberg[6] points out that definitions of strategy assume that an organisation's strategy is always the outcome of internal planning, whereas strategies can actually emerge without any spur from a formal planning approach. From this point of view, strategy is also about what a company actually does rather than merely what it intends to do. The difference can be summarised as *intended* strategies – i.e. those that are planned – and *emergent* strategies – i.e. those that start as unplanned activities.

Emergent strategies can come from anywhere in the organisation, as middle managers and others can develop strategies of this nature that may well help to fulfil the criteria far better than an intended strategy. Managers must also be able to recognise when an emergent strategy is potentially dysfunctional and move to kill it off, and when it is functional and needs to be promoted.

The need to conceptualise a model of strategic management is essential for understanding intended strategies, but this also applies to emergent strategies that have at some point to be given approval and resources allocated. Typically this can be broken down into the components shown in Fig. 3.1, with the traditional approach stressing that a step-by-step approach is required, moving from the determination of the mission through to implementation and review of progress made. This is fine for intended strategies but not for emergent ones, as by their very nature they won't have gone through such a structural approach. However, they will still need (eventually) to be assessed to see how far they fit in with the purpose of the organisation and how resources and capabilities support them.

The significance of the model in Fig. 3.1 for global moves by the company would seem to be that a move of such significance *must* be the result of an intended strategy. The situation facing Honda in America[7] is a much-quoted example of how a market entry decision was finally vindicated, not by the original tactic of using motorbikes, but by the small Honda 50s (50cc bikes) that had been used by Honda workers to run errands in the Los Angeles area and had attracted a lot of attention. Eventually a buyer expressed interest, with the result that Honda became established in the USA

Fig 3.1 THE STRATEGIC MANAGEMENT MODEL

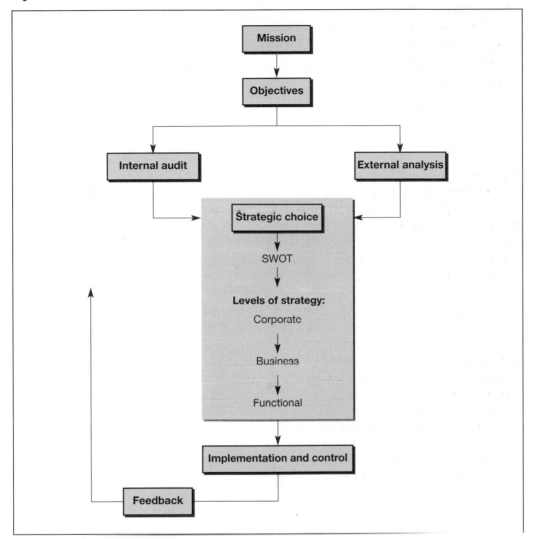

and blossomed from that point. Equally, many universities in the UK have entered into student exchange programmes with EU funding, only to find themselves invited into longer-term commitment with franchised programmes and the building of an overseas campus. Although the mission had been to create a global university/college the means by which it was achieved emerged over time.

It will be useful at this stage to go through the components of the model shown in Fig. 3.1, before looking at global strategy influences.

Mission and objectives

The mission provides the context within which intended strategies are formulated and against which emergent strategies can be evaluated. Objectives for the organisation, if they are in the private sector, focus on profitability and increasing shareholders' wealth, with other objectives taking a lesser priority – i.e. objectives are placed in a hierarchy.

External analysis

The main purpose is to identify opportunities and threats in the organisation's operating environment. The problem here is to determine the horizons for such a review. The broadest overview can be structured using a PEST (Political, Economic, Social and Technological) approach, a more detailed discussion of which occurs in Chapters 5–7; the main problem is that such a wide-ranging view may give little in the way of actionable opportunities, so a narrowing of the scope of the analysis can be undertaken by looking at the specific competitive environment of the organisation.

PEST analysis should incorporate global issues, but a review of the competitive environment will not necessarily involve such an approach. However, the evidence so far presented in Chapters 1 and 2 suggests that this will be a backward step – as, for example, the reduction on the barriers to entry to many if not all markets means that new (foreign) competitors can enter a market very quickly. Equally important is the fact that to obtain competitive advantage may well require a global approach by the company, examples of which are given in Boxes 3.2 and 3.3.

Box 3.1   THEORIES OF STRATEGY[8]

Strategy can be divided into four generic approaches, which Whittington classifies as: classical, evolutionary, processualist and systemic. Using this classification it is possible to see that despite the uniformity found in many textbooks, with reviews of important writers and of their specific approaches to the solving of strategic issues and problems, there are marked differences of view that exist between them, which leads to very different recommendations as to what strategy means for the organisation and its managers.

Classical

This is the oldest and still the most influential, using rational planning methods and according to Whittington covers the work of (amongst others) Ansoff and Porter. Strategy for these writers is a rational process of calculation and analysis, designed to maximise long-term advantage. Good planning consists therefore of mastering internal and external environments and choosing the most appropriate strategy. Failure comes to those who fail to plan, an accusation that can be supported from surveys that show how few organisations in Britain undertake formal planning (except budgeting) and how few UK managers have been trained in suitable and appropriate techniques.

Evolutionary

The approach emphasises the importance of the market place, arguing that its complexity and unpredictability make it difficult to pursue the classical rational planning approaches, as change is the norm and plans often fail to pick this up. Whittington argues that writers within this approach offer a cruel paradox to strategists. Market forces are so prevalent that long-term survival cannot be planned, but only the firms that do profit-maximise will survive. As in economics, where the price taking situation of perfect competition means that only the efficient will be profitable and survive (but the individual company is powerless to set price), so too in the market where managers can ensure only that the organisation is prepared for whatever competition can throw at it.

▶

▶ **Box 3.1 continued**

Processualist

Like the evolutionists, this group agrees that long-term planning is largely futile. Here, strategy emerges from the pragmatic process of learning by mistakes, comparing and spotting opportunities as they arise. Mintzberg is the most influential of the writers in the field, with the encouragement of 'double-loop' learning that can provide one of the planks for the long-term survival of the organisation.

Systemic

This approach supports the idea that managers can plan and carry out their plans and even have a significant impact on the market place around them, rather than just accepting that market forces determine everything. For them, competitive pressures do not ensure that only profit-maximisers survive, but that markets can be manipulated and that profit is not the only criterion against which to judge success. An important point is made by those who are influenced by the systemic approach. Strategies reflect the social system in which they are located and are enacted, so firms from different countries will take a different approach to strategy. This is very different from the more universalist approach of the classical writers, who promote the transferability of their approach to other countries, and can even, as Porter has shown in the *Competitive Advantage of Nations* (1990), seek to identify those characteristics that can show which nations will prosper and which will struggle.

Transferring approaches that work in one country to another will not be easy – the social context of the success of Japan or South Korea could not easily be transferred to the UK, for example.

Whittington, who tends towards the Systemic perspective, is worth quoting in full on the significance of this approach for international competition:

> Recent history has seen a massive growth in international competition, paralleled by the entry into the capitalist world economy of nations with histories and social systems utterly different from those of Anglo-Saxon (UK and USA) business. Even in the Anglo-Saxon world, privatisation and quasi-privatisation have created organisations which must compete, but whose objectives and contexts nevertheless remain much more complex than the simplistics of profit maximisation and perfect markets. The Systematic approach takes these differences seriously. According to the social groups that dominate them, and the immediate social context in which they work, businesses vary widely in the end and means of strategy. To compete and co-operate in this planned environment, we need to be sensitive to the diverse teaching of different business systems. Now, more than ever, history and society matter to competitive strategy.

All four approaches can provide insight and clarification of what is a challenging problem, namely how to formulate strategic plans and responses that will work. Following an approach such as the popular classical approach does not invalidate appreciation of the benefits to be obtained from the evolutionary or processualist approaches. It should also be clear that the 'mix and match' approach has dangers, in that inconsistencies, tensions and even contradictions exist between some of the techniques and suggested 'best-practice' options. However, to be aware of their source and to appreciate their ability to shed light on a problem can permit an educated selection of the approaches reviewed in this book and others.

At the end of the day, managers will be asked to produce plans against which others can judge progress. How the plan is put together, carried out and reviewed and what its impact is on the broader environment is a matter for conjecture and debate and for further research, all of which will contribute to the debate.

Box 3.2

LUCAS VARITY: THE CREATION OF A GLOBAL VEHICLE PARTS MANUFACTURER[9]

In March 1996, George Simpson, the head of Lucas Industries, was rumoured to be taking over the Chairmanship of GEC, a move that was subsequently confirmed. The uncertainty created meant that concern was raised on the future independence of Lucas, as despite the recognition that it had some good products and market strengths, the company had experienced difficult market conditions. Market analysts felt that despite improvements in company performance, there remained doubts as to how it could weather a weak market situation.

Cash flow was not considered strong enough to fund expansion plans, and in an industry that judges success by the size of the company and with the prediction that there will soon be only 20 companies capable of supplying car makers on a global scale, Lucas's future looked less than assured.

In June 1996, Lucas and Varity, a North American company, announced a merger to guarantee a future that could put the new company on a global footing. George Simpson, who was instrumental in bringing the merger forward before his departure for GEC, argued that the significance of regional players, a role which Lucas performed in the UK and Varity in the USA, was nearly at an end, with the emphasis shifting to the global market.

Both groups had undergone major changes throughout the 1980s with Varity emerging from Massey-Ferguson (the agricultural vehicle maker), with common interests to Lucas in brakes, automotive electronics and diesel systems. Equally important was the complementarity of the geographic areas covered, with Varity strong in North America and Lucas in Europe and the Pacific Rim.

To add further to the benefits of the merger, Lucas was particularly strong in the development of electronic brake controls, whilst Varity had been successful in cost cutting and improved automation. One example of this approach can be seen in the new brake plant in Michigan where labour makes up two per cent of costs and stock levels have been reduced to 2.5 days of production.

The combined company had sales of £4.5bn in 1996 with a market value of £3bn. Ownership of the company would be split 62 per cent between Lucas and 38 per cent Varity shareholders. One of the largest of Varity's shareholder is the new Chief Executive of Lucas Varity, Victor Rice, who is spearheading the move by the new company to become a key player in the vehicle parts business.

On the way to a merger, BBA (a UK engineering and textiles manufacturer) launched a hostile take-over bid, that was later withdrawn, but which showed the dangers of engaging in (public) talks where shareholders can be given more than just one option and may take the option of the highest immediate return for their shares, whatever the logic of the original strategic alliance. Further difficulties of merging appeared, such as Cummins, the diesel engine manufacturer (a major Lucas customer), whose attitude to the merger depended on the link-up with the owner of Perkins (Varity), another diesel engine company.

The alliance that Lucas had forged with Sumitomo of Japan in the development of anti-lock brakes was put into question by this change.

With the challenges of overcoming these difficulties, Lucas Varity sees itself as a player in the global market, but as with all companies in this area, being up with the best is still the major challenge. The need to indicate continuous improvement in production can be judged from the task GKN, a UK vehicle parts manufacturer, has had to go through, which reveals the extent of this challenge.

▶ Box 3.2 continued

The arrival of Japanese firms and the spread of their influences as UK firms adopted similar techniques required Hardy Spicer, a subsidiary of GKN, to cope with a more demanding group of manufacturers. To respond to this, GKN introduced team working and inter-departmental business units that meant that big customers could co-operate with the company on the development of new products suitable to their requirements. Despite these changes quality was still below that demanded by customers, a problem that threatened business and forced improved communication, reducing middle management and placing increased emphasis on quality. As a result of these changes faults per million parts fell from thousands in the early 1990s to 75 in 1995 with the long-term aim to reduce this to 10. These figures, although showing substantial improvement, take the company up to the level of an average Japanese plant. To match the best, the aim of reducing faults to 10 would have to be achieved.

Similar challenges face Lucas Varity, as it moves from a successful regional middle-sized company to a major player in the world's markets that will have to compete with the best.

Box 3.3

RESTRUCTURING IN THE DRUGS AND CHEMICAL SECTORS: THE MERGER OF SANDOZ AND CIBA[10]

In late 1995, Sandoz and Ciba announced plans of a merger to create a new company Novartis. The new company is the world's second biggest pharmaceutical company by sales, with a 4.4 per cent share of the global market. In agrochemicals, it is more than twice the size of its nearest rival.

This is but one example of a series of mergers that have taken place in the pharmaceutical industry throughout the 1990s. What reasons can be found for such major upheavals in the industry? The force that has provoked the change has been the need of governments in Europe and North America to control the increase in health care spending, a feature that will be around for sometime to come as ageing populations increase the elderly dependency ratio, with all that that implies for further pressure on health costs and added determination to keep them under control. Major economies such as Japan, Germany, France, Italy and the USA are forecast to see their public sector deficits soar as a result of the change – with Japan, for example, seeing its deficit rise from 13 per cent of GDP in 1995 to over 100 per cent by 2015 (OECD forecast).

Governments are looking closely at how to reduce the pressure on health spending with ageing populations, and expectations that expensive life-saving techniques could become available to a wider group are exerting their toll. Reviews of ways to cut costs have focused on the cost of drugs, with drug buyers introducing cost control measures. Sales growth has slowed, with a result that drug company shares underperformed compared with the late 1980s and many companies looked to boost growth by acquisition.

The change, although forecast for some time, caught many companies unawares. The response was that drug companies sought strategic alliances and invested in bio-technology, with take-overs and mergers aimed at boosting productivity in manufacturing and marketing.

Even with headline-grabbing mergers the world's largest drugs company, Glaxo Wellcome, has only five per cent of the global market. Compare this to many other industries where the largest companies have much larger shares, then many industry observers are predicting continued consolidation.

▶ **Box 3.3 continued**

Faced with such changes, the senior managers of Sandoz and Ciba had to look at what this meant for the future. At Sandoz, managers believed that pharmaceutical companies would need to be strong both in innovation, implying continued investment in R&D, and in off-patent generic drugs. To achieve success in both areas would require different skills and take some time to achieve.

Ciba had seen the trends emerging in the industry and focused on two possible alternatives:

1 what has been termed the 'Anglo-Saxon' strategy (so named after the adoption of strategies by companies in the USA, UK, Australia and New Zealand) where companies focused on what they regarded as 'core businesses';

2 mainland European strategies, which aimed to keep a range of businesses going.

It was the first of these strategies that Ciba adopted, providing the prospect for a merger between themselves and Sandoz.

Taking an active part in the consolidation going on in the industry and with their combined strengths, especially in innovation and in generic drugs, the future of the merged company should be a promising one. However, many companies have found that a merger creates more problems than at first envisaged, even when, like Novatis, the elements making up the new company are both Swiss, i.e. showing a similar identity and approach to business.

In banking, engineering and many other sectors the problems stemming from mergers can lead to many years of frustration and even in some cases of demerger as the only way of solving the problems. In other words, the analysis of the business environment can suggest that an acquisition or merger is the most promising strategy, the companies might in theory complement each other, but making it work is more difficult. Taking Ciba and Sandoz as an example shows the problem. First, they have two headquarters, with their American head offices both situated in New Jersey. Second, the merger of the agrochemical businesses will have restructuring costs. Both of these will make people uncertain of their jobs and, as had happened with other mergers in the industry, lead to an exodus of talented researchers and managers.

A further issue emerges here. To create the world's second biggest pharmaceutical company will trigger responses from companies such as Hoechst and Bayer, who may then hit the acquisition trail. The pressure to keep health care costs down will increase rather than abate, so governments are keen to encourage over the counter (OTC) rather than prescription drugs, as this means the cost is shifted from the taxpayer to the consumer. The logic of the merger is that Novartis is stronger in the OTC area and should be able to exploit this advantage as the OTC movement increases when the markets in Germany and France are deregulated.

Competitive pressures will remain in the industry for many years to come, with new alliances forming, cost-cutting and the demand to understand the needs of the consumer moving up the agenda. Marketing to an OTC market will be more complex than selling to government agencies with a regulated market. Global players with well-known brands widely available will be able to exploit this opportunity.

Internal analysis

As shown in Box 3.2, the realisation of competitive advantage and the reduction (if not the elimination) of threats from more productive and efficient competitors may well require significant changes in systems, procedures, organisation and management. Both the examples given in Boxes 3.2 and 3.3 hint at the need to become more responsive to customer needs.

Strategic choice

Compared to the previous activities, this entails the generating of a series of strategic alternatives against which the company can compare itself via a SWOT analysis. The alternatives have to be evaluated, and the best choice made. In practice, this is a complex task as the views of various stakeholders will make themselves felt at this stage. Once a choice has been made, then corporate, business and functional strategies will spring from this.

Implementation and control

It is here that many organisations find the greatest difficulty as the skill required for implementation differs from those required to identify the most appropriate strategy. This part of the process can involve changing structures, reviewing systems and procedures, working across functions and a whole range of other activities that can support the chosen strategy.

Feedback

Monitoring strategy is seeing how objectives are being met. If they are not, then various courses of action are open to the organisation to rectify the problem. Were the objectives set too high, should they be amended? Was implementation poorly managed or a factor overlooked? The answer to these questions will determine the next phase of action, so as to maintain the move towards corporate objectives.

As we have seen, this type of approach, if taken at face value, will seem to reinforce the approach of rational planning and seeking to fit the organisation to the prevailing competitive environment. The problem is that well-planned approaches often fail spectacularly, and in an increasingly complex world how can an organisation use this approach when its managers are uncertain of the situation they are faced with? This issue is explained further in Box 3.4.

Box 3.4   **STRATEGIC MANAGEMENT IN AN UNPREDICTABLE WORLD[11]**

Many accept that the business environment has become more complex and prone to sudden unexpected changes. When environments are stable, as for example was the general experience of the 1950s and 1960s, organisations could be run using a hierarchical top-down model of planning. For various reasons this is no longer the case. Glass cites three reasons why the environment could be viewed as stable:

1 the organisation will not be disrupted by outside events;

▶

▶ **Box 3.4 continued**

2 the operating environment is stable, and management can develop strategies that take account of the general trends found within it;

3 both for the organisation and the economy there exist certain control mechanisms that can be applied with the clear understanding that the outcome is predictable.

Glass argues that these three situations have been replaced by three new realities, which can be summarised as follows.

● *Reality 1*: organisations are open systems being influenced by and influencing their environment; intended actions can often be influenced by external events or internal changes.

● *Reality 2*: top managers find it impossible to understand fully the existing environment as it changes so rapidly, bringing to the fore new threats and opportunities at an increasing rate; many firms have found that whilst strategy is being formulated the environment has changed irrevocably.

● *Reality 3*: the linear models of cause and effect have broken down, and many actions can lead to quite unexpected consequences.

Accelerated competition and the unpredictable nature of the environment mean that managers find it difficult to understand what it implies for them, so that a firm may well fail to see how a company that appeared to offer no immediate threat starts to take a significant amount of business, or that a competitive advantage was assumed to exist and be unassailable, but was in fact allowed to wither by a lack of investment, or that a move to introduce a new product was undertaken without any due recognition of the possible moves by competitors to counteract the benefit.

The last example suggests that more detailed planning is required rather than less, but Glass's argument is that detailed five-year plans are a worthless exercise if the detail is worthless soon after the plan has been published. Planning from this point of view will have to move from the insistence on detail to a more flexible approach that can adapt itself to changing circumstances with strategic direction or intent setting the basic philosophy but not determining the way in which this can be achieved. After all, according to this approach, new techniques, approaches and technology will be available over time, all of which can be reviewed for an ability to help achieve the desired goal.

Along with writers such as Stacey, Mintzberg and others, Glass proposes that the key to a successful strategy lies in the benefit that the learning organisation brings with it. In essence the 'double loop' learning favoured by these writers requires reacting to a given situation – such as an increase in sales at given times of the year which require an increase in overtime – by questioning the assumption behind the reaction. Would it be possible and desirable to reduce the sales peaks by changing or influencing customer behaviour?

The 'learning organisation', with its emphasis on double-loop learning, can be applied to international markets, where the ability to question assumptions becomes more pronounced as stereotypes and ways of carrying out business come under more strain in the new circumstances. The need for strategy does not decline in these circumstances, with the raising of strategic intent and the promotion of an atmosphere whereby managers can achieve strategy by the use of new tools as they are developed. Senior managers retain the ability to head off an approach that is in danger of pulling strategy away from its moorings.

THE ROLE OF STRATEGIC PLANNING

Reviewing the strategic planning organisation of a firm can often mean looking at the rationalisation of the desire to move into new (foreign) markets. In many circumstances, the motivation to consider these options springs from a number of sources. Firms may experience, perhaps due to a recession in their domestic market, under-utilised resources that can be used to provide a product and service required in a foreign market. A competitive advantage may have been developed from the firm's products, markets and resources, so products can often be tried in international markets because of some unique advantage that they possess. Siemens[12] test marketed a range of machine tool controls in the UK, on the grounds that the UK's value for money approach to factory automation was closest to East Asia than that of any other European country. The need to test market the range lay in the need to meet rapidly rising demands in East Asia, so a successful launch in the UK could be extended to many other countries. However, having spare resources or clear competitive advantage is not in itself enough to guarantee a move into foreign markets. All it means is that the potential exists for this to occur.

Knowledge of a market is often what pushes a firm forward into international endeavours. Knowledge can be objective (i.e. facts and figures concerning a country and the target market), and experiential (which is an understanding of the 'reality' of the situation). The first type of knowledge can be bought, the second type has to be acquired, which means that investment has to be made. Shifting firms towards a more international outlook is, therefore, difficult to achieve if they have been focusing their efforts over many years on their home market.

Investing in the international process takes time, and means that a long-term view and long-term commitment has to be given to it.

Other factors that will influence the likelihood of a firm considering exporting or other involvement in international markets are the influence of the key decision maker in moving a company's thinking away from a domestic bias towards a perception of opportunities elsewhere. Equally important is the consideration of the importance of services to support the product; the more of these that are required, the more complex the relationship between buyer and seller, reducing the stimulus to export.

SMEs find involvement in the international market place more difficult to achieve as resources are scarce, market knowledge is more difficult to obtain or acquire and there is the perception that involvement of this sort can only be short term.

In short, the chances of a firm considering international opportunities will be influenced by, amongst others, its history, the attitude of its senior managers, products, markets and its perceived competitive advantage. Encouraging firms to move into exporting, for example, is not so straightforward a task as simply providing information or seeking out opportunities – a strategy often pursued by governments when wishing to promote trade.

Bradley[13] outlines the importance of company growth stemming from the reaction of managers to the risks involved. Table 3.1 provides a summary, which impacts on the likelihood of a company exporting or seeking some other involvement in the international market place.

Table 3.1 RELATIONSHIP OF COMPANY GROWTH, MOTIVATION TO INTERNATIONALISE, COGNITIVE STYLE AND STAGE OF INTERNATIONALISATION

Attitude towards company growth

• Internal incentives:
    – unused resources
    – special knowledge
    – motivation of management
 	
 • External incentives:
    – increasing demand
    – changes in marketing environment
    – changes in product–technology environment
    – changes in institutional environment

Cognitive style
• Manager's innovativeness and open-mindedness towards new foreign markets   • people high on dogmatism unlikely to exhibit a high propensity to export.
Three stages of internationalisation
1 Potential exporter – firms not having any record or knowledge of ever having received a direct export order   **2** Passive exporters – firms responding to unsolicited export orders   **3** Active exporters – firms exhibiting a continuous pattern of winning foreign businesses through direct sales and marketing effort.

Source: Bradley, F., *International Marketing Strategy*, 2nd edition (Hemel Hempstead: Prentice-Hall, 1995).

Company growth

If the survival of the firm is seen to come from expansion, then opportunities will be sought to achieve this. This is usually the case when market fluctuations are increasing and insecurity causes managers to seek new markets for the firm's products. This is often seen as a rather paradoxical problem for government, which wishes to create macroeconomic stability but wishes also to see dynamic markets – i.e. markets characterised by change and uncertainty. For countries like the UK or the Netherlands, where exporting is a key component of economic growth, creating favourable conditions for this to occur is rather problematic.

A restriction on growth is imposed by resources, including management. Attitudes of managers, and the perceptions they have formed of present and future market conditions, including opportunities for growth, are often critical. The second section of Table 3.1 identifies the cognitive style of managers. Bradley distinguishes between what he calls the 'dogmatic' or 'closed' cognitive style and an 'open-minded' one. Dogmatic managers are unlikely to adapt to a quickly changing situation, and will find difficulties with the complexity of the international market place. Firms who, through their past experience and recruitment have a high proportion of such managers are less likely to export. Open-minded managers tend to thrive in relatively unstructured situations, found particularly in international situations. Such people would tend to push for and exploit international opportunities for growth.

In many, if not all, firms the existence of both types of managers would be expected, and it is quite easy to see that for many firms, where the domestic market has the major part of the firm's business 'dogmatic' managers will survive and even thrive. Open-minded managers, located in parts of the organisation that can push for growth will be able to influence the push into new (foreign) markets. Here, however, the need to support the work of these managers is more than just providing funds. Early setbacks in foreign markets are the norm and as noted previously the need to invest time and commitment over the longer term is essential if the early steps in the market are to be successful.

The three stages of internationalisation in Table 3.1 show the three possible levels of involvement, from no activity at all, to passive activity (i.e. responding to another firm's request), to an active situation where orders are won on a continual basis and sales in foreign markets are a notable part of overall sales.

A significant conclusion to be drawn from the literature on exporting is that to be successful the strategic significance of such a move must be recognised. Moving into markets in an experimental or incremental way lacks the full support of the firm in the commitment of resources and the positive support of its personnel. 'Dogmatic' managers in this scenario would have to be converted to the importance of the export or internationalisation drive. Thus strategic planning and the push towards an international approach go hand in hand. This does not suggest that there is a preferred approach, with the emphasis on the rational planning model, for instance, but that there must be a genuine and concerted effort to achieve growth by this means. Strategic approaches to internationalisation also reinforce the long-term commitment required, rather than the opportunistic short-term excursion into overseas markets that many firms have undertaken.

Brown and Cook[14] found that firms which are successful in the international arena show the following characteristics:

1 firms will be more successful if they concentrate their resources on nominated key (foreign) markets;

2 firms must be prepared to adapt their products;

3 firms should dedicate specialist resources to their chosen foreign markets, and must take a long-term view;

4 strategies based on rigorous marketing research will enhance the likelihood of success.

MARKETING AND CORPORATE STRATEGY

Marketing orientation is the attempt to create a competitive advantage for the firm by starting with identified customer needs and (re)focusing the organisational effort to the satisfaction of them. Box 3.5 on Northern Telecom is a case study in the application of this process, and the benefits that arise from it. This is one example of marketing orientation that exploits the market and product opportunities available, but which places an onus of responsibility on the organisation to review customer needs regularly.

Once a decision has been made on which product–market approach to take, decisions must be taken on the following.

1 Which markets offer the opportunity for successful development?

2 Which markets should be selected for development?

3 How should the firm offer its products in comparison with other competitors?

4 How should we establish a marketing system and organisation for the firm?

5 How should we develop a marketing plan, and then implement and control it?

Having a coherent strategy that can provide direction for the firm's activities in the international market place is important for a number of reasons. To avoid the unsystematic approaches noted earlier, clear objectives, noting the degree of involvement and likely risk of such activity, can provide a framework for the review of opportunities. Figure 3.2, taken from Douglas and Craig,[15] shows that the type of development achieved will itself prompt further developments that move the company into the next phase.

Triggers that move the firm from one phase to another have already been reviewed, but can now be seen to act in a continuous fashion, so that market development (an external trigger) can be seen to offer new opportunities, whilst the international trigger of improving management attitudes towards foreign markets can spur the company forward so that it can take advantage of market opportunities on offer.

Fig 3.2 THE DYNAMICS OF GLOBAL STRATEGY DEVELOPMENT

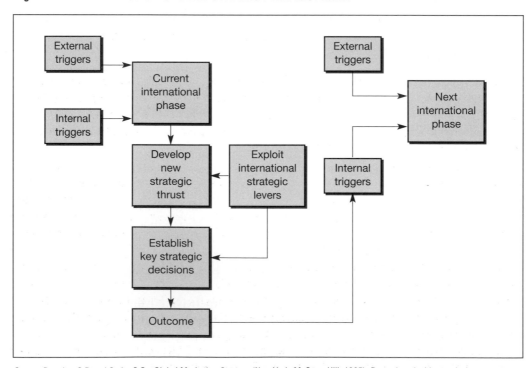

Source: Douglas, S.P. and Craig, C.S., *Global Marketing Strategy* (New York: McGraw-Hill, 1995). Reproduced with permission.

The strategic thrust, as the term would suggest, is concerned with the direction of the company, defining the areas in which the firm will compete along with its strategic priorities. This is itself affected by the phase of internationalisation experienced by the firm with, for example, the first phase concerned with expanding the geographic boundaries of operation, usually by targeting selected countries; the second phase will emphasise the need for consolidation in its chosen market; the third phase sees the full commitment of the company to the international market, as planning is now undertaken with a more global and less national view.

Companies may not wish to move to the last stage, but whatever the situation, a company that has established itself by deliberate intent in foreign markets can transfer its experience and knowledge more easily to other countries or if required develop a more global approach.

Box 3.5

NORTHERN TELECOM[16]

In the early 1980s Canada's Northern Telecom experienced severe difficulties with its business products division:

- a very price-sensitive end-user group, i.e. SMEs, needing from 2 to 100 telephone lines
- resellers who were not making money selling the products, and consequently were not prepared to invest in stimulating interest
- Pacific Rim competitors with lower costs then Northern Telecom
- a strong competitor in AT&T who dominated the much larger US market
- cost and quality problems.

From this situation the business division in the 1990s has proved profitable, won various awards for supplier excellence, the quality of its product and service, and has a dominant market share in the UK and Canada, moving to second place behind AT&T in the USA with a strong global presence. The company overall spends over $1.5bn on research (1995) and has sales in excess of $10bn.

The success of Northern Telecom overall, and its business division in particular, is an example of understanding what had gone wrong and taking corrective action to turn a situation around and regain a competitive edge. Many companies favour starting afresh with something new, but that often ignores the importance of understanding how the situation has arisen, and what can be done to rectify it. Turning round an operation that is in trouble takes particular marketing skills.

The key insight in the development of effective strategies to turn round the situation was the recognition that the total system (i.e. vendor, management, manufacturer, logistics and marketing) was not working. The strategy was simple: make a product that is reliable, easy to use and resellers can make money selling. Seemingly this simple solution (or at least simple to describe) had a key marketing insight incorporated into its heart. What the company was offering was not just a physical product, but a total system. Some of this can still be seen in the reaction of the CEO of Northern Telecom – when commentators describe the company as a telecommunications equipment manufacturer, they are quickly told that the company is in fact a technology supplier.

▶

▶ **Box 3.5 continued**

The reorientation of the division was based on two approaches:

1 the customer was defined as both the end user and a reseller, with particular attention given to the resellers' need to make money. To understand what this would mean in practice, studies were undertaken of resellers' cost structures, with the result that Northern came to the conclusion that the key to a strategy based on reseller profitability was not to charge them less (competitors would soon match this), or to charge premium prices to end users, but to decrease elements of their costs;

2 that a total telephone system should be designed that would give further business opportunities for the resellers.

Development of an easy-to-install reliable telephone system, delivered to the end user in 48 hours has produced the benefits noted earlier. In particular, competitors have found it hard to mount effective imitations and have seen the company take the leading position in many countries. All of this, of course, took time and effort and a very real insight into the needs of the customers (i.e. resellers and end users) that Northern served. For example, cross-functional teams made up of design, manufacturing and marketing personnel were created. To guarantee a 48-hour delivery to end users meant that resellers had little need to hold stock but if this strategy meant that Northern held stock instead then little would have been achieved. The answer lay in the development of a just-in-time (JIT) approach.

What are the lessons to learn from this approach? Good marketing practices can be identified, ranging from market research that enhanced the understanding of consumer behaviour, through a product differentiation strategy to an integrated marketing mix approach. But over and above this, the approach used broke the existing rules, which if they had been followed would not have solved the problem. With design and manufacturing working together with an understanding of the business plan, the vision was shared with employees who were encouraged to seek solutions to the existing problems by understanding the past – i.e. what mistakes had been made and what could be learned.

Competition has not ceased or eased, in fact it has increased, whilst pressure from customers to cut prices has risen. Overall, Northern Telecom is faced with a large number of opportunities amongst which it has to choose which offers the best way forward. The company has chosen to develop four market segments – switching networks, enterprise networks, wireless networks and broadband networks. The aim is to be among the three leaders in each of the segments. Core expertise is important, but in many instances the company develops links with a partner, rather than acquiring an existing company.

What this example shows is that success can come from the application of simple to explain (but not necessarily simple to execute) approaches. As Northern Telecom sets its sight on being a leader in its four chosen segments, the lessons of the past (now good as well as bad) can be applied to the business strategies that have been adopted. As markets are liberalised and as privatisation gathers pace, the opportunities are there for the taking. Not all 'technology suppliers' will be able to take advantage of them, as they follow traditional approaches that will reduce the ability of managers to find answers to new problems. Learning how to apply basic marketing approaches in new ways will become ever more important.

THE INTERACTION BETWEEN MARKETING AND CORPORATE STRATEGY

Figure 3.3, also from Douglas and Craig,[17] shows the importance of setting goals and objectives that incorporate statements outlining the organisation's commitment to the international market place. The mission statement should be amended to encapsulate this change, so that it is clear that the organisation's future survival, growth and profitability depend on these activities.

Mission statements are the embodiment of the organisation's philosophy and self-image, providing guidelines for strategic planning. Mission statements often come with additional statements as to the way in which the mission will be achieved, and incorporate corporate responsibilities and ethical issues that are of increasing importance.

Figure 3.4 outlines the activities required after the mission and objectives and related issues have been resolved. Taking Figs 3.3 and 3.4 together focuses attention on the range of activities that take place under the banner of corporate strategy and international marketing. Having clear objectives for international activities provides a clear direction for the organisation and commits physical and human resources to its achievement. It also requires periodic review to establish how much progress has been achieved against the objectives.

In Fig. 3.3, a definition of the business is also required that is as challenging an activity as the others that precede it. Managers would be well advised to see how far the existing business definition is appropriate for other countries. Markets may only be just emerging for a particular product or service, such as may be found in East European economies; changes may, therefore, be required to broaden the appeal of the product. In other markets, the business definition is not well suited to the market environment, so modifications are required to suit the conditions encountered.

An important activity is that outlined in Fig. 3.4, with the need to review the external market and to adapt the business to the needs of the customers – i.e. a market-oriented approach is pursued. Customer benefits, target segments and the technology used to deliver the benefits can all be reviewed. Again, the example of Northern

Fig 3.3 FIRST STEPS TO GLOBALISATION

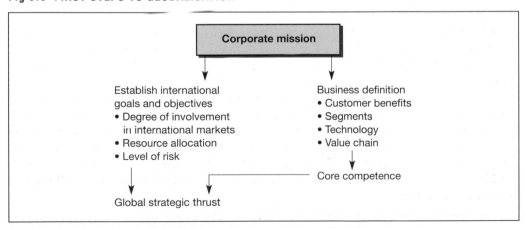

Source: Douglas, S.P. and Craig, C.S., *Global Marketing Strategy* (New York: McGraw-Hill, 1995). Reproduced with permission.

Fig 3.4 THE GLOBAL STRATEGIC PLANNING PROCESS

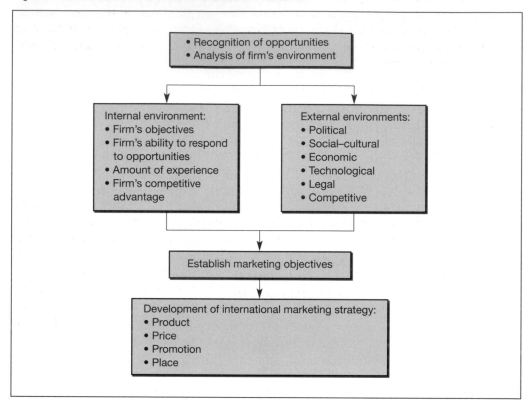

Telecom in Box 3.5 is instructive here. What is being proposed is that significant adaptation not just of the product, but of the whole process involved with its delivery be considered.

Customers' needs may be put in very different ways across different markets, taking into account the physical and business environment and the culture and attitudes of the peoples of the country.

The final aspect of the business definition, following the issues of customer benefits, segments and technology, is the value chain. As with all of these aspects, more detailed reviews are provided in subsequent chapters, but the value chain identifies a number of stages of activities associated with bringing the product to the market place. This covers sourcing, R&D, production (known as upstream activities) and marketing, distribution and service (known as downstream activities). A firm has to decide on the degree to which it should run all of these operations itself, or whether they can be contracted out or brought in. As reviewed in Chapter 4, there are advantages and disadvantages to each approach. What is relevant here is that the entry into the international market place raises the questions afresh as to the extent or advisability of pursing the same value chain strategy in a foreign country as a firm does in its home market.

If all of these aspects are taken together, the familiar ground of a business defined in the traditional way – i.e. as it is in the home markets – should be thought through if a marketing-oriented approach is to be maintained.

The core competence of a firm, which is the specific skills and assets that support the competitive advantage that itself supports the strategic thrust of the organisation, should provide the basis for the review of how this can apply to new situations and across the organisation. Douglas and Craig suggest that a core competence should possess three key elements:

1 it should provide access to a variety of markets;

2 it should provide a contribution to perceived customer benefits;

3 it should be difficult to imitate.

Applying this to the value chain might show how the skills associated with all aspects – say delivery and customer service – can be turned to the advantage of the company by showing how certain activities can be performed better than its competitors.

The final aspect highlighted by Fig. 3.3 is strategic thrust, which defines the area in which the firm seeks to compete, establishing priorities and determining the investment in resources necessary to achieve its goals. A further aspect to strategic thrust is the approach taken up in international markets, either seeking to obtain first-entry status or to follow others who have created or determined the market. Likewise, the company may choose to act aggressively or may avoid confrontation by aiming for neutral markets. Allied to this is the means by which to enter a market (followed up in the case study at the end of this chapter) – with, for example, the need to achieve organic growth or growth by merger and acquisition.

GENERAL ANALYSIS OF STRATEGIC OPTIONS

There are a number of strategies on offer to the manager when looking to enter a market. Some of these have been touched upon already, but a general outline of other issues related to the choices on offer is needed.

It has already been recognised that the international competitive environment is complex and seemingly more volatile that the domestic one. Success comes from an examination of the environment before making the most appropriate response, while combining the appropriate product–market option for the chosen market is a key task. Again, as noted earlier, a marketing orientation is the adoption of an approach that can obtain competitive advantage for the firm by providing the most suitable product offering for the customer.

The marketing manager's task is the planning and carrying out of programmes that ensure (long-term) competitive advantage. The task has two components:

1 to determine specific target markets; and

2 the management of the marketing mix elements that can meet the needs of the target markets.

Selecting target markets

The characteristics of the target market(s) need to be appreciated and acted upon. Czinkota and Ronkainen[18] use what they call the eight '0s' of Occupants, Objects,

Occasions, Objectives, Outlets, Organisations, Operations and Opposition to structure the appraisal of the market. Briefly these can be reviewed as follows.

1 *Occupants* – the customers whose attitudes can be defined in a number of ways, by age, sex, psychographics (attitudes, interests, life-style) or by product-related variables such as usage, brand loyalty, etc. This approach is more usually referred to as 'market segmentation', which focuses on the major influences on the occupants of a market through the decision process.

2 *Objects* – what is purchased to meet a certain need, whether this includes the physical object, services, ideas, places or persons.

3 *Occasions* – when the product is purchased.

4 *Objectives* – the motivations that underpin the purchase, whether tacitly acknowledged or not.

5 *Outlets* – where a product can be purchased or information about it received.

6 *Organisation* – how the purchase or the acceptance of the need to purchase is organised. The focus is on the decision-making unit, which can vary from the small and informal, such as a family or household, up to the large and formal units found in businesses and the public sector.

7 *Operations* – focus on the behaviour of the organisation that is buying the product. An understanding of its behaviour would identify how firms, such as supermarkets, decide to stock certain brands, and what barriers may be expected when trying to gain their acceptance of a new brand.

8 *Opposition* – looks at the competition that is currently found in the market and what might be expected in the future in response to a new entrant. This is a difficult area for consideration as competition can be direct – such as those offering the same product, those that serve the same need (e.g. alternative ways to spend leisure time) – or can come from an unexpected quarter (as, for example, exists for newspapers when they are faced with competition from the computer industry for the provision of on-line information services).

When looking at entering foreign markets, firms have to consider innovation strategies, as it is rarely the case that the existing product will serve the new market. The firm innovates on three dimensions – product innovation, technological innovation and market innovation – revealing that the target market might require more than simply the adjustment of the product to suit local circumstances. Innovation on one dimension requires careful planning, but demands by the market for innovation on two or three dimensions produces a situation where the planning task becomes more complex.

Analysing the eight 'Os' requires the marketer to adjust to the market, at least in the short term. The target market decision is critical for the market, with three general options on offer. *A*, one segment is selected, *B*, a number of segments are chosen, or *C*, the whole market is targeted with an undifferentiated product. (These three generic strategies will be further assessed in later chapters.)

Marketing management

The marketing mix elements can be tailored to the target market after the analysis of its characteristics and the target market decision has been taken. The correct marketing mix, which consists of Product, Price, Place and Promotion (the '4 Ps') mixes the elements together into a viable offering and is critical. Each element of the mix requires further planning – as, for example, with promotion, where the mix of advertising, sales promotion and public relations has to match the life cycle of the product, market sophistication and other variables.

To provide for successful market entry, the marketing manager must understand the strategy and have been influential in its formulation, and work with other senior managers to ensure that the stages of analysis, planning, implementation and control are given due weight and consideration.

SUMMARY

Strategy and strategic planning are important considerations for companies both in their own domestic market and internationally. Various approaches to strategy exist, focusing on the importance of the mission and objectives of the organisation and the involvement of managers in analysis, strategic decision making and implementation. The key role of marketing orientation in creating competitive advantage lies in its ability to free the organisation from some of the constraints of its past, permitting it to look at new ways of meeting customer needs.

Involvement in international markets requires careful thought and the involvement of the organisation over the long term, rather than seeing exporting or other types of involvement as a way of solving a short-term problem. Research has shown that success goes to those who take the long-term view.

Movement into the chosen market will elicit a response from those already serving the market, or if a totally new market will increase the interest of those looking at it as an opportunity for themselves. Yet again the role of competitive advantage comes to the fore, promoting the need for the organisation to understand how it can exploit its strengths at the expense of the competition.

Lastly, the international marketer has a crucial role to place in the process, with the selection of target markets and the combination of the marketing mix elements to exploit identified opportunities. The influence of marketing is a central feature of strategic planning and not an optional extra. At the beginning of the chapter the problem was raised as to the lack of influence of international considerations in the planning process. It can now be seen to be a central feature, with the role of the international marketer made clear.

This introductory chapter on strategy and planning will be followed up by chapters examining the appraisal of all the elements of strategy, planning and implementation.

REVIEW QUESTIONS

1 Why is strategy and strategic planning so important for success in international markets?

2 Outline the rational planning approach to strategy.

3 What alternative approaches exist to rational planning?

4 Why is motivation to pursue internationalisation so important?

5 Describe the steps to globalisation.

6 Why is market segmentation a key tool for the international marketer?

DISCUSSION QUESTIONS

1 Planning is often a complex and time-consuming process that many critics argue is a waste of time. What arguments can be put forward to support this view?

2 How might a supporter of strategic planning in international marketing counter the arguments put forward in Question 1?

3 Strategies may often come 'unstuck', have to be reviewed and even reversed. Using current examples, review the way a company can handle this problem.

4 Is market segmentation the key to success in international markets? Does this approach run counter to the argument for globalisation?

5 Using current government policy measures that encourage companies to export, review the difficulties in persuading companies to take this option seriously. What suggestions can be made to overcome these problems?

Case study

THE MARKETING/PLANNING FRAMEWORK[19]

Since the merger of Schweppes and Cadbury in 1969 into Cadbury-Schweppes plc, there has been a continuous programme of expansion world-wide. The company describes itself as a UK-based but internationally focused food and drinks business, operating primarily in the impulse purchase and informal consumption segment. Furthermore, the company has a stated commitment to:

1 continue to focus operations in the market sub-sectors of confectionery and soft drinks, and specifically to consolidate its soft drinks position world-wide as the largest and most successful non-Cola brand owner and to aim for a top three position in the global confectionery market;

2 aim for profitable growth via a flexible but carefully selected use of organic development, acquisitions and alliances;

3 monitor positively and regularly growth opportunities in adjacent market sections where acquisitions or alliances could bring real gain through synergy.

To achieve the company's objectives in both the beverages and confectionery markets, Cadbury-Schweppes have acquired companies across the world. The largest acquisition of recent years was Dr Pepper/Seven-Up (purchased in 1993) which increased Cadbury-Schweppes' share of the carbonated beverage market in the USA to over 16 per cent. The acquisition had a fundamental impact on the combined business, reducing the importance of the UK market for profits from 46 per cent of the total to 35 per cent, and correspondingly raising the profit earned from operations in North America.

Despite the intentions of the company to expand via organic growth, acquisitions and alliances, the company is a distant third to the greats in the carbonated soft drinks market,

Coca-Cola and PepsiCo. In confectionery, it lies fourth behind Nestlé, Mars and Philip Morris's Kraft, Jacob and Suchard. Although the group is much bigger with the acquisition of Dr Pepper/ Seven-Up, its capitalisation is £5.2bn against Coca-Cola's £78bn, PepsiCo's £34bn and Nestlé's £21bn. However, the opportunities offered in the confectionery market appear to provide more room for manoeuvre as the top three carbonated soft drinks groups control around 75 per cent of the world's market whilst the top six chocolate makers have less than 50 per cent of their market.

To acquire a company large enough to raise their share of the market (from five per cent) world-wide Cadbury-Schweppes would need to consider the purchase of companies such as Hershey (USA), also with a five per cent share, Ferrero (Italy) or Lindt & Spungli (Switzerland). Any one of these would be expensive to acquire and at the moment remain unavailable, controlled either by the founding family or (in Hershey's case) by a charity.

The approach is best described as piecemeal, either by purchasing medium-sized companies or by expensive investment in emerging markets. Large significant acquisitions in either the beverages or confectionery markets will be difficult to foresee in the short term.

The strategic benefit of acquiring Dr Pepper brought with it a strategic response from Coca-Cola, pushing the company from a minor competitor to a more significant one. In responding to the challenge Coca-Cola dropped some Cadbury root beer and fruit juices from its bottling system, and aims to replace the company as the root-beer leader in the USA.

Despite the well-known nature of the Schweppes brand, its market share is small, mainly focused on mixer drinks. Dr Pepper offers the best chance of creating a global brand with significant market share. The company is franchising its beverage brands to other bottlers, particularly after it sold its UK bottling joint venture to its partner Coca-Cola, so making it dependent on production deals with bottlers.

To reduce some of the difficulties of competition from Coca-Cola, Cadbury has obtained long-term agreement for its brands with bottlers in the USA owned by Coke. Dr Pepper, for example, has a five-year cancellation notice, compared to an industry norm of 90 days. The sale of the UK joint venture has also brought a long-term agreement, with a year's notice being given before dropping any Cadbury-Schweppes brand, and there are also agreements to stop rival brands being taken on by the bottler.

With its aspiration to become a significant player in the beverage and confectionery markets, and with significant acquisitions looking to be a distant project, the company has to look to its strengths to stay ahead of the game. One acknowledged area is in its marketing skills, which can be seen in operation through its policy relating to Dr Pepper. After the acquisition certain strategic priorities were identified which focused attention on the need to maintain strong links with the consumer, with products being widely available via vending, restaurant and fast food chains and other outlets. In addition, customer relations were given a high priority so that the needs of the retailers could be more easily serviced. Whilst still focusing on Dr Pepper, the company has a specific aim to realise the benefits of the acquisition, especially if it wishes to create a global brand. These would be to:

1 use the critical mass with bottlers to gain brand portfolio volume;

2 exploit opportunities in the market place;

3 realise synergy benefits in purchasing, manufacturing, markets, selling and administration;

4 develop Dr Pepper internationally, especially in markets where Cadbury-Schweppes is strong, such as Europe, Mexico and Australia;

5 maximise strong cash flow to help reduce debt.

To achieve all of these aims, whilst also supporting the development of new confectionery brands such as Fuse, Darkness and the relaunch of Boost, presents challenges for the management team.

Further development in the production of raw material for chocolate products (i.e. chocolate itself) is also an area where decisions have to be made. Cadbury-Schweppes along with Nestlé and Mars currently make their own chocolate, but there is an emerging trend for users to get out of chocolate making and concentrate on the production of branded products rather than the production of the raw material. Although not an issue for most, the prospect of reviewing this side of the business remains a possibility.

For many observers, Cadbury-Schweppes is, and for some time has been, at a crossroads. To achieve its stated aims in both markets will be difficult. Many in the financial markets expect that Cadburys will have to consider selling its soft drinks division to fund an acquisition of a confectionery company. The next question is who would want to buy the soft drinks operation, followed by the question of the target for the take-over. In any event, pursuing the perceived approach will be slow and expensive, but the marketing skills the company possesses may provide unexpected bonuses in keeping it on track towards its goals.

Questions

1 *Cadbury-Schweppes is a well-known company in the UK and in some other international markets. How far can it capitalise on its expertise in soft drinks and confectionery when entering new markets?*

2 *What was the strategic logic behind the acquisition of Dr Pepper?*

3 *To achieve its stated aims, organic growth rather than acquisition would appear to be the only method possible in the short term. What difficulties might this pose?*

4 *What might be the benefit to customers of the review of its operations?*

5 *What are the possible strategic advantages of having known marketing strengths?*

FURTHER READING

Albaum, G., *International Marketing and Export Management* (Reading, MA: Addison-Wesley, 1992).

Bartlett, C.A. and Ghoshal, S., *Managing Across Borders* (Cambridge, MA: Harvard Business School Press, 1989).

Ghoshal, S., 'Global strategy: an organising framework', *Strategic Management Journal*, 8 (1987), 425–40.

Grant, R.M., *Contemporary Strategy Analysis* (Oxford: Blackwell, 1991).

Ketelhohn, W., *International Business Strategy* (London: Butterworth–Heinemann, 1993).

Mintzberg, H., *The Rise and Fall of Strategic Planning* (Englewood Cliffs, NJ: Prentice-Hall, 1994).

NOTES AND REFERENCES

1   'Brand holds the key to revival of Liberty', *Financial Times* (15 July 1996).

2   Ellis, J. and Williams, D., *International Business Strategy* (London: Pitman Publishing, 1995).

3   Bradley, F., *International Marketing Strategy,* 2nd edition (Englewood Cliffs, NJ: Prentice-Hall, 1995), 33.

4   Ellis and Williams, op. cit., 7.

5   Hill, C.W.L. and Jones, G.R., *Strategy Management: An Integrated Approach*, 2nd edition (Boston, MA: Houghton Mifflin, 1992), 7.

6   Mintzberg, H., 'Crafting strategy' in Mintzberg, H., Quinn, J.B. and Ghoshal, S., *The Strategy Process*, European edition (Englewood Cliffs, NJ: Prentice-Hall , 1995), 114.

7   Hill and Jones, op. cit., 8.

8   Whittington, R., *What is Strategy and Does it Matter?* (London: Routledge, 1993), 10–38.

9   'Uphill struggle without its navigator?', *Financial Times* (15 March 1996); 'Evolution not revolution', *Financial Times* (25 March 1996); 'Component for success', *Financial Times* (8 May 1996); 'The new driving force at Lucas', *Sunday Times* (2 June 1996).

10 Financial Times Survey – 'Pharmaceuticals', *Financial Times* (15 March 1996); 'The road to fiscal ruin', *Lloyd's Bank Economic Bulletin*, 9 (June 1996).

11 Day, G. and Reibstein, D., 'Keeping ahead in the competitive game', *Mastering Management*, Part 18, *Financial Times* (1996); Glass, N., 'Chaos, non-linear systems and day to day management', *European Management Journal*, 14(1) (1996), 98–106.

12 'Siemens tries out no frills control', *Financial Times* (19 July 1996).

13 Bradley, op. cit., 75.

14 Brown, R. and Cook, D., 'Strategy and performance in British exporters', *The Quarterly Review of Marketing*, 15(3) (April 1990), 1–6.

15 Douglas, S.P. and Craig, C.S., *Global Marketing Strategy* (New York: McGraw-Hill, 1995).

16 'The future is calling', *Times* (22 April 1996); 'Northern Telecom remains wedded to technology', *Financial Times* (16 July 1996); Dolan, R., 'Marketing turnarounds', *European Management Journal*, 13(3) (September 1996), 239–44.

17 Douglas and Craig, op. cit., 83.

18 Czinkota, M.R. and Ronkainen, I.A., *International Marketing*, 3rd edition (Orlando: The Dryden Press, 1993), 22.

19 'The acquisition of Dr Pepper/Seven-Up', *The Times 100* (London: MBA Publishing, 1996); 'Cadbury poised to unveil new chocolate countline', *Marketing Week* (5 July 1996); 'Cadbury and Coke end CCSB deal', *Marketing* (6 July 1996); 'Cadbury hopes a diet of chocolate will help it grow', *Financial Times* (12 July 1996).

4

Analysis of global competition

INTRODUCTION

In the fight for markets, firms have to work out the best approach to gaining advantages over their competitors, defending this advantage by constant efforts to improve their capabilities and understanding the strengths of their competitors. This is one way of looking at competition, but a broader view can be taken involving the benefits to be gained from a competitive industry structure that produces firms able to compete effectively in the international market place. A firm's direction is determined by its strategy, but its ability to succeed is defined by its competitive advantage.

An ability to undertake a task or activity, i.e. to produce a particular product or service, is not the same as having a competitive advantage in its production, either in the home market or internationally. If the home market situation provides competitive advantage, can this be transferred to other foreign markets? All firms need to examine what distinct advantage they possess, how it can be exploited and what the costs are of doing so.

This chapter looks at a number of issues as firms face competitive advantage, both from their own point of view and also the challenge they may face from their competitors.

Objectives

This chapter will examine:

- the competitive advantage of nations
- sources of competitive advantage
- leveraging the firm's strength
- avoiding competitive disadvantage
- assessing competitive strategies
- value chains and the strategic role of global markets.

THE COMPETITIVE ADVANTAGE OF NATIONS

The advantage developed by a firm in its domestic market is determined to a significant extent by the national business environment, with benefits being derived from access to resources and skills and competitive pressures derived from other national firms creating the need to invest and innovate.

Porter,[1] in his theory of the competitive advantage of nations, finds four sets of attributes that influence the business environment (a review is provided in Box 4.1). The basic question asked by Porter is: 'why do some nations succeed and others fail in international competition?' He argues that that it is in fact the wrong question if the intention is to provide an understanding of what makes for economic prosperity for a nation or the firms within it. Rather, it is more instructive to look at why a nation becomes the home base for successful international competition in an industry, or how it is that firms in an industry from a particular country can create competitive advantage, and then sustain it over time.

Taking the examples Porter uses to support the theory of national competitive advantage will make the issue global. Why is Germany the home of the world's leading companies in luxury cars and chemicals? Why is Switzerland the home of leading companies in confectionery and pharmaceuticals? Why has the USA produced world leaders in personal computers, software and credit cards?

The need to understand the advantages gained by firms in industries in these countries is valuable for the individual firm in seeing what it is about its own location that can determine its ability to gain competitive advantage. A nation's standard of living over the longer term depends on its ability to improve the level of productivity in the industries in which its firms compete.

The role of the nation in helping to create favourable conditions has been overlooked in many of the theories that were reviewed in Chapter 2. In a sense, therefore, firms may overlook the advantages of their domestic location, an oversight that could severely reduce their ability to leverage competitive advantage.

Following from the review in Box 4.1 (*see* Fig. 4.1), nations can achieve success where they possess advantages in the diamond. In successful national industries, the interplay and self-reinforcement of the determinants are complex and often make it difficult to explain competitive advantage. In most industries, a nation succeeds because it combines some broadly applicable benefits with advantages that are specific to a particular industry or small group of industries.

Box 4.1   **CAN A NATION GAIN COMPETITIVE ADVANTAGE?[2]**

The increase in globalisation and the increasing integration of markets across borders provides a challenge to the nation-state. Despite the erosion of individual governments' ability to control events, they are, according to Kennedy the primary focus of identity, meaning that the government of a nation-state is still the institution people and organisations resident within its borders turn to for solutions. The government of a country must address the question: 'How can we maintain or improve our prosperity?' Porter, although agreeing that the question is frequently put in this way, feels that it misses the point. He

▶

▶ **Box 4.1 continued**

feels that the question should be: 'Why does a nation become the home base for successful international competitors in an industry?'

Macroeconomic stability, cheap labour, abundance of national resources, governments' industrial policies or differences in management techniques are all, according to Porter, less than successful explanations as to why certain countries prosper and others do not. The more relevant question is not based on whether a nation can be competitive – even the most successful nation economically over the last 40 years, Japan, has many industries that are uneconomic and provide a poor service. Rather, the focus should be on the use of resources in the most productive way, depending on both the quality and features of products and the efficiency with which they are produced.

Four broad attributes, that on their own and collectively can determine a nation's competitive advantage, can be identified. They are: factor conditions, demand conditions, related and supporting industries, and the environment in which firms compete. Figure 4.1 shows the relationship between the four attributes.

Fig 4.1 PORTER'S 'DIAMOND' OF A NATION'S COMPETITIVE DETERMINANTS

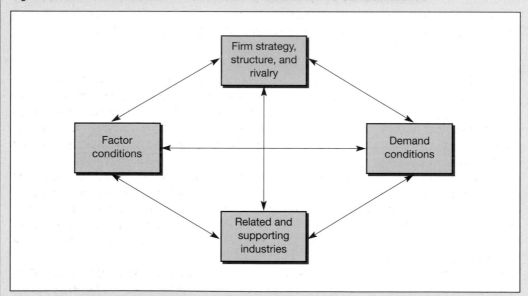

Source: Porter, M.E., *The Competitive Advantage of Nations* (London: Macmillan, 1990). Reproduced with permission.

Factor conditions

Each nation possesses factors of production (land, labour and capital), which can mean that a nation such as Russia has a large endowment of natural resources, while Holland does not. Some countries possess a highly educated workforce (Germany) while others do not (Namibia). Depending on the type and amount of resources available, the nation will tend to favour some industries rather than others. This does not determine the shape of a nation's industry and trade, but it has an influence upon it, as does its ability to maintain its competitive advantage by investing in the modernisation of resources, such as physical capital or the adjustment of its resource environment. Equally, nations can acquire resources, such as an educated labour force, to provide the advantage they seek.

▶ **Box 4.1 continued**

Gaining competitive advantage is not just a matter of looking at the quality and amount of the factors of production available, however; all the parts of the 'diamond' will have an influence. For example, a company that wishes to innovate must have access to skilled labour suppliers who can provide the necessary materials and know-how and the commitment to take the line of action that leads to competitive pressure and advantage.

Demand conditions

Does a nation have strong local demand for its goods and services? Porter argues that if it does then a number of benefits arise that can incorporate an understanding of what buyers want and positive reaction to a change in demand. From this understanding adaptations can take place to develop new or improved products that can then form the basis for successful exports.

Related and supporting industries

If suppliers are providing services at a cost lower than a competitor from a foreign market, then these industries are also helping to achieve internationally competitive production in their own right as well as assisting in the maintenance of a competitive position for the buyer. Suppliers can also provide valuable insight into trends and other issues.

Strategy, structure and rivalry

This looks at the context in which firms are created, organised and managed, along with the nature of domestic firm rivalry. Unlike universalist management theory that argues for a common approach to the management of companies whatever the country, nations do well in industries where the management practices favoured by the national environment are suited to a country's sources of competitive advantage (specific examples are provided in the main text).

A key area of importance is also domestic rivalry, where a strong and dynamic rivalry and competitive advantage would appear to be crucially related. Nations with leading world status often possess a number of robust local rivals that push management to maintain competitive advantage that can then be transferred abroad. The competition may also may be clustered in regions within a particular nation that bring out the best in the competitor's companies.

World leadership is dependent, therefore, on intense domestic competition, rather than local firms improving their domestic market and going international. To be strong internationally would appear to be dependent on having built up strengths at home.

The importance of competition is vital to the creation of competitive advantage. The four determinants noted by Porter feed off and interrelate to each other in complex ways. It is difficult to create conditions for this to occur within a country or for there to be one recipe for success – if there were, many more nations would be able to respond to the challenge. From the supply of skilled labour, with supporting services, through to attractive factor conditions, countries can benefit from the growth of strong firms at both the local and international level. Of itself, this cannot guarantee a future without challenge to a dominant position. Improving prosperity is a challenge for a country's government and its citizens.

Competitive advantage is maintained because the sources are improved and deepened. Porter argues that conditions that provide dynamic rather than static advantages are more important for success. So product innovation (a dynamic advantage) is more important than factor costs (a static advantage). The UK government's aim is to make the country the entrepreneurial capital of Europe. However, a large part of the UK's attractiveness may derive from static advantage, such as low direct labour costs, rather than the ability to meet problems with product innovation and applied research and development, both dynamic advantages. These difficulties have long been recognised, a feature that is picked up by Porter when looking at the UK's national agenda.

Taking the UK example still further, the weakness of car component manufacturers compared to their international rivals has been noted in other chapters, a factor that has resulted in problems in exporting and meant that foreign experts have been brought in to tackle falling standards and a lack of management expertise in matching the best world standards.[3]

DYNAMICS OF NATIONAL ADVANTAGE

Two parts of the diamond – domestic rivalries and geographic industry concentration – appear, from the theory of competitive advantage of nations, to have great influence insofar as they transform the diamond into a system. Domestic rivalry provides the upgrading of the entire national diamond; geographic concentration elevates the interactions within the diamond.

Domestic rivalry produces benefits in other ways, as it stimulates new rivals through spin-offs, creates and attracts factors, upgrades and expands home demand, encourages and upgrades supporting industries and channels government policy in more effective directions.

Competitive industries in a nation will not be evenly distributed, as a nation's successful industries are often linked through vertical or horizontal relationships, all of which tend to reinforce the cluster effect. Once a cluster has been established, benefits travel in many directions, with the maintenance of diversity which overcomes inertia, inward-looking approaches and blocks to competition.

However, industries can lose competitive advantage over time, leading to the loss of national advantage. As indicated above, the ability of firms to adapt to change is a vital part of the process of evolution. Any number of reasons for this loss can be cited, with Porter highlighting particularly factor conditions and home demand conditions.[4]

Factor conditions

Factor conditions decline, for example in investment in human resources or lack of investment in research to improve technology. With developing economies able to manufacture at a cheaper cost than developed economies, production will tend to move to these centres, bringing a challenge for the developed nations' firms as they have to upgrade their technology or lose advantage.

Home demand conditions

1 Advantage can come under threat if home demand conditions move along a path at variance with other advanced nations, with the consequence that local buyers exert a *pull on indigenous firms* that draws attention away from export (world) needs.

2 Home buyers can also present problems for home companies if *foreign buyers become more sophisticated*. This can come from a lack of rivalry in the home market that means that a lack of innovation keeps the industry and the market static. Trade barriers and government regulations can also reduce innovation, factors which mean that firms lose out to more competitive and innovative foreign rivals.

3 *Technological change.* Firms in other nations may gain advantages from the application of technology that requires a period of adjustment from the home nation's companies – a problem that presents opportunities for foreign firms to exploit. Technology, to be applied effectively, also tends to need supporting industries, which a nation may fail to possess. For example, biotechnology and software industries are found in only a few countries, so the development of these industries can support application and updating in other industries. A country with these industries can build competitive advantages.

4 *Rate of investment.* The rate or level of investment is determined to some extent by management goals, which are influenced by capital markets, the tax regime and so on. If investment is reduced compared to international competitors then the ability to innovate can be lost. Shareholders look for short-term investment returns, so R&D can be threatened, an accusation often levelled at UK companies.

5 *Flexibility.* Managers themselves may become complacent, particularly after a period of sustained success, which can undermine the need to change or adjust to new circumstances. Product regulations or decline in the status of the industry locally can also impact on the ability to adjust. What was previously a strength can become a weakness – for example, in investment in machinery, staff development etc. that supported successful past strategy but is now inappropriate to the current situation. A new competitor is not saddled with such costs and could have lower costs associated with innovation.

6 *Domestic rivalry factors.* Consolidation is a noticeable trend in many industries, which in itself can support competitive advantages. As with many periods of consolidation, it can result in anti-competitive positions being built that ultimately result in a reduction in innovation. Equally informal agreements or cooperative approaches can tend to freeze an industry, making it difficult to respond to new rivals. Lack of competition can produce a short-term increase in profitability as sales increase and supporting promotional expenditure is reduced. Longer term, a fall in profits will result as the industry is in a weak position to cope with new competitive pressures.

Building competitive advantage is a feature of many governments' push to improve their nations' economic performance; however, decline and loss of competitive advantage can appear as a hidden trend that catches many companies unawares. Recovery from this situation requires movement on many fronts, with changes in regulations, investment in technology and human resources, and creation of supporting industries that may take many years to achieve. It is very important for businesses to appreciate national benefits: an issue that raises the importance of business involvement in government policy.

The example in Box 4.2 of the automotive industry in the West Midlands area of the UK looks at the problems in dealing with decline, and how to fight back using the area's strength in car and car-parts production.

Box 4.2

THE AUTOMOTIVE INDUSTRY IN THE BIRMINGHAM AND WEST MIDLANDS AREA[5]

After decades when gradual decline seemed the only prospect, the leading motor manufacturers, as well as thousands of suppliers, are preparing for growth into the new millennium. According to economists, the region's motor industry has the potential to grow by six per cent a year over the next decade. This has come about, according to the experts, as the region has become attractive to overseas investors in terms of the critical mass reached, skills that have become available, and in cost and quality terms which have led to much import substitution.

One event shows that the region has turned the corner: the decision of Jaguar (owned by Ford) that it would build the X200 saloon at its West Bromwich plant in Birmingham. This was achieved against fierce opposition from the Ford plant in Detroit to have the work located there. The £400m project, which was backed by £80m of government and European money, is scheduled to create 1300 jobs and safeguard another 3000.

LDV, the Birmingham-based van maker, is looking for international partners to develop new vehicles and global markets, after successfully surviving the collapse of its Anglo-Dutch parent in 1993. Rover, owned by BMW, is undertaking investment programmes for its Land Rover production, while the company's strategy is to move towards niche cars from its mass production past.

Across Birmingham and the West Midlands, such rapid changes are multiplied through the hundreds of large and small suppliers in the region. Rover, for example, cut suppliers from over 2000 in 1991 to 500 in 1996. The challenge for the region's automotive suppliers is whether they can maintain the pace of change as the structure of the industry evolves.

SOURCES OF COMPETITIVE ADVANTAGE

Several approaches have been proposed for the analysis of competitive advantage. The best known has been proposed by Porter,[6] which identifies three competitive or generic strategy types. These are cost leadership, differentiation and focus. This approach depends on the use of strategic targeting, i.e. an industry-wide approach or a niche approach, plus strategic advantage or cost against perceived uniqueness. Cost and differentiation are broad strategies, although they follow different strategic approaches, (as, for example, the case of Rover quoted in Box 4.2, with the move away from mass-car production to niche models). Focus strategies limit the company to one segment of the market, which could itself use either a differentiation or cost approach to gaining success in that segment.

Although Porter argues that firms should not get stuck in the middle – i.e. that the company focuses on cost and quality issues – others have argued that this is not necessarily a problem. In some instances improved quality can lead to higher market share, which itself leads to improved economies of scale.[7]

Douglas and Craig[8] point to a refined framework that consists of three dimensions: customer value, emphasis on costs, and scope of market coverage. This provides a broad framework for possible strategies that highlight core competencies of the organisation and the selection of appropriate markets. Although this approach can be applied to domestic markets, it can also be applied to international markets, which even though more complex to enter and operate within than the home market can also benefit from a clear strategic approach, such as the strategy pursued by British Airways and reviewed in Box 4.3.

Box 4.3

BRITISH AIRWAYS[9]

In a survey of Europe's most respected companies, British Airways came second after assessment by top managers from across Europe. When asked for the best companies world-wide, the same group of managers voted British Airways the fourth most respected company. No other airline came in the top ten.

So what makes British Airways such a good company in the eyes of other managers? The transformation from a state-owned airline facing considerable difficulties to one of the world's most respected companies has been rapid, most notably in the fact that with pre-tax profit of £585m for 1995 it was also the world's most profitable airline. It therefore received high grades in the survey for business and management performance, effective corporate strategy, and was ranked first for impressive improvement in performance.

This level of performance is in the context of a rapidly changing world of aviation, where new alliances are being formed to create global carriers as markets become deregulated, encouraging the entry of new budget-fare carriers. Alongside this has come new (or old) competition from the high-speed railways being developed in many countries, that will contribute to an expected long-term fall in airfares.

Airlines have high costs in terms of purchasing and maintaining their fleets of aircraft, so profits are under threat as fares fall but fleet costs remain high. This scenario would lead in other industries to mergers and acquisitions, but airlines are still governed by government rules and regulations that, for example, mean that in the EU airlines can be only controlled by EU nationals, while only US carriers can make domestic flights in that country. Despite this, there has been a move to pursue an 'open skies' policy, particularly from the Americans, which has encouraged the move to create strategic alliances that in turn has led to the possibility of competition taking place as a result of the extensive nature of the network that the alliance has formed, rather than the effectiveness of the individual airline.

To maintain what can be regarded as the company's competitive position, British Airways has a number of challenges to meet. First, the increase in competition. Second, the way that competition makes itself felt. Third, the squeeze in profits that will occur as competition increases. To this end the airline undertook a review of its operations, announcing a reduction of 5000 jobs in the autumn of 1996 (almost a 10 per cent reduction in the workforce). This headline-grabbing move was given higher prominence than the announcement that an equal number of more skilled jobs, that would be open to those who were multi-skilled, would be created in the three years up to 1999.

▶

▶ **Box 4.3 continued**

A narrower focus on this shows that as the operations of the company have been reviewed – with, for example, luggage handling and ticket processing being compared against companies who might be offered contracts to run these functions on BA's behalf if they could be found to do so more cheaply but as effectively as the in-house operators. Managers were also set targets on costs, aircraft punctuality and the more efficient and effective use of assets.

Why then are labour costs so important to cut and control? Apart from the pressures noted earlier, there are also more long-haul flights, which depress air fares, as the airlines can charge more for short-haul per passenger miles than they can for long-haul. Couple this with the fact that holiday travel is growing faster than business travel, with holiday makers being more price-sensitive than business travellers, then the downward pressure on fares becomes more pronounced.

With fixed costs of fuel, aircraft, etc. being roughly similar for each airline and with staff making up to 25–35 per cent of total cost, then the key focus must be on this issue.

Two approaches are possible:

1 control staff costs by pay freezes or by changing working conditions;

2 contract out services.

British Airways, along with many other carriers, is looking at contracting out baggage handling, checking-in passengers, ticket handling and accounting. Taking this further means that other carriers can franchise the BA name, with nine carriers carrying the logo at the end of 1996. This produced £50m in income for BA in 1996, a figure that is targeted to double – the possibility exists that there could be the creation of a 'virtual airline'.

Following others in the industry could mean that work could go to contractors in India, for example, who could undertake ticketing more cheaply than in the UK. However, not all costs could be reduced in this way – as, for example, cabin crew have to have a high level of language skills, not required on some other airlines, an advantage that the company wished to maintain, but which means having to pay higher wages to attract the right qualified applicant.

Is this reaction reinforcing the view of a well-managed company, that is thinking ahead and responding to change in order to maintain competitive advantage? To take action before profits fall and costs rise would suggest that the change is being well planned. From the unions' side consultation has taken place and job losses are voluntary, although these will be made up with new jobs over a period of time. Doubts remain as to whether contracting out will work or that strategic choices will thrive and prosper. What is happening is a focus on the future that will attempt to preserve the place of BA high up on the respected companies list.

LEVERAGING THE FIRM'S STRENGTH

Cost approaches

Superior cost performance, as seen in discount airline companies, typically involves a pared-down product. Alternatively, companies can offer standard products – as, for example, many DIY retailers offer basic products such as paint at a permanent low price, rather than a one-off discount. This strategy will be effective where customers are price-sensitive, as for example first-time buyers would be when purchasing house-hold items for a new house.

Following a low-cost strategy rather than other possible alternatives is unlikely to have broad appeal in a developed economy. This would not be true of emerging economies, where in Eastern Europe customers have low purchasing power and a need for low-price products.

Cost leadership can, of course, be pursued as a strategy only when the firm has developed a superior cost position, often obtained by economies of scale, with effi-cient cost control and production management techniques. Investment to achieve these advantages is often required, and needs a total commitment by management to cost control. This suggests that the strategy is often product – rather than marketing – driven, and can be pursued in an industry where product differentiation is difficult and economies of scale are obtainable. This can also be used in international markets when they, too, can be entered and developed by similar cost-leadership approaches.

International markets can provide further opportunities for economies of scale, and can lead to a strengthening of the firm's position as barriers to competition can be set up with improved scale performance. This works when customers are price-sensitive across countries, so that they are prepared to accept standardised products rather than additional product features. However, these strategies contain risks (a problem to be recognised in all strategies pursued) as, for example, with the emergence of new process techniques that drive down costs, or the emergence of competition from low-cost competitors – a factor that affects car components manufacturing in the West Midlands and which raises the importance of seeking other strategies to preserve the long-term future of the industry.

Differentiation approaches

Differentiation approaches look at the creation of value to the customers, and involve offering superior products, the development of a robust brand or associated corporate image. Companies have also been able to develop approaches that make them faster in responding to customer requirements than other competitors. Competitive advan-tage is gained by offering targeted customers a product and associated services for which they are prepared to pay a higher price. By offering superior product quality the company can build market share and alongside this a satisfied group of customers.

How, then, is product quality to be enhanced and then guaranteed? 'Quality' can be the compliance with defined standards such as can be found in an individual country or within a multicountry economic area such as the EU. This, though, overlooks the total service that customers require, so firms have to consider how to deal effectively with all the customers' requirements, whenever they come into contact with the organisation.

Box 4.4   TOTAL QUALITY MANAGEMENT[11]

Total quality management (TQM) is a philosophy for change, originally developed in Japan, which systematises the change process, making changes easier to implement. Basic to its philosophy is the idea that the only thing certain in life is that things will change. Change can either happen to the organisation, i.e. a passive attitude is taken, or the organisation can become instrumental in changes that will occur anyway.

TQM looks for the opportunity to change, especially if it means that the organisation is able to do things better. However, this can appear to be a general and rather unfocused philosophy; a company or organisation following this route needs to define quality that can establish targets for improvement. Implied in this is the need to invest in training and development and the ability to get groups co-operating, for example, cross-functionally which can help with the exchange of information and ideas. In effect, TQM requires radical changes in the way an organisation is structured, the way people relate to each other and the interaction with the customer, as TQM requires an outward facing emphasis. Customers form judgements of who is the best to do business with, and can form these after encounters with any part of the organisation.

The key to gaining customer loyalty is the creation of value and the key to value creation is organisational learning. How can organisations learn? This is often achieved through failure – as, for example, if it monitors customer defections that can contain within them information that an organisation needs to compete and prosper.

The example of TQM in Box 4.4 is one way that many organisations have sought to instil the need to look critically at what they do and move to become better, often by looking at world-class standards in manufacturing or via improved distribution services.

Strong brand images that can help when products are basically undifferentiated, such as petrol or cola, or in an industry where image is important, such as in fashion or cosmetics.

Markets play a key role in differentiation approaches, requiring attention to customer needs and interests and the development of an ability to develop new ways to respond. The review of TQM above, although not derived from marketing, has the ability to require all personnel to be 'marketing literate'. So rather than marketing expertise residing with marketing professionals employed in the company, or agencies working for the organisation, it pervades the whole company, providing new ways to meet customer needs and requirements, create new products and enter new markets.

Differentiation strategies have been most successful in industries where customers require additional features. However, in developing economies, as noted previously, a differentiation strategy may appear less attractive when higher prices have less appeal than a low-cost strategy. Equally, in many countries public sector organisations may wish to push for low-cost approaches as public sector deficits are under attack. This can ignore very real changes or the variable speed at which change takes place. Petronas, the national petroleum company of Malaysia,[10] has instituted TQM throughout the organisation in order to compete more effectively against the large multinationals from America and Europe. Public sector restructuring, particularly in the EU countries, has meant that differentiation strategies are pursued to create competitive advantage. In the UK, colleges and universities compete for students both via the Student Charter initiative (part of the Citizens' Charter) that guarantees standards of service, and which is a national initiative, and via a marketing effort that creates a distinctive identity for the university.

Using differentiation strategies in the international market place is more difficult than for cost leadership. A differentiation strategy in the 'home' market based on a quick delivery time, or unique features may be impossible to replicate in another country, either because access to an efficient logistics system is limited or because the system itself is in the early stages of development. Likewise, customers in other countries may have less desire for the features found so attractive elsewhere.

When differentiation strategies can be made to work they provide advantages for the firm, as comparisons cannot be made just on price; other advantages accruing to the company would be the move towards the customer and providing them with a product that they require, rather than one that is assumed to be appropriate, an approach that is taken up in more detail in Box 4.5. The importance of this lies in the emphasising of marketing-related approaches, by identifying the needs of the customer, not just in receiving the product, but as relates to the total requirements associated with the purchase and use of it. This is strategically important as company's can gain competitive advantage from thinking through the implications of this for their business.

Box 4.5

IMPLEMENTING STRATEGY[12]

Organisations that want to succeed in the long term must look at their strategic direction, plus their ability to implement it and meet corporate objectives. Organisations have had to look very carefully at their internal system and procedures to see if improvements in these areas, rather than just focusing on markets and products, could gain competitive advantage for them.

Various approaches are offered by consultants whose aim it is to help companies turn their potential into actual advantage. Three approaches will be reviewed:

1 the balanced scorecard;

2 re-engineering;

3 operations management.

The balanced scorecard

Kaplan and Norton argue that as companies prepare for competition based on information, their ability to exploit intangible assets becomes more decisive than their ability to manage physical assets. The approach focuses on financial measures of performance, plus performance indications of customers, internal business processes and learning and growth. This approach, known as the 'balanced scorecard', enables companies to track financial results, while at the same time monitoring progress in building capabilities. In other words, it provides for the linkage of strategy to short-term measures and targets, so long as there is an emphasis on the four management processes of translating the vision, communication and linking, business planning, feedback and learning.

▶

▶ **Box 4.5 continued**

'Translating the vision' requires companies to turn lofty statements, such as 'being number 1 in the market', into agreed sets of objectives and measures. 'Communication and linking' lets managers communicate their strategy up and down the company, thereby linking it to departments and individual objectives. This is more important than other approaches that stress the utility of objectives, as the balanced approach has learning and growth as well as financial considerations to take into account.

'Business planning' has to acknowledge the benefits of the balanced approach, seeking to allocate resources to achieve long-term mobility. Lastly, 'feedback and learning' provides for feedback to be multidimensional, rather than the more usual one-dimensional feedback approach.

Companies who have used Kaplan and Norton's balanced scorecard approach have employed it as an integrated management system, using it to clarify and update strategy, communicate strategy throughout the company, align unit and individual goals with strategy, link strategic objectives to long-term targets and annual budgets, identify and align strategic initiatives and conduct periodic performance reviews to learn about and improve strategy. Benefits claimed for this approach are that it provides a framework, whilst also allowing strategy to evolve in response to changes in the market and in the surrounding competitive environment.

Re-engineering

A constant challenge faced by companies is the speed at which change takes place, either because customers become more educated and discriminating in their choice of products, or because of technological innovations that produce new threats to a company's way of providing its products to customers, as well as promoting new competitors or substitute products.

In this competitive business environment companies are looking at what makes them successful, a practice now referred to as business process re-engineering (BPR). Ascari, Rock and Dutton see it as having some common elements:

1 an emphasis on rethinking different aspects of the business and existing work practices, an approach that arises from observations that many business practices are outdated and no longer suitable;

2 an emphasis on processes: BPR proceeds on the assumption that a business can be defined as a set of interrelated processes that evolve to satisfy a set of customer-oriented objectives, and has as its goal the aim of obtaining radical performance improvements – which might be cost reductions, speed or quality, or a combination of these.

A study of re-engineering and change undertaken by Ascari, Rock and Dutton shows that focus on the common elements of culture, process, structure and technology becomes critical.

● *Culture*. To be successful with re-engineering, organisations have to recognise the need for flexibility and adapting in today's business environment. The refocusing of the organisation is on the customer as the focal point of cultural change and the recognition by everyone of the importance of this.

● *Process*. This is the review of the sequence of activity that fulfils the needs or requirements of the external (and internal) customer. (This is the way a BPR project is realised.)

▶ **Box 4.5 continued**

To be successful, organisations are required to identify core processes, seek improvement through streamlining and process innovation, while focusing on the customer.

● *Structure.* Structures can enable or constrain communication, knowledge transfer and customer content. They also define how communication takes place between individuals and the degree of individual or collective responsibility. BPR provides cross-functional teams and reaction between functional and process-based structures. According to the researchers of successful approaches, redefinition of jobs, along with flatter hierarchies and employee empowerment and delegation, are key elements.

● *Technology.* Business objectives drive IT requirements, with integration of often fragmented IT systems leading to the emergence of an effective partnership between business staff and IT specialists.

The conclusions reached by the researchers can be summarised as follows:

1 all companies benefit from a continuous re-evaluation of the environment, and how the organisation interacts with it;

2 successful companies may not feel the need to change, but they have to adapt to changing circumstances just as much as less successful firms;

3 focusing on the customer is essential in the redesigning of the business; research has revealed that companies in good or average positions had a customer orientation, whilst those in difficulties showed very little evidence of such a stance;

4 clear goals are essential for change, along with senior management's commitment to the change proposed;

5 organisations should focus on redesigning processes in order to gain maximum improvement; focusing on functions or departments often leads to ineffective solutions.

Operations management

Operations management looks at the resources which are used in the production of goods and services, along with the activities, decisions and responsibilities that facilitate production. Operations management can be defined in a narrow way, or in such a way that much of the product–service development activities, most of the engineering, technical and purchasing activities, along with some of the personnel, accounts and finance activities come within its remit. Slack *et al.* incline to the broader definition, as they focus on the impact on the production of goods and services.

A key role of the operations part of the business is to support strategy, so that resources can be developed to provide the capabilities needed to allow the organisation to achieve its strategic goals. A second role is to implement strategy, whilst a third role is to drive strategy by giving it a competitive edge (advantage).

For an organisation that wishes not just to survive, but to succeed in the long term, the contribution of the operations function is critical. This can be achieved through five performance objectives that can be applied to both the public and private sectors:

1 '*Do things right*': be free of mistakes, providing products that are fit for their purpose, if this can be achieved, then a quality advantage is gained for the organisation;

▶

▶ **Box 4.5 continued**

2 *'Do things fast'*: not doing things to get the job out of the way, but to reduce the time between the customer placing an order or making a request and the delivery of the product or response to the question/enquiry; this helps to increase availability of goods to customers, thereby providing a speed advantage;

3 *'Do things on time'*: adhere to delivery dates, making it easier to give accurate days and times so that the customer finds the organisation dependable;

4 *'Change what you do'*: gain a flexibility advantage to meet changed circumstances or unexpected situations;

Fig 4.2 PERFORMANCE OBJECTIVES AND EXTERNAL/INTERNAL EFFECTS

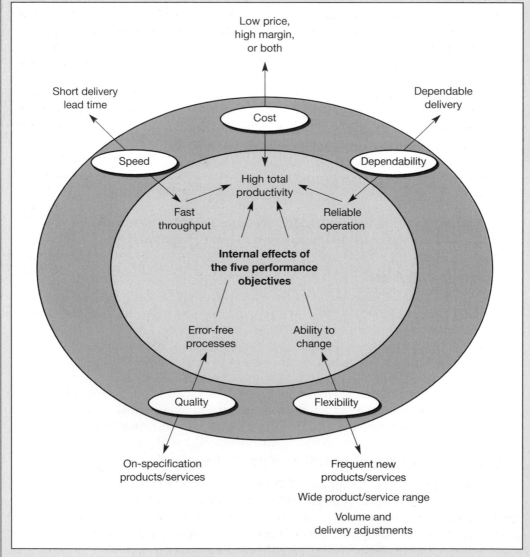

Source: Slack, N. *et al.*, *Operations Management* (London: Pitman Publishing, 1995).

> **Box 4.5 continued**

5 *'Do things cheaply'*: produce goods and services at a cost that enables the organisation to price them in the most appropriate manner for the market, or to show that the taxpayer is obtaining value for money. This provides a cost advantage.

Each of the performance objectives, as shown in Fig. 4.2, has external and internal effects with, for example, the internal effect of high quality, speed, dependability and flexibility helping to reduce costs if undertaken in the most effective way.

The three approaches outlined here have a common focus, which is to look carefully and critically at what the organisation does – i.e. how it presents itself to the market place. Each of the approaches has a particular bias and some critics would point out that many of the ideas and concepts are not new or particularly original. From the marketing point of view, though, they have an important message, which is the need for all parts of the organisation, along with all its employees, to be customer oriented: without this commitment and common purpose a well intentioned strategy will be compromised.

Re-engineering with its links to downsizing has been the subject of much debate, with experts in the field acknowledging that reducing size or flattening the organisation has resulted in experienced workers leaving, and existing workers shouldering the burden, with the result that operations have suffered. None of the approaches, therefore, gives a blueprint of how to go about initiating change. Instead they promote the importance of change while at the same time raising the importance of a considered management approach to the problem.

The achievement of corporate objectives by such approaches and methods of operations management also reveals the multiskilled requirements of managers, whether they be production, research and development or marketing managers. Each area is expected to assist in the achievement of corporate goals and objectives which they do singly and together, either as a part of an integrated team or by the delivery of some facet of the product offering to customers as they make enquiries, seek credit to purchase the product, respond to new products, seek after-sales service, or wish to be provided with a comprehensive and reliable offering by the organisation. Looking at how this is achieved is a key factor in bringing to life competitive advantage for the customer.

AVOIDING COMPETITIVE DISADVANTAGE

It has been accepted that firms should pick one or other of the strategies, i.e. cost leadership or product differentiation. In addition, there are also considerable problems with the actioning of strategies. The main issues can be summarised as follows.

Combining cost leadership and product differentiation

Some firms have effectively combined both cost leadership and product differentiation, with improved product quality and service, which initially raises costs but which can lead to increased market share and hence scale economies. In the UK, J Sainsburys, the grocery supermarket group, has prided itself on keeping costs down due to its market share; this has enabled it to look at the quality of its products and service, attempting to improve year after year, a strategy that can assist with differentiation.

Sustainable cost leadership

Cost leadership means sustainable cost leadership, which as we have seen is problematic if others can copy this approach. Cost leadership could come from sustaining relative market share, an advantage that other firms would not be able to emulate, at least in the short term. It is not certain what the term 'substantial (relative) market share' implies in practice, with various definitions suggesting that it relates to the nearest one, two or even three competitors.

Cost-based approach

Johnson and Scholes[13] point out that Porter uses the terms 'cost leadership' and 'low price' as interchangeable items. However, cost is an input measure and price an output one. Following a cost-leadership approach will not automatically mean that prices will be trimmed. Lowering cost can produce higher margins for investment in R&D and related activities that can provide an edge in the market place – it may be that this feature is the reality in the competitive world that many firms face. Using a cost-based approach can provide managers with the opportunity to compete effectively.

Differentiation

Johnson and Scholes also point to a problem associated with differentiation. 'Differentiation' is used here to refer to the ability of the firm to price products higher than competitors. Here again firms may choose to price products at similar levels to their rivals in order to capture market share. Unique features for a product do not necessarily mean that prices will be raised. Differentiation also brings with it problems of definition. For example, how are competitors to be defined – are they so obvious when an industry can be classified in a broad way, say, food retailing that includes (in the UK), Tesco, Asda, Marks & Spencer and Kwik-Save? It may not be so obvious to spot a direct competitor:

- differentiation can be pursued on different platforms. It could be on products and quality but, as marketers are well aware, consumers are influenced by many factors that can form a comprehensive list. In the case of supermarkets, for example, it includes location and store design to name but two

- using strategies of cost and differentiation across borders depends on the similarity of market structures. Concerns of choice, quality and price would permit similar strategies to be employed, but finding evidence for this via marketing research would be problematic.

FOCUS STRATEGY

A firm can use an approach that pursues broad targeting of customers with a common strategy. As an alternative to this, a firm can adopt a focused strategy that targets a specific market segment, or small clusters of segments. It is the latter approach that will be reviewed here.

'Focused differentiation' means that businesses may compete with each other by offering higher value to the customer at a higher price. The most notable example of this is BMW, which chooses to attract a certain type of customer who is willing to pay more for one of their cars than the saloon cars offered to the market by Ford or General Motors.

There is, of course, a risk associated with this approach, as the company will have to guarantee that there is a determined set of customer needs that are consistent or slowly changing over time and which the company knows it can meet. Equally, the emergence of global markets presents a challenge in so far as a broader approach may become an increasing attraction as new opportunities emerge.

Market segment differences may be gradually eroded over time, a situation particularly noticeable in the motor vehicle industry as even family saloons acquire the features and attributes that were once available only on luxury cars. Continuing with this example, circumstances may change so that a company following this strategy is unable to generate the income to improve its product to keep pace with changes in the market, particularly environmental considerations, such as noise reduction and fuel efficiency. Rolls-Royce, which for many years depended on a 'basic' engine unit, found itself in the early 1990s facing up to the problem of how to finance the development of a new engine. As with many luxury car producers, such as Jaguar and Aston Martin, alliances or take-overs by other car producers come to be the route by which survival can be guaranteed. In Rolls-Royce's case, this meant a link-up with BMW.

Focus strategies can be appropriate where broad market penetration is too expensive, or where the infrastructure is not sufficiently developed to go for a more significant market entry approach.

It is also open to companies to pursue various strategies across markets, so targeting a broad market base in the country of origin can be contrasted with a focused approach in international markets. A strategy that can be effective when demand in foreign markets is more heterogeneous than in the home market or when price sensitivity is less important.

ASSESSING COMPETITORS' STRATEGIES

Reviewing an organisation's position has to be undertaken in relation to its competitors, either when looking at the market or in relation to the competition for resources, as many in the public sector will have to do. This can be achieved via a focused review of the competitive environment, looking at the factors that influence the organisation's capacity to find an effective competitive strategy.

Using the five-forces model developed by Porter provides a structure for this process.

Box 4.6

VALUE-CHAIN ANALYSIS

For an organisation to develop, it must know its strategic capability. Organisations can use various means to do this; traditionally, this has often meant that strengths and weaknesses of its resources have been identified, along with the way they are currently used. The problem is that these are often treated in isolation, leading to significant issues being overlooked. A typical problem is often how an organisation can improve in a certain area, rather than why it is necessary for the company to carry out the activity at all.

The value-chain approach, developed by Porter, identifies the links between activities and the value of them, 'value' in this case being assessed from the viewpoint of the customer of the organisation. Attention is then focused on the competitive advantage gained from the way firms organise and perform activities.

The business of an organisation can best be viewed as a value chain in which the total cost of all activities undertaken to develop and market a product or service yields value. Organisations should understand their value chain, which includes activities of, for example, obtaining raw materials, designing products, building manufacturing facilities and providing customer services. The value chain, shown in Fig. 4.3, shows total value, made up of various activities. Primary activities show the sequence in which the activities are performed by the organisation in converting raw material input to finished products and the transfer of the product to the customer:

1 *inbound logistics* consists of the activities concerned with receiving, storing and handling of raw material;

2 *operations* are the transformation of the raw material input into finished goods – activities here can include assembly, testing, packing and maintenance;

3 *outbound logistics* are those activities relating to storing the product and distribution to customers; this includes packaging, warehousing and testing;

Fig 4.3 THE VALUE CHAIN

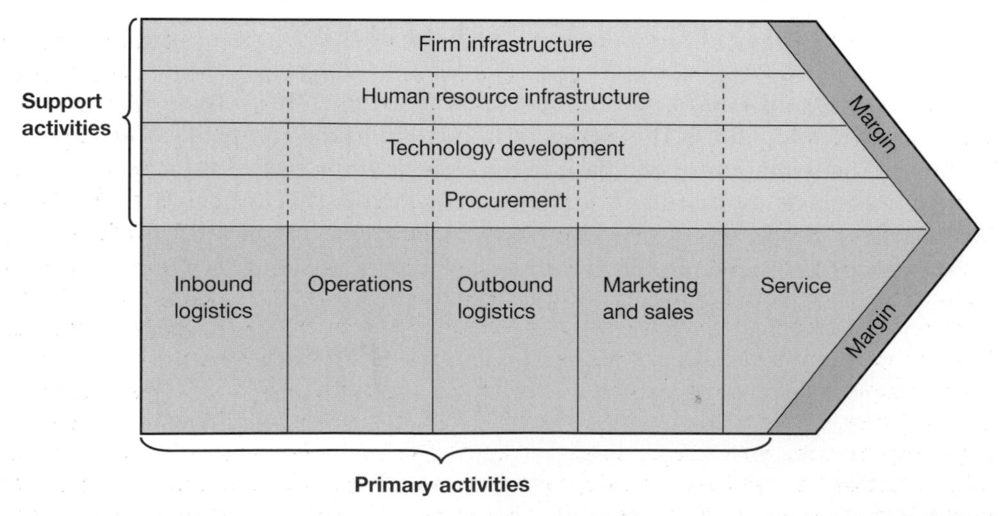

Source: Porter, M.E., *Competitive Advantage* (New York: The Free Press, 1985); © 1985 Michael E. Porter. Reprinted with permission.

▶ **Box 4.6 continued**

4 *marketing and sales* are concerned with activities that relate to informing customers about the product, encouraging them to buy and enabling them to do so;

5 *after-sales services* are activities such as installation, repair, upgrading, spare parts, and so on.

Any one or a combination may be a source of advantage. Support activities are those which provide purchased input, human resources, technology and infrastructure. Each of these cuts across all of the primary activities, where at each stage aid or assistance is provided for the primary activities:

1 *procurement* refers to those activities which acquire the resources input to primary activities, such as the purchase of material;

2 *technology development* – such as techniques, work organisation, etc. – are activities related to product design and to improving processes and resource utilisation;

3 *human resource management* covers the activities of recruitment, training and development;

4 *firm infrastructure* or management planning concerns the systems of planning, finance and quality control which are all activities important to an organisation's strategic capability in all primary activities.

In addition to the categories described, Porter identifies three further types of activity:

1 *direct activities*, concerned with adding value to inputs;

2 *indirect activities*, which enable direct activities to be performed – e.g. maintenance;

3 *quality assurance*, which monitors the quality of other activities via inspection, review and audit.

The value chain will differ between organisations, as each will have its own unique capability profile. Equally, the value chain does not exist in isolation as it is not constrained by an organisation's borders, being connected to a value system, such as those of suppliers, distributors and so on.

In addition to managing its own value chain, an organisation can obtain or leverage competition advantage by managing the linkages with its suppliers and customers. Making best use of these links means giving consideration to the value chains of suppliers and customers, with JIT being but one example of how these can be integrated. It is not surprising that this approach can also be used to good advantage when judging competitors.

In Fig. 4.3, an element referred to as the 'margin' has been incorporated. This is the excess that the customer is prepared to pay over the costs of the inputs and activities.

Although the value chain is a straightforward concept to grasp and can lead to the identification of competitive advantage, as well as eradicating the shortcomings of much SWOT analysis, it is a difficult concept to apply in practice. For example, the linkages between the elements are often hard to track down as, for example, looking at the firm's infrastructure and its support for primary activities. However, it can raise important questions of the value added by activities and how these can be improved, so long as this is in the interests of the customer. So, for example, IT can be applied to the improvement of stock holding and production. Automation can improve quality and raise output, and marketing can benefit from the use of databases, and other software packages that identify customer requirements or potential opportunities to present opportunities to buy.

▶

> **Box 4.6 continued**

It is also possible by the value chain approach to ask the question as to the necessity of undertaking such operations in-house if they can be more successfully undertaken by sub-contractors. References were made in Box 4.3 to British Airways and its desire to reduce costs by sub-contracting out ticketing, luggage handling and other activities. The value chain can result in dramatic changes in the way an organisation operates in the pursuit of competitive advantage.

Threat of entry

This depends on the effectiveness, or lack of effectiveness, of barriers of entry. The problem with the interpretation of this lies in the static analysis that is often undertaken taking an historical or static view of 'how things are now', rather than a dynamic view of how changes will influence business in the future.

Some of the main barriers are associated with economies of scale, or the capital required to enter an industry. Others will be associated with the regulatory regime or government policy, which can be seen in the regulation of the telecoms market in the USA and UK. Still other barriers can be associated with the benefits of effective strategy that has produced a clear preference for the goods and services offered by a particular organisation. To compete against this would take a great amount of investment, for which the new entrant may not have the financial resources or nerve.

Power of buyers and suppliers

This can be viewed as one issue as these groups can have a major impact on strategy. A striking example is the power of supermarkets in the UK, who have a significant impact on price and quality expected of suppliers that has built up over two decades, and for which many suppliers were unprepared. So great is the influence of supermarkets that they also provide responses to major food problems such as the BSE or 'mad-cow disease' scare in 1996, introducing quality schemes for beef throughout the industry.

The importance of supplier power can be felt when there are few of them, the brand which they supply is important for the market place and when switching from one supplier to another would be costly. There are other examples that can be added, but the basic point remains valid: power can lie with suppliers and this has to be given its due recognition in the determination of strategy.

Likewise, buyer power can be high when there are only a few major purchasers in the market, there are alternative sources of supply, or there is a threat of backward integration from the buyers.

Looking at supplier–buyer links, it has been argued that the UK, unlike Japan, has had a competitive situation in relation to these links. Some notable examples, such as Marks & Spencer's relationship to its suppliers, tend to be the exception to prove the rule that competition rather than co-operation can prove beneficial. Since FDI in the UK has increased, however, the move by firms to create supplier networks, particularly in the automotive industry, has been significant.[14]

Threat of substitutes

This can come from various sources, such as the substitution of one product for another (such as electronic organisers for the 'filofax') or from the competition for alternative ways to spend household income, when cars are balanced against holidays or a major extension to the house. The key issues here are how far the threat acts to determine the freedom of the company in the prices it sets, or in the introduction of a new product. The ease of switching is also important when, for example, moving personal accounts from one bank to another was rare as switching costs were high and the advantages of doing so low. With the deregulation of the finance industry, including retail banking, this is now less the case, and switching costs have fallen.

Competitive rivalry

Rivalry is often based on the maturity of an industry, or when a protected and highly regulated industry is privatised and competition introduced. If entry barriers are low and substitutes increase then rivalry will be intense. Equally with mature markets, one of the firms may push to gain market leadership, or when excess capacity exists and exit costs are high, then competition may ensue. It is not clear, therefore, that young dynamic markets will be marked by intense competition. Outbreaks of intense competitive rivalry can also occur as industries reach maturity.

If each of the five forces is viewed as a separate issue then the overall picture may be lost. Sound management judgement will have to be exercised in looking at the principal forces at work that have meaning for the organisation. Competitors – assuming that they also undertake a similar review of competitive rivalry (a fact likely to be the case as organisations go through similar strategic reviews)[15] – are also attempting to deal with a competitive environment. It is vital to know the objectives they have, what strengths they possess and what their strategic thrust will be. Many differences will exist between organisations, ranging from product diversity, international activities, cost, price, and so on. This becomes more of a challenge when competing internationally, as the required information may not be so easily to hand or subject to interpretation.

This problem of competitors' strategy in international markets focuses attention yet again on the need to assess how far a competitive advantage can be sustained on the international stage. Comparisons must be made to ensure that the strategy of the organisation has a good chance of success. In a sense, competitive rivalry analysis can be applied to international markets to determine the feasibility of entering a market, and if appropriate action can then influence the mode of entry, either via direct export or joint venture, or other variants.

Competition can be reviewed by looking at local and international competitors. Local competitors have a domestic focus, a feature that can provide them with key advantages ranging from the possibility of government protection to preference shown to them by the local population, and have key advantages in the supply chain. As with all situations there are weaknesses to locally-based competitors, such as cost, finance and management expertise. From the analysis of such local competitors a new entrant to the market can determine the most effective strategy.

Multinational competition exists in markets such as oil, detergents and cars. Companies operating in these industries, such as General Motors, obtain economies of scale in production and are also able to invest in advertising and R&D to maintain their dominance. They can also obtain access to resources denied to smaller companies, as they source materials from sites across the globe. Working across markets may open the organisation to the need for world-class standards to be applied both to its operations and its products, and can result in further advantages. However, multinationals, with their high profile, are often the subject of hostility from host governments, who look at the profits and power that they have, and in countries such as France at the perceived threat to their culture (particularly American companies). Hostility can come also from environmental and political groups, who look at the exploitation of resources as a threat to the environment and an implied support for political regimes – in 1995, Shell was criticised for environmental pollution due to its activities in the North Sea, and for seemingly supporting the repressive regime in Nigeria.

Both types of competition, local and multinational, have to be assessed, with Cadbury-Schweppes, for example (as we saw in the case study at the end of Chapter 3), looking at global trends and competitors such as Nestlé and Mars, while at the same time looking at local competition in the countries where it operates. Moves in either area can be significant for the success of the company, with domestic rivals moving into the international arena, while multinational rivals may choose to compete with Cadbury in a new market.

THE VALUE CHAIN AND THE STRATEGIC ROLE OF GLOBAL MARKETING

Competitive strategy has shifted from the battle to find a space for the product in the high street, for example, to a need to focus on all the firm's operations (a review of which was given in Box 4.6). A firm can gain competitive advantage which it can defend over time and be profitable despite the fact that the industry structure is unfavourable and other facets of the industry's operations are less than favourable. This gives hope for a well-managed organisation to enhance its performance via a thorough review of everything it does.

Marketing strategies can be developed for all facets of the value chain. In going for an international competitive advantage, the firm can look at all the elements of the business system, which entails cost against value, and in which improvements or changes can be made. The requirement to do this, while at the same time understanding the advantages that competitors have in international markets, is built round the challenge of reduced trade barriers and improved communications, resulting in protected markets coming under threat from new and aggressive competition. For an organisation to survive and prosper it has to look at itself, the industry and the competitors in it, and not just at how it is now, but how it might be in the future. The structured approaches reviewed here are a means by which this can be done.

SUMMARY

Competition is a feature to be found in virtually every country in the world. In emerging markets, the upheaval it has brought has been most notably felt by the state-owned enterprises (SOEs). In the Pacific Rim area, new opportunities have arisen, particularly in the consumer goods industries, while in the developed countries previously protected markets have been opened up to competition. How can an individual firm or organisation survive in this environment?

In some nations, competitive advantage is gained by a number of factors associated with the structure of the industry, concentration and support initiatives, along with government policy; the advantages of geographic location can often be overlooked when focusing on globalisation issues. Whatever the position of the industry under review, it is still possible for the firm to build a strong presence, perhaps from an improving position, if it looks at the rivalry in the industry and its own internal operations. Looking outward is easy to do, but it is by reference to what is often referred to as the 'competencies of the firm' that the two can be married up.

The approaches reviewed in this chapter – the value chain, competitive rivalry and generic strategies – can all be applied to improve performance and build competitive advantage, and can be changed to suit new circumstances such as a move into a new foreign market. As these techniques have gained wide acceptance, they have been applied in many companies, which could threaten their claim to effectiveness. It is in the way in which they are applied, the lessons learned and the action taken, however, that success may be judged. All of these approaches agree that as organisations are unique and opportunities increase, it is a determined pursuit of competitive advantage that organisations should be looking towards for their long-term survival.

REVIEW QUESTIONS

1 Outline the main framework of Porter's theory of the competitive advantage of nations.

2 What are the main elements of the value chain?

3 What is the purpose underlying the generic strategies approach?

4 Identify the difficulties of applying generic strategies.

5 Where can information be obtained to review competitors' strategies?

DISCUSSION QUESTIONS

1 Why is Porter so insistent that firms should not be stuck in the middle between cost and differentiation?

2 Can the techniques reviewed in the chapter be equally applied to the public sector?

3 Could a university or college apply value-chain analysis to itself, and if so what purpose could it serve?

4 If operations can be sub-contracted out on the scale envisaged by British Airways, will the trend produce the same problems as downsizing?

5 How important is marketing in monitoring competitive advantage?

Case study

REORGANISATION IN THE EUROPEAN DEFENCE INDUSTRY[16]

In 1996, Boeing purchased Rockwell's defence business for $3bn, one of a number of deals that had seen consolidation in the industry in the USA. The European industry, on the other hand, remained fragmented along national lines, with the result that companies were seen as being too small to compete effectually in the large defence projects of the twenty-first century.

The Europeans' inertia was explained by the desire of individual countries to maintain their own defence capabilities and the support for the high-tech industries that this policy would reinforce. Meanwhile, each country's Ministry of Defence had its own procurement approaches and weapons requirements, with each country pursuing aims and objectives that were different enough to influence the type of weapons and defence systems that they would go for. Lastly, defence budgets came under attack as countries aimed to reduce their budget deficits to meet the Maastricht criteria for membership of the Single Currency 'club', and the reason to maintain a high defence profile was undermined by the changes in Eastern Europe that had occurred in the late 1980s and early 1990s.

The knock-on effect was felt throughout the whole industry. Cutbacks meant that collaborative projects on the Future Large Aircraft (the European version of the Hercules family of transport planes) and even the Euro-fighter were in doubt. In France, the decision to privatise Thompson meant that companies outside France could see the possibilities of new alliances leading to rationalisation. The Legardère Groupe of France, owner of the Matra defence company, has formed a joint venture with British Aerospace in missiles and another with GEC–Marconi (UK) in satellites.

The Four-nation Euro-fighter, along with the French Rafale and the Swedish Gripen, are all going into production and covering some of the same defence needs; consolidation is needed if competition with American companies is to be pursued. Talks between Dassault and Aerospatiale aim to create the French equivalent of British Aerospace; the alliance between British Aerospace and Saab is another move towards consolidation. However, Europe has to be aware of the delicate political nature of such moves, with countries keen to keep each other involved. This is a desirable feature, but one which has slowed the rate at which change is taking place.

In the USA, where none of these problems exist, the rate of change has accelerated, leading to larger companies adopting an aggressive export approach that has seen Lockheed Martin, for example, offer low-priced F16s to Hungary in order to postpone the decision to have a co-production agreement on the Gripen.

Compared to the Americans even the successful European defence companies look small. US company Lockheed Martin led defence sales in 1995 at $19.4bn, with McDonnell Douglas having $10bn and Boeing/Rockwell $7.8bn. The next largest was British Aerospace with $6.5bn. Out of the top 20 companies, 11 were American, two British, four French, one German, one Italian and one Japanese. Total defence sales in 1995 of US companies in the top 20 equalled $65.84bn, while the combined total for the European companies was $30.32bn. Realignments are not just a feature of Aerospace; in armoured vehicles, Germany, France and Britain have moved to develop a multirole armoured vehicle at a cost of $3bn. A number of Anglo-German groups competed for the contract, Vickers and Alvis (both UK), Thyssen and Henschol (both German) and GKN (UK) and Krauss-Maffie, Nheinmetall and Wegman (German).

The creation of groups that create a pan-European industry could result in pressure for protection from US imports, particularly as now more advanced products could then be exported abroad. Despite this, American firms have spoken of their support for consolidation as future alliances between US and European firms would be worthwhile. This latter possibility has raised the prospect of European firms joining with US firms as an alternative to mergers with German, UK or other European companies. This strategy would make sense if access could be gained to what is often superior technology, and reduce the duplication seen in many areas.

One area where Europe has a model for consolidation is outside the defence industry, but within aerospace. Airbus Industrie, which has moved to become a fully listed company, has saved the civil aircraft business from becoming extinct in the face of US competition, with Boeing and Airbus now fighting for dominance. A similar idea is being put forward for defence contractors. Vertical integration – with, for example, a warplane maker combining with a firm that makes the electronic systems it carries – is also a possibility. In the USA alliances of this type have helped both Lockheed Martin and Northrop Grumman.

In the period where high-tech weapons were only a possibility, where new weapons could be developed relatively cheaply and where the nation-states of Europe had one common enemy in Eastern Europe, with a counter-balancing superpower of the USA, plus some interest in other areas of the globe, small nationally focused defence firms could prosper. As changes have come about in all areas, the possibility of remaining as they are is not an option for the Europeans: if competitive advantage is to be built then major changes have to come about, not only to compete in the world's export markets but also for the contracts that will be up for tender within Europe itself. The need to keep abreast of new technology will also forge the need to create alliances.

Questions

1 *How have American companies managed to build up such a dominant position in the defence industries?*

2 *Identify the constraints that European defence companies still find themselves burdened with.*

3 *It has been suggested that the management of European defence companies has failed to see the need for change. Why might this be so?*

4 *Other than by alliances and mergers, how can competitive advantage be built in Europe?*

5 *US companies will find increasing threats from Europe if rationalisation takes place. How can they respond to this?*

6 *How can markets play a role in the defence industry when targeting export markets?*

FURTHER READING

Davidson, W.H., *Global Strategic Management* (New York: John Wiley, 1982).

Douglas, S.P. and Craig, C.S., 'Evolution of global marketing strategy: scale, scope and synergy', *Columbia Journal of World Business* (Fall 1989).

Johanson, J. and Vahlne, J.E., 'The mechanism of internationalism', *International Marketing Review*, 74 (1990), 11–24.

Prahalad, C.K. and Doz, U., *The Multinational Mission* (New York: The Free Press, 1987).

Takeuchi, H. and Porter, M.E., 'The strategic role of international marketing: managing the nature and extent of worldwide coordination' in Porter, M.E. (ed.), *Competition in Global Industries* (Cambridge, MA: Harvard Business School Press, 1986).

Vernon, R., 'International investment and international trade in the product cycle', *Quarterly Journal of Economics* (May 1966), 190–207.

NOTES AND REFERENCES

1 Porter, M.E., *The Competitive Advantage of Nations* (London: Macmillan, 1990), 11.

2 Kennedy, P., *Preparing for the Twenty-First Century* (Fontana, 1994); Porter, op. cit.

3 'Volkswagen chief hits out at components industry', *Financial Times* (24 September 1996).

4 Porter, op. cit.

5 Financial Times Survey – 'Birmingham and the West Midlands', *Financial Times* (9 September 1996).

6 Porter, M.E., *Competitive Strategy* (New York: The Free Press, 1980).

7 Day, G.S., *Market-Driven Strategy* (New York: The Free Press, 1990).

8 Douglas, S.P. and Craig, C.S., *Global Marketing Strategy* (New York: McGraw-Hill, 1995), 112.

9 de Jonquireres, G., 'Europe's most respected companies', *Financial Times* (18 September 1996); Skapinaker, M., 'Smooth take-off for shake-up', *Financial Times* (19 September 1996).

10 Plenert, G., 'TQM – putting structure behind philosophy', *International Business Review*, 5(1) (1996), 67–78.

11 Reichhold, F.R., 'Learning from customer defections', *Harvard Business Review* (March-April 1996); Plenert, op. cit.

12 Slack, N. *et al.*, *Operations Management* (London: Pitman Publishing, 1995); Kaplan, H. and Norton, C., 'Using the behavioural scorecard as a strategic management system', *Harvard Business Review* (January-February 1996); Ascari, A., Rock, M. and Dutton, S., 'Re-engineering and change', *European Management Journal*, 13(1) (March 1995).

13 Johnson, G. and Scholes, K., *Exploring Corporate Strategy*, 3rd edition (Hemel Hempstead: Prentice-Hall, 1993).

14 Financial Times Survey, op. cit.

15 Warren, K., 'Building resources for competitive advantages', *Mastering Management*, Part 18, *Financial Times* (1996).

16 'Defence companies: getting together', *The Economist* (10 August 1996); Financial Times Survey – Aerospace, *Financial Times* (30 August 1996); 'Building Eurospace corporation', *The Economist* (7 September 1996).

PART 2

Assessing global opportunities

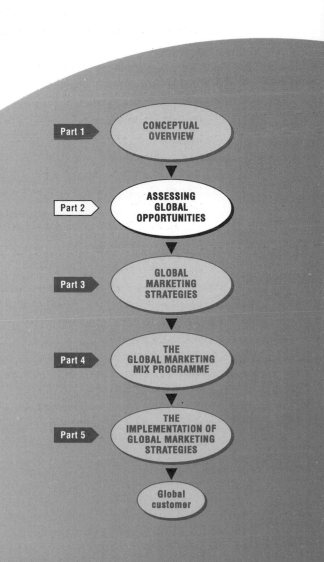

Part 1 — CONCEPTUAL OVERVIEW

Part 2 — ASSESSING GLOBAL OPPORTUNITIES

Part 3 — GLOBAL MARKETING STRATEGIES

Part 4 — THE GLOBAL MARKETING MIX PROGRAMME

Part 5 — THE IMPLEMENTATION OF GLOBAL MARKETING STRATEGIES

Global customer

Part 2 is composed of four chapters that explore and explain the most important factors of the global business environment. This Part considers the environment in which international firms operate. The first three chapters relate specifically to the factors that are external to the firm and which they cannot immediately control. These chapters discuss specific aspects of the environment – economic, social–cultural and political–legal – which is viewed from a global perspective. Readers need to have a good grasp of the environmental issues in order to consider how they affect the firm and the impact the latter has on the environments in which it operates. To be successful, the global marketer needs to adapt to the business environment and resolve conflicts arising out of the economic, political and cultural environments.

Chapter 5 The economic environment

This chapter discusses the most salient features of the economic environment of a country and their significance for a firm when making strategic decisions and employing marketing strategies.

Chapter 6 The social–cultural environment

This chapter looks at the importance of the human and cultural factors of a country for global marketing. Understanding cultural differences among nations and their impact on marketing strategies is crucial to success.

Chapter 7 The political–legal environment

This chapter examines and analyses the key factors in the political arena and how firms need to assess the political risks and the legal strategies for coping with different political systems. The different legal systems and their significance for arbitration and intellectual property rights is also considered.

Chapter 8 Global market research

Making effective decisions implies having a thorough knowledge and understanding of the environment. This chapter covers this important area and looks at the collection, analysis, uses and problems of information that managers need in assessing the risks of any strategic marketing decisions.

5

The economic environment

INTRODUCTION

Economic issues are given an immense amount of media coverage, with newspapers, TV and radio providing around-the-clock reviews of key events. Usually these reviews focus on macroeconomic events, such as growth rates, inflation, unemployment and so on. Focus on the micro issues, with analysis of a particular industry or even one firm, provides a further dimension.

Access to information and informed comment is fairly easy; the problem is to make sense of it to help with the direction and ultimate success of the organisation.

Reviewing the home economy of the organisation presents challenges, but the general literacy of managers in the mechanics of that economy means that informed discussion can usually take place. The same level of literacy cannot be assumed for the review of a 'foreign' economy, even one that at first sight appears to be closely allied to the company's home base. For example, the UK and USA are referred to as free market economies and might be thought to function and behave in similar ways; however, on closer inspection major differences appear that challenge this view. As companies seek to take advantage of the Single European Market (SEM), or the emerging markets of Eastern Europe and Southeast Asia, the differences seem to be more pronounced and require careful interpretation.

This chapter reviews the main trends in the global economy, painting a picture of the general economic issues affecting all countries. From this vantage point, some of the differences between groups of countries can be traced. Following this, a review of protectionism and economic integration is provided to fill out the picture of the economic environment that the international marketing manager will face.

Objectives

This chapter will examine:

- the significance of changes in international trade patterns
- the importance of the balance of payments and the effect of surpluses and deficits
- the use of trade barriers and protectionism, and how they influence national economies
- the movement towards the promotion of economic integration and trade blocs.

THE SIGNIFICANCE OF CHANGES IN INTERNATIONAL TRADE PATTERNS

During the last 15 years three major regional trading areas have emerged – the European Union; Pacific Rim (led by Japan); and NAFTA (comprising the USA, Canada and Mexico). These trading areas account for almost 80 per cent of world output, but have only one-fifth of the world's population.[1] Often referred to as the 'Triad', its significance lies in the fact that these three regions dominate the world's economy. The three parts of the 'Triad' are also increasingly interlinked, with companies trading within and across the three areas, and with the idea of national companies becoming an irrelevance.

Box 5.1

RESEARCH INTO COMPETITIVE ADVANTAGE IN THE ASIA PACIFIC REGION[2]

Many people in developed countries have made the point that low wages in emerging economies provide them with an unfair advantage that will gradually erode the business opportunities, and ultimately the standard of living, of those in the West. This approach stands at variance with the promotion of free trade, supported by economists and others, that rests on the premise that this will bring benefits for all.

The work of David Ricardo, an economist working in the early nineteenth century, as reviewed in Chapter 2, produced the laws of absolute and comparative advantage. According to this, absolute advantage (overall productivity differences between countries) should be reflected in differences in incomes, whilst comparative advantage (variation in productivity differences by sector) will determine the pattern of international trade.

How does the law of comparative advantage help to meet the critics who wish to put up barriers to protect the rich countries from cheap labour imports? Starting with absolute advantage, low wages would lead to low costs and so the poorest country would dominate world trade. The fact that it does not do so draws attention to the issue of productivity. Differences in wages reflect differences in productivity, with emerging markets having both low wages and low productivity.

▶ Box 5.1 continued

Wages and productivity are linked. If wages are less than the value of the output of an extra worker, firms will want to recruit extra labour and hence push up wages. International trade will, it is argued, tend to equalise labour costs per unit of output. If a country's unit labour costs are below world levels, increased demand for its products will drive up either wages or the currency. Countries like South Korea started as low-wage, low-cost economies in the 1960s, but now have wages that are close to those found in many economies in Western Europe.

Research undertaken in 1995 suggests that the unfair advantage of low wages may be illusory. For example, in 1990 wages in Malaysia were only 15 per cent of those in the USA, whilst its productivity in manufacturing was also about 15 per cent of the USA's. Figure 5.1 shows that country differences in labour costs are much smaller than the wage gap would suggest, with the conclusion that unit labour costs in India were actually higher than in the USA. As new technology is applied to production, the fear is that this will give a double advantage to emerging economies, with low wages and the chance to increase productivity. Here again, though, the picture is more complex. Looking at countries that have grown rapidly in the past 20 years suggests that wages grow faster than productivity as workers strive for the standard of living of those in developed economics.

Average unit labour costs tend to converge across countries, but there will still be differences between sectors. This gives rise to comparative advantages, as countries specialise in goods in which they have a comparative advantage (relative productivity is higher). For example, if a developing country has higher relative productivity in textiles compared to the UK, then its unit labour cost will be lower. If it has a lower relative productivity in aerospace compared to the UK, however, then that country has comparative advantage.

The law of comparative advantage predicts that countries will be exporters of goods in which they have a comparative advantage. Using the same research suggests that this is in fact the case, although it is not always the case that countries conform perfectly to the law.

Fig 5.1 THE WAGE GAP: MANUFACTURING LABOUR COSTS FOR SELECTED COUNTRIES (1990)

*including fringe benefits

Source: 'Not so absolutely fabulous' © *The Economist*, London (4 November 1995).

▶ **Box 5.1 continued**

What is the lesson here for those who wish to encourage free international trade and those who worry about its consequences on the national economy?

Markets will be eroded by the lowering of barriers and the export of goods by countries who have comparative advantage. Equally, all countries possess comparative advantage that they can seek to exploit. This is not the same as being able to do so, or to understand the dynamics of the situation, which is where the work of Porter on the competitive advantages of nations sheds light on the circumstances that can lead to a successful exploitation of national advantages.

It is these developments which give rise to the view that globalisation and inter-dependence are the main driving forces within the world economy.

Each country has to prepare for the impact of these changes, not by isolating them-selves from them but by the adoption of viable economic policies that enable their citizens to benefit from the changes (*see* Box 5.1). The UK and other EU countries are closely interlinked in trading terms within the EU, with the UK having the majority of its trade with its sister countries in that trading area. Not only has the trade pattern for the UK swung over into Europe and away from the Commonwealth, but an increasing proportion of GNP is made up of exports and imports. The USA's imports were 18 per cent of its GNP in 1990, compared to just over four per cent in 1970. Likewise, Japan has seen imports increase to 13 per cent of GNP over the same period.[3] The increase in import penetration reveals that competition is now often from foreign companies, a feature which will become more pronounced as the GATT and Single Market initiatives are implemented in full.

For the marketer, the challenge is clear. Competition can come from domestic or foreign companies and increasing integration means that barriers disappear, new leg-islation is enacted and common product standards are accepted. New opportunities emerge and new threats loom. If the impact has been felt first with manufacturing, then the integration of countries into trading blocs and with the increasing activity between them, it is now felt in the service sector and in public procurement.

If companies and their marketers are facing a more complex world, so too are nation-states and their governments. French and German unemployment in early 1996 had climbed to over 10 per cent, with factor market restrictions and low growth rates being blamed. Traditional solutions, via protectionism or state intervention, are no longer the complete answer, as financial markets respond badly to increased state borrowing and to the call for higher trade barriers. A further difficulty arises for coun-tries as they attempt to lure companies to undertake direct investment with them. Siemens, Fujitsu and Daewoo were some of the companies making the headlines in the UK in 1995–6 for their investment in North-East England, attracted by cheaper labour costs, government grants and easy access to the EU. Foreign investment is made on the back of an increasing integration in world markets, but also the desire to look for the best location, a feature that means that German firms would not auto-matically look to invest in Germany as first choice, but review other locations that provide competitive advantage to the company either via location and/or by lower total labour costs and high (potential) productivity. German trade unions' resistance to moves of this sort have not found a sympathetic hearing, leading to concern over how a country can push up its economic performance and hence prosperity.

The importance of economic performance

In 1995, a disagreement broke out in the UK between the Labour and Conservative political parties. The main problem revolved round the issue of how significant the UK economy was in world terms. According to the Labour Party, the economy had slipped to 18th place in an OECD survey carried out earlier in that year. The Conservatives responded by pointing out that these figures were misleading and underestimated the size and importance of the UK. Confusingly both parties had focused on economic 'facts', which were both seen as valid by economic commentators.

Box 5.2

HOW SIGNIFICANT IS THE UK ECONOMY?[4]

The OECD report in 1995 showed that the UK had fallen from 13th to 18th in the world prosperity league. This was measured on GDP per head and appeared to show that despite the reforms of the 1980s and 1990s, with privatisation and other changes to make the economy more competitive, the UK was still continuing the relative decline that had been going on for the past 100 years.

To counter this, the figures could be used to show that the UK was still a significant economy. Using GDP figures, rather than GDP per head, the UK is the world's fifth biggest economy at about $1.1bn, compared with France at $1.5bn, Germany at $2.3bn, Japan at $5.2bn and the USA at $7.0bn (all 1995 figures). Other figures were used to show that improvement in productivity put Britain in ninth place in the world rankings.

More in-depth reviews of the significance of these various statistics, looking at their reliability and long-term implications, occupied the experts and filled many column inches in the press. Two main conclusions can be drawn. One is that when looking at an individual country one statistic is not enough on its own to give the true picture of that particular economy. Is the UK the world's fifth biggest economy, or is it the 18th richest? Both require careful interpretation and on their own are misleading, providing a one- or two-dimensional review. Further country statistics deepen the picture, and can provide a stimulating insight into the economy. Second, relative economic decline will continue, whichever government is in power. Not only that but all Western European countries, along with the USA and Canada, will see their position eroded. The reason is simple: Asia is growing at eight per cent a year, compared with 2.5–3 per cent for most developed economies, and with 1.6bn people Asia is well placed to see some of its countries overtake today's largest economies within 10 years. One prediction is that five of the top 10 countries will be from Asia by 2010: China, Japan, Taiwan, India and Indonesia. By that time the UK will not even be in the top 10 as measured by total GDP.

The challenge for each country is to look at its performance and wealth-creating activities to make sure that they can match the best. Economic power is gradually moving eastwards, and there is very little a medium-sized economy like the UK can do about it. Maintaining the standard of living is altogether a different matter and presents a very different challenge than maintaining a position on a league table, where due to the size of population China and India will inevitably overtake the main European economies.

The case outlined in Box 5.2 provides an insight into the difficulties of using economic data. Other examples could be used to make the same point – was Italy right to claim that it had overtaken the UK economy in the late 1980s by adding on the output generated by the 'black economy' making it 10 per cent richer than had been realised? Is it useful to take the figures for the unified German economy as a guide to the prosperity of both the Eastern and Western parts of that country?

It is important to have a clear approach when looking at economic issues that can provide a useful insight for the marketer. The remainder of this chapter provides a structure to such an investigation, which can lead to more informed decision making.

For the marketer basic facts about an economy such as those used for the UK are merely a starting point for the investigation into market potential. Country analysis will look at a variety of factors that will help to shed light on economic performance as shown by economic growth, inflation, public expenditure, balance of payments and national debt, as well as the economic policies being pursued by the government.

For convenience, countries are often classified. Historically, the classification used to depend on political divisions, with First World countries incorporating the developed economies of the West, Second World countries focusing on the planned Communist economies, whilst the Third World consisted of those developing economies that had a low *per capita* income. Clearly this division is no longer of great use and has now been superseded by the World Bank's classification of high-income economies made up of 22 countries, which in 1991 had a *per capita* GNP of $7911 or more; upper-middle-income economies with *per capita* GNP of between $2555 and $7911, which again comprised 22 counties; lower-middle-income economies with *per capita* income of between $635 and $2555, comprising 43 countries (often referred to as emerging economies); and lastly low-income economies, on a *per capita* income of $675 or less, of which there were 40 such examples in 1991. (These four categories are often reduced to the two of developed and developing economies.)

Key economic indicators that are of use to those researching the market are *per capita* income, quality of life and purchasing power. The World Bank categories are based on the first of these, which is the division of total GDP by the total population of the country. These figures can provide only a snapshot of the total level of activity, and errors and omissions do creep in. The more advanced the economy the more reliable the GDP figures should be, but developing economies find it very difficult to capture figures that provide an adequate picture. Despite such accuracy problems, GDP figures can act as a yardstick by which to measure the performance of countries and the wealth of their citizens. The World Bank publishes these in its *World Development Report* produced each year.[5]

GDP *per capita* information is only the first step to understanding a country. India has a low figure, being one of the 40 countries with a *per capita* figure of less than $635. However, its middle class is estimated to be larger than the population of the UK, with nearly as much disposable income, making it a highly desirable market. Since 1991 economic reforms that have gone a long way to liberalise the economy, and have produced a middle class eager for mobile phones, foreign cars and other luxuries.[6]

With the problems associated with GDP statistics, there are alternative approaches than can assist with appraising a market. The United Nations publishes an annual *Human Development Report,* in which it ranks countries according to various measures such as life expectancy, educational standards and individual purchasing power.[7] This approach does not necessarily coincide with the *per capita* rankings. The UK came 21st on GNP *per capita* in 1993, but 10th on its 'human development' score. Arguably, given the movement to knowledge-based industries and future potential, this assessment provides an indication of future development potential rather than an historic view of what was earned by a country over the past year.

The *per capita* approach also fails to represent purchasing power, that is what money can buy within the country itself. The UN calculates a purchasing power parity index (or PPP), which is able to adjust GDP for the cost of living, which then allows for a direct comparison of living standards in different countries. The index is scaled so that an indicator of 100 is given to the country with the highest PPP, which is the USA. Recent revisions to this index, that have incorporated services consumed in developing countries, have meant that both China and India have larger economies than original PPP figures suggested. India is now calculated as having the sixth largest economy by purchasing power. Other changes when using this approach are that Japan falls from an economy with a *per capita* figure higher than the USA's, to a PPP figure noticeably below it.

Classification of economies by level of development or even by its bias towards one type of economic system (free market, mixed economy or planned) is useful but crude. Many countries do not conform to the classification allotted to them, so even under the old Soviet-style planned economies immense differences could be found between Hungary, East Germany and the USSR. Likewise, today's mixed economies of France, Germany and the UK show further differences. Further afield, how would the Islamic countries of Iran, Iraq and Syria be classified given their differing political and economic goals?

Economic policies

Attention to financial data to see how far a country is worthy of consideration is a starting point for analysis. Also important is a review of the attitude of government towards industry, and how far this will promote opportunities for business. The change in the way India promotes business opportunities has already been mentioned, but there are many examples of emerging markets taking the same route with the help of the World Bank and IMF. Ernst & Young, for example,[8] provide assistance to their corporate customers by publishing a quarterly update on 30 emerging markets, highlighting policy changes in 15 areas, covering corporate structures, foreign investment incentives, tax and market regulations through to labour market reforms and property ownership.

Although each country will have its own bias in economic and industrial policy (an example of which is given in Box 5.3) the requirement is to see how far the policies being pursued provide a friendly environment in which to operate, whatever the level of involvement of the company.

Box 5.3 **LABOUR REFORM IN CHINA[9]**

In the 1980s hiring of labour for foreign companies in China had to be done through the Chinese partner, or through the Foreign Enterprise Service Company. It was not possible to make employees redundant, or to pay bonuses or provide overtime payments. In effect, the government maintained control over the use of Chinese employees.

> **Box 5.3 continued**

In the 1990s a dramatic shift took place, with direct recruitment, managers able to make hiring decisions, layoffs now possible and incentive schemes permitted. This complements the privatisation programme in the country, with the government's expressed aim to sell 98 000 of the 99 000 state-controlled firms.

All of these changes are being made under the control of the Communist Party, which has taken a pragmatic view towards these reforms but which wishes to continue with a one-party state. This approach has produced tensions between the provinces and the central government and, with the reforms implemented mainly in the south, has produced uneven development.

THE IMPORTANCE OF THE BALANCE OF PAYMENTS: EFFECT OF SURPLUSES AND DEFICITS

The review of international trade showed that this activity was of increasing importance for all countries. This can be understood in some detail by reference to the balance of payments, which provides important evidence in seeing a country's predisposition to trade plus its success in paying its way in the world.

The balance of payments summarises all international transactions between domestic and foreign residents. A summary of these accounts for the UK is given in Fig. 5.2.[10] The concept of double entry book-keeping is used for the balance of payments, which is that each transaction is represented by two entries of equal value. Debit entries reflect payment by domestic resident to foreign residents, either for goods purchased or for the purchase of assets overseas. Due, however, to the difficulties of collecting data such as the amount spent by tourists in the UK and vice versa by UK residents overseas, and making sure that all data for UK trade in the SEM is obtained, errors

Fig. 5.2 STRUCTURE OF THE UK BALANCE OF PAYMENTS

Current account
Exports
Imports
Visible balance
Invisible balances:
Services
Interest, profits and dividends
Transfers
Invisible balance
Current balance
UK external assets and liabilities (net transactions)
Balancing item

creep in. The balance of payments account contains a balancing item, which is used to balance total debits and credits, and thus the accounts always balance.

The two main categories are the current account and the external assets and liabilities, often referred to as the capital account.

Current account

This is broken down in two ways: into visible and invisible trade. The visible balance or balance of trade is the difference between the value of exported goods from the UK and imported goods to it. This forms a significant part of the UK's trade, and despite the rise in the importance of services, still accounts for a major proportion of total activity. Historically, the UK had a surplus on this trade, but in the late 1980s and throughout the 1990s this has shown a deficit. However, the invisible or services part of the accounts shows a surplus, which reduces the overall deficit. It is this deficit that creates headlines, particularly if it amounts to many billions of pounds. (The figures for 1994 showed this to be a £1.7bn deficit, which is easily managed.) Deficits have to be paid for, and the larger and more persistent they are the more they will act as a brake on economic growth.

Current account statistics can also reveal the major destination for exports and imports, with the UK having over 60 per cent of its trade with other EU countries.

Capital account

This records new transactions in assets and liabilities during the year. It is not a record of the total of external assets and liabilities and records only the decreases and increases in them. In effect, this account acts to 'balance the books', as any deficit on the current account has to be paid for by borrowing money from abroad.

Balance of payments disequilibria

Large deficits can clearly be understood to be a problem, but so too are surpluses, as can be seen from the current disquiet felt over Japan's balance of trade.

Deficit

Large deficits, measured by the proportion of GDP that they account for, can produce major problems for any economy. During the 1970s and 1980s many developing countries got themselves into debt, which meant that more of their earnings from exports (i.e. hard currency earnings) had to go to pay their debt. This problem is particularly acute in Africa and South America, where export earnings should be used to promote development rather than pay the service or interest payments on the debt. Developed countries can also find themselves with severe problems on the balance of payments; in 1989, the UK, which had a £25bn deficit on current account, brought forward government policies to reduce it, thereby slowing down the economy and bringing on recession.

Pressure on the exchange rate is also a consequence of large deficits, with more people trying to exchange their £s for foreign currency to pay for imports. Increased supply pushes down the rate, making import prices rise, with all that this means for inflation.

Surplus

Superficially this would appear to be an indication of success. In reality, it is no such thing. There are three reasons for this:

1 one country's surplus is another's deficit, as the principles of double entry book-keeping that apply to one country's balance of payments must also apply to the world's balance of payments;

2 large surpluses, such as Japan's with the USA, stimulate calls for retaliatory measures such as increases in tariffs and quotas on Japanese goods;

3 exchange rate readjustments may be required, revaluing a currency such as the yen, that reflects the strong demand for it to pay for Japanese exports.

National balance of payments statistics provide a background whereby both 'home' companies and those wishing to trade with the country can appreciate the challenges if trade becomes tilted too much towards either exports or imports. This is one of the economic indications that can shed light on the health of an economy, and can be of great use to the senior managers of a company in reaching informed decisions (*see* Box 5.4).

Box 5.4   **HOW EXPORTS HELP THE FAST-GROWING COMPANY[11]**

Can we identify the characteristics of a fast-growing European company? Research is vital as new companies are seen as being of great importance for all the countries of the EU over the next decade. In 1995, research was funded by the European Commission to identify 500 exceptional entrepreneurs who were running fast-growing companies. To find companies who fit this definition is far from straightforward. For example, many companies of this type prefer privacy to the full glare of publicity. The terms of reference for what constitutes a fast-growing company placed great emphasis on job creation, rather than increases in turnover. To be eligible, companies had to be growing rapidly, as measured by employment; were required to have grown to at least 40 employees by 1994; and to have started in 1989 with fewer than five employees.

Once identified, the 500 fastest growing were then reviewed and the results published. The results threw up some surprising findings. Most of the companies were founded by experienced men (only one per cent were founded by women), with 10 years in business and an average age of 44. More than half founded their companies with at least one business partner, which supports other research which suggests that teams are either a more creative force than a lone entrepreneur, or that businesses with more than one founder start with greater critical mass and therefore have a much bigger chance of surviving and thriving.

All sectors were well represented, thus supporting other studies that point to the conclusion that there are successful companies and teams rather than successful sectors.

The successful companies were on average 17 years old, but a quarter had been founded in the last century. New management had helped them achieve superior performance, again raising the importance of bringing in experienced managers who will be able to identify opportunities and reverse the spiral of decline.

Exporting was a common characteristic of the rapid growers, but more than three-quarters of their exports were to other EU countries. Two-thirds achieved growth by entering new markets with existing products, but half of those launched new products into new

▶

▶ **Box 5.4 continued**

markets. Growth rates were attributed in the majority of cases to an emphasis on quality and service, rather than to price competition with an emphasis on differentiation.

One conclusion, therefore, is that to help promote growth, further measures to ensure a Single Market in Europe would provide additional opportunities for companies of this type.

These companies are successful exporters from their home country and have adopted strategies that have high risks associated with them. Once they have learned from these experiences, then moving out to non-EU countries becomes a distinct possibility. Success is built on quality and exporting, a lesson that many companies could learn from.

Market characteristics

Economic fundamentals are a helpful way of reviewing a particular country. Issues that have already been covered are GDP *per capita*, quality of life and balance of payments. Equally useful, and implied in the EU's convergence criteria for a single currency, is the amount of public borrowing (PSBR), and how far this can act as a brake on growth as a government seeks to reduce its borrowing by either cutting expenditure and/or raising taxation, a situation in which France, the UK and Italy found themselves in the mid-1990s.

Other economic issues, such as inflation, unemployment and investment, all provide further insight. One area of particular note is that globally real growth in imports of goods and services is running close to three times the rate of GDP growth for the developed economies – 1.75 times the rate of GDP growth for East Asia.[12] This gives 4.4 per cent growth on imports for Germany in 1996 against a sluggish GDP rate, and reinforces the point made earlier concerning the increasing proportion of GDP accounted for by imports in the USA, Japan and elsewhere.

The marketer needs to understand the dynamics of a particular national market if its potential is to be properly assessed. Economic data, important though it is, will be able to provide only a superficial understanding. Market characteristics that can highlight consumer behaviour and the way in which products can be brought to the customer to satisfy demand, also need to be understood. The bulk of this analysis will be undertaken in the forthcoming chapters, but there are issues of a macro nature that can be introduced to provide the context for the more detailed review.

The main dimensions of a market can be captured by considering variables such as those relating to the population and its characteristics. The number of people in a market provides one of the most basic indicators of size, and is a useful indicator of the potential demand for staple goods. However, population figures have to be disaggregated into meaningful and useful categories if the marketer is to be able to exploit market opportunities. For example, many countries in Europe will experience low population growth, whilst countries in Africa and Asia will experience significant increases. Additionally, Italy, France and Germany already have a large proportion of their citizens over the age of 65 and this proportion will increase over the next 20 years. In the UK, the population in 1996 was nearly 59m, with a forecast for this to rise to 62m by 2031. Those over 60 comprised 20 per cent in 1996, but this rises to 29 per cent by 2031 (from 12m to 18m). Consumption patterns for this group will be different, with the possibility of increased savings, more spent on leisure activities that appeal to this age group and so on. Changes of this nature place considerable burdens on those of working age to support the health and welfare services that will be required.

In China, India and many countries in Africa the priorities will be very different. Expanding population will bring with it the need to expand economic activity just to keep pace. Governments may well look to limit family size, as they already do in China. In crude terms, affluent countries will be characterised by ageing populations with low population growth, whilst those in the developing world will be characterised by an expanding population with an emphasis on basic products. All nations will find that population changes over the next 30 years will present them with major challenges, whilst the marketer will need to be conversant with the implications for spotting market opportunity, and of extending life cycles by marketing products that will be maturing later in developing markets.

Alongside population trends, the size of the consumer purchasing unit or household is also a valuable source of information. In the UK there were nearly 23m households in 1993 at an average size of 2.44 persons, a reduction from the 2.91 found in 1971.[13] This reduction is found in other EU countries, where the average size fell from 2.9 in 1977 to 2.7 in 1996.[14] The fall in the average number in each household, but an increase in the general size of the population, points to an increase in the number of households – or, put another way, more people are living on their own, with the UK having 27 per cent of all households of this type in 1993, a factor explained by the divorce rate and by people living longer and thereby producing sole-survivor households.

The UK and other EU countries have quite small households compared with Turkey. As economies such as Turkey's develop there is a tendency for the average household size to shrink; this brings challenges for marketers, with the need to make domestic appliances for single-person households and provide services that meet individuals' changed circumstances.

Consumption patterns

Depending on the sophistication of a country's data collection system, data on consumption patterns is the next step to giving a 'feel' for a market. In Europe, there is ample information available, similarities and differences being easily noted by the use of basic statistics, while leaving out the important task of interpreting their meaning. Italy, for example, consumed 25 litres of beer per head, 58 litres of wine and 0.9 litres of spirits per year in 1993, compared to the Germans who drank 135 litres of beer, 23 litres of wine and 2.6 litres of spirits. Differences of this type can be appreciated from the geography and climate of a country, with the UK being an unsuitable climate for viticulture compared to France, through to historical and social influences on consumption habits.

The percentage of households with washing machines varies far less noticeably, right across the EU, with most countries having between 85 and 95 per cent of households with such appliances. Such statistics are capable of luring the unwary into a trap. What is unknown is the number of times these machines are used, how often they are replaced and how similar they actually are throughout the EU – e.g. are they top-loaders or front-loaders? Marketing campaigns have often foundered on the failure to ask simple questions, assuming that what is bought and used in the 'home' country is replicated elsewhere.

Achieving consistency across the data produced by each country is often difficult. Packaged goods are classified differently in different countries and regions. In some countries, a unit of soft drink means a six-pack; in others it means a single bottle. In some countries the ready-to-eat cereal includes muesli, while in others it does not.[15] With the development of East European economies, the inconsistency in data makes it more difficult to understand consumption patterns and differences between countries.

Nature of the foreign economy

The natural resources of a nation include existing and potential forms of wealth provided by nature, such as minerals, land, water, climate, energy sources, etc. An examination of a country's resources is important to the global marketer for a number of reasons:

1 an economy abundant in resources is an attraction for local production;

2 the country can be evaluated for its future prospects – for example, Mozambique and Angola have an abundance of raw materials that have yet to be exploited; although these countries are presently under-developed their economic prospects look very promising;

3 a country's natural resources are a major determinant of the type of economic structure that can develop there – for example, the abundance of oil in Libya and copper in Zambia has improved the economic prospects of these nations; other nations limited in resources, such as Singapore, have had to depend on international trade to sustain their economies.

The climate also influences a nation's economic development and its potential as a market in the following ways:

1 the existence of a tropical climate in countries in Latin America and the Far East may mean these nations have an advantage in the growth of tropical fruits and vegetables for export to other world markets;

2 climate can dictate the type of consumption patterns and products required – for example, in very hot climates, as in the Middle Eastern countries, air-conditioning equipment would be required;

3 climatic conditions will affect the packaging and distribution of products. For example, electrical goods will need special protection and packaging in very humid conditions.

The topography of a country – its geographic features such as rivers, mountains, forests, etc. – provides not only natural resources but also the potential for tourism. Topography also affects the '4 Ps' of marketing. Mountainous countries will present transportation and distribution problems to a firm. The landlocked nature of countries such as Malawi, Zimbabwe and Paraguay will have an influence on the costs of transportation, and accessibility by land to these markets will depend on the political stability of the neighbouring countries.

Infrastructure

The infrastructure of a nation refers to its transportation, communication, energy, commercial and financial systems. In general, the more developed the economy the better the infrastructural development. The importance of infrastructure in a market may now be summarised:

1 the more developed the infrastructure in an economy, the more its resources will be used. For example, without the development of the Siberian gas pipeline, the former Soviet Union's vast gas reserves could not have been utilised;

2 the transportation infrastructure is important to the international marketer, since it affects the efficient operation of the distribution systems. The existence of good roads, rail and airport systems will facilitate intermodal freight (i.e. containerised cargoes loaded on to trucks, then rail and then transported by air);

3 communications infrastructure is crucial to business success in terms of availability and quality of systems. Telephones, fax systems, telexes, satellites and computers are essential to gain access to markets abroad. The inadequate provision of these facilities will mean that firms will need to adapt their operations. For example, in many countries of Africa and Central America poor communication systems have affected the economic viability of their markets. Firms operating in these markets have had to adjust their delivery and payment policies, and inter-company communications between headquarters and subsidiaries have been adjusted to allow for longer delays.

Urbanisation

Urbanisation refers to the proportion and concentration of population living in the cities. The importance of examining urbanisation for the international marketer may be summarised thus:

- urban areas represent a concentration of potential customers
- urban and non-urban areas have different consumption patterns and thus distinct customer requirements.

The low-income developing countries tend to be less urbanised, and they make unattractive markets as they are difficult to reach, and greater promotional effort is required because of the dispersion of the population and high levels of illiteracy. The degree of urbanisation is therefore a fairly good indicator of the size of the market, and also reflects the type of marketing strategies the firm needs to adopt.

THE USE OF TRADE BARRIERS AND PROTECTIONISM: HOW THEY INFLUENCE NATIONAL ECONOMIES

Despite the importance of globalisation there are still considerable differences between countries' economies, part of which can be explained by the use of trade barriers that seek to protect the interests of certain groups and organisations. The extent of the barriers can be seen by the amount of work undertaken by the European Commission and the World Trade Organisation (WTO), both examined in more detail later in the chapter, to reduce or remove the obstacles to trade that exist between all countries.

Forms

Barriers can come in many forms, but they share a common set of goals. The most frequent are to:

1 protect local jobs by keeping out rival imports;
2 protect infant industries until such time as they are robust enough to stand up to foreign competition;
3 reduce reliance on foreign suppliers;
4 encourage investment in 'home' industries;
5 encourage import substitution;
6 reduce or eliminate balance of payments problems;
7 promote export activity;
8 prevent foreign firms from dumping – i.e. selling goods at below cost price to achieve market share;
9 promote political objectives, as with the erection of barriers against countries involved in the abuse of human rights.[16]

This list is by no means exhaustive, but all countries are involved in some form of trade restrictions against another country's products. To abolish or reduce some of these would appear to make economic sense, but to do so produces problems for the national government. Barriers may be put on products that contain substances taken from endangered animals, or constructed from wood extracted from the rainforests. To remove these would pose a dilemma for all concerned.

A further example of a barrier was that employed by France in 1996, forcing radio stations to ensure that 40 per cent of their pop output is French. The aim is to protect French culture and economic activities,[17] but the counter-claim is that it is an infringement on free trade.

Classification

Barriers come in many guises and can be classified as follows.

Quotas

Quotas restrict the number of units that can be imported or the market share that is permissible. Sometimes the quotas are imposed, at other times they are made voluntarily, such as the quota which existed between the UK and Japanese car producers, who set their market share at 11 per cent of the new car market.

Tariffs

This is when imported goods and services have a tariff added to their price, thus producing a price advantage for locally produced products or discouraging their purchase and consumption. In Poland, an import tax of three per cent is levied in addition to duty rate already levied. In the USA, there has been strong pressure to raise tariffs to help reduce the balance of payments deficit.

Price-fixing

Although outlawed in many countries the most famous example is that undertaken by OPEC (the Organisation of Petroleum Exporting Countries). By controlling output or by fixing the price of crude oil, OPEC hopes to maximise revenue for the member countries. Although strong in the 1970s and early 1980s, its power has waned as other non-OPEC countries began to produce their own oil, alternative energy sources were exploited and as disputes arose between member states.

There are increasing examples of companies acting as a cartel to fix prices, however; cement manufacturers in the EU were fined in 1995 for this offence.

Non-tariff barriers (NTBs)

These comprise rules, regulations and the use of time-consuming forms (red tape) that delay or make more difficult the purchase of foreign goods. This is often a charge levied against the Japanese, who use various rules and regulations, most notably on health and safety grounds, to hinder the import of cars and consumer goods. The example used earlier of the French insistence on 40 per cent of pop music on radio stations coming from a French source is a further reduction on the choice of which music to play.

Financial controls

There are a number of ways in which this occurs. Exchange controls in South American and East European countries restrict the flow of currency by, for example, placing restrictions on access to hard currencies for the purchase of imports. This can be supported when, as in the case of Russia in the early 1990s, the US dollar was used as an alternative currency for trading purposes for internal trade, thereby undermining the role of the rouble. Foreign investment controls place limits on investment or the transfer or remittance of funds. The controls can encompass requiring investors to accept minority ownership positions, limits to the remittance of profit out of the country, or prohibiting royalty payments to the parent company.

Barriers to trade

Barriers to trade will always be found, some created as a deliberate attempt to protect the home market, others acting to hinder trade, but not intended specifically for that purpose. Attempts to overcome many of the problems associated with barriers to trade can be grouped under two headings:

1 economic integration;

2 GATT (the General Agreement on Tariffs and Trade).

Economic integration has been one of the major economic developments since the Second World War, gaining considerable momentum in the 1980s. Integration of this type ranges from the free trade agreement between member states to the more ambitious economic and political union.

Free trade area

As its title suggests, this is an agreement amongst a number of nations to remove all barriers to member states. An early example of this was EFTA (the European Free Trade Association), which helped first eight countries and then five (after the UK, Portugal and Denmark joined the EEC in 1973) to trade freely with each other. With Sweden, Finland and Austria joining the EU in 1995, the remaining two countries participate with the EU via the European Economic Area (EEA).

A more recent example is NAFTA (the North American Free Trade Agreement), which came into being in 1989, originally with the USA and Canada and now with Mexico agreeing to eliminate tariffs and other barriers over a 10-year period.[18] The challenges of incorporating the two closely aligned and developed countries of the USA and Canada plus the developing economy of Mexico is proving difficult, as companies are accused of relocating in Mexico to take advantage of cheap labour[19] and to gain access to the Latin and South American markets.

Customs union

In a free trade area member countries are free to set their own tariffs and other barriers with non-member counties. A customs union changes this so that common barriers are established with non-member states. With a customs union member countries have to cede at least some of the control of their economic policies to the group at large. Many of the regional trade associations (RTAs) had ambitions to achieve economic integration, but effectively settled for a customs union due to the difficulties associated with the loss of economic control over an individual country's economy. An example is the Caribbean Community (CARICOM).

Common market

This is characterised by the abolition of barriers between member countries, a common external trade policy and the mobility of factors of production across member state boundaries. The key example of this was the European Community (EC) which, with its Single European Market (SEM) initiative, focused attention on the movement of goods and services, people and capital by various directives that came into force on 1 January 1993 or later (*see* Box 5.5). This was an attempt to harmonise standards, smooth the way for companies to operate freely throughout the Community and thereby increase trade, reduce costs and promote economic growth.[20]

Economic union

Under the Maastricht Treaty of 1991 the then 12 member states created a European Union, a move towards full economic union. Economic and monetary union (EMU) was set to be achieved by 1999, enshrined in the introduction of a single currency, (the Euro), by that date. The treaty also proposed political co-operation on defence and foreign affairs.

> **Box 5.5**
>
> ### EU DIRECTIVES
>
> On 1 January 1996 the Investment Services Directive (ISD) came into force. This is a striking example of the changes that have been made to promote a working economic union environment. The aim is to give investment firms a 'passport' to trade in all member states if they are authorised to do so in one, an approach that has speeded up harmonisation in all areas.
>
> The ISD contained two key measures. The first is that firms will be able to operate in any EU member state provided they are regulated in one of them. When operating outside of their home country they will be subject to rules on the conduct of business devised by the local regulators for all banks and brokers.
>
> The second measure is to allow staff exchanges and futures and options markets to trade throughout the EU. This should in effect allow brokers to conduct business from offices located anywhere in Europe. On the first day of trading under this new directive, NatWest Securities commenced trading on the Swedish Stock Exchange from its offices in London without having to go through local (Swedish) brokers.
>
> It is not always the case that directives of this sort make life easier. ISD will challenge working practices and may undermine confidence in smaller firms to produce the same level of service as the larger ones, leading to the possibility of a shakeout.

THE MOVEMENT TOWARDS THE PROMOTION OF ECONOMIC INTEGRATION AND TRADE BLOCS

Economic integration can take any of the forms outlined above, but as with international business generally there is never a stable period. The EU has changed radically in just 10 years, from a slow-moving attempt to produce economic integration to the Single Market and Maastricht initiatives that provided a much needed impetus. New and yet more adventurous initiatives have been proposed, whilst new groupings emerge. In 1995, for example, the Black Sea Economic Co-operation summit was held representing the 11 nations bordering on that area, with the intention of sharing economic resources to develop infrastructure and reduce political tensions.

New forms and agreements have emerged that give a new twist to economic integration. In 1996, the EU and Turkey formed a customs union that revealed the level of integration by the 15 states of the EU as well as the desire of others to join. This desire to join the EU has led to a significant increase in applications, perhaps taking the number in the EU to between 18 and 26 countries early in the next century. The EU's ability to accommodate these countries is a different matter, but successful economic integration acts as a magnet, attracting admirers as well as critics.

The success of the EU in bringing together first six and now 15 countries makes it important to give further consideration to the structure and purpose of such a group and to identify its stated goals.

European Union

The Single European Act 1987, which was popularised under the more easily under-stood title of the Single European Market (SEM), was born out of the frustration with the continual fragmentation of the European Community, which reduced the ability of firms to move freely across borders and to reap the benefits of the economies of scale that an integrated market of 320m people (in the then 12 member states) would provide. The Cecchini report[21] sought to quantify the benefits of a single market, and by implication noted the drawbacks that continued fragmentation brought with it. According to the report the gains from a single market would be: an increase of 4.5 per cent to the GDP of the Community; a reduction of inflation, with average consumer prices falling by 6.1 per cent; an improvement in the balance of public finances of 2.2 per cent of GDP; a reduction in unemployment of up to 1.8m. Whether these improvements will actually come about is a matter of intense debate, but they do point to the supply-side improvement that would be encouraged by integration.

Comparing the US and European markets, it was easy to see the problem. Whirlpool, a company operating in the domestic appliance market, experienced noticeable differences between the USA and markets in Europe. In Western Europe the industry is fragmented along national lines, which is partly a reflection of traditional differences between national products, but which has produced dominance by 'home' producers such as Thomson (France), Bosch-Siemens (Germany) and so on. Companies such as Whirlpool would prefer to create a European-scale operation which would reduce the costs associated with selling and administration, but which could accommodate the various customer preferences seen in each country. Prior to the SEM, different technical standards applied in each of the 12 member states, pushing up costs and making it difficult to trade across borders; different tax regimes also existed that created price differentials from market to market.

It was against this background that the Single European Act was introduced. The Act set out certain changes which were to be introduced by the end of 1992.

1 *Border controls*. These were to be reduced to allow for the speedy passage of goods and people. Businesses would benefit, as they would find a borderless Europe reduced waiting time whilst documents were checked.

2 *Mutual recognition of standards*. This was an issue where the greatest danger lay, as it could have derailed the whole process. Mutual recognition meant, for example, that a standard developed in one country should be accepted by another, provided it met basic requirements on such issues as health and safety. (This approach not only affected product standards but also the movement of people, as a qualification gained in one country would be recognised in another.)

3 *Public procurement*. Put simply, this would open up procurement to non-national suppliers. The aim was to reduce costs by allowing low-cost supplies into national economies and increasing competition. Public sector organisations would then be able to choose the best supplier irrespective of nationality.

4 *Financial services*. Insurance, banking and other financial services would now be offered across Europe.

5 *Freight transport*. The restrictions on cabotage, which is the right of freight delivery companies to pick up and deliver goods within another member state's borders,

would be abolished. This was estimated to reduce the cost of haulage by up to 15 per cent.

The implications of these changes are enormous. The benefits to the member states would be in the reduction of costs, and thereby in the reduction of price and the greater choice that would be offered. The other aspect of the change would be the shift in power and influence to the European level.

Maastricht Treaty

After the move towards the creation of the Single Market, the Maastricht Treaty was drawn up in 1991 to strengthen the community. Its main objectives are as follows.

1 To build closer co-operation on foreign policy and justice/home affairs on an inter-governmental bias.

2 To enshrine the principle of subsidiarity, limiting the Community's involvement in national affairs. In areas where both the Community and member states have power to act, the Community will do so only if the objective of the proposed action cannot be achieved sufficiently by an individual member state. In addition, an action by the Community in any field must not go beyond what is necessary to achieve the Treaty's objectives. If there is a dispute the European Court of Justice will judge whether action is necessary. This principle should ensure that:

(a) the Community will not stray into areas where it is not needed;
(b) where EU action is needed, it will go no further than is required;
(c) the European Court of Justice will be able to clamp down on those that do not implement agreed EC rules;
(d) the scope for EC activities in such areas as education, training and health will be defined by setting out the sort of action the Community should take;
(e) EU action in such areas as the environment, which affect all countries, can be taken;
(f) he European Commission can be more accountable to the European Parliament;
(g) new rights for EU citizens can be established;
(h) movement towards economic and monetary union can be facilitated.

The Maastricht Treaty also established a new framework, which was encapsulated in the change in name from the European Community to the European Union. This is made up of three areas of co-operation:

1 Treaty of Rome (that set up the community); Single European Act, Maastricht Treaty;

2 foreign and security policy;

3 justice and home affairs.

In summary, the purpose of the Treaty was to gain increased political co-operation under the EU, which would provide for a closer union in which decisions would be taken as near to the people as possible.

Economic and monetary union

Forming a key part of Maastricht, and the subject of much debate, is economic and monetary union (EMU), a topic arguably of great interest to companies and marketing managers. The Treaty sets out a number of convergence criteria for monetary union:

1 low relative inflation – each country's inflation rate should not exceed the average of the three lowest inflation rates by more than 1.5 percentage points;

2 budget discipline – the government deficit should be lower than three per cent of GDP and government debt should be lower than 60 per cent of GDP;

3 low relative interest rates – each country's long-term government bond yield should not exceed the average of the yield of the three lowest inflation economies by more than two percentage points;

4 stable exchange rate – Exchange Rate Mechanism (ERM) participation without devaluation in the last two years.

Many countries, such as Italy, Greece and Portugal, struggled to meet these 'convergence criteria', whilst the UK was worried about the loss of political sovereignty and France was affected by strikes in response to public sector cutbacks to meet the criteria by the end of 1998. The arguments[22] in favour of monetary union and those against can be summarised as follows.

Benefits of monetary union

1 Elimination of costs, i.e. the costs of changing from one currency to another.

2 Elimination of currency risk premiums, i.e. the cost of using forward market contracts to reduce the risk of exchange rate movement.

3 Greater price stability.

4 Supports for the SEM programme, promoting a true single market.

5 A single currency would make European tax and spending more acceptable.

Drawbacks to monetary union

1 Loss of national autonomy in monetary policy is potentially damaging because economic shocks are not uniform in impact across the EU. Research suggests that France, Belgium, Luxembourg and Germany could act as an optimal currency area – i.e. an economic shock such as an oil price rise would have a similar affect, requiring a uniform response. Scandinavia, the UK and the Mediterranean countries would be affected differently, requiring unique policies to overcome the problem.

2 Inflexibility of markets, particularly the labour market, could cause severe difficulties when responding to economic shocks.

3 Absence of tax and public spending stabilisers at the federal level.

4 Economic and psychological costs of transition to the new currency could undermine the SEM programme. Public opinion in Germany moved against the idea of a single currency when they realised that the deutschmark would be abolished.

Box 5.6 **FREE TRADE BETWEEN ASIA PACIFIC COUNTRIES**[23]

Eighteen Pacific Rim governments have agreed to free all trade and investment in the region by 2020. The Asia Pacific Economic Co-operation (APEC) forum plan calls for the members, who together account for half of all world trade, to open their markets by cutting tariffs, liberalising services, public procurement and investment, and harmonising industrial standards. Although no firm timetable has been laid down, it has been recognised that those countries which are already industrialised and with more open markets need not move as swiftly as those members who are less developed with greater protectionist barriers.

The diversity of APEC is striking. The 18 members are Canada, the USA, Mexico, Chile, China, South Korea, Japan, Taiwan, Hong Kong, the Philippines, Indonesia, Papua New Guinea, New Zealand, Australia, Brunei, Malaysia, Singapore and Thailand. With such diversity in economic development, as well as in the way business is undertaken in each country, it is not surprising that each member of APEC is still fairly cautious in committing themselves to a specific agenda to introduce free trade.

The APEC approach is one example of co-operation between the countries of this region. A further example is the increasing co-operation between the central banks of the Asia Pacific countries. The 11 members – Australia, China, Hong Kong, Indonesia, Japan, South Korea, Malaysia, New Zealand, the Philippines, Singapore, Thailand – are also members of APEC, but have now joined forces to create the Executive Meeting of East Asia and Pacific Central Banks (EMEAP). A tangible benefit of this co-operation will be seen when central banks gain greater access to cash to help defend their currencies at times of uncertainty. To do this the banks have exchanged bilateral securities repurchase ('repo') agreements. Further work on banking regulations, capital markets, bank payments systems and so on are all being considered.

The effect of these developments on individual countries varies according to their geography. In the USA, for example, the challenge is to strike a balance between the EU, which is well advanced in terms of integration and significance, and APEC, which has the aim of free trade rather than economic integration as seen in Europe. The USA cannot ignore the increasing dominance of the Pacific area in world economic affairs, but neither can it forget the influence of the very wealthy and mature market economies of the EU.

Even with the Asia Pacific countries, there are challenges. Japan has traditionally seen Europe and North America as key markets for its exports, has worked as part of the G7 group of countries and has joined international agencies such as the IMF, World Bank and WTO, which have been dominated by the wealthy Western countries. The rise of the Pacific Rim countries, therefore, presents Japan with a dilemma. How will it work with newly wealthy neighbours as well as maintaining the links with the developed countries of the world?

In the last decade, private sector investment by Japanese companies in the region has meant that the Japanese now have a higher market share in cars, consumer electronics and industrial machinery than the Europeans and Americans. Asia overtook the USA as Japan's biggest export market in 1991, while in 1993 its trade surplus with the region surpassed its surplus with America.

The move into Asia has raised questions on many other issues. With the collapse of the Soviet Union and moves by Russia towards a market economy, questions are now being asked about the need for a military alliance with the USA. Politicians in Japan are now seeking to find a way to be independent of the USA, but complementing the efforts of the USA and the major European countries to encourage economic growth and development.

The EU has moved from what in reality was a customs union, added members from a free trade area, and then progressed towards economic and political union. It therefore encompasses all the issues relating to the benefits of integration and acts as a spur to others to look at some form of integration (*see* Box 5.6). For the international marketer these movements create new opportunities and challenges. Large markets provide opportunities not previously experienced when separate national markets acted independently, but the worry is that the creation of a powerful trading bloc, such as the EU, could act to focus activity inwards whilst seeking to discourage competition from entry. In the EU's case, this was seen as 'Fortress Europe', causing American[24] and Japanese companies to bring forward plans for investment.

The harmonisation of standards and increased factor mobility can all assist the marketer in achieving corporate goals. Despite this, many trading blocs remain diverse and heterogeneous, particularly where a mix of 15 nations is brought together. In other cases, such as in South America, countries belong to more than one group, giving rise to confusion that may be reduced when the benefits of co-operation are realised.

For firms within a bloc, competition will be enhanced and mergers and acquisitions will increase as firms seek to take advantage of the increased opportunities. Not often remembered is the European Commission's admission that up to half of all the companies in the EU would probably disappear as competition and acquisitions took place to prepare for the SEM.

Table 5.1 MAJOR TRADING ASSOCIATIONS AND GROUPS

ANCOM	Andean Common Market: consists of Bolivia, Colombia, Ecuador, Peru (or Andean Pact) and Venezuela
APEC	Asia Pacific Economic Co-operation
ASEAN	Association of Southeast Asian Nations: consists of Indonesia, Malaysia, the Philippines, Singapore and Thailand
CACM	Central American Common Market: consists of Costa Rica, El Salvador, Guatemala, Honduras and Nicaragua
CARICOM	Caribbean Community: consists of Antigua, Bahamas, Barbados, Belize, Dominica, Grenada, Guyana, Jamaica, Montserrat, St Kitts–Nevis, Anguilla, St Lucia, St Vincent and the Grenadines, Trinidad and Tobago
ECOWAS	Economic Community of West African States: consists of Benin, Burkina Faso, Cape Verde, The Gambia, Ghana, Guinea, Guinea-Bissau, Ivory Coast, Liberia, Mali, Mauritania, Niger, Nigeria, Senegal, Sierra Leone, Togo
EEA	European Economic Area: consists of the EU plus Norway, Iceland and Liechtenstein
EU	European Union: consists of Austria, Belgium, Denmark, Finland, France, Germany, Greece, Ireland, Italy, Luxembourg, Netherlands, Portugal, Spain, Sweden and the UK
GCC	Gulf Co-operation Council: consists of Bahrain, Kuwait, Oman, Qatar, Saudi Arabia and the United Arab Emirates
LAIA	Latin America Integration Association: consists of Argentina, Bolivia, Brazil, Chile, Ecuador, Mexico, Paraguay, Peru, Uruguay and Venezuela
MERCOSUR	Southern Common Market: consists of Argentina, Brazil, Paraguay and Uruguay
NAFTA	North America Free Trade Agreement: consists of Canada, Mexico and the USA

The key question asked when Norway voted to stay out of the EU (but remained in the European Economic Area) was whether it was possible to remain independent and survive. In a world where the nation-state is increasingly under threat the consensus is that some loss of sovereignty is inevitable in order to reap the benefits of the larger and fast-moving market place. Perhaps it is instructive to look at Norway's compromise when seeing it as a beneficiancy of the EEA, but still able to retain political independence with its own currency, thereby protecting its way of life and the subsidies that go to support it.

With the creation of larger free trade areas (*see* Table 5.1) international managers and marketers have to keep abreast of the possibilities that open up for them. As is often the case there will be a variety of responses to these challenges, but those that appreciate and respond to them will be well placed to exploit the benefits as they arise.

THE INTERNATIONAL FINANCIAL SYSTEM

There are a number of transnational institutions whose task it is to influence world trade and the financial systems that support it. Organisations such as the International Monetary Fund (IMF), the International Bank for Reconstruction and Development (IBRD, the World Bank), the World Trade Organisation (WTO) and the Organisation for Economic Co-operation and Development (OECD), all achieve various degrees of publicity for their work. From the point of view of international marketing strategy, it may not be at all clear how the influence of these organisations will be brought to bear. The following review highlights their main functions and work, which is then followed by examples drawn from Eastern Europe and other emergent markets, all of which show the influence of the IMF and World Bank in helping these economies switch from a centrally-planned to a market economy. Businesses seeking opportunities in these markets or any others where they play a major role have to be aware of the impact they have, and how this can affect entry strategies into these countries.

General Agreement on Tariffs and Trade/World Trade Organisation (GATT/WTO)

The GATT was set up in 1948 and was originally planned to be a temporary agreement to complement the international commercial agreement known as the International Trade Organisation (ITO), but this collapsed on the refusal of the USA to endorse it. However, the membership gradually increased over the years as countries perceived the benefits to be gained by working together to reduce barriers to trade.

The organisation is independent of the United Nations, but has a loose affiliation to it.

The main objective of the GATT is to reduce, or, if possible, eliminate, trade restrictions and to create an international forum in which trading nations can discuss trade issues, resolve trade conflicts and plan trading policies. As a multilateral agreement, the GATT had no binding authority over its members, but acts to persuade members to:

1 eliminate tariffs and quotas among the members of GATT;

2 improve the trading environment through negotiation on trade matters;

3 follow the most favoured nation (MFN) rule, by which all members treat each other equally and without discrimination;

4 treat exports from developing countries preferentially.

The members of the GATT meet in annual sessions to discuss and resolve trade issues and to hold conferences (or Rounds) which last over a number of years and focus on specific restrictions. The last conference, known as the Uruguay Round, lasted from 1986 to 1994, and involved issues related to food and drink, intellectual property rights, textiles, services and farm subsidies. The complexity of these issues and the threat to some groups' (such as farmers) incomes provided many stumbling blocks along the way, but the main trading groups of the EU, Japan and the USA finally passed the Uruguay Round proposals in December 1994, providing a huge boost to world demand and prospects.

In addition to the agreement to reduce protective measures, a new organisation was born which came into existence on 1 January 1995, replacing the GATT. The World Trade Organisation (WTO) provides a more formal response to trading issues, looks at the implementation of the 1994 agreements and focuses on those areas, mainly services, that were not the subject of previous rounds.

The success of the GATT is important for business as it has created opportunities that companies should recognise and be prepared to exploit. Although the advanced economies are expected to be the main beneficiaries, there will be losers as adjustments and structural change takes place.

International Monetary Fund (IMF)

First established in 1944, the main purposes of the IMF were to produce stability in international exchange markets, to promote monetary co-operation and to provide short-term financial help (liquidity) to member countries.

The role of the IMF has developed over the years and attracted more and more nations as the advantages of belonging to it have become apparent. The main advantage is in attracting bank loans, as a country that does not belong will be viewed as a credit risk.

Over the past 10 years the focus of the IMF has been on helping the ex-Communist countries introduce financial reforms and to help developing countries improve their prospects for growth by bringing in a more market-oriented approach.

For the advanced economies, the role of the IMF has been reduced, particularly as a global financial market has emerged. The richest countries, known as the Group of 7 or G7 – made up of the USA, Japan, Germany, France, Italy, the UK and Canada – have set up meetings or summits to review items of interest. However, the long-term importance of the G7 is uncertain as economic development in Far Eastern countries has shifted the balance of economic power towards that region.

International Bank for Reconstruction and Development (IBRD)

More commonly referred to as the World Bank, and not to be confused with the EBRD (*see* Box 5.7), this was set up about the same time as the IMF to provide loans to developing countries for long-term economic projects. The Bank is the major provider of long-term loans at low rates to these countries and is in effect the largest provider of aid assistance.

Box 5.7   **EUROPEAN BANK FOR RECONSTRUCTION AND DEVELOPMENT: A SUMMARY**

1 *Capital*: the bank has 10bn Ecu of capital supplied by its 43 member countries.

2 *Objectives*: to provide advice, loans and equity investment and debt guarantees to qualified applicants designed to:

   (a) foster the transition towards democracy and open-market-oriented economies;

   (b) promote private and entrepreneurial initiatives in the countries of Central and Eastern Europe.

3 *Mandate*: the EBRD mandate gives it a particular concern for the promotion of democratic institutions and human rights.

4 *Funding*: the EBRD is a combination of merchant and development bank approaches, with not less than 60 per cent of its funding directed to either:

   (a) private sector enterprises; or

   (b) state-owned enterprises (SOEs) implementing a programme to achieve private ownership and control.

Not more than 40 per cent will be directed to public infrastructure or other projects.

5 *Lending*: the bank will lend money to projects that:

   (a) develop the private sector;
   (b) implement the privatisation of SOEs;
   (c) encourage foreign direct investment (FDI);
   (d) create and strengthen financial institutions;
   (e) restructure the industrial sector;
   (f) create a modern infrastructure;
   (g) promote SMEs;
   (h) improve the environment.

The bank offers a full range of funding on a market, rather than on a subsidised or concessionary, basis including:

1 loans (secured/unsecured, etc.) with a maximum of final maturity of 10 years for commercial enterprises or of 15 years for infrastructure projects;

2 equity;

3 guarantees and indemnity.

It is able to mobilise additional commercial funds from private sector banks and with the assistance of other international financial institutions.

Funds are mainly provided by the subscriptions of member states, and as poorer countries have often found it difficult to meet the IBRD conditions, the Bank set up the International Development Association (IDA) and the International Finance Corporation (IFC) to provide longer-term loans at very low rates to those countries with severe difficulties.

The IMF and World Bank had a clear demarcation, with the former focusing on short-term loans, whilst the latter provided long-term assistance. As a consequence of the involvement of the IMF in resolving the Third World's debt crisis and the reforms and restructuring of Eastern Europe, it has been increasingly involved in providing long-term loans to debt-ridden nations. Likewise, the World Bank has provided loans against promises of macroeconomic reform, giving it a focus not too dissimilar to the IMF.

The convergence between the two organisations points to the possibility of a merger at some time in the future. However, due to the volume of work that each of them has this is not likely to happen very quickly.

Organisation for Economic Co-operation and Development (OECD)

This is made up of 26 members drawn from the rich industrialised countries, which explains the term 'rich man's club' that is often used for the OECD. Although gradually expanding as more countries reach higher levels of economic sophistication and income, it still focuses on the interests of a minority of the world's population.

The OECD conducts numerous research projects dealing with economic and industrial development of both advanced and developing countries, international trade, foreign investments and other areas. The main influence is to persuade governments of the wisdom of a certain course of action, and to facilitate this process it provides periodic economic forecasts and surveys both of its members and other countries, an event that is awaited with some interest by both government and by the financial community, as a favourable report can act as a valuable endorsement of macroeconomic policy.

The international financial environment

To be successful, companies will have to look to foreign markets to undertake business, either by the purchase of raw materials and components for the sale of their products, (*see* Boxes 5.8 and 5.9). When a firm moves into the international market place it will be exploiting the opportunities that exist, but at the same time will be entering into a fiercely competitive environment. An additional factor has to be taken into account here, and that is that trade will be undertaken in a currency other than that of the home country, and many companies will be required to go beyond their own working capital and lines of credit to service contracts in their new market.

For the marketer these are important considerations, as failure to appreciate them could have a major impact on the company's success in overseas markets as well as having potentially damaging consequences on the financial well-being of the company. This section will focus on the financial issues facing the marketer and point to the help available to manage financial risks.

Foreign exchange market dynamics

It is important for importers and exporters to identify the risk that their businesses face when trading internationally, and to be aware of the methods available to mitigate or reduce these risks. The risks can be grouped under six headings:

1 country risk, incorporating political and economic stability, war, import/export regulations;

2 importer risk, involving non-payment of invoices, delayed payment or insolvency of the buyer;

3 industry risk, focusing on demands for particular produces, recession in an industry, competitive behaviour within an industry and fashionable or seasonal goods;

4 exporter risk, involving problems in providing correct documentation or failure to supply goods in accordance with the sales contract;

5 transportation risk, associated with the mode of transport – e.g. containership loss at sea plus storage facilities at ports;

6 foreign exchange risk, along with fluctuating rates that affect pricing and profit.

Box 5.8 **INVESTING IN EASTERN EUROPE AND THE CIS[25]**

ABB, the Swiss–Swedish engineering company, has built a network of 60 companies in the region over the five years 1990–5. The rewards of the investment, in what many regard as a high-risk market, are growing sales and low cost supplies of top-class products for the international market.

ABB has woven itself into the region's industrial fabric, particularly in power engineering where it feels that there is great potential in reviewing and replacing out-dated power stations. The company's plants can be found in Poland, Kazakhstan, Croatia and Bulgaria, and during 1995 and 1996 an average of one new company every month was added to the company's portfolio.

Orders in the region have increased from $225m in 1990 to $1.65bn in 1995, and are projected to rise further to over $3bn by the year 2000. If this total is reached eight per cent of the group's total sales will come from the region. Perhaps more importantly, the move is helping ABB secure lower-cost sources of components such as turbines and switching gear which are up to 40 per cent cheaper than from the equivalent Western supplier. These savings play a part in helping to achieve the cost-cutting that can help to win international market share.

Despite this success, risks still have to be managed. To do this, acquisition costs have been kept low, with the company rarely spending more than $20m on any single acquisition, and with the 60 companies in total having cost no more than $300m to buy. Enterprises might be bought cheaply, but the investment in management resources has been high, with investment in technical skills to permit the use of a single quality standard across all factories, plus training managers in marketing, finance and management skills. In addition, the company has transferred technology, including machine tools and computer programmes.

Investments in Eastern Europe have not been the cause of job cuts in Western Europe – cutting costs to compete in the global market would have done that anyway. The new investments alongside the existing expertise of the rest of the company create new opportunities to become more competitive and hence, the company argues, create new job opportunities in the longer term.

Buying into privatised companies over such a diverse number of countries has not been an easy proposition, with each country having its own version of privatisation. Emerging

▶

> **Box 5.8 continued**

markets going through this transition adopted various approaches, either with outright sales to corporate investors or by retaining a controlling interest, or by partial sales to managers, workers or the general public. Some governments have dragged their feet on privatisation, but have been persuaded by IMF/World Bank stipulations to enter into the process.

In a similar vein, East European countries have a variety of market regulations that make operating in these markets more difficult than it would be in a developed economy. Nevertheless, some of these countries have made significant progress, with the Czech Republic and Poland joining the OECD in 1996, and this explains ABB's strategy of using managers from their plants in these two countries to train their counterparts in Russia and Ukraine.

ABB was one of the first companies to take advantage of the changes in Eastern Europe and the CIS, and despite the difficulties, has made a success of the move because as it fits in with its overall strategy of cost reduction.

Box 5.9   FINANCING COMPANY INVESTMENT IN EMERGING MARKETS[26]

Firms in developed economies finance their investment first from profits and then from borrowing. As a last resort, they will raise money by issuing new shares. This preference is not seen in emerging markets, where many firms prefer the equity solution to their financing problems.

The choice between debt and equity depends on three main factors:

1 the rates at which the two are taxed;

2 the potential cost of bankruptcy;

3 agency costs – i.e. conflict of trust between managers, shareholders and creditors.

In many cases, the firm's choices will be partly influenced by government, and this is especially true of emerging markets, where companies are encouraged to use equity. Likewise bond markets from which firms can raise debt finance are weak in these economies, making it difficult and expensive to raise funds from this source.

Recent research on the 100 largest firms (by net assets) in Brazil, India, Jordan, Malaysia, Pakistan, South Korea, Thailand, Turkey and Zimbabwe shows that between 1980 and 1990 they obtained about one-third of their total financing from internal sources. In Germany the comparable figure was 67 per cent. Firms that relied most on outside finance tended to be in the bigger emerging markets.

Various reasons for this dependency can be put forward, but government policy in these countries has tended to favour equity over debt finance. In some countries this has been caused by governments seeking to encourage their citizens to buy shares or to exchange coupons for shares in newly privatised companies. Other influences are lower corporate tax rates if enough shares are traded publicly, ceiling on debt to equity rates and other direct and indirect influences. The problem is that an influence in a certain direction will distort decisions and reduce options. Many governments in Eastern Europe are seeking to improve the transparency and efficiency of their financial markets, thereby promoting the possibility of firms exploiting both equity and debt finance.

▶

▶ **Box 5.9 continued**

Focusing on emerging markets as an homogeneous entity is fraught with complications and contradictions, as is the implied assumption that developed economies share the same approach to financing. Comparison between the USA, Japan and Germany by Michael Porter points to the short-term view in the former country and to a longer-term view taken by the other two countries, a factor in the relative decline of the USA. Emerging markets have more than one model to follow, with the influence of Germany and Japan's approach being particularly felt throughout Eastern Europe and the Asia Pacific region

Careful consideration should be given to the planning of activities involving the movement of products across international political boundaries. Most of these risks can be reduced, but this will lead to higher costs for the company or result in the shifts of some of the burden to the business partner abroad – a factor that could severely compromise the competitive position of the company.

With foreign exchange an export company dealing with an organisation in France will either invoice in their own currency (e.g. in sterling), the currency of the purchaser (e.g. French francs) or in an acceptable third currency (e.g. US dollars). If the first course of action is chosen the risk of the pound moving against the franc will put the risk on to the purchaser, the second approach will reverse the risk (i.e. the risk is now with the seller), while the use of a third currency will make commercial sense only if both sides regularly use US dollars for trade with other companies. As all three of these currencies move against each other every day, the risk is there for all to see.

In some countries, the rise of their currency against most of the major trading nations has meant that the major exporting companies have had to reconsider their strategies. This is particularly noticeable in the Japanese economy, with the increasing value of the yen obliging many of their major companies to look for production opportunities overseas, as has happened with car manufacturers and electronic firms locating in the USA, Europe and elsewhere to overcome this problem.

Foreign exchange issues therefore figure at the individual company level, either in the problem of risk in everyday exchange movements, or in the longer-term picture that impacts on location issues.

Newly emergent markets in Eastern Europe present different problems in relation to foreign exchange, with currencies that are hardly known outside of their own countries and which are not freely convertible on the exchange markets. The Bulgarian lev, the Armenian dram and the Albanian lek are three such currencies that will be unfamiliar to most and cause problems for those wishing to trade with these countries, particularly as a market for the buying and selling of currencies will be in its infancy. In Armenia, the dram was introduced in 1992, but has had to compete with the US dollar and German mark, as well as the Russian rouble, as methods by which to transact business.

Georgia is a country that currently shows risks under all six categories outlined above, which will compound the problem of doing business with that country. However, this has not stopped deals being struck, which may in the short term prove to be unprofitable, but over a longer period of time be beneficial. *Overseas Trade*[27] pointed out early in 1996 that in both Russia and Belarus a range of opportunities existed for those companies who were willing to read beyond the headline figures of falling output, high inflation and exchange rate uncertainties.

Exchange risks have to be seen in relation to other issues and the opportunity and potential seen in the market place. A marketer must appreciate the need to be fully appraised on all of these areas, as each one could compromise the competitive position of the firm. Exchange risk can be seen as affecting short- and long-term considerations that move from the management of risk through to the influence on market entry in countries such as Belarus and ultimately to the location of production facilities.

SUMMARY

The chapter has touched on the most important aspects of the economic environment, from increased global trade, economic performance, assessing market potential through to the financial markets that support trade.

Increased import penetration is seen in all countries, increasing competition but at the same time opening up new opportunities for companies to source their supplies from the most appropriate supplier.

The economic performance of countries will be judged more by improvements in standards of living than crude measures such as GDP statistics. Countries will have to adapt to a market that has expanded and increasingly fails to recognise political borders. Governments will find that their room for manoeuvre has been reduced, encouraging the move to co-operation with countries within trading blocs.

Trading blocs aim to promote trade, but at the same time act as impediments to it. 'Fortress Europe' is a major concern for many US and Japanese firms, who see common barriers being exerted if the WTO/GATT initiatives fail to have the expected effects.

IMF/World Bank initiatives, particularly in the emerging markets, pave the way for the move to a market economy, and along with merchant banks and other financial sector companies seek to set up a legal, financial and corporate governance framework that supports this move.

Companies trading across political borders experience problems with exchange rate movements which, being outside of their control, increase risk. Exchange risk management becomes an important issue. Assistance with this problem is provided by the financial sector who provide a range of services to cover exchange rate exposure, payments risk, insurance and the use of alternative trading methods.

As exporting becomes more important for all countries, the challenge is to encourage more firms to consider this option, as research suggests that such a strategy assists rapid development of the company and thereby of the host country.

REVIEW QUESTIONS

1 Outline the economic fundamentals that provide information to the marketer.

2 What other available information will the marketer seek to provide a rounded picture of an economy?

3 Review the types of economic integration seen in the world today.

4 What is risk management in terms of foreign trade?

5 What is the role of the WTO in world trade?

DISCUSSION QUESTIONS

1 What are the salient features of a global economy, and how does it affect the marketing manager?

2 What are the difficulties associated with the assessment of market potential in an emerging market in Eastern Europe?

3 All countries will feel the impact of increased globalisation. Outline the main challenges facing France, Germany or the UK in meeting these.

4 The introduction of the single currency (the Euro) in the EU will reduce foreign exchange problems. How will this threaten the UK's financial services sector?

5 Is it important for the global marketer to be aware of, and literate in, the financial environment of international trade?

6 How far is it relevant to produce balance of payments statistics for the UK, when integration has effectively created a single market in Europe, and many companies trade freely across borders throughout the world?

Case study

ECONOMIC INTEGRATION AND GLOBAL STRATEGIES

WPP Group, the UK-based marketing services group, employs over 22 000 people in 40 units. In the 1980s it took over such groups as Oglivy and Mather and J. Walter Thompson, expanding to become the largest group of its type in the world, but saddled with huge debts. The size of the debt was predicted to bring the group down, but throughout the 1990s the performance of the group has been such that its sales have increased to over £7bn, its debt has reduced to £145m and its profits have increased by 35 per cent (1996). The value of the company stood at £2bn, making it one of the largest companies in the UK.

The turnaround in the financial performance is mirrored by the strategy adapted by WPP. The company's clients, such as Ford, IBM and Unilever, were the inspiration for the holding company's move beyond financial control of its 40 units. Each of these clients is seeking to co-ordinate its activities on a global scale, and WPP is following suit, by shadowing their approach. Training, personnel and technology have been centralised to gain benefits and to invest in new developments, such as Internet-based companies, when head office feels the time is right.

WPP is one of a number of companies that have adopted an approach based on the premise that the world (and marketing) has become borderless and that strategies that fail to recognise this will be less than optimal in their impact. Studies have, however, shown that in certain industries, such as white goods, businesses pursuing global strategies were losing out to smaller regional competitors. Economic environmental changes, and regional trading blocs development must be interpreted by managers to see what response they should make.

At the industry level, response to globalisation can be felt in structural forces as well as collective actions of businesses.

Structural forces: three drivers can be identified

1 economies of scale in value-adding activities;
2 differences in comparative advantages across countries;
3 standardised market demand across countries.

All of these function with some force in global industries, while their influence is heavily reduced in national and multidomestic industries. If these drivers have a high influence, then a global business strategy consisting of integrated operations and cross-subsidisation of international market share battles can help the firm adopt viable structural considerations.

Firms can also be influenced by the strategies of other companies, with a common approach adopted by others that pushes the individual enterprise to develop a strategy consistent with their approach. The social forces at work in an industry can influence firms in such a way that their strategy to a certain extent ignores technical pressures. An examples of this was the move by Japanese financial firms in the late 1980s who invested in North American real estate, copying the strategy of those first into the industry. Structural considerations had little impact on decision making.

Competition on a global scale is shaped via structural drivers, whilst competition actually occurs through imitative behaviour that might be justified by structural considerations. This combines the economic organisation of an industry and the strategy as devised by the business and its managers. It is, therefore, possible to see that there can be a number of industries in which structural conditions favour globalisation, but business still competes at national or multidomestic levels. Industries of this type offer first-mover advantages for those firms who can develop a global approach. Over-globalisation is another possibility. In this situation, management may have assumed the benefits of globalisation, but the industry is incapable of supporting it. In either circumstance, business strategy fails to support the approach used by companies.

Research by Burkinshaw, Morrison and Hullard (1995) looked at the strong performers in these industries who had adopted a globally integrated strategy. It found that a positive relationship between the global approach that focused on the integration of business activities and performance supported work that found that the majority of industries were under-globalised.

Regional strategies are also seen to be of increasing use, particularly when demand and competitive advantage considerations point in that direction.

WPP, in following the global strategies of its clients, is looking at the potential offered by other clients flowing in a global direction. However, some clients of Oligvy and Mather, part of the group, are troubled by the conflict of interest that can arise from part of the group serving what are in fact competitors. Recognising this problem, WPP announced that it was vital to keep its brands as separate as possible. Another issue for the group is to strengthen its operations across the globe by setting up or acquiring other agencies. To this end, a second agency in Brazil was acquired, with plans to support expansion in China and Latin America. The idea of these moves is to allow local participation to make a central idea relevant, with the maximum impact on a local market.

Economic developments in China, South and Latin America and elsewhere, with the emphasis on privatisation and adapting market economies, are predicted to continue, creating new opportunities and threats for firms like WPP and its clients. Trading blocs and the role of international agencies such as the WTO are all expected to continue the move towards regionalisation and globalisation.

Questions

1 *If many industries are under-globalised, what opportunities does this offer WPP?*

2 *According to research, economies of scale play a major role in determining the drive (or lack of it) to globalisation. How far can WPP gain economy of scale advantages?*

3 *Could the advent of Internet marketing adversely affect the strategy of WPP?*

4 *How likely is it that companies such as Coriant (formerly Saatchi & Saatchi) will follow WPP's strategy?*

FURTHER READING

Daniels, J.D. and Radebaugh, L.H., *International Business Environment and Operations* (Reading, MA: Addison-Wesley, 1995).

Howell, J., *Understanding Eastern Europe* (London: Kogan Page, 1994).

Kennedy, P., *Preparing for the Twenty-First Century* (London: Fontana, 1993).

Larisley, S., *After the Gold Rush* (London: Century, 1994).

Norgan, S., *Market Management: A European Perspective* (Reading, MA: Addison-Wesley, 1994).

Vaitilingam, R., *Guide to Using Economies and Economic Indications* (London: Pitman Publishing, 1994).

NOTES AND REFERENCES

1   Ellis, J. and Williams, D., *International Business Strategy* (London: Pitman Publishing, 1995), 88.

2   'Not so absolutely fabulous', *The Economist* (4 November 1995).

3   Ellis and Williams, op. cit., 89.

4   McRae, H., 'A seismic shift to the East', *Independent on Sunday* (5 October 1995); Smith, D., 'Labouring under a delusion', *Sunday Times* (5 October 1995).

5   World Bank, *World Development Report 1995* (Oxford University Press, 1995).

6   'Spending spree on the cards in India', *Times* (4 January 1996).

7   Ibid.

8   'Emerging market profiles', Ernst & Young (Winter 1995).

9   'Doing business in China', Ernst & Young (1994).

10 BPP, 'The monetary and financial system' (London: BPP, October 1995).

11 'Europe's dynamic entrepreneurs', *Financial Times* (16 November 1995).

12 'The state of the market', Chartered Institute of Marketing (Winter 1995).

13 Advertising Association, *Marketing Pocket Book 1996* (NTC Publications, 1995), 12.

14 Czinkota, M.R. and Ronkainen, I.A., *International Marketing*, 3rd edition (Orlando: The Dryden Press, 1993), 64.

15 Cramp, B., 'Border crossing', *Marketing Business* (July/August 1995).

16 Rugman, A.M. and Hodgetts, R.M., *International Business* (London: McGraw-Hill, 1995).

17 Appleyard, B., 'Blame it all on the Beatles', *Independent* (2 January 1996).

18 Czinkota and Ronkainen, op. cit., 89.

19 Ibid., 90.

20 Cecchini, P. *et al.*, *The European Challenge 1992: The Benefits of a Single Market* (London: Wildwood House, 1988).

21 Ibid.

22 Goodhart, C., 'EMU: a future that works?', *Prospect* (December 1995).

23 Ohmae, K. (ed.) *The Evolving Global Economy* (Cambridge, MA: Harvard Business School Press, 1995); 'Japan in Asia', *Financial Times* (14 November 1995).

24 Hufbauer, G.C. (ed.), *Europe 1992: An American Perspective* (Washington, DC: Brookings Institute, 1990).

25 'Woven in the fabric', *Financial Times* (10 January 1996); Palmer, G., *The EIU Privatisation Manual* (London: The Economist Intelligence Unit, 1994).

26 'That's the way the money comes', *The Economist* (11 November 1995); Porter, M., 'Capital disadvantage: America's failed investment system' in Ohmae, K. (ed.) *The Evolving Global Economy* (Cambridge, MA: Harvard Business School Press, 1995).

27 'Bear necessities', *Overseas Trade* (London: Brass Tracks, December-January 1996).

The social–cultural environment

INTRODUCTION

The examples used in the preceding chapters show a world that has become increasingly integrated as international business opportunities have been created both at a regional trade bloc level and globally. Whereas previously many firms and organisations could choose to ignore competition either because it simply didn't exist or because of protective barriers, this in many instances is no longer the case. If opportunities are sought in international markets, this needs an understanding of customer requirements as well as learning how to manage operations across countries with a multicultural workforce.

As transportation and technological links have made the world seem a much smaller place, organisations can overlook the importance of being able to understand both the needs of the customer and the requirements of personnel working within and between countries.

Samsung,[1] the South Korean conglomerate, runs businesses right across Europe, from Hungary where TVs are produced to Portugal with microchip production and Germany where cameras are produced. Other operations exist in the UK and in Slovakia. How can a Korean company be successful in these vastly different cultural climates?

The approach taken by Samsung is to produce a synthesis of management styles, taking the best from both the European and Korean approaches. For example, in Germany the emphasis can be given to the individual worker as the company recognises that individual ability is high. In South Korea, on the other hand, emphasis is placed on teamwork to fulfil a project. A further difference emerges when looking at the bureaucratic approach favoured by the company in its home base; an autocratic approach to management prevails. In Europe, this approach would not find favour, so in the UK the company's management structure is flat and authority devolved. Creating an indigenous management style is also part of the company's strategy to make its European operations self-sufficient, based on the need to have fast response times to market changes. Self-sufficiency encompasses people, material and technologies.

The example of Samsung shows the way that competition has produced the movement of people (managers from Korea to set up operations), goods that appeal to local markets and capital to set up operations. Underpinning this is the requirement to appreciate and understand the social–cultural environment that will assist with the move towards a successful strategy. Samsung, although not always guaranteed to achieve its aims, shows good practice in understanding the differences and using them for the advantage and those of employees, suppliers and customers.

For all the examples of good practice there are many *faux pas* made by companies who fail to explore the effect of their advertising campaigns, management approaches and relations with suppliers and retailers, consequently losing a great deal of money, either because they have to withdraw from a market or seek to rectify problems: fast-changing markets are not matched by changes in behavioural patterns, values and attitudes. This chapter will analyse these issues and look at successful ways of meeting the challenge that culture presents to every firm and of every facet of business.

Objectives

This chapter will examine:

- the meaning and role of culture
- elements of culture in global markets
- cultural analysis of international markets
- approaches for assessing cultural differences and similarities
- global markets as a change agent
- the challenge of cultural change.

MEANING AND THE ROLE OF CULTURE

The cultural environment shapes people's values, attitudes, perceptions and patterns of behaviour. Cultural elements include language, religion, social organisation, aesthetics, education and so on. Figure 6.1 shows the connection between these and the consumer decision process, while Fig. 6.2 shows the breadth of the task facing marketing managers in the area of cultural analysis.

There are numerous definitions of culture, offered by sociologists, anthropologists, historians and others. A number of common elements can be discerned – that culture is learned, shared and transmitted from one generation to another.[2] Culture is passed on both by family units and social institutions, state and religious organisations. According to Hofstede,[3] the word 'culture' can be used in the sense of 'the collective programming of the mind that distinguishes the members of one category of people from another'. The category can be a nation or region or ethnic group. To Czinkota and Ronkainen,[4] culture is also multidimensional, consisting of a number of common elements that are interdependent, so that changes that occur in one of the dimensions will affect the others. Despite this interdependence, culture is very slow to change, as it is, according to Hofstede's definition, a collective programming that provides a degree of continuity.

Fig 6.1 CULTURAL INFLUENCES ON BUYER BEHAVIOUR

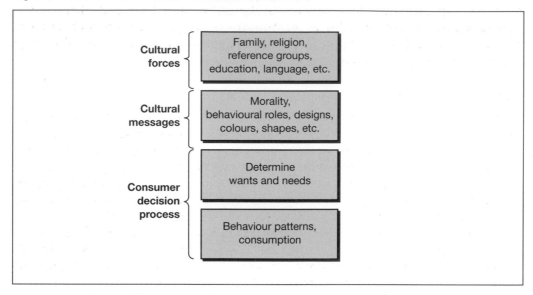

Moving from one culture to another is, therefore, problematic as adjustments have to be made to be able to communicate and get things done in different circumstances. Business operations across borders, either from the point of view of manufacturing or from the need to understand customer requirements, will have to adjust to the new cultural circumstances. Managers and operatives require new skills and the ability to adjust to the new circumstances within a company trading internationally.

Fig 6.2 MARKETING AND CULTURE

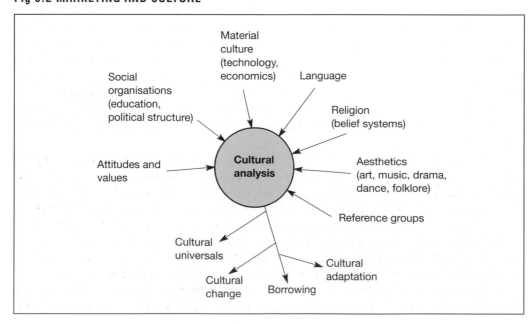

A society's cultural values and behaviour patterns are learned and not biologically determined, shared with other members of the group and interrelated – i.e. one element of culture is connected with another (for example, marriage and religion, material goods and social status, and so on). According to Orlando and Cateora,[5] cultural knowledge can be classified into two types.

Factual knowledge

Factual knowledge of a culture refers to the facts that a marketer can study and understand – for example, the meanings attached to different colours and tastes. So in the UK, the colour black is normally worn at funerals, whereas in Brazil it is purple. There are also cultural differences with respect to giving gifts. In Japan, one never gives items with four in the name, as the pronunciation of the word sounds like death; similarly you can give flowers to a Japanese person, but not white ones, as white has connotations with death. In France, yellow flowers are not normally given, as they suggest infidelity.

Other types of fact are quite straightforward, such as the number of Protestants in Germany or the UK. However, the difference between a Protestant within German culture and a Protestant in UK culture can assume significance when it is interpreted within a cultural context. This is attributed to differences in the practice of the religion; therefore, factual and interpretative knowledge about religion in Germany is essential to gaining an understanding of German culture.

Interpretative knowledge

The second type of knowledge about a culture, interpretative knowledge, refers to the nuances of a culture's values, traits and patterns – for example, the culture's attitude to time, the meaning of life, etc. To interpret this type of knowledge requires experience and a degree of empathy. Since this type of knowledge is prone to misinterpretation, the global marketing manager may need to operate closely with indigenous people in the target market to appreciate and understand the culture fully.

In dealing with a particular market, the global marketer is really dealing with its culture. The product design and style must fit in with the aesthetics of the culture. The promotional message is acceptable only if the symbols are meaningful or recognisable to the consumers. The success of a product in a foreign market therefore depends on whether it is culturally accepted or resisted. For example, trying to promote products using semi-clad women in Islamic countries would result in failure, as this type of advertising is an affront to the culture. Similarly, trying to sell pig's brain soup as a delicacy in a Chinese restaurant in Britain does not fit in well with British food culture.

In the analysis of different cultures the marketer must be careful to avoid applying their own cultural values and rules of behaviour. This is referred to as the 'self-reference criterion trap', in which a person unconsciously applies his or her own cultural values, knowledge and experiences in evaluating a situation. For example, in some cultures not to be on time for a business appointment is quite acceptable and normal. This would be considered rude and insulting if this behaviour were manifest in a UK context. Similarly, to refuse refreshments in the Middle East or Asia would be considered offensive, whereas this is acceptable in most West European cultures.

The existence of self-reference criteria in a marketing manager can lead to market failure because it could prevent the person from developing an awareness of the cultural differences, and recognising how important these differences are. The end result is that the marketing manager will either take no action or react in a manner which will be considered as being at worst offensive or at best insensitive.

Box 6.1

EXPORTING TO FRANCE[6]

In France, business meetings are generally conducted in a formal atmosphere, with first names being rarely used in business relationships. Senior executives in France often call their staff by their surnames. Similarly, the formal *vous* is more usual in business, with the familiar *tu* reserved for friends or relatives. This reflects the fact that French companies are far more hierarchical than their UK counterparts, with team working and social mixing out of hours being less familiar than in the Anglo-Saxon-dominated cultures of the UK and USA.

The French and British have differing senses of humour; the French rarely laugh at themselves and hate being on the receiving end of practical jokes. The general rule for exporters is to be as formal as the French when conducting business, but no more.

Appointments should be punctually kept, but it is not the norm to expect tea or coffee to be offered on arrival. The French appreciate it if people try to speak French, even if only a little, and always warm to comments about economic success in France.

In France, information is supplied to business people visiting the UK, with the following provided as useful tips for meetings:

1 take English documentation to meetings;
2 take a legal advisor for important negotiations;
3 be punctual;
4 speak English or take an interpreter;
5 adapt the product to British tastes;
6 on meeting, shake hands firmly and say 'How do you do';
7 if you are called by your first name, do likewise;
8 always accept the offer of coffee at the start of a meeting;
9 do not take nice words as a sign of agreement;
10 talk about the weather to fill awkward silences.

Scottish companies can exploit the long relationship with France that goes back to 1295 and the 'Auld Alliance' between the two countries against England, with a particular recognition of the 'Made in Scotland' label which suggests added value.

ELEMENTS OF CULTURE IN GLOBAL MARKETS

The example of exporting to France (*see* Box 6.1) reveals the danger of assuming that a nation's culture is homogeneous and all-pervading. If the UK is dominated by Anglo-Saxon attitudes there are areas and regions where its influence is weak and even challenged. This can apply to Wales and Scotland and even to areas with a higher than average proportion of an ethnic minority, such as the Asian populations of the Midlands. In these circumstances, different values and ways of behaving will apply.

With the possible exception of countries such as Japan, few countries are dominated by a culture that goes unchallenged. Intracultural differences have to be understood as well as cross-cultural variations. Examples of intracultural differences can be found in Spain, America, Canada and Iraq.

With increasing contact made between countries with the advent of the Internet, improved travel and communications and product movement, cultures are influenced in many and various ways. Some accept these interactions willingly, while others react negatively, seeing a threat to a way of life or a challenge to fundamentally held beliefs. When the Taliban took control of Afghanistan in 1996 they sought to impose strict Islamic law, keeping women indoors and banning various activities and games. Likewise, Iran has for many years sought to maintain adherence to Islamic laws and traditions.

Business activities, however, act to change or amend a culture by the introduction of new products and ways of doing business. 'Cultural imperialism' is an accusation often levelled at companies whose products change long-established systems, a factor that could pose a threat to future business with a country that feels particularly threatened by this. International marketing managers have, therefore, to be particularly aware of this problem. An appropriate place to start is with a review of the elements of culture (and sub-cultures, where appropriate) that can shed light on how they interact with each other.

'Cultural universals' are activities that occur across cultures and involve gestures, music, personal names, courtship, trade and other elements; they can be unique in a given culture as to how they link and interact with other elements. Looking at the major elements which are listed below shows that they cover both physical items, such as material culture, as well as intangible items, such as values and attitudes.

The main elements of culture that will be reviewed are religion, language, education, aesthetics, social organisation and material culture. The need to adapt to these elements will vary between cultures and depend on the degree of involvement of the company in a particular market. So, for example, a firm exporting to a foreign country might have to consider only the cultural implications of the marketing mix ('4 Ps') elements of price, product, place and promotion. A firm involved in FDI would also have to consider business and management practice. Even if little is required in the way of adaptation, consideration has to be given to understanding the potential impact on the activities of the firm. The Introduction showed how the way Samsung understood the very real differences in the operation of its various production sites in Korea and in Europe led to the development of a new strategy to benefit both the European and Korean operations.

Culture and international markets

Religion
Religious values influence a culture's outlook on life. This is reflected in the society's morality, attitude to life, gender roles, etc. The major religions of the world, in terms of numbers of adherents, are Christianity, Islam, Hinduism, Buddhism, Shintoism and Anumism, accounting for over three-quarters of the world's population. Religious values do influence consumption patterns, as the following examples reveal.

- In most Western European countries the Christian ethic of hard work and success is a dominant value, and the measure of achievement is the acquisition of wealth. In contrast, Hinduism, as practised in India, is fatalistic about the acquisition of wealth.

- Certain religions prohibit the use of certain goods and services – for example, Hinduism prescribes abstinence from beef consumption, Muslims are prohibited from drinking alcohol or eating pork, whereas Jews are prohibited from eating pork and shellfish. Potential opportunities, therefore, exist in these markets for the sale of non-alcoholic drinks and vegetarian products.

- Religion also influences gender roles, customs such as dress and marriage and social institutions. The Muslim woman's role is restricted, in the main, to the household.

- Religious divisions can affect the potential stability of the market. For example, the Muslim separatist movements in Indian Kashmir have created instability in those countries, and the conflicts in the Middle East, are based on religious factors. Marketing in these regions can be a threat but, equally, opportunities do exist.

- Religious holidays affect working patterns, so that, in the Muslim world, during the month of Ramadan virtually all types of work slow down, particularly business. It would not be desirable to conduct business in this month in these countries. Religion is often a total way of life for people in these countries whereas, in Western societies, it is an aspect of life and business interruptions are minimal. Indeed, interruptions to retailing have become less common with, for example, the introduction of Sunday shopping in Germany in 1996; a country that had long resisted the change to opening hours on that day.

Language

Language is an essential element of culture for it reflects its nature and riches, and it is language which distinguishes one culture from another. In countries such as Canada and Switzerland, two or more languages are spoken. This also affects countries like China, Nigeria and India, with a huge diversity of populations, but it can also be found in many smaller countries such as Belgium.

Although language could be said to reflect the nature and values of a culture, this is not always the case. English is the official language of many countries, such as Australia and Singapore, but the two countries are culturally diverse. English tends also to be the business language, while French is often seen as the language of diplomacy.

In business communications, the translation from one language to another can result in inaccuracies. A literal translation may change the entire meaning. For example, some of the more famous translation blunders are 'Body by Fisher' which translated as 'Corpse by Fisher', or 'Braniff's 747 Rendezvous Lounge', which was translated into Portuguese as 'Braniff's 747 "Meet your Mistress" Lounge'. The nuances of meaning for particular words may also be lost in translation. For example, the advertisement by Quantas, the Australian airline had the catchphrase 'Don't be a Wallaby, Fly Quantas'. This would be extremely difficult to translate into another language and retain its subtle play on words.

The same language may have different terms for the same word – for example, in American and British English, we have:

British English	American English
Petrol	Gasoline
Biscuits	Cookies
Plimsolls	Sneakers
Pavement	Sidewalk

To 'Table the Report' in America means postponement, but in the UK it means to bring the matter to the forefront. The global marketer needs to be very aware and careful when handling language in business transactions, or it can result in very costly mistakes.

Communication goes beyond the formal written and oral structure of language. Language is also symbolic communication in terms of space, time, friendship, etc., and marketers need to be aware of these 'silent languages'. In the UK, a person with a large office could mean that that person was important in the hierarchy. But in Japan many executives share offices. Many countries conduct business negotiations at a leisurely pace, as in Japan, but a UK or US sales person will be eager to conclude the business agreement before socialising. This could create unease for the negotiators involved.

Another important 'silent language' for business practice is the language of time. In the UK and European countries, meeting at the appointed time is considered reliable and polite. In many cultures, meeting at 10 a.m. means 'about' that time. The Indonesians show respect by arriving late for meetings.

Much business communication also depends on non-verbal messages. The difficulty with 'silent languages' is that the differences are not obvious and they can be difficult to interpret. Much of this can be attributed to the fact that such languages operate within a context to convey the message (*see* Fig. 6.3). In a high-context culture (Japanese and Arabic cultures) the communication depends on the context or non-verbal aspect of communication – i.e. interpreting what is meant rather than what is actually spoken. In a low-context culture (US and German) communication

Fig 6.3 CULTURAL CONTEXTS

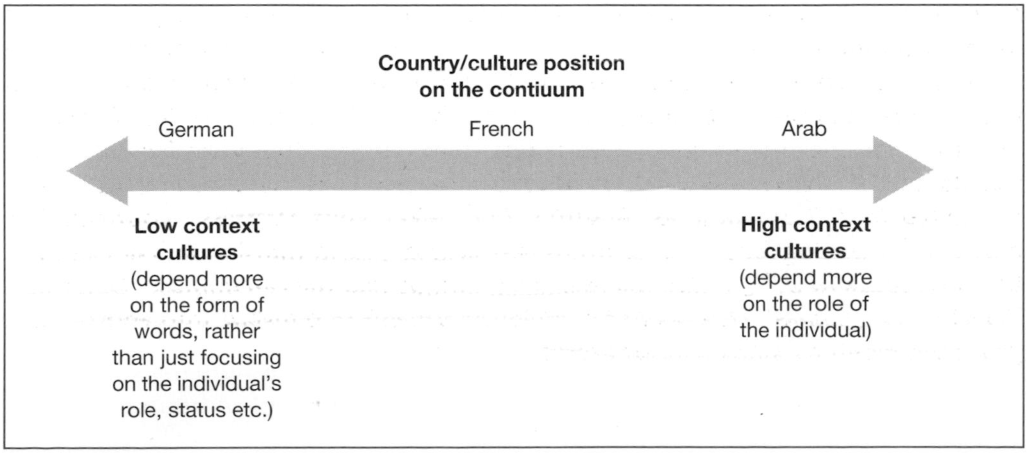

Country/culture position on the contiuum

German   French   Arab

Low context cultures
(depend more on the form of words, rather than just focusing on the individual's role, status etc.)

High context cultures
(depend more on the role of the individual)

depends more on explicit, verbally expressed communications. English stands midway between the extremes of this continuum.

Managers from low-context cultures will need to be trained to develop skills to listen for unspoken messages, whereas individuals from high-context cultures moving into low-context environments will need to be trained to be precise in both written and spoken messages. Obviously, this has serious implications for business meetings and negotiations for those in low-context cultures where business is done quickly and for those in high-context cultures where business is conducted at a slower pace.

Education

The process of learning and sharing cultural values is transmitted through the educational system. The educational system can take many forms, and it is important for the marketer to understand the differences because it can indicate the type of consumer market available. For example:

- the literacy rate will affect the marketer's promotional strategies; a high illiteracy rate may mean the exclusion of printed instructions and more drawings
- an economy with a poorly developed educational system may hinder the firm's operations in the market through the lack of trained personnel within the firm and in support services, such as research and advertising agencies.

Aesthetics

The aesthetics of a culture refers to designs, forms, colours, shapes, sounds – things conveying the concept of beauty and good taste. These are reflected in the music, arts, architecture, etc. of a society. The aesthetics of a culture can affect a firm's marketing strategy.

Colours, for example, are often used as a mechanism to identify brands and for product differentiation. Colours tend to have different connotations and more symbolic value in international than in domestic markets. Red, for instance, is a good-luck colour for many oriental cultures, while white and green are associated with death in Muslim countries.

The design of products and packages should take into consideration the local preferences. McDonald's often have a uniform policy regarding the design of their facilities, but in Vienna they modified their design to fit in with local tastes.

Brand names are also affected by aesthetics. The general policy of many companies is to have one in the local language. With global integration firms are trying to project a global brand image, such as Coke or Kodak. Marketers, therefore, need to be aware and sensitive to local aesthetic preferences.

Social organisation

Social organisation defines the way people relate to each other – the roles of men and women in society, social class, the family, group behaviour, marriage and rituals are all examples of the elements of social organisation. These different elements have an effect on marketing as each institution has an influence on the overall patterns of life such as social behaviours, value systems and the social hierarchy.

The family unit is a fundamental unit of social organisation in many societies. In many countries, such as the UK and most of Europe, the typical household is the nuclear family, consisting of two parents and their children. In other countries, such as India, parts of Africa and the Far East, the family unit is the extended family consisting of two or three generations – grandparents, parents and children. Information on household units can be useful to marketers, as they need to know who the decision maker is in the large unit, whether families travel in a unit or individually, whether they buy large packs, etc. The information gathered from questions such as these will contribute to an effective promotional targeting.

Social organisation also influences the role and status of people in society. Men and women may adopt different roles in the family and in social institutions. In many countries, the role of women is restricted to the family and to bringing up the children. In the UK and other advanced industrial societies, gender roles are becoming more blurred and less predictable; increasingly, women are competing with men in the workplace. In some less developed economies women and men play different but complementary roles, and these roles are strictly defined on the basis of gender. In many Middle Eastern countries, women tend to purchase products and it would be inappropriate for firms to target men in their promotional campaigns.

There may also be a social hierarchy or class system. Members of a society are generally ranked according to some criteria based on income, power, religion, wealth, etc. In different countries, the distribution of people among societies and social mobility will vary. In the UK, the opportunity for social mobility is high, made possible by education and occupation; a good level of education increases the potential for class mobility. In contrast, in Hindu India, the 'caste' system is so rigid that social mobility is very limited for a member of a lower caste. In the caste system, the classes are ranked according to purity, spiritual quality and power, and this is normally defined by birth. An understanding of the social stratification system would enable marketers to segment their markets effectively, as well as 'position' their products appropriately. Promoting a product as a sign of upward mobility would not work in the Indian market.

Values and attitudes are also important determinants of consumer behaviour, and global marketers should develop an understanding of them. Social norms are the modes of behaviour and the accepted roles and standards in a society. A belief is a person's opinion about something – for example, someone may believe that BMW cars stand up under rugged use. This may be based on real fact, opinion or faith. Marketers are interested in people's beliefs regarding products and services because these beliefs make up the product and brand image, and people act on these beliefs. An attitude is a person's point of view towards something (e.g. religion, music, food, politics, etc.) and usually involves liking or disliking. Someone may have the attitude that the Japanese have the best quality products, and this will lead to a consistent behaviour pattern towards Japanese products. Attitudes are difficult to change, and marketers can benefit by fitting their products into existing attitudes, rather than trying to change people's views. Values are shared beliefs or group norms – for example, belief about what is good ethical business practice is normally rooted in religious or social values. The global marketer must identify different values held by foreign consumers and businessmen in order to communicate effectively.

Attitudes towards foreign products. Some societies regard the purchase of foreign products as unpatriotic. This may hamper a firm wishing to enter the market.

Attitudes towards achievement. In some societies achievement is well rewarded and this motivates people to work even more. Marketers would normally prefer to operate in these 'achieving' societies, as one of the tangible rewards is access to goods and services. In contrast, in a society in which success is unlikely to be well rewarded there is lack of motivation and people may not be motivated to produce and consume, as in some less developed economies and socialist economies. In the latter case the rewards may simply be more status, rather than financial or material gain.

Attitudes towards change. In industrial societies attitudes towards change tend to be more positive, whereas in more traditional societies change is viewed with some suspicion. Attitudes towards change affect the speed of product acceptance and firms will tend to find that in industrial nations there will be a greater number who will accept innovations more easily; thus the firm is unlikely to suffer the financial risk of poor product performance in those countries.

Only a few examples have been discussed, but they demonstrate the importance and relevance of attitudes to understanding consumer behaviour in foreign markets.

Material culture

'Material culture' refers to the technological and economic aspects of a society. The way technology is utilised in the creation of goods and services is also related to how a society organises its economic activity. Cultures which have high levels of technology are likely to have a general population who will have a broad understanding of technical know-how, so that operating a washing machine or maintaining a car or lawnmower is not difficult. But in low-technology cultures, as in many less developed countries, this will not be the case. The economic aspects of culture refer to the production, distribution and consumption of goods and services. These affect the level of economic development and hence living conditions.

Material culture and living conditions have a major impact on the quantity, quality and type of products demanded. There are many marketing implications of a country's material culture. Consumer goods such as fridges or vacuum cleaners will sell in the UK, Europe and other advanced industrial nations, but the demand for these electrical items will be very limited in less affluent societies where the material culture has not developed sufficiently. However, there are also differences in health needs, food preferences, leisure activities and living standards and styles. In the UK, front-loading washing machines are preferred; in Japan, houses are typically small, and this will dictate the size of furniture and home appliances. A UK producer wishing to export to Japan will need to consider all these dimensions.

Cultural assessment

To enter a foreign market, a marketer needs to analyse the different elements of culture in order to develop an effective marketing strategy. However, the marketer should not fall into the trap of analysing each of the elements of culture independently from the rest, for they are inextricably linked to form a total picture. Naturally, some elements will be more relevant and directly influence the marketing planning, but this should not detract from analysing the elements of culture as a single entity.

Table 6.1 provides a summary of the major cultural determinants of consumer behaviour which should assist the marketer in identifying those traits which will be

Table 6.1 OUTLINE OF CROSS-CULTURAL ANALYSIS OF CONSUMER BEHAVIOUR

● *Determine relevant motivations.* What needs are fulfilled with the product in the minds of members of the culture? How are these needs presently fulfilled? Do members of this culture readily recognise these needs?
● *Determine characteristic behaviour patterns.* What patterns are characteristic of purchasing behaviour? What forms of division of labour exist within the family structure? How frequently are products of this type purchased? What size packages are normally purchased? Do any of these characteristic behaviours conflict with behaviour expected for this product? How strongly ingrained are the behaviour patterns that conflict with those needed for distribution of this product?
● *Determine what broad cultural values are relevant.* Are there strong values about work, morality, religion, family relations, and so on, that relate to the product? Does the product connote attributes that are in conflict with these cultural values? Can conflicts with values be avoided by changing the product? Are there positive values in this culture with which the product might be identified?
● *Determine characteristic forms of decision making.* Do members of the culture display a studied approach or an impulsive approach to decisions concerning innovations? What is the form of the decision process? Upon what information sources do members of the culture rely? Do members of the culture tend to be rigid or flexible in the acceptance of new ideas? What criteria do they use in evaluating alternatives?
● *Evaluate appropriate promotion methods.* What role does advertising occupy in the culture? What themes, words, or illustrations are taboo? What language problems exist in present markets that cannot be translated into this culture? What types of salespeople are accepted by members of this culture? Are such salespeople available?
● *Determine appropriate institutions for this product in the minds of consumers.* What types of retailers and intermediary institutions are available? What services do these institutions offer that are expected by the consumer? What alternatives are available for obtaining services needed for the product but not offered by existing institutions? How are various types of retailers regarded by consumers? Will changes in the distribution structure be readily accepted?

Source: Consumer Behaviour, 3rd edition, by James F. Engel, Roger D. Blackwell and David T. Kollat. © 1978 by Holt, Rinehart and Winston. Reproduced with permission.

critical to the development of an effective marketing plan. Merely knowing the education system or type of class system is not sufficient; what must be analysed is whether the product or service to be introduced conforms to the cultural patterns of that society, and does not conflict with the existing values. This is an issue taken further in Box 6.2 with an example from the entertainment industry.

Culture and management

For marketers to achieve their stated objectives in international markets it is often necessary, as we have seen, to enter into FDI or some other intermediate stage. Either the marketing function requires awareness of effective management approaches in different cultural contexts and/or other production and management functions need to be aware of the challenges that face them. Managers in many organisations need to develop a global perspective which will bring a heightened awareness of cultural influences.

| Box 6.2 | THE ENTERTAINMENT INDUSTRY[7] |

In 1995, Hollywood earned more money in other countries than was made in North America, catching up with the situation already found in the music industry.

The development of the music industry has occurred without the effect on individual cultures' identity that some had predicted. Ownership is concentrated in a few companies, but musical taste varies widely across the globe. Can the film industry expand internationally, aided by the development of multimedia and market deregulation, without sacrificing cultural diversity? The music industry was worth $40bn in 1995, and is dominated by five companies – Polygram, Sony, Warner Music, BMG and EMI. The first four of these are owned by parent companies with interests in the electronics industry, such as Philips which owns Polygram and Sony, or part of a bigger media group, such as Warner Music, which comes under the Time Warner wing. EMI is the only one that can still be classified as a specialist music company.

The five companies control more than two-thirds of the market, but this has not been at the expense of local taste, despite the notable influence of groups such as U2 (of Ireland), who have an international following. New talent is considered the life-blood of the industry and for many different reasons new groups often prefer independent record labels before moving to the larger established companies. Links are therefore necessary between the two, with Creation Records having an investment by Sony, who own 49 per cent, and are well aware that groups like Oasis can spring from such labels.

EMI maintains a degree of independence for its Asian labels (with their own names, for example) for fear that foreign ownership could dissuade customers. The importance of the Asian market along with Latin America cannot be underestimated: their economic growth increases their overall importance and raises the demand for local groups. Estimates suggest that by the year 2000 the Asian market will account for 29 per cent of the total market (up from 22 per cent in 1996), while the markets of North America and Western Europe will fall from 69 per cent to near to 50 per cent by the same time. The film industry will experience a similar shift, as the rest of the world expands faster than the developed market.

Hollywood studios realise the significance of the shift and are looking to 'localise' filming by making more films outside of North America. They have plans to open more production centres in Europe, partly to offset the high production costs associated with Hollywood productions. A move globally might suggest that as with the music industry, more account must be taken of local tastes and culture.

Managerial behaviour and practices can be influenced by cultural differences – there will be differences in long-term perspectives, delegation, organisational structure and in other areas such as leadership, recruitment and control.

The cultural influences on business, an issue already touched upon, can be seen in the advice given to French and UK business people wishing to do business with each other (*see* Box 6.1 on p. 142). Taking the example of leadership,[8] the differences can be seen in the current practice of Japan, USA and the People's Republic of China.

Japan
Managers in Japan are seen as social integrators who are themselves part of the group, therefore common values and the development of team spirit provides the basis for

co-operation. The manager's role in such circumstances is to create the right environment for such an approach to flourish, being willing to help undertake the same work as their junior colleagues.

Harmony is an important aspect for the Japanese, with face-to-face confrontation being avoided by leaving things ambiguous. Individuals are required to reduce their self-interest to that of the group and the organisation they work for. Peer-group pressure as well as the manager's influence is very important in keeping individual team members in check. This approach is aided by the fact that close personal relationships are developed both inside and outside the work place, with the blurring of work and personal life.

China

Here, the leader is head of the group with a directive style of leadership, with the leader's commands being obeyed as fully as possible. Leaders are responsible to their immediate superiors for the production and performance targets that are still a feature of much of Chinese industry. (This is meeting a challenge in the face of rising free market approaches, with the needs of the customer also coming to the fore.) Leading in China is aided by common values and an emphasis on harmony. Unlike in Japanese companies, where communication feeds top-down as well as bottom-up, communications are mainly top-down.

The USA

Managers here are expected to be decision takers, with a clear vision of where they and their team are heading. Integration here is complicated by the importance of individualism which can act as a counter-weight to co-operation.

Managers in this culture will be expected to confront dissenters who may deflect the effort of the team or group. Unlike in Japan, managers will at least attempt to separate their private and working lives. Communication is generally top-down, with the emphasis on written communication rather than the Japanese preference for face-to-face contact.

These differences in the leadership role of managers are also carried over into areas such as planning. The work of Hofstede takes these differences between cultures and subjects them to closer study, a summary of which is provided in Box 6.3.

Box 6.3

NATIONAL CULTURE DIFFERENCES[9]

National cultures can be distinguished from organisational cultures. The former can be studied in over 50 countries and described with the help of five dimensions. The differences shown set limits to the application of management theory across cultural (national) borders.

Hofstede's study involved sending a questionnaire about values to 60 000 employees of IBM in more than 60 countries. The results showed that there were dimensions which correlated with nationality. The five dimensions of culture that Hofstede identified were power distance, individualism versus collectivism, masculinity versus femininity, uncertainty avoidance and long-term versus short-term orientation.

▶

▶ **Box 6.3 continued**

Power distance

This is the acceptance by less powerful and less influential members of organisations and groups, such as families, that power is distributed unequally; this results in both the leaders and led accepting inequality.

Individualism versus collectivism

This is the degree to which individuals are integrated into groups, with individualistic societies having loose ties between individuals whilst collectivist societies have cohesive groups, often based on extended families.

Masculinity versus femininity

The IBM study revealed that women's values differ less among societies than men's, with men's values moving along a dimension from very assertive, with an emphasis on competition in some societies, to modest and caring in others, placing them closer to women's values. As male values move to the more assertive, women's values adjust, becoming themselves more assertive, but not to the same degree as the men's, showing a wider gap between the two.

Uncertainty avoidance

The focus here is on society's tolerance for uncertainty and ambiguity, indicating the extent to which its members react to structured or unstructured situations. Cultures that are uncertainty avoiding will seek to reduce the possibility of unstructured situations occurring by strict rules and regulations. At the religious level, these tend to involve an adherence to universal beliefs and truths.

In uncertainty accepting societies, the opposite tends to be true, with people more accepting of diversity of opinions and belief, and placing less stress on showing emotions than in uncertainty avoidance societies.

Long-term versus short-term orientation

This dimension deals more with virtue, with values placed on long-term orientations such as thrift. At the opposite end, short-term orientation is characterised by respect for tradition and fulfiling social obligations. Hofstede regards this dimension as problematic insofar as it has not been subject to sufficient research to allow the development of a table of differences to be developed showing its impact on the family, school and workplace (Tables 6.2–6.5 show the differences of the other four dimensions).

What does all this mean for management approaches? Hofstede supports the view that management practices in a country are culturally dependent, leading to the conclusion that what works in one country will not be guaranteed to work in another. What is true for managers is also, if Hofstede is to be believed, true of management theorists, where preferences and solutions have also to be seen as culturally dependent. (Perhaps a similar line of argument can be developed for marketing and marketing management, requiring significant adaptations in varying cultural contexts.) Hofstede cites the examples of performance appraisal, management by objectives, strategic management and humanisation of work to draw attention to the difficulties encountered. For the purpose of this book, strategic management is the most pertinent with its assumption of a weak uncertainty avoidance environment, in which diverging strategic ideas are actively sought out. Its

▶

▶ **Box 6.3 continued**

Table 6.2 DIFFERENCES ACCORDING TO POWER DISTANCE

Small power distance societies	Large power distance societies
In the family:	
Children encouraged to have a will of their own	Children educated towards obedience to parents
Parents treated as equals	Parents treated as superiors
At school:	
Student-centered education (initiative)	Teacher-centered education (order)
Learning represents impersonal 'truth'	Learning represents personal 'wisdom' from teacher (guru)
At workplace:	
Hierarchy means an inequality of roles, established for convenience	Hierarchy means existential inequality
Subordinates expect to be consulted	Subordinates expect to be told what to do
Ideal boss is resourceful democrat	Ideal boss is benevolent autocrat (good father)

Table 6.3 DIFFERENCES ACCORDING TO COLLECTIVISM/INDIVIDUALISM

Collectivist societies	Individualist societies
In the family:	
Education towards 'we' consciousness	Education towards 'I' consciousness
Opinions pre-determined by group	Private opinion expected
Obligations to family or in-group:	Obligations to self:
– harmony	– self-interest
– respect	– self-actualisation
– shame	– guilt
At school:	
Learning is for the young only	Permanent education
Learn how to do	Learn how to learn
At the workplace:	
Value standards differ for in-group and out-groups: particularism	Same value standards apply to all: universalism
Other people are seen as members of their group	Other people seen as potential resources
Relationship prevails over task	Task prevails over relationship
Moral model of employer–employee relationship	Calculative model of employer–employee relationship

origin is the USA and it is accepted in countries that show stronger uncertainty avoidance, such as France and Germany. In these countries its influence is reduced, as the role of senior management is to take strategic decisions, rather than encourage broader participation. However, it is not true that cultural interaction cannot promote change, with the acceptance of MBA programmes and the Single European Market bringing changes in the perspectives of all concerned.

▶

▶ **Box 6.3 continued**

Table 6.4 DIFFERENCES ACCORDING TO FEMININITY/MASCULINITY

Feminine societies	Masculine societies
In the family:	
Stress on relationships	Stress on achievement
Solidarity	Competition
Resolution of conflicts by compromise and negotiation	Resolution of conflicts by fighting them out
At school:	
Average student is norm	Best students are norm
System rewards students' social adaptation	System rewards students' academic performance
Student's failure at school is relatively minor accident	Student's failure at school is disaster – may lead to suicide
At the workplace:	
Assertiveness ridiculed	Assertiveness appreciated
Undersell yourself	Oversell yourself
Stress on life quality	Stress on careers
Intuition	Decisiveness

Table 6.5 DIFFERENCES ACCORDING TO UNCERTAINTY AVOIDANCE

Weak uncertainty avoidance societies	Strong uncertainty avoidance societies
In the family:	
What is different, is ridiculous or curious	What is different is dangerous
Ease, indolence, low stress	Higher anxiety and stress
Aggression and emotions not shown	Showing of aggression and emotions accepted
At school:	
Students comfortable with:	Students comfortable with:
– Unstructured learning situations	– Structured learning situations
– Vague objectives	– Precise objectives
– Broad assignments	– Detailed assignments
– No time tables	– Strict time tables
Teachers may say 'I don't know'	Teachers should have all the answers
At the workplace:	
Dislike of rules – written or unwritten	Emotional need for rules – written or unwritten
Less formalisation and standardisation	More formalisation and standarisation

Hofstede's analysis can be criticised on the grounds that it is static, while the comments in the last paragraph suggest that each culture is dynamic and subject to changes, such as immigration, European integration, and so on. Further observations have suggested that Hofstede's dimensions are themselves dominated by Western cultural thinking and fail to appreciate the influence of Eastern culture.

▶

▶ Box 6.3 continued

Finally, the spread of Western culture through the internationalisation and globalisation of markets, along with improved transportation and communication links, has helped to promote the rise of individualism, which causes unease in countries such as Japan and China. Despite these observations, Hofstede's work helps to identify the problems associated with managing operations across markets and should be a first step in appraising the problems encountered.

CULTURAL ANALYSIS OF INTERNATIONAL MARKETS

The influence of culture on a company's operations is difficult to quantify. What is undeniable is the probability of making mistakes based on misunderstandings and misinterpretation of actions and agreements. The example of GKN–Westland, referred to later in this chapter shows the challenge of overcoming this if the company is to succeed not just in Europe, but internationally. One benefit to arise from the effort to understand cross-cultural issues is that cultural issues do not just apply to companies working together, or in international marketing. Many organisations are finding the need to collaborate in their own markets and with companies drawn from the same country; many of the skills used to achieve international objectives will also be of benefit when looking at the varying organisational cultures that collaborative ventures bring together.

Focusing on international marketing, it is useful to divide up the study of cultural issues into macro and micro. Macro studies identify the climate in a country, particularly its attitude to business and products, whilst micro studies focus on the cultural impact on the target market or segment. The aim of both studies is to find the universals or the modes of behaviour that exist in all cultures, an advantage which will allow marketers to provide a standard marketing programme.

Macro studies do not take the culture as a given (*see* Box 6.3), but it is often the case that managers do view cultural aspects as given, ignoring in fact that cultures change over time, some faster than others, and that the recognition of such change cannot be overlooked or ignored.

Macro analysis reveals that companies face unpredictable situations, given the rapid changes in economic and technological developments that are influenced by and then in their turn influence social and cultural progress. Facing a changing macro-cultural environment, organisations will need to become more flexible, prepared to review systems, procedures and studies the ability to adapt to local circumstances.

Cultural complexity along with hostility (or lack of it) and heterogeneity all play a role in forming a view or opinion on the reception that the firm's product, marketing effort and operations will have in the targeted county. Of course, the role of transnational groups and organisations should also be considered, as nation-states are not discrete entities with little communication with other parts of the globe. International communication links mean that the activities of Shell in Nigeria and

Colombia become known across the world, affecting opinion and, therefore, operations beyond the area of activity. The activities of Greenpeace and Friends of the Earth, although not necessarily sanctioned in many countries, may hold sway over opinions in countries where companies operate: the disposal of off-shore drilling rigs by Shell in the North Sea has had an impact not just on that company's operations but also on those of all North Sea exploration companies.

Micro analysis identifies how cultural influences affect individuals in the market place. What is relevant here is the way people are likely to react to goods from abroad. In Islamic countries, certain products are deemed unsuitable as they threaten traditional beliefs and attitudes – a toy such as the Barbie doll is considered unacceptable in a country like Iran, promoting Western (immodest) dress and immoral life-style. Japan has often been seen as a difficult country to export to not because of import regulations, but because of the attitude of its people towards what are regarded as inferior foreign goods. Likewise, the French are considered to be sensitive to companies and products that undermine their culture, so hamburgers and fast foods are seen as a threat to the 'café society', a situation seemingly borne out by the steep decline in such establishments in the last 20 years. The challenge for companies is to adapt accordingly, to try and develop an identity that blends in with local preferences, as Nissan seeks to do by promoting its operations in the USA and the UK as being an integral part of these two countries. In addition it can seek to convince consumers that its products are a better choice for them to make.

Marks & Spencer's experience in France shows that it has been able to convince shoppers, particularly in Paris, that food products such as sandwiches, offer a unique combination originally unfamiliar to the French consumer – a tactic that has put the Paris M&S stores at the forefront of good taste. However, the company's experience in Canada, where it was assumed that tastes would be similar to those found in the UK, has not worked out.[10] The success of the French M&S stores has shifted the perception of customers away from the view that UK food products are inferior, towards one where they are seen as innovative and exciting, so that other UK food suppliers have been able to enter the market successfully – a remarkable achievement given the problems of 'mad-cow disease'.[11]

In a similar way the success of Australian wine in the UK was achieved on the back of understanding (i.e. adapting) the product to suit local tastes and preferences. French wine producers, on the other hand, took the view that their wines were superior and failed to adapt them, so that one of their biggest export markets was lost. Lacking a level of local production that could satisfy needs, and with the growth of eating out and socialising outside of the home, UK consumers were prepared to experiment with wines from many different countries, resulting in a market where wines from Bulgaria, Argentina, Canada and South Africa can be found; the market now has a sophistication it lacked 10 years ago. The preparedness to try new products is an important issue for companies to consider – a country can over time move from high resistance to innovation to acceptance, leading to new opportunities.

If there is a general lesson to learn from the wine industry, it lies in the preparedness of companies to examine tastes and preferences and explain the product or service in ways that are easily understood. Products that appeal to people, suit their way of life and support cultural values will be accepted more easily than those that do not take such considerations into account.

Techniques for assessment of the micro-cultural level are fraught with difficulty, with the intangible dimensions involved making it more difficult to apply analytical approaches. What is clear is that the international marketing manager and policy maker needs to move away from self-referencing criteria in order to understand how another culture operates, issues followed up in Boxes 6.4 and 6.5. Intense cultural understanding is not required – all that is necessary is an understanding of the culture's impact on demand and use of a product; what influences the purchase decision; how organisations are structured and communicate; and how employers relate to each other.

Box 6.4

GLOBAL ETHICS[12]

Culture differs in fundamental ways between countries and can often cause particular difficulties for marketers and managers. Take, for example, the situation when a manager of a large US-based speciality products company in China caught an employee stealing. The manager followed company practice and turned the employee over to the authorities, who executed him – the normal punishment for such activity.

Software piracy is calculated to affect 35 per cent of the US market, whilst it is 57 per cent in Germany and 80 per cent in Japan. In Asian countries it is estimated to be close to 100 per cent. Why is piracy so high in Asian countries? The Software Publishers' Association makes the connection between piracy and culture; they carried out research asking whether one should use software without paying for it. The majority of respondents in countries such as Italy and Hong Kong agreed that this was wrong, but respondents in other countries regarded the practice as less unethical. Confucian culture puts stress on the individual sharing what they create with the group and society, a factor that could explain the Chinese attitude towards intellectual property rights as an attempt by developed countries to monopolise technically advanced products.

Donaldson argues that there are often two responses to the problem. One is based on cultural relativism which argues that one country's ethics are no better than any other's, leading to the conclusion that there are no international rights and wrongs. Bribery to gain contracts or issues related to pollution are then left to individual managers to resolve according to the prevailing cultural norms.

The opposite to relativism is cultural imperialism, which argues that what is right within the home context is right for the operations of the firm in whatever country they operate. US companies transferred sexual harassment programmes to their operations in Saudi Arabia; the result was less than conclusive, as the major lesson concerned with coercion and sexual discrimination was lost amidst the confusion of the Saudi personnel as to what was actually intended. Donaldson summarised the theory behind this approach as based on absolutism, which supports the notion that there is a single list of truths which can be expressed with one set of concepts and calls for the same behaviour whatever the context.

Between the two versions lies a third way which attempts to balance the extremes and looks at the real world of business decision making. Ethical behaviour can be guided by the following principles:

1 respect for core human values, which determine the absolute moral threshold for all business activities;

▶

▶ **Box 6.4 continued**

2 respect for local traditions;

3 the belief that context matters when deciding what is 'right' or 'wrong'.

So, for example, in Japan people engaged in business often exchange gifts, a custom that has gone on for many years. Executives from Europe or North America instinctively feel that providing a gift is near to bribery, however, as they have become more accustomed to doing business in Japan, they have realised that the custom is part of its culture and in effect it will be more difficult to be a successful business without accepting such a practice. Companies have adapted to the need for such gifts in Japan, but maintained an overall policy on bribery. Without this understanding, successful international marketing strategies could have been severely jeopardised.

Box 6.5
IDEOLOGY AND ECONOMIC POLICY[13]

According to Brouthers and Lambe, a standard approach to economic reform can be traced for the former Eastern bloc countries. Essentially it entailed a six-point strategy, the components of which were:

1 macroeconomic stabilisation, requiring both a budget that is close to being balanced and tight controls over credit;

2 liberalisation of the prices of most goods;

3 current account convertibility of the currency;

4 a social safety net;

5 privatisation of state property;

6 laws to accommodate and facilitate the development of a market economy.

Each of these components are difficult areas to manage effectively, but many economists argued that a common approach should be taken despite the differences between countries like the USA, Russia, Belarus, and so on. This standard model may not, according to research, be able to deal with such diversity.

The standard assumption is that there is one best type of economy for all countries. A contingency approach takes the view that there is no one best type of economic model, and in addition that there is no 'single best' form of capitalism – there are at least three general models of capitalism as alternatives to the command economy.

Countries have different economic goals, which some writers have argued springs from different national ideologies that are themselves a product of the country's history. National ideologies can be placed in categories ranging from individualism to communitarism.

Individualism

This is an ideology that stresses the freedom of individuals to make decisions that are in their best personal interest; in addition, there is a right of business to develop and

▶ **Box 6.5 continued**

implement strategies that reflect shareholders' desires to maximise profits. The role of government in a society such as this is focused on protecting property, enforcing contracts, promoting competition and regulating the market where competition is unreliable.

Communitarism

This stresses the role of government in defining the needs of the community and seeing that these needs are met. Relationships between individuals in such a society are governed more by consensus than by contract. Stakeholders in a communitariam society are different from those in an individualistic society – employers, for example, are considered to be important stakeholders in a business, followed by customers and then shareholders.

Businesses are expected to pursue improved employee wages and employment stability above profits, equally businesses are expected to have collective strategies to strengthen each other's activities.

Japan has a position closest to the latter model, whilst the USA is closer to the former. This focused attention on the pursuit of different objectives by organisations within a country.

Middle ideology

Between these two types are countries who value aspects of both ideologies, valuing extensive social welfare programmes and government legislation protecting workers' rights. Governments in these countries support joint public–private ownership forms, with one consequence being that firms tend to have a longer-term profit orientation than firms located in countries with a preference for other ideological forms.

The consequence of having varying ideologies is that they influence (and are influenced by) economic types, leading to a variety of alternative economic systems. This contingency view, when applied to areas such as Eastern Europe, produces the recognition that the best economy for one nation may not be the best for another. Countries in the process of reforming their economies, or about to embark on this journey, have a number of alternatives to choose between.

According to Brouthers and Lambe the contingency approach to economic development has implications for the theory of comparative advantage. Instead of factor abundance being the driving mechanism, in the emerging global economy, a strategic synergy between the generic economy type chosen by a government and the appropriate factor usage chosen by the firm determines the basis for advantage. Their prediction is that factor regulation could replace factor abundance as a 'new' theory of comparative advantage.

THE FIRM AND CULTURAL CHANGE

From the preceding discussion it is apparent that the greatest challenge lies in organisations realising the need to understand, adapt and change if they are to be successful in their efforts to enter and develop foreign markets. The need to encourage cultural sensitivity spreads beyond senior managers and international marketers. Links are made at many levels when a firm is involved in the international market place and rapid progress has to be made to bring employers (and suppliers) up to speed on the needs and requirements of a particular country's market.

Beyond that, many organisations need to form alliances and mergers to compete internationally, bringing with it the need to look at operational issues and how teams can be formed from groups drawn from different countries and cultural backgrounds (a need that is not peculiar to foreign co-operation).

GKN–Westland,[14] the UK helicopter producer, is involved in collaborative ventures with companies like Augusta of Italy for various products as well as competing against it for other contracts. To create successful links between these two companies and others involved on similar projects, a cross-cultural management programme entitled Network for Aerospace Management in Europe (NAME) was set up. One part of the programme involved the training of young managers, covering the following topics:

1 creating awareness of how to manage successfully cross-cultural aspects of business life;

2 understanding the process of change and identifying the personal role in the change programmes;

3 creating awareness of the key factors for the success of cross-cultural teamwork;

4 working together as a team to tackle management of change issues.

The aim of the programme is to build up co-operative working and understanding, and to provide individual participants with particular skills. Seven were identified:

1 to value differences and cultural diversity;

2 to tolerate ambiguity and manage change;

3 to build effective partnerships;

4 to function in flexible organisation structures;

5 to prefer working with others and in teams;

6 to give and receive feedback openly and honestly;

7 to generate understanding and tolerance.

The programme highlights the importance of cultural awareness and not simply a preference for language training. Seminars and courses were held in various European locations to gain first-hand experience of the culture and means of operations, whilst trying to sensitise the participants to the benefits to be gained by working together and appreciating the strengths of each approach to work and organisation. In GKN–Westland's case the need to collaborate in both the military and civilian helicopter market is not an option but a necessity. Even companies who do not have the same impetus to collaborate on product development will be forming partnerships both in their home markets and in foreign ones – with suppliers, retailers, marketing agencies, and so on. Valuing cultural diversity and finding a way to overcome the barriers to successful partnership has become a necessity for many firms. The benefit lies in the enhancement of skills that can be further harnessed for further improvement in product design, quality and delivery.

Programmes such as NAME do, however, have to be seen as offering a challenge to those involved. Trompenaars[15] has provided examples of just such cases, where people may be open and friendly, but limit this to specific areas of their lives and are not keen to allow people to trespass into other areas. Other cultures may on first encounter be private and take some time to open up, but eventually accept people into all areas. A further difference can be found in the authority a manager can use in areas outside of the work role, with influence on the broader community as can be found in many Eastern cultures. To appreciate these differences is to be aware how they can affect the success of marketing operations – and, indeed, the success of the whole enterprise.

SUMMARY

Culture influences thoughts and actions and is of great interest to the international marketer. By looking at the elements of culture and adopting both the macro and micro levels of analysis, certain issues have been highlighted. These are the ability to see it as evolving rather than static, and to appreciate the need to overcome the self-referencing criterion challenge. Careful thought and planning offer dividends.

A further aspect of the importance of culture is the operational area where companies have to work with other organisations to achieve their aims. Appreciating cultural diversity is more than just offering language training, it is building up the employers' skills to understand and use the different perspectives that each participant will bring with them.

Czinkota and Ronkainen[16] quote the survey undertaken by *Fortune* in 1986 showing that the common characteristic of successful American international companies is patience, building an understanding of both the new market and the operational issues. A more recent version[17] concerning Marks & Spencer makes the same point: the move from the saturated UK market became essential, but each new market was reviewed separately to make sure, after the poor performance of the Canadian venture, that each was properly understood, an approach that the Chairman described as 'snail-like'. Snails, it appears, can often win races.

REVIEW QUESTIONS

1 Why is culture so important an issue for the international marketing manager?

2 Outline the main elements of 'culture'.

3 Why is corporate culture a major issue that must be dealt with?

4 Describe Hofstede's main ideas on culture and the business.

5 What criticisms can be made of Hofstede's approach?

DISCUSSION QUESTIONS

1 Identify products that have been failures in foreign markets, and seek to isolate the cultural factors that led to this failure.

2 Companies who have developed a cultural awareness training programme for their staff still find adverse comments made by some staff about their international partners. Does this mean that these programmes are to be judged a failure?

3 Is cultural diversity a threat to globalisation?

4 Marks & Spencer takes a long time to review new markets and yet can still make mistakes. Is such an approach justifiable if such mistakes can still be made?

5 If culture is a fluid and changing reality, is there any point in studying it? (This question, like many others asked in this book, could reveal a cultural bias!)

Case study

MARKETING IN EMERGING MARKETS[18]

Since the fall of Communism, Western companies have sought to take advantage of the emerging markets of Eastern Europe and Asia, particularly the large markets of Russia and China. Companies such as the French casual clothes company NAF-NAF have opened stores in Moscow, while the American cosmetics company Avon has seen sales increase dramatically in China.

Consumer attitudes in these countries have changed rapidly, particularly amongst the young, where demand for stylish and fashionable clothing has been strongly backed by hard-currency disposable income. Having first though accepted any brand, consumers soon learned to be more selective, valuing high-quality, good-value products that were consistently available.

Consumers in Russia prefer Western goods imported or locally made rather than products made by Russian companies. In 1996, there were some 15 urban areas in Russia where consumers had sufficient income to buy goods of Western style or quality to encourage Western companies to invest in local production facilities and the building up of distribution networks. This last issue raises many problems, particularly as most of the goods are brought directly to wholesale markets near Moscow and then use independent Russian business executives to get the goods to retail centres.

In China, Avon has been able to exploit the demand for cosmetics, a demand that it has seen emerging in many markets in Asia. The company has responded by becoming multicultural itself, with managers of six nationalities sitting on the company's 11-strong 'Global Business Council', an approach that has helped the company benefit both internationally and in its US home market. Korean and Vietnamese immigrants have been targeted by the company, successfully overcoming cultural problems, and helping the new immigrants adjust to the new host culture.

Avon's approach of using 'Avon Ladies', of which it has two million globally, seems to work in markets such as China and with newly arrived immigrants, but has difficulties dealing with the life-styles of many American women, who have full-time jobs and are not at home to receive a call. To compound the problem, the company's customers are ageing, with younger people preferring to use the branded goods of L'Oréal or The Body Shop. To counter this, efforts have been made to sell in the workplace rather than the home and to use mail and telephone ordering. As an appeal to younger shoppers, the cosmetic lines have been toned up as well as adding clothing, jewellery and gifts.

With other changes to improve its appeal to women in the developed markets of Western Europe and North America, such as supporting anti-cancer campaigns, the company is facing increased competition in its traditional markets that will mean only slow growth in sales. As a result of this, the developing markets of Asia have become a priority. In 1996, 38 per cent of the firm's sales and 49 per cent of its pre-tax profits came from developing countries.

The company has entered markets as diverse as China, South America and India, where sales have increased dramatically. Developing countries, as in Russia, have a poorly developed infrastructure which the company is well placed to overcome with its history of selling door-to-door and by word of mouth. The company can also offer advantages to women in such countries who are keen to work but not prepared to sacrifice their role in the running of the household.

In Russia, Avon spent $500 000, with 16 000 representatives selling $30m of products in 1996. The products are sourced from the UK, with a target of $50m in sales that if achieved would provide a sound basis for the establishment of local production.

In South Africa, starting from scratch Avon, bought a local cosmetic company to help it understand the market, with the intention to have 10 000 representatives in 1997. A secondary catalogue has been introduced to many of the markets, selling goods of 30 companies who have no local sales force which has seen sales further increase.

The majority of Avon products cater for local preferences on such issues as skin tone and packaging, however the company wishes to focus on a number of global brands, creating six lines, which it is hoped will account for 60 per cent of sales by 2000. By the consolidation of its brands, there has been an improvement in quality and a reduction in suppliers, saving the company $35m a year. The aim is to improve brand recognition and counter the threat of the well-known brands such as Chanel.

The efforts of companies such as Avon to appeal to a younger group as well as maintain its position with its older customers can be seen against a rising world population, due to reach six billion by 2000, with nearly half being under the age of 20. This 'market of the future' is one that has many challenges as it is mainly located in developing countries with high poverty levels and unemployment. Companies who can show that their presence adds to the development of these economies by creating much needed jobs locally will gain distinct advantages in goodwill and local representation. Avon's approach with its local representatives may well help it to prosper in such circumstances.

Questions

1 *Is Avon pursuing a similar strategy internationally to that which it pursues in its home market?*

2 *Is it true to say that pursuing any international strategy will have a significant impact on total corporate strategy?*

3 *Why, despite Avon's success in emerging and developing markets, is it seeking to rationalise its brands?*

4 *What are the cultural challenges that Avon can expect to meet in African markets compared to the developed markets of North America?*

5 *Identify the cross-cultural challenges that Avon will have to deal with in managing its operations.*

FURTHER READING

Bennett, P. and Kassarjan, H., *Consumer Behaviour* (Englewood Cliffs, NJ: Prentice-Hall, 1972).

Cundiff, E.A. and Tharp Higler, M.E., *Marketing in the International Environment* (Englewood Cliffs, NJ: Prentice-Hall, 1984).

Engel, J.F., Blackwell, R.D. and Miniard, P.W., *Consumer Behaviour*, 7th edition (Chicago: The Dryden Press, 1993).

Keegan, W.J., *Global Marketing Management,* 4th edition (Englewood Cliffs, NJ: Prentice-Hall, 1989).

Robock, S., Simmonds, K. and Zwick, J., *International Business and Multinational Enterprise*, 4th edition (Homewood, IL: Irwin, 1989).

Terpstra, V., *The Cultural Environment of International Business* (Ohio: South-Western Publishing, 1978).

NOTES AND REFERENCES

1 Jackson, T., 'The sum of its European parts', *Financial Times* (21 October 1996).

2 Czinkota, M.R. and Ronkainen, I.A., *International Marketing*, 3rd edition (Orlando: The Dryden Press, 1993).

3 Hofstede, G., 'The business of international business is culture', *International Business Review*, 3(1) (1994).

4 Czinkota and Ronkainen, op. cit.

5 Orlando, F.I. and Cateora, P.R., *International Markets*, 7th edition (Homewood, IL: Irwin, 1990).

6 *France: An Overseas Trade Supplement* (London: Brass Tracks, September 1996).

7 'Hollywood goes global', *Financial Times* (27 September 1997).

8 Weihrich, H. and Koontz, H., *Management: A Global Perspective*, 10th edition (New York: McGraw-Hill, 1994), 567.

9 Hofstede, op. cit.

10 Bayes, R. 'M&S set out to storm German high streets', *The Times* (11 October 1996).

11 'Meal in a box down £1m a day', *The Times* (2 January 1996).

12 Donaldson, T., 'When is different just different, and when is it wrong?', *Harvard Business Review* (September–October 1996); Mammon, A. and Richards, D., 'Perceptions and possibilities of intercultural adjustment: some neglected characteristics of expatriates', *International Business Review*, 50(3) (1996), 283–301.

13 Brouthers, L.E. and Lambe, C.W., 'National ideology, public policy and the business environment: a contingency approach to economic reform in Hungary, Poland and Eastern Europe', *International Business Review*, 4(3) (September 1995).

14 '*Network for aerospace management in Europe*', GKN–Westland (1997).

15 Trompenaars, F., *Riding the Waves of Culture* (London: Nicholas Brealey, 1993).

16 Czinkota and Ronkainen, op. cit.

17 Bernoth, A., 'Booming market shows its spark', *Sunday Times* (10 November 1996).

18 Financial Times Survey – 'International youth', *Financial Times* (2 February 1996); 'Scents and sensibility', *The Economist* (13 July 1996); 'Consumerism's new citadel', *Financial Times* (31 July 1996).

7

The political–legal environment

INTRODUCTION

The political–legal and regulatory environment is an issue for marketing managers to take very seriously, as changes in this area can turn a successful strategy to worthless paper. Examples gleaned from the world's news gathering services will reveal changes that range from small amendments in the regulatory framework to major shifts in government policy that can affect a whole industry. In 1996 in the UK, for example, restrictions on the marketing and selling of knives were introduced; in Australia, automatic weapons were banned; in Belarus an attempt was made to hinder the sale of many foreign-produced products. These are a few examples of the movements in the legal and regulatory environment that can, intentionally or otherwise, impact on the organisation.

Marketing managers have to be particularly aware that these movements can have both predictable and unpredictable impacts on a firm, and it is their job to ascertain what they might be. In the international arena, the complexity or uniqueness of the decision-making and political processes will provide a further challenge. What has so far been outlined is a reaction to events; making predictions on trends through environmental scanning is another facet of this review (applicable to all parts of the PEST analysis), as is the influence that can be brought to bear on decision makers, for example at the EU and national government levels.

Influencing the decision makers is a vital skill that can be exercised through trade–industrial groups, professional bodies, and so on.

The political–legal environment is therefore a fascinating and complex area that will be reviewed in this chapter.

Objectives

This chapter will examine:

- sources of political risk and political conflict
- methods of political risk assessment
- risk-reduction strategies
- international transfers
- legal systems and international marketing
- international treaties
- conflict resolution.

SOURCES OF POLITICAL RISK AND POLITICAL CONFLICT

In order to carry on in business in a foreign country, permission is required from the host country's government. Governments can have very different views on how business should be conducted within the country's borders. Everything from the product itself, to the promotional mix and the behaviour of the company's operatives can be governed or regulated. It is not only the reaction of a government to business that is of interest here, but its stability and indeed the longevity of the political system itself that will be under review by a company wishing to do business.

The dominant political philosophy – be it democratic, socialist or Communist – as well as the type of government – constitutional monarchy, dictatorships, party rule (socialist and Communist) will all be of interest to the company. However, as will be reviewed in later sections, taking a broad-brush approach is often counter-productive. When Eastern Europe was ruled by Communist Party government, it was never the case that Hungary and Russia, for example, looked at the issue of profit and the role of private business in quite the same way. Equally, it has never been true that the UK and France, although referred to as democratic capitalist countries, have run their economies in quite the same way.

Classification of items – or, in this case, countries – can be a useful starting point to structure analysis.

Political risk can be found in every nation and a manager's attempt to find a friendly and welcoming environment with little or no political risk can reduce options to such an extent that viable business opportunities can be lost. Some way has therefore to be found to assess the political stability of a country and the likelihood of a successful business venture.

Stable political systems and their governments provide continuity. If this is threatened by, say, the rise of nationalist parties then uncertainty is found, with businesses unsure what the consequences of these changes may mean. As reviewed in Chapter 6 on culture, firms should be aware of the problem of applying their own notions of what constitutes 'acceptable political behaviour' to another country. It is too easy for, say, a UK firm, to believe that the political traditions of that country provide it with a sound, pragmatic and stable system and that this is the way for all countries to go. This clearly would cause difficulties in the appreciation of how decisions are reached in another country. Government change has been a regular feature of political life since the Second World War in Italy; it might be thought that this would provide a poor background for business. However, the Italian system does show continuity over time, such as the long dominance of the Christian Democrats and the fact that decision-making power and influence rests with officials. This has allowed the system to function in a way that managers from the UK or elsewhere, would at first find difficult to understand. However, once the system is understood it can provide a way to reach those who make or influence policy and who provide the foundation for continuity.

METHODS OF POLITICAL RISK ASSESSMENT

Firms can use various ways to assess political instability. Some ways of assessing this are set out in Box 7.1, with a review of Taiwan. Categorisation of political risk can be done via analysis of ownership risk, operating risk and transfer risk. Each of these three areas can be assessed separately and independently, with various strategies involved to deal with threats. Operating risk will have to be assessed with foreign-owned firms working in the City of London, and who need to calculate the likelihood of Irish nationalist action disrupting the City, for example. A similar situation would also apply in Spain, caused by the possibility of action by Basque separatists.

Box 7.1   TAIWAN: COUNTRY RISK SUMMARY, JUNE 1996

Table 7.1 summarises the risk ratings as of June 1996.

Table 7.1 COUNTRY VIEW

Country risk rating	Overall rating	Overall score	Medium-term lending risk	Short-term trade risk	Political and policy risk
Current	A	10	A	A	B
Previous	A	10	A	A	B

Every country is rated by category, ranging from 'A' (the lowest risk) to 'E' (the highest risk) and is assigned a grade for its overall short-term trade risk, medium-term lending risk and political and policy risk. Overall scores can range from 0 ('A' category) to a maximum of 100 points ('E' category) for the highest-risk countries.

Political risk

The main opposition party is beginning to fragment, which should benefit the ruling Kuomintang (KMT). Working-level talks with China have yet to resume, but business ties are continuing to flourish.

▶

▶ **Box 7.1 continued**

Economic outlook

The economy will expand less quickly in 1996 and 1997 than it did in the first half of the 1990s, but growth will remain respectable by developed country standards. Inflation will stay at 3.5 per cent or below and the New Taiwan dollar should begin to recover some lost ground against its US counterpart (*see* Table 7.2).

Table 7.2 ECONOMIC FORECAST SUMMARY 1996–8

	1996	1997	1998
Real GDP (% change)	5.8	5.7	6.3
Consumer prices (% change; av)	3.3	3.5	3.2
Exchange rate NT$:US$ (av)	27.4	27.1	26.6
Current account (US$ m)			
Merchandise exports fob	115 082	124 949	138 023
Merchandise imports fob	–99 891	–109 874	–123 044
Trade balance	15 191	15 075	14 979
Current account balance	7 699	7 370	7 075
% of GDP	2.8	2.4	2.1
External financing (US$m)			
Financing surplus	6 693	6 328	5 766
Total debt	29 787	32 225	33 786
Total debt service	2 099	2 269	2 601
Debt-service ratio (%)	1.5	1.5	1.5
Financial markets			
Stock-market index (end-period)	6 900	7 450	

Financial market trends

The stock market has factored in the new, slower rate of growth and is enjoying the political stability created by the return of Lee Teng-hui to the presidency. Inflows of foreign capital and a recovery in the semiconductor market should allow for further gains in stock prices in 1997.

Debt outlook

New data from the OECD on the stock of debt have led to some minor revisions to data, particularly regarding debt service. The debt-service ratio is now expected to be only 1.5 per cent in each of the next two years (*see* Table 7.3).

Table 7.3 KEY INDICATORS 1996–2001

Key indicators	1996	1997	1998	1999	2000	2001
Real GDP growth (%)	5.8	5.7	6.3	6.2	5.9	5.6
Consumer price inflation (%)	3.3	3.5	3.2	3.3	3.2	3.1
Commercial bank prime rate (year-end, %)	8.5	8.4	8.5	8.5	8.3	8.0
Exchange rate NT$:US$	27.4	27.1	26.6	26.0	25.5	25.0

▶

▶ **Box 7.1 continued**

Relations with China will slowly improve, with occasional setbacks. On commercial issues, the governments are likely to find a new *modus vivendi*, although direct links in trade and finance are still some way off. The recent 'war games' in the Taiwan Straits mean that the KMT will lower the profile of its campaign for international recognition somewhat, in order to smooth ruffled feathers in Beijing.

A split in the opposition DPP will strengthen the power base of the ruling KMT. Any threat from the CNP will also diminish. The KMT's anti-corruption drive will have to be stepped up to enhance the party's image.

Economic growth will average 5.95 per cent per year in 1997–2001, led by private consumption and, from 1998, investment. From 1999 imports will outpace exports and the current account surplus will fall as a share of GDP.

Watchlist

The tiny majority (83 seats of a total of 164) which the KMT has in the legislature will make for difficulties in the passage of important legislation, putting a premium on the need for compromise in the national interest. The imminence of elections to the legislature (1998) will prevent the KMT government from taking unpopular decisions affecting spending or taxation.

Connected with a growing unease in the government about increased economic dependence on China, plans to develop Taiwan into an Asia Pacific Regional Operations Centre might be scaled down.

Political infighting will preclude efficient planning and implementation of the high-speed railway link from Taipei to Kaohsiung, and the public transport project in Kaohsiung itself, which is already embroiled in corruption claims.

The Central Bank of China will continue with its expansionary monetary policy. As economic and political factors lie behind the reluctance to invest domestically, lowering the cost of borrowing will not have the desired effect on domestic investment demand.

Source: EIU Country Risk Service, *Taiwan: Country Risk Summary* (London: The Economist Intelligence Unit, June 1996).

Ownership risk is still apparent in countries that wish to transfer assets and legal property (and intellectual, land and property rights) to a host country organisation. Although rarer than it was in the 1970s and early 1980s, the threat still remains in some African countries and the independent states that used to be part of the Soviet Union. Companies may also find themselves targeted by those who wish to extort money by means of kidnapping, armed robbery and other non-legal means. Coups d'etat, civil wars and ethnic disputes spilling over borders, as happened in Zaire (now the Democratic Republic of Congo) in 1997, are possible, and the risk of disputes of this latter kind can be found in Europe, where ethnic–national minority groups are present in many East European countries; this is a situation that can provide a level of uncertainty that could lead to instability.

Changes in government policy or in government can also give rise to nervousness on the part of the business community, particularly if this threatens growth potential through changes in interest and exchange rates. Although less damaging than other actions, problems can spring from nationalistic sources, and may escalate – in developed countries such as Austria and France, the increase in the share of the vote captured by right-wing nationalist parties is an example.

Expropriation, where a firm has its assets confiscated and receives no remuneration, is less likely to be top of a country's political agenda than was the case previously. Domestication is more probable, where a government demands the partial transfer of ownership and management roles to local organisations, with the imposition of regulations that ensure, amongst other things, that profits are retained in the country and that production is sourced locally. This can be found in many developing countries and emerging economies. It has already been noted that Belarus requested that local products should be given priority in the shops, but this attitude can be found in many regulations (although perhaps to a less dramatic degree) adopted in other emerging markets. This approach may be linked to past experience in managing the economy as well as a cultural predisposition to such an arrangement, but it can cause particular challenges for the marketer.

If, for example, the firm is required to have nationals to run production, distribution and even marketing, but their experience of working with Western systems and approaches is low, problems will emerge. If locally produced components, raw materials and semi-finished products are also part of the policy of domestication and are of poor quality the marketing stance of the company will be threatened. Perhaps the most telling problem will be the shielding of domestic production from foreign competition, which can lead to the continuation of inefficient practices.

Domestication as opposed to joint venture alliances provide great difficulties for the international firm. A joint venture can benefit both partners and lead to an effective entry strategy into an expanding market; domestication can lead to an inefficient firm or industry that will reveal problems when opened up in later years to competition.

Exchange controls are often thought to have been eradicated in a deregulated world market operating 24 hours every day of the year. Further inspection of the situation will reveal that many currencies do not possess full convertibility, whilst many countries such as Bulgaria experience severe financial problems, that have placed great stress on the currency (lev), leading to bank restrictions and controls. Box 7.2 explores what is meant by deregulation, which can also be applied to situations such as exchange controls.

If not imposed across the board, exchange controls can be targeted on the import of so-called luxury goods, components and other supplies that are deemed to be unnecessary for the country's development. This was the case with India in the 1980s, and can still be found in emerging markets. These are particularly difficult to deal with as they either discriminate against particular firms (for example, luxury car producers), or affect production when supplies cannot be obtained. Even foodstuffs may be subject to controls for no obvious reason. What is a totally valid point of view to the government of the country imposing the controls – e.g. that valuable foreign exchange should not be 'wasted' on non-essentials – translates into regulations that hinder production and other activities.

Box 7.2 **REGULATING IN A DYNAMIC WORLD**[1]

In newspapers, the TV/radio news and academic journals the impression is given that turbulence has significantly increased over the past 50 years, fundamentally challenging everything we do and think. What is true of the individual is true of the organisation,

▶ **Box 7.2 continued**

with new ways having continually to be found to deal with globalisation and increased competition. However, there is a need to have an historical perspective, as it would otherwise appear that such turbulence is something new and inexplicable and therefore without precedent. Globalisation has been seen before – in the later part of the nineteenth and early part of the twentieth centuries, when it was pursued to obtain both economic and political objectives, particularly in the Western colonial countries.

Mintzberg's analysis of the literature on strategic planning reveals that commentators since the early 1960s have been explaining change by reference to turbulence and showing how this has created a dynamic economic context. Mintzberg's comment that those who speak of 'turbulence' and 'unexpected change' should talk to those who lived through the Great Depression and the two world wars provides a riposte to those who believe that this is new. The manifestation or symptoms (e.g. the advent of the Internet) may be new, but the cause may not be. When seeking to build an historical perspective it is useful to remember that counter-movements or trends can also be identified at the same time, containing the ability to derail the move to globalisation. One is the plethora of trading areas – over 100 – that now exist.

Deregulation does not mean that regulation disappears, it can often mean that it takes a different form. Likewise, the role of the nation-state has also been questioned, in its apparent inability to control business in an interdependent world. A much-quoted example is the all-pervasive Internet evolution that can apparently thwart government attempts to control developments. This has not deterred the government of Mainland China from seeking to limit its influence to maintain control of the Communist Party, and neither has it stopped developments in tracking activities, as shown with the successful prosecution of a Catholic priest in the UK for promoting paedophile pornography on the Internet.

Examination of regulatory agencies, changes in legislation and the increase of statutory instruments (changes in the law allowed by enabling legislation) by UK government ministers reveals a desire to influence business to achieve national or transnational objectives. Deregulation can be seen as the recognition by a country's government that other foreign-based companies have the right to trade within the country. Once permission is given to trade within a territory, however, regulations then have to be adhered to in order to continue to function.

Referring to Mintzberg again can be a useful way to see change and dynamic environmental change in perspective. He provides three reasons why those who comment on strategy have identified the current age as problematic:

1 planning attempted to eradicate turbulence, particularly in the 1960s and that giant corporations were content to compete in only a limited way. When new competitors appeared who refused to play by the rules, the dominance of these oligopolies disappeared and change became the norm;

2 each age thinks of itself as being superior in relation to previous ones, often by citing them as 'well-intentioned but wrong'. We have it tougher and harder than other times, and we have to seek new ways to overcome the obstacles;

3 the third explanation, and one that Mintzberg prefers even though it contradicts the first, is that planning aimed to promote stability and that when it failed to do so any

▶

> ▶ **Box 7.2 continued**
>
> perturbation set off a wave of panic and the assumption that turbulence had arrived. So in countries such as the USA and the UK, competition from Japan produced the response that everything was changing rapidly and companies could no longer control the situation. Now in countries such as South Korea that are heavily protected agreeing to deregulation has begun to produce the same reaction.
>
> Turbulence from this point of view was change, a normal part of evolution that planning could not handle.
>
> Looking at industry evolution, which moves from the early embryonic stage, through growth, shakeout, maturity and decline, it is possible to see how in a situation of maturity companies can experience stable market conditions, perhaps for some period of time. Eventually, however, these will give way to new circumstances calling for new innovative thinking.
>
> What is true of industrial development has to be true of the regulatory environment. If the pursuit of social and political goals can be achieved only through regulation, such as for preserving the environment, then new ways will be found to achieve this as circumstances themselves change. The agencies involved in the regulation of activity, looking at the way this has changed to suit the prevailing situation, must appraise the continuing need to influence business and output decisions. As further developments manifest themselves so further changes are required of both the regulators and of their political masters.

Taxation can also be levied with the good intention to raise money for the government to finance essential public services and the development of the country's infrastructure. The problem is that companies may be targeted if they are thought to be earning excessive profits. Firms extracting oil from the North Sea were subject to high tax levels by the UK government in the 1980s, bringing in up to £12bn a year. The problem was that activities and further exploration was threatened. Tax revenue fell to £1bn in 1995–6, partly explained by this situation.

Price controls can be found in countries who wish to help the population by for example, keeping food prices down. This can be an emotive political issue, particularly when the population is poor. In Egypt in 1995, food riots broke out when the price of bread increased. Staple foodstuffs are not the only areas where control may be used to help reduce inflation, but controls of this nature have been found to be less effective than focusing on monetary controls such as interest rates and reining in public expenditure to reduce taxation. The World Bank and the IMF, and many governments, prefer to run economies in this way, but price controls in sensitive areas will pose a problem for the marketing manager as the price aspect of the marketing mix will be reduced in importance, and then raised in importance when reduced revenue hits profitability and challenges the strategy of operating in that market.

RISK-REDUCTION STRATEGIES

Business, despite the political risks, will still be driven to exploit the opportunities that a particular market offers. Managers will therefore have to identify the most appropriate ways to assess risk and develop effective means to meet challenges when they occur. Although extreme political risk does exist in some countries by far the majority will show only moderate risks for the company. Effective ways to be accepted by the host country need to be developed if accusations of exploitation in its negative sense are to be avoided. Companies can introduce local involvement by their hiring policy, sourcing locally and making a contribution to the community in which its operations are located. Firms can also be proactive by direct talks with government ministries, regulatory agencies and regional governments.

Various sources can be used to identify country and political risk, as shown by the examples provided in Boxes 7.3 and 7.4. However a focus on how easy or difficult it is to do business in a particular country is imperative. In Mexico regulations tend to be more extensive and less transparent than companies would expect. The UK firm BIP Group Ltd, a manufacturer of plastics, estimated that the company needed 30 per cent more accountants and 60 per cent more buyers on the staff in Mexico than it would have expected in its home country.

Box 7.3

INDIA[2]

India is seen as the world's largest parliamentary democracy, a situation unlike that found in other developing countries which have tended to favour centralised and non-democratic governments. However, the situation is more complex than the description 'parliamentary democracy' would suggest. For example, both radio and television networks are directly run by the government, and it is only with the introduction of satellite and cable TV that a threat to this monopoly has emerged.

Films are censored, whilst newspapers have freedom of expression and openly criticise government bodies and their officials and political masters. Whilst this freedom is familiar to companies from Western democracies, the centralisation and power of the government is not. The government has it within its power to declare a state of emergency, not just in time of war, but also to maintain law and order; these powers give the government rights over constituent states and individual citizens, as can be seen in Jammu and Kashmir.

Government politicians also possess power over what are often fragmented opposition parties, making use of government facilities and officials to organise campaigns. Elections are often subject to the violation of rules and open to fraud, all leading to the promotion of powerful interest groups to influence policy in their favour.

In the area of economic management, the government prepares five-year plans, issues licences for setting up factories, applies import controls to protect domestic industries. Although in recent years these restrictions have been eased, and some abolished, the market is not one based on free trade. As a result of such government intervention, commentators such as Tayeb (1996) argue that the country has been disadvantaged compared to other Asian nations. In the 'Tiger economies' government control and intervention is easily identified, but the effect has been to promote trade and commerce and to encourage firms to move into export markets, thereby promoting the need to hone marketing skills, control costs and invest in R&D. The Indian solution has, so it is argued, produced none of these benefits, but served to protect monopoly practices in the home market, thereby protecting inefficient practices and stopping the exploitation of the country's comparative advantages.

However, India does have a new willingness to encourage business and has created a basis for growth in some industries. Further progress will depend on changing the regulatory regime, a move that is not guaranteed to work given the vested interests who will find their protected status under threat.

Box 7.4   INDONESIA[3]

In order to maintain stability, many governments seek to silence opposition and dissent, feeling that this will adversely affect the business environment. Countries such as Myanmar (Burma), Malaysia, Indonesia and South Korea have often been targeted by human rights' activists who point to abuse of political and military power by the government.

Indonesia has been governed by Suharto since 1966. When he took power the country was poverty-stricken, stretching across 13 667 islands, with many ethnic groups and several religions. Over more than 30 years the country has seen a population explosion, now standing at over 200m, but with economic growth averaging six per cent a year, producing an increase in GDP per head from $100 in 1970 to $900 in 1996.

Growth has helped to reduce the number living in absolute poverty from 70 per cent to 15 per cent of the population, and has pushed the country into the lower-middle-income category. The government has argued that economic progress of this magnitude has been assisted by statutes. Suharto has ruled with the support of the Army, which is guaranteed a political role by the constitution. Only three parties are allowed to operate – the government party (Golkar) and two (small) opposition groups. This situation has produced stable political circumstances but has given little opportunity for alternative opinions to be expressed as would happen in most Western democracies.

Political expression often manifests itself in rioting that leads to the intervention of the Army to restore peace. With ethnic tensions and religious conflict having caused serious unrest in the early 1960s, the imposition of political stability is a price that many consider worth paying to maintain progress. However, the further use of the military to solve political issues is causing companies and friendly governments to worry over the country's long-term stability.

Starting up operations in the capital, Mexico City,[4] takes 90 working days due to the necessity to register with government agencies. Other restrictions and regulations cause companies to change the way they operate, such as the restrictions on part-time staff where use is forbidden by federal law. Regulations affecting environmental contamination are unclear, offering the possibility for corruption. The Mexican government, realising the problem caused by this approach and spurred on by the North American Free Trade Agreement (NAFTA), has been reviewing the regulatory framework. 'One-stop' approaches are becoming common, with a single office dealing with all the regulations a company could need to abide by. Offering huge potential, Mexico is a country where companies wish to do business. In the environment of change and deregulation, active companies are taking a role in influencing the process.

INTERNATIONAL TRANSFERS

In an era of globalisation the issue of why countries attempt to control movement of capital, goods and people is an area where dissension exists. The EU and WTO,[5] for example, point to the need to reduce such restrictions and in some instances, such as in the EU, draw up agendas based on the identification of common barriers to exporting and other forms of international business. Some of the reasons for this have already been noted, with the need to protect domestic industry, to protect jobs and even to promote local products. Others can be added, notably to help with the balance of payments, to defend national security and even to provide a base on which to achieve political aims in both the domestic and international arenas, examples of which are given in Boxes 7.5 and 7.6.

Box 7.5

REGULATION IN AMERICA[6]

An estimate of the cost of complying with Federal regulations was made by Thomas Hopkins of the Rochester Institute of Technology. This put the cost at $668bn in 1995, compared with $1.5trn in Federal spending (*see* Figs 7.1 and 7.2). This calculation only included complying with rules, rather than seeking to calculate the possible loss of productivity caused by new regulations. Using Hopkins' estimate, it is possible to argue that regulation costs a typical American household $7000 more than it pays out in tax.

Fig 7.1 RULES OVER TAXES

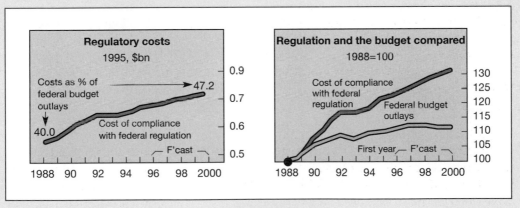

Source: 'Over-regulating America' © *The Economist*, London (27 July 1996).

In the 1980s and 1990s regulation has grown, with rules governing clearer air, help for disabled people, a higher minimum wage and more stringent product-liability laws. Eastman-Kodak, for example, a photography company, has seen its tax staff grow by two-thirds over the decade 1985–95, partly because of the tax breaks allowed by new regulations. The company's annual tax return has doubled in weight to 35lb over the same period.

Federal agencies scrutinise every aspect of a company's activity: the Equal Employment Opportunity Commission (for the personnel department); the Occupational and Health Administration (the factory floor); plus the Environmental Protection Agency which covers many activities. Regulation at the Federal level is repeated at state, county, city and at semi-autonomous level from agencies charged with controlling pollution.

The increase in regulations in the USA is running counter to the requirement to cut the Federal budget deficit and reduce the size of the government sector, and is now supported by the rise of the cost of compliance as seen in Fig. 7.2.

▶ **Box 7.5 continued**

The costs are made up of price and entry controls, paperwork, and environmental and risk reduction. This gives rise to the possible conclusion that free market capitalism in America is as heavily regulated as that found in Japan.

Fig 7.2 DISTRIBUTION OF REGULATORY COSTS

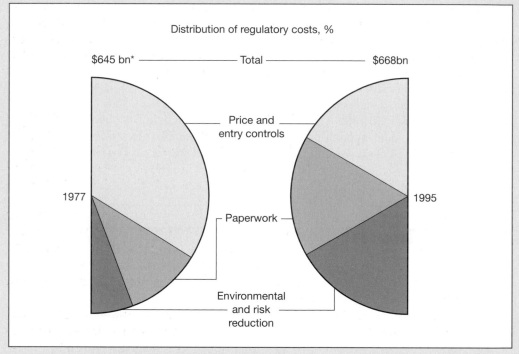

Distribution of regulatory costs, %

$645 bn* ——————— Total ——————— $668bn

Source: 'Over-regulating America' © *The Economist*, London (27 July 1996).

Box 7.6   THE HELMS–BURTON LAW[7]

The dominance of the USA in international matters produces anxieties in those countries which, for whatever reason, evoke the displeasure of the superpower whose influence can be felt at the IMF, World Bank and the United Nations, in peace-keeping roles in Bosnia as well as direct military intervention in countries such as Somalia.

One of the most long-standing disputes between the USA and another country is that with Cuba, one of the few remaining Communist states. From military intervention to economic sanctions the USA has sought to isolate the country to defeat the Communist government of Fidel Castro. With the withdrawal of economic support from Russia and Eastern Europe, the country was thought to be vulnerable, but has continued to survive. US political representatives have identified investment in Cuba in, for example, the tourist industry, as bolstering the government. To this end the Helms–Burton law was

> **Box 7.6 continued**

passed to punish those who invested in Cuba, permitting private lawsuits against foreign firms who take such action (a provision that has now been suspended).

Countries such as Canada and Mexico were expected to follow the Helms–Burton law by refusing to invest and trade with Cuba. These countries and the EU have refused, resenting the spread of US law to the international arena. Although resisted by many countries, this use of a nation's laws to influence others, particularly when it is the world's largest economy and single superpower shows the possibilities of exerting political and legal power to re-direct trade. In this case, however, individual countries have taken the line that trade with Cuba, not sanctions, would bring the required changes. Cuba now has new trade agreements, and has even seen its leader meet the Pope.

Seen in this way it becomes more understandable, if not less difficult, for managers to appreciate that governments have an agenda that may require action that impinges on businesses. The imposition of tariffs raises revenue for governments, which given the difficult circumstances facing countries such as Russia[8] where lack of taxable income has threatened public finances, action of this nature can be explained, if not defended.

Areas where other influences on trade and business can be identified are assistance for exporters, such as the Export Credit Guarantee Department (ECGD) in the UK, which offers cover at a competitive rate to insure against various risks. Areas may be created to attract investment from abroad, as was noted with FDI flows that can be influenced by the creation of Special Economic Zones in especially deprived areas, which can be found in most countries.

When Italy rejoined the ERM in November 1996, a major problem was at what level it would join. Eventually, this was set at 990 lire to the deutschmark, but business and government wanted it to be at least 1000. This is a further example of how exchange rate competitiveness that favours exports and hinders imports is a major concern for countries who wish to use trade to assist economic development.

Regulations concerning the transfer of people and technology are of great importance to managers. Restrictions on the movement of people have been considerably eased since the cold war tensions declined after 1989. Changes in South Africa also produced the abolition of sanctions against that country. In many instances countries wish to promote tourism, thereby allowing short-term visits. In the case of longer-term commitments, particularly from personnel moving to work in a new location, gaining a work permit can be a very bureaucratic procedure. However, since the rise of FDI and the support by governments for this development, movement of personnel has come to be seen as an accepted part of the package, at least in the short term.

Changes in the EU brought about both by the Single Market programme and the resulting mergers and FDI have been a notable development, with the aim to create a situation where movement of personnel is not hindered by barriers created by regulations or problems of disparities between qualifications.[9] The result has been to permit the movement of those professionally and occupationally highly qualified workers, who can raise the performance of a company and thereby help to improve the host country's economic welfare, but to clamp down on those allowed in for reasons other than work, the reasoning being that many immigrants would place unnecessary burdens on the state benefit system. In the UK, for example, as in many other countries, it has become progressively harder for immigrants to be permitted entry.

The transfer of technology to developing countries covers all aspects from machinery to knowledge of managerial and technical processes. As shown in the case study at the end of this chapter, developing economies such as Vietnam are keen to exploit the possibilities offered by such transfers. As buyers of technology, they lay great store in making sure that it meets their requirements, and in the case of Vietnam have five-year plans that reveal the priority areas for development. Problems remain for firms involved in technology transfer, particularly to a third party, that may put their own businesses in jeopardy.

Developed economies tend to be both buyers and sellers of technology, with little interference on the part of governments in the process. Disputes can and do arise, which are settled in court (or by reaching an out-of-court settlement). The example of Volkswagen reveals how difficult situations can arise. In this case, General Motors of the USA claimed that the head of production and purchasing of VW, who had been recruited by the company from GM, had been involved in industrial espionage, transferring knowledge of how to reduce costs and improve efficiency using GM's 'blueprint'.

LEGAL SYSTEMS AND INTERNATIONAL MARKETING

Countries are different not just in the rules and regulations that they apply, but also in the laws and legal systems that they employ. The dispute between GM and VW exemplifies this problem, the international firm being forced to deal with many different legal systems to win or defend itself in any dispute. In this example, the German and American legal systems differed enough to cause problems in reaching agreements. The development of an international legal system is in its infancy, and is in reality a hotch-potch of agreements and institutions that affect international businesses only in some areas.

Countries sign treaties and conventions that directly and indirectly cover business matters. When the UK signed an agreement on defence matters with the United Arab Emirates (UAE) in 1996, the benefits were seen by defence contractors, who are now able to exploit the opportunities this agreement provides by selling armaments and services. Any dispute will be settled by recourse to the courts of the two countries.

In general terms, the world's legal systems can be divided into:

1 common law-based systems;
2 code law-based systems.

Common law

Countries operating this system do not attempt to foresee every circumstance in the application of a law, by so constructing it that all circumstances then known can be catered for. Cases can be decided by reference to common practice, tradition and interpretation. Common law systems operate on precedence; previous decisions provide the current law until distinguished, overruled or set aside. Such legal systems are flexible and evolve over a long period of time.

Code law

Code law systems do try to frame their laws so that they can include all applications of that law. Codes can thereby be developed covering commercial activity.

In the EU, both codes can be found in operation, leading to the possibility of misunderstanding and conflict. Bradley[10] uses the example of industrial property rights to show how problems can emerge. In common law countries such as the UK, the ownership of a right, such as the use of a brand name, comes from its use. In code law countries, ownership comes from the registering of a name. UK firms may then find themselves in a position that they have protection in the UK, but no protection for a brand abroad. Box 7.7 on Dr Martens shows how a company can build up a defence across countries using different systems, thereby exploiting its brand name and, in this case, its high brand recognition.

Box 7.7

DR MARTENS[11]

In the UK, the Trade Mark Act 1994 defines a trade mark (™) as:

> any sign capable of being represented graphically, which is capable of distinguishing goods or services of one undertaking from those of other undertakings. A Trade Mark may, in particular, consist of words (including personal names), designing letters, numerals or the shape of goods or their service and their packaging.

This means that in the case of the Dr Martens shoe company, that DR MARTENS, DOC'S, DM'S, DOC MARTENS (etc.) as well as AIRWAIR (etc.) can be protected as trade marks.

In addition to the configuration of the product, the trade dress can also be protected through three-dimensional trade mark and design protection. Protection can also be obtained for advertising slogans, packaging and new elements, as in the case of new sole patterns on Dr Martens' shoes.

With sales and franchise operations in many other counties complications arise in attempting to protect marks, particularly in countries that do not use the Roman alphabet. In such cases, with the local population being unable to understand Roman script and perhaps with difficulties in pronouncing the name, a translation into the language needs to be found.

In order to retain the validity of the mark, it has to be used correctly, with use having to be proved in any of the markets within which the company operates, in which application and registration has been filed or granted. Beyond this, a brand owner may well wish to secure ™ protection in markets where trade is not currently taking place, nor where it is anticipated to be so for some time. The purpose here is to prevent third parties from using or applying to register the mark, a tactic which is defensive in intent but permits a more offensive approach in the company's other markets across the globe.

In practice, the separation between the two systems is never that clear-cut. In the UK, there are also codes of law to be found, and aspects of the two systems can be seen in the gradual application of EC approaches in a UK context. However, the possibility for problems comes from the evolution of the UK legal systems and its need to adapt to the code-law emphasis of much of the EC approach. The EC merger law in Box 7.8 shows how the two approaches can be compared by looking at the EC and the USA.

Box 7.8   EUROPEAN COMMUNITY MERGER LAW[12]

The merger regulation

Regulation on the control of concentrations between businesses, the so-called merger Control Regulation, became effective on 21 September 1990. This regulation attempts to establish a division between those community-scale mergers for which the Commission is responsible and those mergers which primarily affect the territory of a single 'member state', where the national authorities are responsible.

The Community-scale dimensions of a merger are defined by three criteria. First, a threshold of at least 5bn Ecu (approximately $6bn) for the aggregate worldwide sales activity of all the businesses concerned. This amount reflects the aggregate economic and financial powers of the enterprises involved in a merger. This is the enterprise's net sales in the preceding financial year of its ordinary activities. Second, a threshold of at least 250m Ecu (approximately $300m) for the aggregate Community-wide turnover each of at least two of the businesses concerned. Only enterprises with a specified level of activity in the Community are regulated. Third, Community control does not apply if each of the businesses concerned achieves two-thirds of its turnover within one and the same member state. Mergers whose impact is primarily national are therefore excluded from this regulation.

The regulation is designed to apply only to Community-scale concentrations. Such concentrations arise when two or more previously independent businesses merge or one or more businesses acquire control of the whole or part of one other business. Control may be obtained by the purchase of shares or assets, by contract, or by any means that permits the possibility of exercising decisive influence on a business. The creation of a joint venture could be a concentration when it performs on a lasting basis all the functions of an autonomous economic entity and does not constitute a means by which to co-ordinate the competitive behaviour of the joint parties.

Extraterritorial application of EC antitrust law

Unlike US antitrust statutes, Articles 85 and 86 of the Treaty of Rome do not have a foreign-commerce clause which might suggest application of the law to non-Community parties. Article 85 prohibits anti-competitive practices which occur only within the EU and affect trade between member states. Article 86 dominant-position violations are those within the EU or a substantial part thereof. However, both articles have been applied to foreign parties whose operations have occurred within the EU.

The adoption and implementation of a merger-regulation law by the EC was to fill a perceived gap in the law governing competition. The maintenance of competition is an important element in the EU unification process. The emphasis on competition policy is somewhat different from that in the USA where policy leads to a watchdog focus. US policy is concerned with market power, the number of competitors, pricing behaviour, and other microeconomic market conditions. The EC regulation is concerned with a dominant position. The EU policy emphasis is one of opening national markets and removing national barriers within member states. With this basic mission in mind, the Commission

▶

> ▶ **Box 7.8 continued**
>
> consistently examines a merger and its potential for creating a barrier of constraint on economic movement within the entire Community. This is the overall goal, competition policy which acts to enforce the removal of economic barriers and restricts the development of new barriers within the community. Enforcement of the merger regulation law is a key determinant of this mission.

Countries may adopt laws that affect the marketing effort. Examples of this approach have already been seen earlier in this chapter and in others, where export quotas and tariffs are enshrined in law. In India, for example, the import policy for the period 1992–7 reveals that a negative list of imports exists, with three items banned and 86 items restricted.[13] Anti-dumping laws can also be found banning products that are sold at less than full cost, or laws (and corresponding rules and regulations) that require a licence and that may also require what may be regarded as too high a level of health and safety standards. In the USA, the Department of Commerce Import Administration (IA) enforces laws and agreements that seek to prevent unfairly traded imports, particularly on the issues of foreign pricing and government subsidies that according to IA distort the free flow of goods and harm US business. In particular, IA undertakes to:

1 administer the US anti-dumping and countervailing duty laws;
2 assist domestic industries to decide whether there is sufficient evidence to petition for anti-dumping and countervailing duty investigations;
3 partner in negotiations to promote fair trade.[14]

Other areas where legal issues arise, with each country having its own rules and regulations that can influence all the aspects of the marketing mix, are promotion, packaging, pricing, standards and health and safety issues, all impacting on what may have been a uniform marketing approach.

Legislation, and the rules and regulations that spring from it, can influence advertisers. In the UK, Belgium and Italy superlatives in advertising are permitted, but not in Germany, whilst in the Netherlands the use of superlatives are permitted as long as they are backed up by factual information.

With other aspects of advertising there are not just cultural differences, but differences enshrined in legislation that can restrict how competing products are mentioned, the use of what is considered pornographic images, or even the amount of advertising that is allowed for any specific media (e.g. television).

Although it is necessary to understand how the legal environment affects business decision making, it is also necessary to understand the importance of influencing the framing of laws and regulations, as was suggested earlier in the chapter. Pressure groups lobby political representatives to introduce new laws, amend existing ones and even to remove arcane and out-of-date statutes. Companies and their respective trade associates, and professional associations, maintain offices in centres where they can have the most influence on any proposed changes. This can be done at many levels, from inter-governmental and transnational approaches, through to regional development agencies (RDAs) working on behalf of business in a particular location. These pressures can be exerted in the home country to permit exports or in the host country to change an aspect of law that is felt to be a hindrance to business.

Pressure to review the US government's stance on cryptography (that helps protect commercial interests, personal privacy and assist with law enforcement) came from a committee set up by Congress to study the role of cryptography in the digital world. Trade representatives played a role in helping to provide evidence for the committee, which considered that the US should not bar the manufacture, sale or use of any encryption in the US but, as importantly, argued that export controls should be gradually relaxed, but not completely abolished,[15] an outcome that would help the US maintain its lead in this area and help build up the competitive advantages of its firms.

INTERNATIONAL TREATIES

International agreements are of various types, ranging from bilateral and multilateral agreements on trade, to formal regional groupings, to those agreements that work on the international level, such as those covered by the World Trade Organisation (WTO). The economic rationale behind these was covered in Chapter 5, but as has been seen throughout this chapter the legal and regulatory effects may facilitate, or constrain, the marketing effort.

Examples taken from the EU, NAFTA and the WTO can show how responses can be made to their efforts to regulate and harmonise business activities either within actual borders (the EU) or to provide a common approach (the WTO).

The European Community

To see how EC directives influence business decisions it is instructive to take an example of a US company's response to this issue – the CE Mark. Allen Bradley[16] is a company that manufactures and sells industrial control and automation products. In surveying and then interpreting EC directives the company produced a paper for the use of its customers, thereby helping to inform them of the significance of EC directives in general, and electrical and electronic control and automation systems in particular. In addition, the paper also showed the position of the company in relation to the directives, the expected impact on its products, the company's response and the support that Allen Bradley would provide to customers in their efforts to meet the directive's requirements.

In providing information for the company's customers, the paper explained the relevance of EC directives in establishing requirements for a wide variety of products, processes and services, marketed both in the EU and the European Economic Area (EEA). The requirements will impact on the marketability of products in these areas and without compliance, trade with (and within) the EU would become very difficult and eventually impossible. A number of directives apply to control products with differing dates for compliance, such as January 1996 for electromagnetic compatibility and January 1997 for low voltage. From January 1997, all products had to meet the directives that apply to them and carry the CE Mark (CE marking is a compliance symbol which shows that a product has met the requirements of the directives; without this, goods cannot be marketed within the EU after a certain date).

CE marking requires evidence to be produced that satisfies the European Commission that the product does comply with the relevant directives, without which the CE Mark cannot be used. In summary, the product has to comply with all the technical standards before a Declaration of Conformity (DOC) is issued. If the product is not produced in the EU, authorised representatives in the EU must be set up who will take full responsibility for ensuring conformity and availability of technical documentation.

Allen Bradley's products will conform in that DOCs will be produced; products will bear the CE Mark and conform to all regulations, and all technical information will be available for inspection. In addition, machinery builders and others who have responsibilities in the application and installation of electrical/electronic products will be assisted by the company providing information that will help them to gain compliance with EC directives.

The strategy underlying this approach can be seen as having many levels – (a) it shows the commitment to the EU market, (b) it provides reassurance for existing customers, and (c) it can attract new customers who can be reassured regarding the quality of the products. At another level, the effect of directives can be seen on the organisation of the company in dealing with the market and in the way it has to be organised to meet the demands placed upon it.

NAFTA and WTO

Rules of origin
NAFTA has 'rules of origin' requirements that stipulate, for example, how much of a car needs to be made in Mexico for it to qualify as 'NAFTA' and be able to enter the American market without attracting tariffs.[17] In the automotive sector, no country in NAFTA can increase customs duties on any organisation's product, whilst each country will aim to eliminate custom duties progressively (except where prior agreement has been reached). Equally, all non-tariff changes will be subject to review by the three member countries, whose aim it is at least to implement GATT rules on trade.

Detail of the agreement
The detail of the NAFTA agreement covers the full range of products and services, with everything from wood to dockyard cranes subject to scrutiny. WTO has seen membership increase to 126 countries in 1996 (*see* Figs 7.3 and 7.4), with at that stage 30 countries waiting to join. The Uruguay Round of GATT, of which further examples are given in Box 7.9, that preceded the creation of the WTO, agreed to cut tariffs on manufacturing and look at liberalising trade in agriculture and services. Non-tariff businesses were also included for the first time, as was a new system to settle disputes. Any dispute on trade is reviewed by a panel within nine months, and the decision of the WTO can be overridden only by consensus, unlike the previous situation where any member could veto the verdict. Many obstacles still exist, however, with quotas on textiles and clothing being reviewed only by 2005, but this protects mainly developed countries' markets and hinders progress by developing countries' exporters.

Fig 7.3 GATT/WTO MEMBERSHIP

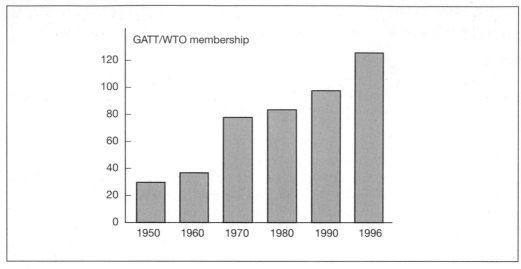

Source: 'Spoiling world trade' © *The Economist*, London (6 December 1996).

Fig 7.4 REGIONAL INTEGRATION AGREEMENTS

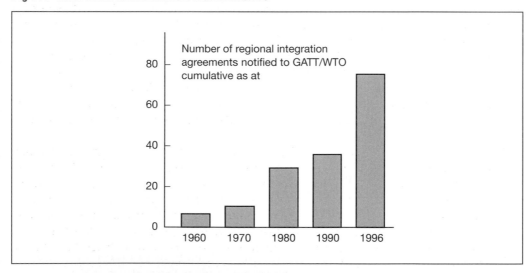

Source: 'Spoiling world trade' © *The Economist*, London (6 December 1996).

| Box 7.9 | URUGUAY ROUND RESULTS[18] |

On 15 December 1993, the 125 countries participating in the Uruguay Round concluded negotiations on market access for goods and services. The trade accord was signed by ministers from most of those countries on 15 April 1994, in Marrakesh, Morocco.

The final package has two parts – the Final Act and the schedules. The Final Act is a 500-page document establishing the World Trade Organisation (WTO), and amending or

▶ Box 7.9 continued

updating existing GATT trade rules. Annexed to the Final Act are 22 500 pages of individual national concessions (schedules) on market access for goods, services and agriculture.

Market access

The overall objective for the Round was a one-third average reduction in tariffs as well as removal of many non-tariff barriers (NTBs). The final reduction was nearer to 40 per cent. The USA estimates that the Uruguay Round will give a $6trn boost to the world economy over the next decade.

General Agreement on Trade in Services (GATS)

One of the most important accomplishments of the Uruguay Round was the establishment, for the first time, of a set of rules governing trade in services. GATT economists estimated in 1990 that services, such as banking, insurance, tourism, construction, or telecommunications, accounted for as much as 20 per cent of total goods and services' world trade. The GATS agreement establishes a multilateral framework for trade in services and provides a specific legal basis for future negotiations aimed at eliminating barriers that discriminate against foreign services providers and deny them market access. The principal elements of the GATS framework agreement include the most favoured nation (MFN) treatment, national treatment (each government shall treat foreign services and service suppliers no less favourably than its own), market access, and free flow of payments and transfers. The rules are augmented by Annexes addressing the special situations of individual service sectors (financial services, telecommunications, air transport, and movement of labour). The GATS' strong provision on national treatment specifically requires GATS countries to ensure that domestic laws and regulations do not tilt competitive conditions against foreign firms. Complementing the GATS rules are binding commitments to market access and national treatment in service sectors that countries schedule as a result of bilateral negotiations. These commitments became effective upon entry into force of the WTO.

The GATS agreement provides for the progressive liberalisation of trade in services through a series of successive rounds which may be commenced at five-year intervals to allow governments to work towards improving their national commitments and gradually to reduce MFN exemptions. In addition, governments decided to set up special working parties on Trade in Services and the Environment and on Professional Services. The working party on Professional Services will work to ensure that technical standards and licensing requirements do not constitute unnecessary barriers to trade. It has been agreed that the group will give priority to the development of multilateral disciplines in the accountancy sector.

Post-Uruguay Round GATS negotiations

At the end of the Uruguay Round, governments decided to continue GATS negotiations in four areas:

- *Basic Telecommunications*: *Duration* – began May 1994, set to conclude in April 1997. *Goal* – to produce national commitments and a basic set of rules for liberalisation.
- *Maritime Transport*: *Duration* – began May 1994, set to conclude June 1996. *Goal* – to improve commitments on the use of port facilities, auxiliary services and ocean transport.

▶ **Box 7.9 continued**

- *Movement of Natural Persons*: *Duration* – May 1994–June 1995. *Results* – although the negotiations produced only modest improvements to offers on the table at the end of the Uruguay Round, nearly all important WTO members have now agreed to facilitate cross-border movement of senior business executives.

- *Financial Services*: (concluded 28 July 1995): *Goal* – To improve the schedules negotiated during the Uruguay Round for opening financial services markets. *Results* – Only 30 of the 76 nations with commitments in the financial services sector improved those commitments during the post-Uruguay Round negotiations.

- *US Policy*: The US judged the offers, especially by Asian countries, to be insufficient and did not join the agreement. US financial services are already wide open to foreign participation. The agreement will take effect for 17 months starting 17 August 1996. Thereafter, governments will be free to review or improve on their commitments, opening the way for possible future US participation.

Intellectual property rights

The Final Act contains the most extensive agreement on intellectual property ever negotiated. The Trade Related Aspects of Intellectual Property Rights (TRIPS) agreement covers patents, copyright, the rights of performers and producers of sound recordings, trademarks, and geographical indications, including appellations of origin, industrial designs, layout designs of integrated circuits (semiconductor chips) and trade secrets. TRIPS establishes improved standards for the protection of intellectual property and sets out, for the first time in international law, the procedures and remedies that governments must provide under their domestic law so that rights can be effectively enforced. The agreement protects computer programs as literary works and databases as compilations under copyright; establishes a term of 50 years for the protection of new and existing sound recordings; and sets a minimum term of 50 years for the protection of motion pictures and other works where companies may be the author.

Textiles and clothing

The Uruguay Round Agreement on Textiles and Clothing establishes a process whereby during a 10-year period, textiles and clothing products will be progressively integrated into the WTO rules. Since 1974, most industrialised countries have restricted imports of textiles and clothing through bilateral quotas negotiated under the Multifibre Arrangement (MFA). Quotas would normally have been illegal under GATT rules, but when the MFA was set up MFA members agreed to derogate from this rule. The agreement provides a mechanism for the gradual phasing out of bilateral quotas and at the same time includes an improved safeguards mechanism. Implementation of the agreement is to be overseen by a Textile Monitoring Body (TMB). At the end of the transitional period, only normal WTO rules will apply in this sector.

Reform of trade in agriculture

The Agreement on Agriculture strengthens and clarifies the rules for agricultural trade, and reduces subsidies and other specific policies – such as barriers to market access – which distort it. The agreement envisages the tariffication of all non-tariff measures, with the resulting tariffs to be subject to a 36 per cent reduction over six years. A related measure is

▶

▶ **Box 7.9 continued**

the Agreement on the Application of Sanitary and Phytosanitary (S&P) Measures. The agreement sets out rules intended to prevent S&P measures – measures taken to protect human, animal or plant life or health – from being used as disguised barriers to trade. It provides for increased transparency in the process of establishing new S&P measures by requiring advance notice and opportunity for comment on proposed measures.

Non-tariff barriers

The Uruguay Round package includes a number of agreements aimed at reducing or eliminating NTBs to trade. These include specific agreements on safeguards, anti-dumping, subsidies and countervailing measures, import licensing procedures, technical barriers to trade and customs valuation. The agreements strengthen existing GATT rules, and for the first time extend GATT disciplines to NTBs in the areas of investment, rules of origin and pre-shipment inspection.

Subsidies and countervailing measures

Countries often counter subsidised exports by imposing special duties (countervailing measures) on the subsidised product or other exports from the subsidising country. The new agreement establishes clearer rules in this area, by defining which subsidies are legal and which are not. It creates three categories of subsidies and remedies:

1 prohibit subsidies;
2 permissible subsidies against which action can be taken only if they cause adverse trade effects;
3 non-actionable subsidies which cannot be countered by duties, and which include certain types of government assistance for industrial research, regional development, or adaptation of existing plant and equipment to new environmental requirements.

Trade-Related Investment Measures (TRIMS)

The Final Act recognises that certain investment rules and regulations can restrict or distort trade and provides for the phasing out of GATT-inconsistent investment measures such as requirements on particular levels of local procurement by enterprises or restrictions on the volume or value of their imports. Countries must eliminate prohibited TRIMs within a specific time period – two years for developed countries, five years for developing countries, and seven years for the least developed countries.

Trade and environment

With the adoption of the Uruguay Round Final Act, governments adopted a decision on Trade and Environment which called for the setting up of a WTO Committee on Trade and Environment. The committee has been asked to explore the link between trade and environmental policies, notably how tighter environmental protection measures are compatible with WTO rights and obligations. Mandated to analyse the relationship between trade and environmental measures, it can make recommendations should any modifications of the multilateral trading system be required. The committee's work is, however, restricted by two parameters. One is that WTO competence for policy co-ordination is limited to trade, and the second is that problems of policy co-ordination must be resolved in a way that upholds the principles of the multilateral trading system.

Liberalising trade in goods and services, admitting new countries such as China to the WTO, extension of the WTO's influence over FDI, competitive policy and labour standards[19] are new areas for the WTO. Moves into these areas will be important developments that affect operations of business – not just marketing, but employment law, health and safety, take-overs and mergers, and so on.

Regional trade agreements, such as NAFTA are, as has been seen, on the increase, bringing a situation where nearly every member of the WTO is a participant in at least one regional trade agreement. The possibility exists that the importance attached to regional integration and agreements can move the issue away from liberalising world trade towards the promotion of the interests of particular groups of countries that can serve to erect new, perhaps less hidden, barriers to trade via the regulation of the market place.

SUMMARY

Political risk assessment and the regulation of markets and government business practice present a formidable challenge to organisations.

Country risk assessment is a useful tool in appraising market potential and future opportunities. Despite this, risk assessment requires a greater awareness of the underlying foundation of a country, as seen in the Czech Republic with its ethnic German population, which may give rise to uncertainty over the future relationships between it and Germany. If this risk can be found in member states of the OECD, it can also be found in many other countries, and businesses should be aware of its potential to influence the political decision process, leading to the possibility of putting up barriers and restrictions on people and organisations which pose a potential threat.

A country's economic policy is affected by political issues and considerations, so that price controls and direct intervention in company affairs to reinforce the government's commitment to the pursuit of particular objectives are situations that can have a significant impact on a company's fortunes.

Legal frameworks differ between countries, with two major systems being identified. The important issue is to understand the differences, whilst at the same time recognising that overlaps bring the two closer together.

Specific laws and regulations need to be recognised and action taken so that the marketing effort can remain on course. A broad view of this is essential as the interpretation of laws is also an area where court decisions can produce an effect on the business environment. In Germany, a large wholesaler of pharmaceuticals in 1995 was held to be contravening the Cartel Law, when it refused to offer pharmacists products offered by an importer of pharmaceuticals. This sounds straightforward enough, but the result was that imports which had been manufactured under licence from German companies, but still produced in the EU, and could be produced more cheaply outside Germany, could now compete with the German-made variety. Pharmacists can now be offered the less expensive (imported) version of the same product – a ruling that will produce a reassessment by all participants from the importer, licensors (i.e. the German drug companies), the wholesaler and the pharmacists.

To understand and appreciate the complex legal and political environment is therefore essential for all businesses. New opportunities can be created, such as those now found by Allen Bradley, that develops a positive atmosphere to exploit the potential on offer.

REVIEW QUESTIONS

1 What is country risk assessment?

2 Why is political stability an important issue for marketing managers?

3 What are the two main legal codes, and how do they differ from each other?

4 Outline the organisations or institutions that can affect the regulation of businesses.

5 How can business influence the political and regulatory environment?

DISCUSSION QUESTIONS

1 How useful is country risk assessment? Using an actual example, outline why taking its analysis at face value could be counter-productive.

2 Are markets becoming deregulated and more open to trade?

3 The UK is a member of the EU, WTO, IMF, OECD and many other international organisations. How can it reconcile the demands of each of these to have a say in the deregulation of trade?

4 Is the EU's approach to deregulation the same as that found in NAFTA?

5 It is argued that countries such as China and India can afford to ignore the WTO – why is this?

Case study

CANADIAN EXPORTS TO VIETNAM[20]

The Canadian government provides advice to actual and potential exporters from that country, identifying locations that have potential and pointing out any difficulties and issues that they should be aware of.

Vietnam is a country that has great potential, requiring capital and consumer goods, upgrading of its infrastructure and the provision of services to support a modernising economy. Where once the country was blacklisted, due to action taken by IMF and World Bank, it is now co-operating with them to restructure its economy and seek the benefits of growth that other Asian economies are currently experiencing.

Despite its potential, the country has to be assessed by firms in a thorough and clear-sighted way. To facilitate this the Canadian government provides guidance on the environment facing exporters to Vietnam, which can be summarised as follows:

Factors for consideration

Population by the year 2002 will have grown from 71m to 85m, a population equal to that of Germany. However, there is at present only limited consumer demand, and with difficulties in distributing goods to the main centres of population, partly accounted for by the problems associated with physical infrastructure. Despite this, Vietnam, like China, has a stable government that has sought to encourage investment, but given little attention to the purchase of goods and services from abroad and as a consequence the rules and regulations governing agents and distributors are under-developed.

The long-term potential of the country is great, but there are difficulties in reaching satisfactory deals. Among the major problems are limited access by citizens to foreign exchange, and the fact that the type of goods Canadian companies traditionally export, which incorporate aspects of advanced technology, are not yet right for the market. Lower-technology-based products are considered to offer more opportunities, at least in the short term.

Skill availability, raw material availability, replacement parts and power supply are some of the factors to consider.

Trade controls

The Ministry of Trade exercises, through the Council of Ministers, control over all imports and exports to and from the country. The Ministry has responsibility for co-ordinating with the State Planning Committee the strategy and objectives for the country's economy, incorporating planning for exports and imports. As a result of this, the Ministry is responsible for quotas, licences, inspection and control of all foreign trade activities. It is the company's responsibility for identifying restrictions that apply to their products and services.

In Vietnam, not every enterprise is authorised to be involved in foreign trade. Trading partners who are able to participate in trade can be found at the state, provincial and semi-private levels. Private firms and individuals are not permitted to import goods directly. Each of the organisations permitted to carry out trade possess varying degrees of experience in this area, with many preferring to deal in counter-trade. If the Canadian company's cash flow cannot bear the cost of such an investment, it will find it difficult to penetrate the market.

The government of the country encourages the transfer of technology, partly by guaranteeing the rights and interests of the company. However, the transfer of technology must achieve improvement in product quality and production efficiency. The National Office of Inventions of the Ministry of Science, Technology and Environment has the authority to approve technology contracts.

Tariff and customs duties change frequently, requiring companies to consult the relevant government departments on actual and proposed changes.

Joint ventures can be exempt from import duties on raw materials, spare parts, accessories and materials imported for export production. If, however, the imported items are sold in the country then the exemption no longer applies.

Import/export licence applications are made to the Ministry of Trade, while the Vietnam Superintendent and Inspection Company (Vinacontrol) can provide exporters with quality control inspection certificates; health and safety certificates are provided by the Sanitary Bureau Office, while insurance certificates are the responsibility of Baoviet. Bureaucratic delays can, therefore, be expected, so the appointment of agents or representatives are a necessity to ensure that goods and documentation can be processed speedily.

Market surveys

As the financial capability to import foreign goods into the country is weak, any company wishing to trade with Vietnam should identify the export priorities of the government so as to identify the sectors that have been given foreign exchange to purchase essential items. This cannot be achieved at a distance, as a meeting with the relevant government agencies and ministries is essential. To organise meetings and to see the relevant ministries and civil servant, local consultancy companies will prepare information and arrange matters so that the company is fully briefed.

Lastly, companies can obtain information from the Vietcochamber, and ministries and people's committees can advise them on what the priorities are for their jurisdiction.

To exploit the potential of the market, low sales levels in the short term are to be expected, with the need to take a long-term view, looking to build market share and total sales over a period of years. Short-term commitments are, therefore, not recommended.

Questions

1 *Identify the regulatory issues associated with trade to Vietnam.*

2 *Is the advice given by the Canadian government to the country's firms equally applicable in other circumstances – e.g. in exporting to Germany?*

3 *In your view, would the laws and regulations governing trade in Vietnam determine companies' entry strategy?*

4 *Why is it essential to meet government officials, rather than rely on secondary research?*

5 *Firms have been advised to take a long-term view with regard to Vietnam. Is this true just for emerging markets, or for all markets?*

FURTHER READING

'Managing for Global Excellence', Business International (1996).

Lee, J.A., 'Cultural analysis in overseas operations', *Harvard Business Review*, 44 (1996), 106–14.

Ricks, D.A., *Blunders in International Business* (Cambridge, MA: Blackwell, 1993).

NOTES AND REFERENCES

1   Neilson, T.H., *Chaos Marketing* (McGraw-Hill, 1995); Hill, C.W. and Jones, G.R., *Strategic Management Theory* (Houghton Mifflin, 1995); Mintzberg, H., *The Rise and Fall of Strategic Planning* (Prentice-Hall, 1994).

2   Tayeb, M., 'India: a non-tiger of Asia', *International Business Review*, 5(5) (1996), 425–45.

3   'Indonesia: what price stability?', *The Economist* (3 August 1996).

4   Financial Times Survey – 'Mexico', *Financial Times* (28 October 1996).

5   Reel, Q., 'Lack of leadership slowing WTO's pace', *Financial Times* (25 November 1996).

6   'Over-regulating America', *The Economist* (27 July 1996).

7   'Cuba and the USA', *The Economist* (7 September 1996).

8   Reel, op. cit.

9   Cecchini, P. *et al.*, *The European Challenge 1992: The Benefits of a Single Market* (London: Wildwood House, 1988).

10   Bradley, F., *International Marketing Strategy*, 2nd edition (Englewood Cliffs, NJ: Prentice-Hall, 1995).

11   'Development of the Dr Martens brand through trade mark protection', *The Times 100* case studies (December 1996).

12   Ryba, W., 'The new European Community merger law: competition policy and its application', *Business and the Contemporary World*, 4(4) (Autumn 1992).

13   India Information Service, *Indiaserver* (1995).

14   US Department of Commerce, *Import Administration* (December 1996).

15   *Web Week*, 2(8) (17 June 1996).

16   Allen Bradley, *Guidelines for Marketing in the EU* (October 1995).

17   'Spoiling world trade', *The Economist* (7 December 1996).

18   World Trade Organisation, *Briefing Book on International Organisations* (United States Information Service).

19   'All free traders now', *The Economist* (7 December 1996).

20   'Exporting to Vietnam', Canadian Government (October 1995).

8

Global market research

INTRODUCTION

The marketing function is to produce and sell products/services that consumers want, and therefore firms have to assess what consumers want by undertaking marketing research. The differences in the international business environment makes conducting global marketing research more difficult and complex than domestic market research. Insufficient preparation and lack of knowledge of global markets increases the risk of doing business abroad, and it is certainly one of the most important causes of failure in the international market place. Information about overseas markets trends to be less than accurate and can be attributed to difficulties in collecting information, a firm's limited experience in overseas research and whether the firm is seriously committed to the international market. Given the rapid changes in the world economy, the complexity of markets and the unpredictability of consumers, market research is crucial if the firm wants to reduce the risks of undertaking business in international markets. The purpose of this chapter is to examine the particular nature, problems and techniques of global marketing research.

Objectives

This chapter will examine:

- the role of marketing research
- the international market research process
- problem formulation issues
- the major issues and problems concerning primary and secondary data
- the issues of equivalence in cross-cultural market research
- the marketing information system.

One of the major differences between the domestic and international market place is the highly complex environment in which the firm has to operate. To minimise the risk of poor or incorrect decision making requires a good knowledge base. It is in this respect that global market research is critically important to global marketing managers. Research by Ricks[1] has shown that poor knowledge of foreign markets is a major factor in blunders committed in the international market place. Market information is therefore a key element in the company's international success and the aim of this chapter is to examine the role of market research in its contribution to the decision-making process. In addition, we will examine the market research process, issues concerning primary and secondary data, the limits to equivalence when one undertakes cross-cultural market research and the role of the marketing information system.

THE ROLE OF MARKET RESEARCH

The availability of sound market information is fundamentally important for a company operating in the international market place as it is an important tool to help reduce risk in the decision-making process. *Marketing research* can be defined as the systematic collection, objective search for, and analysis and interpretation of information relevant to the identification and solution of any of the firm's marketing problems.

Global marketers require market data for a number of reasons:

- marketers not only need validated information but it must also be systematic and objective
- data assists marketers in problem identification
- data influences which international markets to enter
- data monitors the changes in the environment and the need to make changes if necessary to the firm's marketing programme and resource allocation priorities
- data influences the type of marketing mix strategies to deploy, e.g. the positioning strategy to adopt
- data enables the company to assess the effectiveness of its core marketing strategies.

The role of market research is not without its critics, who argue that marketing research lacks accountability, is costly in terms of time and money, that there is too much ritual in the research process and statistics, and finally that it can only recommend action and lacks precision.

We can separate market research into three distinct activities as illustrated in Fig. 8.1[2]; these are:

1. *industry research* – provides information to decision makers concerned with corporate-level strategies; the main focus of the information is on the competitive environment in which the company operates – i.e. technology, number of competitors, etc.;

Fig 8.1 RESEARCH ACTIVITIES UNDERTAKEN BY COMPANIES

Corporate responsibility or enterprise strategy research

1 Consumers right to know studies
2 Ecological impact studies
3 Social values and policies studies
4 Cross-national managerial practice studies

Market or business strategy research

1 Market potential studies
2 Market share analysis
3 Market characteristics studies
4 Distribution channel studies
5 Sales analyses: products, territories, sales force
6 Competitive product studies

Industry or corporate strategy research

1 Corporate and business unit portfolio studies
2 Manufacturing cost studies: economies of scale, learning curve
3 Strength of channel relationships
4 Shared costs or activities of business units
5 Resource studies: financial, depth of management
6 Labour force climate
7 Economic and political trend analyses
8 Competitor studies: strengths and weaknesses

Marketing research

1 Buyer behaviour studies
2 Product testing
3 Packaging studies
4 Price elasticity studies
5 Buyer motivation studies
6 Media research
7 Copy research

Source: Toyne, B. and Walters, P.G.P., *Global Marketing Management: A Strategic Perspective*, 2nd edition (Boston, MA: Allyn & Bacon), 365. © 1993. Reprinted by permission of Prentice-Hall, Inc.

2 *market research* – provides information to those concerned with formulating business strategies of the firm; the main thrust of the information is on the markets in which the various strategic business units are operating in, and the emphasis is on the analysis of competitor actions in specific markets and the factors affecting market sales and market shares, supply and demand trends, etc.;

3 *marketing research* – provides information to those concerned with ensuring an effective and efficient operation of the firm's marketing function and activities, the focus of the research is on the potential users of the firm's products and services and the factors that affect the purchase decision – essentially, this involves an analysis of the factors that influence the '4 Ps'.

In general, some companies treat all three activities as distinct whilst others would consider them a comprehensive unit. International marketing intelligence is undoubtedly more comprehensive than domestic marketing research.

| Box 8.1 | COMPETITIVE INTELLIGENCE[3] |

Information about competitors and market conditions are critical for business decisions yet many US companies make decisions based on incomplete information about the competition. As one noted author, Larry Kahaner, said: 'one no longer is living in the age of information but in the age of intelligence'. The concept of competitive intelligence (CI) has been used quite extensively in the corporate world, and it is essentially the gathering of every bit of information that can be obtained legally that will assist an organisation do better than its competitors. The advent of the Internet and computer databases has made information easily available and a cheap commodity, with the consequent effect of data saturation. An effective CI will filter much of the data glut and give company strategists and executives a more focused approach to collecting and analysing public information about competitors and using it to make effective decisions. CI involves using an array of techniques and databases from the Internet to data on the competitors' new products, manufacturing costs and executive profiles. Although CI has long been accepted in Europe and the Asian countries, it has only recently taken hold in the USA. The recent use of CI by corporate America is partly driven by the globalisation of world markets, where better intelligence is required to counter foreign threats and penetrate international markets, and also partly by the rapid pace of technological change and the global climate of deregulation and restructuring. US companies such as Xerox, Nutrasweet, the brokerage firm of Charles Schwab, etc. all have CI programmes. However, it is not always clear how to draw the fine line between CI and illegality, such as snooping through a competitor's trash on public property to expressing an interest in a job in a rival firm to find out the competitor's plans. However, there is a clear dividing line when CI becomes illegal – that is, when proprietary materials or trade secrets are stolen. Whatever the ethical issues, competitive intelligence is critical for a firm's competitive advantage in a global market, and there is no doubt that CI is spreading, with the consequent growth of specialist firms and consultants engaged in this trade.

THE INTERNATIONAL RESEARCH PROCESS

The international research process consists of a number of sequential activities, as shown in Fig. 8.2. The different stages will be examined briefly and particular stages will be discussed extensively under separate headings. The six main stages in the research process are as follows:

1 identification and formulation of the research problem;

2 selection of an appropriate research design;

3 selection of appropriate samples;

4 data collection techniques;

5 analysis and interpretation of the data and information collected;

6 reporting of results and follow-up.

We can see that the international research process is similar to the domestic process; however, there are differences:

Fig 8.2 THE GLOBAL MARKETING RESEARCH PROCESS

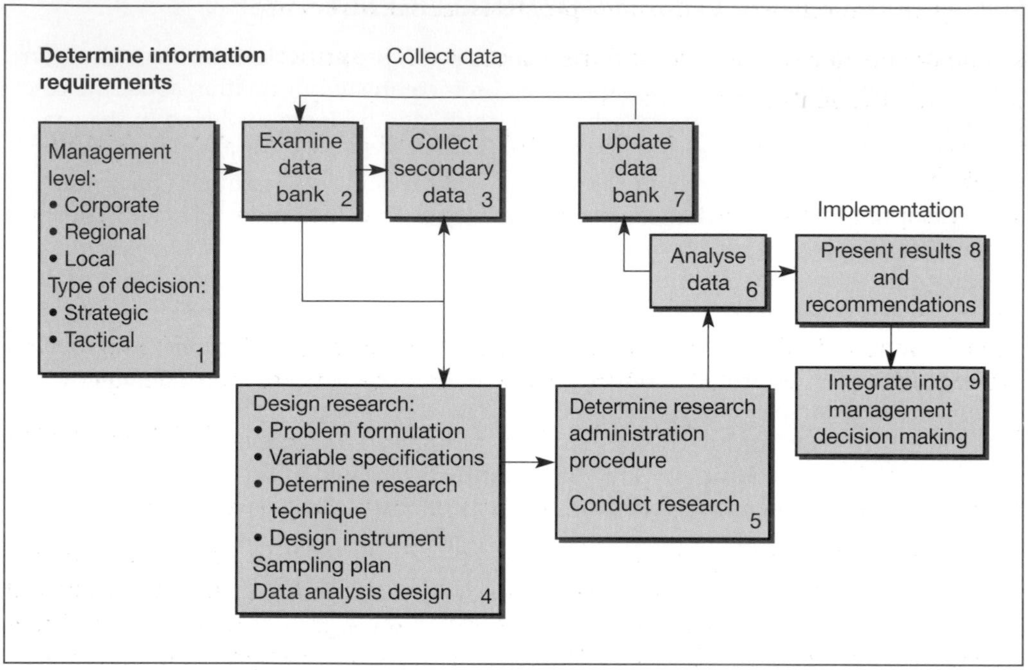

Source: Douglas, S.P. and Craig, C.S., *International Marketing Research Process* (Englewood Cliffs, NJ: Prentice-Hall, 1983), 27.

- the research focus may be across several national markets rather than a single market, and therefore the formulation of research goals when developed through different cultural contexts is unlikely to be the same as for the domestic research process
- as the company operates in several markets the problems encountered may be unique for each particular market(s)
- given the local differences in each national market, the research techniques may have to be adapted to accommodate the particular country
- there may be unique problems associated with the collection and analysis of secondary and primary data in each national market
- reporting the results may turn out to be more complex than in the domestic market.

We will now discuss each of these steps briefly and outline the issues of concern in the international research process.

Problem formulation

Problem formulation is one of the most fundamental steps to be undertaken. It could be said that this process is at the heart of the research programme, and the researcher needs to translate the management problem into a research problem. This translation problem requires the researcher to understand intimately the issues confronting the management team and to rephrase it in meaningful terms. The net effect should be that the management problem should not only be analytically understood but that the type of information required to help resolve the management problem can be specified. Furthermore, researchers need to be absolutely aware of the following issues for they present different and unique problems for the researcher:

● who are the decision makers and the resources they control?

● what are the goals of the research?

● what courses of action are available to solve the management problem under investigation?

● do we appreciate the consequences of different courses of action being undertaken?

Research method and design

The research methodology will depend on the nature of the problem to be solved and the level of current knowledge. There are two broad categories of methodologies:

1 experimental research – allows the researcher to manipulate and control some of the variables;

2 non-experimental research – this simply involves measuring data.

The *research design* is the specification of the methods and procedure for acquiring the required information – i.e. it is a plan or framework for undertaking the study and collecting the data. This ensures that the project is relevant to the problem and that effective procedures are employed. Whether the research design is an exploratory, descriptive or a causal one, researchers will need to be aware of the problems that are peculiar to conducting research across country markets and cultures. It is critical for researchers to be aware of these issues, otherwise the findings are likely to be worthless if they are not anticipated in the research design. The issues that are important for the research design are:

1 *construct equivalence*, which relates to the question of whether the researcher is studying the same phenomenon in countries A and B;

2 *measurement equivalence*, which is concerned with whether the phenomenon in countries A and B is being measured in the same way;

3 *sample equivalence*, which is concerned with whether the samples used in countries A and B are equivalent.

What follows is a brief discussion of each of these categories, and although all three issues are interrelated they will be discussed separately; it is also assumed that the research is conducted across several markets. Much of the discussion is based on the works of Douglas and Craig[4] and Toyne and Walters.[5]

Construct equivalence

This relates to how the researcher perceives the subjects of the research – i.e. whether the concepts used in cross-cultural research have similar meanings across the social units studied. The researcher may not have an identical or equivalent perspective because of the differences in socio-cultural, political and economic attitudes. The researcher may also suffer from the 'self-reference criterion' problem. There are a number of aspects to consider under this heading.[6]

Functional equivalence – this deals with how one should interpret the activity–function relationship of human behaviour – i.e. what function does it serve? For example, in some Middle Eastern countries inviting you to the host's home is considered a form of politeness as well as the opportunity to get to know you before settling down to business; refusal may constitute a snub. The same activity in some Western countries is construed as a polite gesture, and is a less formal and guarded occasion after business has been concluded. To take another familiar example, cycling is considered a leisure activity in many of the developed economies, whereas the same activity in many developing nations such as India and China is primarily for transportation purposes. The function served by a particular activity needs to be considered within the country context, and he/she needs to clarify what function is served by the activity and the name given to it.

Conceptual equivalence – this is concerned with the concepts used to identify the activity–function relationships in the markets under study. The assumption is that many concepts are culture-bound and may therefore not be appropriate for research in the countries in which research is being conducted. Transferring models and concepts from one culture to another is possible and desirable, but what needs to be emphasised is that a researcher cannot simply assume there are no problems in such transfers and that they are universal constructs which transcend country differences. The definition of product quality, for example, is likely to be different for a European consumer to one in the emerging markets of Eastern Europe or China. To take another example, consumer dissatisfaction has been used for assessing cross-cultural differences in consumer attitudes; a study examining the complaining behaviour between US and Dutch consumers looked for conceptual equivalence of the dissatisfaction concept, in terms of whether it had the same meaning both individually and socially. There was a 29 per cent variance attributed to national factors; the Dutch, for example, perceived making complaints as unpleasant or inconvenient. Conceptual equivalence takes on a prominent role when interpreting differences in the research results.

Definitional equivalence – relates to categories that researchers use, for there can be equivalence problems with these concepts; for example, group data (age groupings, occupational groupings, etc.). Mayer[7] illustrates the point, saying that attempts to standardise age groupings on a global basis were stopped because the same age groupings in different countries were found not to exhibit the same attitudinal or behavioural patterns.

Temporal equivalence – refers to the situation when research is conducted independently or simultaneously in more than two markets. Comparability is compounded by political, economic, cultural and seasonal factors. For example, a European firm marketing a product internationally might find that it is not in the same stage of the product life cycle in all the markets it wishes to enter. It may be in the mature stage in Europe, the growth stage in the USA and the introductory stage in some Asia Pacific markets. Undertaking research in more than one market is therefore no guarantee that the data is comparable.

Market structure equivalence – refers to possible construct error in markets exhibiting similarity in market indicators. For example, consumption patterns are influenced by product awareness and availability, which in turn are affected by channel accessibility, promotional coverage, etc.

Measurement equivalence

This refers to the methodology used to collect data and information. There is a close relationship between constructs and measurement, where the latter is the operationalisation of the former. However, the construct equivalence is no guarantee of measurement equivalence. For example, some advertisements utilise the ideas of loyalty, sex appeal or affection that are considered universal concepts. However, to determine the form that these different concepts display in different cultures is difficult. If researchers use identical measures for such concepts, it is likely that the data provided will be unreliable for making a realistic assessment of the market.

International researchers use one of two general types of measures in their studies, the *emic* or *etic* approach. The *emic* approach believes that behavioural or attitudinal phenomena are expressed in a unique manner in each culture. The logical extension of this position is that comparative analysis is not possible. The *etic* approach is focused on identifying universals. According to Usunier,[8] market research measurement instruments that are adapted to each national culture (the emic approach) offers more reliability than tests applicable to several cultures (the etic approach) or 'culture-free tests'. Other equivalencies that the researcher must be aware of under this category are the following.

Gradation equivalence – this refers to equivalence in the units of measurement such as weight, volume, etc. In cross-cultural studies the validity of a rating scale is affected by the metric equivalence of the scale. Pras and Angelmar[9] found that difficulties were encountered when an attempt was made in determining lexical equivalents in different languages of verbal descriptions on the scale. In the marketing context, equivalence is required in entities such as product quality and safety procedures, and these invariably differ from country to country. What is even more difficult to ascertain are perceptual cues such as form, shape or colour. Colour has different interpretations in different cultures – red is considered quite sacrilegious in some African countries while in many Far Eastern cultures it is a good luck colour (*see* Chapter 6). Naturally this has implications for the researcher in terms of gradation equivalence.

Translation equivalence – this refers to the verbal and non-verbal languages which have to be considered when using a research instrument in different markets with various languages or when it is used for secondary sources. Although the researcher needs to translate verbalised statements, it is the non-verbal stimuli that need to be looked at most carefully. Both verbal and non-verbal translations are necessary requirements to establish the construct validity, and can be subject to much error.

As noted above, translation equivalence is important when developing instruments to collect primary data; however, it is equally important when translating secondary data. It is often assumed, for example, that British English has the same meanings and connotations as American English. This is not so, for if we consider the most obvious measurement unit of a billion, in the USA it is 1000m while in the UK it is a million million.

Scale equivalence – when the researcher is evaluating the results presented in a secondary data document, the scale used is critically important if the results are required to make comparisons. For example, in attitudinal measurements, some countries like the USA uses a 5–7 point scale whilst others use a 10–20 point system.

Data collection techniques

The selection of research techniques will depend on a number of factors:

1 the extent of objectivity desired – if the firm requires objective data then standardised techniques would be preferable;

2 if the firm requires a high degree of structure in its data collection, then it will require fewer open-ended questions and less time;

3 the firm needs to determine whether the data collection is to be in a controlled environment or not;

4 The cultural preferences of the firm will also determine the research technique, which in turn is influenced by national preferences – for example, US companies are inclined to select survey techniques with much statistical manipulation of data, while Japanese firms prefer to rely on the 'soft' approach. This entails obtaining data directly from the channel members ('soft data') and also from sales figures, stock levels, etc. ('hard data').[10]

Data collection predominantly uses the processes of *observation* or *communication*. The former involves observing present and past behaviour (e.g. past data includes looking at secondary data), whilst the latter involves asking questions and receiving a response. The communications process is achieved by the use of telephone and mail surveys, or by personal interview. In general, the choice of data collection techniques is closely related to the process of measurement and is a two-way relationship. That is, the measurement considerations affect the choice of techniques, and at the same time the content and structure of the measurement instrument can be influenced by the data collection technique. The best data collection technique is a function of what needs to be researched, who has to be contacted, the sample size and how members of the sample can be reached. The main ways to obtain information from primary sources are observation, experiments and surveys, which is considered the most powerful method of hypothesis testing for cross-cultural surveys.[11] We will now briefly discuss each of the major instruments.

Observation

Observation requires the researcher to be a non-participant when observing behaviour and activity. This method is particularly useful for researchers who are not familiar with a market situation and can reduce the lead time in developing an understanding of it. A further benefit is that there is a less opportunity for the observer to impose any self-reference criterion. This makes the assumption that the observer understands what he/she is observing, and can interpret it. The other advantages are that it is not obtrusive and it is very appropriate when other techniques may affect how the subjects might respond. For example, a UK cosmetics producer can obtain information on how its EU competitors are doing by hiring an agency to observe their promotional campaigns in various markets. The disadvantages of this method are that the subjects may behave differently if they become aware that they are being observed; the task of observing may also become complex because of the multiplicity of languages involved. There may be also bureaucratic obstacles to clear if one wants to observe behaviour in a retail outlet.

Experiments

Experimenting involves testing the impact of a given marketing decision. A chocolate producer may choose a small area to test market the product first and gauge consumer reaction before launching it nationally. In theory, experimental techniques are applicable to all markets; in the global context, however, this is much more difficult to achieve as it is difficult to control the experiment's reliability. This difficulty is compounded when the experiments are conducted in different cultures because of the comparability problem discussed earlier.

Surveys

Surveys involve asking questions directly, usually conducted via questionnaires which are administered by telephone, mail or personally. Surveys are used to gather information that may be difficult or impossible to collect by the other methods. The type of information gathered includes behaviour patterns, knowledge and attitudes. This method presupposes that the subjects can understand and respond to the questions posed. If the researchers have a low knowledge base about the target population and the product market, then an open-ended approach to collecting data would be more suitable. On the other hand, if there is a high knowledge base about the research topic, then a structured and standardised approach would be more appropriate. We will now briefly examine some of the major survey techniques.

Mail survey

Mail surveys are generally used in many industrial market research projects and are an effective technique that is frequently used. On a per-unit basis this method is very cost-effective. When applied to the global market this technique can have severe limitations – varying levels of literacy, poor postal service infrastructure or unreliable delivery, the questionnaire may be in the wrong language, the address database may not be comprehensive and up to date, and there may be a low response rate because of poor motivation.

The development of telecommunication and computer technology has given international marketers an additional aid to their arsenal of techniques. Computer-aided surveys have been used on a frequent basis to conduct research on consumer behaviour. This method has been used mainly in highly industrialised economics where there is access to computers and the level of computer literacy is high. The advantage of this method is that subjects produce fewer errors and biases when compared to other survey techniques. The development of the World Wide Web or Internet has accelerated the process of using technologically-driven aids in international market research.

Telephone surveys

Telephone surveys presuppose that the relevant country market has a well-developed telephone and communications infrastructure. The advantage of this technique is that it is time-saving, has a higher response rate because of the greater motivation to answer telephone calls and finally is economic in that a researcher can remain in one location and conduct regional research to a cluster of country markets such as in Europe. The disadvantages are that there is a limited ownership of private telephones, lack of comprehensive telephone directories and there is the unknown quantity of ex-directory numbers. In addition, the nature of this method means that any data obtained will be highly biased, and the anonymity of the researcher may induce a low response rate for fear of revealing information to competitors; in some cultures there may also be low response rates as it may not be customary to speak to strangers.

Personal interviewing
Compared to other survey methods personal interviewing is a very expensive approach. However, it is perhaps one of the most cost-effective techniques in the sense that the interview format is very flexible and therefore encourages a high response rate, and it can address complicated and complex issues on the spot. The result is a higher quality of data, the only caution being that the interviewer's social position and language should be congruent with the target group. Personal interviews are also used in situations where there is poor telephone and postal infrastructure and where the literacy level is low.

A major problem with surveys in the global context is the difficulty of obtaining valid, reliable and comparable data. There are cultural constraints in using the various types of survey methods – for example, there may be a dearth of telephone lines in the particular regional market, as mentioned above; women participants may be inaccessible to be surveyed; with respect to new products, subjects may lack responsibility in terms of saying one thing when their buying behaviour reflects the opposite opinion. Generally, conservative views prevail for new products.[12] In spite of these difficulties, survey methods are a useful method of collecting large quantities of data that can be statistically analysed.

Box 8.2
VIEWING LABS[13]

The debate on what constitutes an ideal research environment in market research is perennial, especially on whether one should use a viewing lab or a member of the public's front room. The use of one-way mirrors or viewing laboratories have generally been the dominant mode for qualitative research in Europe and the USA; however, UK marketers and research firms appear not to have fully taken on board viewing labs to catch up with the rest of the world. Traditionally, UK researchers have focused on the use of the living-room methodology, using the arguments that it is natural and responses will be more forthcoming. The proponents of viewing labs argue that they have advantages such as allowing more involvement for both clients and researchers, although clients do view the proceedings unobserved. Furthermore, viewing labs are advantageous in the early stages of research before a product or campaign has been undertaken. The use of labs also allows clients to get closer to the consumers as well as hearing first hand what they think of the company's brands. In the UK, companies such as Barclays, Nestlé, Honda and Guinness have all used viewing labs to get consumer views and suggestions. One of the main disadvantages of this methodology is that it is an artificial environment when compared to the 'real' living-room of the consumer. This point is countered by some researchers, who argue that whether in the home or lab surroundings, discussing a product is unlikely to feel 'normal' in any environment.

Sample design
The researcher needs to obtain results which represent the true market situation, and this means that the study must reach the representative members of the population

under investigation. This is usually specified in the formulation stage of the research process, and is important as the data from the sample can then be used in making inferences about the larger population. It is rare that that the entire population will need to be examined. The researcher also needs to be clear about the following when designing the sample:

1 the size of the sample, which will partly be dictated by the availability of resources;

2 where the sample is to be selected;

3 the process of sample selection – this will determine whether the researcher can make inferences about the larger group.

As with the earlier stages of the research process, the issue in the cross-cultural sampling process is the selection of samples that can be considered comparable across country markets. It has been said that reaching perfect comparability is almost impossible.[14] Some of the unique problems encountered in cross-cultural studies are:[15]

● to identify and operationalise comparable populations

● to select samples which are not only representative of their populations but are comparable across countries.

With respect to the first problem, a population can be defined by external criteria such as income, age, etc., or by internally dictated traits which are inherent in the subjects under study, such as personality or psychological traits. Both techniques encounter comparability problems – for example, if we take demographic definitions such as income groupings, education, occupation, etc., they tend not to correspond exactly from one country to another. It may be the case that specific income groups have different life-styles in different cultures. In some cultures in less developed markets it may even be necessary to add tribal membership to the demographics, as this can be extremely important.

Using household addresses to estimate potential market behaviour can be highly misleading; in a polygamous society where husbands have more than one wife, for example, this could pose difficulties in assessing the reliability of the data. With regard to the second point about representative samples, it is not always possible to select comparable samples from each population: it is time-consuming, costly and difficult. Furthermore, there may be such extreme variations from representative samples from each population that comparative analysis is virtually impossible. A sample which has 50 per cent men and 50 per cent women will have different implications in societies where women have lower status to those where they have equal rights. To overcome some of the problems, it is quite common for international researchers to restrict the scope within the sample and focus on selected demographic variables so that comparisons can be made based on the selected variables, thereby sacrificing representativeness.

Data collection

It is important to check the quality of the data collection process to ensure data quality. In some markets, the administrative procedures, such as the processing of questionnaires, which may be haphazard, may not be up to the requisite standards. It is also sometimes useful to check the data if it appears inconsistent with the general perception of the samples under study. This can be achieved by comparing secondary data.

There are organisational issues related to data collection which companies will need to address, such as the following.

1 Whether the research should be *centralised* or *decentralised*. The answer is determined partly by the strategies adopted by the company – i.e. whether the firm adopts a standardised or customisation approach to world markets – and also by the size of the company and the extent of its overseas operations. The decentralised approach involves establishing local affiliate research centres where the entire research is done locally and the final report is sent to the headquarters. In some instances, headquarters may set the parameters of the research project. With a centralised approach, the research focus and design are determined by headquarters and then sent to local affiliates for implementation. Naturally, there are arguments for and against each approach but these are not discussed here.

2 Whether research should be done *in-house* or *outsourced*. Many companies who do not have a substantial proportion of their sales from overseas cannot justify in-house research, for a number of reasons:

   (a) the high cost of maintaining a research staff cannot be justified;

   (b) they do not have in-house expertise to design and conduct research;

   (c) they lack familiarity with foreign markets;

   (d) they lack linguistic competencies, which necessitates the outsourcing of the research unless it is secondary data desk research.

Analysis and interpretation

Once the data is collected, it must be coded and tabulated before analysis. Analysis and interpretation will be required in order to answer the research questions that were initially formulated. The measurement instruments, data collection techniques and sampling procedures will determine the type of analysis that can be undertaken. The quality of analysis will also be a function of the research tools used.

Reporting results and follow-up

The research report is the culmination of the research process and the focus of the presentation is communications. The report must be complete in the sense that it contains all the information required as formulated in the research objective; and it must be concise. At times, these two attributes will conflict, in that a well structured and designed report may contain irrelevant or tangential information which does not meet its objectives. In addition, such a marketing report will have no impact in changing the organisation's current level of knowledge and understanding. Follow-up really involves the management team, who must now examine the report's recommendations and make their decisions based upon the analysis presented. If the report recommends adaptations to the marketing promotional campaign for some of the markets the firm is involved in, for example, this must be communicated to the relevant departments, otherwise the research effort becomes an ineffectual exercise.

SOURCES OF INFORMATION FOR GLOBAL MARKETING

Having discussed the research process and highlighted some of the issues of concern, we now turn our attention to examining in more detail some of the issues and problems confronting international market researchers. Companies undertaking foreign market research need to access a variety of information services and sources. We can classify information according to the internal and external sources:

- *internal sources* include company documentation and records and the knowledge gained by company individuals who in the course of their work obtain data from their contacts with customers, suppliers, government personnel and even competitors
- *external sources* include primary and secondary sources.

Primary sources are information obtained by experiments, observation, surveys and other techniques, and the research is specifically commissioned by the company involved. As discussed earlier, conducting primary research is complicated by different environmental factors and market conditions. In many instances, primary research is essential for the formulation of a marketing plan. For example, in global segmentation strategies, the firm will need to have data on how segmentation variables such as life-styles, income, etc. can be applied to different country markets. In these instances, primary research is necessary.

Secondary sources refer to published information from home government publications, commercial banks, foreign embassies and consulates, trade papers, magazines, business and trade association publications, books and other published research studies. International institutions such as the World Bank, IMF, EU, United Nations, etc. all provide statistical data with a wide coverage of topics for many countries. A major development in secondary information has been the development and availability of on-line and CD-ROM databases. Specialist information can now be accessed with this new technology at a competitive cost even to the small firm that is trading internationally. The type and volume of information available through on-line data has expanded spectacularly; the Internet has only added to this information base and the danger is now of information saturation – finding the right information has become crucial for researchers. In a rapidly changing environment, these sources of information are critical to companies wishing to build market databases on potential markets. Relevant information is a strategic asset and can contribute to a firm's competitive advantage.

Secondary data issues

There are advantages, disadvantages and problems when using secondary data for research purposes. The criteria for selecting and evaluating international informational sources are as follows.

1 *Accuracy*: the quality of the information depends on its accuracy. It may be the case that different sources may report different values for variables such as demographic data, GNP, household incomes, etc. of a particular country market. This difference may be attributed to a number of factors:

(a) *definition problems* – various sources may use different measures, for example, measuring the number of 'retail outlets' involves identifying what constitutes a retail outlet. This could lead researchers to different statistics;

(b) *timeframes* – the timeframes used for data collection may differ. It may be the case that adjustments are made to the data before the publication date (for highly sensitive statistics such as trade, inflation or balance of payments figures). These may be understated or overstated by government departments for political reasons;[16]

(c) *collecting data* – in many emerging markets the mechanism for collecting data may be inadequate or the population have a low literacy level. In such cases it is not uncommon for estimates to be listed rather than the actual data collected. Low *per capita* income countries tend to have weaker data sources when compared to higher income *per capita* countries;

(d) *purpose* – the purpose for collecting data may also influence the accuracy. If respondents feel that the data that is collected is then used by governments to assess tax bands, it is likely that the data will be incomplete. Income earnings or factory production figures, for example, may be distorted to avoid paying the requisite tax band.

Great caution is therefore needed by researchers, especially to understand how a statistic is defined in the particular country, and which data is best suited for the research being undertaken.

2 *Reliability:* the reliability of information is affected by the objectivity of the information base. If the interested party (supplier or government) wishes to encourage consumers or investors to behave in a particular way, the information is unlikely to be accurate. Tourist organisations may not report epidemics or political instability, for example, for fear of hurting the tourist industry. In the UK, the government has been accused of providing incomplete and even inaccurate information concerning the spread of 'mad cow disease' or BSE. Furthermore, if the measurement is repeated in a different context or time, will the same results prevail?

3 *Timeliness:* this refers to being up to date and is a defining quality of good data. Data that is too old may be irrelevant for the current problem. An indicator of timeliness is when the data was last published. Some data variables change rather slowly (such as *per capita* income, income distribution, population density, etc.); some data change rapidly (such as political opinion polls, where a week is considered old information).

4 *Availability:* data is not always available in equal quantity, aggregation and detail from all country markets. Developed economies with the necessary resources tend to have much more detailed data compared to emerging markets. The scarcity of data, especially in developing economies, is a very serious problem for global marketers. For example, the Asia Pacific markets are considered key markets for growth in the next millennium, and detailed information is required in this region. Yet there is a consensus that countries such as China, Vietnam and Taiwan do not have reliable data for various reasons – from government influence to lack of information infrastructure.[17]

5 *Comparability*: this is another measure of data quality. Comparable data may not be available to make cross-national comparisons. Some countries may not use the same categories when displaying the distribution of income or data may be available only in some of the markets. There are a number of factors which may explain the lack of comparability:

   (a) different definitions are used – for example, the concept of 'youth market' can vary in different markets from the 10–14, the 15–24 or the 13–20 age group;[18]

   (b) there is a dearth of data- and information-gathering agencies in many emerging markets and this may be a contributing factor in the variation of data quality and quantity;

   (c) for many indicators, such as productivity data, inflation and employment figures, it may be the case that different base years have been used.

   For the researcher to make a judgement about the value of the data, they need to assess who collected the data, how was it collected and for what purpose.

6 *Relevance of data:* even good quality information may be worthless to the decision makers in the company if the contents are irrelevant. The data must assist management to formulate their strategic marketing plans and to make decisions. This relevance criteria is an important variable in evaluating the type of information.

7 *Costs of data*: the firm needs to assess the costs of acquiring data against the value it derives from improved decision making resulting from better information flow. Some types of information come at a nominal price or even free, but the firm needs to guard against processing costs – i.e. it still has to gather, analyse, store and discard unwanted data. Finally, the firm needs to evaluate the costs of gaining information that is cheap but not relevant to its needs: it may even be worthwhile for the firm to undertake primary research to gain the specific data for its strategic marketing needs.

Primary data issues

Primary data collection is undertaken only when the sources for secondary data are inadequate. There are a number of problems faced in primary research, such as inaccurate sampling leading to errors, respondent biases in the interview stage of the process and researcher bias. It could be argued that the latter two are the major cause for non-comparability of results from different country markets. We will now examine some of these problems in more detail.

Respondent bias
Different cultural markets will inevitably produce different responses to interviews or surveys. There are three types of respondent bias:[19]

1 *Social bias* – we can distinguish three types of social bias when collecting primary material:[20]

   (a) *courtesy bias* relates to respondents in some cultures, who give researchers answers they feel are desired by the interviewers; this is particularly strong in Middle Eastern and Asian cultures – Japanese culture, for example, is deeply imbued with the concept of not offending another person or making them 'lose face';

(b) *social desirability bias* refers to the response of some subjects in giving answers that reflect their social standing, educational level, etc.; this phenomenon is quite strong across countries with certain social groupings, especially the upper classes or well educated groups;

(c) *topic bias* deals with the sensitivity of particular topics or areas in different cultures: certain subjects like sex, women's role in society or public display of affection are taboo in some Middle Eastern cultures and in countries like China and India; therefore, in some of these cultures women may not be able to respond to interview or surveys personally. Under these circumstances a mailed questionnaire for researching the female market would be more appropriate. Another aspect of the response style of cultural groups concerns the accuracy of their responses. Certain groups might understate their responses to certain questions whilst others would exaggerate.

2 *Non-response bias* – there are cultural patterns of non-response at both country and individual levels. In one study the response rate of several countries under investigation varied from 15 to 40 per cent. There is a strong tendency among former socialist economies to be reticent when interviewed, given the previous culture of conformity. There is also variation in individual item non-response and this varies according to different countries. For example, US respondents were more likely to answer personal questions compared to UK respondents. Japanese and Indian respondents were more reluctant to answer questions related to sexuality or which had a sexual connotation.

3 *Researcher–respondent interaction bias* – most primary research requires researcher–respondent interaction. There are two aspects to this problem, the first concerns the location in which the interaction takes place. In some cultures it is virtually impossible to interview a respondent alone, either at home or in some neutral place, for the subject is always accompanied. In such a situation the presence of 'others' can affect the response outcome for there may be an inclination to give 'appropriate' answers. Second, the social status of the researcher and respondent could affect the outcome. For example, a researcher from the upper strata interviewing a lower-strata subject may find the response biased and misinterpretation of the objective of the study can occur.

Researcher biases

One of the main problems concerning the researcher is the self-reference criterion problem, particularly in interview situations using open-ended questions. This can lead to misinterpretation of data and ineffective communication between the researcher and respondent. The researcher will tend to perceive behaviour in other cultures in terms of their own culture (*see* Chapter 6), and this can lead to systematic bias in the report findings. An attempt to overcome this problem is to build into the research design the perspectives of the researcher in order to minimise the bias, or hire a local research agency if one is available.

Linguistic and translation problems

There are a number of problems in primary research. The first concerns the translation of the questionnaire which could be grammatically correct but does not incorporate local nuances or convey the appropriate message. Second, the researcher needs to make a decision about which language to use for the questionnaire or interview. In Switzerland, there are three possible languages to use – German, French or Italian. In Singapore, there are two main official languages – Chinese and English. Apart from which language to use in the market concerned, the researchers need to be fluent in the language of the targeted market, as without this mistakes and misunderstandings will occur.

Literacy levels

The low level of literacy in many emerging markets means that to some extent the marketing research techniques used in many industrialised economies cannot be utilised in these markets[21] and pictorial response charts may have to be used.

Sampling frames

There is a problem in obtaining valid and reliable sampling frames in international markets, partly because of the lack of secondary data and marketing infrastructure and partly because data is collected in a more informal manner. Consequently, the construction of the sample will rely heavily on experience and judgement which could inevitably lead to distorted results

THE MARKETING INFORMATION SYSTEM

The collection of primary and secondary information is not just a marketing issue to provide decision makers with relevant information but it is also an organisational one. The function of the marketing information system (MIS) is to systematically provide information resources to the company to evaluate the markets it wishes to enter – i.e. provide information for effective decision making – and it should be a cost-effective resource base. The MIS should contain the following inputs using the '12C' environmental analysis model as illustrated in Fig. 8.3 (overleaf).[22] This detailed information base should provide a solid platform for the company to assess the degree of its competitive advantage in the global market place, and enable it to make cross-country comparisons and identify threats and opportunities so that the firm can design appropriate marketing strategies. In addition, this market intelligence system should keep management abreast on a daily basis of international markets, competition, countries and products. In sum, the MIS should provide the company with cost-effective, timely and relevant information.

One of the implications of the information explosion in the global market place is that knowledge or information is being perceived as an asset in its own right. With respect to the marketing process, the role of information is changing from being a support tool to being a strategic asset that can generate wealth. One effect of this reconstituted role of information is that some organisations have restructured so that they have 'flatter', less hierarchical and less centralised decision-making structures. Such organisational structures are supposed to facilitate the flow and exchange of information between different departments. The more information-intensive the company, the greater marketing's role will be in other functional areas of the company.[23]

The basis for competitive advantage will, therefore, no longer lie in the product itself but in the relationships that the company cultivates with its consumers, markets

Fig 8.3 THE '12C' FRAMEWORK FOR ANALYSING INTERNATIONAL RELATIONS

Country
- general country information
- basis SLEPT data
- impact of environmental dimensions

Currency
- stability
- restrictions
- exchange controls

Choices
- analysis of supply
- international and external competition
- characteristics of competitors
- import analysis
- competitive strengths and weakesses

Channels
- purchasing behaviour
- capabilities of intermediaries
- coverage of distribution costs
- physical distribution infrastructure
- size and grade of products purchased

Concentration
- structure of the market segments
- geographical spread

Commitment
- access to market
- trade incentives and barriers
- custom tariffs
- government regulations
- regulations on market entry

Culture/consumer behaviour
- characteristics of the country
- diversity of cultural groupings
- nature of decision making
- major influences of purchase behaviour

Communication
- promotion
- media infrastructure and availability
- which marketing approaches are effective
- cost of promotion
- common selling practices
- media information

Consumption
- demand and end-use analysis of economic sectors that use the product
- market share by demand sector
- growth patterns of sectors
- evaluation of the threat of substitute products

Contractual obligations
- business practices
- insurance
- legal obligation

Capacity to pay
- pricing
- extrapolation of pricing to examine trends
- culture of pricing
- conditions of payment
- insurance terms

Caveats
- factors to beware of

Source: Phillips, C., Doole, I. and Lowe, R., *International Marketing Strategy* (London: International Thomson Publishing, 1994), 142.

and suppliers. The implication of this scenario is that market intelligence has a key role to play in these relationships and is thus an important strategic asset for the company. The traditional role of marketing as a distinct functional area in the company will become outmoded and obsolete, dissolving the boundary between marketing and the other functional areas.

SUMMARY

The global market research process is complex because of the problems of collecting data in different foreign markets. The international research process has seven stages and is identical to the domestic research process. The objectives are similar for both processes – that is, to provide information to decision makers. However, the global research process has unique problems which can cause potential errors at each stage of the research process. These are lack of familiarity with country markets; the need to achieve comparability in research design, analysis and interpretation; issues of equivalence – construct, functional, conceptual, definitional, market structure, gradation, translation, scale and sampling.

The three major techniques for data collection are observation, experimental and surveys. Data can be divided into primary and secondary sources, the latter being used predominantly by firms relatively new to international markets. To obtain specific information requirements firms normally engage in primary research. There are problems associated with each source of information. With respect to primary data, the major sources of error are the biases made by both researcher and subject. With secondary data, the global marketer needs to be sure that the source of the data is accurate, reliable and comparable. The information that is collected must be evaluated for timeliness, quality, accuracy, comparability, relevance and cost-effectiveness.

Firms need to develop a marketing information system in order to provide ongoing information to decision makers and to pass the information throughout the whole organisation. In addition, information has taken on a strategic importance in shaping the firm's marketing strategy.

REVIEW QUESTIONS

1 What is the difference between global and domestic marketing research?

2 What are the different modes of information acquisition?

3 Identify two aspects of construct equivalence that need to be taken into account when developing a market research instrument for the global market.

4 List the major sources of information for global marketers.

5 What is measurement equivalence, and how can this problem be overcome?

6 What are the major problems of primary data collection?

7 What are the benefits of secondary data collection?

8 What are the advantages and disadvantages of centralised versus decentralised global market research?

9 What is a global marketing information system (MIS)?

10 What is the difference between observation, experimental and survey methods of data collection?

DISCUSSION QUESTIONS

1 Discuss the notion that global market intelligence is more comprehensive than domestic market research.

2 Discuss the criteria for evaluating information in global marketing research.

3 Has marketing intelligence become a strategic asset for the firm? How can the company deploy this asset in the most effective manner?

4 Discuss how the cultural environment can affect the global marketing research task.

5 Is the comparability problem the only major obstacle in global market research?

Case study

AFRICAN SAFARI EXPLORATIONS LTD

Jane Borges was one of three directors for European Consultants Universal Ltd (ECU Ltd), a London-based company which has been in operation since 1989 providing business and marketing consultancies for clients in Europe, Africa and Asia Pacific. One of her recent clients was a medium-sized travel agency called African Safari Explorations Ltd (ASE Ltd). ASE Ltd was based in Harare in Zimbabwe and also had an office in Johannesburg in South Africa. It was interested in Europe's image of Zimbabwe and South Africa as tourist destinations, as it wanted to develop a marketing campaign to increase the number of tourists to these two countries. ASE Ltd was fairly well-known in the African travel industry for its unique travel packages which included ballooning over the game reserve, backpacking in the remote and natural Chimanimani region in the south-east of Zimbabwe, bordering Mozambique.

John Timbers, the director of ASE Ltd, was convinced that a segment of the European travel market would be interested in living healthier lives in natural surroundings with basic amenities. This 'adventure' into the wilds of Zimbabwe would appeal to the nature-loving Europeans who lived predominantly in an urbanised and industrial environment. In addition, this type of tourist package fitted in with the concept of 'ecotourism'. Furthermore, given the former colonial ties of the two countries, English was the main language of communication and this would appeal to the European consumer. Although it was not a new idea to develop 'natural' or 'back to basics' tours for the European consumer, it was certainly a novel idea to develop such holidays in Africa. ASE was interested in determining whether or not a viable European market for such a product might exist. It asked Jane Borges to evaluate the interest among European tourists in 'natural' holidays. There was certainly research done in France and Germany for European 'natural' destinations and it had identified the following market segments – naturalists, outdoor enthusiasts, excitement seekers and families. The European research had found that most 'natural' holiday goers had taken a 'natural' holiday before and about 70 per cent had no children. The largest segment going for 'natural' holidays were the outdoor enthusiasts who were much older and had no children.

Source: Chee Associates (1998). All rights reserved. This case was written by Harold Chee from a consultancy project undertaken by the author in 1995. Names have been changed to protect the identity of the parties to this project.

Questions

1 *What type of research would be needed in this project?*

2 *What are some of the international dimensions that may cause difficulties in implementing such a research proposal?*

FURTHER READING

Churchill, G.A., Jr., 'A paradigm for developing better measures of marketing constructs,' *Journal of Marketing Research*, 16 (February 1979), 64–73.

Churchill, G.A., Jr., *Marketing Research: Methodological Foundations*, 6th edition (Fort Worth: The Dryden Press, 1995).

Hofstede, G., *Culture's Consequences: International Differences in Work Related Values* (Beverly Hills, CA: Sage, 1980).

Hofstede, G., *Culture and Organisations: Software of the Mind* (London: McGraw-Hill, 1991).

Zikmund, W. G., *Exploring Marketing Research* (Chicago: The Dryden Press, 1994).

NOTES AND REFERENCES

1 Ricks, D.A., *Blunders in International Business* (Cambridge, MA: Blackwell, 1993).

2 Toyne, B. and Walters, P.G.P., *Global Marketing Management: A Strategic Perspective*, 2nd edition (Cambridge, MA: Allyn and Bacon, 1993).

3 Crock, S. *et al.*, 'They snoop to conquer', *Business Week* (28 October 1996).

4 Douglas, S.P. and Craig, C.S., *International Marketing Research* (Englewood Cliffs, NJ: Prentice-Hall, 1983); 'Establishing equivalence in comparative consumer research' in Kaynak, E. and Savitt, R. (eds), *Comparative Marketing Systems* (New York: Praeger, 1984).

5 Toyne and Walters, op. cit.

6 Mayer, C.S., 'Multinational marketing research: the magnifying glass of methodological problems', *European Research*, 6 (1978).

7 Ibid.

8 Usunier, J., *International Marketing: A Cultural Approach* (Hemel Hempstead: Prentice-Hall, 1993).

9 Pras, B. and Angelmar, R., 'Verbal rating scales for multinational research', *European Research*, 6 (1978), 62–7.

10 Czinkota, M.R. and Ronkainen, I.A., *Global Marketing* (Orlando: The Dryden Press, 1996).

11 Winter, L.G. and Prohaska, C.R., 'Methodological problems in the comparative analysis of international marketing systems', *Journal of the Academy of Marketing Science*, 11 (1983), 421.

12 Nishikawa, R., 'New product planning at Hitachi', *Long Range Planning*, 22 (1989), 20–4.

13 Dwek, R., 'Through the looking glass', *Marketing* (11 September 1997).

14 Green, R.T. and White, P.D., 'Methodological considerations in cross-national consumer research', *Journal of International Business Studies* (Fall–Winter), 81–7.

15 Toyne and Walters, op. cit.

16 Ibid.

17 Lassere, P., 'Gathering and interpreting strategic intelligence in Asia', *Long Range Planning*, 26(3) (1993).

18 Terpstra, V. and Sarathy, R., *International Marketing*, 6th edition (Chicago, IL: The Dryden Press, 1994).

19 Toyne and Walters, op. cit.

20 Douglas and Craig, op. cit.

21 Malhotra, N.K., 'Methodology for measuring consumer preferences in developing countries', *International Marketing Review*, 5(3) (1988).

22 Phillips, C., Doole, I. and Lowe, R., *International Marketing Strategy* (London: International Thomson Publishing, 1994).

23 Keegan, W.J., *Global Marketing Management,* 5th edition (Englewood Cliffs, NJ: Prentice-Hall, 1995).

PART 3

Global marketing strategies

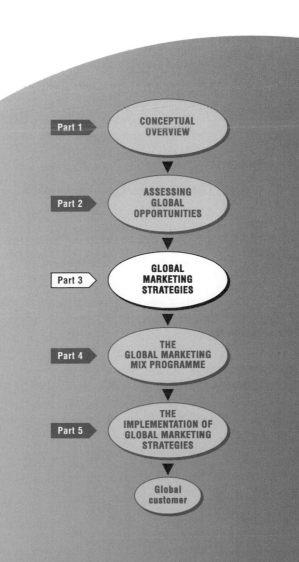

Part 1 — CONCEPTUAL OVERVIEW

Part 2 — ASSESSING GLOBAL OPPORTUNITIES

Part 3 — **GLOBAL MARKETING STRATEGIES**

Part 4 — THE GLOBAL MARKETING MIX PROGRAMME

Part 5 — THE IMPLEMENTATION OF GLOBAL MARKETING STRATEGIES

Global customer

Part 3 of the book consists of four chapters and focuses on choosing the appropriate global strategies and managing the various sub-strategies.

Chapter 9 Global competitive marketing strategies

This chapter explores the myriad of marketing strategies available to a firm once it has entered the global market place. It looks at how firms reformulate their competitive posture and strategic thrust in the international market place. Whether a firm should pursue a concentrated or a diversification strategy is one of the topics considered. An analysis of the basis of a firm's competitive advantages is undertaken and the ensuing positioning and segmentation strategies are identified and examined. Once in the global market, a firm sometimes has to redefine its business and competencies, and the implications of such an analysis are examined with respect to the type of competitive strategies that might be pursued from low-cost to focused niche strategies.

Chapter 10 Market-entry decisions

This chapter considers the three key phases of internationalisation and focuses on the key strategic marketing issues facing the company in each of the different phases. It also examines the internal and external factors that influence which type of entry mode should be pursued. Finally, a consideration of the portfolio models is undertaken to illustrate how firms can use this technique to choose country markets and allocate resources across countries, products and target segments.

Chapter 11 Market-entry strategies

This chapter has extensive coverage of the major means by which foreign involvement may be undertaken, ranging from fulfilling an unsolicited export order to strategic alliances.

Chapter 12 Export management

This chapter discusses the strategic dimensions of import/export operations. It focuses on the needs of small and medium-sized firms and examines the factors encouraging export operations and the various institutions assisting exporting.

Global competitive marketing strategies

INTRODUCTION

There are various perspectives and theoretical bases available to global marketers when formulating global competitive marketing strategies. When adopting such strategies, the firm will be defining the way it will be competing in the global market and it will also play a crucial role in determining performance in the international market place. There are many strands of global competitive marketing strategies, and by adopting some aspects, the firm will not only incorporate a broad strategic direction, but also specify how some activities must be co-ordinated world-wide if the firm is to exploit and sustain its competitive advantages. The purpose of this chapter is to explore the various facets of competitive marketing strategies and how they may be integrated to form the firm's global marketing thrust.

Objectives

This chapter will examine:

- the process of formulating a global marketing strategy
- how firms gain competitive advantages in the global market place
- globalisation, multidomestic and regional strategic approaches
- the types of global segmentation available
- the issues in market concentration versus diversification strategies
- and contrast market-based and resource-based strategies
- competitive generic strategies and their strategic implications.

Once a firm has entered the global market, it must formulate global marketing strategies which are not only consistent with overall corporate strategy but should also be feasible and suitable for implementing an effective marketing mix strategy. A firm may have to take many different types of strategic decisions with respect to global marketing.

1 The extent it should internationalise its operations in an environment which has seen the globalisation of both markets and competition. It is anticipated that by the millennium only a few major players will survive in each world industry.[1] Internationalising its operations is an important and critical decision for many firms, and may be the result of having a proactive policy or simply a reactive one based on a specific business opportunity. The phases of internationalisation are fully discussed in Chapter 10.

2 Once the decision to internationalise has been taken, the company then needs to decide which country/market to select and what type of entry strategy to pursue in the chosen market. The decision making underlying this important topic cannot be stressed enough, and this is reflected in two chapters being devoted to these issues (*see* Chapters 10 and 11).

3 Once in the chosen market(s), the company then has to make a number of strategic decisions concerning the global marketing mix in terms of applying particular global product, place, pricing and promotional policies; these strategic issues are treated extensively in Chapters 13–17.

4 In addition to the above major management decisions, a company also has a number of other strategic issues to address which will impact on their marketing strategy. These include decisions on whether to pursue market concentration or diversification strategies, the type of competitive generic strategies to adopt, product/market strategies, etc. The focus of this chapter is to examine the above issues in some detail.

The philosophical and conceptual framework for the global strategic planning process was discussed in Chapter 3; this chapter will extend and elaborate on those concepts and briefly examine the process of formulating global marketing strategies. It is not the intention here to delve deeply into the vast and complex subject matter of strategic planning analysis. We will examine some types of strategic marketing decisions; other strategic issues will be introduced and treated in greater detail in the chapters that follow.

The globalisation of the world economy and intense competition for markets has created both opportunities and challenges for many companies, with the result that firms need to engage in strategic planning on a global scale in order to be more effective and efficient in resource utilisation, and to sustain competitive advantages. The planning activity allows the firm to understand the environment and develop strategies that will match markets with products. The planning process involves forecasting future conditions, formulating objectives and strategies and mobilising the firm's resources to achieve its objectives. However, planning in the international environment is a much more difficult task because of the different elements involved as illustrated in Table 9.1, indicating the increased complexity of both strategic market planning and its implementation.

Table 9.1 DOMESTIC VERSUS INTERNATIONAL PLANNING

Domestic planning	International planning
1 Single language and nationality	1 Multilingual – multinational – multicultural factors
2 Relatively homogeneous market	2 Fragmented and diverse markets
3 Data available, usually accurate and collection easy	3 Data collection a formidable task, requiring significantly higher budgets and personnel allocation
4 Political factors relatively unimportant	4 Political factors frequently vital
5 Relative freedom from government interference	5 Involvement in national economic plans; government influences business decisions
6 Individual corporation has little effect on environment	6 'Gravitational' distortion by large companies
7 Chauvinism helps	7 Chauvinism hinders
8 Relatively stable business environment	8 Multiple environments, many of which are highly unstable (but may be highly profitable)
9 Uniform financial climate	9 Variety of financial climates ranging from over-conservative to wildly inflationary
10 Single currency	10 Currencies differing in stability and real value
11 Business 'rules of the game' mature and understood	11 Rules diverse, changeable and unclear
12 Management generally accustomed to sharing responsibilities and using financial controls	12 Management frequently autonomous and unfamiliar with budgets and controls

Source: Cain, W.W., 'International planning: mission impossible?', *Columbia Journal of World Business* (July/August 1970), 58. Reprinted with permission.

GLOBAL MARKETING AND GLOBAL STRATEGIC PLANNING

Global marketing is inextricably linked to, and constrained by, the firm's corporate global strategy. If the firm wishes to be competitive by pursuing a penetration pricing strategy to enter a market, for example, it must ensure that its global manufacturing strategy involves low-cost production.

In turn, marketing plays a vital role in the corporate strategic planning process, since it is the link between a firm and its markets. The marketing process assists in the identification, analysis and selection of environmental opportunities, as well as in the development and implementation of strategies to utilise these opportunities. Marketing-supplied information is used in the formulation of corporate strategies, and so marketing plays a key role in the shape of the global corporate strategies that emerge; it would therefore be difficult to separate global marketing strategy from overall corporate strategy. We will now briefly summarise the global strategic planning process as illustrated in Fig. 9.1 (overleaf) which is seen as a series of stages. A global strategy is a statement of the means by which an international firm or multinational company (MNC) can achieve its objectives and we can define a global corporate strategy as:

219

Fig 9.1 STRATEGIC MANAGEMENT PROCESS IN A GLOBAL CONTEXT

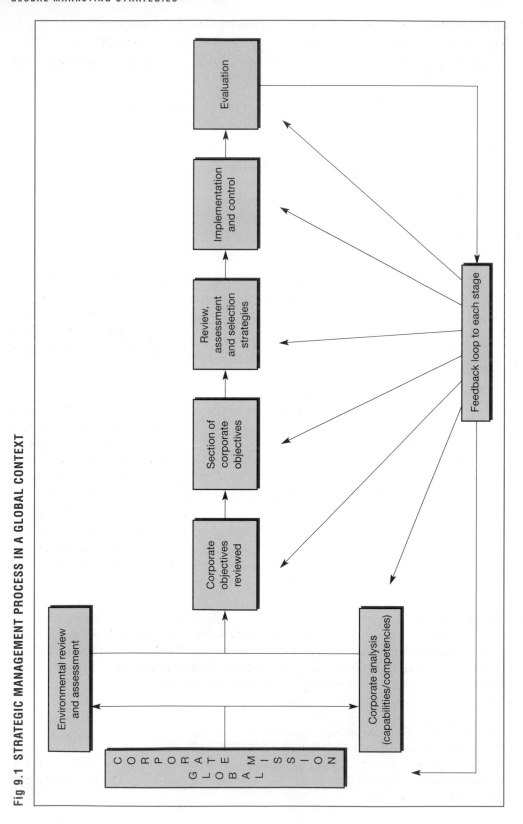

- a unified plan – i.e. it ties together all parts of the global company
- a comprehensive plan – i.e. it covers all major aspects of the company
- an integrated plan – i.e. all parts of the strategy are compatible with each other and fit well together.

A global strategic planning process addresses key questions such as:

- What is our business?
- What should our business be?
- What are our products and services?
- Where are our markets?
- What should our objectives be?
- How can we accomplish our objectives?
- How can we effectively implement our strategies?

Although the concepts of marketing strategic and tactical planning have already been discussed in Chapter 3, we will now turn to a brief discussion of some of the stages of the global strategic planning process to highlight some of the relevant issues that may affect the formulation of competitive strategies. Readers may wish to refer back to that chapter for a revision of the concepts. Figure 9.1 depicts a global strategic management process model.

Definition of the firm's purpose and mission

The definition of the firm's mission involves asking questions such as: What activities should the firm engage in? What products or services should the firm provide? Where are the markets? What types of technologies should be used? Who are the customers? Answers to all these questions form the company's purpose and mission. The firm's global corporate strategy, objectives and mission will therefore define the role played by the marketing function in the organisation. The corporate marketing mission defines

> the major markets the company is interested in satisfying, the way these markets will be segmented and satisfied, and the competitive position taken in particular market segments. By defining the particular markets the firm is interested in, the competitive position to adopt and the segmentation of the markets, the firm is establishing the framework from which the marketing strategic decisions are to be made.

Global environment analysis

The environmental analysis (discussed in Chapters 5–7) provides clues to major events which could affect a firm's strategy. The process involves information gathering, forecasting and recognising the potential threats and opportunities for the firm. For example, firms in the 1990s would be foolish to ignore the impact of the 'green' factor on corporate strategies.

Internal environmental analysis

This is essentially an organisational analysis from which the firm develops its competitive advantages (i.e. its strengths and weaknesses). This involves an assessment of the firm's operations and performance, its resources and capabilities, management expectations, competencies, etc.

Competitor analysis

This involves an analysis of many aspects of the company's competitors. The assumption underlying this type of analysis is that a firm's relative position within the industry, and hence its long-run profitability, is determined by the degree to which it is able to establish a sustainable advantage over its competitors. The analysis is a detailed appraisal of many aspects of competitors' current strategies and capabilities – such as marketing/selling strategies, products, overall costs, financial strength, general manager ability, etc.

The last three stages will necessitate strategic planners to focus simultaneously across a range of markets rather than on a county-by-country basis. The latter approach could result in a distorted observation of the real performance of the company across world markets. The former approach would provide a more accurate assessment of the type of resource requirements, risk levels, etc. To help marketers in this process various portfolio techniques have evolved to assist in this type of analysis. Global portfolio assessment provides an overview of how the firm can:

1 classify its foreign markets, since this classification will provide a good indication of the importance of those markets to the firm and its role in attaining the company's objectives, which has a bearing on the strategic decisions of the company;

2 determine its allocation of organisational and marketing resources to the market place;

3 determine the degree of modification required to the marketing mix.

The review of the firm's portfolio of markets will therefore identify which business activities should be maintained, reduced or eliminated. Some of the major techniques available to assist firms evaluate their current business activities include the Boston Consulting Group growth-share matrix, the General Electric–McKinsey and A.D. Little portfolio models.

Global objectives

After an analysis of the firm's internal and external objectives environments, the firm will formulate its long-term objectives which will then be translated into short-term objectives and goals.

Generation of alternative strategies

Alternative strategies are also generated to achieve the firm's global objectives.

Global strategy choice

This phase involves evaluating the different alternative strategies and choosing the one that will take best advantage of the opportunities and minimise the environmental threats.

Implementation

This phase involves putting the strategy into action. It involves developing the appropriate organisational structure to support the strategy, the management of human resources and other functional strategies.

Control

Control is the process of evaluating strategy implementation and managing the personnel responsible for it. Control is accomplished through feedback and any strategy that is not working effectively will be dealt with at this stage.

Box 9.1   McDONALD'S COMPETITIVE STRATEGY

The burger market is intensely competitive, and McDonald's, the global fast food company, not only faced a slow-growing market but also tough competition from both the UK-owned Burger King and Wendy International. In response to this, McDonald's competitive strategy was to cut prices in order to stimulate sales, which marked a shift from its previous strategy of introducing more high-priced items. This strategy was approved by the US franchisees and the campaign began in April 1997. In addition to price cuts, the sales campaign incorporated improved service.

Source: Tomkins, R., 'McDonald's price cuts win approval', *Financial Times* (3 March 1997).

This strategic planning a process is a continuous one, each phase being closely related to and dependent on the other phases. Thus a global corporate strategy is a statement of a firm's purpose, direction of growth and long-range objectives. Before we explore some of the different types of generic strategies, we will examine the concept of competitive advantage which is one of the major foundations for a firm's global marketing strategy.

GENERIC STRATEGIC OPTIONS IN THE GLOBAL MARKET PLACE

Having discussed some of the key aspects of the strategic management planning processes, we now turn our attention to some of the generic international strategies that companies can adopt. 'Generic strategies' are so called because they can be applied across markets and across different industry and product sectors. Furthermore, there exist different master and sub-strategies which companies can pursue to compete effectively in the international markets. Firms will tend to pursue several types of strategies from different categories rather than just selecting from one category. In fact, we can say that many firms have so many strategy options available to them that they are spoilt for choice.

Global marketing strategy is not synonymous with global standardisation, the former relating to the application of a common set of strategic principles across most international markets. There may be similarity in products or in the marketing processes, but this is not a requirement. A global marketing strategy looks at the world market as a whole and not on a country-based framework. A *standardisation* strategy is one where firms attempt to achieve similarity across many markets with respect to both their marketing mix and marketing strategies, whereas a *globalisation* strategy involves the integration of many types of country strategies which are subsumed in one global framework. Globalisation is based on the belief that the world is becoming more homogeneous and that national differences are disappearing. Firms therefore need to globalise their strategies across markets in order to take advantage of underlying market, competitive and cost factors. The globalisation of a firm's marketing operations can take several forms, ranging from the globalisation of the firm's marketing mix to global logistics, R&D and manufacturing outsourcing.

Global market segmentation

As discussed earlier in the chapter, the formulation of a global marketing strategy is derived from the development of the global corporate strategy. The initial step in the development of a global marketing strategy is to choose the markets the company wishes to enter. Once the target market(s) is selected, the firm needs to segment its markets and target them to provide benefits to itself and its customers. It will also need to establish the type of entry and competitive strategies it will pursue in the designated markets. It is to these different strategies that we now turn our attention.

Global segmentation is the process of identifying potential consumers at the national or sub-national level who are likely to exhibit similar buying behaviour patterns or respond to the same marketing mix stimuli. After the identification of the segments, the global marketer needs to *target* the international markets, which means selecting the appropriate segments for focusing the marketing effort. Targeting is an important step, as it reflects the fact that the company should identify only consumers who have the potential to respond and whom they can reach most effectively. To reach their chosen target markets, companies need to establish the *positioning* for their product offering – i.e. the position the product occupies in the consumer's mind along some criteria spectrum.

If segmentation is used effectively, then it will allow the company to exploit the benefits of standardisation, while at the same time enabling it to meet the particular needs and expectations of a specific target group. The reasons why firms segment markets is because it enables them to:

- allocate resources appropriately and efficiently
- evaluate the competition and opportunities
- focus its marketing strategies and positioning
- fine tune its marketing mix programme.

Traditionally, global marketers have used environmental bases such as geographical, economic, political and cultural variables for segmenting international markets, as well as other bases such as psychographics (attitudes, values and life-styles), demographics (age, gender, income, occupation, education, etc.), behaviour (usage rates, user status, etc.). There are many bases for segmenting the international market and the major challenge for the global marketer is to choose the most appropriate.

In general, a combination of bases is used in order to produce significant results. For instance, using economic variables alone would not generate sufficient information on which to base a firm's targeting decisions. However, the suitability of some of these approaches has been questioned and new criteria for segmenting international markets have been emerging. Markets which exhibit a high degree of homogeneity with respect to the marketing variables, for example, could be perceived as a segment. In addition, such a grouping could respond to a standardised marketing approach.[2] One of the effects of globalisation on the distribution system is the converging of channel structures, so that we see the emergence of regional and global chains. Markets can therefore be segmented by outlet types for defined groupings – for example, producers of toys can segment their market not only by the number of children but also how their products can be reached by global chains such as Toys 'Я' Us.[3] If we look at the product variable (attitudes towards product attributes, stages of the product life cycle, etc.) we also find global segments emerging regardless of the economic constraints. Producers of durable electronic consumer products such as cassette recorders, microwaves, etc., for example, found sales of their products were buoyant in low income markets; it may be the case that buying behaviour was based predominantly on status or emotional needs. The implications of such buyer behaviour for a global marketer is that product modifications will be minimal and that global segments are emerging across markets of contrasting economic and cultural factors. It is not surprising given that a global segment had already existed for teenage groups for some time. It has been said that the teenage segment is converging even more now because of common tastes in music and sports, and the process has been helped by global communications and increased travel by that market segment.

Identifying groups of consumers with similar needs and wants constitutes the segmentation process, whilst *targeting* involves identifying those segmented groups with the highest potential and selecting one or more of them. According to Keegan,[4] there are three major criteria for assessing opportunities in the targeted markets:

1 *current market size and growth potential*: the key question is whether the current market segment is large enough to sustain long-term profitability. A small segment in one market may not be a profitable proposition but a small segment in a several international markets would be more attractive in the intermediate to long term;

2 *potential competition*: if there is intense rivalry in the market segment then an avoidance strategy may be the best policy to adopt. However, there are many cases whereby firms have made a competitive offensive and gained market share. In the colour film market, the classic rivalry between Kodak and Japan's Fuji company saw the latter entering the US market and, in spite of Kodak's well-entrenched position, still managing to gain market share, albeit a small one;

3 *compatibility and feasibility*: once the company has established that the market segment is viable and there are limited barriers to entry, it needs to decide whether the option is feasible. That is, does the company have the resources to reach the segment, and is the targeted segment compatible with the company's objectives and consistent with its distinctive competencies?

Box 9.2   **GE'S SALES DRIVE**

General Electric, the world's fourth biggest maker of white goods and the eighth-largest supplier of white goods in Europe, is looking to double its sales of domestic appliances in Europe over the next three years. The company wants to increase its annual white goods sale in Europe from about $1bn to $2bn in 2000. If it achieves its goals then its share of European white goods (which include fridges, cookers and washing machines) would rise from about four per cent to eight per cent. It is still well behind the market leaders – Electrolux of Sweden with 20 per cent market share and Bosch–Siemens of Germany with 16 per cent. General Electric's efforts follow a European campaign by Whirlpool, GE's main US rival in white goods and the world's third biggest domestic appliance maker, which cost tens of millions of dollars. The campaign was considered a failure, and this was attributed to Whirlpool's pan-European marketing strategy which ignored the differences between consumers in different countries. GE's strategy is based on a series of domestic appliances that cater for 'a diversity of product types' within the European market. GE also hopes to improve its chances in Europe by placing orders with independent white goods' producers for GE-designed machines and a GE badge.

Source: Marsh, P., 'GE in drive to double sales in Europe', *Financial Times* (3 March 1997).

Targeting strategy

We can identify three types of global target marketing strategies – undifferentiated, differentiated and concentrated marketing.

1 *Undifferentiated global marketing* is really mass marketing to multicountries and the firm engages in a standardised marketing mix. This approach involves a standard-ised product and communications strategy as well as an extensive distribution system. Nike shoes have adopted an undifferentiated approach to their world mar-kets with a global theme of, 'Just Do It'.

2 *Concentrated marketing* involves creating a marketing mix to reach a single segment of the international market. This approach has been used by many clothing and cos-metics companies – Giorgio Armani, Valentino, Boss and other fashion houses, for example, have successfully targeted the luxury and prestige segment of the market.

3 *Differentiated marketing* involves targeting two or more distinct market segments with varied marketing mixes in order to capture a wider market – Ford Motor Corporation targets the upper end of the market with its Mondeo model whilst the Fiesta and Escort are the mass market brands.

Having segmented the market and targeted one or more segments, the company needs to reach the target groups. This is achieved by a positioning strategy whereby the firm creates an image of its product offerings relative to the competitors in the minds of the consumer – Sony is synonymous with quality and BMW is associated with German engineering and sophistication. There are many different positioning strategies that a firm can employ, as with the domestic market, including the following.

1 *Positioning by benefits or solving problems*: many products and services offer solutions to specific consumer problems – DHL positions its world-wide parcel delivery ser-vice as completely reliable; aspirin is positioned as a fast relief for your headache, American Express cards are positioned as being widely accepted.

2 *Positioning against your competitor's product*: this strategy involves comparative pro-motion against other leading product brands, and mainly concerns consumer products such as cars, toothpastes, air travel, car hire, etc. – British Airways is posi-tioned as the 'world's favourite airline'.

3 *Positioning by user category*: this involves positioning the product in respect of the consumers by an emphasis on the type of consumers who use the product/service – some holiday tour packages such as the 18–30 age group are obviously aimed at the younger and less affluent segment, whereas Caribbean holiday cruises are for the niche market for older and more well-off segments of the population. Or take the example of 'multivitamins for men' or soft drinks for vegetarians.

4 *Positioning by product features*: this involves emphasising the product attributes such as convenience in use, sturdy construction, etc. – Canon photocopiers and fax machines stress the durability and reliability to solve any office problem.

5 *Positioning by usage or use occasions*: this relates the product to specific occasions or usage situations – the Marriott hotel chain emphasises that they cater globally for the business traveller's needs.

Recent work in this area seems to suggest that global product positioning can be more effective if the products approach either end of the 'high-touch–high-tech' continuum.[5]

1 *High-tech positioning*: high-tech products are usually purchased on the basis of concrete features and so consumers tend to seek more technical information. Examples of products in this category include cars, electronic goods, computers, etc. Three categories of high-tech products can be distinguished:

   (a) *technical products* – consumers buying these products require a great deal of product information and share a common language such as bond, stock or 486 microprocessor. The marketing implications are that the promotion should emphasise product features and be very informative. Financial services, chemicals, computers, etc. are in this category.

   (b) *special-interest products* – are characterised by a shared experience and high involvement among the buyers. These products are less technical and more leisure oriented. There is a common language with users and items such as Nikon cameras, Nike sports products, etc. are typical.

   (c) *products that demonstrate well* – the product features and benefits of goods in this category are self-evident; the Polaroid instant camera, which has been a very successful global product, is an example.

2 *High-touch positioning*: high-touch products require more emphasis on image and less specialised information, and the consumers for such products are highly involved. There is also a shared common language with users of such products. There are three categories of high-touch products:

   (a) *products that solve a common problem* – the benefits in this product category are understood globally and solve everyday problems, such as soap powder to wash clothes or drinking orange juice to quench a thirst.

   (b) *global village products* – have a global positioning based on the cosmopolitan nature of the product, for example, designer labels in fashion and cosmetics, lower-priced items such as mineral water. Products can also have global appeal by virtue of their country of origin labels: Toyota is associated with Japanese quality whilst Levi's, Calvin Klein and Coke are associated with America.

   (c) *products that use universal themes* – some products have global appeal as discussed above, but there are additional themes which can be transferred to the international arena such as play (recreation/leisure) or heroism (images of romance and courtship).

Global segmentation strategy

A firm operating in the international market can serve the same market segments on a global basis (global market segments), a national basis (national market segments) and on a combined basis (mixed market segments of global and national) as illustrated in Fig. 9.2 (overleaf).[6]

Fig 9.2 TYPES OF GLOBAL SEGMENTATION STRATEGIES

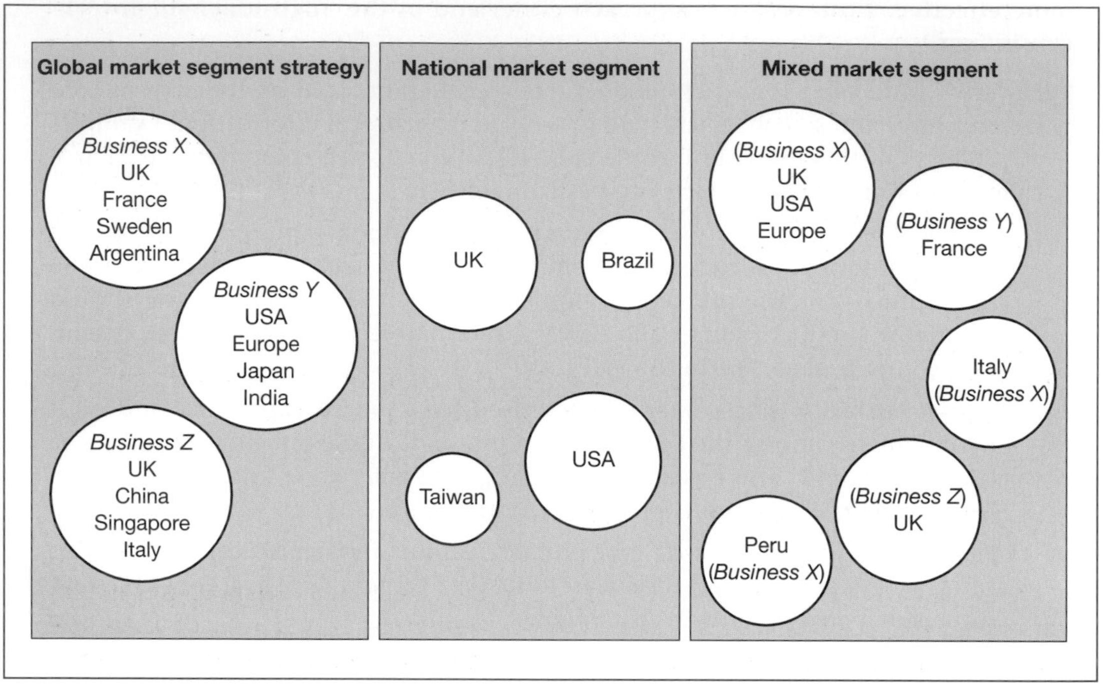

Global market segments

This type of segmentation strategy is usually employed in global industries, and the firm:

1 concentrates on segmenting markets that ignore national boundaries;

2 seeks to identify and serve market segments whose needs cannot be divided into distinct groups of buyers;

3 concentrates on what is common rather than what is different across foreign market segments.

To succeed with a global market segment strategy, a firm would need to develop global competitive strategies:

● global brand names

● universal after-sales service standards

● global product positions

● co-ordinated pricing decisions

● emphasis on using similar channels which would ultimately translate into excellent customer care.

National market segments

These are companies serving the same segments in multiple markets but on a national basis. Using the national market segmentation strategy implies competing with both domestic and global competitors. The competitive advantage of this type of strategy is derived from:

1 marketing strategy flexibility – this means that the company needs the flexibility to exploit local knowledge to serve and respond to local needs if it is to succeed locally. Product development, market research, distribution, pricing, etc. are therefore predominantly determined locally;

2 global marketing support infrastructure – a firm using the national market segmentation strategy supports local activities such as market research, product development and transfers its experiences from other international markets to the local market, thereby benefiting the national market. A key success factor in the national segment strategy is the establishment and deployment of a marketing information system.

Mixed market segments

These are firms using a combination of global and national segments. It is very rare for a firm to pursue a pure global or national segmentation strategy.

GEOGRAPHIC MARKET CHOICE

Once a company has made the decision to internationalise its operations in the pursuit of growth, it needs to determine how many markets to enter and the level of marketing resource allocation. According to Keegan,[7] a company should attempt to seek as many markets as possible, provided this is consistent with the company's resources. In an ideal situation, a firm should target the global market for its products and gain first mover advantage. Spreading itself out like this will result in pre-empting the competition from establishing its own home base from which to venture into the global market. The danger of such a strategy is that it may exceed the company's resources. However, for many companies, entering a single market first will enable it to establish a solid base from which to launch on to the global market. There are, of course, resource allocation implications for pursuing geographic market expansion policies, which in turn will determine the distribution of the firm's resources among particular country markets and products. To ascertain the scope of the desired global market coverage, three strategies are available:[8]

1 *market concentration* – this involves selecting a limited number of markets. There is some debate as to what constitutes a concentration strategy. According to Piercy,[9] a small company which serves up to six export markets is pursuing a concentration strategy; for larger well established firms the figure of 10 would constitute the maximum number;

2 *market diversification* – this focuses on a larger number of markets and normally implies no more than 10–12 countries with equal distribution of marketing resources;[10]

3 *a combination* of the above two.

When the firm decides to choose between concentration and diversification strategies, it will be influenced by a number of factors – such as company-related factors, mix considerations and the market itself, as illustrated in Table 9.2 (overleaf). If a particular market is stable and exhibits high growth rates then the market is an attractive

Table 9.2 FACTORS AFFECTING CHOICE BETWEEN CONCENTRATION AND DIVERSIFICATION STRATEGIES

Factor	Diversification	Concentration
Market growth rate	Low	High
Sales stability	Low	High
Sales response function	Decreasing	Increasing
Competitive lead time	Short	Long
Spillover effects	High	Low
Need for product adaptation	Low	High
Need for communication adaptation	Low	High
Economies of scale distribution	Low	High
Extent of constraints	Low	High
Programme control requirements	Low	High

Source: Ayal, I. and Zif, J., 'Marketing expansion strategies in multinational marketing', *Journal of Marketing*, 43 (1979), 84.

one, and the company is more likely to opt for a concentration strategy. On the other hand, if there is a global demand for the firm's products then a diversification strategy is likely to be adopted. With respect to the marketing mix, a firm adopting a standardised marketing strategy is likely to pursue a diversification strategy. In general, concentration strategies are attractive for small firms because of the low investment required for marketing facilities. There is less market research to be done and less management control is required. On the other hand, a market diversification strategy requires larger investments in the initial stages and is a consequent high risk for the company. The objective is to attain a higher rate of return through market development than market penetration; in the long run this strategy results in market consolidation as unprofitable markets are abandoned.

Fig 9.3 GEOGRAPHIC EXPANSION STRATEGY ALTERNATIVES

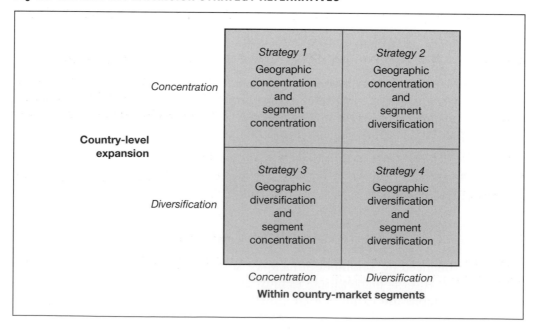

Figure 9.3 illustrates the different combinations of expansion policies together with the firm's segmentation strategy. The firm can adopt a segment concentration approach, which means that it limits its activities to one or a few market segments within each country market. A segment diversification strategy entails extending its business and marketing activities across a number of market segments. Each geographic segmentation combination has implications for the firm's strategic direction, resource allocation and marketing mix programme.

Strategy 1 – Geographic and segment concentration

With this strategy, the firm concentrates on a few market segments in a small number of countries. Six main conditions are necessary for this strategy to be appropriate:

1 the market segments must be large;
2 there are high or stable growth rates;
3 competition in the segments is intense;
4 the market segments are widely dispersed;
5 the segment requires large marketing resources to educate the consumers of the products value;
6 the firm wants to establish an effective distribution system, develop brand loyalty or even exploit scale economies.

Strategy 2 – Geographic concentration and segment diversification

This strategy involves the firm in concentrating on many market segments in a limited number of countries. It is most appropriate in the following situations:

1 the product appeals to more than one segment;
2 the company can attain economies of scale in both distribution and promotion;
3 the consumer profile uses a variety of retail outlets and different shopping habits.

Strategy 3 – Geographic diversification and segment concentration

The firm in this quadrant would typically have a few market segments in a large number of countries. This strategy is suitable for global companies with specialised products which can appeal to the same segment of customers in many countries. It is most appropriate:

1 when the company can attain production economies;
2 when the company has an effective distribution system in each country market – a prerequisite for this type of strategy to be successful.

Strategy 4 – Geographic and segment diversification

This strategy involves the company focusing on many market segments in a large number of countries and it is most appropriate:

1 for large global market companies whose product lines appeal to a numerous national markets;

2 for companies with fewer resources, provided that distribution costs can be kept down, there is limited resource allocation (i.e. management time is devoted to channel members), and if the company is willing to accept superficial coverage of the market.

Strategy 5 – Combination strategies

Although not shown in the matrix diagram (Fig. 9.3), this strategy involves companies using two or more of the above strategies at the same time. This would be most appropriate for diversified multi-divisional companies.

RESOURCE-BASED AND MARKET-BASED OPTIONS

Part 2 of the text covered an analysis of the firm's external environment. It is assumed that the reader will also have carried out an internal audit of the organisation, which entails an analysis of the firm's resources and core competencies; only then is it possible for the firm to develop options for strategy development. This chapter will focus on the strategic options that may arise from an analysis of the company's resources (resourced-based options) and from an analysis of the market opportunities (market-based options). It must be emphasised that the two approaches are not mutually exclusive, and in fact complement each other.

Resource-based options

Resource-based strategies (RBOs) are options based on the differential endowment of strategic resources of the organisation. RBOs have been established for some time[11] and the strategy has gone through faddish phases – for example, in the 1970s and 1980s it was not favourably received. An RBO is most relevant when the opportunities in the market place are limited or the firm has few resources for expansion. RBOs are derived from the resources within the organisation, especially in functional areas such as finance, operations, human resources, etc. The strategic resources comprise an organisation's assets, capabilities, information, business attributes, organisational processes, etc. Essentially, RBOs are developed from:

1 *the resource-based capabilities* of the organisation – i.e. the assets of the company. The assets of Microsoft Corporation, for example, are predominantly its human resources – that is, its intellectual capital;

2 *the core competencies* of the organisation, which are the technologies, skills and knowledge base of the firm.

The most critical resources have the following characteristics:

1 superior in use – for example, organisational routines which drive the business activities;

2 difficult to imitate;

3 difficult to substitute for;

4 more valuable within the business than outside.

The assumptions underlying the RBO model are that:

1 the strategic resources that the firms control in the industry are heterogeneous;

2 heterogeneity is assumed to be long-lasting, as the resources are not perfectly mobile across firms;

3 the firm's goal is to earn above normal returns.

Lynch[12] provides a useful framework for analysing the resources of an organisation and the subsequent development of options (*see* Fig. 9.4). A useful starting point is to consider the value chain in the development of these options as it contributes to the development of competitive advantages. Any strategic option should add value to an organisation – i.e. the value of the output should exceed the cost of the inputs. A firm's activities can be divided into upstream and downstream activities and value can be added in the value chain of activities as follows:

1 *upstream value-added activities* – these are activities that add value early on in the value chain. The procurement of inputs, for example, could mean that the firm engages in bulk buying and efficient purchasing, which would keep costs down. In addition, innovations in the process function would also reduce the costs of production. The end result may be to have standardised products, as one of the strategic resource options may be to focus on lower costs;

Fig 9.4 RESOURCE-BASED STRATEGIES

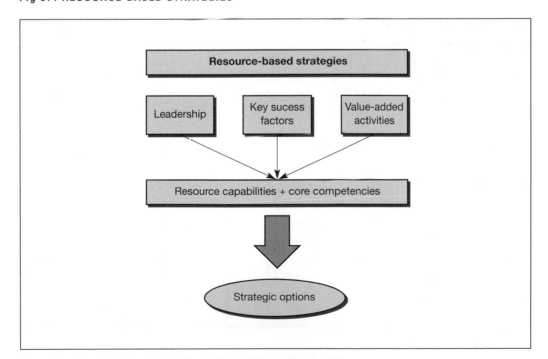

Source: Adapted from Lynch, R., *Corporate Strategy* (London: Pitman Publishing, 1997).

2 *downstream value-added activities*: these add value later in the production cycle. The major activities involved here would include product differentiation processes, market positioning, R&D, etc.

Depending on the firm's activities, some may be predominantly located in upstream activities (such as mining companies who are involved in extraction processes); other companies are mainly involved in downstream activities (such as marketing and advertising functions, particularly the service sector companies). A consideration of the value chain of an organisation is important as it helps firms determine and identify their competitive advantages. Understanding where and how value can be added will enable the firm to generate RBOs.

Therefore, to develop its competitive advantage, a firm needs to carry out an analysis of both its internal and external external environments and of its competitors (*see* Fig. 9.5) – i.e. an analysis of its resources, business practices, organisational structure, leadership skills, architecture (relationship network within and around the organisation), etc. The assessment of its internal environment (its strengths and weaknesses) will enable the firm to establish whether it has distinctive competencies and resources with which to exploit the market opportunities. Sustaining competitive advantage in the RBO model is derived from the company's distinctive product or ability to sell the product at a lower cost. This in turn is tied directly to the distinctiveness in the firm's inputs (resources) used to make the product. Strategy is therefore derived from the

Fig 9.5 DETERMINATION OF A FIRM'S COMPETITIVE ADVANTAGES

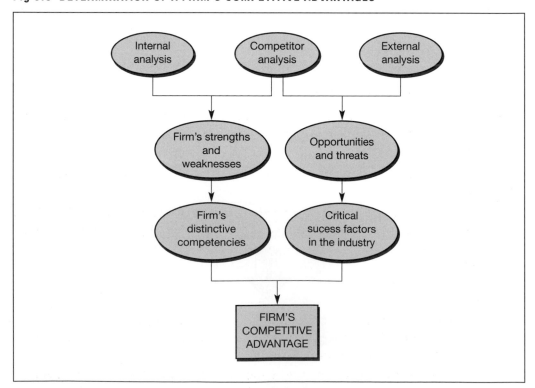

Source: Dahringer, L.D. and Mühlbacher, H., *International Marketing* (Reading, MA: Addison-Wesley, 1991); reproduced with permission.

firm's conscious move to capitalise on its unique heterogeneous resources – i.e. the main drivers of competitive marketing strategy are internal to the business, but the main thrust is on the intangible skills and resources that will constitute the principal engine of competitive choice. Honda, the Japanese car manufacturer, is well known for its excellent after-sales service, for example, and this constitutes one of its distinctive competencies. To identify its competitive advantages, a firm needs to link its unique competencies with those factors which are critical for success – these are known as key success factors. The firm should be aware of factors in the environment which may be critical for success. For example, a UK manufacturer of English china exporting to Japan may find that a critical factor to succeed in that market is to have networking skills.

Since sustainable competitive advantage is critical to any firm competing in the global market place, we will elaborate on this concept. A firm's *competitive advantages,*[13] then, are its unique competencies which are in demand in the market and which competitors are unable to provide at that point in time. For example, if similar products or services are offered and the quality of the competitors' products is poor or the items are expensive then these aspects – high quality or low cost – constitute the firm's competitive advantages. Competitive advantages can be derived from:

1 the firm's products which are competitively priced – for example, high-quality television sets, calculators, watches, etc.;

2 the firm's markets;

3 the firm's technological orientation – i.e. technically superior products: the Sony Corporation prides itself on the excellence of its high-quality technical electronic products;

4 product quality;

5 delivery;

6 flexibility of service, etc.

From these distinctive competencies, the company can begin to develop its global marketing strategies. There are a number of observations to make about competitive advantages.

1 When these advantages are unique to the firm they tend to be the strongest competencies.

2 When a firm does not have a unique competitive advantage on which to build strategy, it can create niches in the market. This is done by examining what the differences are between itself and its competitors, which it can then exploit in various ways.

  (a) Develop new products.

  (b) Develop customer segments that have not yet been exploited. The Japanese car manufacturers offered US consumers a compact car which had not been previously available. The Japanese manufacturers used this competitive advantage to gain a strong presence in the US car market.

  (c) Develop competitive advantages which are not available to firms operating only in domestic markets, as the following examples illustrate.

(i) *Cost-leadership advantages*: these can be derived from many sources. The global company can attain economies of scale advantages since the demand for its products will be from many international markets. The firm will derive economies from its manufacturing process and thereby gain a low-cost advantage over its competitors. If the firm operates in different countries, the firm can also take advantage of cost differences in resources and labour to reduce its administrative and manufacturing costs, and thus develop a further competitive advantage over its rivals. The firm can also spread its R&D costs across many national markets. This will result in lower costs per unit of output, which is then transformed into customer benefits.

(ii) *Access to global resources and information*: the global firm can develop its competitive advantages by having access to global resources and information. A competitive advantage can stem from operating in markets where technological innovation is taking place. The global firm will be in a position to acquire this information to improve its technical operation and product offerings. The firm can also gain competitor information when it operates in the domestic markets of its foreign competitors. The global firm will then be in an advantageous position to understand its competitors' strategies and business practices. American and Japanese firms operating in the EU markets, for example, will be able to evaluate their European rivals and gain much valuable information. The global firm has access to other resources which may give it a competitive advantage, such as financial resources obtained from foreign markets where they are abundant and inexpensive. Other resources could include access to experienced international marketing personnel, access to reliable and effective market information, etc. The global firm can also reduce duplication of effort and resources in its various markets and thereby gain economies – for example, when developing and testing new products it need not carry out these processes in more than one country.

Market-based options

Market-based options (MBOs) are those that arise from exploiting marketing opportunities and build on the analysis of the customers and competitors. MBO strategies do not preclude an analysis of the firm's internal resources and the value chain – in MBO strategies, the primary emphasis is on the *external* industry–market factors as being the main drivers of the company's global competitive strategies. The firm's strategy is developed as a response to the industry–market imperatives, and the MBO model makes the following assumptions:

1 firms within the industry are identical in terms of the strategic resources they have and control;

2 the major drivers of the firm's global competitive strategies are industry–market factors rather than organisational resources or characteristics;

3 the firm's goal is to attain above-normal returns.

Fig 9.6 MARKET-BASED STRATEGIES

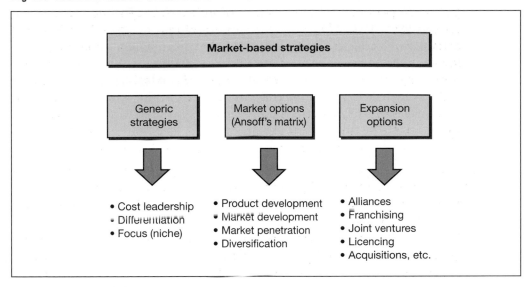

Source: Adapted from Lynch, R., *Corporate Strategy* (London: Pitman Publishing, 1997).

Under the MBO model, a firm's sustained competitive advantage is obtained by implementing strategies which differentiate products or offer them at lower prices, erect barriers to entry, benefit from scale economies or exploit experience or learning-curve effects. In other words, under the MBO model competitive advantage is attained by exploiting the firm's internal strengths through responding to environmental opportunities, neutralising external threats and avoiding internal weaknesses. MBOs can be divided into three broad categories as illustrated in Fig. 9.6:

1 generic strategies (discussed extensively in this chapter);

2 market options (i.e. the Ansoff matrix, explored later in this chapter);

3 expansion options (e.g. joint ventures, strategic alliances, licensing, etc., discussed at length in Chapter 11).

Generic strategies

This section will focus on the different types of competitive strategies that firms can pursue in the global market place. Competitive strategies are the approaches that a company adopts in order to compete more effectively to strengthen its market position. The principle of *competitive strategy* is that a firm should aim to create and gain a sustainable competitive advantage over its competitors; only in this way can a firm attain above-average profits and improve its market position. Michael Porter[14] of Harvard University has pioneered much of the work on competitive strategies. For a firm to achieve a competitive advantage over its rivals in a particular industry, he suggests two generic competitive strategies:

1 *lower cost* – whereby a firm can produce and market a similar product more efficiently than its rivals;

2 *differentiation* – the ability of a firm to provide a product whose attributes differ significantly from the competitors' products in terms of better quality, more special features or technical superiority.

Porter views these two strategies as mutually exclusive. A firm which pursues both will be 'stuck in the middle' and will be guaranteed low profits (this will be discussed later in this chapter). Porter proposes that the firm's competitive advantage in the industry is also determined by its *competitive scope*, i.e. the breadth of the firm's target market. Before the firm selects one of the two generic competitive strategies it must first determine its target market. The firm can choose either:

1 a broad target – aim at the mass market; or

2 a narrow target – select a market niche.

Combining the two competitive strategies with the two types of target markets will give us four variations of generic strategies, as illustrated in Fig. 9.7. With a broad mass market we have *cost leadership* and *differentiation* strategies. When the two competitive strategies are focused on a narrow target they are called *cost focus* and *focus differentiation*.

Cost leadership

Cost leadership is a low-cost competitive strategy that is targeted at the broad mass market. The basis for competitive advantage under this strategy is that the low-cost leader has lower overall costs than its competitors. A number of advantages accrue from this strategy for the low-cost producer:

Fig 9.7 GENERIC STRATEGIES

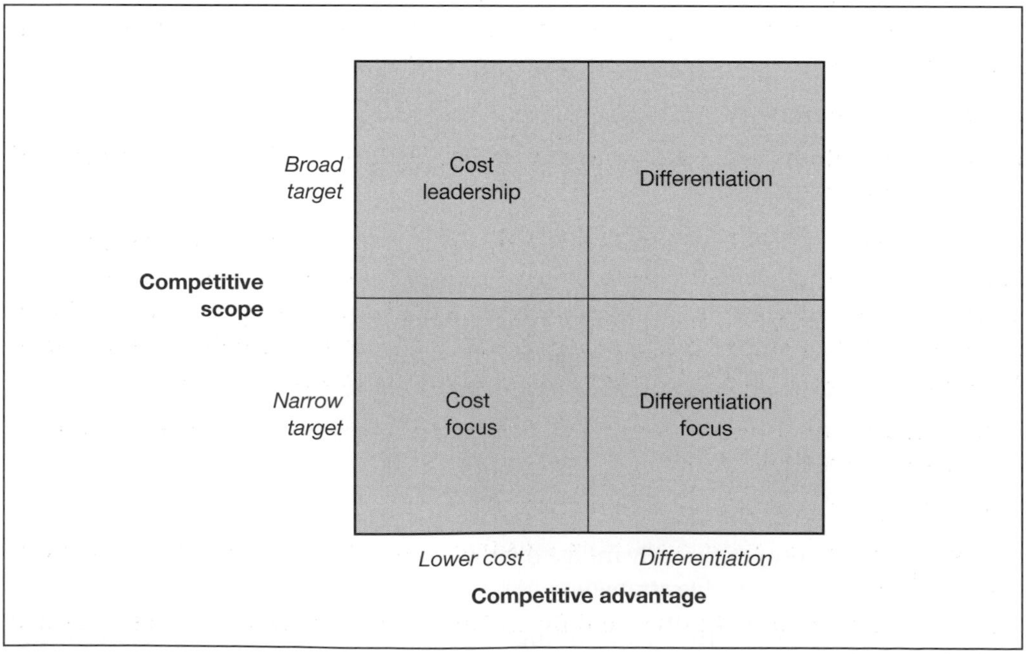

Source: Adapted with permission of The Free Press, a Division of Simon & Schuster, from *Competitive Advantage: Creating and Sustaining Superior Performance* by Michael E. Porter. © 1985 Michael E. Porter.

1 it can under-price its competitors, gain market share at their expense, and yet still make the same level of profit as they do;

2 it can earn a higher profit margin selling at the going market price;

3 in the event of a price war, which invariably occurs in a mature industry, the low-cost producer will be in a position to withstand the competition better, because of its lower costs relative to its competitors;

4 its higher market share will give it a stronger bargaining power over its suppliers;

5 its low price will deter entrants to the industry, as they are unlikely to march the leader's cost advantage.

As a result of these advantages, the low-cost producer is likely to earn above-average returns. To achieve a cost advantage, a firm's cumulative cost across its activity cost chain must be lower than its rivals. This entails the low-cost producer:

● being more efficient in its existing production activities, as well as managing its cost control more effectively than its competitors

● constantly finding ways to cut cost producing activities out of its production chain.

Firms pursuing this strategy will pursue cost savings in their functional areas. For example, R&D will be targeted at improving operational and logistical efficiencies. Marketing and promotional costs will be minimised. Procurement of inputs will be made from suppliers who offer lower prices and discounts. Standardised mass production will be followed whenever possible, to attain lower production costs per unit. Generally, these low-cost firms will also have a very cost-conscious organisational culture.

Companies can achieve cost leadership by eliminating unnecessary cost-producing activities, as well as restructuring their value chain activities to gain their distinctive competencies and hence competitive advantage. Thus adopting a low-price, low-cost strategy generally implies a market positioning based on:

● a 'no-frills' product

● a standardised offering, i.e. the output of one business differs little from that of other businesses.

The market demand for these products is fairly elastic, given that the low-cost producer addresses a mass market of price-sensitive customers. The cost leader will pursue a policy of vigorous cost reductions in all its production activities, tight cost and overhead control, and a close relationship with its customers. If the following conditions prevail, then the competitive power of a low-cost leadership strategy is greatly enhanced:

1 the product is essentially identical to all the other competitors in the industry, i.e. a fairly standardised product;

2 price competition dominates the market;

3 there are many buyers who are price-sensitive, and they have the power to bargain prices down;

4 there are limited opportunities to differentiate the product which would add value to customers;

5 product usage is fairly similar for all buyers, therefore price and not product features will determine buyer consumption;

6 consumers will seek the best price wherever possible, as they have low switching costs when they change from one retailer to another.

There are a number of risks attached to pursuing a low-cost strategy.

1 Competitors may find a way to produce at a lower cost; this may occur in a number of ways:

   (a) technological breakthroughs may lead to lower costs, which new companies may utilise to give them a cost advantage over the cost leader;

   (b) competitors may find it relatively easy to imitate the cost leader's low-cost methods;

   (c) low-wage countries such as Thailand, China, Poland, etc. offer companies the opportunity to produce their products at a low cost, thereby removing the cost leader's advantages.

2 A company that is driven by the intense desire to reduce costs in its value chain activities, and that values its technological stability, may lose sight of its customers' needs; the product may become obsolete as buyers' preferences turn to better features, quality, performance, etc. The low-cost producer's obsessive pursuit of cost minimisation may lock the firm in its present technology and product profile, thus leaving it vulnerable to new and lower-cost technologies and new product preferences. In some industries the South Koreans are pursuing low-cost leadership strategies to beat their Japanese, American and European competitors; Samsung in electronics and Hyundai in car manufacturing are examples.

Differentiation strategy

The firm pursuing a differentiation strategy hopes to achieve a competitive advantage by creating a product or service that is perceived throughout its industry as unique. The basis for competitive advantage is a product whose attributes differ substantially from the products of competitors. *Differential advantage* occurs when the firm is able to:

- *charge a premium price* which exceeds the cost of differentiating the product

- *gain buyer loyalty* because the customers are attached to the differentiating features

- *gain greater sales* as new buyers are won over by the differentiated product.

Differentiation does increase the firm's profitability, because the premium price is well above the price charged by the cost leader. Buyers pay it because they believe the product's differentiated features and qualities are worth it. For example, Porsche cars are highly priced because ownership of such a product confers status on the buyer; similarly, in jewellery the name Cartier stands out because of the unique quality buyers perceive in it, and also for its ability to confer status and prestige on its wearer. To take another example, Armani clothes are not a lot more expensive to produce than some of its competitors, but they command a premium price, simply because customers believe the prestige of owning Armani clothes is something worth paying for.

The firm can differentiate its product in a number of ways. To some extent, the potential for differentiation is determined by:

- the technical features of a product
- the characteristics of its market.

Complex products such as motor cars, washing machines or package holidays offer greater scope for differentiation. On the other hand, standardised industrial products, such as widgets or memory chips, offer limited differentiation opportunities. However, even with such products, it has been argued that there are possibilities to differentiate them; for example, customers could be supplied with product seminars, quick customer response or even market data. Differentiating this augmented part of the product is certainly an important aspect.

The differentiation variables are those absolute product-service characteristics which are relevant for consumer preferences and choices, and include colour, size, shape, design, material, etc. In addition, the performance of the product in terms of durability, reliability, safety, consistency, speed, etc. are equally important differentiating variables. Those products and services which complement the product in question are also important as sources of differentiation, these would include after-sales, speed of delivery, credit availability, etc.

Finally, *intangible* characteristics are also important differentiating variables, and can be very powerful in determining customer choice, especially when it is extremely difficult to ascertain the performance of such products-services as education, restaurants, cosmetics, etc. Consumer choice is, therefore, not only determined solely by observable performance criteria, but also by emotional, aesthetic, moral and psychological considerations. For example, the desire for prestige, exclusivity, status and individuality are very important motivation factors in choices relating to consumer products.

As stated earlier, product differentiation can be achieved in a wide variety of ways:

- superior service, i.e. reliability (DHL in overnight package delivery)
- special features (Black & Decker hand tools)
- design, performance and conferring status (BMW cars)
- consistency (McDonald's fast food)
- quality manufacture (Toshiba, Marks & Spencer)
- technological innovation in electronic products (Philips and Sony)
- top of the range image and reputation (Armani and Calvin Klein in men's and women's wear)
- prestige and distinctiveness (Rolex, Tag Heuer)
- spare parts' availability (Japanese car companies)
- product reliability (Boeing)
- buyer value (IBM, who provide back-up services and technical support)
- reputation and professionalism (Price Waterhouse Consultancy Services).

A company that pursues a differentiation strategy will endeavour to differentiate along as many dimensions as possible. The more distinctive and unique its product, the greater it is protected from its competitors, while at the same time widening its market appeal. The competitive power of differentiation strategy is greatly enhanced in the following situations:

- when buyers' needs are diverse
- when it is impossible to differentiate the product in many ways, and the buyers perceive these difference as adding value to the product
- when very few companies are choosing the same approach
- when the firm's products cannot be easily and cheaply imitated – it is much more difficult for competitors to imitate a product if it is based on quality, superior technology and good customer support services; these attributes are not easily matched and can become major assets of a fairly enduring nature.

However, there are a number of problems with a differentiation strategy.

1 Perhaps the major problem for a firm pursuing a differentiation strategy is its ability to maintain its perceived uniqueness in the long term. If rivals can quickly imitate the successful products this will undoubtedly reduce the differentiator's advantage. There are many examples of imitators in the car and computer industries in which differentiating firms who were first in the industry were not able to maintain their lead. This has not been helped by the spread of consumer awareness about the quality of competing products. Armed with this knowledge, consumers are not afraid to switch to low-cost products.

2 A low-cost producer can defeat a differentiation strategy, if buyers do not see much value in a firm's product uniqueness, in other words, buyers are not willing to pay a higher price for the perceived extra attributes.

3 Another danger is that the firm must constantly be aware of changing consumer demands and tastes, otherwise its rivals will outperform them. The clothing industry is an example of rapidly changing tastes where firms must be aware of rapidly changing demands.

4 These are some pitfalls which a differentiator must avoid, otherwise its differentiation strategy will be unsuccessful:

   (a) the inability to identify what buyers consider as value;

   (b) an excessively high premium price;

   (c) over-differentiating, so that the firm has to charge a very high price relative to a competitor's products and which exceeds the buyer's requirements or needs.

Cost leadership versus differentiation

Questions have been raised about how a firm can simultaneously differentiate its products and lower its costs. This strategy is relatively controversial, in that some theorists would argue that competing simultaneously with both strategies is inconsistent.

The idea behind this type of hybrid strategy is to create customer value by meeting or exceeding their expectations on the features–quality–service–performance attributes, while at the same time offering it at a reduced price. The competitive advantage of this hybrid strategy comes from matching competitors on the key attributes and yet beating them on cost. There is thus a delicate balance on the emphasis between low cost and differentiation which ultimately produces superior customer value.

Hill and Jones[15] believe that the low-cost–differentiation strategy is not only possible to attain but effective. This possibility has arisen because of technological developments, in particular flexible manufacturing technologies. These technologies allow a firm to pursue a differentiation strategy at a low cost, thus taking advantage of the benefits of both.

Box 9.3   INTERNET SHARE TRADING

Merrill Lynch, the biggest US brokerage firm, has decided to launch a strategy to counter potential loss of business to discounters in electronic trading. The company plans to become a first full-service broker to offer Internet share trading to all its customers in 1998. Internet trading has grown in popularity but has remained the exclusive province of discount brokers that offer low fees but little or no financial advice. Dean Witter Discover, the third biggest US brokerage firm, was the first full-service broker to offer Internet trading and the service is offered at discounted prices. Fees for on-line services have dropped to as low as $9.00 per trade. Currently there are about 1.5m on-line brokerage accounts but this figure is expected to surge to 10m by the year 2001.

Source: Branstein, L., 'Merrill Lynch plans Internet trading', *Financial Times* (3 March 1997).

Differentiation strategies have usually been associated with high costs because to meet the different market requirements it meant producing and offering more than one model. In contrast, low-cost producers could produce batches of standardised products, thus reaping the benefits of volume production and economies of scale, resulting in lower costs per unit. The key to this hybrid strategy is to use flexible manufacturing which enables a firm to manufacture a range of differentiated products at a comparable cost to the cost leader. According to Hill and Jones,[16] small production runs are associated with high retailing, material and marketing costs. However, the use of flexible manufacturing cells and robotics reduces overall costs. They also cite an example where a firm reduced marketing and production costs by limiting the number of models on the production line with certain given options instead of allowing the consumer to select. For example, car manufacturers target principal market requirements with, say, an economy package and a luxury package. These packages reduce the manufacturing costs because long production runs of the different packages are possible. This in turn also reduces the promotional costs as these are targeted at fewer segments. Furthermore, the deployment of just-in-time (JIT) inventory systems has also reduced costs as well as improving the reliability and quality of products.

The adoption of this hybrid strategy enables a firm to contain costs and at the same time provide a comparable product on the service–features–quality–performance attributes, i.e. incorporating upscale product attributes at a lower cost than its rivals. The hybrid strategy works best in markets:

● where because of buyer diversity, product differentiation is the norm

● customers are price-sensitive.

Companies such as Coca-Cola, IBM, McDonald's, etc., are pursuing both strategies simultaneously. The competitive power of these hybrid strategies is that the firm can position itself:

● to produce a medium-quality product at a price varying from average to low, or

● to produce an excellent product at a medium price.

It could be argue that many consumers may prefer a mid-range product in preference to a very expensive differentiated up-market product or to the very cheap, 'no-frills' basic product.

Focused strategy

A focused strategy is directed towards a market niche, i.e. serving the needs of a limited customer group or segment. The niche can be defined by:

1 *geographical uniqueness*, e.g. serving the Welsh market or the greater London area – for example, producers of a regional beer such as Newcastle Brown concentrate their efforts in the North-East of England;

2 *type of customer*, e.g. those earning over £100000 a year – for example, Ralph Lauren clothes focus on the upper-end segment;

3 *segment of the product line*, e.g. concentrating on women's high fashion clothes or focusing on health foods only.

Once the segment is chosen, a firm can pursue a focus strategy through differentiation or a low-cost approach.

1 *Cost focus* is a low-cost competitive strategy which attempts only to serve that particular niche of the market to the exclusion of others. It competes against the cost leader in segments where it has a cost advantage. Regional firms in engineering or cement markets, for example, tend to have cost advantages relative to the low-cost national companies.

2 *A differentiation focus* strategy depends on there being a buyer segment that would like unique product attributes. In this case, the focused firm will compete with the differentiator on only one or just a few segments. For example, Michelin tyres focus on the upper-end segment – i.e. those buyers who are not price-sensitive and want the best quality available. The BMW company competes against car manufacturers such as Ford or Toyota in the luxury car segment of the market only, and not in other segments.

Focused companies tend to serve their narrow target market more effectively than their competitors. They develop a specialised knowledge of that segment and sometimes tend to innovate more quickly than the large differentiator. Those firms who develop a focused approach tend to build market share first in the selected segment, and then serve more market segments at a later stage and gently undermine the differentiator's unique competence. A classic example of this is the Japanese car manufacturers' focused approach to the sub-compact car segment in the US car market. After establishing their market positions, they gradually moved to other car segments, so that today Infiniti and Lexus are beginning to challenge the niche markets of BMW and Mercedes. The competitive power of a focus strategy is that it either has lower costs than its competitors in serving a particular market segment, or can offer its niche members something unique and different from its competitors. The focus approach can become an extremely powerful strategy if some or all of the following conditions are present:

- there is growth potential in the segment which is large enough to be profitable
- major competitors are not interested in the segment
- special skills and resources are required to serve the segment effectively.

Indeed, the focusing strategy works best when:

- buyer needs are diverse and hence the market has many different segments; this allows the focused firm to select a particular niche which is suited to its unique competencies and capabilities
- multi-segment competitors do not find the specialised needs of the niche easy to satisfy or it is costly to do so
- no other competitors are attempting to specialise in the same segment.

A firm's focus strategy does carry risks.

1 *Competitors may develop competencies to match the focused firm in serving the selected market niche* – for example, Nissan and Toyota's new top-of-the-line models were designed to compete in the Mercedes and BMW niches.

2 *Changes in consumer needs and technology may erode the focuser's niche market* – the focused firm tends to find it difficult to move easily into new niches.

3 *The product costs of a focused firm are generally much higher than those of a low-cost producer* – this will threaten profit margins and even the viability of the firm. In cases when the focuser needs to invest heavily to develop or sustain its competitive advantage, profitability is likely to fall. However, as discussed earlier in this chapter, the emergence of flexible manufacturing systems can eliminate some of the costs and hence allow the focused firm to compete with larger competitors, where their cost disadvantage is reduced.

4 It may be the case that *the market niche is so attractive and profitable that it attracts new competitors*, and thus reduces profits and the returns to the firm.

Stuck in the middle

Looking at Fig. 9.8 (overleaf) we notice that firms in the upper-left-hand end of the curve are very profitable despite a small market share. This is because they offer unique products or their markets are specialised and they can charge premium prices. Firms at the upper-right-hand end of the curve are equally profitable. This is because they differentiate their products or they charge lower prices because they have attained lower costs of production and so are able to gain a large market share. However, it is the firms in the lower-middle part of the curve that will face difficulties. These firms are said to be '*stuck in the middle*'. They have low profits and modest market share. They do not have much going for them. They are unable to obtain or sustain a competitive advantage, and have arrived in this position through bad strategic decisions, ignorance or through being subject to adverse environmental changes.

Fig 9.8 THE GENERIC STRATEGIES MODEL

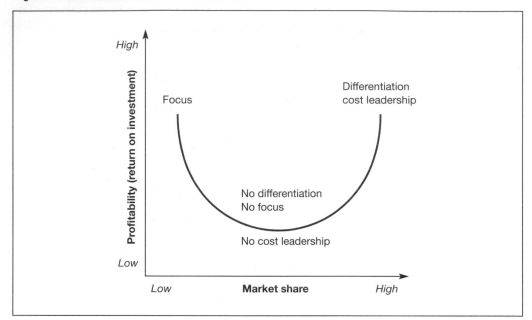

Even though firms may pursue one of the three generic strategies previously discussed, it is very easy to fall into the middle position:

1 a differentiator with unique product features that tries to reduce its R&D expenditure may lose its competitive advantage as its distinctive competence disappears;

2 a focused firm can get stuck in the middle when it begins to behave as a broad differentiator;

3 if a differentiator's market is attacked by low-cost products or very highly specialised products, then the differentiator can end up stuck in the middle; with the advent of flexible manufacturing processes, differentiators and cost leaders could have problems in the future, hence the need to monitor the environmental changes and their impact on the firm's strengths and weaknesses.

Research has shown that it is possible for a firm to pursue differentiation and low-cost strategies simultaneously.[17] Porter considers this to be only a temporary state, as eventually the firm will choose one of the generic strategies, despite the risks, otherwise they will be stuck in the middle, with no competitive advantage.

Generic global marketing strategies

A firm which adopts a global competitive strategy will attempt to:

● develop international competitive strengths that would not have been available had it remained a purely domestic firm

● perceive its key opportunities and threats on a world-wide basis; however, this does not preclude the firm having a national strategic orientation in some parts of its operations.

Fig 9.9 INTERNATIONAL GENERIC STRATEGIES

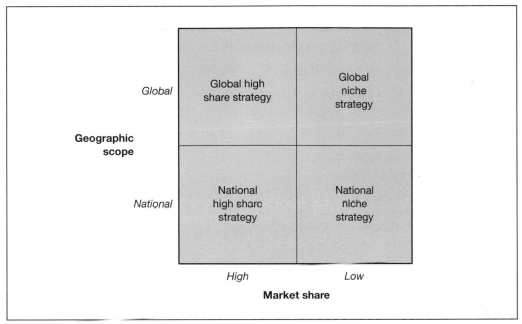

Source: Grosse, R. and Kujawa, D., *International Business* (Homewood, IL: Irwin, 1992). Reproduced with permission.

There are four main strategic choices open to the company (*see* Fig. 9.9).

Global high share strategy firms seek:

1 to identify high-volume segments in global markets;

2 to produce a wide range of products and services in one or more industries: for example, in the computer industry[18] IBM competes in many segments such as personal computers, minicomputers, mainframes and home computers, whilst most of its competitors focus on only one of the segments – Burroughs (mainframes), Apple (micros), Digital Equipment Corporation (minis); examples of other companies adopting this strategy are Sony, Nestlé and Exxon.

To compete against the global niche firms, a global high-share firm must find spill-over benefits from its other activities. They can obtain reduced prices for inputs, which are then used for two or more products in their portfolio, whereas single-product firms are unable to attain this. This global orientation may give the company several competitive advantages:

1 economies of scale due to high world-wide production volume;

2 the ability to implement global sourcing policies, thereby obtaining cheap raw materials and inexpensive labour;

3 the ability to provide a global service for its customers – e.g. some banks have internationalised their services so that customers can obtain them world-wide;

4 the ability to project a consistent and global corporate image;

5 the provision of a global portfolio of strategic business units.

The major drawbacks of this strategy are the huge commitments of capital and management expertise required. It is, perhaps, the most difficult strategy to achieve.

Global niche strategy firms target a particular industry segment for competition globally; this type of strategy is pursued by firms who:

1 wish to avoid head-on competition with the global high share firms;

2 do not have the resources for a global share strategy;

3 do not have to adapt their products to local conditions;

4 are small, but have one or more global competitive advantage.

The global niche strategy can be based on a low-cost or differentiation basis. A *low-cost global nicher* can obtain economies of scale in a wide variety of functional areas such as procurement, distribution, R&D and distribution because they are selling in more than one country. Had the firm remained domestic these scale economies would not have been possible. McDonald's, the fast food restaurant, is normally cited as an example of a global nicher. A global focus can also be based on a firm which *differentiates its products*. Some firms may concentrate on producing expensive or high-quality products, or high performance or excellent customer services, or a combination of these. Mercedes' global niche strategy is based on producing very high-quality and expensive cars. BMW competes in the global segment of the motorcycle market as it does in its car division. These are based on its excellent product quality, technological superiority and other differentiating features.

Finally, the nicher gains substantial scale economies in production across countries; however, these benefits will be lost if too much adaptation is required in the different market segments.

National high share strategies are adopted by multinational firms that target high national market share through exploiting nationally-based competitive advantages.

This type of strategy depends on national entry barriers to counter global competitors. These barriers can take the form of quotes, tariffs and institutional barriers in the host market which may deter other foreign companies, or preferential laws that favour national competitors who could be domestic- or foreign-owned. Barriers can take the form of:

1 government support against competitors through tariffs on imported goods that may compete with it, a reduced tax burden, etc. MNCs are able to obtain these concessions from the host government in exchange for their investment and job creation activities;

2 obtaining government purchase contracts for the firm's products and services; these contracts tend to continue into the future;

3 government protection for firms that they control through ownership; these protected firms tend to be in utility industries such as in railways, electric generating industries, mining industries, telecommunications, etc. – the risk associated with this strategy is that the competitive advantages are subject to changes in government policies and thus the competitive advantage is not sustainable (in the last 10 years, the British government embarked on a major programme of privatisation of state

industries and thus removed some of the competitive advantages previously enjoyed by firms such as British Telecommunications (BT) and British Airways).

A classic example of a protected niche is that of ICL, a British computer company, which is now predominantly owned by Fujitsu. In the past ICL was able to use national barriers to provide itself with competitive advantages against global competitors. These national barriers were preferential treatment by the UK government to obtain government contracts and assistance. However, with intense technological changes and diminishing barriers, ICL had to move to a global niche strategy to survive.

National niche strategies are pursued by firms that exploit the advantages of specialisation on a national basis to help defend their segments against local and international rivals. A firm may pursue this strategy when:

1 its global product strategies are not compatible with local demands;
2 much product adaptation is required from country to country.

These market differences may limit the benefits of a global niche strategy, and in this instance a national niche strategy would be preferable and superior. Competitive advantage is derived by the firm emphasising its adaptability to local needs; for example, car manufacturers have adapted their products to suit specific market needs – in hot and humid climates cars are equipped with air conditioners and the wiring in the car is protected from the high humidity. It is partially similar to the national high share strategy in that national barriers are also used to defend against international competitors.

Confrontational or offensive strategies

As discussed earlier the principle of competitive strategy is that if a firm wishes to earn above-average profits it must create a sustainable competitive advantage. A firm can implement a competitive strategy either offensively or defensively. Firms use *offensive* moves to build strategy, and this usually occurs in locations away from the firm's current position in the market place. *Defensive* moves are used to protect competitive advantages and usually take place on the firm's current market position. There are a number of ways to mount strategic offensives.[19]

A frontal assault is based on attacking the competitors' strengths. It involves a head-to-head confrontation in areas from product to promotion. The attacks should challenge the rival with an equally good or better product and at a lower price. This could take many forms, from new models to match the competitor's, price-cutting, to adding new features, etc. If the attacker goes for price-cutting, it must be supported by a cost advantage or financial strength. The aim of the attacker is to whittle away at the rival's competitive advantage and narrow the competitive gap. To be successful, the aggressive firm must have superior resources and to be able to persevere, and at the very least should take some market share from the targeted rival.

A flanking manoeuvre is a firm that attacks the market where the rivals are weak. Some of the areas of weaknesses which challengers could attack are:

1 rivals with poor customer service, thus winning some of the disenchanted customers;

2 geographic regions where rivals have poor market share;

3 buyer segments that are being ignored or neglected by rivals;

4 rivals who lag on product quality, features and performance – the aim is to offer a better product and cause brand switching;

5 rivals who have weak promotions and broad recognition;

6 market leaders who have gaps in their product lines, the aim being to create new market segments.

This strategy of attacking rivals where they are most vulnerable has a greater chance of success than the frontal assault. The flanker is likely to be successful if it is willing to expand slowly and to be patient, and the rival has no ready defence. The most celebrated example of this approach is the Japanese car manufacturers who followed this tactic during the 1960s. Nissan and Toyota attacked the sub-compact car segment that was ignored by the US car manufacturers at the time.

Encirclement involves launching a competitive offensive on several fronts in an attempt to divert the rival's attention and to force it to channel resources on several fronts simultaneously. The challenger must have greater product variety as well as serving more markets. Examples of successful encirclers are Honda who took on every market segment in the motorcycle industry except for the top-of-the-range segment controlled by Harley-Davidson. It was Seiko's strategy in the watch market, where it had over 400 watch models. To succeed with this strategy requires vast resources and capabilities to attack multiple segments.

A **bypass attack** is the most indirect assault; it involves bypassing the rival and attacking unoccupied markets. The tactics involve:

1 early entry into uncontested geographic markets;

2 the creation of new market segments with new product features and performance attributes to meet buyers' needs;

3 leapfrogging into next-generation technologies which will form the basis of its new competitive advantage.

The aim of this strategy is to change the rules of the game in favour of the challenger.

Guerrilla offensives consist of 'hit and run' tactics in different market segments of the competitor. The aim is to demoralise opponents by the use of small, intermittent and random assaults on rivals, using tactics such as special promotional campaigns or reducing prices considerably to win a client's account. The challenger should attack:

1 weakly defended segments;

2 areas where competitors have overextended themselves – e.g. enhancing customer services where rivals are underperforming.

The strategy is best suited for a small firm or new entrant to the market. This mode of attack will not threaten the large established rivals and hence reduce the likelihood of retaliation from them.

Pre-emptive strategies involve the challenger gaining competitive advantage first, which will then prevent or discourage rivals from duplicating. A prime advantage does put rivals at a competitive disadvantage and is difficult to circumvent. There are several ways to gain a prime position with these pre-emptive tactics:

1 secure the best geographical locations in a shopping mall or the motorway interchange;

2 monopolise the sources of raw materials, quality suppliers, etc. – De Beers bought the production of all the major diamond mines;

3 build a positioning image that is unique and difficult to copy, such as Coca-Cola or Tiffany jewellers.

Defensive strategies

The main aim of defensive strategies is to protect a firm's competitive position; the use of defensive tactics is to:

1 lower the risk of being attacked;

2 lessen the impact of an attack;

3 divert attackers so that they aim their effort at other competitors.

Defensive attacks do not increase a firm's competitive advantage but they help to make its competitive advantage sustainable. The effect of defensive tactics is that they reduce short-term profitability so as to ensure that long-term profits are not compromised. There are several ways a firm can protect its position against attacks by new entrants or established rivals.

Raise barriers involve trying to block a challenger's avenues of attack. Some of the options include:

(a) increasing the firm's product line in every profitable segment and hence closing the gaps;

(b) signing exclusive agreements with distributors;

(c) raising buyer switching costs by offering free or low-cost training to users;

(d) reducing unit costs by exploiting scale economies;

(e) introducing brands–models that match the characteristics of the challenger's models;

(f) removing access to alternative technologies through licensing or patenting;

(g) having exclusive contracts with key suppliers to block challengers' access;

(h) avoiding suppliers that serve competitors;

(i) challenging rivals' products or practices in court;

(j) increasing warranty coverage;

(k) encouraging the government to raise competitive barriers such as pollution control standards, health and safety measures etc. so as to disadvantage rivals;

(l) making it difficult for rivals to get buyers to try their products–brands by tactics such as giving price discounts to buyers who are considering trying the rival's brand, and having high levels of sales promotion (samples and coupons).

Signal strong retaliation – a good defensive strategy is to increase the perceived threat of retaliation for an attack. The objective of this tactic is to dissuade the challenger from attacking at all by increasing the expectation that any challenger would be fought off vigorously and that the ensuing conflict would be an extremely costly exercise. The firm can signal their intentions in the following way:

(a) announcing that the firm is prepared to defend its market share;

(b) announcing plans to increase production capacity and building ahead of time;

(c) commiting the firm to match the challenger's prices and terms;

(d) enhancing the firm's image as a strong defender, by making counter-moves to the offensive challenges of weaker competitors;

(e) announcing in advance information relating to new technological innovation or new product development in order to delay and deter potential moves by the challenger.

Lowering the profit inducement involves reducing a challenger's expectations of future profits. If high profits are earned in an industry, challengers are more likely to take on high defensive barriers as well as combating strong retaliation attacks. Potential attacks can be deflected by:

(a) keeping prices low and forgoing current profits; this would be a disincentive for new entrants;

(b) leaking to the media the problems faced by the industry;

(c) using accounting methods which obscure the true profit picture.

Timing strategy

The firm which manufactures and sells the product first is called the *first mover* and the advantages attached to a first mover are:[20]

- obtaining higher market shares than late entrants
- enjoying long-term profit advantage over their competitors
- establishing a reputation as a leader in the industry
- retaining the loyalty of first-time buyers
- making it more difficult for firms to imitate their product by being the first in the market
- having moved down the learning curve they can become a cost leader and hence perhaps have an absolute cost advantage over their rivals.

However, there are disadvantages associated with being a first mover:

- late movers may be able to imitate easily the technological know-how and skills, which in turn reduces their R&D costs
- customer loyalty to pioneering firms is not as strong
- given that there is rapid technological change, the first-mover's technology may become obsolete, allowing challengers to gain advantages of new technologies and processes

- rivals reduce their risks by waiting for the market to develop and establish itself, and also to exploit new market segments which have been ignored by the prime mover.

Given these pros and cons, it becomes important to understand that *when* to make a strategic move is just as crucial as *what* moves a firm should make.

PRODUCT–MARKET OPTIONS[21]

In developing its portfolio strategy, a firm can choose a number of strategy alternatives to generate global growth as illustrated in Fig. 9.10. This grid (also called the Ansoff Matrix) shows there are several strategies open to the firm.

Withdrawal strategy

Paradoxically, a firm may withdraw from some businesses in order to grow. It may be the case that to sustain its competitive advantage a firm may need to consider withdrawing from the market place and consolidating its position; this can occur in a number of instances:

1 *reduce an extensive product range*: it may be the case that a firm has a broad product range and some items are simply not economical to continue without endangering the company's survival. Some cosmetic firms have withdrawn some product lines such as lipsticks, and TV companies have removed programmes with a small audience;

Fig 9.10 ANSOFF'S PRODUCT–MARKET EXPANSION GRID

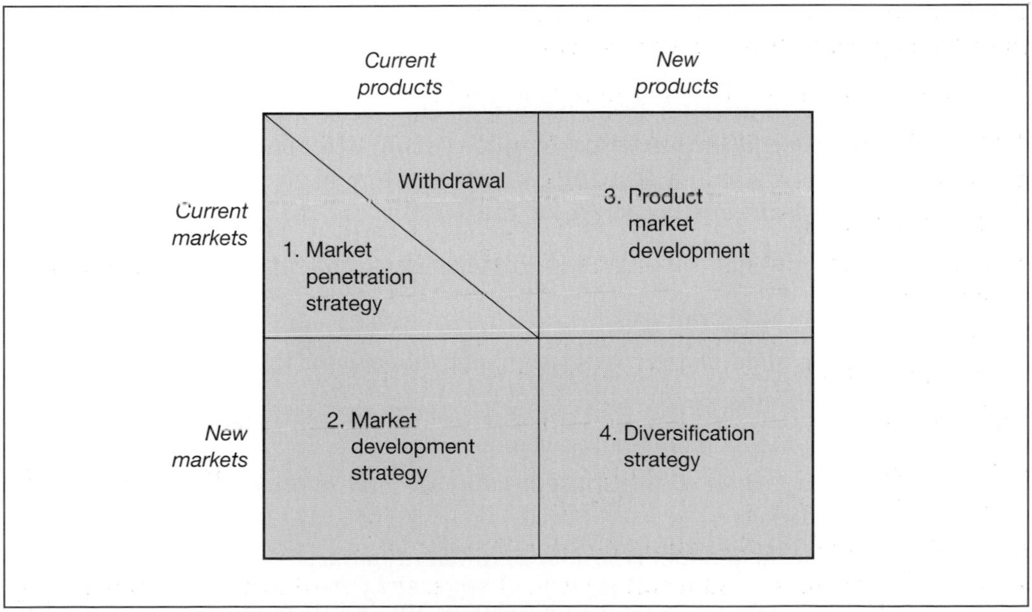

Source: Adapted and reprinted by permission of *Harvard Business Review* from Ansoff, H. S., 'Strategies for diversification', (September–October 1957). © 1957 by the President and Fellows of Harvard College. All rights reserved.

2 *the end of the product life cycle*: in some industries there will be products which have reached the decline stage of their cycle with no possibility of renewed demand. Under these circumstances, the product or service is likely to be removed and new products or services will be developed. Certain airline routes have been discontinued due to limited demand which may also be due to reasons outside the firm's control (such as routes to Afghanistan in the 1990s). To take another example, compact discs have virtually replaced the production of LP records.

Product–market penetration

This strategy involves the firm in trying to increase the share of its product in the overseas markets which it already serves. It can achieve this by employing several types of tactics:

1 *product-line stretching*: the firm adds new items to its existing product line in a market segment which it has already penetrated. The aim is to attract more customers from rivals and current non-users of the firm's products – i.e. to reach a broader market. Coca-Cola has added new items to its basic product and now offers Diet Coke and Cherry Coke in some of its world markets. Similarly, the Japanese car manufacturers first penetrated the European car market with medium-sized cars, and have now extended their product lines to target the luxury segments;

2 *product proliferation*: this involves offering many different product types. Seiko offers a variety of watches with different features, functions, etc.;

3 *product improvement*: this involves updating and augmenting the existing product, and could entail the application of the latest technology to improve the product's capabilities, improving customer services, etc.

Generally, market penetration is easier if the market is growing because new customers are still entering the market and still seeking the appropriate product. Firms which have a relatively large market share in a growing market are more likely to lose some market share to predator firms because of their attractive position. The larger companies could defend their position by price cuts to deter entry; firms with a relatively small market share in a growing market are more likely to take an aggressive strategy and attack the market share of the big players, as Burger King did with McDonald's in the fast-food sector.

Market development strategy

This strategy involves developing new *geographic* markets for the firm's current product lines. This type of expansion is most suitable:

● where minimal product modification is required

● where profit margins are diminishing because of intense price competition in the firm's existing markets

● if the life cycle of the product is similar in different markets.

Many Pacific Basin economies such as Singapore and South Korea are adopting this type of expansion strategy.

The firm could equally attract new customers with its current product range by seeking new *segments* of the market or new *uses* for its products. Firms could also slightly repackage or reposition their products. Johnson's baby oil, for example, was re-positioned as a product for women who wanted to retain their youthful looks.

Product–market development strategy

This strategy involves the firm maintaining its existing overseas markets but developing new product markets within them. A firm selling a software package to the industrial segment in market X might go after a consumer segment in the same market. The product development undertaken here would be substantial and the reasons for adopting such a strategy could be to counter competition, exploit new technology, protect overall market share, etc.

Diversification

Diversification strategies involve the firm entering new product markets outside its present business or related product markets. The firm may wish to pursue the former strategy in the following circumstances:

1 when opportunities in the new product market are highly attractive;
2 when the firm wishes to reduce the impact of a negative environmental trend in its existing industry – for example to reduce the economic impact of a decline in cigarette smoking or the ageing of the UK population.

Where the firm expands into products and markets which have no relationship to the firm's current product, markets or technology the strategy is called a *conglomerate* or *unrelated diversification strategy*. Coca-Cola purchased a movie company as a strategic move to counter the possible decline in the customer segment for its products which is presently the youth group. When an organisation enters unknown markets and products, they incur higher risks. Such companies tend to act as holding companies, and the two best known companies in this respect are General Electric (USA) and Hanson PLC (UK) which have operated with considerable success. Firms can justify such strategies on financial and management synergies.

Firms could enter a *related* diversification strategy, which means that there is some existing connection with the firm's current value chain activities; these can be divided into two types:

1 *forward or backward integration*, whereby the outlets or sources of supplies are joined with the firm. This is prevalent in the semiconductor industries where manufacturers of microprocessors join forces with semiconductor producers to ensure a continuous supply;
2 *horizontal integration* is another type of related diversification strategy. When BMW (Germany) acquired Rover cars (UK) there was some complementarity between the two companies in terms of their markets and technology.

EXPANSION-METHOD STRATEGIES

Under this category of strategies, the focus is on the methods by which the market strategies are to be achieved. For example, to develop new products a company can allocate expenditure on internal R&D, have a joint venture or even acquire a new company and its product portfolio. In the global context, these options widen for the firm and these expansion methods are discussed extensively in Chapter 11.

SUMMARY

A global corporate strategy is the means by which an international firm achieves its global objectives. It is a unified, comprehensive and integrated plan. The process of establishing a global strategy involves defining the firm's purpose and mission, and environmental analysis, establishing global objectives and alternative strategies, implementation and control. A global corporate strategy is inextricably linked with international marketing.

The process of formulating a global marketing strategy is essentially similar to the formulation of the global corporate strategy, but the objectives of the latter will define the role played by the marketing function. This role is referred to as the 'corporate marketing mission', which establishes the target markets, the segmentation of these markets and the competitive position taken in them.

Global marketers need to assess and make choices about markets. The marketer needs to assess potential customers by segmenting them into groups. The bases for segmenting are numerous and varied, ranging from environmental criteria to psychographics, demographics and behavioural characteristics. New forms of segmenting international markets are emerging, such as marketing mix variables. Targeting is based on segment size and potential, competition, feasibility and compatibility. The three major categories of targeting strategies are differentiated, undifferentiated and concentrated. Companies reach their target groups by positioning their product offerings. There are three categories of segmentation strategy – global, national and mixed-market strategies. Firms also have to decide on the strategies of concentration versus diversification.

Strategy options can be divided into resource-based and market-based options. The former relies on the analysis of the company to ascertain its capabilities and competences before it can formulate its options, the latter relies on responding to the external environment, in particular competitors and other exogenous factors.

A firm has a competitive advantage when it is able to compete successfully against its competitors. To attain this, a firm needs to link its distinctive competencies with the critical factors for success. Competitive advantages can be derived from a number of sources such as product quality, flexibility of service, the firm's technological orientation, etc. These advantages are strongest when they are unique to the firm, and firms can develop these advantages in a number of ways. International firms have more potential to develop competitive advantages compared to domestic firms because of the opportunities in the international market place, such as cost leadership advantages, access to global resources and information, and the transfer of functional experience.

Porter proposes three 'generic' competitive strategies to outperform other firms in a particular industry: these are cost leadership, differentiation and focus. A cost leader is a firm which can produce a comparable product more efficiently than its rivals. Differentiation occurs when a firm can produce unique products which add value for the customer in terms of quality, features and performance. Furthermore, when lower-cost or differentiation strategies are focused on a market niche, they are called cost focus and focused differentiation. Each of these different strategies has its advantages and disadvantages. A firm needs to manage its strategy constantly, otherwise it risks being 'stuck in the middle'.

A firm's behaviour or actions in the market place are defined by its competitive market strategy, and this includes its approach as to whether it should go for a high global market share, a global niche or a protected niche.

A firm needs to adopt a variety of offensive tactics to create competitive advantages and to apply defensive tactics to sustain the advantage gained. The use of timing tactics is also a useful strategic ploy in many market situations.

There are four alternative strategies open to the firm which develops a portfolio strategy, namely product market penetration, market development, product market development and diversification.

REVIEW QUESTIONS

1 Describe the functions of each of the main stages of the strategic planning process.

2 What is the role of the firm's corporate strategy in determining its global marketing strategy?

3 What is a cost leadership strategy?

4 What is the difference between a differentiation and a focus strategy?

5 List the advantages and disadvantages of cost-leadership and differentiation strategies.

6 What are the main types of offensive strategies?

7 Outline the main defensive strategies the company may adopt.

DISCUSSION QUESTIONS

1 What are the key elements of the global corporate strategy process? Discuss the factors which are of importance to an international firm during this process.

2 Discuss the relationship of international product life cycles and competitive strategy in international marketing.

3 How can companies pursuing one of the three generic strategies become 'stuck in the middle'?

4 What is the difference between cost focus and differentiated focus?

5 Is it possible for a company to pursue cost leadership and differentiation strategies simultaneously?

6 When are offensive strategies appropriate and what factors determine which option should be used?

7 What strategies can a firm employ if it wishes to penetrate a current market further?

Case study

CREATING COMPETITIVE ADVANTAGE[22]

Consumer software technopolists tend to design products for home use which are cheap and where standards are less rigorous compared with the standards required for a networked office. It is in the home that Intuit dominates, largely as a result of its programme called Quicken. The Californian firm has controlled 75 per cent of the financial software market for more than 13 years, shaking off aggressive competition from Microsoft.

Intuit's revenues have quadrupled in the last few years and by June 1996 amounted to $538m. The company has purchased many other companies and investments in new concerns which have kept it in the red.

The secret of Intuit's success is simplicity. When founder Scott Cook began selling Quicken in 1983 there were 43 competing products, and many of these were very sophisticated. Early success came when Quicken developed an on-screen universally familiar way for paying bills by cheque. The program remains one of the easiest to use as it is tailored to the needs of ordinary users.

Intuit has held sway over Microsoft even though the latter has developed a competing product called Money. Despite the fact that it has given Money away free of charge, Microsoft has managed to corner only a quarter of the market. Microsoft attempted to buy Intuit for $2bn. Part of the deal involved Microsoft giving away Money to other companies to maintain a form of competition. This strategy failed to win the battle for Intuit.

However, victory over Microsoft is no guarantee for future success. A continually changing market place presents the biggest challenge. In the immediate future providing on-line services, such as enabling people to pay bills, manage share portfolios and purchase insurance over the Web, rather than the software itself, will be the determining factor for success.

Consultants Booz-Allen and Hamilton maintain that over the next few years one in six US households will conduct their banking business over the Internet. These relatively wealthy bank customers will provide almost a third of bank profits. This fact is attracting many companies including banks to the emerging on-line financial services market. This new competition, as well as that from Microsoft, will be a deciding factor in whether Intuit holds sway.

Several of Intuit's products link it to its Web-based Quicken Financial Network (QFN). By offering data on insurance schemes, mutual funds and introducing sellers and buyers, Intuit acts as a middleman. Some of the services are offered on monthly subscription while others are free. The company expects to make money not only from the subscription but also from its site advertisements. Intuit's Open Exchange, connecting users to their bank accounts, is used by more than 38 US banks, which pay Intuit a licence fee. Scott Cook expects Internet transactions to account for half of Intuit's revenues within a few years.

Relations between the bank and Intuit are complicated by the fact that roles are confused. On the one hand, Intuit wants banks to utilise Open Exchange while, on the other, Intuit is in competition with banks who are developing Web-based banking services. Booz-Allen and Hamilton say that over 1000 US banks are already doing so. These banks will find that QFN will be the point of contact between on-line customers and their financial institutions, and if customers come to banks via QFN it will be difficult to sort out who the competitors are.

Intuit's advantage over banks is its ability to give impartial advice to customers on, for instance, pensions, investments and current accounts. Moreover, Quicken's customers appear to be loyal.

Microsoft is aggressively promoting Money which is linked to a personal-finance Website and part of the Microsoft network that is central to the company's attempt to get into the media. Microsoft has brought in 61 institutional partners on its Open Financial Connectivity to rival Intuit's Open Exchange. Its attempt to buy Intuit was somewhat counter-productive because it made banks take note of smaller firms.

Intuit cannot afford to lose the on-line financial services battle. Microsoft and the banks have deep enough pockets to keep going while they work out alternative strategies. Intuit's winning ticket may be that it is hungrier than its rivals.

Questions

1 *What do you consider are Intuit's major competitive advantages?*

2 *Discuss and evaluate the strategies that Intuit has pursued to remain competitive.*

FURTHER READING

Day, G.S., *Market Driven Strategy* (New York: The Free Press, 1990).

Yip, G.S., *Total Global Strategy* (Englewood Cliffs, NJ: Prentice-Hall, 1992).

NOTES AND REFERENCES

1 Yip, G.S., *Total Global Strategy* (Englewood Cliffs, NJ: Prentice-Hall, 1992).

2 Baalbaki, I.B. and Malhotra, N.K., 'Marketing management bases for international market segmentation: an alternative look at the standardisation/customisation debate', *International Marketing Review*, 10(1) (1993), 19–44.

3 Czinkota, M.R. and Ronkainen, I.A., *Global Marketing* (The Dryden Press, 1996).

4 Keegan, W.J., *Global Marketing Management*, 5th edition (Englewood Cliffs, NJ: Prentice-Hall, 1995).

5 Ibid.

6 Toyne, B. and Walters, P.G.P., *Global Marketing Management: A Strategic Perspective* (Cambridge, MA: Allyn & Bacon, 1989).

7 Keegan, op. cit.

8 Ayal, I. and Zif, J., 'Marketing expansion strategies in multinational marketing', *Journal of Marketing*, 43 (1979), 89.

9 Piercy, N., *Export Strategy, Markets and Competition* (London: George Allen & Unwin, 1982).

10 Ibid.

11 Hamel, G. and Prahalad, C.K., *Competing for the Future* (Boston, MA: Harvard Business School Press, 1994).

12 Lynch, R., *Corporate Strategy* (London: Pitman Publishing, 1997).

13 Rothschild, W.E., 'Surprise and competitive advantage', *Journal of Business Strategy*, 4(3) (1984), 10–18.

14 Porter, M.E., *Competitive Strategy: Techniques for Analysing Industries and Competitors* (New York: The Free Press, 1980); Ibid., *Competitive Advantage* (New York: The Free Press, 1985); Ibid., 'Changing patterns of international competition', *California Management Review*, 28(2) (1986).

15 Hill, C.W.L. and Jones, G.R., *Strategic Management*, 2nd edition (Boston, MA: Houghton Mifflin, 1992).

16 Ibid.

17 Hayes, R.H. and Wheelwright, S.C., *Restoring Our Competitive Edge* (New York: John Wiley, 1984); Phillips, L., Chang, D.R. and Buzzell, R.D., 'Product quality, cost position and business performance: a test of some key hypotheses', *Journal of Marketing,* 47 (1983), 26–43.

18 Grosse, R. and Kujawa, D., *International Business* (Homewood, IL: Irwin, 1992).

19 Kotler, P., *Marketing Management*, 7th edition (Englewood Cliffs, NJ: Prentice-Hall, 1991); Macmilllan, D., 'Pre-emptive strategies', *Journal of Business Strategy*, 14(2) (1983), 16–26.

20 Hill and Jones, op. cit.; Thompson, A.A., Jr. and Stickland, III, A.J., *Strategic Management: Concepts and Cases*, 7th edition (Homewood, IL: Irwin, 1993).

21 Ansoff, H.S., 'Strategies for diversification', *Harvard Business Review* (September–October 1957), 113–24.

22 'Intuitively competitive', *The Economist* (21 December 1996).

10

Market-entry decisions

INTRODUCTION

Some firms enter the international market place by choice, and others because of the necessity to remain competitive. The increased global competition and pressures in the domestic markets are forcing firms to consider going abroad seriously. The firm contemplating international operations needs to consider its strategic thrust, as this will define the areas in which it will operate and determine its strategic priorities. There are immense pressures for firms to engage in international business and operate in foreign markets in order to survive. Participating in the global market place is equally rewarding, but firms need to be prepared and adjust to the needs and opportunities in international markets. This entails a thorough analysis of potential country markets and developing parameters to guide their choice of entry strategies. A wide range of options is open to the firm wishing to enter foreign markets, and these will be discussed extensively in Chapter 11. The focus of this chapter will be to briefly discuss the different phases of and triggers to internationalisation, how firms select the appropriate country markets by the use of portfolio techniques and the entry criteria for determining the type of entry methods a firm should select in specific country markets.

Objectives

This chapter will examine:

- the major triggers to internationalisation
- the major phases of the internationalisation process
- the application of portfolio techniques in the global market place
- portfolio techniques as a tool to help firms to evaluate their choice of country markets
- the major criteria that determine a firm's choice of entry mode.

PHASES OF INTERNATIONALISATION

Whatever the factor that has triggered the firm to enter the international market, it will need to determine its strategic and investment priorities. The firm's expansion strategy in the global market will depend on the phase of its internationalisation. According to Douglas and Craig,[1] we can analytically define three phases in the internationalisation process:

1 the initial market entry;

2 national or local market expansion; and

3 global rationalisation.

This process is evolutionary for many firms, although in some cases companies may combine one or more of these stages at the same time.

Box 10.1 — KINGFISHER —

Kingfisher, the UK high street retailer, is further internationalising its activities by expanding in France through a £59.3m deal to buy a 20 per cent stake in BUT, a furniture and electrical goods retailer. Kingfisher has the right to take control after two years at a price to be determined. In 1995, BUT made £23.9m profits on sales of £1.1bn including fees from franchises. The chief executive of Kingfisher saw the deal as 'a real opportunity, and a sensible way to build on the success of Darty [France's leading electrical goods company which is a Kingfisher subsidiary]'. Darty has been seeking a stake in BUT for some time. BUT has 232 mixed-format stores in France and it claims to be in the number 4 spot in French electrical goods with 5.1 per cent of the market, and is France's second largest furniture retailer. BUT and Darty are very different types of retailers with BUT being very promotional oriented. An analyst agreed that Kingfisher had bought a very good business, but it was difficult to justify it in terms of return on capital.

Source: Hollinger, P., *Financial Times* (11 January 1996).

Initial market entry

This is the first phase of internationalisation, and management's role here is to decide on the rate and extent at which it will expand its international strategy – i.e. the firm needs to decide on the extent of the company's geographic markets. There are many factors propelling firms to enter global markets. These can be internal triggers such as fulfiling management objectives of profit and growth, exploiting the firm's unique product–technology competencies, excess capacity of resources, management attitudes, etc. The external triggers include environmental trends, industry factors or competitive pressures. Whether alone or in concert, these different factors will be a stimulus for firms to explore international markets and determine the firm's strategic thrust.

There are several reasons for European firms to seek business opportunities elsewhere. In the past many firms have concentrated within the EU countries and certainly within the European orbit. In recent years the rapid evolution of the global market has not only made international marketing a very desirable alternative for growth, but also a necessity for corporate survival. The motivations for globalisation are diverse and vary from market to market for different industry sectors and for firms. Some of these factors which may stimulate firms to market abroad are now examined.

Market saturation ｜\

Market saturation can provide the trigger for firms to seek new opportunities abroad. Saturation occurs when the home market has slackening growth rates or there is limited potential for growth. The implication of a saturated home market is that the firm's resources are unused and thus there is production and managerial slack; this should act as a spur to go international. In the EU countries, the market for a variety of goods is becoming saturated faster than new markets are being found. This combined with the overall slow growth of the population of EU countries means that firms must develop new markets to survive. For example, the market for cars and electronic consumer goods is fast approaching saturation point in many EU markets, hence the attraction of markets in the Asia Pacific region and in Eastern Europe.

Economies of scale ｐ.)

To attain economies of scale, a large market is essential. If the domestic market is not large enough to absorb the entire output then the firm could enter a foreign market and gain considerable cost economies. It is through operating on a global scale that significant economies of scale and operational efficiencies can be realised. Firms in certain industries such as computer chips, cars, electronics, etc. need to compete globally to sustain their competitive position. The critical success factor for such industries is market share on a global scale. Attaining scale economies enables the firm to reduce its cost of creating value, and thereby gain a cost advantage with respect to its competitors.

End of the product life cycle ｔ.ｾ

A product may be near the end of its product life cycle in the domestic market but could experience a growth cycle in a foreign market. Sales of many consumer durables have begun to stagnate in EU markets, yet there is a growth market for these products in the emerging markets of Asia Pacific, Latin America and Eastern Europe.

Risk diversification ｒ\

If there is an economic downswing in the home market then firms that already trade internationally will be able to shift their focus and efforts to markets which have not yet been affected by the downturn in business. The assumption is that a recession will not affect all foreign markets at the same time or with the same intensity. This market-spreading strategy reduces the risk and cushions the firm from declining growth and profits in any one market.

Sourcing economies

In some industries, labour constitutes a high proportion of production costs. Currently, the emerging markets in Eastern Europe and the Asia Pacific region are a source of cheap and fairly skilled labour; this should be an incentive to many firms to expand their foreign operations. Many European, US and Japanese corporations have already established a foreign presence in countries such as Indonesia, Malaysia, China, Poland and Russia. Global sourcing has given many firms the competitive edge in international markets and contributed to the globalisation process. For example, the textile industry has shifted their location of production to the East Asian countries such as Southern China and the Philippines. The electronics industry has also sourced world-wide so that a substantial proportion of the world's disk drives are produced in Singapore. In spite of the advantages of sourcing, there are costs in using such labour in these markets. They include training costs as well as problems in transferring technology to these overseas sites. Both of these problems have been experienced in China, Hungary and Russia. In spite of these problems, companies are still attracted by the benefits of sourcing from these countries. Some nations offer tax incentives and subsidies to foreign firms to invest in their economies as a means to create jobs, obtain technological know-how and obtain scarce foreign currencies. In these circumstances, a foreign firm would reap the benefits of reduced production costs from cheap labour and from access to raw materials. It would also establish a presence in the market and gain invaluable market information for future opportunities. The UK has been one of the major EU countries to offer incentives to foreign firms to invest in the UK. Today, there are many Japanese, South Korean, Taiwanese and German companies based in the UK.

Box 10.2

THE WDA[2]

The Welsh Development Agency (WDA) is making strenuous efforts to attract inward investment, which it sees as the lifeblood of the region. Attracting foreign direct investment into the UK is a highly competitive business. The WDA has to compete with other UK regions such as Warwickshire, Cumbria and Northumbria. By February 1996 it had scored considerable success in attracting investment, in spite of losing Samsung and Siemens to North-East England. It won its first South Korean manufacturer, Halla, who invested £17m in a factory at Merthyr creating about 300 jobs. Then a Japanese company, Surface Technology Systems opened a £5m purpose-built plant making plasma systems for integrated circuits at Newport, Gwent. The Welsh economy depends heavily on foreign investment; there are over 360 overseas-owned plants employing about 70 000 people, representing about a third of the manufacturing force. The chairman of the WDA, Mr Rowe-Beddoe, said that low pay was not the motivating factor for inward investors to Wales. In fact, the major motivator is the UK as a whole and its advantages as far as Europe is concerned – convenience to customers, proximity to raw materials and component suppliers, highly skilled labour, infrastructure, quality of life for the workers and executives, etc. – that were major factors determining inward investment in the UK. According to the chairman of the WDA it is this 'package' that made the WDA a competitive agency.

Foreign marketing advantages

A home-based company may have built up competitive marketing advantages such as a strong sales force, product uniqueness or an efficient marketing organisational infrastructure. This should spur firms to expand internationally, and these marketing advantages can act as entry barriers to potential competitors in the overseas markets. For UK/EU companies, it may be the case that many international markets are less competitive than EU markets, in which case this would be a good opportunity for many of them to enter the market and even establish near-monopoly market positions.

International market opportunities

The 1990s has witnessed the emergence of new markets in different regions of the world. EU firms have generally not made their presence felt in Asia Pacific countries as much as Japanese and American firms have done. Asia Pacific countries are achieving high growth rates which are exceeding those of EU countries and are providing unprecedented opportunities. The political and cultural barriers to conducting business in this region are beginning to fall rapidly, and two potentially huge markets, those of China and India, should provide ample opportunities for market expansion in the late 1990s and into the twenty-first century. The emergence of Russia and the Eastern European countries, as well as the Latin American subcontinent, constitutes a potential major market for EU firms in the coming decades. Most of these markets are yet to be tapped by EU firms and those that plan their international strategies accordingly will gain considerable competitive advantages.

National policy

International marketing may be encouraged by national governments as a means of overcoming trade deficits. The UK's consistent deficits have made exporting a matter of urgency; the UK government offers grants, export advice, credit facilities and insurance to firms who wish to embark on international business. Indeed, the strategic thrust of the Asian 'Tiger' economies of Singapore, Taiwan, Hong Kong and now China is export oriented. The governments of some of the African emerging markets, such as Zimbabwe, South Africa and Botswana, have given export processing a priority in their economic development strategies.

Global competition

In many EU economies, European firms face fierce and intense competition from foreign firms, in particular from American and Japanese multinational corporations. The car and high-tech industries are particularly vulnerable and one of the ways to meet foreign competition is to enter the home markets of their foreign competitors and dent their competitiveness there. This in turn is likely to affect competitors' ability to penetrate overseas markets effectively. This strategy is best exemplified in the tyre industry, when the French company Michelin entered the US market and threatened Goodyear's market. Goodyear decided to expand to Europe and attack Michelin's home-market base and undercut the price of their products. This was an effective strategy and Michelin soon withdrew from the US market. In addition, firms in some industries such as steel, cars, electronic goods, etc., need to compete globally to sustain their market position. An added advantage of competing internationally is that firms can be kept abreast of the latest developments in technology, market focus, promotional strategies and so on.

To overcome trade barriers

One of the major reasons for entering foreign markets is to overcome potential trade barriers. It has been said that many Japanese firms have set up production facilities in the UK and other EU countries to overcome EU external trade barriers to non-EU members. Sony Corporation, for example, have set up facilities in Wales and Germany.

Geographical diversification

For firms who have a narrow product line, it may be a more desirable alternative to go international than engage in product-line diversification which could be costly and unsuccessful and eventually jeopardise the company's survival.

Utilise excess capacity

Firms which have excess capacity of resources, such as proprietary knowledge, production capacity, financial resources, etc., which are not being optimally used in the domestic market have been spurred to examine international market opportunities.

Information technology revolution

The rapid developments in telecommunications technology, satellite linkages, electronic mail, faxes, teleconferencing, etc., have made possible rapid and efficient multicountry communications, reducing the geographic distances between countries. This has been a major factor in encouraging firms to operate globally – it is almost as easy to conduct business between London and Paris as between Frankfurt and Singapore. Furthermore, the current development of the so called 'Information Superhighway' (the Internet) will alter the way business is conducted both nationally and globally. The rapid interchange of information between global markets will reduce business obstacles across different markets. Companies will be able to view the global economy as a single unit and it will also allow them to manage sophisticated systems. Companies operating different plants in several countries can now co-ordinate their activities with considerable ease. Passenger enquiries to American Airlines in Europe, for example, have all their calls routed to the Republic of Ireland.

The firm's strategic priorities in the initial market-entry phase is to ensure a strategic fit between the firm's current product offerings and the opportunities in the different country markets. The goal is to limit adaptation to its product–service offerings. The strategic focus is to extend the geographic markets and incur minimal marketing or production costs. The only major costs should be distributional to ensure delivery to the customers. The management focus is to determine which country markets to enter and market segments to serve, and how to enter those markets, i.e. the entry mode. The initial entry decision is critical as it entails resources and commitment that will be difficult to undo in the short run. The firm is faced with three major interrelated decisions:

1 *which countries to enter* – this will be evaluated on the basis of the opportunities and threats in the business environment of the country and the specific product market or service. This will be discussed later on in the chapter;

2 *timing of entry* – this refers specifically to whether the firm should enter one market and build its experience there before entering other markets, or whether it should enter several country markets simultaneously. The decision will depend on whether

the firm has adequate financial and managerial resources. Entering several markets at once will also give the firm a first-mover advantage (*see* Chapter 9), with the resulting scale economies and pre-empting future competitors' moves;[3]

3 *mode of entry* – this refers to the way the international operations are to be conducted – i.e. a joint venture or licensing arrangement. This will be discussed at some length in Chapter 11.

A firm that has entered the international arena for the first time will have been guided by customer needs, competitive forces and industry trends in the domestic market. The firm will lack international exposure and hence the necessary experience and knowledge of global markets. The firm's focus will therefore be to leverage its domestic core competencies internationally in order to gain economies of scale. Some of its competencies could be based on innovative product, technological expertise, strong brand or image, quality product, cost efficiency or on other proprietary assets. Well-known brand names such as Chanel, Benetton, The Body Shop and IKEA are proprietary assets that are leveraged internationally. Some of Japan's major companies began their internationalisation process by the introduction of innovative products in other countries with superior production technology and skills. US companies such as Proctor & Gamble leveraged their superior marketing management skills globally to gain a competitive advantage over their international and domestic competitors.

The majority of firms in the initial phase of internationalisation are small and medium-sized, or they are large companies from the emerging market countries. Hyundai and Daewoo are two firms from South Korea who have entered and invested substantially in EU countries and Eastern Europe. Acer, a Taiwanese computer firm, has also entered the EU market, emphasing its lower-priced models and product quality.

Local market expansion phase

This is the second phase of internationalisation. The focus on national orientation may be due to a number of factors:

1 to counter local competitors and respond to their initiatives;
2 to effectively and efficiently utilise its local marketing infrastructure, networks, etc.;
3 to increase market penetration, modifying the marketing strategy to broaden the local customer base;
4 to accommodate local management's thrust for growth and expansion;
5 to overcome local market constraints such as telecommunications and media networks, transportation systems, etc.

During this stage, management's focus is to seek expansion and growth in the country markets where the firm has already established its operations. The firm has developed familiarity with the local environment, established networks with suppliers, distributors and other business organisations, and built up its marketing and distribution infrastructure. The firm's goal will be to leverage these assets across a range of products to achieve economies of scope and develop local market potential. It will also need to foster demand by developing new products or targeting new market segments. Its strategic focus is therefore to move away from its domestic competencies and skills and develop local market know-how, competencies and expertise.

To leverage core competencies, the major priorities are to build on the firm's assets and organisational structures. Product lines can be expanded by building on the company's technological skills or proprietary assets such as brand names. New products or product variants can be made under the same brand name such as Honda motor cycles, Honda cars and lawnmowers. The Swiss watch manufacturer, Swatch, leveraged its brand name to expand its product line and introduced a line of low-priced sunglasses. A company's domestic mass-merchandising skills can also be utilised on new products developed specifically for the local market; Proctor & Gamble, for example, has applied its considerable international marketing expertise to products in the local markets.

The key area for management in this phase is to expand the local market developing suitable products and strategies for local needs, and this may involve product adaptation to expand the market base. Pricing tactics must be designed so as to take account of price elasticities and substitute- and competitor-product prices rather than the usual cost-plus approach, if the firm really wants to stimulate local market penetration. Promotional and distribution tactics will also be adopted and orientated to local market development.

This phase of internationalisation is often associated with a country-by-country approach, with the firm consolidating operations within each country market. When a company has several country markets with each country organisation operating as a profit centre, it can be said to be pursuing a *multicountry* or *multidomestic strategy*. Multidomestic competition exists when competition in one national market is independent of competition in another national market. A number of assumptions underlie the multidomestic strategy approach, including:

- national markets differ widely in consumer tastes, competitive conditions, political–legal structures, etc. (*see* Chapters 5–7); hence the need to decentralise strategic decision making

- product attributes will vary among nations according to consumer preferences.

Given that the marketing focus is to customise strategies to fit the circumstances of each host country, the implication is that there is little or no co-ordination across markets. Each country market functions as an independent business centre with its own range of product lines targeted to different customer segments and utilising different marketing strategies. Distribution is adapted to the practices and cultures of each host country. The production strategy will involve plants scattered across many host countries, and the source of supply for raw materials and components will be localised. In some cases, local sourcing may be a requirement of host governments. Organisationally, it is likely that subsidiary companies will be formed in each host market and operate more or less autonomously to fit the host country conditions. The impact of all these different specific operations, strategies and goals is that a company with many country markets will have little or no co-ordination between its different markets. The consequences of such a patchwork of diverse host country businesses is inefficiencies in the system. This factor, combined with the globalisation drive to integrate markets globally, will force many companies to rationalise and improve their global co-ordination.

Global rationalisation

This is the third and final phase of internationalisation. Management's focus in this phase is to realise potential synergies arising from operating on a international scale. The triggers for a global orientation are:

1 to take advantage of the multinational character of its operations and exploit the opportunities for transferring its skills, products, brands, etc. from one country market to another;

2 to eliminate the cost inefficiencies and duplication among the different host country subsidiaries;

3 to develop and enhance the linkages among the national marketing and business infrastructures with the aim of developing a global marketing infrastructure;

4 to capture a growing market of global consumers in both the industrial and consumer markets,

5 to be fully prepared for increased global competition.

The strategic thrust for a company in this phase is to improve the co-ordination and integration of strategy across the different country markets; and to fundamentally shift the focus of the development of its strategy from a country-by-country basis to a global one. In addition, what should guide the firm's strategic formulation is global market expansion. At this stage in the internationalisation process, the firm should try to attain synergies and improve the efficiency and co-ordination of its various marketing activities. This will involve transferring skills or assets such as technical know-how, products, marketing and management expertise, brand image, experience skills, marketing ideas, etc. across different country markets. By leveraging its assets and position in different country markets and globally, the company can obtain global synergies. The firm can rationalise its operations in the following way.[4]

Increasing the operational efficiency of its world-wide networks

If the firm rationalises its operations and improves the co-ordination between them, this is likely to increase the company's efficiency. The company could consolidate its upstream activities such as production, R&D, procurement, etc., and the end result will be a reduction in the duplication of activities which will enable the company to realise some economies of scale. The firm that can produce a product in a few choice locations can reap global volume-scale economies that are not available to smaller domestic firms. The scale economies will lower the costs of value creation and will help the company to become a low-cost player in the global industry.

On the other hand, the firm could develop and refine a global logistical system whereby components or parts can be produced in specific locations; these are then shipped to assembly or production locations in other parts of the world. In other words, the firm needs to configure the global value chain so as to increase its value-added functions. This means it must perform different value-creating activities in the locations where the mix of factors of production and costs and skills is most favourable. The major factors determining the most favourable location for global manufacturing are access to a ready infrastructure (transportation systems, conducive political climate, etc.), energy costs, access to an appropriately trained workforce, labour costs and proximity to the consumer and industrial markets.

In the late 1980s the Ford subsidiary in Europe moved its European car production facilities to the UK from Germany because labour costs were not only lower, but the productivity of the British workers was higher than their German counterparts. Ford thus moved their operations from a high-cost and high-skill location to a low-cost and high-skill location. The company was able to lower its costs of value creation. Sony Corporation of Japan was able to become a low-cost producer in the global television market when it centralised its manufacturing facilities, thereby gaining scale economies, and it also deployed global marketing strategies.

The process of re-nationalisation can be undertaken on both a global and regional basis, and with the current trend for trade blocs such as the EU and NAFTA, it is not surprising that some firms have already opted for this strategy. Some companies, such as Scott Paper, have adopted pan-European strategies whereby production, logistics, financial and marketing operations serve the regional customers. Plants are located at strategic points in the EU; this means all the plants can use the same technology and management experience can be transferred to different country locations within the EU.

Transferring core skills overseas: A company's core skills of technology, management, marketing, R&D and know-how can be transferred and shared across the firm's global operations. The company's core skills allow it to perform one or more value-creation functions that enable it to differentiate itself from its competitors and charge a premium price. Companies such as IBM and Kodak have gained from transferring their core skills in R&D and technology. Some firms, for example, Coca-Cola, Procter & Gamble and H.J. Heinz, have based their global competitive advantages on marketing skills and know-how and have profited enormously. Many service organisations have a global competitive advantage over local competitors because of better management techniques and trained managers; the Sheraton chain of hotels and management consultancy companies are examples.

Development of a global strategy

The second aspect of management's strategic thrust in this phase is to develop a global marketing strategic perspective. This mindset, which forms the basis of this text and will be discussed at length in the rest of the book, will assist marketing managers to allocate resources appropriately across country markets, target segments, product businesses and the firm's various international operations. This global strategy needs to be implemented effectively if the firm is to see the desired results. This may entail the establishment of mechanisms to co-ordinate and control resources, information, etc. across country markets and product businesses.

SELECTION OF FOREIGN MARKETS

The globalisation of the world economy has intensified competition across a range of industries, and many companies need firm guidelines and approaches to enable them to evaluate international market opportunities. Companies will need an approach to assist them to determine which markets to invest in, and what the optimal combination of country markets and market segments should be.

Portfolio analysis

Portfolio analysis is one of the major techniques used to evaluate a company's competitive position in the global market. The firm needs to review its current and potential portfolio of global markets to determine the roles they should play in the company's overall strategic marketing plan. In the last two decades, a number of portfolio techniques have been developed to assist firms to assess their current activities; these are the growth–share matrix and the market attractiveness–business position matrix. Global portfolio assessment:

1 provides an overview of how the firm classifies its foreign markets and is a useful graphical device for examining the competitive position of the firm's businesses or products;

2 forces management to set priorities and make decisions;

3 determines the degree of modification to the marketing mix required for a particular market;

4 allocates its marketing resources for a particular market.

The portfolio analysis will identify which business activities should be maintained, reduced or eliminated. Two of the major portfolio techniques to help firms evaluate their current business activities will be discussed.

BCG growth–share matrix

A simplified version of the Boston Consulting Group (BCG) portfolio matrix is shown in Fig. 10.1.

Fig 10.1 THE BCG GROWTH–SHARE MATRIX

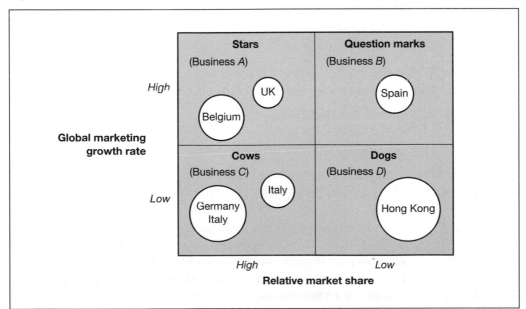

The aim of the matrix is to assist marketing managers in determining the role of each business unit or product of a company on the basis of:

● its market growth rate and market share relative to its competitors

● its cash flow potential.

The BCG matrix highlights the cash flow, investment and profitability characteristics of various businesses and the benefits of shifting financial resources between them to optimise the whole portfolio's performance. Market share is on the horizontal axis relative to the firm's largest competitor, and market growth of the industry is on the vertical axis with x per cent growth rate arbitrarily used to separate the markets into high and low growth. Each circle represents a product with sales equivalent to the area of the circle. Four basic strategies of the BCG matrix can be adopted with a given product. The simplest strategy for a global firm to follow is to divest its dogs and harvest the cash flows from its cash cows to assist the growth of the stars and help the position of the question mark businesses. The implications for global marketing strategies in terms of the matrix are as follows:

1 for cash cows, maintain market share whilst at the same time generating large cash flows;

2 for star businesses, build market share and therefore improve their competitive position;

3 for question marks, use them to increase market share if firms are willing to invest in these types of businesses;

4 for dog businesses, divest, or if the objective is to generate short-term cash flows, then harvest the business.

In the international context, the strategy selected will depend on:

● the product's present market position

● the company's resources relative to major competitors

● the likely reactions of its competitors

● the product's life-cycle stage

● other information such as social, legal and political pressures, etc.

Although the BCG matrix was designed for the domestic market, it can be used in the international market but it must be interpreted and used with caution. The growth–share matrix can help managers to evaluate their international marketing strategies:

1 if a UK company has a cash cow in Brazil, but due to government regulations it is not allowed to transfer funds from Brazil to its star businesses in Germany or Japan, then the global marketing strategy will be seriously affected;

2 the growth–share matrix can highlight the company's competitive position – it may be strategically sensible to retain a business unit in a country with a slow market growth rate in order to defend its position and pre-empt entry by its competitors;

3 the matrix technique can also assist the firm in establishing where funds should be generated, where they should be re-invested and which country markets to target, we can illustrate this by looking at Fig. 10.2.

Fig 10.2 CASH COWS, STARS, QUESTION MARKS AND DOGS

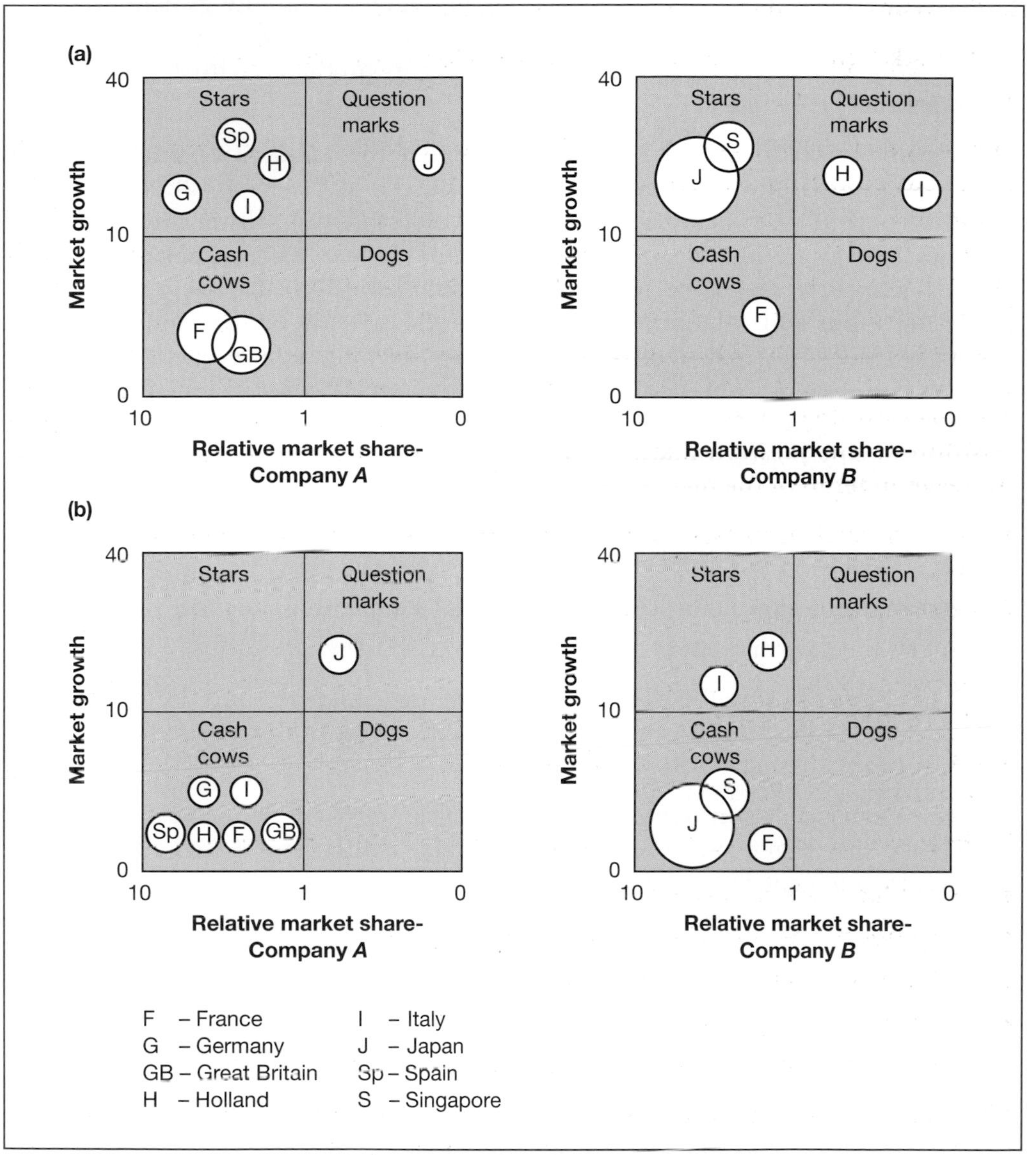

(a)

(b)

F – France   I – Italy
G – Germany   J – Japan
GB – Great Britain   Sp – Spain
H – Holland   S – Singapore

Source: Adapted from Gilligan, C. and Hird, M., *International Marketing* (London: Croom Helm, 1986), 177.

We will now illustrate how the portfolio technique is applied. We will assume that the analysis is based on one product area, with the circles in the matrices representing country rather than product sales. The objective of the analysis would be to assess the company's current global product–country market portfolio, the competitors' portfolios and the projection of future portfolios. Figure 10.2 illustrates the product–market portfolios of two companies.

1 *Company A* (Fig. 10.2a) is the market leader with a relatively weak portfolio. It has mature products in the UK and France (cash cows), and it has a number of high-growth products in parts of Europe (stars). It has a small presence in Japan.

2 *Company B* is the smaller of the two companies, but it has great potential as it has a substantial presence in Singapore and Japan which are rapidly growing markets. What emerges from the above brief description of the two companies, is that Company *A* is facing a decline in demand for its products, whilst Company *B*'s products are in demand.

If Company *A* were to forecast the likely outcome of the competitive situation in 2–4 years' time, we could have the situation as illustrated in Fig. 10.2b. Company *A* would then need to implement a strategy to avoid its demise. Using the BCG framework in the way we have just illustrated, companies can assess their competitors' product–market strength and forecast (albeit simplistically), the likely outcomes of future portfolios and what strategic moves to make. Using our example, it may be necessary for Company *A* to enter the Japanese and Singaporean markets and thus prevent Company *B* from gaining a significant competitive position in the future. What strategic options it would choose to achieve this objective would depend on its overall company objectives, resources and competencies. Company *A*'s core marketing strategy could be to price aggressively or promote heavily to achieve a market position in those markets or it could form strategic alliances with local firms. This example illustrates two key advantages in using portfolio analysis:

● it gives a firm a global perspective of the global competitive situation

● it guides the development of a global marketing strategy.

The limitations of using the portfolio approach are similar to those in the domestic market. Some of the problems with using the BCG matrix in the international evaluation of markets are that:

1 government regulations which block the transfer of funds or increase operational costs, etc. may turn a cash cow into a dog, thus the matrix cannot account for changes in the environmental parameters, and risk dimensions are excluded from the analysis;

2 there are other factors which affect the portfolio analysis, such as profitability, the effects of diversification, etc. and not simply product sales;

3 the model does not incorporate the costs of entering various markets.

These additional factors are difficult to introduce into the matrix. It is not the intention here to give a comprehensive review; the reader is advised to consult the relevant literature on this topic for an in-depth analysis of the technique.

The market attractiveness–competitive position matrix

Portfolio analysis can also be used to establish market priorities – that is, how one business unit or product can be compared with another in terms of investment and competitiveness. The BCG growth–share matrix technique can provide only a partial insight to this aspect. The market attractiveness–competitive position matrix (sometimes known as the country attractiveness–competitive strength matrix) should assist the manager to focus simultaneously across a range of foreign markets to determine:

● resource requirements

● entry costs to foreign markets

● profitability levels.

This model can be useful as a tool to determine country market selection (*see* Fig. 10.3). The vertical axis measures market attractiveness and the horizontal axis measures the company's competitive strengths; on both axes the factors are weighted and ranked on a scale as shown. The variables which are assessed in Table 10.1 will depend on the product sold, and the choice of variables will depend on the industry sector. Since many of the variables cannot be quantified, a subjective evaluation will have to be made.

Fig 10.3 MARKET ATTRACTIVENESS–COMPETITIVE POSITION MATRIX

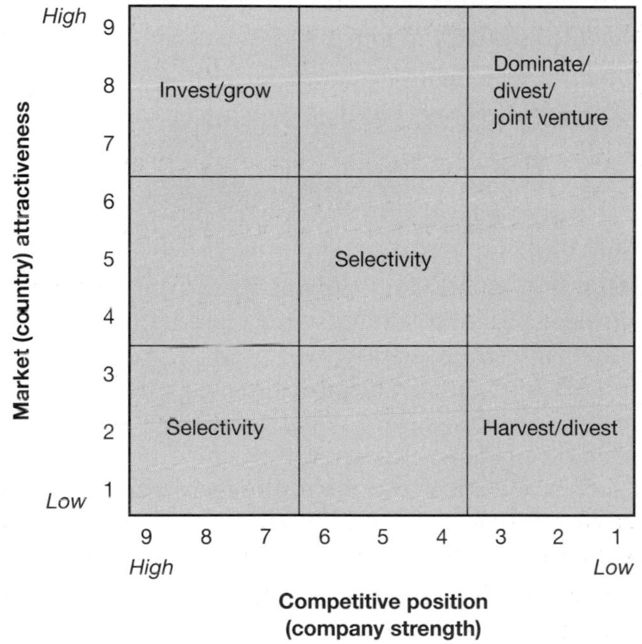

Source: Harrell, G.D. and Kiefer, R.O., 'Multinational strategic market portfolios', *MSU Business Topics* (Winter 1981), 5–15.

Table 10.1 DIMENSIONS OF COUNTRY ATTRACTIVENESS AND COMPETITIVE STRENGTH

Country attractiveness	Competitive strength
Market size (total and segments)	Market share
Market growth (total and segments)	Marketing ability and capacity
Market seasons and fluctuations	Product fit
Competitive conditions (concentration, intensity entry barriers, etc.)	Contribution margin
Market prohibitive conditions (tarrifs, NTBs, import restrictions, etc.)	Image
	Technology position
Government regulations (price controls, local content, compensatory exports, etc.)	Product quality
	Market support
Economic and political stability	Quality of distributors and service

Source: Albaum, G. *et al.*, *International Marketing and Export Management*, 2nd edition (Reading, MA: Addison-Wesley, 1994), 113.

In using Fig. 10.3, each country would be located in one of the cells, based on the ratings from 1 to 9.

1 *Invest/grow markets*: countries falling into the upper-left-hand corner of the matrix are good market positions for additional investment. Countries in this cell have high attractiveness ratings and the firm has the best competitive advantage to exploit the market opportunities.

2 *Harvest/divest/license/combine markets*: countries falling into the lower-right-hand corner of the matrix call for strategies that harvest the profits or sell the business. Countries in this cell are not attractive, and the firm also lacks the competitive strengths to maintain its market position. Any cash that is generated from the business is maximised and is required to maintain market share. However, the firm could still generate income without much investment outlay by a licensing strategy.

3 *Dominant/divest/joint venture markets*: countries falling into the upper-right-hand corner of the matrix are attractive, but the company lacks the competitive strengths to exploit the market potential. This may be due to the firm not having the right products or market expertise. The firm could strengthen its position by having a joint venture with either a local firm or competitor in the market. Generally, no investments should be made. These markets pose difficult choices for the firm.

4 *Selectivity markets*: the situation is more complex for the other areas of the matrix and the firm will need to assess carefully each case before making a decision. In some cases, products in certain markets will produce good cash flows but market share may be difficult to maintain. Competition tends to be extreme and intense. These markets are good candidates for milking, and maintenance strategies should be adopted that build cash flows. However, if a company has a unique competence or competitive advantage such as a technological breakthrough, it could even attempt to build market share.

Figure 10.4 illustrates the use of the country attractiveness–competitive strength matrix. This matrix shows how the Ford Tractor division assessed its international operations: Brazil would seem to indicate a fairly sizeable market but the firm's competitive position in Brazil is only moderately good. The Honda company also uses the matrix to assess its market portfolio. This type of portfolio analysis is useful to the marketing manager because:

1 it enables the firm to assess whether it has tapped the growth markets or whether it has committed itself extensively to slow-growth markets;

2 it enables the firm to determine whether it has exploited opportunities in new markets before its competitors;

3 it enables the firm to determine the major role of each foreign market in its international plans – it may be the case that country *X*'s primary role is to provide growth, or to prevent the expansion of rival firms.

However, it should be noted that the market attractiveness–competitive position matrix is only one of a number of tools to use in assessing a firm's overall international marketing strategy, and other analytical methods will need to be used in conjunction with it. Global portfolio analysis is used essentially to assist firms:

Fig 10.4 A KEY COUNTRY MATRIX

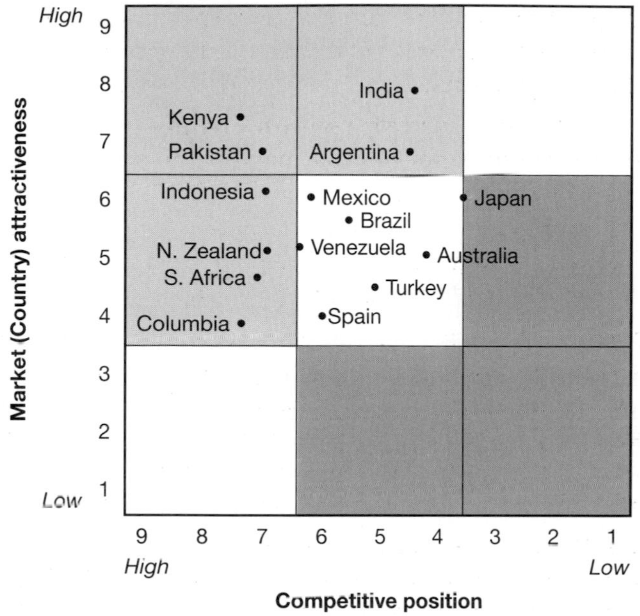

Source: Harrell, G.D. and Kiefer, R.O., 'Multinational strategic market portfolios', *MSU Business Topics* (Winter 1981), 13.

- to allocate their resources among different geographic and product markets
- to determine the extent of their global operations.

Naturally, the two points are related. If the firm spreads its resources too thinly over a wide product market, it may lead to competitive disadvantages in the form of a limited research and development programme or poor-quality service. After making an assessment of its country portfolio, the firm must then choose a competitive market strategy to implement its portfolio strategy. There are numerous types of strategies available to a firm, ranging from the co-operative to confrontational; these were discussed in Chapter 9.

DECISION CRITERIA FOR CHOICE OF ENTRY MODE

The country choice decision discussed earlier in the chapter is closely linked to decisions regarding how a firm should conduct its operations in global markets – exporting, joint ventures, etc. Although the two decisions are separate and distinct, it is safe to add that specific country–market characteristics as well as the firm's expansion strategies do ultimately affect the mode of entry choice. A country's political situation, infrastructure, market size, etc. is likely to affect the company's management attitudes regarding the amount of resources the firm is prepared to commit to the given country–market. A country with a slow growth rate is unlikely to attract large resources, and the management team may prefer direct exporting or having a local partner agreement in the form of distributors.

The choice of mode of entry into foreign markets is for many firms a fundamental and critical decision in international marketing, since the type of entry mode will influence the rest of the marketing programme.[5] For example, if the firm opts for a licensing agreement then its ability to influence product development, promotion or pricing will be severely curtailed. On the other hand, if the firm makes a decision to manufacture in the host country, then it will be able to exert a high degree of control in terms of its marketing and production decisions, but this will entail higher costs and greater risks. The choice of entry method may also involve the firm in a long-term commitment from which it might find it hard to extricate itself without some cost. The market entry decision thus involves a trade-off between control, costs and risks (*see* Fig. 10.5). Many firms from small concerns to large multinational enterprises should be able to find appropriate channels to reach foreign markets with the diversity of alternatives available, and these are discussed in Chapter 11.

The variables affecting the entry mode choice (*see* Fig.10.6) can be categorised into two broad groupings:

- environmental variables
- firm specific variables.

There are numerous other variables which can impact on the firm's mode of entry choice, but this chapter will focus only on the major ones. The importance and specific nature of these variables will depend on the company, the market it competes in, and the company's product or service. The mode choice is a multidimensional task, and each entry decision is not made in isolation from others. How these different variables impact on the mode of entry choice will now be discussed.

Fig 10.5 TRADE-OFFS IN THE MARKET-ENTRY DECISION

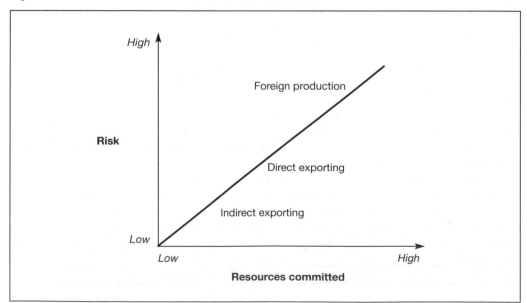

Fig 10.6 AN ENTRY-MODE CHOICE FRAMEWORK

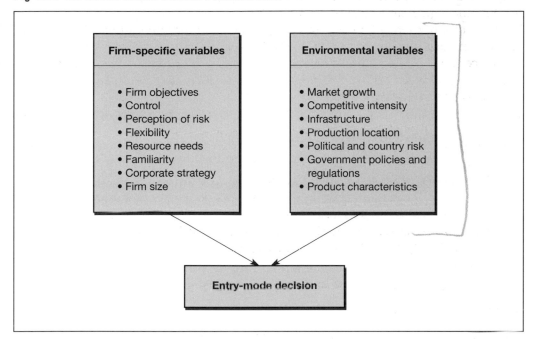

FIRM-SPECIFIC VARIABLES

The firm's objectives, strategies, varying international experience and attitudes towards key characteristics such as control, risk, flexibility, etc. will influence its choice of market-entry techniques.

The firm's objectives

The degree of involvement in and commitment to international markets will depend to a large extent on the firm's strategic motivations, goals and objectives. If these are established clearly before any overseas ventures, it will provide direction and focus for the firm's efforts in terms of assessing global opportunities and resource allocation requirements.

Firms who have limited objectives for international expansion are likely to favour indirect exporting methods. These entail the use of export houses, agents or distributors, and require limited financial and management resources as well as minimal commitment to the venture.

On the other hand, a firm which perceives the international markets as a source of long-term growth and profits is likely to take a more proactive and aggressive approach. The entry-mode choice is likely to involve a direct market-entry option, such as joint ventures or even overseas acquisitions in order to establish a strong market presence. If the firm's goal is to be a market leader, then these options would be suitable. For example, Nestlé, the giant Swiss multinational company, tends to enter foreign markets through acquisitions, joint ventures or other forms of foreign direct investment.

Control

The firm's need for control management is another critical factor determining the entry-mode choice. Control involves the firm having authority over operational and strategic decision making. For example, it enables the firm to:

- co-ordinate activities across markets
- control product quality
- have an input into the logistical and marketing activities in the target market
- adapt its products and services to meet local needs
- respond to pre-emptive moves by competitors in the host markets.

By controlling the decision-making process, the firm is able to determine its international destiny. A firm that wants to have more control over its foreign marketing activities, such as its pricing or promotional strategies, will most likely opt for a direct exporting entry mode such as an overseas sales subsidiary. If producing overseas, it may have a licensing or joint venture agreement. Such a high degree of control will entail higher levels of resource commitment; these will include not only financial resources but also greater management time to co-ordinate the various activities and ensure product quality.

On the other hand, a firm opting for less control in the initial stages of overseas expansion would perhaps select an indirect method of entry such as the use of a UK export merchant in the first instance. In this case, resource and management commitments would be minimal. The firm would have no control over the way the product is marketed and developed.

Resource requirements

The firm's resources refers to the financial, physical and human resources that it commits to its overseas markets. Setting up an overseas operation such as a joint venture requires not only capital resources but also management time and effort. Although the resources and risks are shared between the partners in a joint venture, much management time is taken up with managing the venture and smoothing out any operational difficulties. On the other hand, firms may opt for indirect exporting methods such as using an export management company – this mode involves a low level of risk, and low levels of resources to be committed to the venture. Some would argue that minimal resource commitments by firms would not be conducive to developing their international markets and operations: they may lose out on opportunities in the global market.[6] According to Driscoll,[7] firms tend over time to increase the resources committed to foreign markets as the level of uncertainty declines. This is due to firms gaining experience and knowledge of the markets.

The opportunity cost of committing resources to one specific market is not investing it in other markets. The risk involved in committing resources is that they may be expropriated by governments. Two critical questions arise regarding resource allocation:

- What level of resources should the firm commit to the venture?
- Does the firm have the requisite resources for international markets?

With respect to the last question, human resource requirements can hinder the international growth of the firm as well as determining its entry mode. In general, if the firm lacks skilled and experienced international personnel, it should avoid direct and high-risk entry strategies. The administrative burdens of market entry, such as documentation and management expertise, will vary depending on the entry technique chosen. To avoid such costs the firm could choose indirect exporting, such as using export houses or export management companies, which imposes limited burdens on the firm.

Risk

Firms perceive the foreign market as a riskier venture than the home market, and the degree of risk a firm is willing to accept will depend on a number of factors, such as its commitment to international markets, its corporate strategy, level of overseas experience, etc. There are many different types of risks, but we can conveniently group them into four broad categories as identified by Ghoshal[8] and illustrated in Fig. 10.7. A thorough analysis of risk management will not be attempted here as they are comprehensively discussed in Chapters 5 and 7.

Macroenvironmental risks

These are beyond the control of the firm and arise from unstable economic or political conditions. They can manifest themselves as wars and internal conflicts, as in Sri Lanka. The exchange rate risk is another variable which increases the degree of risk associated with entry methods. A profit margin of five per cent of gross sales could be wiped out by a currency devaluation exceeding five per cent, as many companies experienced in late 1997 and early 1998 in Indonesia and Malaysia, when these countries' currencies depreciated substantially against the US dollar. One possible method of entry to avoid rapid fluctuations in exchange rates is by means of direct production. Profits can then be repatriated when the exchange rates are at an appropriate level, otherwise the firm could re-invest the profits and wait for the desired rate of exchange before transferring the funds back to the home country.

Fig 10.7 COMPONENTS OF RISK

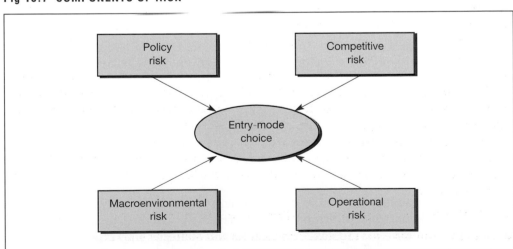

Policy risks

These arise from government decisions, and may include restrictions on FDI and the repatriation of profits, the imposition of tariffs and regulatory restrictions. The implications of macroenvironmental and policy risks on the choice of entry strategies will be discussed under the Environmental variables section of this chapter.

Operational risks

These arise from the firm's own strategic actions in international markets. The firm may be introducing a new product–service to an untested market, or there may be cultural resistance to accepting the product, such as introducing Kellogg's Corn Flakes for breakfast in China.

Competitive risks

These arise from the competitors' actions in both the domestic and international markets. For example, a competitor may launch a pre-emptive strike against the firm to gain market share, or it may launch a new product–service.

All four categories of risk will influence and affect the firm's decision on *whether* it should enter a given market, and *how* it should enter it. Firms which have limited resources and a low tolerance for financial risk may prefer indirect entry methods. Indirect entry modes, such as franchising, would be more attractive because a firm would share the financial risk with the host country firms. The international expansion of firms like The Body Shop and Benetton have been made possible because of such shared risks.

Another particular type of risk which can impact on the entry-mode decision is known as dissemination risk.

Dissemination risk[9]

This is the perceived risk by firms that their contractual partners may expropriate their know-how. This know-how, be it marketing- or technologically-based, may be the firm's source of competitive advantage, and dissemination of this knowledge asset may harm its competitive position or even threaten its survival. Although this type of risk may be combated through comprehensive contract clauses, they are in practice difficult to specify, if at all. This type of risk is a crucial determinant of a firm's choice of entry.

When planning an entry strategy, the firm thus needs to carry out a thorough analysis of the different types of risks. The impact of the various types of risk are not necessarily cumulative, nor are they static. Risks change over time, and at different rates. The macroenvironment and policy risks are not under the control of the firm, and management will need to determine the trade-off between an acceptable level of risk and the potential benefits of the particular market. The firm's attitude to risk is a critical factor in determining the choice of country markets, mode of entry and the allocation of resources to be committed.

Flexibility

This refers to the ability of a firm to change its entry methods quickly and with minimal cost when market conditions change. The firm's ability to adapt to meet changing circumstances is critical: a firm's goals and strategies may change over time, as will the markets in which it operates. If the firm expects to be in the overseas markets for a long period, this flexibility to expand its operations in a growing market or to contract its overseas operations in adverse conditions is important.

For firms that wish to maintain this flexibility in the initial stages of market expansion overseas, it would be prudent to choose an entry option with limited involvement to gain the necessary experience and confidence before committing themselves to a long-term entry strategy in which flexibility is difficult to attain.

There is an inverse relationship between flexibility and resource commitment. Firms who engage in substantial resource investment, such as in production facilities, will find it difficult to exit immediately in adverse environmental conditions. This type of strategic inflexibility increases the firm's costs of entry, as well as the possibility of losing out on 'first-mover' advantages in other markets. A firm's desire for flexibility will undoubtedly influence its entry options.

Familiarity with global markets

If the firm's management has little or no experience of international markets, it is likely that the company will select an entry option that limits its international involvement and hence its resource commitment. This lack of experience or familiarity with customer characteristics, environmental conditions, etc. will lead management to perceive foreign markets as risky and full of uncertainty. On the other hand, if managers are familiar with international markets, the converse situation arises. The experiential knowledge reduces the firm's costs and uncertainties of operating in global markets, and furthermore the company would be more inclined to commit resources to the international programme.

Corporate strategies

The firm's strategic approach to foreign markets will also affect its entry model choice.

Multinational corporations may have global strategic motivations which can result in them not selecting the most optimal entry method. A firm can be said to have a global strategic motivation when it wishes to 'fulfil strategic objectives set out at the corporate level for the purpose of attaining overall corporate efficiency maximisation'.[10] A firm may enter a particular market to source raw materials for its world-wide activities. Its entry strategy may not be an optimal one, but it may better fit the company-wide or the long-term strategy of the firm. In general, it could be argued that firms with strategic motivations are more likely to opt for high-control entry modes.

Most small UK firms lack export orientation and therefore their strategy is defined in terms of the UK market. It is more than likely that such firms will engage at most in indirect market entry strategies. On the other hand, a small company in Belgium might undertake a direct market-entry strategy believing that its survival and growth depended on exporting regularly.

In situations where a company has to exploit market opportunities rapidly before their competitors, it is possible that it will select an entry mode that will take advantage of established business networks, distribution channels, market knowledge, etc. The firm could therefore select anything from a joint venture operation, strategic alliance or acquisition of a local company. On the other hand, if the firm wanted to explore a particular market in a piecemeal fashion, it would probably start off with indirect exporting and then go on to more direct forms of investment.

A firm which wanted to enter multiple markets rapidly to gain 'first-mover' advantages before its competitors, would probably enter into collaborative agreements such as joint ventures, licensing or strategic alliances. These options will compensate for the firm's lack of resources and complement their existing competencies and skills.[11]

The strategic goals and motivations of a firm thus play a crucial role in determining its entry mode in foreign markets.

Company size

Company size will influence a firm's objectives in international markets, as well as being a good indicator of its ability to access resources. A small firm may wish to be heavily involved in foreign markets with a high level of control over its operations, but being small makes it difficult for it to access both financial and human resources (i.e. management expertise and skills). The small firm may have limited choice, and will have to adopt an indirect exporting mode of entry in many cases. However, this is not a permanent constraint, the development of specialist international services such freight forwarding, marketing agencies, etc. in combination with developments in logistics management and IT, have all facilitated international expansion by smaller companies.

ENVIRONMENTAL VARIABLES

There are a number of key environmental factors which impact on the entry-mode decision and these will now be discussed.

Economic environment

Market growth

One of the major considerations for firms in selecting an entry method is whether there is a demand for its products–services. Country size and market growth rate are fairly good indicators of demand conditions. Management is more likely to commit resources to a larger country with a high market growth rate. They may consider establishing joint ventures or setting up their own subsidiary. With such a resource commitment, the firm will exert greater control and be able to guide the market development process more directly.

Smaller markets, which may exhibit lower purchasing power, with fragmented demand segments or which are geographically dispersed, will not command major resource commitments from the firm. The most likely entry options would entail the use of agents or distributors, or at most some licensing agreement. While these approaches may not capitalise on the market opportunities, they do allow the firm to enter the market where demand is uncertain or small with minimal resources; at the same time, it enables the firm to commit more resources to larger and more attractive markets.

Intensity of competition

When competition is intense in host markets, it may lead to price wars and subsequently reduced returns on investment; in addition, the opportunities to determine pricing strategies are reduced. Other things being equal, the greater the intensity of competition, the more the firm is likely favour entry methods that involve low resource commitment.

Market infrastructure

Another major factor which has an impact on the entry-mode choice is a country's economic and market infrastructure. If a market has a poorly developed physical infrastructure – distribution facilities, transportation systems, communication systems and so on – this will ultimately increase a firm's costs of entry. Although promising, the markets of Eastern Europe and China have a major drawback in this respect. The most feasible entry option would be indirect exporting – the use of distributors, perhaps. Again, the decision needs to be considered in conjunction with other factors such as market size, market growth, etc. before a final choice is made.

Production location

Cost factors are the major determinant in the exporting versus local production decision. It may be the case that a market is not large enough to support an economic scale of production. Apart from cost considerations, there are many advantages associated with local production, such as immediate market feedback and adaptation of products–service to meet local needs. Firms may produce locally to overcome trade barriers to the market – many Japanese companies and Southeast Asian firms have set-up local production facilities in the UK and the EU in recent times, for example.

On the other hand, studies[12] have shown that if firms perceive a great distance between the home and host markets in terms of culture and business practices then they will not choose a direct investment entry option, but rather a joint venture agreement which gives the firm greater flexibility to withdraw as well as having to commit minimal resources.

Production and country risk

If a market's political and economic environment is volatile and unpredictable, this will increase the firm's perceived risk and uncertainty. The favoured mode of entry would be one where resource commitment was minimal, with a large degree of flexibility in order to respond to potential risks of nationalisation, expropriation or civil unrest. Many Western firms investing in Russia and some of the Eastern European markets face political and economic instability on a constant basis, this is not helped by a bureaucratic business culture, habit of broken contractual agreements, etc. Under these circumstances, exporting would perhaps represent the preferred option.

Government policies and regulations

Government policies and regulations have a major impact on the firm's mode-of-entry options. In some cases, governments' actions do in fact restrict the mode-of-entry options open to foreign firms. Some host governments prohibit 100 per cent ownership or place limits on ownership of strategically important industrial sectors such as transportation, telecommunications and defence. Under these circumstances, the firm may have to choose contractual entry options such as joint ventures, licensing or contract manufacturing.

Protectionist policies in the form of tariffs, quotas and duties also influence the mode-of-entry decision. The effect of such barriers to trade, is that it encourages the deployment of contractual and investment entry options. Japanese companies, especially in the car and electronic sectors, have opted for investment-based entry strategies in the EU, establishing production facilities to circumvent import quota restrictions.

Indirect trade barriers, in the form of product or trade regulations and preferences for local suppliers, affect a firm's entry choice. The effect of product and trade regulations is to encourage companies to form local production facilities in the host market, jointly with local companies if necessary. By doing this, the foreign firm gains instant access to information in the local market and can easily adapt their products–services to meet local regulations and standards. Where there is a strong tendency to prefer local suppliers, foreign companies can form joint ventures or other contractual agreements with local firms to overcome this barrier.

Product characteristics

The company's product (industrial or consumer) will determine the level of service support required. If technical products are sold to industrial end-users then technical support will be required. For fast-moving consumer products, merchandising the product will be needed. Where the product requires after-sales service this will also affect the choice of method of entry – it is most likely that a direct exporting strategy will be advantageous to the firm here. Komatsu, the Japanese construction equipment company, is committed to a high-quality service world-wide, and this approach has involved direct marketing in most of the markets the company has entered.

For products with low weight–value ratios, such as watches and portable laptops, direct exporting- or investment-based strategies would be suitable. Management would have greater control over product quality as well as gaining scale economies.

In cases where the product–service incorporates proprietary technology, the firm is unlikely to participate in joint ventures or any entry mode that entails loss of control over production or sharing of proprietary information. The most likely type of entry choice would be a strict licensing agreement with constant monitoring.

SUMMARY

Firms entering international markets gain a number of benefits which are not attainable in the domestic market. Some of the major motives for global expansion include growth and profit goals, diversification of risks, exploiting unique product and technological competencies, gaining economies of scale, to utilise unused excess capacity of resources, etc.

Global portfolio analysis provides the firm with a framework to assist managers to determine the allocation of resources and which national markets to maintain, expand, enter into or divest. The growth–share model is particularly useful in identifying the impact of the internally generated cash flows on these decisions. The market attractiveness–business position matrix can be used to understand the implications of the investment decisions in different country markets.

The choice of entry methods depends on two broad categories of variables, firm-specific and environmental. The former group includes the firm's goals and objectives, its desire to maintain control and flexibility, resource commitment, whether it is risk averse or not, familiarity with overseas markets, company size and corporate strategy. The environmental factors include market size and growth, infrastructure, political and country risks, location of production, government policies and regulations and product characteristics.

REVIEW QUESTIONS

1 What are the benefits of international marketing?

2 What is global portfolio analysis?

3 What are the problems in using the BCG growth–share matrix?

4 What are the drawbacks of adopting a portfolio approach in international marketing?

5 Identify the major dimensions used to analyse the competitor's strengths and weaknesses.

6 What are the firm-specific and environmental variables that influence a firm's mode-of-entry choice?

DISCUSSION QUESTIONS

1 Should the UK/EU governments encourage and facilitate UK/EU export activities?

2 The BCG portfolio matrix technique was designed for domestic firms. Discuss how successful it is when applied to international companies.

3 Why do firms need to have different levels of market entry?

4 Table 10.1 (p. 275) illustrated variables which measured country attractiveness and competitive strengths. What changes would you make to the variables? Explain why you made these changes.

5 Is there a relationship between a global marketing plan and the foreign market-entry strategy?

6 There are many factors that have an influence on the type of market-entry mode that a firm might select. Are any of these more important than the others? Justify your conclusion.

Case study

VOLKSWAGEN SWITCHES WORK TO LOW-COST UNIT IN SLOVAKIA

Volkswagen, Europe's leading carmaker, is rapidly expanding its operations in Slovakia as part of its effort to develop plants in Eastern Europe to offset its high-cost structure in Germany.

Volkswagen Bratislava, its Slovak subsidiary, more than doubled car production to 20 000 in 1995 from 8000 in 1994 and 3000 in 1993. Car output was planned to rise by a further 50 per cent to 30 000 in 1996, said Mr Karl Wilhelm, Technical Managing Director.

VW has moved all production of its four-wheel-drive Golf Syncro family hatchbacks and estate cars for the European market from Wolfsburg, its main plant in Germany, to Bratislava.

Output of the technically sophisticated four-wheel-drive cars was to be increased to around 20 000 in 1996 from 13 500 in 1995, while the company planned to assemble about 5000 front-wheel-drive Golfs and 5000 Passat large family cars for sale in Slovakia and in other markets in Central and Eastern Europe. VW is also developing the Bratislava plant for the assembly of gear boxes and the machining of some gearbox components in order to lower costs at its main German gearbox plant at Kessel. The German carmaker began gearbox assembly in Bratislava in 1994. Output rose from 46 000 in 1994 to 185 000 in 1995 and was planned to rise further to 260 000 in 1996.

In 1995, it also moved a machining line from Kassel to Bratislava and is to produce around 600 000 gearbox parts for use at both the Slovak and Kassel plants.

Mr Wilhelm said that the Bratislava plant was being used as 'an extended workbench' for the Kassel operation. 'They have cost problems. Machining these components in Bratislava cuts the cost of a gearbox by DM5 per unit and makes Kessel more competitive. This is interesting for both plants and gives them a long-term future.'

The workforce at the Bratislava plant is growing rapidly as a result of the transfer of operations from Germany and increased from 817 in 1994 to 1950 by the end of 1995. VW has now developed a low-cost assembly plant with body welding, paint shop and final assembly operations. Parts arrive every night directly at the plant by train from Braunschweig, Germany, through the Czech Republic.

Mr Jozef Uhrik, Commercial Managing Director, said that the plant's big advantages were the high skill levels of the workforce and low wage costs, as well as its location close to the borders with Austria – it is only 60km east of Vienna – and Hungary.

The Bratislava operation is being developed for the assembly of niche vehicles that can be produced much more cheaply in a flexible, labour-intensive plant than on the highly automated, capital-intensive assembly lines of VW's big German plants. The plant has no robots.

The average age of the workforce is just over 28 years, and more than half of the workforce has Abitur (A-level) qualifications or higher, while wage levels are less than a tenth of those in Germany. The plant consistently ranked in the top third of VW operations worldwide for quality, according to internal company audits, said Mr Uhrik.

VW has also been able to take advantage of the restructuring of the Slovak arms industry, one of the big centres for weapons production in the former Eastern bloc, by attracting more than 300 skilled workers from former armaments factories. The 2000-strong workforce has been selected from more than 16 000 applicants.

Source: Done, K., 'VW to double Slovak output', *Financial Times* (19 December 1995).

Questions

1 *Discuss the major reasons for VW's move to Bratislava.*

2 *What factors have influenced VW's mode-of-entry choice to Bratislava?*

3 *What are the advantages of the entry mode that VW has chosen?*

FURTHER READING

Agarwal, S. and Ramaswami, S.N., 'Choice of foreign market entry mode: impact of ownership, location and internationalisation factors', *Journal of International Business Studies* (1st Quarter 1992), 1–27.

Anderson, E. and Gatignon, H., 'Modes of entry: a transaction cost analysis and propositions', *Journal of International Business Studies*, 17 (1986), 1–26.

Buckley, P.J. and Casson, M.C., *The Economic Theory of the Multinational Enterprise* (London: Macmillan, 1985).

Buckley, P.J. and Ghauri, P. (eds), *The Internationalisation of the Firm* (London: Academic Press, 1993).

Douglas, S.P. and Craig, C.S., 'Evolution of global marketing strategy: scale, scope and synergy', *Columbia Journal of World Business* (Fall 1989), 47–59.

Dunning, J.H., *International Production and the Multinational Enterprise* (London: George Allen & Unwin, 1981).

Erramilli, M.K. and Rao, C.P., 'Service firms' international entry mode choice: a modified transaction–cost analysis approach', *Journal of Marketing*, 57 (1993), 19–38.

Hill, C.W.L., Hwang, P. and Kim, W.C., 'An eclectic theory of the choice of international entry mode', *Strategic Management Journal* 11(2) (1990), 117–28.

Hymer, S.A., 'The international operations of national firms: a study of direct foreign investment'. Doctoral Dissertation, Massachusetts Institute of Technology (1960). (Reprinted Cambridge, MA: MIT Press, 1973.)

Johanson, J. & Wiedersheim, P.F., 'The internationalisation of the firm – four Swedish cases', *Journal of Management Studies*, 12 (1975), 305–22.

Kindleberger, C.O., *American Business Abroad: Six Lectures in Direct Investment* (New Haven, CN: Yale University Press, 1969).

Kogut, B. & Singh, H., 'The effect of national culture on the choice of entry mode', *Journal of International Business Studies*, 19 (1988), 411–32.

Root, F.R., *Entry Strategies for International Markets* (Lexington, MA: Lexington Books, 1987).

Yip, G.S., 'Global strategy ... in a world of nations?', *Sloan Management Review* (Fall 1989), 29–41.

Young, S., Hamill, J. and Davies, J.R., *International Market Entry and Development: Strategies and Management* (Hemel Hempstead: Harvester Wheatsheaf, 1989).

NOTES AND REFERENCES

1 Douglas, S.P. and Craig, C.S., *Global Marketing Strategy* (New York: McGraw-Hill, 1995).

2 Adburgham, R., 'Dragon's fire rekindles development in Wales', *Financial Times* (23 February 1996).

3 Ayal, I. and Zif, J., 'Market expansion strategies in multinational marketing', *Journal of Marketing*, 43 (1979), 84–94.

4   Douglas and Craig, op. cit.

5   Wind, Y. and Perlmutter, H., 'On the identification of frontier issues in multinational marketing', *Columbia Journal of World Business* (Winter 1977), 131–9.

6   Douglas and Craig, op. cit.

7   Driscoll, A., 'Foreign market entry methods: a mode choice framework', in Paliwoda, S.J. and Ryans, J.K., Jr (eds), *International Market Reader* (London: Routledge, 1995).

8   Ghoshal, S. 'Global strategy: an organising framework', *Strategic Management Journal*, 8 (1987), 425–40.

9   Driscoll, op. cit.

10 Kim, W.C. and Hwang, P., 'Global strategy and multinationals' entry mode choice', *Journal of International Business Studies*, 23(1) (1992), 29–53.

11 Hamel, G. and Prahalad, C.K., 'Do you have a global strategy?', *Harvard Business Review* (July–August 1985), 134–48.

12 Anderson, E. and Coughlan, A.T., 'International market entry and expansion via independent or integrated channels of distribution', *Journal of Marketing,* 51 (1987), 71–82.

11

Market-entry strategies

INTRODUCTION

Once the firm decides to enter the foreign market it must then establish which entry mode to select to optimise its operations. The internationalisation of the firm is not a sequential process from the initial exporting approach to direct investment. In fact, it is not a practical strategy to enter all markets with a single entry method; many large companies adopt multiple entry strategies, each reflecting different levels of commitment and resources as well as the dynamic nature of international markets which makes it difficult to adopt a single entry method that will work effectively in all markets. This chapter will examine in some detail the various approaches to international markets and discuss the advantages and disadvantages associated with each mode of market penetration.

Objectives

This chapter will examine:

- the major types of international entry methods
- the different types of direct and indirect forms of exporting
- the different types of foreign manufacturing and ownership entry strategies such as licensing, contract manufacturing, joint ventures and strategic alliances
- the advantages and disadvantages of the various forms of entry strategies
- and evaluate strategic alliances.

The choice of method of entry into foreign markets for many firms is a fundamental and critical decision in international marketing, since the entry technique will influence the rest of the marketing programme. If the firm opts for a licensing agreement, then its ability to influence product development, promotion or pricing will be severely curtailed. On the other hand, if the firm makes a decision to manufacture in the host country, it will be able to exert a high degree of control in terms of its marketing and production decisions, but this will entail higher costs and greater risks. The market-entry decision involves a trade-off between control, costs and risks, as illustrated in Fig. 11.1. Furthermore, the choice of entry method will involve the firm in a long-term commitment from which it might find it hard to extricate itself without some cost.

Fig 11.1 TRADE-OFFS IN THE MARKET-ENTRY DECISION

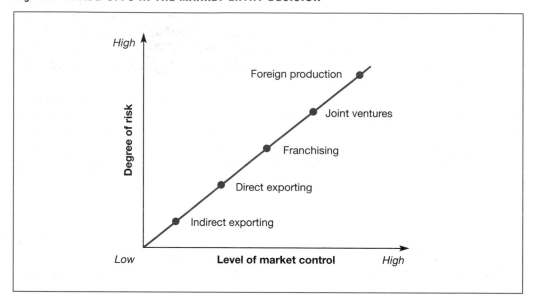

Box 11.1 A. & M. BOLTON[1]

Michael Bolton is chairman of A. & M. Bolton, a shoe company based in Leicester. It started from very humble beginnings 44 years ago and its path to success has not always been smooth. The firm had to deal with a series of recessions and to cope with cheap imports from the Asia Pacific countries. The company's shoes are sold at the lower end of the market, selling at an average of £10 in England under the brand name of Early Days. Although still a family concern, it is a very successful company and the chairman attributes its success to design, quality, service and dedication to the business. Today, it supplies some of the UK's leading department stores such as Harrods, John Lewis and Fenwick. It also exports to Hong Kong and the Middle Eastern countries. The company supplied some overseas markets early in its development and in fact it has been shipping its products to one Hong Kong firm for 30 years. A. & M. Bolton has been using an export assistance firm to deal with the complex task of supplying its products globally. The company is looking to boost its export sales, and initially, it hopes to win new contracts in the southern part of Europe, mainly Cyprus, Greece and Malta.

Box 11.1 shows that many SMEs, and indeed large firms too, cannot simply jump into the global market and expect to be successful. With the globalisation of the market place, fewer firms have the time to adjust to the new realities, let alone decide how to respond to it. The effect is that many firms are now so exposed to international competition that in order to survive they need to participate in the world market place whether they want to or not. The international arena offers many opportunities and participation can be very profitable. However, there will problems and decisions that a firm will need to consider when it wishes to involve itself in the international market place. What choice does the firm have in terms of servicing these overseas markets? Should it export directly, use an intermediary or join with a partner to take advantage of extra resources and utilise the partner's competencies? Many firms from small concerns to large multinational enterprises should be able to find appropriate channels to reach foreign markets given the diversity of alternatives shown schematically in Fig. 11.2. These range from indirect exporting to foreign production and ownership strategies.

Chapter 10 focused on the reasons for international expansion, the choice of market presence, portfolio techniques to assess market choice and the criteria for making an effective choice amongst the different types of entry strategies. This chapter will focus on the range of options open to companies in developing a successful international programme. An analysis of the advantages and disadvantages of the different methods of international entry will also be undertaken.

Indirect exporting

In general, this means that the firm sells to an intermediary (middleman) within the UK, who in turn re-sells the goods to a customer abroad. The manufacturing firm does not need to undertake the export operations within the company such as documentation,

Fig 11.2 MARKET-ENTRY STRATEGIES

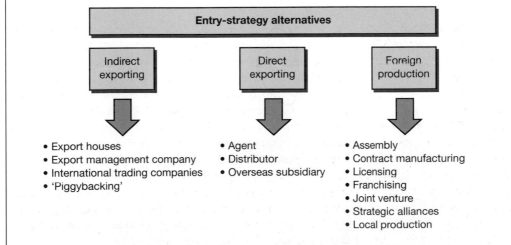

freighting, etc. These are carried out by others, and in many instances they take place without the knowledge of the manufacturer. Indirect exporting may occur through:

- export houses
- export management companies
- overseas buying offices
- international trading companies
- 'piggyback operations' (joint venture marketing operations).

Direct exporting

The firm sells to a customer abroad, who may be the final user of the product–service or an intermediary, the latter being a distributor or agent. In this case, the firm has to undertake market research, transportation, and handle documentation and the various other export procedures. In general, the move to direct exporting indicates a genuine commitment to exporting with the resulting benefits of market feedback and greater control of process, although it is a more expensive alternative. Direct exporting takes place through:

- sales by foreign distributors
- sale agents
- overseas sales subsidiaries.

Foreign manufacturing

The firm is involved in production and distribution of the goods in the market concerned. This can take many forms:

- assembly operations
- contract manufacturing
- licensing operations
- franchising
- joint ventures
- strategic alliances
- local production.

INDIRECT EXPORTING

Export houses

There are about 800 export houses in the UK and they account for approximately 20 per cent of the UK's export trade. An 'export house' can be defined as any company which is not a manufacturer, whose main activity is the handling or financing of the UK export trade or international trade that is not connected with the UK. There are three main categories of export houses:

1 export merchants buying the goods outright and selling them on their own account;

2 confirming houses, where they act as agents for the buyers;

3 export agents, where they act as agents for the exporter.

Export merchants

As export merchants, they are essentially acting as domestic wholesalers operating in foreign markets through their own sales agents or salesforce. Their profit is derived from the difference between the buying and the selling price. Some export merchants tend to specialise in certain markets (e.g. Canada), or in certain classes of goods (e.g. footwear).

Advantages of trading through export merchants

1 The firm can take immediate advantage of the merchant's knowledge of foreign markets and contacts in those markets;

2 there is no need for the firm to have its own export organisation since the merchant will handle the mechanics of exporting – shipping, documentation, etc.;

3 merchants generally pay the firm as soon as the goods come under their control; this relieves the small firm from the need to finance the export transaction and avoids any credit risk;

4 the firm does not generally pay the merchant for its services since it is paid by the overseas customer;

5 some merchants have developed expertise in specialist fields such as barter dealings.

Disadvantages of trading through export merchants

1 By channelling its business through the merchants, the firm will have no direct contact with its overseas customers; this means it is not building up goodwill in the market which can form the basis for expansion;

2 the firm will have little or no control over its market;

3 to some extent, the firm will be producing in the dark as it will have no idea of the market's true needs and potential;

4 the merchant may take on many product lines and it may be the case that a particular firm's product will receive little attention, or in some cases may even be dropped if a more profitable line appears;

5 the small firm is unable to influence the market and create further sales; if the market does expand significantly, it will be more profitable for the small firm to deal directly.

Confirming houses

Export houses can also act on behalf of an overseas principal. They confirm as a principal an order which a foreign buyer has placed with a UK manufacturer. The confirming house finances the transaction and accepts the credit risk, and it can extend credit to the importer for a period of 60, 90 or 180 days. In return, the confirming house receives a commission from the buyer. In many cases, the house arranges shipment, documentation and insurance of the goods.

Advantages and disadvantages of trading through a confirming house
Trading through a confirming house is more or less the same as through export merchants, with similar advantages and disadvantages. However, there are some further points to note. The additional advantages of the confirming house are that:

1 the credit is carried by the confirming house, which also pays in the home currency, and promptly;

2 the exporter will tend to have a closer link with the overseas customer, since the confirming house is only an agent;

3 for the importer, the advantages are that they can place orders to exact specifications.

Export agents

The export house can also act as a manufacturer's export agent and will sell abroad on behalf of the UK manufacturer. In general, the export agent will act as the manufacturer's export department and undertake most or all of the exporting tasks – e.g. attending to the physical and clerical tasks associated with exporting, stocking goods at home or abroad, following up delivery dates, providing after-sales service if required, carrying credit risks, etc.

An export agent will usually cover a particular sector of industry. Remuneration is in the form of a commission from the UK manufacturer, although an alternative form of remuneration is possible – e.g. on a cost plus profit margin basis.

Advantages and disadvantages of trading through an export agent
The export agent will offer the same advantages as the export merchant. In addition, the small-firm manufacturer will:

1 retain much greater control over the market because the sale is in the company's name;

2 immediately gain an 'export department', at minimal cost;

3 as the goods are sold in the manufacturer's own name, it will be building up goodwill in the overseas market for future expansion.

The disadvantages of an export agent are the same as those for the export merchant. In addition, the following should be noted:

1 if the manufacturer's product provides a poor return, then the export agent may ignore or drop the product;

2 the firm may not get the opportunity to develop export experience and capability if the export agent undertakes all the export procedures; if the firm wanted to change to direct exporting it would be at a distinct disadvantage;

3 the export agent may be prepared to accept only a world-wide brief or a regional agreement – i.e. that the supplier will allow the agent to develop sales within a given area, which may prove to be restrictive; this is a key issue, and the supplier must ensure that the company's target markets coincide with those of the export agent.

Summary
Export houses can be the key to profitable exporting, especially for those companies
which: Good for

- have limited capacity for developing their export trade
- are venturing into export for the first time
- have 'unbranded' products
- wish to receive prompt payment.

Export management companies

The export management company is a specialist intermediary in that it acts as an
export department for the exporting firm – in effect, it is acting as the exporter's
agent. Export management companies are particularly useful for SMEs.

A number of advantages accrue to an exporter using an export management
company:

1 they gain instant market knowledge and business contacts via the export management company;

2 as an export management company deals with a large number of firms simultaneously, the exporter gains from management cost and transport economies;

3 the exporter's products are part of a whole range of products handled by the export
management company, and this is likely to have a greater impact than the products
of just one firm;

4 payment is based on performance; hence the export management company will
tend to generate high sales.

However, there can be shortcomings:

1 the export management company may lack the degree and depth of market coverage that the exporter's goods need;

2 the exporting firm may not receive the degree of attention expected as the export
management company is dealing with many firms in unrelated product areas;

3 the exporter will not gain international knowledge and experience, and this is critical when sales increase substantially and the firm wishes to embark on an overseas
marketing strategy;

4 export management companies tend to specialise in geographic markets or product
types, and the exporter may have to resort to using several export management
companies.

Overseas buying offices

Many of the major department stores in other industrialised nations have buying
offices in the UK, whilst others appoint UK export houses as their buying agents. This
option can be important for a firm wishing to become established in an overseas
market. Major department stores of Japan, Germany and the USA have buying offices
in London.

International trading companies

International trading companies tend to be large scale manufacturers and merchants, and they are involved in wholesale and retail distribution. They normally act as agents for principals in overseas markets. They are particularly important for Korean and Japanese trade, but less so in Europe.

There are a number of advantages in using international trading companies:

- they can act as a traditional agent in the overseas market and can supply you with technical back-up if required
- they tend to handle documentation, shipping, etc., and pay in the country of origin.

Perhaps the major disadvantage is that they carry competing products and are unlikely to give the firm's product the attention it may need to succeed in overseas markets.

Joint marketing or 'piggyback exporting'

This occurs when a firm enters into a collaborative arrangement with a major manufacturer in a similar field, in other words when one manufacturer (the 'carrier') uses its established overseas distribution network to market the goods of another manufacturer (the 'rider') alongside its own. This arrangement is termed 'piggyback' or joint manufacturing, and there are two possible arrangements:

- the carrier can act as an agent by selling the rider's products on a commission basis, or
- the carrier can act as a merchant and buy the products outright to re-sell them.

This is an ideal method for firms wishing to enter the international market and it is most suited to those situations where:

- the marketing, distribution and service costs are high
- the carrier may sell the rider's products because they complement its product range, and therefore give the carrier a wider competitive offering to the market
- the marketing requirements are high and sophisticated
- overseas customers have a desire for innovative products which the carrier cannot supply from its own range
- the opportunity for lowering unit distribution costs exists.

Advantages of 'piggyback operations' for the rider

1 It provides the rider with a simple and low-risk method of entering the foreign market;
2 it provides an immediate access to an overseas market, especially for firms with limited resources;
3 the expenses of distribution are shared by both parties.

Advantages of 'piggyback operations' for the carrier

1 It is an easy and profitable way of broadening its product range;

2 it provides the carrier with an attractive sales package which could increase its profit levels;

3 it is also an easy way for the carriers of cyclical or seasonal products to keep their distribution channels operating throughout the year.

Problems with 'piggyback operations'

1 The exporting company may become dependent on the carrier and therefore may find itself under the control of the bigger company;

2 it is quite difficult to find a suitable 'piggyback' partner;

3 the rider's product may take second priority to the carrier's product line;

4 problems could arise from branding and promotional policies in that the rider's products could be sold under the carrier's label, and this could limit potential overseas expansion;

5 the carrier's sales and service staff may need to be trained to handle the rider's product(s) or arrangements may be needed to provide warranty and service back-up.

In the UK in the 1980s 'piggybacking' was used quite frequently by small high-tech electronics and biotechnology companies who wanted to enter foreign markets rapidly. 'Piggybacking' is also used by large companies – Sony is a carrier for a number of EU and US firms in the Japanese market. Another example is Colgate–Palmolive, which acts as carrier for many firms, including Wilkinson Sword (with razor blades) and Weetabix (with Alpen breakfast cereal).

Dudley[2] describes a number of possible ways of approaching a 'piggyback' arrangement:

- collaboration with a UK firm which has an international marketing organisation
- collaboration with firms in the foreign markets
- a mutual collaborative venture in which you would sell your partner's goods in the UK while your partner's company will sell your products in its own country and perhaps its export markets
- a corporate venturing arrangement.

Collaboration with a UK firm

One of the features of large international companies is that their divisions or international subsidiaries tend to be separated from their UK divisions. One possible effect of this is that UK R&D will focus on the needs of the home market. This means that in many instances UK-based divisions have a strong product range while their export or overseas operations are short on this aspect. This is an ideal opportunity for the firm to see if its products can fit into the international firm's product range or to find gaps in its own range. The firm could try to persuade the international firm that its product fits the latter's requirements; however, persistence will be needed. This may necessitate finding out which firms are responsible for particular global regions and making efforts to get in touch with them, or visiting the subsidiary if at all possible, and persistent enquiries. Consultancies and banks may be of help in such enquiries.

Collaboration with firms in the foreign markets

Many foreign firms face similar problems to those outlined for the UK international firms above. Again this would be a good opportunity to get in touch with a major foreign firm and persuade it that your firm's product fits its range. The advantages of this approach for the firm are as follows:

1 its product will not be competing with those of other exporters for marketing priority but only with the major firm's own products;

2 the firm will have available a highly professional marketing staff as well as having its marketing costs shared by the major firm;

3 its product will be seen as part of the major company's product range, as opposed to being a foreign product. This has obvious advantages.

The problems with this arrangement are that:

1 the firm will have very little management say in the marketing policy and decisions;

2 it may also have to accept a lower profit margin when compared to other possible methods of distribution.

Mutual collaborative arrangement with a foreign company

In this type of arrangement you handle your partner's UK marketing while your foreign partner handles your marketing in the foreign market. This type of joint marketing arrangement assumes that both companies' customer and product ranges are in the same market, e.g. in the health food sector.

Corporate venturing arrangement

Recently, many small high-technology-based companies have managed to persuade large firms to invest in them. In this way, they gain financial and managerial resources, and access to the major firm's international marketing infrastructure. In return, the large firms obtain innovative product development and production capacity. Firms may contact merchant banks or consultancies to assist in this type of arrangement.

DIRECT EXPORTING

Disadvantage

Direct selling takes a lot of preparatory work, and a lot of time and travelling to make and develop the right contacts. Also, once business is built up the firm must be prepared to visit the markets they are operating in at short notice to solve any problems as and when they arise. Direct selling is particularly useful in the engineering and capital goods sectors.

Agents and distributors

The most common method of direct selling adopted by companies coming to the EU for the first time is that of appointing an agent of some kind, or a distributor. The choice will depend on the firm's product, the market and the firm's marketing strategy. Agents and distributors are the traditional channels through which exporting takes place: at least 70 per cent of European firms and approximately 60 per cent of US firms use distributors for some or all of their export activities.

Agents

An agent is an individual or organisation that acts on behalf of a principal to bring the principal into a contractual relationship with third parties to whom the principal's products–services can be sold – i.e. they act as intermediaries between the supplier and end-user. Agents may be classified in many different ways and each will have specific characteristics. In general, agents do not normally own the goods which they are selling, nor do they carry stock or take responsibility for credit risks, unless they are *del credere* agents (*see* below). Agents tend not to be involved in promotional marketing, though they may distribute catalogues and price lists if required. Agents receive commission which ranges from two per cent to 15 per cent depending on the value of the transaction; in transactions which involve very large sums of money the commission will vary between 0.25 per cent and two per cent. Agents can also set up licensing agreements if required, and they are particularly useful in dealing with government contracts. It is usual for an agent to work for a number of principals offering a cohesive group of products, but not so as to be in direct competition with each other. Agents also tend to deal predominantly with industrial and capital goods.

Types of agents

There are many different types of agent; some of the more important ones in international marketing are discussed below.

Commission agent. This type of agent fits most of the characteristics described above, i.e. they do not hold stocks and they pass the orders to the principal who then delivers the goods direct to the customer. Such an agent is particularly useful for industrial products and where there are entry problems into a particular market. This type of agent is also useful for markets with limited or spasmodic orders.

Service after-sales agent. Many technical products are such that it is necessary to provide a maker's guarantee. This task is undertaken by such an agent and involves stocks and parts being carried in the market. Furthermore, the agent will provide servicing and repair facilities and charge the customer. Details of the arrangements between the parties will vary, and such an agent will expect to be paid a higher commission rate.

Stocking agent. This agent will hold stocks of the product, in effect acting as a wholesaler for the overseas principal. They do not take title to the goods, and they will receive a commission on sales plus a fixed sum to cover storage and handling facilities.

***Del credere* agent.** This type of agent accepts the credit risk, agreeing to pay the principal in the event of a default by the customer. Great care is required in defining the rights and responsibilities of this type of agent, and they will obviously expect to be paid a much higher commission.

Advantages of using agents

1 The firm obtains the services of an experienced local national, who is familiar with local business practices and customs, is fluent in the language and perhaps fully conversant with the exporter's industry; in the initial stages, this will reduce the need for specialist export personnel in the exporting firm;

2 the agent can provide information on the market and recent developments; this will enable the firm to plan effectively;

3 if the exporter is visiting the territory, the agent can make the necessary arrangements and provide the right introductions;

4 the firm gains overseas market experience from the use of an agent;

5 the cost to the firm of using an agent is virtually nil, and the results of using such a channel is almost immediate in terms of sales.

Disadvantages of using an agent

1 The company has only a part share of the agent's time because they normally work for other principals as well, this means the company is competing for their work and if your products are difficult to sell or they represent only a small part of an agent's turnover, then little time may be devoted to selling your products;

2 an agent dealing with a highly technical product may find it difficult to keep abreast of the latest technical innovation and its merits; the agent may then not clinch a sale as they are unsure of the unique selling qualities of the product;

3 in general, most agents are weak on marketing skills, and rarely involve themselves in promotional work;

4 as agents do not take title to the goods they risk very little except perhaps time, and this could have the effect of not inducing them to invest their best efforts on your products;

5 the agent's customer base for your products may not necessarily be the right one for you if you are tying to create a particular image for your product – you may want a higher class type of customer for your product;

6 the agency contracts between agents and principals are quite difficult to sever without paying large sums of compensation; this situation could arise if the market conditions change and there is a need to alter the distribution methods – e.g. from agency to the use of export houses;

7 commission agents may order in small quantities, which can lead to uneconomic freighting arrangements;

8 as sales develop, there is a danger that the commission costs will become disproportionately high when compared to other methods of distribution such as setting up an overseas marketing subsidiary;

9 in general, agents are not prepared to cover credit risks;

10 agents are particularly poor on providing a high level of distribution and customer service.

Despite the disadvantages of using agents they are considered to be useful in many respects, especially in markets where there is unlikely to be long-term potential due to economic instability or under-development. Also they are useful in markets where orders are small or spasmodic.

Box 11.2

SECO ENGINEERING[3]

Seco Engineering was a small business company based in the UK making hand-held industrial polishing machines. Like many small firms in the UK, exporting meant responding to *ad hoc* orders. This reactive strategy was in part due to lack of knowledge of overseas markets, and especially overseas customer needs. Once a firm decides to export, the first step is to find agents or distributors who will in effect be the company's representative. This is a very responsible task, for the company's reputation and its sales will rest on making the right choice of distributor–agent. Usually, a firm should talk first to a prospective agent or distributor, or even to their customers, to make an assessment of their suitability. Seco found its German distributor by sending a two-page letter in German to about 100 companies. The companies were selected from paging through the business directories in the local Chamber of Commerce. The Managing Director of Seco said that the whole process was more than just trying to find the right distributor. He believed that sending out the letter in German helped to generate a lot of goodwill for the company. He said that afterwards Seco received a positive response from people at trade fairs in Germany.

In addition to selecting the right intermediary, it is also important to make the overseas representative feel part of a team. This is essential for morale and for boosting sales. Seco sends one of its directors to visit customers and sales reps abroad every month.

Distributors

Distributors are customers who have been given exclusive or preferential rights to purchase and re-sell a specific range of products from a supplier organisation. Normally, they are given sole rights and operate in specific geographical areas or markets. In effect, the distributor is a wholesaler whose remuneration comes from the difference between the purchase and resale price. They differ from agents in a number of respects – they contract to hold stocks, have preferential rights, and the contractual relationship with the supplier is one of principal-and-principal, not one of principal-and-agent. Successful distributors tend to be those who can provide a package of products to the customers; in this way they can offer choice and thus gain a competitive advantage.

Approximately 80 per cent of UK export trade goes via distributors, and it is the method most used by exporters. Distributors can offer exporters a number of valuable services such as stock holding, promotional support, after-sales service, market feedback, sales forecasting and sales reports, and sales and distribution management.

Advantages of using a distributor

1 They have an intimate knowledge of the market to help the exporter plan and develop their marketing in that market;

2 distributors will take all the credit risks in the market;

good sells try to push

3 their livelihood depends on the sale of stocks, and therefore they will push for high sales volume;

4 the exporter can supply distributors in bulk, and thus use cost-effective freight rates;

5 distributors tend to have experience in selling and distributing the product, and this reduces the supplier's work load;

6 distributors carry most of the risk for product failure in the market; however, this can have the effect of making them cautious about taking on new lines;

7 distributors will be able to look after the supplier's staff during visits to the market;

8 distributors tend to achieve higher levels of sales than agents.

Disadvantages of using distributors

1 The product will be competing for the distributor's time and attention, and if it sells slowly it may be given low priority;

2 as they carry the risks of failure of products, distributors may be reluctant to take on new products from you;

3 distributors and exporters are very suspicious of each other's profit margins;

 4 terminating a distributor's agreement is very difficult, as the distributor has invested more heavily in the project than an agent;

5 a continuous problem is the level and share of promotional expenditure;

6 a distributor may become concerned that you will perhaps decide to set up subsidiary in the market if business sales are substantial;

7 distributors tend to change their product range at frequent intervals, and your product may not be pushed because it is not considered competitive any more; this can give rise to conflicts of opinion as to what constitutes a 'competitive product'.

Distributors do play an important role in most distribution strategies, and they are particularly useful in markets which are geographically far from the home market. They are indispensable in markets which have technical or regional problems that the supplier firm is unable to deal with – e.g. distributors based in Kenya or Brazil can deal with local regional problems more effectively than the supplier firm.

Overseas subsidiary

The exporter may choose not to have any form of intermediary, but may:

1 use his own resources; or

2 set up an overseas branch officer; or

3 set up an overseas marketing subsidiary.

Own resources

The use of a company's own salespeople occurs in markets where suitable agents are not available or difficult to find (e.g. in Eastern Europe), and for highly technical products where it may be difficult to impart the subtle and complex technical knowledge to a third party. The advantages of this approach for the company is that the salespeople can project the company image and obtain immediate market feedback which will facilitate market and production planning. The exporter will not need to share any profits as there are no intermediaries. The major drawback of this approach is that the firm may need to develop a full export organisation.

Overseas branch office

Alternatively, the firm could set up an overseas branch office, using local personnel who will be trained in the firm's products and organisational culture and supervised by resident executives. The usual method of setting up an overseas branch office is that the local agent is bought by the company and becomes the local company. Overseas branch offices are normally set up because the overseas operation has become too large for the local agent to handle. It forms a useful base from which to operate an after-sales service and enhances both effective communications with customers and the firm's competitive position. The advantage to the exporter is that the overseas branch office is viewed favourably by the local authorities because it employs local personnel. The other major advantages are that the firm can deal with local problems immediately; selling and marketing are handled more effectively than if they were in the hands of an intermediary, and company policy on various issues can be imposed. For the importer, the advantage is that they are dealing with a home-based company. The disadvantages for the exporter are that they encounter foreign problems such as legal rules, repatriation of profits and labour problems; conflicts may arise between head office and the local directors of the overseas branch office, and the firm's capital investment is subject to greater risk due to political instability.

Overseas subsidiary company

Finally, the firm could adopt the third method of entering foreign markets: the setting up of an overseas subsidiary company. This is possible only if the scale of business can support a higher level of operations. It provides a firm with a base in the market for the elaboration of marketing operations and carrying of stock. The advantages and disadvantages of this method are in most cases similar to most of those of an overseas branch office, the additional points to note being that the firm could gain tax advantages and reduced tariffs, or no barriers at all are imposed.

FOREIGN MANUFACTURING

A common and widely practised form of entry is the local production of a company's products. There are a number of factors which may affect the choice to manufacture locally rather than supply the foreign market from domestic sources. Some of these factors are positive in that they encourage a firm to produce abroad, whilst others are forced upon the firm in order for it to compete or survive in the foreign market at all. The existence of tariff barriers or quotas could prevent a firm entering a particular market, and political consideration will also play a part in the firm's decision to produce locally. In some markets, governments may prefer local suppliers, and in these situations the exporting firm will be forced to manufacture locally in order to sell its products. Another factor is transportation costs – if the distance between the target market and the firm's home base is substantial, then direct entry in the form of setting up a local production unit is highly desirable for both cost and control reasons. Transport costs for heavy or bulk goods may make the firm's home-produced products uncompetitive in the local market.

A firm could also be encouraged to produce locally because the market is growing or is large enough to warrant local production, such as in the EU. The number of Japanese firms which have established local production units in the UK has grown quite rapidly since the 1980s to include Nissan, Honda, Sony and Toyota. These companies will take advantage of the growing EU market and at the same time avoid tariff barriers.

Another advantage for producing locally is that the firm will respond more favourably to local needs concerning delivery, service levels and product adoption, as well as obtaining better market feedback. In certain foreign markets, production and distribution costs could be lowered substantially – for example, in 1989, manufacturing wages in Japan were on average $13 an hour, in the USA they were $10.50, while in most of the Southeast Asian countries the rates were below $2.00.[4]

The actual type of local production depends on the arrangements made and could vary from constant manufacturing, assembly plants and licensing or joint ventures, to total ownership of foreign production facilities. The source of the company's goods in the market is foreign production but the level of involvement in the production and the marketing aspects will vary with each approach.

Assembly

The assembly process consists of the last stages of the manufacturing process and most of the product's components are manufactured in the domestic plants or other foreign countries before they are transferred to the particular foreign market for final assembly. An assembly operation could be said to be a half-way stage between indirect exporting and foreign manufacturing, and it is usually labour-intensive rather than capital-intensive. The notable examples of foreign assembly operations are the motor vehicle and pharmaceutical industries. Most European, Japanese and US car manufacturers, such as Ford, Honda and Nissan, ship cars as CKDs (completely knocked down) and assemble them in local markets. This type of operation is particularly advantageous when:

1 the firm can take advantage of lower labour costs in the foreign market, which results in a lower final price of the product;

2 the local government puts pressure on the setting up of assembly operations by banning the import of a fully assembled good; this also creates employment in the local market;

3 a tariff barrier is in existence, thereby making the product uncompetitive in terms of price. In this situation, the firm would be better off to begin assembly operations to protect its market. Many developing nations started to impose higher tariffs on products imported in assembly form; this explains why Hitachi[5] began to replace exports of colour TV sets from Japan to developing countries with local assembly operations because of pressure from the local governments, as the developing nations were starting to impose higher tariffs on colour TVs imported into the respective countries;

4 the transportation costs on fully assembled products are high and it would be more advantageous for the firm to ship the components to be assembled locally and thus have lower freight costs;

5 the final product is perceived as 'local', which can also help in its marketing;

6 initial experience of the foreign market during assembly operations will be useful at a later stage, should a full manufacturing operation be established.

Contract manufacturing

Contract manufacturing is an alternative to assembly operations in which a company's product is manufactured or assembled in the foreign market by another producer operating under contract.

The company placing the contract would still be handling the distribution and the marketing of the product – this would be particularly so in the case where the firm's competitive advantage lies in its marketing expertise and experience.

Contract manufacturing can be said to be a half-way house between licensing and direct investment in production facilities. It differs from licensing with respect to the legal relationship of the parties involved, in that the producer simply produces on the basis of orders from the foreign firm.

The attractions of this sort of operation are many and varied:

1 the international firm's investment is kept to a minimum. This can be a particularly attractive low-cost strategy in that the firm can withdraw should the market not develop as expected. It is also a useful strategy for firms to adopt when there are political uncertainties about the market, or the firm does not have the necessary capital for full-scale investment. The firm avoids most of the foreign market problems which may arise from a lack of familiarity with the economy concerned, such as legal or labour problems;

2 the product which is produced in the country can be marketed as locally made; this would be perceived in very positive terms by both consumers and the government, especially if the firm is attempting to procure government contracts;

3 compared to exporting, there will be savings in transportation costs;

4 it is possible that production costs could be lower in the foreign market because of cheaper labour or material costs;

5 it allows a firm to enter a market otherwise protected by trade barriers such as high tariffs;

6 the firm could concentrate its efforts on developing markets without having to divert resources to establish its manufacturing plant in the market as an entry strategy, since this type of arrangement is not always satisfactory to the foreign firm. It is normally employed where marketing expertise is critical in the success of the product.

There are many drawbacks to this approach:

1 it may be difficult to find satisfactory and reliable manufacturers in the foreign market;

2 extensive technical training may be required for the local producer's staff;

3 quality control of the product is usually difficult to achieve;

4 it is also possible, at the end of the contract, for the local producer to become a potential competitor, having acquired the necessary production and marketing expertise; this possibility could be minimised by the international firm pursuing a strong branding policy.

Despite its drawbacks contract manufacturing should still be considered, especially where the market is not sufficiently large to justify investment in manufacturing operations. It is also likely to be of interest to firms whose product and production technology have no patent protection. The approach can also offer considerable advantages especially in markets which are politically unstable or where foreign assets are occasionally expropriated, conditions that tend to exist in the smaller economies of Africa, Asia and Latin America.

Many multinational companies tend to have contract manufacturing arrangements – e.g. Procter & Gamble has such an arrangement in Italy where it has several products manufactured by local firms, and Del Monte has chosen this method as a low-cost form of production in Central America.

Licensing

Licensing can be seen as an extension or development of contract manufacturing in that it covers a longer term and it involves the licensee in a wider sphere of responsibility and activities (*see* Fig. 11.3).

Licensing entails the sale of a patent (concerning a product or a process), manufacturing know-how, technical advice and assistance, or the use of a trade mark or trade name on a contractual basis, by which the international firm (licensor) grants a licence to a national company (licensee) and receives royalty payments in return.

Fig 11.3 THE LIFE-CYCLE BENEFITS OF LICENSING

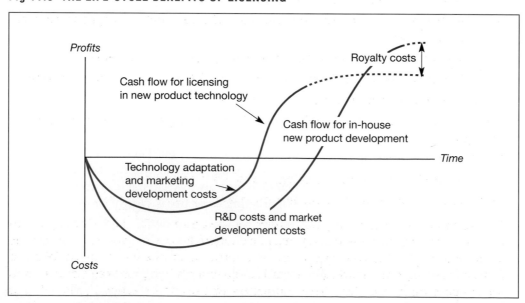

Source: Lowe, J., and Crawford, N., *Technology Licensing and the Small Firm* (London: Gower, 1984).

The payment for a licence can take many forms:

- an initial payment where the agreement is signed to pay for the initial transfer of components, design or know-how
- an annual percentage fee based on profits or sales
- an annual minimum payment, or
- an exchange of patents or knowledge, i.e. cross-licensing.

The know-how or rights received by the licensee may be used in specific markets or in several countries. In addition, the licensee takes a greater responsibility for marketing as well as for production.

Many UK industries – particularly general engineering, food processing equipment and vehicle parts – operate licensing agreements as part of their market-entry strategy to expand world-wide sales. Many European and US companies have used this approach in the 1990s to enter some East European markets. Licensing agreements have considerable attractions for the licensor.

1 They require little, or even no, capital outlay; this may be attractive for small firms entering the world market.

2 Licensing permits a quick and fairly unproblematic way of entering foreign markets.

3 The firm gains immediate access to local market knowledge, distribution and existing consumer contacts.

4 Licensing permits market entry and development which would otherwise be closed on account of:
   (a) high tariffs on finished imported manufactured products;
   (b) high costs of setting up wholly-owned subsidiaries;
   (c) distant overseas markets where the extra costs and logistics of shipping finished products would make the products uncompetitive;
   (d) home manufacturers who do not have the production capacity to meet overseas orders;
   (e) expensive freight charges on bulky or heavy products of low value;
   (f) difficulties in the repatriation of profits, dividends and, sometimes, royalties;
   (g) local suppliers have an entrenched position.

5 Many governments look favourably upon licensing largely because of the implications for:
   (a) local employment; and
   (b) long-term benefits from technology transfer to the host nation.

In this respect, the licensor should fear no expropriation of investment.

6 In many markets, particularly the former socialist economies, licensing is perhaps the only way in which the markets may be entered: Pepsi-Cola and Fiat entered the Soviet market in this way, and China is another example where many Western firms have entered the market via licensing agreements, ranging from electronics to food processing industries; these companies will no doubt enjoy the benefits of being a preferred component supplier and having uninterrupted royalties on sales.

7 Licensing can also provide an opportunity to produce revenue from processes–technology which the firm no longer uses in its key markets; the firm can continue to increase its income by charging fees for technical–engineering assistance and the sale of components to the licensee.

8 From the licensee's point of view, the attractions are no R&D costs and access to the new technology know-how of the licensor to strengthen its comparative position.

The disadvantages of licensing are less numerous, but they have a much more significant influence on the licensor firm's operations.

problem

1 No matter how clearly the initial contract agreement was spelled out, disagreements may arise on the responsibilities of each party, the marketing effort of the licensee, territorial coverage, etc., this situation is further aggravated when market conditions change and the terms of the original agreement become less relevant and appropriate.

2 When the agreement finally expires, the licensor may find it has indirectly established its future competitor, who has used the expertise gained to set up as a rival organisation.

3 Strict product quality control is difficult to achieve, and this matter is not helped by the fact that the product will tend to be sold under the licensor's brand name.

4 Governments can impose conditions on firms remitting royalties.

5 The returns from licensing can be limited when compared to direct investment; typically, a licence fee averages 1–20 per cent of sales, but 3–6 per cent is more typical of industrial products – it is sometimes argued that direct investment, which requires more effort and resources, can provide larger profits in the long run.

6 Another drawback is the great difficulty of finding a suitable licensee with the necessary technical expertise in the target market.

7 The licensee has a weak bargaining position, in particular for undisclosed technology, until the technology has been supplied.

8 There may be difficulties in successfully communicating complex and, sometimes, subtle technologies from one company to another, and across cultures.

Overall, licensing offers many companies significant advantages and it is an attractive strategy for entering foreign markets. Licensing agreements have ranged from industrial products to the licensing of film personalities and cartoons such as Garfield and Snoopy.

Franchising → _do mkt programme + brand_

Franchising is a particular form of licensing in which the franchiser makes a total marketing programme available, including brand name, product, method of operation and management advice (*see* Table 11.1). The franchise agreement tends to be more comprehensive than a normal licensing arrangement, in that the franchise agrees to a total operation being prescribed.

Table 11.1 FORMS OF FRANCHISING

Job franchising	Wholesaler–retailer	Spar, Londis, VG, Service Master
Investment franchise	Manufacturer–retailer	Petrol service stations
	Manufacturer–wholesaler	Pepsi-Cola, 7-Up
	Other	Holiday Inns, Avis Rent-A-Car, Coca-Cola
Business format franchise	Trade marks, trade names	Kentucky Fried Chicken (KFC), Prontaprint
	Licensor–retailer	McDonald's, Wimpey International

Source: Bradley, F., *International Marketing Strategy* (Englewood Cliffs, NJ: Prentice-Hall, 1995), 392.

Franchising is mainly a US phenomenon and it accounts for approximately 34 per cent of all retail sales in the USA. It is less developed in Europe, although more common in the UK and France – in these two countries, franchising accounts for about 10 per cent of retail sales.[6]

1 Many companies have successfully exploited franchising as a method of market expansion in the international sphere. US firms tend to dominate this field of activity ranging from fast foods (Kentucky Fried Chicken, McDonald's, Burger King), soft drinks (Coca-Cola, Pepsi-Cola, 7-Up), car rental (Hertz and Avis) and others (Holiday Inns, Tandy Corporation). Perhaps one of the best known examples of international franchising is Benetton who have a unique system of franchising in that the franchisees pay no fees or royalties and their obligation in the agreement is to carry only Benetton clothes and adhere to specific marketing guidelines.[7] In recent times the rapid expansion of the UK company The Body Shop seems to indicate the immense potential for franchising in both Europe and other parts of the globe. Franchising seems to be more suited to:

(a) service industries;

(b) markets with high levels of economic development;

(c) product concepts which require limited training and can be easily applied.

2 The advantages of franchising as a means of rapidly entering the international market are that:

(a) it is a much more rapid way to expand business activity over a larger area with minimum investment than other forms of market-entry strategy – this is due predominantly to the role of the franchisee who has a vested interest in making a success of the venture as well as having local knowledge of the market;

(b) it is very profitable for the franchiser, who receives income in the form of royalties and fees and from the purchase of product components–ingredients;

(c) by purchasing exclusively from the firm in many cases, the franchiser retains maximum control over the product concept.

3 Some of the major disadvantages of franchising, especially from the franchiser's viewpoint, are that:

(a) the firm could possibly attain higher profit levels by running the operations itself;

word to find franchisees

(b) to expand rapidly and over a wide geographic area requires many franchisees who are not only competent but who are also financially in a position to take on a franchise – these are difficult conditions to fulfil;

(c) there are difficulties in monitoring the quality of the franchise operations, and this requires a constant and systematic supervision of the franchisee; McDonald's in France had to go to court to end a particular franchise because it felt the required standards and quality were not being met, and this turned out to be a very expensive and time-consuming affair.

Box 11.3

THE BODY SHOP[8]

The Body Shop International first opened in Brighton in 1976 with a £4000 bank loan, and six months later the second shop opened in Chichester. Its first shop in Europe opened in 1978 and the key to expansion was franchising. In 1984, the company went public and today there are over 930 branches of The Body Shop in over 42 countries, trading in over 20 languages. The company has franchises in most of the Western European countries but currently has none in Eastern Europe. The company's mission appears to be both educational and the furthering of the societal concept. The latter refers to the firm's wish to consider not only its customers and company needs, but also the long-term interests of both consumers and society as a whole. The implications of such a philosophy is that the company needs to make its products both consumer and environmentally friendly. Indeed, it was one of the first companies to market natural cosmetics which were not tested on animals and the company's products have a refill facility.

Franchising has been the major growth engine for The Body Shop; however, the majority of franchisees are not company-owned. In spite of this, the company closely monitors and controls all activities, and the corporate image is fiercely protected.

Joint ventures

A joint venture is a project in which two or more parties invest. It normally results in the formation of a new company in which the parties have shares, though neither party has effective control over the decision-making process (*see* Table 11.2). A joint venture differs from licensing in that the firm:

1 takes an equity share; and

2 has a managerial role.

In this collaboration, the parties share profits, risks and assets. In some joint ventures each party holds an equal share, while in others, one partner may have a majority of shares, thus the equality of partners is not a necessary condition. The contribution of each partner may also vary, and can take many forms from funding, technology, equipment and know-how to marketing organisation.

Forms of joint ventures

In practice, there are many forms of joint ventures (*see* Fig. 11.4).

Table 11.2 FORMS OF JOINT VENTURE

Spider's-web strategy	• Establishing a joint venture with a large competitor • Avoid absorption through joint ventures with others in network
Go-together then split strategy	• Co-operating over extended period • Separate • Suitable for limited projects (construction)
Successive integration strategy	• Starts with weak inter-firm linkages • Develops towards interdependence • Ends with take-over – merger

Source: Ullander, G., and Taffon, S., 'Joint ventures and corporate strategy', *Columbia Journal of World Business*, 11(1) (1976), 104–14. © 1976. Reprinted with permission.

1 The 'spider's-web' type of joint venture consists of many firms, as found in the car and electronics industries. The major drawback of this form of joint venture, is that there is real danger that the firm could be taken over and that it could form a link with a competitor. Wright's research in 1976 into Japanese joint ventures with US firms, found that 65 ventures were terminated or transferred to the Japanese interest.[9]

Fig 11.4 THE SPIDER'S WEB: JOINT VENTURES IN THE CAR INDUSTRY

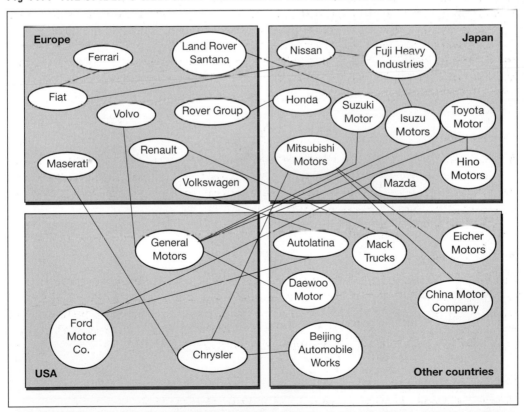

Source: Reprinted from *Long Range Planning* (October 1988), Devlin, G. and Blackley, M., 'Strategic alliances: guidelines for success', 14–23. © 1988. With kind permission from Elsevier Science Ltd.

2 The second type of approach is where the firm gets together with its partners and after a period of time they separate. The separation may be due to the company having achieved its objectives and moving on; or the venture may not have been a success Research by Franko of 170 multinationals[10] showed that over one-third of 1100 joint ventures either ended in 'divorce' or one partner increased its power in the relationship.

3 A third form is where the parties move closer together and may eventually integrate. Figure 11.4 shows a complex spider's web joint venture network and Fig. 11.5 shows the network for the semiconductor industry.

Fig 11.5 ALLIANCE NETWORKS IN THE SEMICONDUCTOR INDUSTRY

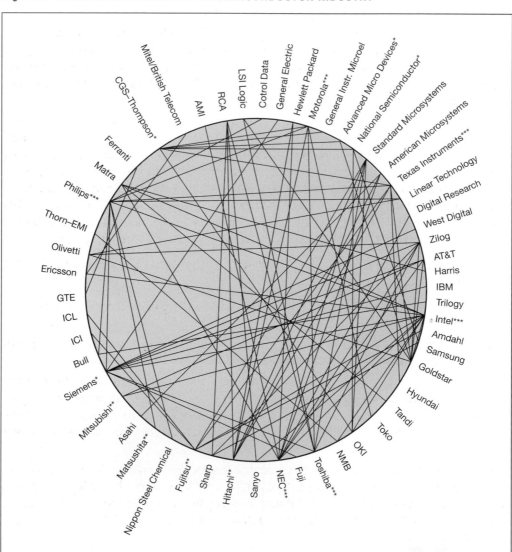

Source: Reprinted from *Long Range Planning*, 25(1) (1992), Gugler, P., 'Building transnational alliances to create competitive advantage', 90–9. © 1992. With kind permission from Elsevier Science Ltd.

As joint ventures have increased in the variety and form they take, it is necessary to be clear on how joint ventures are defined. For the purposes of the present discussion, it will be assumed that the participant holds enough equity to have some management voice, but not enough to dominate the venture.

The alternative to a wholly-owned joint venture can be seen as the manufacturing operation abroad. Joint ventures are commonly used because they offer important advantages to the foreign firm.

1 A firm can expect higher returns compared to royalty payments.

2 Greater controls may be exerted over production and marketing operations.

3 The risk is shared on a new venture, especially when it involves long-term capital investment; given that economic and political conditions in many countries are volatile, this particular advantage takes on increasing importance.

4 More international experience may be gained and therefore greater familiarity with the local environment, in particular the cultural aspects; this may enable the joint venture to be more aware of cultural sensitivities and also benefit from greater awareness of changing market conditions and needs in order to improve its marketing strategy.

5 Many firms embark on joint ventures as ways of overcoming import limitations – for example, many Japanese car producers opted for joint ventures to protect their existing volume of cars sold in EU markets as well as gaining further access (Honda's joint venture with the former Austin Rover Group provided the Japanese firm with access to many European markets). Many Japanese firms, varying from car producers to the electronics industries, have entered the US market in this manner and many US firms, e.g. General Foods, have entered the Japanese market through the joint venture route to gain access to the distribution channels.

When compared to wholly-owned subsidiaries joint ventures have further distinct advantages.

1 Many foreign governments look more favourably upon joint ventures for a number of reasons:

   (a) governments may fear a loss of control over their economies if a large portion of their industries become foreign-owned;

   (b) governments may feel that if their nationals have a share in the joint venture, they will get more of the benefits of technology transfer and more profit – for these reasons, India is a particularly restrictive market, and in Japan for many years until the early 1980s it was difficult to own more than 50 per cent of a subsidiary.

2 In the former socialist markets, joint ventures were the most viable vehicle to gain entry; in these markets the foreign firm will in many instances be taking a minority position with the local firms, and many Western firms have entered the markets of the former USSR and China with this method, e.g. Volkswagen Motor Corporation in China.

Compared to wholly-owned subsidiaries a joint venture has the following benefits:

- it requires less capital and management resources
- with a local partner the firm is less likely to be taken over by the government
- a local partner can exert political influence, so the joint venture may benefit from government support, grants and tax advantages
- the joint venture may benefit from better relationships with labour unions, local government and other local organisations as it is not perceived as a foreign firm.

There are also strategic considerations when evaluating joint ventures.

Market knowledge

A major advantage of having a local joint venture partner is that it can provide instant and better market knowledge and feedback, while the home firm is providing important contacts or skills of value to the foreign firm. This pooling of resources is very valuable for joint venture partners – for example, if the firm has a competitive edge in the technology available but lacks sufficient capital, market knowledge or access to a well-established distribution network, it will be difficult for the firm to enter on its own. By joining forces, the technology will be utilised more effectively and market penetration will be easier. Allied Lyons formed a joint venture with Suntory to enter the tough Japanese market to sell its alcoholic beverages; Kodak formed a venture with a Japanese distributor to develop and strengthen its marketing. Firms entering the US market have also collaborated with US companies – e.g. when Volvo joined with General Motors for the US truck segment. The formation of the European Single Market in 1992 saw European firms enter into joint venture agreements in preparation for the intense competition which will evolve out of the larger market. Some have entered into these arrangements for offensive and some for defensive reasons to protect existing market share. The UK distillery company Guinness has a joint venture with Moët–Hennessy in France; in the car industry, Volkswagen, the German firm, has a joint venture with the French firm Renault to produce gearboxes.

Oligopolistic markets

Another major strategic advantage of joint ventures is for firms entering predominantly oligopolistic markets, where few firms dominate the industry. A foreign firm may find the cost of entering such a market too high, and will look to join with a competing firm. Coca-Cola joined with Cadbury-Schweppes in the UK, and Bols and Heineken formed a joint venture in preparation for the 1992 Single Market.

Not all joint ventures are successful and many multinationals do have reservations about them. Some of the major disadvantages are as follows.

1 Compared to licensing, joint ventures require:
   (a) more capital and management resources;
   (b) an increased risk factor with an equity approach.

2 Compared with wholly-owned production operations joint ventures suffer from the following major drawbacks:

(a) conflict of interest may arise from national differences in management philosophy, culture and business objectives – conflict can arise over how profits are to be shared, management style, marketing policies, production personnel, R&D, levels of earning to be reinvested and transfer pricing;

(b) the business objectives of the parties concerned may differ – for example, many foreign multinational companies used joint ventures in Japan to gain access to the distribution network, whereas the Japanese partners were interested in the acquisition of new technology; this has been the root cause of many failures in Japan;

(c) integrating joint venture operations between different nations can be difficult and unsatisfactory even in a 50–50 partnership;

(d) there is the feeling that the other partner may be getting the better deal; one partner might feel that it is giving more technical know-how, management skills and other resources, whilst receiving less in terms of market knowledge and half the profits;

(e) frequently many joint ventures suffer from the fact that they are not exactly 'joint'. One partner is likely to hold more than 50 per cent of the equity, and the minority partner in the arrangement will be under pressure to accept the majority partner's decision;

(f) a major difficulty for an international firm is to integrate the venture into a synergistic international operation; this is more likely to occur when the international firm wishes to carry out a standardisation strategy in terms of product, quality, design, etc. and the local partner may disagree with the objectives;

(g) since the financial interests of both parties are effectively limited by the nature of the agreement, it is possible that the joint venture may be starved of further resources.

For joint ventures to be successful, a number of points should be observed.

1 It is essential to find the right partner in terms of commonality of orientation and goals, and there should be complementary and relevant benefits to both partners. If both parties have a competitive advantage in technology but limited marketing expertise, there would be little sense in having an alliance as there would be no mutual benefit to the parties.

2 The negotiations must address key issues from the outset, such as profit distribution, marketing objectives, plans for the dissolution of the venture (should the need arise) and, perhaps most importantly, a provision for changes in the original mission statement. This is imperative because firms operate in dynamic and volatile business environments, and must adapt to changing market conditions. The implications of responding to these changes is the need to be able to change outdated objectives and business practices which could affect the partnership if they were allowed to continue.

Killing[11] categorises joint venture operations into dominant and shared partnerships and outlines the conditions for each type to function well. In dominant-type partnerships, the suggestion is that the international partner should be dominant, especially when control of technological know-how is critical, and the local partner should play a passive role. However, when the international partner's knowledge and skills are easily transferable or are required only for a short period, then the local partner should be dominant.

Shared partnerships will work well only if both partner's skills and competencies are needed over time. In such cases, partners should be chosen who complement the skills of the other party, and there should be some autonomy in the joint venture with an exit clause if required.

Box 11.4

CATERPILLAR IN CHINA[12]

Western firms are generally not very familiar with planned economies such as China. However, in the last 10 years or so, China has become a market that cannot be ignored. It presents a great source of natural resources, as well as a potentially lucrative market for consumer and industrial goods. The Chinese economy has witnessed some of the most accelerated growth rates in the last 10 years; it is now the world's third largest economy behind that of the USA and Japan. Although there are several modes of entry, many Western firms find that joint ventures are the preferred choice. The Chinese government also encourages joint ventures between Western investors and Chinese partners. Licensing would require a Western firm to transfer its technology to a Chinese partner and possibly forgo control over its technology, and there is an added worry about China's intellectual property protection and whether it affords sufficient protection for a foreign firm's technology. Given that China's intellectual property regime is under-developed, most Western firms tend to rule out the licensing option and opt for high-control modes such as joint ventures or wholly-owned subsidiaries. Caterpillar has been selling its products to China since 1975, and in the past did use licensing to overcome entry barriers to particular markets. Licensing also offered more certainty of securing hard currency than a joint venture. Caterpillar signed its first technical licence in China for power-shift transmissions in 1984, with two factories in Sichuan and the Ministry of Machine Building Industry (MMBI) and the China Machine Building International Corporation. In 1985, Caterpillar bid for a project covering 10 factories to produce components and complete machinery. At the same time Caterpillar's rival, Komatsu also put in their bid. The contract was won by Caterpillar in spite of the lower bid from Komatsu. Caterpillar's success was attributed to non-price factors. In particular, its sales campaign dealt with two critical issues:

1 it offered a counter-trade programme through its Hong Kong office, whereby it would buy manufactured goods from the factories, under the wing of the State Commission of Machiners Industry, and hand the foreign exchange from its overseas sales over to the factory, so that it could pay for its semi-knocked-down kits, components and equipment;

2 with hints from the MMBI, Caterpillar circumvented Beijing and targeted the factory officials instead to back its bid; the company's proposals were backed by all 12 factories.

The agreements were finally completed in 1987 and included five technology transfer contracts, a counter-trade pack and a used equipment sales agreement. The know-how and counter-trade agreements last for eight years. Any improvements made in China's

▶

▶ **Box 11.4 continued**

plants would be transferred to other Caterpillar plants world-wide and vice versa. The agreement also provides for training Chinese workers in the USA and on-site assistance from the company's engineers.

Compensation was divided into an upfront fee and royalties over the contract's eight-year term (all in US dollars). Normally, the Chinese preferred royalties to be based on net sales or net value-added, Caterpillar were able to secure an agreement where it was based on unit of output instead. This ploy was used by Caterpillar to avoid the uncertainties of using China's complex pricing system.

To protect its technology, which was estimated by Caterpillar's management to be about 10 years ahead of best Chinese factories, the company's designs, factory production and management techniques are protected by confidentiality clauses for the term of the contract. An unresolved issue with the Chinese was the possibility of the Chinese factories exporting equipment based on Caterpillar designs. However, Caterpillar's management were not unduly concerned as they felt that it would take China some time to attain the quality demanded by overseas markets, as well as the fact that China has a great internal demand for such equipment.

Strategic alliances

One of the most significant trends in international marketing/business has been the growth in cross-national collaboration or strategic alliances. This term is sometimes used interchangeably with corporate coalitions, strategic partnerships and competitive alliances. Strategic alliances have become a popular mode for global expansion, and Ohmae[13] and Perlmutter and Heenan[14] have gone so far as to argue that globalisation of the world market has forced firms to form strategic alliances for corporate survival. The rapid growth of these alliances perhaps underlines the changes in the global market place: the world market is now characterised by fierce competition, rapid technological obsolescence, high R&D costs, shorter product life cycles, and so on. Companies, particularly global ones, need to rethink their current methods and market growth strategy. It is in this context that strategic alliances have become the major instrument of growth, since they have a more flexible structure to enable companies to maintain their competitive position and compete successfully on a worldwide basis. Collaborative arrangements have existed for many years in the form of joint ventures and marketing–distribution agreements. But strategic alliances differ in their contractual forms and the purpose for their establishment.

Strategic alliances are co-operative arrangements between two or more companies. These companies tend to be competing firms from different countries, although they could be from the same country. The partners in an alliance seek to add to their competencies by combining their resources with those of other firms with a commitment to reach an agreed goal. Partners tend to be of comparable strength and resources, though this is not always the case. Strategic alliances have been mainly concentrated in manufacturing and high-tech industries. Some of the more notable examples are Plessey and GEC (UK), GEC and Siemens (Germany), Texas Instruments (USA) with Hitachi (Japan), and Ford (USA) and Mazda (Japan). Strategic alliances are also occurring increasingly in the service sector, such as insurance, banking, transportation and airlines. Swissair has alliances with Delta and Singapore Airlines. In the computer software sector, we have companies like Wordperfect collaborating with Lotus.

NATURE OF GLOBAL STRATEGIC ALLIANCES

According to Keegan,[15] strategic alliances tend to exhibit the following characteristics (*see also* Table 11.3):

- they tend to be contractual rather than equity arrangements
- in general, they tend to have limited life spans
- when technology transfers are involved, this is by other means rather than through subsidiaries or via direct investment
- ownership is not clear-cut and its quite difficult to identify company 'boundaries'.

Strategic alliances are also quite different from joint ventures; joint ventures essentially focus on a single national market, or if the joint venture is based abroad, it usually involves partners of unequal strengths and resources (as in the case of a developed country multinational company and a local firm in a developing country). The differences according to Young *et al.*[16] and Perlmutter and Heenan[17] are that:

1 strategic alliances involve collaboration between two or more parties of comparable strengths and resources, although this is not a necessary condition; furthermore, the parties tend to be from industrialised countries;

2 the parties will often be competing in the same geographical and product markets, whilst at the same time collaborating with each other;

3 in a traditional joint venture relationship the contributions to the venture are unbalanced – a multinational corporation may contribute capital and technology, whilst the local firm contributes local market knowledge and business contacts; the contributions of partners in a strategic alliance may still be asymmetrical, but are more balanced;

4 co-operative ventures are motivated by factors such as market access and economies of scale; these are equally important in strategic alliances, but the underlying motivations are guided by strategic and competitive considerations – an alliance can influence the competitive nature of an industry, in terms of providing access to new technology, or affecting a firm's cost structure or enhancing competition by facilitating entry of new firms in a particular market area;

5 the relationship is reciprocal, in that each party possesses specific competencies and strengths that it shares with the other partner; learning is implicit in this type of collaboration if the alliance is to be of any benefit;

6 the strategic and global focus are perhaps the most distinguishing features of strategic alliances, in that they can potentially influence market behaviour; strategic alliances thus represent a change in competitive tactics, not competitive goals.

Key success factors

According to Perlmutter and Heenan[18] and Lynch,[19] there are a number of factors that can positively impact on an alliance. These are mission, governance, strategy, organisation, culture and management, as summarised by Keegan in Table 11.3.[20]

Table 11.3 SUCCESS FACTORS IN GLOBAL STRATEGIC PARTNERSHIPS (GSPs)

1 Mission	Successful GSPs create win-win situations, where participants pursue objectives on the basis of mutual need or advantage.
2 Strategy	A company may establish separate GSPs with different partners; strategy must be thought out up front to avoid conflicts.
3 Governance	Discussion and consensus must be the norms. Partners must be viewed as equals.
4 Culture	Personal chemistry is important, as is the successful development of a shared set of values.
5 Organisation	Innovative structures and designs may be needed to offset the complexity of multicountry management.
6 Management	GSPs invariably involve a different type of decision making. Identify potentially divisive issues in advance, and establish clear, unitary lines of authority that will result in commitment by all partners.

Source: Keegan, W.J., *Global Marketing Management* (Englewood Cliffs, NJ: Prentice-Hall, 1995), 401. Adapted by permission.

Objectives and types of alliance

The objectives of strategic alliances are many and varied but the most important include:

1 *to gain market entry*: some firms find that this type of alliance is a better way to enter a market than going through a distributor, agent or licensee;

2 *to remain competitive on a global scale*: R&D costs in today's competitive environment may be beyond the resources of a single firm and the establishment of an alliance provides the necessary financial resources and technological expertise to remain competitive;

3 *to attain economies of scale*: these can be gained more rapidly in a partnership than as a single firm;

4 *to learn from their partners*: partners use these collaborations to acquire new technologies or skills to enhance their internal skills and technologies, whilst guarding against transferring competitive advantages to more ambitious partners.

There are many thousands of alliances between companies of different sizes and strengths. We have large companies collaborating with smaller ones to complement their respective competencies, with smaller companies providing market insight and entrepreneurial capabilities and the larger companies providing much-needed capital resources. There are many different kinds of alliances from formal to informal ones, vertical, horizontal and conglomerate links, equity and non-equity agreements, local and national alliances, etc. According to Jeannet and Hennessey,[21] strategic alliances can be categorised in three main ways.

Production-based alliances

The aim in this type of alliance is to improve manufacturing–production efficiency through economies of scale and/or learning benefits; or through exploiting country comparative advantages. JVC and Thomson have an alliance where both hope to learn from each other. They both make VCRs, but Thomson needs manufacturing and product technology, while JVC needs to learn how to operate in the fragmented European market. GM (USA) made an alliance with Toyota (Japan) to manufacture and market small cars in the US market. GM would obtain the manufacturing know-how from Toyota; in return, the Japanese company expected access to the US market. Toyota may have gained more from this alliance in that its long-term objective of moving into the US market was achieved at the expense, perhaps, of GM car sales.

Distribution-based alliances

Mitsubishi (Japan) has a strategic alliance with Caterpillar Tractors (USA) where both companies will share the Far Eastern distribution network, and Caterpillar will supply the Australian market out of Japan and thereby save on transport costs. An additional motive was that this alliance was formed to compete more directly with Komatsu (Japan).[22] A similar sort of agreement exists between Hitachi (Japan) and Fiatallis (Italy) whereby Fiatallis will sell Hitachi's hydraulic excavators in return for Hitachi's use of Fiatallis's distribution network.

Technology-based alliances

Technological partnerships are aimed at reducing costs and sharing the risks. This comes about through technology transfer and from the pooling of R&D. The alliance struck by AT&T with Philips (Netherlands) was for the exchange of digital technology for wider market access.

Risks of strategic alliances

There are many types of risks associated with strategic alliances:

1 there may be differences in corporate culture and management philosophy and practice, which may threaten the survival of the alliance;

2 strategic alliances involve a degree of shared decision making. This could result, for example, in disagreements over types of objectives, and the need for compromise may not result in the most optimal choice. There could also be a slowing down in decision making. Major decisions in global alliances will require top management participation, and this may be costly in terms of top management time;

3 there may be conflict between partners: differences in solving problems are common, one partner preferring a technical to a marketing solution. There may be disagreement over distribution of benefits, allocation of inputs, etc.;

4 there may be imbalance in benefits. There is a danger of one-way flow of technological know-how if procedures and guarantees are not enforced and adhered to. Some would argue that US companies are losing out to Japanese partners in terms of transferring technology to a potential rival;[23]

5 these alliances do involve mutual dependency, in that each partner is dependent on the other's inputs and contributions. There is a risk that one partner's input may be inadequate, which may be construed as a lack of commitment and motivation by the other;

6 over time, there is an evolving balance of power between the parties. According to Hamel *et al.*[24] there is a threat of 'strategic encroachment' where one party attempts to be the dominant partner in the venture and exploit any technical know-how to achieve its competitive objectives;

7 there are co-ordination costs involved in strategic alliances. These costs refer to the effort and time spent in managing diverse interests between the parties, and in trying to integrate alliance activities to form a coherent strategy.

Many of the problems discussed above do exist in other types of collaborative agreements; however, it is the strategic and global dimensions which make the difference, because of the impact on global competitiveness. Strategic partnerships are thus a response to global competition in order to enhance a firm's global competitiveness. These international coalitions are established to enter markets, gain access to a whole series of resources and skills and achieve global strategic objectives.

Ownership of foreign production

Investment in foreign markets can take many forms but two important distinctions are normally made – portfolio investment and foreign direct investment (FDI). The former refers to the purchase of shares in companies, but control does not follow. Since portfolio investment is not directly concerned with the management and control of the foreign company, it will not be discussed any further here.

Foreign direct investment refers to the type of investment taking place in which participation in the management and control of the enterprise is involved. Ownership ranges from 100 per cent downwards, and though this can amount to a small percentage of the equity of the company being acquired (as little as 10 or 25 per cent ownership), the primary concern is the degree of managerial control that the firm can exercise. FDI represents the highest level of investment a company can make in an overseas market, and involves immense financial commitment, as well as management skills, marketing expertise, manufacturing know-how, transfer of technology, etc. Once established, it will be difficult for the firm to withdraw as this will entail heavy costs.

Foreign direct investment is often chosen as an alternative to exporting, for a number of reasons:

1 the firm may have to establish a presence in the local market to defend itself from local competition;
2 exporting to the foreign market is not attractive because of government policies and barriers to trade, therefore the firm needs to establish a base in the market;
3 the firm could serve the market better by adapting its products to local needs;
4 the foreign firm can compete more effectively in the local market because it can gain competitive advantages in terms of costs or technology;

5 there may be efficiency gains if the operations are close to the source of the raw materials.

There are two major strategies to establish foreign production facilities:

1 by acquisition, which involves buying out an existing local firm; or

2 by developing a new company from scratch.

Acquisition

The acquisition route involves the purchase of all or the majority of the shares of the local company to gain control. There are a number of advantages of this method. It is the fastest way for the firm to enter a market, and it has the added advantage of acquiring a trained labour force, local management, access to a distribution network, local knowledge and contacts with the market and local authorities. The ownership and management of well-known brands is in itself a major advantage, especially since shelf space is scarce in supermarkets and this has meant that consumers now focus on one or two major brands in the market and these have become highly valued commodities in acquisitions.

It was for these reasons that Nestlé, the giant Swiss multinational company, acquired in 1988 for $1.3bn the UK manufacturing producer Rowntree Mackintosh, who had world brands such as 'After Eight' and 'Kit Kat'. Nestlé also agreed to pay $1.3m for Buitoni, an Italian food company. Many large firms tend to offset the high cost of entry against the market potential of their acquisitions which is viewed as an essential part of a world strategy. Boots Company, the UK chemist chain, paid $555m to buy a US company, Boster Fravenal Laboratories, which was nearly 50 times the book value. Electrolux, the giant Swedish company, acquired White Consolidated Industries (USA) for $150m, and Hoechst (Germany) agreed to pay $2.8bn in cash for the US company Celonse. In some cases, a company has no option but to acquire companies as a means to enter a market which would otherwise be closed. Electrolux (Sweden) acquired a US company, National Union Electric, for immediate access to the US market via National Union Electric's distribution network of over 36 000 dealers.

There are two major disadvantages of the acquisitions strategy:

1 there will be problems of integrating a newly acquired company, and these will be compounded if it is a company which has different management and business practices; this could turn out to be expensive and time-consuming;

2 most governments tend to offer foreign investors low-interest loans and tax holidays for building new plants; these may not be available for firms pursuing an acquisition strategy.

Box 11.5 MIDLAND BANK PLC[25]

In early 1992, Midland Bank PLC was one of the top 100 companies quoted on the UK Stock Exchange, with a market value of over £1.6bn, and with over 100 000 shareholders and over 50 000 employees world-wide. However, the period from 1988 to 1990 were depressing years for the bank under the stewardship of Sir Kit McMahon who reigned

▶

> **Box 11.5 continued**

from 1985 to 1990. During his period in office, Sir Kit adopted innovative strategies in an attempt to revive the bank, and to break the mould of UK banking. Due to a number of unsuccessful international ventures, the Midland Bank was in serious problems. The first of its mistakes was the acquisition of a California-based Crocker Bank in the 1980s. Crocker Bank turned out to have a portfolio of bad loans to developing countries, and the Midland had to write off those loans from its UK domestic banking profits. The effect of such an action was that the Midland had a very poor cost structure and thus weakened its competitive position. In 1989 and 1990 the bank's Treasury Division had forecast a drop in interest rates; the opposite occurred with the result that the bank lost over £200m. To add to the bank's problems, Sir Kit's attempt to establish a multinational senior management team to change the bank's corporate culture into an international one backfired. Many employees left the bank preferring to work in a more traditional institution. Finally, Sir Kit was not able to bring to fruition a marriage between the Midland and the Hong Kong & Shanghai Bank (HKSB). In 1987 the HKSB had bought just under 15 per cent of Midland's shares, this was much needed capital for the Midland after its mistakes in the 1980s. As for the HKSB, they were cash-rich and wanted to put most of their financial resources out of Hong Kong before the take-over by China in 1997. Sir Kit resigned in 1991 and Brian Pearse was in charge with a mandate to restructure the bank, and it was quite clear that the Midland was by now up for sale. There were two potential buyers for the Midland, the HKSB and Lloyds Bank. The Lloyds bid was based on the notion that a concentrated business would lower aggregate costs and push up aggregate profits. On the other hand, the rationale behind HKSB's bid was that the acquisition of Midland Bank would give it leverage in the global market, and that the combined revenues of the merged businesses would be much higher than if the businesses were single entities. HKSB's global strategy was to have a presence in the Asia Pacific region where it was already a dominant player outside Japan and with close links to China. HKSB's ownership of the New York bank Midland Marine would ensure that it captured business between the USA and the Far East. The acquisition of the Midland Bank would give HKSB a foothold on the UK–European and European–US axis. The purchase of the Midland was thus essential to achieve HKSB's 'global reach' of operating in the 'Triad' regions of the world economy. The HKSB would serve the Asia Pacific region, the North American bloc would be serviced by Midland Marine and the European region would be spearheaded by the Midland Bank. The HKSB achieved its aim when in June 1992, it acquired the Midland Bank for £3.9bn, thereby making it one of the largest banking groups in the world.

New production facilities

The alternative approach is to establish new production facilities. Although costly and time-consuming this does have advantages. It may be the only method available to enter a market which does not have a local company willing to sell, or whose government makes it difficult for local firms to be sold to foreign companies, as in Japan. Building a new plant means that the foreign firm can develop in the way it wants to. It can incorporate the latest equipment and technology. It also avoids the problems of changing the business practices of the former organisation, which could lead to resistance on the part of workers and managers. Other advantages which may accrue are favourable grants and tax-free periods, maximum control over the product and reduced transportation costs as the product is now produced locally.

There are, however, disadvantages associated with this entry method:

1 there are heavy costs involved;

2 there is an increased risk in the event of political upheavals;

3 there is a lengthy period before the venture starts to generate income and profits;

4 the firm will have to abide by local laws concerning taxation, unionisation, etc. which may be detrimental to the firm's goals and organisation;

5 firms may be under pressure to increase the percentage of components that are sourced locally, and this may create serious problems, especially if the supply products are of dubious quality.

In general, there are arguments for and against wholly-owned ventures. The points in favour of solo operations are that:

- the firm will acquire greater experience in international operations
- all profits will accrue to the firm
- conflicts of interest which will invariably arise in joint partnerships are eliminated
- there is the possibility of developing a synergistic international system.

The limitations of solo operations, in particular those firms with 100 per cent ownership, are that:

- the venture is extremely expensive in financial and management resources
- the firm may lose out on the advantages of having local contact and local knowledge of the market
- with such an amount of capital tied up in one market, the risk of expropriation is much greater.

SUMMARY

This chapter has extensively discussed the different methods of foreign market entry. There is no one 'best way' to enter a foreign market, for this will depend on the firm's internal factors such as its capabilities, assets, resources, objectives and experience of the global market; and on the opportunities available in the foreign market.

Entry strategy decisions are frequently made by companies and since this type of strategic decision will affect later successes in international markets, they will have to be made very carefully. Not only is the firm faced with a multitude of market-entry options it also has to attain an effective strategy leading to optimum results, and this calls for the highest managerial skills at ongoing market-entry configurations. The globalisation of markets has intensified competition for market dominance, and this means that firms can no longer rely on the neat categories of exporting, licensing or joint ventures to attain their goals, but may need to adopt entry strategies which are a mixture of a number of different methods or even new structures such as strategic alliances, as discussed in this chapter.

These added complexities of market-entry management are made even more difficult by the need to consider the rapidly changing international marketing environment. The constant changes in legal–political–economic environments will affect the costs of various entry methods and the firm will need to re-examine its entry decisions on a continual basis. This may necessitate changes to the original programme to take account of the present situation. This need for flexibility in the firm's choice of entry methods will present an important challenge for managers in global marketing in the future.

The major types of international entry methods can be broadly divided into three categories. Indirect exporting involves the firm selling to an intermediary within the country who, in turn, re-sells the goods to a customer abroad. Direct exporting involves the firm selling to the customer abroad, who might be the final user of the product or service; or to an intermediary who is either a distributor or agent. Finally, in foreign manufacturing the firm is directly involved in production and distribution of the goods/services in the market concerned.

Indirect marketing offers the lowest level of market control and degree of risk. It is also a very useful method for firms with limited resources who wish to enter foreign markets quickly and easily. There are several methods in this approach including casual exporting, export houses, export management companies and joint venture marketing operations ('piggyback'). The firm can begin by making domestic sales to companies with buying offices in the UK.

Export houses are another form of indirect exporting. They have three major functions – as merchants, buying and selling on their own account, as export agents who represent a UK firm, and as buying houses who represent the buyer abroad. They offer instant market access as well as being a low-cost method of entry.

Export management companies offer specialised exporting and marketing services. This is a cheap method of market entry, and the firm need not set up an export department.

'Piggybacking', or joint marketing operations, is a form of co-operative marketing between two firms whereby each firm carries the products of its partner firm to the export markets. There are mutual advantages in this set-up, whereby the carrier complements their product range whilst the rider gains instant and inexpensive access to the market.

Direct exporting occurs when the firm directly sells its products in the host market. The firm sells directly to an import house or to a wholesale retail agent, and undertakes to find the representatives in the foreign markets, organising the logistical arrangements and choosing its target markets. An alternative arrangement is to use the foreign sales representatives or establish branch offices.

There are many types of foreign production strategies. One form of foreign production is assembly operations, whereby components or ingredients are shipped from the home base to be manufactured locally. This type of operation is advantageous to the foreign firm in reducing its overall costs through the lower transport, tariff and raw material costs in most cases. The foreign firm can also respond better and more quickly to local requirements.

Contract manufacturing uses a local firm's production facilities and the foreign firm avoids heavy capital investment and saves on tariff and transport costs, and also gains a favourable response from foreign governments by being perceived as a local supplier.

Licensing involves a local firm producing and marketing the foreign firm's products. The foreign firm saves on major capital commitment and gains a competitive edge on supplying the goods at low cost, which serves as a quick and easy entry to foreign markets. In some countries, licensing is the only way to enter these markets, but this method of entry can create potential competition and the firm's ability to control operational activities is reduced.

Joint ventures are a costly method of entry compared with most others apart from wholly-owned production facilities. They enjoy the advantages of local production and control over production and marketing operations, and reduce local hostility to the presence of foreign companies. This type of approach can suffer from internal conflicts over management objectives, philosophies and business practices.

Strategic alliances involve co-operation in production, marketing and distribution activities. Rival firms may be involved in this type of partnership. Most of the advantages of joint venture accrue to this type of alliance, and in today's competitive international environment it has become an important survival strategy.

Wholly-owned foreign production involves the firm in a major commitment. The firm gains complete control of operations and it is possible to implement a more synergistic strategy. But the firm encounters foreign market operational problems and economic and political risks. Wholly-owned operations can be acquired by buying out an existing organisation or by establishing and developing a completely new company. Although acquisitions allow quick entry, they do not give the advantages of tax holidays, investment grants, etc. as in the case of establishing a new company. The disadvantages of starting a new company are the huge capital investments and lengthy period required before revenues are generated.

REVIEW QUESTIONS

1 What are the functions of export intermediaries?

2 Compare and contrast the functions of an agent and a distributor.

3 What are the advantages and disadvantages to both the rider and the carrier in 'piggy-back' operations?

4 What are the pros and cons of establishing a joint venture?

5 Discuss the benefits and drawbacks of strategic alliances.

6 Why do firms prefer the acquisition route to foreign-owned production operations?

DISCUSSION QUESTIONS

1 What conditions favour foreign direct investment (FDI) as a market strategy?

2 Why do firms need to have different levels of market entry?

3 What should a firm consider when it decides whether to license or to enter a strategic partnership? Explain your reasons.

4 Explain why joint ventures are generally popular entry strategies.

5 Explore the proposition that in strategic alliances it is possible for competitors to collaborate with each other in order to sustain their competitive advantages.

STRATEGIC ALLIANCES[26]

The countries of the EU lose out in competition to the giants of aerospace, heavy engineering and defence industries from the USA, which has companies such as Lockheed Martin, Boeing and General Electric, and Japan, which has Mitsubishi Heavy Industries and Hitachi. Although large conglomerates, EU companies are the wrong size and shape to bring the strength needed in each of their individual businesses.

To counter this problem European firms are forming alliances. This is perhaps Europe's way to modernise some of its heavy industries without shedding too much blood.

US firms have also caught the alliance bug. Alliances have increased in the USA from 750 during the 1970s to 20 000 in 1987–92, according to management consultants Booz, Allen & Hamilton. Alliances are especially popular in the media and telecommunications businesses on both sides of the Atlantic.

Europe's heavy engineering industries are known for alliance-building. Airbus, owned by a consortium of France, Germany, the UK and Spain, has a third of the world market for commercial airliners. Recently, two of Airbus's partners, UK Aerospace (BAe) and Aerospatiale of France, formed a joint venture with Italy's Alenia. This merges the three countries' regional aircraft businesses in a company called AIR (some are referring to it as Minibus).

Collaborations are very much part of Europe's defence industry. The latest are agreements on satellites and missiles between Daimler–Benz Aerospace (DASA) and Aerospatiale. In the electrical engineering sector, GEC Alsthom was the result of an alliance, and France's Framatome and Germany's Siemens formed an alliance to design nuclear reactors.

Even rail transport is subject to alliance-forming. Recently, Siemens and GEC Alsthom discussed an alliance to market the high-speed trains produced by companies in Asia. Analysts say that these sorts of agreements could result in technical collaboration and eventually an Airbus on rails. The Swiss–Swedish engineering firm ABB Asea Brown Boveri agreed to place its train-building programme in a joint venture with AEG doing the same work – the deal has been agreed with the European Commission.

Airbus was formed 25 years ago because, singly, European companies could not afford the costs of developing the intercontinental jet. The situation was much the same at the end of the 1980s, seen in the fact that the A330/A340 aircraft cost $3.6bn to design, too large a bill for one company to foot. Eurocopter, the company formed to sort out shrinking defence budgets with high development costs, was the result of an alliance with DASA and Aerospatiale and is Europe's most successful and biggest joint venture.

The other reason for forming alliances is that even with the European Single Market, nationalist sentiment acts against much needed cross-border take-overs. The US market for defence and aerospace is three times larger than the European market, but, according to Aerospatiale, in Europe there are three–four times as many companies chasing the business. Restructuring in Europe has been less dramatic because of political protection, says Christopher Bartlett, Professor at the Harvard Business School.

Political factors are most evident in defence and aerospace. This is one of the reasons making it difficult for state-owned Aerospatiale, with its involvement in France's nuclear weapons, to merge with Germany's DASA.

Jordan Lewis, a US consultant, believes that alliances allow companies to take advantage of each other's strengths without paying the price of a full-scale merger or take-over. Costs involve the payment of goodwill (the difference between net asset value and market price), can be exorbitant and have to be written off. Booz, Allen and Hamilton found from research in the USA that the return on investment was higher in alliances – 17 per cent as opposed to 12 per cent in conventional firms. Also attractive is the fact that allies can be selective in what they want to ignore in an ally's business. This is suitable for Europe's very diversified conglomerates.

Joint ventures and alliances on the whole are more effective when limited to specific projects. America's General Electric and France's SNECMA collaborated on a range of aircraft engines that required different technical skills from each party. Alliances allow for companies to use complementary strengths – for example, in railway engineering AEG's technology is of interest to ABB. Daimler–Benz, with an eye to ABB's markets, paid $900m for an equal stake in this alliance for AEG. It is pointed out by critics that alliances are a way to avoid market-driven take-overs.

Defence companies may be hamstrung by politics, but then why should each country in Europe have its own car or train manufacturer? On the occasion when politicians have permitted cross-border mergers the results have been very successful – ABB proved this. ABB came into being partly because Swedish and Swiss governments saw the limitations being imposed by their national champions.

Decisions are made faster and there is better communication in a single structure. Essential strategic steps become messy compromises if a single structure is not in place, and decisions involving factory closures and layoffs may not be made because agreement is difficult to reach.

Sceptics of alliances say that the rationalisation of heavy industry in Europe was subject to mergers but came unstuck at national borders. UK Aerospace (BAe) was formed by many mergers after the 1960s. During the chairmanship of Edward Reuter, Daimler–Benz's 'shopping expeditions' resulted in DASA having 80 per cent of Germany's aerospace industry. Although there is little possibility of mergers within national borders the commercial logic remains. Daimler–Benz is always seeking alliances because of its many small businesses that are not big enough to compete on their own. It is expected that this logic will prevail and create another round of cross-border mergers.

Could the joint ventures of today lead to such a consolidation in the future? Successful alliances may present a challenge to their founders by taking on lives of their own. There are discussions of turning the Airbus consortium into an independent company to speed up the decision-making process and to save on purchasing. The merger between ABB and AEG railway engineering is an alliance in all but name. A similar thing is happening to a 1990s joint venture in small jet engines that connects the technology of UK's Rolls-Royce with the financial clout of Germany's BMW. The joint venture has its own payroll and testing facilities. Up until now the research results have been passed back to Rolls-Royce, but in the future these results could be sold to the highest bidder. Furthermore BMW and Rolls-Royce might find themselves competing with Rolls-Royce in the next series of jet engines.

All the corporate parent can expect to receive in the future is a dividend. Daimler is beginning to look like a car maker with a portfolio of financial stakes in several joint ventures, moving away from the integrated technology-based company envisaged by Mr Reuter.

National conglomerates may be broken up by grand European alliances and reconstituted as pan-European specialists able to compete in world markets, but not before parent companies and national champions alike give them more room for manoeuvre.

Questions

1 *What are the key factors to consider when selecting a partner for a strategic alliance?*

2 *'The success of a strategic alliance depends on the partners contributing equally.' Comment on this statement.*

3 *How can a partner in an alliance ensure that it continues to obtain value from such a co-operative venture?*

4 *Are alliances merely a device to avoid market-driven take-overs, as mentioned in the case study?*

FURTHER READING

Anderson, E. and Coughlan, A.T., 'International market entry and expansion via independent or integrated channels of distribution', *Journal of Marketing*, 51 (1987), 71–82.

Buckley, P.J. and Ghauri, P. (eds), *The Internationalisation of the Firm* (London: Academic Press, 1993).

Contractor, F., *Licensing in International Strategy: A Guide for Planning and Negotiations* (Westport, CN: Quorum Books, 1987).

Contractor, F. and Lorange, P., *Cooperative Strategies in International Business* (Toronto: Lexington Books, 1988).

Czinkota, M.R. and Johnston, W.J., 'Exporting: does sales volume make a difference?', *Journal of International Business Studies* (Spring–Summer 1983), 147–53.

Geringer, J.M., 'Partner selection criteria for developed country joint ventures', *Business Quarterly*, 53(1) (1988).

Harrigan, K.R., 'Joint ventures and global strategies', *Columbia Journal of World Business*, 19(1) (1981), 7–16.

Kim, W.C. and Hwang, P., 'Global strategy and multinationals' entry mode choice', *Journal of International Business Studies*, 23(1) (1992), 29–53.

Kogut, B., 'Joint ventures: theoretical and empirical perspectives', *Strategic Management Journal*, 9(4) (1989), 319–32.

Lorange, P. and Roos, J., *Strategic Alliances* (Oxford: Blackwell, 1993).

McDougall, P., 'New venture strategies: an emperical identification of eight "archetypes" of competitive strategies for entry', *Strategic Management Journal*, 11(6) (1990), 447–67.

Root, F.R., *Entry Strategies for International Markets* (Lexington, MA: Lexington Books, 1987).

NOTES AND REFERENCES

1 *Sunday Times* (Business Section) (14 January 1996).

2 Dudley, J.W., *Exporting* (London: Pitman Publishing, 1984).

3 'Telling tales from abroad', *The Guardian* (16 Janaury 1996).

4 Matsuura, N.F., *International Business* (London: Harcourt Brace Jovanovich, 1991).

5 'Hitachi sales will replace exports with local output', *Japan Economic Journal* (23 January 1979), 9.

6 Commins, K., 'US franchisers see explosion in European market place in the 90s', *The Journal of Commerce* (13 July).

7 Bruce, L., 'The bright new world of Benetton', *International Management*, 42(11) (1987), 24–30.

8 Harris, P. and McDonald, F., 'The Body Shop International: an ethical success' in Harris, P. (ed.), *European Business and Marketing* (London: Paul Chapman, 1994).

9 Wright, W., 'Joint venture problems in Japan', *Columbia Journal of World Business* (Spring 1979), 25–31.

10 Franko, G., 'Joint venture divorce in the multinational company', *Columbia Journal of World Business* (May–June 1971), 13–22.

11 Killing, J.P., 'How to make joint ventures', *Harvard Business Review* (1982), 120–7.

12 *Business International*, 34(28) (13 July 1987), 217–19.

13 Ohmae, K. 'The global logic of strategic alliances', *Harvard Business Review*, 67(2) (1989), 143–54.

14 Perlmutter, H. and Heenan, D., 'Cooperate to compete globally', *Harvard Business Review*, 64(2) (1986), 136–52.

15 Keegan, W.J., *Global Marketing Management,* 5th edition (Englewood Cliffs: Prentice-Hall, 1995), 38.

16 Young, S., Hamill, J. and Davies, J.R., *International Market Entry and Development: Strategies and Management* (Hemel Hempstead: Harvester Wheatsheaf, 1989).

17 Perlmutter and Heenan, op. cit.

18 Ibid.

19 Lynch, R.P., *Business Alliances Guide: The Hidden Competitive Weapon* (New York: Wiley, 1993).

20 Keegan, op. cit.

21 Jeannet, J.-P. and Hennessey, H.D., *Global Marketing Strategies* (Boston, MA: Houghton Mifflin, 1995).

22 Sims, J.T., 'Japanese market entry strategy at work: Komatsu vs Caterpillar', *International Marketing Review* (Autumn 1986), 21–32.

23 Reich, R. and Mankin, E., 'Joint ventures with Japanese give away our future', *Harvard Business Review*, 86(2) (1986), 78–86.

24 Hamel, G., Doz, Y.L. and Prahalad, C.K., 'Collaborate with your competitors – and win', *Harvard Business Review*, 67(1) (1989), 133–9.

25 Stephen, R., 'The year of the dragon: internationalization and corporate death: the case of the Midland Bank' in Preston, J. (ed.), *International Business: Text and Cases* (London: Pitman Publishing, 1993); 'HKSB versus the world', *International Business Week* (31 July 1995).

26 'Slugs or caterpillars', *The Economist* (2 September 1995), 83–5.

Export management

INTRODUCTION

Exporting is often the first contact with foreign markets that the majority of firms will experience. Seen as one of the quickest and perhaps most successful ways to internationalise, many firms will often find it a more difficult entry method than they at first imagined, experiencing many pitfalls on the way from the challenges of documentation and export finance through to the more significant challenges of matching foreign customer expectations. However, a country's economic well-being often depends on a healthy export sector that assists with the balance of payments, boosts economic activity and can lead at the micro level to the successful growth of the firm, both in profits, sales and brand recognition.

Companies ranging from large concerns such as Reyrolle (part of the Rolls-Royce International Power Group) that supplies equipment to the power industry, to smaller companies such as Zeta Communications[1] that makes voice and data networking devices to improve transmission between phones, faxes and computers (both of the UK), have achieved recognition of their success in exporting. Although success in export markets does not guarantee success for a company overall, it does provide opportunities for growth and the spreading of risk over a number of markets, in Zeta's case, 50 per cent of its turnover was exported, providing a cushion against its home market experiencing economic difficulties – a position that few SMEs are able to attain.

Promoting these success stories is often a tempting policy for governments given the macroeconomic benefits that spring from exports. However, there are many failure stories, showing that a premature entry into exporting by firms who are unprepared for the task of competing on an international scale and unaware of the many new administrative tasks that await them can be hazardous. This chapter will review the strategic operational considerations, and provide detail on the documentary, financial and logistical issues that should be recognised at the start.

Objectives

This chapter will examine:

● export behaviour
● export logistics and documentation
● government policy and exporting
● the strategic export marketing plan
● imports
● barter and counter-trade
● free trade zones.

EXPORT BEHAVIOUR

In previous chapters, some of the reasons why firms choose to enter foreign markets have been reviewed. In the case of exports, often seen as the first stage in the internationalisation process, this strategy is pursued when the home market is suffering recessionary pressures, economies of scale require expansion away from the home market, or an opportunity has arisen through an unsolicited enquiry. If these are the spurs to exporting then it is not clear that it is the best method to enter the new market. The fact that exporting, rather than licensing, is selected can be put down to inexperience by the firm, a fear of the financial and other resource commitments that come from alternative entry strategies, or that the risks – either political or economic – are seen as an impediment to a higher level of commitment. Whatever the reason, the bulk of firms enter the market via exporting with the majority being content to stay as exporters. As noted in the Introduction, there are many failures in exporting ventures, arising from simple operational incompetence through to the more problematic issues associated with the product. This last issue is of critical concern to firms as product adaptation is often a major consideration, along with quality standards, delivery time, packaging and advertising.

In a review of strategy and performance of UK exporters[2], Brown and Cook summarise best practice as identified by academic researchers:

1 for a firm to be successful it should concentrate its scarce resources on to nominated markets, rather than seeking to attack a large number;

2 the firm should be prepared to adapt its products to meet foreign market requirements;

3 specialist resources should be allocated to exporting, and the firm should see itself in these markets for the long term;

4 a strategy based on rigorous marketing research is more likely to be successful.

Whilst few practitioners and academics would disagree with this summary, few exporters actually follow this prescription. Brown and Cook undertook research on UK companies that had been awarded the Queen's Award for Export Achievement. (Awards are given to around 100 companies a year.)

The firms are judged against the following criteria:

1 a substantial and sustained increase in total exports over three years;

2 a substantial increase in the percentage of exports sales to total business over three years;

3 a percentage of exports to total business that is considerably higher than the average for that industry;

4 a very significant increase in export sales over a shorter period than three years, with every likelihood that this can be maintained;

5 an entry and breakthrough into what is regarded as a difficult market;

6 the greatest value of export sales by any group or company in a given year.

Each company completes a pro-forma on which a panel of judges bases its decision. Typically about 10 per cent of all applicants achieve the award.

Using these, successful companies would show how far they matched good practice and what their chances were of maintaining their performance into the future.

In summary, the research identified the following:

1 the respondents showed a bias towards the smaller firm, but 70 per cent of all firms responding had exports accounting for 60 per cent of turnover;

2 the most popular reason for exporting was to gain more sales, followed by long-term survival;

3 over half of the companies (57 per cent) reported that they did not have a market research budget, another 30 per cent had budgets of £10 000 or less;

4 most companies undertook research by using exploratory forays by managers, sales personnel, etc., and by using government agencies; a minority of companies used in-house researchers.

5 only one in three companies saw major benefits in market concentration;

6 one in two companies extended their UK product policy to export markets;

7 over 60 per cent of companies either priced differently in each market, or sought to assess customer value; 15 per cent of companies based price on cost;

8 the use of export sales staff and/or export support staff was absent in 40 per cent of the companies, while those companies who did use export sales staff more often than not expected them to cover more than one market; one in five companies organised their sales effort on product lines;

9 promotional techniques favoured brochures, followed by exhibitions and advertising; 60 per cent of companies had an overseas advertising budget, and most attempted at least to modify the advertisement;

10 export success factors showed that quality and design were deemed to be the two most important items, with market research being given low support, whilst the agent or distributor was accorded a middle order ranking;

11 price was thought to be a major reason for failure in a market, with quality, delivery and finance problems coming in some way behind.

The conclusions drawn from this research suggested at the time (1990) that many firms had a tactical rather than a strategic response to exporting and appeared, to the researchers at least, to be production- or sales-led in their approach rather than marketing orientated.

The more recent study by Styles and Ambler,[3] outlined in Box 12.1, notes that delivery dates and matching customer specifications had all increased in importance since a similar survey carried out in 1979. The other interesting difference between the two studies is the focus in Styles and Ambler, not on what they term the neo-classical ('4 Ps') approach, but on the relational paradigm, which identifies the importance attached to offering a product that is unique, of good quality, supported by good supply chain relationships. Firms also tend, not surprisingly, to export in the first instance to those countries that they feel they have a closer understanding of, or cultural affinity with (the psychic distance is shortened), such as EU and North American countries, rather than Asian economies. Having developed competences in exporting, firms were then likely to use their expertise to enter other markets.

Box 12.1   WHAT MAKES A COMPANY SUCCESSFUL IN EXPORT MARKETS?

Most researchers have found that focusing on the marketing mix as a prerequisite for success in export markets offers little in the way of useful guidance for firms wishing to enter a foreign market for the first time.

Using the winners of the 1992 Queen's Award for Export Achievement, Styles and Ambler focus on three broad groupings of variables:

1 market environment;

2 the firm and its management;

3 key elements of strategy.

Market environment

Market environment studies conclude that firms who are new to exporting tend to choose those countries that are psychologically closest, extending further afield as they gain experience. 'Psychic distance' is identified by these studies as a key variable – the differences in language, education, business practice, culture, and so on. The better a firm can adapt to the local environment, the better the chances of success. Infrastructure and government barriers reduce the likelihood of success.

The firm and its management

The firm's management affects success via manager's commitment, experience (and competences) in international markets, which will in large measure determine export performance. Personal contacts and inviting channel members to participate in decision making have also been found to assist in understanding the needs and requirements of customers. Personal visits to foreign markets assist with export performance. Market research, which is seen as significant in understanding markets, was found by a number of researchers to have either no direct bearing on success or only a weak link with it. This was found in studies both in Denmark and the UK.

▶

▶ **Box 12.1 continued**

Key elements of strategy

Product benefits, in so far as the product is perceived to be unique and of quality, are identified with strong export performance. However, the importance of adapting products to local market requirements is less clear, with some studies suggesting that standard products can be at least as successful as those adapted to local market needs. With respect to price, some research has identified that price competitiveness is of some significance, while others show it to be less so. The outcome of these studies depends upon the focus of attention – if it was profitability, premium pricing became more of a vital issue, whereas with export sales premium pricing acted most significantly as a brake.

Export marketing literature, according to Styles and Ambler, relates to the '*neo-classical*' paradigm – i.e. the marketing mix; however, in the summary of success factors outlined above marketing mix issues have been relegated in comparison with those based on the relationship of the company to the chosen market and the relationships with channel members and appreciation of customers' needs. The *relational paradigm* (RP) sees the market as a network of value-laden relationships – between the brand, customers and other influence groups such as advertising and market research companies. The role of the marketer is to develop the network, to gain short-term profits, but also to gain the benefit of relating the brand to buyers' needs and to persuade buyers that the brand meets their requirements.

The RP has implications for exporters. The marketing mix points to firms making rational decisions based on the collection–interpretation of marketing research data. The RP approach points to the initial development of relationships, with marketing mix decisions taking place only afterwards.

The RP also suggests that exporters rely on information obtained through interactions, followed by more analytical approaches, rather that these approaches being developed in line with each other; relationships are therefore of primary importance.

By undertaking a study of 67 of the 127 winners of the 1992 Queen's Award for Export Achievement, organised by questionnaires sent to the manager responsible for export markets, the top factors for success were shown to be consistent quality, company reputation and meeting delivery dates – the core competencies of the firm. Matching customer specifications came fourth in importance.

Comparing these findings to a similar survey undertaken by Mitchell in 1977 revealed that marketing mix elements were given a lower level of importance. Indeed the average company marketed the same product in foreign markets as they did in the UK (supporting other research that suggests that success does not depend on product adaptation). The markets of Western Europe and North America were priority markets for these companies, suggesting the importance of the 'psychic distance' theory reviewed earlier.

Styles and Ambler argue that the relational paradigm is a valid approach to the investigation and explanation of export marketing. Export marketers should look at four areas:

1 *success factors*: attention to personal contact, communication and working relationships;
2 *decision making*: appoint local representatives to help develop local insights and develop a mobile marketing plan;
3 *information*: rich information should be gathered from local contacts, and should be given a higher priority over secondary data;
4 *choice of market*: should initially be based on those which are closest in 'psychic distance'.

Do these two approaches conflict and contradict each other? Studies that highlight the importance of market research, marketing orientation and adaptation of the product can be supported by other studies that reveal the necessary investment that has to take place to develop competences in exporting. A hybrid model can bring the two together, although it has to be noted that the relational paradigm has not been the subject of as intense a level of research and debate as the 'neo-classical' approach.

Styles and Ambler identify what they refer to as 'key dynamics' of the model:

1 key elements of the firm are its management characteristics and core competences, which determine its ability to acquire and use information; this is problematic for small firms who may not be able to devote human resources to this activity (but they note that findings on this are inconsistent);

2 a firm's relationships are responsible for providing information and resources for the firm which can contribute to better decision making;

3 marketing strategy factors, particularly choice of market, segmentation, and the marketing mix, are outputs of the firm's internal characteristics as well as the relationship built up with supply and channel members;

4 all of the above exist in a market environment, with elements such as government barriers to trade, infrastructure and market attractiveness affecting performance;

5 the outcome of the model is export performance, which is shown by sales, market share, profits, growth, strategic objectives and brand equity.

Export performance in this model is therefore related to the environment, core competences and management commitment to exporting, development of channel relationships, development of market strategy, and plans to exploit the chosen market. None of this may come as a great surprise to experienced companies, but it has significant implications for companies both new to exporting and less experienced in this activity, and agencies of national government and regional and local development organisations. Success in export marketing will not be guaranteed by appropriate marketing strategies and plans unless core competences, and the support of senior managers, is given due recognition.

Focusing on external characteristics will not guarantee success, neither will the development of internal characteristics assist if the 'hard-systems' approach of market orientation summed up in marketing plans is left out of account. Taking the two together assists in training for firms, support and advisory services and government policy in this area. Management considerations are also stressed by this hybrid model.

The importance of experience points to a gradual process of adaptation to export markets, that brings with it more complex structures such as foreign-based production facilities to accommodate more varied market situations and prepare the company for more direct involvement. Firms at the first stage of exporting (i.e. looking at the possibility of market involvement) require knowledge, help and advice to understand the market situation and their response to it. Box 12.2 outlines the advice offered by HKSB for firms new to exporting.

Box 12.2

HKSB GUIDANCE ON DOCUMENTS REQUIRED
FOR FOREIGN TRADE[4]

Commercial invoice

A commercial invoice is a claim for payment for the goods under the terms of the commercial contract. It is addressed to the importer by the exporter. An invoice will normally include a detailed description of the goods together with unit prices, totals, weight and terms of payment, as well as packing details and shipping marks. It serves as a checklist so that a particular consignment can be identified and is the main evidence in any assessment for customs duty.

Packing list

Where there are several packages in one consignment, an invoice is usually accompanied by a packing list which details the contents of each package and may also show their weights and measurements.

Insurance policy or certificate

The terms of a contract between the importer and the exporter should define the responsibilities for arranging insurance cover while the goods are in transit and what risks are to be covered. The insured risks will be detailed under Institute Cargo Clauses, and those applicable to a particular transaction will be noted on the certificate or policy. In order to obtain the widest possible cover, the Insurance Terms Institute Cargo Clauses 'A' should be specified.

Bills of Lading

Still the most important commercial document in international trade, the Bill of Lading (B/L) is used to control delivery of goods transported by sea. In negotiable form, title to the goods may be transferred by endorsement of the B/L. The various types of Bills of Lading are described below.

Marine B/L

A Marine B/L is a document signed by the carrier of goods or agent of the carrier setting out the conditions of carriage and acknowledging that goods have been shipped on board a particular vessel bound for a particular destination. If issued by the carrier's agent, the name of the carrier should be evidenced on the document. The B/L serves as evidence of the freight contract between the shipper and the carrier, and will indicate whether the freight costs have been paid or are still to be collected.

Clean B/L

A clean B/L is one which has no superimposed clause or statement declaring some defect in the condition of the exported goods or the packaging, or some other aspect of the consignment.

Received for shipment B/L

Evidence of receipt of goods for shipment, requiring a later-dated clause or stamp 'shipped on board' to raise it to the status of a 'receipt for goods shipped'. Conventional B/Ls of this type are usually only used in bulk trades where cargo is received and delivered alongside.

▶

▶ **Box 12.2 continued**

Combined transport B/L or multimodal transport document

The majority of general cargo is now 'containerised' – packed in containers either at the factory or consolidated with other merchandise at a receiving point operated by the ocean carrier or specialist operator. These locations are remote from ports, with the result that the ocean carrier's liability commences when the goods are received either at the shipper's premises or container freight station. Hence the concept of 'multimodal transport'. Cargo will be delivered to the consignee at the (inland) place named as the destination.

Sea waybill

Like a B/L, a waybill provides a receipt for goods and evidence of a contract for their carriage by sea. However, it is not a negotiable document and cannot be used to convey title to the goods. The shipper can vary the consignee and delivery instructions at any time prior to delivery. It is a simple alternative where the transferable nature of a B/L is not required.

Air waybill

An Air Waybill is a receipt for goods carried by air and is often referred to as an 'Air Consignment Note'. Like the Sea Waybill, it is non-transferable and not a document of title. It is usually produced as a 'House Air Waybill' where cargo consolidation is involved.

Road consignment note

This is used for international transport by road. It is not a document of title and is not transferable. It is more commonly known as a Certificate of Movement by Road (CMR) or Truck Waybill.

Railway consignment note

This is used for international transport by rail. It is not a document of title and is not transferable.

Parcel post receipt

A post office receipt for goods dispatched by mail. The receipt is evidence of despatch only.

Certificate of Origin

This is a declaration which states the country (or countries) of origin of the goods and is commonplace in countries wishing to identify the origin of all imported goods (or their components) or where there are quotas or other import restrictions in force. It should be completed by the supplier and may have to be authenticated by a Chamber of Commerce or other authorised body in the exporter's country. In some instances, the certificate must also be legalised by the embassy or other representative of the country concerned. The certificate should include the name and address of the exporter, the manufacturer (if different), the importer, a description of the goods and, if required, the signatures and seals of the authorising organisation.

> **Box 12.2 continued**

Certificate of Inspection

Importers can safeguard their interests, and ensure that the goods comply with the specifications stated in the contract of sale, by arranging for the goods to be inspected by an independent body before they are dispatched. The Certificate of Inspection will give details such as weights, numbers and quality, packaging and identifying marks, shipping details and the signatures and seals of the inspecting organisation. UK exporters may be required to obtain Certificates of Inspection from a specific inspection agency, such as SGS or Cotecna, for exports to certain countries.

Certificate of Health

Agricultural and animal products may require a certificate stating that they comply with the importing country's health regulations. This certificate must be authorised and signed by the health authority in the exporter's country. In the UK, this is usually undertaken by the Ministry of Agriculture, Fisheries and Food (MAFF).

Carnet

A carnet is a document that makes customs clearance of certain temporary imports and exports easier by replacing:

1 normal customs documents in the exporter's country;
2 normal customs documentation and security in the country into which the goods are imported.

ATA (*admission temporaire*/temporary admission) is the main carnet in use. This is an international customs document issued by Chambers of Commerce in most major countries. It can be used for practically all kinds of goods and can provide for a simple entry and exit to and from a single foreign country or for numerous multidestination journeys during the validity of the carnet. This validity can never exceed one year.

When applying for the carnet, the trader must provide the issuing chamber with an equivalent security either in cash or bank draft or, most often, through a counter-guarantee from a bank or financial institution. This security must be for an amount equal to the highest rate of duty and taxes applicable to the goods in any country of destination and transit

EXPORT FINANCE AND LOGISTICS

As identified in the previous section, the importance of ensuring that the customer receives their goods on time and in a fit condition has become of increasing importance to exporters. The pitfalls associated with documentation are outlined in Box 12.3. Although focusing on the practical issues of finance and logistics, it should be borne in mind that both of these should be part of a broader framework of activities and planning that the company has undertaken. This issue will be further developed below, but should be seen as part of the learning process that companies go through in building a successful exporting business.

Box 12.3

THE PAPER CHASE[5]

The secret of handling documentation is making sure you know what is required and then filling the forms out accurately. Delays will be caused if the right documents are not in the right place at the right time, or if they are inaccurately completed.

Paperwork is a crucial part of exporting. A study undertaken for the European Commission highlights that documentation accounts for between four per cent and seven per cent of export costs, increasing to as much as 15 per cent if the documents contain errors.

For the sake of efficient exporting and maintaining a competitive edge it is important for management to give sufficient time and resources to processing paperwork. Having enough time to prepare the documents themselves is another important factor.

Commercial

Export documentation falls into distinct categories. The first is the commercial or contract forms, such as the order enquiry, quotation, pro-forma invoice, the order and order acknowledgement. These are concerned with what goods are needed, how they will be transported, delivery terms and payment details, and represent the contract between the customer and supplier.

While most goods do not need export licences, certain items, such as antiques, works of art, military equipment and hi-tech products, do. This means that a special licence has to be issued by DTI's Export Control and Non-proliferation Division.

Customs

The next category is customs documents. For business with EU customers, depending on the value, exporters will cover these goods on their quarterly VAT declarations for sales under £150 000. Over this figure, companies will have to fill out a C1501 Supplementary Declaration for Despatches, commonly known as an Intrastate, on a monthly basis. These have to be sent to HM Customs within 10 working days of the month's end.

Low value

For goods outside the EU, the value of goods is reported through a Single Administrative Document, which is the basic customs document, the 'low-value' procedure or the 'simplified clearance' procedure.

The low-value option relates to shipments below a certain value and exporters can present evidence using a carrier's receipt, so long as the goods are not liable to UK excise duty.

The simplified clearance procedure means that companies can pre-register with HM Customs and receive a unique Customs Registration Number (CRN). This can be used to declare all shipments within 14 days, and must be accompanied by a document stating the CRN plus the consignment number to identify the load.

Transport documents are another important group. These include bills of lading, waybills, ATA carnets or movement certificates. For moving goods by air, road or rail, the main documents are the relevant waybills or consignment notes. ATA carnets may also be needed to move goods temporarily between countries without paying tax or customs duties. This applies to such things as exhibition materials and customer samples. Movement orders are linked to goods moving between EU and non-EU countries.

▶ **Box 12.3 continued**

Goods moving by sea can be more complex, especially container movements. These may require several sets of documents to meet the various regulations at different stages of the journey. Clear instructions are needed from the start. Exporters who have difficulties can sort them out through their own shipping department or their freight forwarders. A copy of all transport documents is also needed for VAT purposes to support a zero-rated invoice.

Export finance

When an exporter sells to a foreign buyer, to facilitate business that buyer will often be allowed a period of credit prior to paying for the goods. This may encourage trade but it will pose a problem for the exporter in that a cash shortage may then result. Export finance is the way that the exporter can obtain a solution to this problem, by approaching a financial institution. The challenge of dealing with the financial arrangements for exporters can also be seen in Box 12.4, which provides a summary of the various ways in which payments will be organised, in this case for UK exporters, showing that open accounts are the most likely method of receiving payment from EU and North American trading partners. In a real sense, therefore, the risk is taken by the exporter in providing a period of credit and receiving payment. Solutions to the risk involved do exist, but this adds to the cost, and perhaps the price of doing business abroad.

In the case of export finance, there are short- to long-term requirements to which different financial organisations can provide solutions. Short-term finance can be provided by overdraft facilities, while longer-term finance needs can be achieved via loans and bond issues. The following is a summary of the main provisions (noting that this review does not cover all possible solutions currently available, but only the major facilities offered by banks and other financial institutions; although focusing on UK exporters, solutions similar to those reviewed here are available for most countries).

Box 12.4 METHODS OF PAYMENT

The method of payment that is used in exporting will depend very much on what the seller and buyer agree on, plus the banking arrangements that normally apply between the representative countries of the buyer and seller.

The methods of payment are:

1 payment in advance;

2 irrevocable letter of credit;

3 payment on the shipment of goods;

4 documentary collection;

5 open account.

Before proceeding to explain each of these methods, it is important to look at the issue of shipping documents, which include invoices, insurance certificates, insurance cover notes and either a waybill or a bill of lading. The last of these is significant as it acts as a receipt

▶

▶ **Box 12.4 continued**

to show that the goods were accepted for shipment, plus an undertaking to deliver the goods to a particular destination and also as a document of title, where the holder of the bill can claim the goods from the shipping company.

Although different arrangements apply when goods are transported by air or by road, in all cases the goods pass from the exporter to the foreign buyer by means of documentation. This bureaucratic issue, when combined with the method of payment, has particular influence on marketing considerations.

Payment in advance

As the title suggests the exporter is paid in advance of the goods being shipped, so that there is no problem of default or need to provide credit terms. Looking at this issue from the point of view of the foreign buyer (i.e. the importer), they have to accept the risk of the exporter keeping their end of the deal by shipping the specified goods as the importer is financing the deal prior to receipt of the goods. A further consideration is that there may be restrictions placed on foreign exchange transactions of this nature, a change that can happen quickly as noted in Chapter 7 on the regulatory environment.

Irrevocable letter of credit

This is issued by the buyer's bank and is a conditional guarantee of payment by that bank for the exporter – the guarantee will be conditional upon things such as the date of shipment, the quality of the goods, and so on. To make certain that the letter of credit is virtually without risk, it can be confirmed by the exporter's bank.

Many companies have problems with letters of credit as the documentary procedures outlined earlier are often not adhered to, giving rise to problems that result in hold-ups to payment.

Payment upon shipment of the goods

The two parties can agree in these circumstances to pay once the goods have been received, with the exporter given security as the goods will be released only once payment has been received.

Although the risk to the exporter of failing to receive payment for goods sent has been reduced, the problem still exists that payment may not be forthcoming, leaving the exporter with goods in transit or to be stored.

Documentary collection

This situation calls for the assistance of the exporter's bank, in order to deal with shipping documents, bills of exchange or other methods of settlement. In other words, the bank takes over the responsibility to collect money for the customer and credit this to the exporter's account once received.

There are standard international rules that govern the role of banks in this situation, and provide a guaranteed level of assistance, at a price, to the customer.

Open account

This is a situation where the exporter sells to the importer, without prior receipt of funds or other safeguards. This is the same arrangement as applies in domestic trade, whereby a period of credit is permitted to the buyer, with the exporter waiting until the agreed date for payment. This is now customary for UK companies trading with the EU and the USA.

▶

> **Box 12.4 continued**

Even here, though, the issue of documentation still plays a vital role. If a UK supplier to a German buyer sells goods to them with a period of 60 days' credit, then the goods will be transported from the UK to Germany (along with the relevant shipping documents). After 60 days the German firm will pay the debt.

In these circumstances the goods and the title to them (i.e. the shipping documents) have passed to the buyer, which means that before payment is due, the goods can be re-sold. Open account offers the least secure way to effect payments and is dependent upon trust being built up between buyer and seller. Open-account arrangements tend, therefore, to be popular only when such long-term relationships have been built up.

From the point of view of marketing, the methods of payment have a role to play in gaining business. When the company of a country or area is new or risky then other arrangements will be preferred by the exporter, as long as this is okay by the foreign buyer. However, the apportionment of risk is important here. Using payment in advance puts the risk on the importer and in such a situation business may fail to take place. Using other methods entails using the offices of a third party, typically a bank, whose services will have to be paid for, in some cases such as letters of credit, by both parties. Where open-account trading is the norm, such as in the EU, business partners may insist on it, which could prove difficult if long-term relationships have not yet been established.

In many cases, the need for insurance to cover failures (i.e. non-payment) becomes of paramount importance, which is where specialist firms and government agencies come to the aid of exporters. (*See* Chapter 16 for more details.

Credit risks

The risks which an exporter must consider have been listed above, but two of them will have a major impact on the credit policy of the exporter.

Buyer risk is similar to that encountered in domestic sales, except that the credit period on export sales is often longer. Also, suing someone overseas is often a much harder, longer and therefore more expensive process than suing a customer in the domestic market.

Country risk includes problems in the buyer's country, but also obstacles in the UK, such as the cancellation of an export licence on military goods, or problems in a third country through which payment must be made. In 1994, Poland placed restrictions on the import of items in strategic areas in the form of licence requirements and quotas. The law that introduced these changes also gave the right to the Council of Ministers to impose bans or introduce quotas on a range of products from alcohol to used cars and trucks.

Credit insurers

With these risks, companies require a method of insuring against non-payment:

1 cover for short-term business (up to 180 days) is provided in the UK by private sector insurers, most notably by NCM Credit Insurance Ltd (*see* Box 12.5), but also by trade indemnity and overseas companies;

2 cover for business on terms of two years or more is provided by a department of government known as the Export Credit Guarantee Department (ECGD).

Box 12.5 ## EXPORT INSURANCE

NCM cover

As the largest company operating in this sector in the UK it is worthwhile reviewing the type of cover offered.

Buyer risks
- insolvency of the buyer
- buyer's failure to pay within six months of the due date for goods which have been accepted
- buyer's failure to take up goods dispatched, where such failure is not caused by the exporter's actions.

Political risks
- delays in transferring money from the buyer's country
- any action by the government of a foreign country which prevents performance of the contract
- political events or economic, legislative or administrative measures arising outside the UK which prevent or delay the transfer of payment
- cancellation or non-renewal of an export licence or the imposition of new restrictions on exports after the date of the contract.

ECGD cover

Guarantees to banks
The ECGD issues guarantees to banks, against the strength of this security; the bank provides, often at favourable interest rates, finance to support the export contract.

The facility will be a buyer or supplier credit, depending on whether it is the exporter of the importer who borrows from the bank. With a buyer credit, the buyer draws a loan from the bank in the UK and the proceeds go direct to the exporter. The ECGD guarantees to the bank repayment of the principal and interest. A supplier credit, on the other hand, provides a loan from a bank in order to allow the company to sell on deferred payment terms.

Specific guarantees
These are provided to exporters who want to finance sales either out of their own funds or by way of ordinary borrowing.

Third-party guarantees
The ECGD also supports the issue of third-party guarantees or bonds by indemnifying the bondgiver.

Other help
The ECGD also helps firms by offering project participant insolvency cover, tender to contract cover and overseas investment insurance, all of which focus on capital projects rather than cover for credit risks.

The range of services on offer is intended to boost the confidence of those involved in international trade, with the aim of expanding export business by taking on new buyers and breaking into new markets without the fear of crippling loss. With the ECGD, there is a particular emphasis on expanding exports, but it must also break even in its operations in pursuit of that goal. In 1995, there were criticisms from a House of Commons Select Committee, which pointed to an inability to fulfil this objective.

Despite the cover available from NCM and the ECGD only 20 per cent of UK exports by value are insured, so that many exporters appear to be happy to take the risk on the payment of monies due from their customers. On occasions some customers may fail to pay their bills, in which case the company will either have to write the amount off or pursue the non-paying customer through the courts, which could be a lengthy and costly exercise.

Trade finance

This covers both the provision of a loan to an importer and the credit given to an exporter by a financial institution to surmount the problems of either a cash shortage or the need for a period of credit.

Supplier credit

This is where a bank provides finance to the overseas buyer, so that the exporter can be paid immediately on the shipment of the goods.

Buyer credit

The most straightforward way of financing export sales is through an overdraft facility with the exporter's own bank. This is a simple and convenient way to finance all the elements of the contract such as purchasing, manufacturing, shipping and credit, either in sterling or foreign currency. The bank is generally more favourably disposed towards granting a sterling overdraft if the exporter has already obtained an export credit insurance policy. In the case of a foreign exchange overdraft the exporter will be expected to earn foreign currency to pay if off, the interest charged by the bank for the facilities being at a rate above the Eurocurrency London Interbank Offered Rate (LIBOR). This method of financing exports is unlikely to be of use to a firm that is expanding its exports, especially as the rates charged could be higher than for other forms of financing.

Another method of obtaining short-term finance is by asking the UK bank to advance funds against the face value of a bill of exchange. The exporter sends the bill to the bank which then gives an agreed percentage of the value to the exporter and undertakes to present the bill to the overseas buyer for collection. This method is used only when a bill is unaccompanied by any document relating to the exported goods.

The drawback with this method is that only a limited amount of funds are released. If a larger sum is required an alternative method must be used: this is known as the negotiation of bills. In this situation the exporter's bank agrees to purchase the bills – in this case, they are normally accompanied by shipping documents on presentation. The bank may even purchase the documents under a cash-against-documents collection, whereby the bills are sent to the overseas buyer and the bank then collects the money.

In both cases, there is a risk of buyer default. The exporter must therefore take into account that if this occurs the bank will then charge the exporter interest and any collection fees. Alternative methods of raising short-term finance include acceptance credits and documentary acceptance credits. Again, it is clear that the variety of help on offer to exporters and importers is such that a good deal of research must be undertaken prior to the arrangement of any short-term credit facilities to assess how appropriate it is for the company.

Factoring

Most of the methods of financing described so far are appropriate for most companies whether large or small. However, if export turnover is large enough, generally above £250 000, then factoring may be the most appropriate method. Factoring means selling trade debts for immediate cash, or to put it another way, the exporter shifts the problems of collecting payment for completed orders over to organisations or factors that specialise in export credit management and finance. Most factors offer three basic services:

- an accounting credit checking or debt collection service
- credit insurance against bad debts
- the provision of immediate cash against invoices.

The factor works in a similar way to any financial institution. It provides a customer assessment service which identifies a foreign company's creditworthiness, and then establishes credit limits. The exporter sells within these limits and delivers and invoices to customers in the usual way.

The advantages to the exporter are that the export debts are sold to the factor, relieving the firm of the task of credit checking, some documentation and collection, as well as the problems of bad debts and currency loss. Factoring companies do not usually purchase trade debts on terms exceeding 120 days, although in some circumstances this can be increased to 180 days. Factoring may be of particular use to those companies trading on open-account terms. For this service, the factor will charge from 0.75 per cent to 2.5 per cent of the sales value, depending on the risk and the workload involved.

The advantages to the exporter are clear, but there are noticeable disadvantages that have to be judged with care. Factors will wish to reduce their own risk and so may choose carefully which debt they will factor because of their assessment of the overseas buyer and/or the country in which that buyer is located. The charge of 0.75 per cent to 2.5 per cent may not seem excessive but it may well amount to more than the cost of doing the job oneself and, as importantly, it reduces contact with the customer and provides no in-house experience for the company itself.

Forfaiting

This is a method of providing medium-term export finance which originated in Switzerland in the 1950s. More properly known as forfait financing, it is a description of a quite simple system whereby exporters of capital goods can obtain medium-term export finance (or in some cases short-term assistance), usually for periods of between one and seven years.

The system can be explained as follows. An exporter of capital goods has an overseas buyer who wishes to have medium-term credit to finance the purchase. The buyer must be willing to pay some of the costs at once, and pay the balance in regular instalments for the next five years. The buyer will issue a series of promissory notes which are the preferred instrument of payment, rather than bills of exchange, as it frees the exporter from all recourse obligations.

The promissory notes might mature every six months over the five-year period, and in most cases the buyer will normally be required to find a bank which is willing to provide an unconditional bank guarantee. The exporter must find a bank that is willing to be a forfaiter, which is the business of discounting medium-term promissory notes. Discounts are normally at a fixed rate notified to the exporter, so when the goods have been delivered and the promissory notes have been received they will be sold to the forfaiter who will purchase them without recourse to the exporter. The forfaiter must now bear the risk of non-payment, etc.

The principal benefits are that there is immediate cash for the exporter, and along with the first cash payment by the buyer, forfaiting can finance up to 100 per cent of the contract value. This system also has speed and flexibility, with each agreement being tailored to the requirements of each contract. Alongside these benefits go the drawbacks, one of which is the cost of using this approach. However, according to Paliwoda (1990) the high cost is a result of the combined benefits offered by the forfaiter, who provides both the services of a bank and an insurance company in the assumption risk. Finding a bank to act as a forfaiter may not be straightforward: for example, the bank may not be satisfied with the credit standing of the buyer, or the availing (guaranteeing) bank may not have a first-class name.

If there is a large item of capital equipment to be sold to an overseas buyer, an exporter may find it more beneficial to sell the product to a leasing company, which then provides it to the buyer on a lease agreement. This allows the buyer to use the equipment without having to pay for it first, and it can also enable the exporter to receive immediate payment.

GOVERNMENT POLICY AND EXPORTING

DTI and OTS

Government economic policy focuses on the importance of exports as a valuable source of income. This is seen in the UK's Department of Trade and Industry (DTI) objectives.[6] Its general aim is to 'help UK business compete successfully at home, in the rest of Europe and throughout the world'. One of the 11 objectives on the DTI's Home Page is that the DTI (and therefore the government) will 'work for trade liberalisation world-wide and help businesses to take full advantage of UK and overseas market opportunities. The principal method by which this is carried out is through the Overseas Trade Services (OTS), a joint responsibility between the DTI and the Foreign and Commonwealth Office.

The services provided by the OTS cover market advice, assistance in taking the first steps into the export market, and specialist advice and assistance. Information can be provided on import licence regulations, import duties, import regulations, standards, and so on. Information on overseas markets can be undertaken by consultation of the OTS's market intelligence library; when an exporter undertakes an extensive market research project a grant can be made of up to 50 per cent of the cost.

Specialist agencies can offer other assistance:

- Export Representative Service – provides a locally vetted contact who can act as a representative for the exporter
- Market Prospects Service – after information has been obtained about the exporter and its operation, a report is drawn up looking at possible contacts in targeted countries
- Export Intelligence Service – looks at export opportunities that can match those of exporters who have expressed an interest in the search for business opportunities
- Technical Help for Exporters (a trade mission) – provides information on technical standards.

These and many other services are provided by the OTS who, with the help of Business Link (a one-stop shop of information provided for businesses in a particular area) aims to provide as comprehensive a level of assistance as possible.

Looking at the DTI objectives on international trade and exporting, it is clear that the UK government works at different levels to assist exporters. The OTS works at the company level, via embassies and government officials, to provide a helping-hand. At ministerial level, working with international agencies such as the WTO, the aim is to promote freer trade. This approach is often matched by the need of professional associations and business representatives to lobby organisations such as the European Commission, to influence directives and policy. Government policy uses the combination of business involvement and ministerial pressure to create as favourable environment as possible.

How effective are the services offered by the OTS? The National Audit Office (NAO), which reviews all aspects of public sector operators, reported on the OTS in 1996.[7] In its review the NAO found that the OTS was valued by users and generated useful levels of new export business. It did report, however, that there was room for improvement in the relevance of some information and in raising awareness, and there was a need to monitor performance. One of the areas researched were the services to the four Southeast Asian countries, looking at services such as Outward Missions and Export Promotions; differences were found between these markets and other areas of the world, showing that a uniform approach across countries was inappropriate.

Amongst other findings was that awareness of the OTS and its services was high amongst experienced exporters, but low amongst small to medium-sized companies, a group targeted as important both in job-creation possibilities and in exporting terms.

The range of services offered in the UK is matched by governments in other developed countries. In the USA, the Department of Commerce via the International Trade Administration provides similar services to those of the OTS. Similar problems exist, as for example on the number and varieties of services on offer and the fact that the level of awareness of the services is considered too low.

It is not only advice on exporting and export markets that is made available to the indigenous companies of a particular country. The World Aid Section (WAS) of the

OTS provides information on multilateral development agencies, who in 1996 spent over $40bn on the procurement of goods and services. Multilateral development agencies, such as the World Bank, UN agencies and regional development banks (e.g. the Asian Development Bank), provide opportunities for exporters. WAS provides information and briefings on these issues.

Also related to aid is the Overseas Development Administration's Aid and Trade provision, which takes the form of grant and export credit cover.[8] This complements the ECGD provision offered by this arm of government.

Government policy takes effect, as has been noted, at many levels. The importance for marketing management in all types of companies is that an awareness, under-standing and use of the services offered is essential to facilitate the operations of the company in foreign markets. The complexity of exporting has already been noted, and the services offered by government export services are a way of helping to over-come some of the difficulties involved. However, it is incumbent on firms to incorporate these issues into their export plans, as it is firms that trade internationally and on firms' good management that governments depend for the success of these services. Building up management competences in exporting is an area where policy has to be implemented via training and management development initiatives.

EXPORT PLANNING

If the achievement of macro objectives lies with the individual company, and there is a need to transfer good practice to all companies, whether currently exporting or not, then the issue of export planning becomes a critical aspect.

Various benefits are claimed for export planning. Trade advisory bodies in the USA, for example,[9] suggest that the development of a plan is vital to communicate a com-pany's ideas to others in a clear and understandable way. Additionally, it can help the company going through the process of planning to analyse its strengths and weak-nesses, identify export responsibilities and help to reach a clear understanding of:

1 reasons and commitment to exporting;

2 long- and short-term goals;

3 product and company readiness;

4 primary and secondary target markets;

5 export strategy;

6 details of pricing, payment and delivery;

7 financing of the export operation.

In essence, therefore, this is business planning incorporating the extra issues associ-ated with exporting.

It is important to recognise that exporting has more variables associated with it than trading in the domestic market. External environment complexity, appreciating who the competitors are, understanding the behaviour of new customers, export finance and documentation are all facets of business that the company new to export-ing will have to contend with.

Box 12.6 shows an export plan template developed by Bay Trade and Latrade advice and information centres covering the San Francisco and Los Angeles areas.[10] The template is not, as noted earlier, greatly different from the business plan template that the majority of organisations use in developed countries for internal management decision making, as well as presenting a case to a bank, or financial institution or government agency for funding and reporting purposes.

Box 12.6　　　DEVELOPING AN EXPORT PLAN: AN OUTLINE TEMPLATE

Table of contents

1 Executive summary

2 Introduction
　(a) Purpose of the plan
　(b) Export readiness factors
　　(i) Short-term and long-term goals for exporting
　　(ii) Statements of why company is ready to export (i.e. management commitment, financial and personnel resources, etc.)
　　(iii) Product description and function
　　(iv) Statements of why product is ready to export (i.e. domestic product success, and targets a need)
　　(v) Brief description of the industry structure, competition and demand

3 Market research
　(a) Product classification
　(b) Basic customer profile
　(c) Target industry (identify and evaluate)
　(d) Target country (identify and evaluate)
　　(i) Primary
　　(ii) Secondary
　　(iii) Special challenges of country (i.e. culture, climate, resources, etc.)
　　(iv) Product modifications needed
　(e) Target market (identify and evaluate)
　　(i) Primary
　　(ii) Secondary
　　(iii) Special challenges of country (i.e. culture, import controls, etc.)
　　(iv) Product modifications needed
　　(v) Competition and demand (identify and evaluate)

4 Export strategy
　(a) Entry into market
　(b) Trade leads
　(c) Overseas representation
　　(i) Managing distributors
　　(ii) Motivating distributors
　(d) Promoting the product
　(e) Servicing products and warranties

5 Sales and delivery
　(a) Product pricing
　(b) Method of payment
　　(i) Terms
　　(ii) Conditions
　(c) Product delivery
　　(i) Shipping
　　(ii) Storing
　(d) Forecast of sales within first year

6 Trade rules and regulations
　(a) Rules and regulations that affect product per country and market (i.e. export licences, tariff laws, etc.)

7 Financing
　(a) Available financing resources
　(b) Methods

8 Plan implementation schedule
　(a) Time frame for implementing elements of plan
　(b) Time frame for evaluating implementation

Appendix
　(a) Background information on company
　(b) Background information on target countries
　(c) Background information of target markets

The possibility of making mistakes is high given that documentation, financial arrangements and the challenge of operating in a strange (new) market place produce stress on the company that the domestic trade experience will not have revealed. Other than the importance of documentation and finance reviewed above, the issue of export logistics as outlined in Box 12.7 shows that the export plan will force the company to consider attention to detail and to understand the situation.

Box 12.7

EXPORT LOGISTICS: A SUMMARY

When preparing to ship a product overseas, the exporter needs to be aware of packing, labelling, documentation, and insurance requirements. Because the goods are being shipped by unknown carriers to distant customers, the new exporter must be sure to follow all shipping requirements to help ensure that the merchandise is:

- packed correctly so that it arrives in good condition
- labelled correctly to ensure that the goods are handled properly and arrive on time and at the right place
- documented correctly to meet EU and foreign government requirements as well as proper collection standards
- insured against damage, loss, pilferage and, in some cases, delay.

Because of the variety of considerations involved in the physical export process, most exporters, both new and experienced, rely on an international freight forwarder to perform these services.

Freight forwarders

The international freight forwarder acts as an agent for the exporter in moving cargo to the overseas destination. These agents are familiar with the import rules and regulations of foreign countries, methods of shipping, EU government export regulations, and the documents connected with foreign trade.

Freight forwarders can assist with an order from the start by advising the exporter of the freight costs, port charges, consular fees, cost of special documentation, and insurance costs as well as their handling fees, all of which help in preparing price quotations. Freight forwarders may also recommend the best type of packing for protecting the merchandise in transit; they can arrange to have the merchandise packed at the port or containerised. The cost for their services is a legitimate export cost that should be figured into the price charged to the customer.

When the order is ready to ship, freight forwarders should be able to review the letter of credit, commercial invoices, packing list, and so on, to ensure that everything is in order. They can also reserve the necessary space on board an ocean vessel, if the exporter desires.

If the cargo arrives at the port of export and the exporter has not already done so, freight forwarders may make the necessary arrangements with customs brokers to ensure that the goods comply with customs export documentation regulations. In addition, they may have the goods delivered to the carrier in time for loading. They may also prepare the Bill of Lading (B/L) and any special required documentation. After shipment, they forward all documents directly to the customer, or to the paying bank if desired. Three issues will be reviewed: labelling, documentation and shipping.

▶

▶ **Box 12.7 continued**

Labelling

Specific marking and labelling is used on export shipping cartons and containers to:

- meet shipping regulations
- ensure proper handling
- conceal the identity of the contents
- help receivers identify shipments.

The overseas buyer usually specifies export marks that should appear on the cargo for easy identification by receivers. Many markings may be needed for shipment. Exporters need to put the following markings on cartons to be shipped:

- shipper's mark
- country/area of origin
- weight marking (in pounds and in kilogrammes)
- number of packages and size of cases (in inches and centimetres)
- handling marks (international pictorial symbols)
- cautionary markings, such as 'This Side Up' or 'Use No Hooks' (in English and in the language of the country of destination)
- port of entry
- labels for hazardous materials (universal symbols adapted by the International Maritime Organisation).

Legibility is extremely important to prevent misunderstandings and delays in shipping. Letters are generally stencilled on to packages and containers in waterproof ink. Markings should appear on three faces of the container, preferably on the top and on the two ends or the two sides. Old markings must be completely removed.

In addition to port marks, customer identification code, and indication of origin, the marks should include the package number, gross and net weights, and dimensions. If more than one package is being shipped, the total number of packages in the shipment should be included in the markings. The exporter should also include any special handling instructions on the package. It is a good idea to repeat these instructions in the language of the country of destination. Standard international shipping and handling symbols should also be used.

Exporters may find that customs regulations regarding freight labelling are strictly enforced; for example, most countries require that the country of origin be clearly labelled on each imported package. Most freight forwarders and export packing specialists can supply necessary information regarding specific regulations.

Documentation

Documentation must be precise. A slight discrepancy or omission may prevent UK merchandise from being exported, resulting in the firm not getting paid, or even lead to the seizure of the exporter's goods by UK or foreign government customs. Collection documents are subject to precise time limits and may not be honoured by a bank if out of date. Much of the documentation is routine for freight forwarders or customs brokers acting on the firm's behalf, but the exporter is ultimately responsible for the accuracy of the documentation.

▶ **Box 12.7 continued**

The number of documents the exporter must deal with varies depending on the destination of the shipment. Because each country has different import regulations, the exporter must be careful to provide proper documentation. If the exporter does not rely on the services of a freight forwarder, there are several methods of obtaining information on foreign import restrictions:

- country desk officers of the OTS are specialists in individual country conditions
- industry specialists in the OTS can advise on product classifications
- foreign government embassies and consulates in the UK can often provide information on import regulations.

Shipping

The handling of transportation is similar for domestic orders and export orders. The export marks should be added to the standard information shown on a domestic bill of lading and should show the name of the exporting carrier and the latest allowed arrival date at the port of export. The exporter should also include instructions for the inland carrier to notify the international freight forwarder by telephone on arrival.

International shipments are increasingly being made through Bills of Lading under a multimodel contract. The multimodal transport operator (frequently one of the modal carriers) takes charge of and responsibility for the entire movement from factory to the final destination.

When determining the method of international shipping, the exporter may find it useful to consult with a freight forwarder. Since carriers are often used for large and bulky shipments, the exporter should reserve space on the carrier well before the actual shipment date (this reservation is called the booking contract).

The exporter should consider the cost of shipment, delivery schedule and accessibility to the shipped product by the foreign buyer when determining the method of international shipping. Although air carriers are more expensive, their cost may be offset by lower domestic shipping costs (because they may use a local airport instead of a coastal seaport) and quicker delivery times.

Insurance

Export shipments are usually insured against loss, damage and delay in transit by cargo insurance. For international shipments, the carrier's liability is frequently limited by international agreements and the coverage is substantially different from domestic coverage. Arrangements for cargo insurance may be made by either the buyer or the seller, depending on the terms of sale. Exporters are advised to consult with international insurance carriers or freight forwarders for more information.

Damaging weather conditions, rough handling by carriers, and other common hazards to cargo make marine insurance important protection for UK/EU exporters. If the terms of sale make the UK/EU firm responsible for insurance, it should either obtain its own policy or insure cargo under a freight forwarder's policy for a fee. If the terms of sale make the foreign buyer responsible, the exporter should not assume (or even take the buyer's word) that adequate insurance has been obtained. If the buyer neglects to obtain coverage or obtains too little, damage to the cargo may cause a major financial loss to the exporter.

It should be remembered that this one example shows the additional cost factors of the use of a freight forwarder, insurance, labelling, shipping and financing. This is in addition to the issue of risk, which in order to gain a foothold in the market the exporter may have to accept by, for example, using an open account.

Describing exporting by looking at all the extra considerations and responsibilities associated with this activity, can act to dissuade rather than attract. Exporting, however, offers fresh opportunities for growth and expansion, and can be seen as a strategic focus that can help to boost profitability. Export planning, using government advisory services, and an understanding of good business practice will overcome the initial concerns; the help and assistance offered by financial institutions and specialists in the movement of goods will provide the infrastructure that export planning and management can use to good strategic advantage.

IMPORTS

Many of the issues of concern to exporters are also relevant to the importer. As seen in Chapter 7 on the regulatory environment, import regulations in countries such as India require as much care to the importer as they do for the exporter.

Financial issues, such as credit and means of payment, as described from the exporter's point of view, apply just as much to the importer. The sections on Barter and Counter-trade and Free Trade Zones below show specific rules and regulations apply that impact on the importer. Labelling, meeting standards and restriction or prohibition of certain imports, such as drugs, are all aspects requiring attention.

Country and regional trading bloc regulations, which affect most if not all of the world's economies, have to be taken into account. The NAFTA agreement, also covered in Chapter 7 on the regulatory environment, shows how the establishment of a free trade area (FTA) requires agreement on what can and cannot be excluded from import control. Importers, therefore, who wish to trade successfully in a country require the same acumen as exporters when it comes to regulations, finance and credit arrangements. From the point of view of a country's economic well-being, importers are as important as exporters, bringing in much-needed supplies – such as commodities, components, semi-finished products and luxury goods, etc. Industry relies as much on an efficient import procedure as it does on an exporting one. Jobs, investment and wealth creation come as much from importing activities as from any other. From a marketing management point of view the need to get this process right, with clear objectives and planning, is just as important as any other aspect of marketing.

BARTER AND COUNTER-TRADE

Academic publications and the trade press often offer confusing accounts of barter and counter-trade. Four features distinguish the two. First, barter transactions are exchanges of goods and services without money, whereas counter-trade involves partial or full compensation in money. Second, one contract will formalise a barter transaction, whereas more than one contract will generally be required to formalise counter-trade. Third, counter-trade requires a longer time for the completion of transactions compared to barter, and involves greater risk. Fourth, counter-trade requires a greater commitment of the firm's resources, and greater risk. Some forms of counter-trade can require firms to provide capital to invest in joint venture production facilities. Counter-trade, therefore, can be simply described as a commercial arrangement for reciprocal trade between companies in two or more countries.

Counter-trade has arisen because of shortages in both foreign exchange and lines of credit, because some world markets for raw materials are rather weak, and because of competition between mainly Western exporters of manufactured goods. The DTI lists four main reasons why countries may want to counter-trade:

1 to finance trade which a lack of commercial credit or convertible currency would otherwise preclude;

2 to exploit a 'buyers' market' position to obtain better terms of trade or similar benefits;

3 to protect or stimulate the output of domestic industries (including agriculture and mineral extraction);

4 as a reflection of political and economic policies which seek to plan and balance overseas trade.

Estimates put the size of counter-trade as high as 10–15 per cent of world trade, with 100 countries having some sort of rules on its organisation. Another estimate suggests that five per cent of UK trade is made up of counter-trade transactions.

As noted at the beginning of the section counter-trade is a difficult concept to pin down as it varies according to circumstances; excluding barter, the following five varieties are the most common.

Counter-purchase

Here, the exporter agrees to purchase goods and/or services from the overseas country, so that there are two contracts, one being for the export order which is paid for in the normal way and the second one being for the counter-trade order. The goods in the counter-trade order might be totally unrelated to the goods in the principal export order.

Buyback

This is a form of barter where the exporter of capital equipment agrees to repayment from the proceeds of the output from that equipment. The duration of these contracts is usually in excess of three years and may extend for a much longer period. This has advantages for both sides, especially for the country buying the equipment, as it generates export markets.

Offset trading

Here, the importing country is seeking to develop its own industrial capability, usually in advanced technology. An offset agreement involves the export of goods where the exporter agrees to incorporate into these goods certain material or components sourced from within the importing country. An example of an offset agreement involving two advanced economies was Boeing's deal to sell AWAC aircraft to the UK for £860m in 1993, in return for which Boeing agreed to place orders in the UK worth 130 per cent of the contract price.

Switch trading

This situation arises when one of the two parties involved in barter or a counter-purchase arrangement has goods that the other does not want. In this case switch trading can be used, often with the help of a switch specialist. The example used by Albaum[11] is useful to quote here in full:

> A German firm agrees to trade machine tools worth Dm/M to Brazil in exchange for coffee having an equivalent open market value. The equipment is shipped to Sao Paulo, and the coffee is ready for shipment to Hamburg – but, the German firm really does not want the coffee. So, with the help of a switch specialist, the coffee is sold to a Canadian company for DM 925,000. The German company gets its hard currency, *less* a five per cent commission paid to the switch specialist. Since the German company would know in advance that the coffee would have to be sold at discount it could build this into its price for the equipment.

Evidence account

Companies that conduct a large amount of continuing business in a country may be required to arrange counter-purchases equal to the value of their export. In this solution, a company would find it impractical to arrange a counter-purchase for each separate consignment, so an evidence account can be kept showing how over a year a balance has been kept between its imports into the country and the exports it has taken out.

There are, of course, risks for the exporter in counter-trade, which are in addition to those risks associated with normal exports. An exporter could be persuaded to accept goods for which there is a weak market, or there might be hidden costs in accepting certain goods, such as higher transport costs than anticipated. Likewise, the importing country might place a higher value on the goods than is realistic, and there are the additional problems of arranging insurance. Despite these considerations, the ECGD, OTS and the banks, as well as specialist consultants and trading houses, all offer advice to help overcome these problems.

What are the marketing issues that are associated with barter and counter-trade? Ideally, marketing managers should be as aware of the challenges facing them with this form of exchange as they are with traditional exporting.

With the case of barter, marketing objectives can be met by this form of exchange when new markets can be entered only by this method, or existing markets penetrated further. Barter requires fewer company resources than, say, establishing the firm in a new market would often require, and thus can support short-term objectives.

Counter-purchase, on the other hand, involves different risks, as the products may not necessarily fit with the organisation's marketing expertise and thereby increase risk and cost. The company may well feel these are worth taking when given the opportunities offered of breaking into a new market or building up market share. The requirement to trade in unrelated goods received by the Western company can either be dealt with in-house or taken over by specialists in this type of transaction.

Marketing managers should take more than a passing interest in these arrangements. Offset trading approach can assist with market entry, market penetration and development. In many industries, such as the defence industry, offset deals are common (as noted in the review of this form of arrangement above). One major consideration when trading via this method with development economies is that it could set up competitors who might well challenge the dominance of the supplier at some future date.

Overall, therefore, counter-trade requires very careful balancing of the possibilities it opens up against the costs and risks involved. Legal considerations will play a larger role than they do with barter, plus a longer-term involvement by companies when offset trading is used. The question remains as to how far barter and counter-trade will continue to expand, given the rapid development of many countries, the move from centrally-planned economies and hence a possible lower requirement for arrangements of this nature. The existence of large numbers of economies with 'soft currencies', economic difficulties and reduced opportunities for trade, will probably continue to offer scope for the continued use of such measures.[12]

The changes in counter-trade can be seen in the advice offered by the US Counter-trade Association,[13] which points to the increasing costs associated with the marketing of counter-stations, particularly those associated with developing countries. Western exporters, they argue, will find it necessary to look at alternative approaches to meet their counter-trade commitments. Promotion of tourism with the buyer's country, training of the buyer's workforce, and investment in labour-intensive projects are all examples.

Advice on counter-trade is also provided by Kuwait's Ministry of Finance to help fulfil its broader economic objectives. In its Economic Development Plan[14] the following objectives are listed:

1 to contribute to the government's privatisation programme;
2 to promote the growth and diversification of the country's private sector;
3 to promote the creation and growth of high-skill jobs for Kuwaiti nationals in the private sector;
4 to promote investment in and development of quality education and scientific research activity;
5 to promote the transfer and continual upgrading of state-of-the-art and knowledge-intensive technologies appropriate for the state of Kuwait.

The government intends to use the offset programme as a vehicle to achieve its economic objectives:

1 to promote mutually beneficial, collaborative business ventures between Kuwait nationals and foreign contractors, with an emphasis on investment in the private sector;
2 to achieve sustainable economic benefits, including those of increasing export sales of locally-produced goods and substituting foreign-produced goods with locally produced ones;
3 to enhance the ability of the private sector to sustain high-tech industries through the expansion and creation of educational and training opportunities;
4 to facilitate the transfer of state-of-the-art technology to the private sector;
5 to support the country's foreign aid programme.

The government's desire is that the benefits of trade should be shared in a equitable way between foreign companies and Kuwait. As at January 1997 all foreign contractors awarded an individual supply contract with the government equal to (or greater than) 1KDC (Kuwaiti dinar) incurred an offset obligation.

From the two perspectives of the US Counter-trade Association and the Kuwait government, counter-trade is a vital issue for companies to understand. From the US point of view, the focus is on the individual business, raising its awareness both of the activities that comprise barter and counter-trade as well as the need to look at trends in this area. Without this awareness, many companies will be ill-prepared for the realities of exporting. From Kuwait's point of view, counter-trade is a way of boosting long-term economic prospects in restructuring the economy and creating a vibrant private sector.

As with payment and financing, there are financial and specialist organisations who can provide advice and help on these issues. However, as Kuwait's Ministry of Finance observes, the promotion of the regulations on counter-trade provides little in the way of an excuse in pleading ignorance of their existence.

FREE TRADE ZONES

The importance of Free Trade Zones (FTZs) has already been noted in previous chapters. Box 12.8 provides a summary of these zones from two very different countries – Turkey and the USA.[15] FTZs are defined as a zones or regions within a country that are deemed to be outside of the customs border of that country, and where the regulations related to foreign trade and other financial and economic areas are either inapplicable or only partly so. Basically, the zones are established to create incentives for business and to lead to an increase in trade volume and exports and use of labour. These arrangements are not particularly new (the USA passed a Foreign Trade Zones Act in 1934).

Box 12.8 **FREE TRADE ZONES**

Free Trade Zones in Turkey

Free Zones Law No. 3218 was issued in 1985 with the objective of increasing export-orientated investments and production in Turkey, accelerating the inflow of foreign capital and technology, procuring inputs for the economy in an economic and orderly fashion, and increasing the utilisation of external finance and trade possibilities.

Free Zones Law No. 3218 was put into effect in 1985; the Mersin and Antalya Free Zones became operational in 1988, the Aegean and Istanbul Ataturk Airport Free Zones in 1990, the Trabzon Free Zone in 1992 and the Istanbul–Leather, Eastern Anatolian and Mardin Free Zones in 1995.

Incentives and advantages offered in Turkish Free Zones
- Turkish Free Zones are tax-free zones; income generated through activities in the zones are exempted from all kinds of taxes, including income, corporate and value-added tax

▶ **Box 12.8 continued**

- the validity period of an operation licence is a maximum of 10 years for tenant users, and 20 years for other users who wish to make their own offices in the zone; if the operation licence period requested is in excess of 20 years, the period can be prolonged to 99 years

- Free Zones' earnings and revenues can be transferred to any country, including Turkey, freely without any prior permission and are not subject to any kind of taxes, duties and fees

- there is no limitation on the proportion of foreign capital participation in investment within the Free Zones

- in contrast to most Free Zones of the world, sales into the domestic market are allowed in Turkish Free Zones

- currencies used in the Zones are convertible foreign currencies accepted by the Central Bank of Turkey

- infrastructure of the Turkish Free Zones is comparable with international standards

- red tape and bureaucracy have been minimised during application and operation phases by authorising only one agency in charge of these procedures

- the geographical location of Turkey provides significant advantages to the Turkish Free Zones

- Turkish Free Zones are adjacent to the major Turkish ports on the Mediterranean, Aegean and Black Seas; in addition, they have been established within easy access from international airports and highways

- there is no procedural restriction regarding price, standards or quality of goods in the Turkish Free Zones

- for a period of 10 years following the commencement of operations in the zones, strikes and lockouts shall not be applicable; any disputes occurring within the context of collective bargaining during the period shall be resolved by the Supreme Arbitration Council

- in the Turkish Free Zones, the Municipality Law, Passport Law, Foreign Investment Law, Foreign Investment and Encouragement Law, and all other articles of laws contrary to the provisions of the Free Zones Law shall not be applicable.

Free Trade Zones in the USA

General Purpose Zone
A General Purpose Zone is, as the name suggests, the general zone site or sites established for multiple users.

Special Purpose Sub-zone
A Special Purpose Sub-zone is a site ancillary to the General Purpose Zone which is given foreign trade zone status for the benefit of a particular user who cannot be accommodated at the General Purpose Zone site. Sub-zone status is commonly granted to existing manufacturing facilities, and because it is ancillary to an existing General Purpose Zone does not require separate state enabling legislation.

▶

> ▶ **Box 12.8 continued**

Benefits

A business operating in a foreign trade zone may obtain a number of benefits.

- *Duty deferral.* One of the primary benefits is duty deferral, the ability to avoid paying duties on imported merchandise until the merchandise leaves the foreign trade zone and enters the commerce of the USA. Merchandise imported into and re-exported from a foreign trade zone is not subject to duty.

- *Lower duty rates.* Lower duty rates are also achievable through foreign trade zones. As discussed more fully below, a foreign trade zone user that assembles or manufactures in a zone may elect to pay duty on imported components either at the duty rate applicable to the components or at the duty rate applicable to the finished product. US added value is not subject to duty at all. In an inverted tariff situation – that is, a situation in which the duty rate on the finished product is lower than that on the imported components – the foreign trade zone results in a lower overall duty to the foreign trade zone user.

- *Quota restrictions avoidance.* Quota restrictions generally may be avoided by admitting goods into a foreign trade zone. Over-quota merchandise may usually be held in a zone until the next quota period begins, and may often be used as a component part of a product that is not over quota. Some marking restrictions may also be avoided by bringing goods into a foreign trade zone.

- *Export savings.* Domestic goods moved into a zone for export are treated as exported when they enter the zone; consequently, exporters may accelerate drawbacks by moving goods to be exported into a zone. Imported goods that are brought into a zone to be destroyed, such as defective products, are treated as exported and subject to drawback.

- *Tax and licensing savings.* Some savings are also available through the avoidance of state or local laws that are inapplicable in a foreign trade zone because of federal pre-emption.

The benefit can vary from country to country depending on the existing regulations and tax regimes, and the type of zone established. The existence of FTZs provides opportunities for exporters (and others) to seek benefits, whilst at the same time helping to achieve the host country's macroeconomic–microeconomic objectives. Advantages to the company of establishing itself in a zone can come from savings in shipping charges, duties and taxes which accrue to the company bringing in unassembled machinery and assembling it in the zone. Many other benefits can be gained, but the marketing manager can, through awareness of the opportunities and benefits that can be obtained from location in a zone, help to achieve the company's objectives. (The benefits to the economy are not considered here; many Free Ports in the UK failed to realise their objectives and were abolished or scrapped, and there is some disagreement on their actual value in providing long-term investment and job creation.)

SUMMARY

Many companies who participate in international trade do so via exporting (and importing) and while a significant minority move to more direct involvement in foreign trade, the majority remain committed exporters. The review undertaken in this chapter has therefore focused on the issues that new exporters and those familiar with the operations of exporting will face. By reviewing the literature on export practice, the skills required to succeed in the market were identified which, together with the importance attached to export and marketing planning and knowledge acquisition, quality of the product offered and the importance of building personal contacts and first-hand understanding of the customer's needs, can lay the foundation for success.

From this review, the specific logistical, documentation and financial considerations were outlined, showing the need for companies to be aware of the operational requirements of exporting and the help and assistance that they can receive from private sector institutions (mainly banks) and governmental bodies. The influence of government policy can be observed in other areas of the export process, particularly in counter-trade, barter and the establishment of Free Trade Zones (FTZs), where macroeconomic and microeconomic objectives can be pursued.

The importance of these issues, from the marketing manager's point of view, can be traced from the strategic level (via counter-trade, for example, offering diversification and market development possibilities) through to the operational stage where a failure to observe the proper rules, regulations and procedures can result in unnecessary delay or even failure in the market place – when, for example, incorrect documentary procedures result in problems in the receipt of goods and delays in payment.

Throughout the issues covered here, the appreciation of the risks and costs and recognition of rules, regulations and other stipulations is paramount. Marketing management of the export (and import) effort relies on those involved being fully briefed on these points and aware of trends and possible changes in these areas.

REVIEW QUESTIONS

1 What factors have been identified as leading to success in exporting?

2 Review the documentary requirements associated with exporting outside the EU.

3 Outline the present government support for exporters.

4 List the elements of the export plan and identify the differences between exporting and marketing planning.

5 What are the differences between barter and counter-trade?

DISCUSSION QUESTIONS

1 How can national governments:
   (a) increase the number of firms actively exporting?
   (b) improve service to exporters?

2 Should we treat firms who import as being of equal importance as those who export?

3 Are Free Trade Zones (FTZs) compatible with free trade?

4 Is it acceptable that countries should use counter-trade to assist with their economic development?

5 Why do the majority of firms remain at the export stage, rather than moving to more direct involvement in foreign trade?

Case study

UK EYES EASTERN PROMISE[16]

The UK government in early 1997 launched a drive to double trade with the fast-growing Czech, Hungarian, Polish, Slovak and Slovenian markets over two years. It also aimed to stimulate 100 investment projects by alerting UK companies to opportunities in these Central European countries.

The DTI's 'Open for Business in Central Europe' campaign was launched in London by Mr Malcolm Rifkind, the then Foreign Secretary, and Mr Ian Lang, the then Trade Secretary.

'Central Europe is now an economic tiger on our doorstep,' said Mr Lang. 'Some earlier investors got their fingers burnt. Others were put off by legal and other problems. But these markets are now ready for a new look.'

Trade has grown by up to 35 per cent a year in these markets over the two years 1995–6, although from a low base. Trade with the former Soviet bloc accounted for only two per cent of UK imports and 2.6 per cent of exports in 1995. But trade with Central Europe increased much faster than UK trade generally. UK exports to Poland, the largest single market with 39m people, broke the £1bn ($1.67bn) barrier in 1996.

The DTI identified agribusiness and the motor, consumer goods, electronics, telecommunications and healthcare industries as the most promising sectors.

UK companies have lagged behind their EU competitors in both trade and investment with this region of 65m consumers, whose foreign trade is forecast to exceed £125bn by the end of 1998. Germany's trade with the former Soviet bloc is bigger than its trade with the USA. Central Europe has seen an influx of German banks and medium-sized companies looking for a low-cost manufacturing base and export markets.

The UK is well placed for further growth in Central Europe. London-based banks and institutions, including the European Bank for Reconstruction and Development (EBRD), have high levels of specialised knowledge. London is a hub for financial and other deals providing work for UK accountants, lawyers and consultants, often working with the government's Know-How Fund.

The UK's record of attracting inward investment is another under-utilised asset. When Czechinvest, the Czech inward investment corporation, decided to seek Japanese investment it came to London rather than to Tokyo to lobby Japanese companies which had already invested in the UK. In contrast, UK-based companies with German, Italian or other EU subsidiaries often prefer to use their continental companies to expand links with Eastern and Central Europe.

UK multinationals such as Unilever and Cadbury-Schweppes – which has a plant in Poland and another in Russia – along with BP, Pilkington, British Oxygen, British Vita and others, have led the way. Tesco, which took over the US K-Mart group's Hungarian stores for $77m, and Marks & Spencer spearheaded a drive by UK retailers. Marks & Spencer has opened large franchised stores in Budapest and Prague and is seeking a partner and sites in Poland.

The target countries are all 'fast-track' reform economies which were quick to re-orientate their trade from COMECON to Western markets. All aspire to joining the EU. Tight macro-economic policies have cut inflation to single figures in the Czech Republic and Slovakia, while Poland combines high growth with declining inflation. Hungary is emerging fitter from two years of austerity accompanied by rapid privatisation and record foreign investment, while Slovenia's open economy is poised to gain from peace in the Balkans.

Privatisation of state assets, rising foreign investment and new entrepreneurial companies have created dynamic and largely private economies eager for investment and access to foreign markets and technology.

Questions

1 *Outline the problems that face UK exporters to these Central and East European (CEE) countries and which can explain why exports were at a low level in 1995.*

2 *How can government campaigns such as 'Open for Business' help to boost exports?*

3 *Links and opportunities can come from unexpected quarters. Other than those mentioned in the case study what other assets that countries like the UK possess can be exploited to create export opportunities?*

4 *Does the theory of 'psychic distance' explain the reluctance to export to these countries by the UK, and the dominance of German companies?*

5 *What cover and assistance would companies look for to back up their export efforts to CEE countries?*

FURTHER READING

Reading for this topic falls into two broad types:

1 Reading on rules, regulations and government policy. Trade associations who have a direct interest in exporting have valuable data. Information can best be gained via access to the Home Pages of the relevant government department of the country concerned, which will review the developments associated with export/import controls, trade areas, counter-trade, and so on. Guidance and information on documentation is obtainable from banks specialising on this issue.

2 The second category looks at the strategies pursued by exporters, and how effective they are. The following are some of the many sources available on this issue.

Aaby, N.E. and Slater, S.F., 'Management influences on export performance: a review of the empirical literature 1978–88', *International Marketing Review*, 6(4) (1989), 1–26.

Axinn, C.N., 'Export performance: do managerial perceptions make a difference?', *International Marketing Review*, 5 (1988), 61–71.

Cateora, P.R., *International Marketing*, 8th international student edition (Homewood, IL: Irwin, 1993).

Cavusgil, S.T. and Kirpalani, V.H., 'Introducing products into export markets: success factors', *Journal of Business Research*, 27 (1993), 1–15.

Cavusgil, S.T. and Zou, S., 'Marketing strategy – performance relationship: an investigation of the empirical link in export market ventures', *Journal of Marketing*, 58 (1994), 1–21.

Chetty, S.K. and Hamilton, R.T., 'Firm-level determinants of export performance: a meta-analysis', *International Marketing Review*, 10(3) (1993), 26–34.

Ford, D. and Leonidou, L., 'Research developments in international marketing', in Paliwoda, S.J. (ed.), *New Perspectives on International Marketing* (London: Routledge, 1991).

NOTES AND REFERENCES

1 Fazey, I., 'Bar code marker picks up the prize', *Financial Times Exporter* (Winter 1995).

2 Brown, R. and Cook, D., 'Strategy and performance in British exporter', *The Quarterly Review of Marketing*, 15(3) (1990), 1–6.

3 Styles, C. and Ambler, T., 'Successful export practice: the UK experience', *International Marketing Review*, 11(6) (1994), 23–47.

4 HKSB, *International Trade* (Hong Kong Shanghai Bank Trade Services, November 1995).

5 'The paper chase', *Overseas Trade* (London: Brass Tracks, April 1996).

6 'Strategic objectives', DTI Home Page (1996).

7 National Audit Office (NAO), press release summarising its report on Overseas Trade Services (3 April 1996).

8 Taylor, A., 'UK runs out of export aid cash', *Financial Times* (17 January 1997).

9 'Developing an export plan', LA Trade and Baytrade (1995).

10 Ibid.

11 Albaum, G. *et al.*, *International Marketing and Export Management* (Reading, MA: Addison-Wesley, 1992).

12 Huszagh, S. and Huszagh, F., 'International barter and counter-trade' in Thorelli, H.B. and Cavusgil, S., *International Marketing Strategy*, 3rd edition (Oxford: Pergamon Press, 1993).

13 American Counter-trade Association, *Forms of Counter-trade* (1995).

14 'Guidelines for the counter-trade offset programme', Government of Kuwait (1997).

15 Wyatt, R.C., 'Doing business in the United States: Foreign Trade Zones', Internet page of AM-SEC-COM (1996); 'Free Trade Zones in Turkey', Internet page of Turkish Ministry of Trade (1996).

16 Robinson, A., 'Britain eyes Eastern promise', *Financial Times* (15 January 1997).

PART 4

The global marketing mix programme

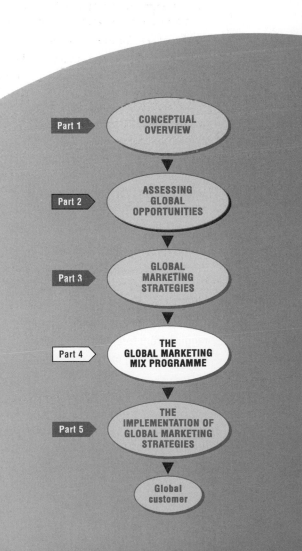

Part 1 — CONCEPTUAL OVERVIEW

Part 2 — ASSESSING GLOBAL OPPORTUNITIES

Part 3 — GLOBAL MARKETING STRATEGIES

Part 4 — THE GLOBAL MARKETING MIX PROGRAMME

Part 5 — THE IMPLEMENTATION OF GLOBAL MARKETING STRATEGIES

Global customer

Part 4 consists of six chapters and provides a detailed focus on the functional orientation of global marketing strategies. It acknowledges the uniqueness of each firm, product and country in global marketing and that marketing tactics developed in one market are not necessarily appropriate in other markets.

Chapter 13 Global product strategies

This chapter covers issues relating to product standardisation/adaptation, product line management, Keegan's product matrix, etc.

Chapter 14 Global service strategies

This section has been included because it was felt that service products were sufficiently different from physical products, with unique characteristics and problems that warranted a separate chapter. The uniqueness of services are examined and the marketing implications of these differences are discussed.

Chapter 15 Global channel strategies

This chapter gives extensive coverage of this important area in global marketing. Distribution is seen as the last frontier for firms to conquer if they want to attain superior competitive advantage in international markets. Distribution is the interface with the final customer and an efficient channel system translates into good customer service. Topics covered in this section include the structure and management of distribution systems, the impact of globalisation on channel configuration, Japanese distribution structures and grey markets.

Chapter 16 Global pricing strategies

This chapter examines the determinants of global pricing, transfer pricing, export terms, etc., and the strategic implications of various pricing strategies.

Chapter 17 Global promotional strategies

This section provides wide coverage of the issues confronting a global marketing manager, ranging from foreign environmental impact on promotional strategies to global personal selling, public relations, etc.

Chapter 18 Negotiation strategies

This key skill in selling has been briefly touched upon in many books and it was felt that a detailed inclusion of this very important topic would be valuable to the reader. A thorough understanding of the types of and differences in negotiating tactics is given; these can be a key competitive advantage in the international market place.

13

Global product strategies

INTRODUCTION

What product or service to sell abroad is among the first decisions that a firm makes in order to develop a marketing mix. Product decisions are a critical aspect of a firm's marketing programme as they define the firm's business, its customers and its competitors and influences the company's pricing, distribution and promotional strategies. The firm could export its existing product, adapt it to meet the requirements in the foreign markets or it could develop new products for those markets. The firm with global ambitions needs to develop product policies and strategies which are commensurate with its resources, meet market needs and respond to competitive challenges. There are a number of decisions that need to be made with regard to the area of product policy which are compounded by operating in multiple foreign markets. The product policy tasks facing a company are formidable and must be considered before its product offering is designed:

1 What range and type of products should be sold to the world market?
2 Can current products be sold abroad as they are or do they need to be customised?
3 What products should be added, adapted or eliminated from the firm's product line?
4 Should the company pursue new product innovation/acquisition strategies?
5 What type of brand strategies should be used?
6 How should the products be packaged and labelled?
7 What type of post-sales service and warranty back-up should be provided?

This chapter will focus on a number of key issues such as product innovation, which involves looking at the product development process; product diffusion and adoption in international markets; the controversial issue of product standardisation versus product customisation or adaptation; product attributes such as design and branding strategies; packaging, labelling and warranty provisions; and the management of international product lines.

Objectives

This chapter will examine:

- the product concept and the classification of products
- global product strategies
- the criteria determining whether products should be standardised or customised
- the arguments for and against the standardisation and adaptation of products
- the criteria for product design
- product attributes such as global branding, global packaging, etc.
- the process of new product development for global markets
- the adoption and diffusion of new products
- the product deletion process
- global product line management.

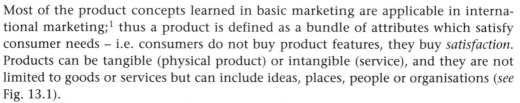

PRODUCT CONCEPTS

Most of the product concepts learned in basic marketing are applicable in international marketing;[1] thus a product is defined as a bundle of attributes which satisfy consumer needs – i.e. consumers do not buy product features, they buy *satisfaction*. Products can be tangible (physical product) or intangible (service), and they are not limited to goods or services but can include ideas, places, people or organisations (*see* Fig. 13.1).

The product is at the centre of the firm's marketing strategy in international markets, as it is in domestic markets. The term 'product' refers not only to physical but also to non-physical aspects. The core product stands for the benefits that consumers attain when purchasing a good or service. For example, when people visit an amusement park the core benefit is escaping from reality. Global marketers therefore need to define precisely the core benefits that the product will provide to consumers.

The actual product consists of its features, brand, quality, styling and packaging. BMW saloon cars are the actual product, but the brand name, the high-quality engineering and stylish features all contribute to delivering the core product or benefit which is a very efficient, high-quality, tasteful, status symbol product. The augmented product consists of attributes such as installation, after-sales service, warranty, delivery and credit facilities. A computer firm can provide free installation or back-up services; a car manufacturer can give generous warranty terms and excellent after-sales service. The augmented part of a product can constitute a major selling part for a firm over its competitors, and indeed many global companies conduct their competitive strategies at the augmented level. All these different levels of the product constitute the 'total offering'.

Fig 13.1 THREE LEVELS OF PRODUCT

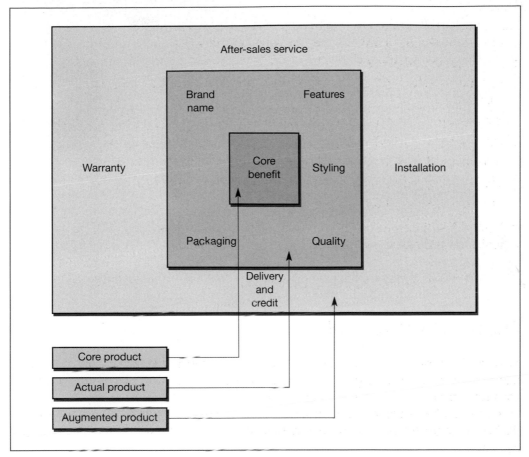

Source: Kotler, P. and Armstrong, G., *Principles of Marketing*, 6th edition (Englewood Cliffs: Prentice-Hall), 119; © 1994. Adapted by permission.

These elements of the total offering can be managed to give the firm a competitive advantage in the global market place, and therefore increase the perceived benefits relative to the perceived costs. The provision of after-sales service facilities or superior warranty terms may give the firm a competitive advantage over its rivals. This increases the level of perceived benefits relative to perceived costs, and as long as this is the case, consumers will buy the product. Many Japanese companies have focused their strategies on providing excellent marketing support services (i.e. augmented product) such as superior after-sales service and guarantees; these offerings have given them marketing advantages over their competitors. A product can be described as a 'value-added commodity', and the added-value bundle includes product attributes such as design, branding, after-sales service, etc. irrespective of whether such attributes are real or not, or whether they are physical or psychological.

CLASSIFICATION OF PRODUCTS

Products can be classified in a number of ways as Kotler illustrates.[2] One classification is based on users in which products are divided into consumer and industrial goods. These two aspects will be the focus of this chapter and 'service products' will be discussed separately in Chapter 14 since service goods have unique characteristics and strategies and therefore warrant a separate discussion.

The rapid internationalisation of the world economy in the last couple of decades has resulted in numerous joint ventures, strategic alliances and acquisitions of foreign companies. The net result of these expansive strategies has been the acquisition or development of new products for the particular national market. Whichever national market the firm is based in, it still faces the crucial question of the extent to which the local national product is broadly suitable for expansion. In practice, many firms move into international markets by selling their name and expertise in the form of the brand or the patent on the product or the production process rather than selling the physical product itself. In the international market context, we have a continuum from local to global products.[3]

A *local product* is one that is profitable but is considered to have potential only in a particular local market. Niche beer products such as Newcastle Brown beer in the UK tend to be produced predominantly for the local market; Japanese electronics companies tend to produce many products mainly for home consumption because of the unquenchable demand by Japanese consumers for electronic goods. The major problem with developing local products is that the firm is unable to leverage some of the advantages derived from global production such as economies in R&D, marketing and production.

An *international product* is one that is considered to have potential for extension into other international markets. It is a product that is developed for one national market and then sold with virtually no change to international markets – i.e. a standardised product. Chanel perfume and cosmetics, Cartier jewellery or Laura Ashley design fabrics and accessories are all examples.

A *global product* is a product designed for the international market and incorporating all the differences into one product design. One of the triggers for developing global products is the high cost of R&D, shorter product life cycles and intense global competition. ITT produces a 'world chassis' for its TV sets which enables the assemblage of TV sets for all the three TV systems of the world (PAL, SECAM and NTSC) without the need to change the circuitry on various modules. The Ford motor company designs a uniform 'core' product which can then accept a variety of standard parts and components to assemble a range of products with variable characteristics. With a global product, a firm can adapt its global design to meet unique national market needs.

GLOBAL PRODUCT POLICY

A firm needs to answer a number of key questions: What type of products to sell in international markets? How should it develop these products for the global market?

With respect to the latter question, the firm could:

- simply export its domestic product
- modify the product for different national markets
- design new products for the international market
- acquire products through joint ventures or take-overs.

The type of global product policy pursued by a firm should reflect its global marketing orientation and strategy. A firm's goals and objectives, management attitudes to global markets, availability of resources and organisational design will all have an impact on its product strategies. There are a number of product development approaches or orientations that a firm can pursue, and these will be briefly discussed here.

Ethnocentric approach (market extension)

International product development is based on extending the domestic product internationally. The major assumption underlying this approach is that, as Levitt[4] says, consumer needs and market conditions are becoming homogeneous as a result of globalisation. Domestic product strategies for domestic consumers do represent 'best practice', and should thus be applicable to overseas markets. The advantage of this approach is that it facilitates rapid market entry and minimises costs in various functional areas. The major drawback of this approach is product rejection in international markets, because the product does not meet local consumer needs and/or mandatory local product standards. The ethnocentric approach is a viable option under certain conditions, in particular where the international market product use conditions and consumer needs are comparable with the domestic market. The classic example of this approach is Coca-Cola, a product produced initially for the domestic market but then extended to overseas markets with very minor modifications in some markets in its packaging or taste.

Geocentric approach (global)

Under this approach the firm views the world as a single market. Product development is based on having a high degree of international uniformity, and the firm will seek to identify homogeneous international demand segments in terms of needs and purchasing power that can be targeted with its standard product. Geocentric orientation implies a high degree of centralisation and co-ordination of activities. The benefits of this approach are reduced R&D costs as duplication is avoided, the uniformity of many products will rationalise the product lines, economies of scale will be achieved and there is rapid world-wide distribution of the product. The difficulty of this approach is that its success depends on careful and continuous global market research which is expensive and time-consuming. There will also be marked differences between markets which may necessitate the firm having to abandon some or, alternatively, relinquish its international standard product programme.

However, it could be argued that this would be an ideal product orientation for any firm that wished to survive and be competitive in a dynamic and rapidly changing global market. Companies such as Sony, McDonald's and ICI tend to have a geo-centric orientation.

Regiocentric approach

This approach seeks product uniformity within a cluster of markets. The market clusters could be based on geographic proximity, language or membership of a regional union such as the EU or NAFTA. The major benefit of this approach is that the firm can obtain economies of production, marketing, etc. when compared to a polycentric orientation. However, if the market cluster is too large this could slow down the diffusion of the product and limit the possibilities for leveraging the firm's advantages. According to Majaro,[5] the cluster approach is based on the need to achieve optimum penetration of a group of markets without the need for a company to spread itself too thinly. These clusters of countries will have highly standardised marketing mixes which can be managed economically. Argentina and Brazil, for example, are different markets but there are enough common factors between them (i.e. consumption factors) for a firm to adopt a cluster approach. A cluster approach thus involves channelling a company's resources into one or more market segments, and by concentrating its resources and efforts in these markets hoping to capture large market shares. Ford Europe's product lines are very different from its North American counterpart and it has a pan-European product, developing uniform product lines for its European markets. The Swedish white goods giant Electrolux sold refrigerator products with about 40 brand names and produced 120 basic designs; the company has now embarked on a regional product standardisation programme to gain economies and reduce production costs. It could be argued that the regiocentric approach may be the strategy of the future, given that there is a strong movement towards regionalisation in the world economy.[6]

Polycentric approach (multidomestic)

In this orientation the firm identifies only differences in each national market. Each market where the firm operates is treated as if it were unique and will have its own strategy and objectives. Product development is geared to adapting the product's attributes to suit the local market conditions. A major assumption underlying this approach is that international markets differ with respect to consumer needs, levels of socio-economic development, conditions of product use, etc. Philips, the giant Dutch electronics company, had a multidomestic orientation to its various markets in the EU, customising its products to suit each market. Recently, it has begun to adopt a regiocentric approach to product development. Seeing each market as being different and unique will ultimately result in lower profits as duplication of effort and strategies will occur.

STANDARDISATION VERSUS ADAPTATION (CUSTOMISATION/LOCALISATION)

One of the key issues that has dominated international marketing and international product development for the last 30 years or more has been the degree to which a company needs to adapt or customise its product offerings in the international markets (*see* Table 13.1). *Standardisation* means offering a common product on a world-wide basis whereas *customisation* (or *adaptation*) means making changes to the product to satisfy local needs.[7] This may involve modifying the product, its packaging, logo or brand name. These two design strategies are critical to a firm's success in the international markets, for a well-designed product can affect the product's appeal in terms of its acceptability and usefulness, and can gain the firm a competitive advantage. In the literature, there are numerous examples to illustrate the success or failure of standardisation policies. Successful standardisation policies have been carried out by companies such as Coca-Cola, Levi's and Sony. On the other hand, standardisation policies have also led to failures: the US company Campbell's attempted to sell its standard US tomato soup formulation in the UK. This was a disastrous venture; after carrying out some research they found out that the UK consumer prefers a more bitter tasting soup than US consumers.

In many cases, firms do sell the same product in foreign markets as they do in domestic markets, perhaps with only very slight modifications, such as changing the packaging or having the instructions translated into the local language. UK car

Table 13.1 FACTORS FAVOURING PRODUCT STANDARDISATION VERSUS ADAPTATION

Standardisation	Adaptation
• High costs of adaptation	• Differences in technical standards
• Primary industrial products	• Primary consumer and personal-use products
• Convergence and similar tastes in diverse country markets	• Variations in consumer needs
• Predominant use in urban environments	• Variations in conditions of use
• Marketing to predominantly similar countries (i.e. the Triad economies)	• Variations in ability to buy – differences in income levels
• Centralised management of international operations when mode of entry is mainly exports	• Fragmentation, with independent national subsidiaries
• Strong country of origin image and effect	• Strong cultural differences, language, etc. affecting purchase and use
• Scale economies in production and marketing	• Local environment-induced adaptation: differences in raw material available, government-required standards and regulations
• Standardised products marketed by competitors	• Adaptation strategy successfully used competitors

Source: Terpstra, V. and Sarathy, C.R., *International Marketing*, 6th edition (Orlando: The Dryden Press, 1994), Table 8.1, 264. Reproduced by permission

manufacturers modify their right-hand-drive to left-hand-drives for the continental market. These are still relatively minor modifications; many firms are reluctant to change the basic product and ideally would like to sell a standardised product across most of their world markets because of the reduced costs of large-scale production and marketing operations. Firms need to confront this issue of whether the same product is suitable for the global market or whether it should be adapted to meet local requirements.

A major proponent of the desirability and feasibility of product standardisation has been Levitt,[8] who argued strongly and persuasively that unless firms standardised their marketing mix they were unlikely to be competitive in world markets. On the other hand, there are some who question the potential economic gains from standardisation and whether it is possible to standardise many aspects of the marketing mix.[9] The standardisation versus adaptation debate is partially hampered by the lack of precise definitions regarding these two terms. This has given rise to interpretation problems. Standardisation can mean that:

- a product should be 100 per cent uniform in all global markets
- a product is uniform if it is essentially similar in its key elements
- a product is still standardised even if there is local customisation around a 'standard core' product;[10] for example, modifications in electrical goods to meet local voltage requirements would not be considered to have changed basic product characteristics.

To take another example, detergent manufacturers alter the chemical composition of their products in different markets in order to adapt to the hardness or softness of local water which affects the product's performance. The rationale for this interpretation of a standardised product is that such limited adaptations will have minimal impact on marketing and production costs. If the changes do have a significant effect on costs and benefits, then the product may be said to have been localised.

Therefore, it is not the absolute but the relative degree of standardisation that matters, and is of more practical relevance. The primacy of the debate should not focus on whether it is standardisation versus adaptation but which approach can gain the firm a competitive advantage in the global market place. This chapter will adopt the relative interpretation of standardisation, and the pros and cons of standardisation will be evaluated in that light. Whether a firm should standardise or localise its marketing programme it can be guided by a number of criteria in making its choice.[11]

CRITERIA FOR STANDARDISATION VERSUS ADAPTATION DECISIONS

Nature of the product

Industrial products – medical equipment, heavy machinery and computers – tend to require less adaptation than consumer goods. Durable consumer products – cameras, washing machines, etc. – are more amenable to standardisation. Non-durable products such as food and soft drinks tend to require greater adaptation, as these products are influenced more by customs and tastes. Selling food with pork ingredients to Muslim markets, for example, would be unacceptable. The gradual success of McDonald's hamburgers and Kentucky Fried Chicken in Japan and some markets in the Far East in which complex food habits and traditions exist is an exception. However, these cultural differences in tastes may diminish over time as we witness many consumer goods, such as cosmetics, soft drinks like Coca-Cola, etc., successfully breaking through the cultural barriers in world markets.

Market conditions

The needs of a market will be influenced by the level of economic prosperity and cultural preferences, factors that will influence a marketer's decision as to whether adaptation of the product is required. The need for transportation is world-wide, but the form of transportation will vary according to economic needs and the existence of a transport infrastructure. If cars are to be exported to an economy which is poorer than the UK and its roads are not as well developed, it is likely that the car will have to be adapted. There will perhaps be fewer features, excluding stereo systems or central locking devices; the product may also need to be made sturdier to cope with unsurfaced roads, perhaps by strengthening the suspension system.

Cultural perception of foreign products can also dictate whether the product is to be standardised or adapted. This is known as the *country of origin effect*,[12] where products from a particular country are perceived as of high quality. In this situation, the firm should standardise its product for that particular market. If the image of the country's product is a negative one, it would be better to adapt that product. British-made cars for the mass market, for example, have a very poor quality image overseas.

Market environment

A number of factors in the foreign business environment can influence the firm's decision to adapt or standardise the product. First, the physical environment of resources, climate, etc. can affect the firm's decision to adapt or standardise the product. In very hot climates, products such as cars may have to have air-conditioning units installed. Again, refrigerators have to be redesigned to fit the smaller Japanese home. Second, the competitive environment will influence product design: in very competitive markets, adaptation may be necessary to gain a competitive edge over rivals. This could take many forms, from providing colour choice to after-sales service facilities. Third, the legal environment of different markets will have a direct impact on product standards, safety, labelling and so on. A UK appliance firm will need to adapt its product's electrical system from 240 volts to 220 volts for the European market, for example.

Market development

The choice to adapt or standardise a product is not only related to the product's life cycle but also to the stages of the market's socio-economic development. A successful product such as a hand calculator may be at the maturity stage of its cycle in a highly developed economy like the UK. However, if the manufacturers intend to sell the product to a new market, and thus at the growth stage of the product's life cycle, in a less developed economy like Zambia, it is very likely that adaptation may be required for that market, as a simplified model may be more appropriate.

Infrastructural systems

This refers specifically to institutions and functions which will assist and support the marketer's needs to service customers. It includes intermediaries, logistical support such as transportation, warehousing, financial intermediaries, advertising and media agencies. The lack of reliable and efficient intermediaries like retailers may hamper the provision of good after-sales service; this may necessitate adapting the product, re-designing it slightly to require less after-sales servicing.

Cost-benefit analysis

Finally, the firm needs to weigh the costs and benefits of adapted and standardised products. Product modifications can lead to profitable opportunities but they presuppose the firm has the necessary resources and that the size of the market is large enough to make such adaptations worthwhile – in other words, the costs of the adaptation must be outweighed by its benefits.

BENEFITS OF PRODUCT STANDARDISATION

There are many factors encouraging the standardisation of products.

Economies of scale

The mass production of goods creates economies of scale and leads to large savings:

- the impact of disruptions to production flows is minimised
- tooling and set-up costs associated with manufacturing a variety of different products are avoided
- production costs per unit fall when more goods are produced
- stock control and distribution costs are greatly reduced as a smaller inventory is required
- as the firm learns how to manufacture a standardised product over time, production rates are increased, wastage is reduced, etc. and overall costs are reduced – this is the *experience curve*.

R&D costs

The standardisation of products reduces the necessity for continuous R&D on product variations and product design, thus lowering the firm's overall R&D costs.

Marketing economies

Standardised products facilitate standardised promotion, resulting in savings on advertising. When firms employ the same promotional campaign to different markets, such as Esso's 'Tiger in your tank' advertisement, there are substantial savings made, thus increasing the return on advertising.

Global consistency

Economic globalisation has made it possible for firms to sell a unified product on a world-wide basis. The need for a consistent international image is a strong argument for product standardisation. The following developments have helped this trend.

Consumer protection legislation

Most countries have introduced consumer protection laws. As a result, goods have to be sold under new regulations which mean the weight, volume and ingredients of standardised products can be displayed in a uniform manner.

Trade groups

Within trading blocs like the EU, trading regulations are increasingly standardised to simplify trade between member states. Multinational firms can take advantage by offering standardised product packaging and labelling.

Global trends

The globalisation of the world economy aided by the communications revolution has encouraged the standardisation process, making it possible for companies to present a uniform product offering and a consistent presentation to customers in any part of the world. Consistency in product style, features, design, brand name and packaging all contribute to a uniform product image world-wide, which helps to increase sales. A consumer accustomed to a particular brand is likely to buy or consume the same brand overseas if it is available. The global exposure that brands receive today as a result of extensive travel and mass media requires consistency which is feasible only through standardisation. Companies are therefore developing global brands – Marathon/Snickers, Philips/Whirlpool, Kodak film. Sheraton Hotels in London/Paris/Harare all provide a standardised product or service.

Global manufacturing

As firms begin to develop and produce global products from world-wide production locations there is a strong argument for having standardised components. The firm can gain from economies of scale and it can multisource its components; the latter is particularly useful if there is a supply disruption in one production location – the firm could then switch to alternative supplies from its other factories wherever they may be in the world.

Market homogeneity

For some products a world market – e.g. the youth market for jeans, fast food and pop music – is already available without the need for product modification.

In conclusion, the major basis for product uniformity has been cost minimisation, but there is little in the way of empirical data to substantiate the cost savings claims made by the proponents of product standardisation.[13] The advantages of product standardisation will vary according to the particular product attributes in question;

for example, the product's brand name and warranty provisions are not likely to lead to major cost economies but will certainly enhance the company's coherent image in world markets. It is more likely that major cost economies will be achieved in the areas of packaging and the product's physical characteristics.

FACTORS DISCOURAGING PRODUCT STANDARDISATION

The factors encouraging product standardisation, as discussed above, were mainly based on minimising costs rather than maximising profits. However, there are other factors at work which are conducive to product modification, namely the attainment of higher profits. If the cost of adaptation is outweighed by the benefit in the form of higher returns then this would be the strongest inducement for product modification.

Consumer tastes

Consumer tastes and preferences are highly specific and often vary between and within nations. Levitt[14] postulates that the effect of globalisation will result in lower prices and better-quality goods and services, and that customers will be attracted to these lower-priced goods and hence drop local preferences. However, lower prices and heavy promotions are necessary but not sufficient conditions for successful market penetration. In spite of closer EU integration, market differences do not disappear rapidly, and there are still substantial consumer differences between member states. Research done by Hoover Europe[15] on customer preferences for washing machines showed large variations and distinct preferences on dimension, machine capacity, external styling, etc. With respect to dimensions, it was found that the British, French and Italians preferred a narrower machine, whilst the Germans and Swedes wanted a wider one. Apart from the economics of standardisation, firms do really need to consider other major influences on local consumption patterns. Styling is important in some national markets, and colours may have specific religious or patriotic meanings. In Egypt, green is the national colour and a company needs to ensure that perhaps packaging is not in that colour. In China, red is associated with happiness and good luck, and colours may have to be modified accordingly. On the other hand, red has negative connotations in some African countries. The firm needs to be aware of the significance of colour in a culture when planning its product development strategies and may have to adapt its product offerings.

Levels of socio-economic development

Disparities exist between countries' living standards, labour costs and levels of manufacturing expertise, and these factors will encourage product modifications. Markets with a low *per capita* income are likely to have lower purchasing power and differences in the users' skill levels when compared to consumers in the industrialised markets. This may mean that products will have to be customised to reflect market realities – products such as cars or electronic goods may have made easier to use with less maintenance required.

Market parameters

It is often the case that modifications to products have to be made to comply with the parameters of a market. With the growth of consumer protection legislation, it is now commonplace for governments to impose minimum legal requirements on manufacturers. In 1986, for example, Switzerland banned the use of phosphates in detergents. Perfumes sold in the Middle East must not be ethanol-based to comply with the national laws against alcohol. Vitamins which legally must be added to margarine in the UK and Holland are forbidden in Italy.

Government influence

All governments seek to protect their own economies and this may necessitate the modification of products. Tariffs may force a manufacturer to buy components and produce goods at specific locations, rendering standardisation impossible. Protectionist governments often insist on some components of a product being manufactured locally (the 'local content' rule), and this may require product modification by the firm. Government taxation policies often impact on the product offering – for example, the EU tax on engine size and cigarettes affected product design. In the UK, cigarettes used to be taxed on the number of cigarettes in the carton; producers re-designed their products and made cigarettes longer with the same number in each box in order to gain market advantage.

Some of the government regulations on products, packaging and labelling are mandatory, especially for pharmaceutical goods and food. Products are also modified by technical constraints. Variations in electricity voltage between UK and continental Europe have major implications for product manufacture and marketing. Additionally, imperial calibration, whilst declining in importance, is still a significant product modifier in the UK market.

Use conditions

Products may fulfil similar functions in different markets, but the conditions under which the product is used will vary from market to market. The influence of climate on product modification can be considerable. Hot tropical conditions clearly will make different demands on a product and, indeed, its packaging compared to a cold climate. Products may therefore have to be modified to cope with such climatic conditions – Avon produces a moist lipstick for hot climates, for example. The formulation of petrol has also to be changed to cope with extremes of temperature.

Corporate history

With some long-established firms it may be the case that autonomy has been devolved to their overseas affiliates to design their own product strategies and to tailor their products for the local market. It could then be difficult for headquarters to implement a uniform product strategy, and national affiliates will attempt to be very 'national' in product approaches perhaps to avoid centralisation of policies. Under these circumstances, the headquarters may have to continue its multidomestic product approach until it can change the corporate culture to one of a global mindset.

It can thus be seen that there are a number of factors which encourage product uniformity, but there are many situations in which it is neither feasible nor desirable to have complete product uniformity. Comprehensive standardisation of all facets of a product, even if feasible, may not be an appropriate strategy. If branding was globally uniform, it might not be an optimum policy to standardise other product areas, such as warranties, since conditions will differ according to market conditions.

PRODUCT STRATEGIES

What approaches are available to firms to maximise the standardisation of their international product strategies? The modular approach[16] is based on developing a standard range of components that can be used world-wide and assembled in a number of configurations. In this way, the greatest efficiency is attained – i.e. when component parts are mass produced at specific locations and there is a limited number of variants of each component. This approach offers a large degree of product adaptation because the major components can be assembled in different combinations. This approach enables firms to be flexible to meet specific market needs without having to undertake a major customisation programme. One way to achieve this is to develop a universal product strategy – this is attained by developing a 'core' product which can accept a variety of standard parts and components. From this approach, a range of products can be assembled which have variable characteristics. The Ford Motor company, as we saw above, has produced a 'core' car which can then be adapted for different markets with a variety of different components and standard attachments.

Keegan's product/promotions matrix model[17] offers five specific approaches to product policy along the standardisation-adaptation continuum (see Fig. 13.2).

Strategy I (straight extension strategy: product–communications extension)

This involves introducing a standardised product with the same promotion strategy throughout the world market. By applying standardisation on a global basis to both

Fig 13.2 THE PRODUCT–COMMUNICATIONS MODEL

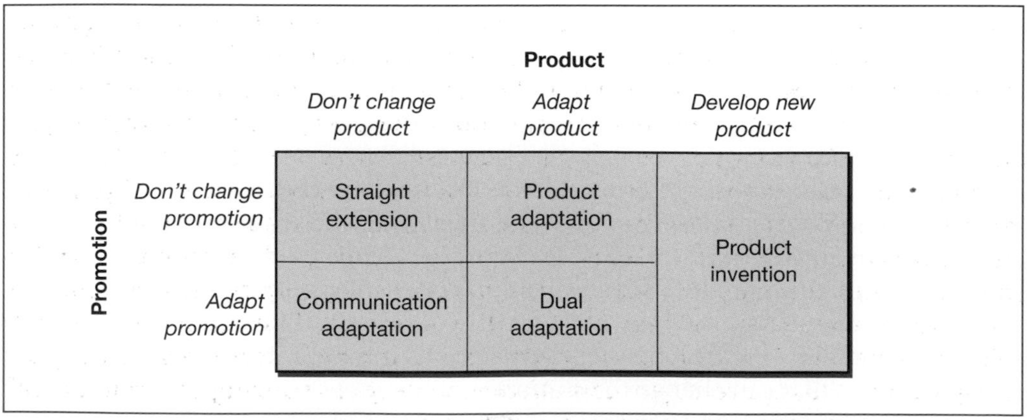

Source: Keegan, W.J., Global Marketing Management, 5th edition (Englewood Cliffs: Prentice-Hall); © 1989. Adapted with permission.

product and promotion, major savings can be made on market research and product development. To achieve this, a company will seek to promote its product using a universal message which will transcend linguistic and cultural barriers. If a company can develop such a promotional message, the same advertisement can be used anywhere in the world simply translated into the language of the target market. Companies in the soft-drinks industry such as Coca-Cola and Pepsi-Cola have been fairly successful with this strategy, and certain product categories – such as cameras, machine tools and electronic goods – have been more successful with this strategy than others. However, it has not worked with many consumer products. For example, CPC International[18] tried to sell its Knorr dehydrated soups to the US market adopting the dual extension strategy. It was not a total success for the conditions of use were quite different in the US market. Dehydrated soup required 15–20 minutes' preparation time compared to the almost immediate benefit of canned soup which required only to be heated and served. Preparation time was a crucial factor in soup purchases in the US market and in spite of the basic product and communications extension it was a market failure.

Strategy II (product adaptation and communications extension)

By modifying only the product, the manufacturer intends to maintain the original product function in diverse markets. Electrical appliances manufactured in the UK will be modified to cope with the differing domestic electrical voltages in continental Europe, as we have seen. It is also possible that a product may have to be modified to overcome deeply ingrained cultural traits. A company will blend different coffees for the French who drink their coffee black, for the British who drink their coffee with milk, and for Latin Americans who prefer their coffee with a chicory taste. It is also possible that a product will have to be changed to meet legal requirements, such as car exhaust emission levels. Finally, a product can be adapted to function under different physical environmental conditions – Esso has a standardised promotional campaign of 'Put a tiger in your tank', but they change the chemical composition of petrol to cope with the extremes of climate. Detergent and soap producers adapt their product formulation to deal with hard or soft water.

Strategy III (communications adaptation and product extension)

Use of this strategy involves leaving a product unchanged but fine-tuning promotional activity to take into account legal, cultural and linguistic differences between markets. This strategy is usually employed when a product fulfils a different need or serves a different function in similar conditions of use. Bicycle and motorcycle producers have adapted their communications strategies for the less developed economies of Africa, Asia and Latin America, where these products are used primarily for transportation, whereas in the developed economies of Europe and the USA these same products are perceived as being for recreational and sporting purposes. Garden equipment and lawnmowers are promoted as agricultural implements in some less developed markets where farming is on small plots of land. The equipment was suitable, and relatively cheaper than competitor products which were specially designed for agriculture. This is a relatively cost-effective strategy as changing communications messages is not as expensive as product modification.

Strategy IV (product and communications adaptation)

The modification of both product and promotional activity is potentially a very expensive strategy, but often necessary if the product is to be used in a slightly different way in a new market. Indeed, this strategy applies to the majority of products in the world. A US greeting card company had to adapt both product and promotion when they entered the European market. There were two major aspects of European buyer behaviour when it came to greeting cards. Cards were perceived as a means to send a written message (whereas in the US cards tend to contain prepared messages known as 'sentiments'). Second, European consumers handled the cards more frequently, and the US company had to add cellophane wrappings for the European market. This company is now one of the dominant players in the European card industry.

Strategy V (product invention strategy)

If an existing product cannot be adapted to a new market or promoted in a manner reflecting its needs, a company may need to develop a new product. This is a common method used by multinationals to enter many less industrialised economies, where existing products may be too technologically sophisticated to operate in a market where power supplies may be intermittent and local technological skills in short supply. General Motors designed a very basic vehicle that it sold only to developing countries, which was not expensive and was designed to function in varied conditions. Companies can also develop new products for which there is a need at an affordable price – for example, where there is an urgent need for low-cost, high protein food. In this instance, this type of product invention strategy means better customer value, because of higher consumer benefits at a low price.

Box 13.1   **AIRBUS INDUSTRIE[19]**

Airbus Industrie narrowly outsold Boeing in 1994 but in 1995 its market share fell by more than half to about 18.9 per cent, placing it in third position world-wide. The two major rivals to Airbus are the US companies, Boeing and McDonnell Douglas Corporation, who have rejuvenated themselves to the point where they could push Airbus into being an insignificant player. There is now talk of turning Airbus into a profit-oriented manufacturing company to reverse its bad fortunes. In addition, new product developments are on the drawing board in an attempt to crack Boeing's monopoly in the jumbo-jet market, which is the industry's most lucrative segment. Airbus hopes its new design A3XX will help it to compete effectively. The A3XX will be a double-decker with 550 riders in three classes or up to 800 in all economy. It is anticipated that the plane will enter service by 2003. Airbus believes that jumbos will be the growth vehicles of the future and expects that 25 per cent of industry revenues will be derived from planes carrying 500 passengers or more. This segment currently does not exist.

PRODUCT ATTRIBUTES

This section will examine how different product attributes may need to be adapted in the diverse global marketing environment.

Global branding

This section is intended to draw out and illustrate the complexities of selecting appropriate brand names in the international sphere. To be successful in diverse international markets, companies have to make appropriate branding decisions: this process is made more complex by language, nationality and cultural considerations. The basic objective, nevertheless, remains the same – to create a brand name which will appeal to similar emotions in different parts of the world. If a company is to succeed internationally, it is essential for the company to select brand names appropriate to a disparate market. Whether a company brands individual products or links the company name to its products are merely different strategies to achieve the overriding goal of attaining a large international market share and sales (*see* Table 13.2 overleaf).

Branding strategies

According to Jain,[20] four basic strategies are open to the global marketer:

● a uniform brand name world-wide

● a uniform brand name world-wide modified for different markets

● a different brand name for the product to suit different markets

● corporate umbrella branding, where the company name becomes the brand name.

In addition to Jain's strategies, there is regional branding, which could be used by firms particularly if they are targeting markets that are close to each other and share common traits – i.e. life-style or consumer habits.

Uniform brand name world-wide

This approach corresponds to the notion of a global brand[21] which can be defined as one that is marketed to the same positioning and marketing approaches in every part of the world. A global brand is a set of beliefs and perceptions about a product ascribed to it by consumers. A product is an objective and physical entity and is not a brand. A global brand is created by marketers.

Companies which produce and market one major product on a global basis use this strategy to secure world-wide identification of brand with the producer. Repeated customer identification with the brand reinforces familiarity with the product. Note, for example, the universality of Coca-Cola, Avis, American Express, Sony, BMW, Heineken Beer, Philips and McDonald's. There are enormous advantages to be gained from adopting a global brand, namely greater product identification which should enhance sales, and association with quality or technical superiority. It also eliminates confusion with competing products.

Table 13.2 BRANDING: ADVANTAGES AND DISADVANTAGES

Advantages	Disadvantages
No brand	
Lower production cost	Severe price competition
Lower marketing cost	Lack of market identity
Lower legal cost	
Flexible quality and quantity control	
Branding	
Better identification and awareness	Higher production cost
Better chance for product differentiation	Higher marketing cost
Possible brand loyalty	Higher legal cost
Possible premium pricing	
Private brand	
Better margins for dealers	Severe price competition
Possibility of larger market share	Lack of market identity
No promotional problems	
Manufacturer's brand	
Better price due to more price inelasticity	Difficulty for small manufacturer with unknown brand or identity
Retention of brand loyalty	
Better bargaining power	Brand promotion required
Better control of distribution	
Multiple brands (in one market)	
Market segmented for varying needs	Higher marketing cost
Competitive spirit created	Higher inventory cost
Negative connotation of existing brand avoided	Loss of economies of scale
More retail shelf space gained	
Existing brand's image not damaged	
Single brand (in one market)	
Marketing efficiency	Market homogeneity assumed
More focused marketing permitted	Existing brand's image hurt when trading up/down
Brand confusion eliminated	
Advantage for product with good reputation (halo effect)	Limited shelf space
Local brands	
Meaningful names	Higher marketing cost
Local identification	Higher inventory cost
Avoidance of taxation in international brand	Loss of economies of scale
Quick market penetration by acquiring local brand	Diffused image
Variations of quantity and quality across markets allowed	
World-wide brand	
Maximum marketing efficiency	Market homogeneity assumed
Reduction of advertising costs	Problems with black and grey markets
Elimination of brand confusion	Possibility of negative connotation
Advantage for culture-free product	Quality and quantity consistency required
Advantage for prestigious product	LDCs opposition and resentment
Easy identification/recognition for international travellers	Legal complications
Uniform world-wide image	

Source: Onkvisit, S. and Shaw, J., 'International dimension of branding', *International Marketing Review*, 6(3) (1989), Table 1, 24.

Uniform brand name world-wide modified for differing markets

Companies attempting to enter a foreign market often modify brand names to be more compatible with that market. In the 1960s, Nestlé marketed instant coffee in the UK as 'Nescafé Gold Blend' and in Germany as 'Nescafé Gold'. It is also common for a company to try to win over a new market by creating an image of being from that area. Following years of emphasising the 'Scottishness' of the company name, most British consumers perceive Campbell's soups as British rather than American. Producers also need to take into account the effect of media when branding. Where national TV crosses frontiers, as is commonplace in Europe, consumers may be exposed to two different brand names for the same product.

Different brand name for the product to suit different markets

Shrewd producers will be aware that language barriers often prevent translation of brand names. Additionally, a brand name which is used in one country may be totally inappropriate in another – Vauxhall Nova, for example, is branded as the Opel Corsa in Spain because Nova sounds like 'no go' in Spanish. It is also a contributory factor in the branding of the car – Rolls-Royce realised that it was impossible to name a new model of car 'Mist' as this means dung in German. Volkswagen brand their car names on famous winds, such as 'Golf' which means Gulf wind in German; this was inappropriate for the US market where it was renamed the Rabbit, or for the Latin American market where the Spanish name Caribe was adopted. This type of brand strategy is suitable when the original brand name is inappropriate or cannot be translated into the local language, and as a way of playing down its foreignness. However, VW, in an attempt to leverage global brands, has now renamed its Rabbit Golf in the US market.

Corporate umbrella branding

A corporate name is a form of trade mark. Trade marks can take the form of letters, symbols, logos, initials, etc. Brands identify the product but trade marks identify both product and company. Some firms have benefited from this double impact of trade mark, e.g. Levi-Strauss Co. Other firms, such as the UK's Imperial Chemicals Industries (ICI), promote their products under the corporate name; Unilever, the Anglo-Dutch multinational firm, on the other hand, does not promote its corporate name but rather its branded products.

Regional branding

Regional branding occurs when a brand is used in more than the national market. Germany, Austria and those parts of Switzerland where German is spoken constitute a market of nearly 100m consumers, and a unique brand and strategy could be used for the 'region'. Many countries of Eastern Europe such as Hungary, the Czech Republic and Slovakia also speak German, and this could mean an even larger consumer market. Regional branding could be justified on the grounds of the gains from better co-ordination and effective control of the promotional strategy.

BRAND PIRACY

Counterfeiting is costing companies lost revenue, and consumers pay premium prices for fake products. It is estimated that fakes account for about $500m annually in world trade. Violations of trade marks and brands are difficult to track and control. Piracy can take a number of forms, from imitating an established brand such as Chanel perfumes to faking the original product. This involves using a brand name or symbol which is very similar to the famous product. Several European companies sold jeans under the brand names of 'Lewis' (France) and 'Levys' (Germany), both of which sound similar to Levi-Strauss products. A final form of faking is pre-emption of brand names. In some countries, the local laws allow individuals to register in their names a number of well-known brands, which are then sold to the original company when it moves into the local market.

   The countries most involved with abuses of trade marks are found mainly in the Far East, e.g. Taiwan, Malaysia, India and Indonesia, as well as in Brazil and Mexico. Industrialised economies have an equal share of counterfeit activities. The most recent case of widespread abuse of intellectual property rights happened in China in the 1990s, with wholesale pirating of compact discs and the 'Windows 95' software package. The major factors contributing to piracy are that many major foreign brands are highly valuable commodities in many developing economies and possession confers high status on the owner. Furthermore, it is relatively easy to gain access to the technology required to produce these goods. Given the lack of coherent international laws pertaining to brand piracy, this problem will continue for some years to come. However, we can identify three basic types of protection against the counterfeiting of intellectual property:

● trade marks – which protect a sign, symbol or name

● patents – which protect new methods and processes

● copyright – which protects expressed ideas.

In spite of these protective laws, countries have not been able to agree with respect to the legal rights for intellectual property owners, and how to enforce these laws.

Box 13.2   THE ROLE OF BRANDS[22]

The recent development of private labels seemed to pose a huge threat to the established brands. Now companies like Proctor & Gamble, Microsoft and Coca-Cola are proving that having a strong brand name may be the ultimate competitive weapon. Indeed, Doug Ivester, president of Coca-Cola USA, never thought that private labels were really much of a threat to Coke. His rationale was that Coke, being a premium label, did not abuse its branding threat by over-charging consumers. This made it extremely difficult for private labels to undercut it. At the beginning of 1996, Coke was at the top of *Fortune*'s Most Admired list, and 12 of the top 15 companies on the list were household brand names, including Johnson & Johnson and Proctor & Gamble. In fact, total sales of private-label goods, which rose in the early 1990s, have peaked. Another indication that branded goods are back on the offensive is the amount spent on advertising. Advertising is still considered one of the best ways to build brand equity. McCann-Erikson estimate that advertisers

> **Box 13.2 continued**

spent \$174.1bn in 1996, up 7.8 per cent from 1995. Apart from the fact that brands can attract higher incomes, they can bestow credibility and attract instant attention in a new market or industry sector. The role of brands has gone through different stages of development in the industrialised economies. In the 1940s and 1950s, brands were perceived to be symbols of the good life. During the 1960s and 1970s, the brand mirrored the economic prosperity of the times, but also implied the sharing of wealth, when the message of the advertisements echoed themes like 'You could become ... when you buy ...' However, in the late 1970s, with the oil crisis and political and economical turbulence, there was an erosion of confidence in the institutions of government and business. In the 1980s, brands had become symbols of one-upmanship – BMW was 'the ultimate driving machine' and possession of one implied that one was a winner and the others were losers. Consumers had been turning against brands in the late 1980s, but towards the mid-1990s consumers wanted to 'trust' again and to reduce the risk of getting stuck with faulty or sub-standard products. With consumers being overloaded with so many messages and product offerings, the role of brands will become even more critical, and the future for many businesses in a highly competitive environment is brand equity and the associations with it.

Box 13.2 illustrates the importance of product development and its attributes in order to gain a competitive advantage in the global market place. Success is not simply based on developing the physical characteristics of a product; the augmented parts of the product (i.e. branding, warranties, etc.) are just as important.

GLOBAL PACKAGING

Global packaging performs the same functions as in the domestic sphere, namely to protect and promote the product. The package should attract customers and make a positive impression. It should result in greater convenience in terms of handling and ease of transport. Well designed packages should contribute to consumer recognition of the product or company – for example Kellogg's Corn Flakes has a unique package which is immediately recognisable. In international markets, packaging requirements will differ for various markets because of legal and economic factors. The shape, colour, symbols and aesthetics of a package must be also in harmony with the cultural norms of the host market.

The packaging decision is also subject to whether standardisation or adaptation is more appropriate. However, this decision is perhaps less crucial than for the product. The protection and promotion functions of international packaging will vary according to the different conditions prevailing in the different markets.

Protective functions

Climate

Different climatic conditions may require a change in the package to ensure sufficient protection. If products are destined for markets with wet climates then the packaging should be able to withstand humidity. Again, if goods are destined for mountainous regions they may require sturdy material and careful packaging.

Handling

The product's success can also be enhanced if it is packaged to withstand sustained handling as it goes through the chain of intermediaries. In Japan, for example, the distribution channel tends to include many intermediaries which means frequent handling and therefore requires sturdy packaging.

Safety

Safety is an important criterion especially in developed economies. The package should be designed to be safe when used as a protective cover as well as after use. At a time when ecological and pollution issues are paramount, the packaging should reflect these concerns and be environmentally friendly so that its disposal does not lead to pollution.

Promotional functions

The promotional aspects of packaging tend to overshadow its protective functions because the former has a powerful influence on the purchase decision. Indeed, the promotional function needs to respond to the various environmental variables if it is to be successful, as the following examples illustrate:

1 the visual aesthetics of packaging will appeal more to consumers in advanced economies, whereas consumers in less developed economics will appreciate the physical quality of the package;

2 there are also cultural differences with respect to aesthetic perceptions – Hong Kong consumers place a low value on floral design on soap packages, whereas American consumers associate it with feminine goods;

3 package size will also differ by metric or non-metric standards and by custom – larger packs are more common in countries with high *per capita* income as consumers shop less frequently and buy larger quantities; in economies with low *per capita* income, consumers buy smaller quantities more frequently;

4 the colour of a package can be influenced by local preferences; gift packages should avoid certain colour combinations – red, as we have seen, is a good combination in the Far East, while white is associated with mourning;

5 numbers of items in a package are equally important and can affect a product's success – a US golf ball manufacturer exported his products to Japan, packed in groups of four; unfortunately, the word 'four' when pronounced in Japanese sounds like the word for 'death', and the product was not well accepted;

6 the size and shape of the package can affect its handling and transportation – products which are large or heavy will be difficult to move through the distribution system;

7 different legal requirements will affect the firm in different ways – the way ingredients are listed will differ according to different markets; or markets such as Canada with two or more common languages require bilingual instructions, and some EU countries now have trilingual or multilingual labelling on many products.

WARRANTIES

A warranty is a guarantee by the seller that the product will perform as stated. Warranties have two main functions:

1 a promotional role, which can give the firm a competitive advantage – potential buyers will feel reassured about buying from a firm which provides a warranty, especially when buying expensive technical products;

2 a protective function, derived from limiting the firm's liability, especially from unreasonable claims.

Warranty policy decisions raise questions about whether the firm should standardise its warranty world-wide or whether the warranty should be adapted for each market. The nature of the warranty will depend on a number of factors:

1 *global competition* – a firm's warranty policy should be similar to that of competitors in the local market if it is to compete effectively;

2 *conditions of product use* – if the product is subject to more stress and abuse in certain markets, then the warranty may have to be shortened; for example, cars in many less developed economies where the quality of the road infrastructure is poor. Here, as the product will be subject to more stress than in the UK, the firm is likely to offer a shorter and less liberal warranty than to UK customers;

3 *nature of the product* – some firms offer warranties which are limited to basic performance only; certain products are amenable to this type of warranty (e.g. pens and cars). Volkswagen and Parker offer basic warranties on their products, and in this situation a standardised warranty could be offered on the world market;

4 *firm's capability* – some warranties require servicing facilities as it would be impossible for the firm to have facilities in every country it serves, the firm may offer different warranties in different markets.

In general, the pressure towards standardised warranties is limited, simply because they do not offer the same rewards as are possible with standardised products.

GLOBAL SERVICING

Some products, particularly consumer durable and industrial goods, require servicing on a regular basis. Servicing is required because:

- the firm needs to comply with the warranty policy it offers
- it can serve as a promotional tool – certain products like mechanical equipment require periodic servicing, and a firm that can offer such a service will gain a competitive edge over its rivals.

The objective of a service policy is to enhance consumer satisfaction and develop repeat purchases. The issue of standardising a service does not arise, as the conditions and needs of different markets make it an impractical task. To provide a service operation requires commitment by the firm in terms of huge investments in facilities, personnel, supply of spare parts, training, etc.

Global servicing arrangements can be organised in three main ways:

1 *home operations* – the firm can operate from the home base using its own trained staff;

2 *distributors* – the firm can be represented in the foreign market by a distributor who can provide the necessary service back-up; in general, the firm will often be involved in providing training to the distributor's personnel, or company personnel will spend time with the distributor's firm;

3 *direct service* – here the firm sets up an organisation in the foreign market to deal directly with the customers; this is particularly useful for firms in the capital goods industry in those markets which are geographically close to one another, such as the EU markets.

What will determine the choice of method will be the comparative costs of each of the three methods, the type of servicing required (as complex tasks may necessitate a direct service), and other competitive factors determining the type of service required. In very competitive markets a comprehensive and high level of service may be needed.

In conclusion, good service may be a critical factor in being successful in the world markets. Japanese companies have gained competitive advantages with their excellent after-sales service facilities, sometimes providing service or spare parts within 36 hours.

NEW PRODUCT DEVELOPMENT

There are many ways in which a firm can add products to its international product line.

1 Exporting its domestic products.

2 Acquisition strategy. The firm can acquire a foreign company or a home-based company. When Nestlé acquired the UK company Rowntree in the late 1980s, it acquired a large portfolio of products for which there was a potential overseas market. The same was true when Ford acquired Jaguar. Although acquisitions are a relatively easy option, they are still a fairly expensive method of product development. Companies that have engaged in acquisitions probably believe that, in the long run, it is still cheaper than having to invest and build brands.

3 Copying products. Firms can increase their product portfolio by copying products developed successfully by other firms. Many of the newly industrialising countries

(NICs) of Taiwan, South Korea, Hong Kong and Singapore began their successful export strategy by producing imitations of standardised mature products. In many cases, manufacturers from NICs produced improved versions of the original product. Japanese firms led the move from imitators to modifiers and now innovators.

4 Internal product development. The process and problems of new product development are similar for all firms, whether they are operating in the domestic market or overseas. Six stages are involved (see Fig.13.3):

   (a) idea;

   (b) screening;

   (c) business evaluation;

   (d) prototype;

   (e) market test;

   (f) market introduction (commercialisation).

A new product could be new to the firm, host market or international market. The success rate for new products is generally low. In Japan, for example, the success rate is approximately two out of 100 and in the USA it is two out of 10.[23] At each stage of the product development process management faces the decision of whether to abandon the project, continue to the next stage, or seek additional information before proceeding further.

Fig 13.3 THE NEW PRODUCT DECISION PROCESS

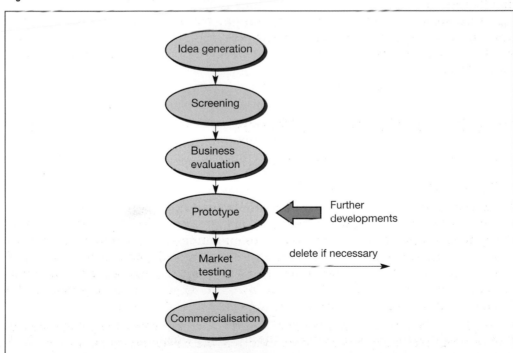

Idea generation

New product development begins with ideas that emanate from many sources: the salesforce, customers who write letters asking 'Why don't you ...', marketing employees, R&D specialists, competitive products, retailers and inventors outside the company. 'Consumer hotlines' are a source of many new product ideas as are 'brainstorming' sessions and incentives or rewards for good ideas. The idea for 3M's Post-It adhesive-backed yellow notes came from an employee. As a church choir member, he used slips of paper for marking songs in his hymn-book. Because the pieces of paper fell out, he suggested developing an adhesive backed note. An added dimension for the global firm is that ideas can be derived from all its international markets. These new product ideas can be purchased from other companies or by licensing. Joint ventures are also a means of generating and developing new product ideas.

Screening

The critical screening stage involves separating ideas with potential from those incapable of meeting company objectives. Some organisations use checklists to determine whether product ideas should be eliminated or subjected to further consideration. These checklists typically include such factors as product uniqueness, availability of raw materials and the proposed product's compatibility with current product offerings, existing facilities and present capabilities. In other instances, the screening stage consists of open discussions of new product ideas among representatives of different functional areas in the organisation. Toy maker, Hasbro Inc., screens new product ideas by looking for three traits in a toy: lasting play value, ability to be shared and ability to stimulate the imagination. Screening is an important stage in the development process because any product ideas that proceed further will cost the firm time and money.

Business analysis

Product ideas that survive the initial screening are subjected to a thorough business analysis. This involves an assessment of the new product's potential market, growth rate and likely competitive strengths. Decisions must be made about the compatibility of the proposed product with such company resources as financial support for necessary promotion, production capabilities and distribution facilities.

Concept testing – the consideration of the product idea prior to its actual development – is an important aspect of the business analysis stage. Concept testing is a marketing research project that attempts to measure consumer attitudes and perceptions relevant to new product idea. Focus groups and in-store polling can be effective methods for assessment of a new product concept.

Prototype

Ideas with profit potential are converted into a physical product. The conversion process is the joint responsibility of the development engineering department, which turns the original concept into a product, and the marketing department, which provides feedback on consumer reaction to product design, package, colour and other physical features. Numerous changes may be necessary before the original mock-up is converted into the final product. Some firms use computer-aided design (CAD) to reduce the number of prototypes developers must build, thus hastening the development stage.

The series of tests, revisions and refinements should ultimately result in the introduction of a product with great likelihood of success. Some firms obtain the reactions of their own employees to proposed new product offerings. Employees at Levi-Strauss test new styles of blue jeans by wearing them and reporting the various features.

Failure to determine how consumers feel about the product or service, and how they will use it, may lead to the product's failure. The classic example of this was the Sinclair C5 electric buggy developed in the UK as a serious on-the-road single-seater car, intended for city or country use. In reality, drivers felt too low to the ground and that they would be safer in heavy traffic on a bicycle.

Market testing

To determine consumer reactions to a product under normal conditions, many firms test market their new product offerings. Up to this point they have obtained consumer information by submitting free products to consumers, who then give their reactions; other information may come from shoppers asked to evaluate competitive products. Test marketing is the first stage at which the product or service must perform in a real-life environment.

Test marketing is the process of selecting a specific city or television-coverage area that is considered reasonably typical of the total market, and then introducing the product or services with a complete marketing campaign in that area. If the test is carefully designed and controlled, consumers in the test market city will respond to the new offerings without knowing that a test is being conducted. After the test has been under way for a few months, and sales and market shares in the test market city have been calculated, management can estimate the product's likely performance in a full-scale introduction.

In selecting test market locations, marketers look for an area which is a manageable size. In addition, its residents should represent the overall population in such characteristics as age, education and income. Finally, the media should be self-contained so that the promotional efforts can be directed to people who represent the target market of the product or services being tested.

Some firms omit test marketing and move directly from product development to full-scale production. The companies cite four problems with test marketing:

1 it is expensive;
2 competitors who learn about the test market often disrupt the findings by reducing the prices of their own products in the area, distributing money-off coupons, installing attractive in-store displays, or giving additional discounts to retailers to induce them to display more of their products;

3 long-lived durable goods, such as dishwashers, hair-dryers and compact disc players, are seldom test marketed due to the major financial investment required for their development, the need to establish a network of dealers to distribute the product, and the parts and servicing required;

4 test marketing a new product or service communicates company plans to competitors prior to its introduction.

The decision to skip the test marketing stage should be based on the conclusion that the new product or service has an extremely high likelihood of success. The cost of developing a new detergent, for example, from idea generation to national marketing has been estimated at £15m. Even if a company experienced losses on a good or service that failed at the test marketing stage, it would save itself from incurring even greater losses and embarrassment in the total market.

Commercialisation

The few product ideas that survive all the steps in the development process are ready for full-scale marketing. Marketing programmes must be established, outlays for necessary production facilities made, and the sales force, marketing intermediaries and potential customers acquainted with the new product.

A systematic approach to new product development is essential. The traditional method for developing new products, called phased development, follows a *sequential* pattern whereby products are developed in an orderly series of steps. Responsibility for each phase passes from product planners to designers and engineers, then to manufacturers, and finally to marketers. This method works well for firms that dominate mature markets and develop variations on existing products. It is less effective for firms in industries affected by rapidly changing technology, in which the slow process of phased development is a liability. In the electronics industry, for example, bringing a new product to market nine months late can cost the product half of its potential income.

Instead of proceeding sequentially, many firms have adopted the *parallel* approach, which uses teams of design, manufacturing, marketing, sales and service people who are involved with development from idea generation to commercialisation. Venture teams are an example of the parallel approach which reduces the time needed for developing products.

The key factors contributing to product failure are as follows:

1 *technical problems* – some products are badly designed, have poor performance and quality or are too complicated to understand;

2 *market research* – poor market research is a crucial factor in terms of perhaps overestimating what the market requires, or not acquiring sufficient knowledge of the consumers' buying motives;

3 *timing* – product introduction was either too quick or too slow;

On the other hand, new product success can be attributed to the following factors:

1 the product has a competitive advantage in terms of technical superiority or even price advantages;

2 the product satisfies a need;

3 the presence of a positive management philosophy and effective organisation facilitates successful new product developments.

ADOPTION AND DIFFUSION OF NEW PRODUCTS

The acceptance of new products by the public is a major concern for global marketers. To ascertain whether a new product is accepted by a fairly large number of buyers, the firm would need to conduct an analysis of the expected product adoption and diffusion in the global market. The adoption of new products goes through sequential stages whereby consumers follow a step-by-step process of deciding whether to accept or reject it. There are five stages in product acceptance:

- *awareness*: consumers are exposed to the new product/service
- *knowledge*: interested consumers will seek additional information on the product
- *evaluation*: involves the development of either a positive or negative attitude towards the product
- *trial*: the product is bought by consumers to see if it meets their expectations
- *adoption*: if the experience is satisfactory the product is accepted and it will be bought on a frequent basis.

The sequence of adoption does not mean that all consumers have to pass through the different stages. Some may skip and move straight from awareness to trial and adoption. Furthermore, the time taken between different stages will also differ among consumers. The nature of the product will be an important determinant of the time lapse between the different stages – very expensive items such as a car or computer will take much longer to decide on than trying out a new soft drink.

There is also a relationship between the number of consumers adopting a product and the time period involved.[24] As shown in Fig.13.4 (overleaf), only a small proportion of consumers accept the product in the early stages, followed by a marginally larger percentage and eventually by the majority. The 'bell-shaped' curve is indicative of the adoption time – the framework was based predominantly on studies done in the field of agriculture relating it to farmers' acceptance of new practices. Not much work has been done on the adoption of marketed products, but it is reasonable to expect that there is such a distribution tendency although it might not replicate the adoption pattern so neatly. If we accept this assumption, this framework can be utilised to assess the demand for a new product in an overseas market, and how this demand will change with time. If the adoption curve for a particular product indicated a mass market in only seven years' time, then the firm would not even contemplate building production facilities in that particular overseas market. From the curve we can identify five categories of consumers – innovators, early adopters, early majority adopters, late majority adopters and laggards. It is only when the early and late majority adopters enter the market that the potential of the market develops.

Diffusion refers to how a new product captures a target market – i.e. this process emphasises the aggregate individual decisions to adopt a new product, whereas the

Fig 13.4 NEW PRODUCT ADOPTION SEGMENTS

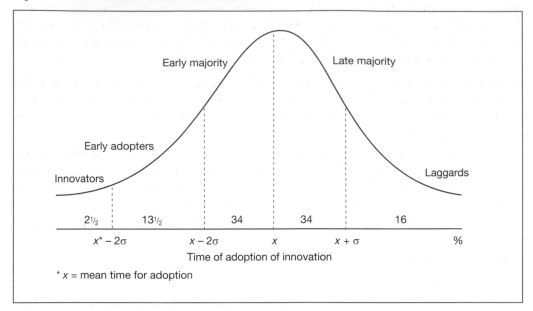

adoption process refers to the acceptance of new products by individuals. While the precise time for diffusion cannot really be estimated, an approximate time can be assessed for a particular product. The diffusion concept is essential in global marketing, and research has shown that this process is influenced by:

- organisational factors – effective communications especially between parent and subsidiaries
- product-related characteristics
- market-related characteristics.

Product-related characteristics

We need to consider five characteristics.

Relative advantage

This refers to the degree of advantage or superiority of the new product offering over the present ones. If the new offering is perceived to offer more advantages or benefits, then it is likely to diffuse more rapidly. This tendency will be increased by word of mouth recommendation from the innovators to other consumers.

Complexity

Diffusion will occur faster if the new product is easy to use or understand. Complex products require detailed instructions and involve educating the consumer – the more complex the product, the longer the diffusion process. At one stage in the early days of the video cassette recorder (VCR) the instructions were quite complex to learn, and the uptake of VCRs was slow.

Compatibility

If the new product offering is compatible with the current ones, then there will be rapid diffusion. Compatibility involves the social-cultural dimensions of the market, and consistency with existing values and behaviours. New innovations or products can be assessed on three levels to judge their compatibility:

- *Continuous innovation* has the least disruptive influence on current consumption patterns. Generally, this type of innovation involves the alteration of a current product offering rather than a new product. A new soft drink or new model of television would fall into this category.

- *Dynamically continuous innovation* is a more disruptive type of offering than the previously mentioned one. But it does not alter the established consumption pattern and it could involve either an alteration of a current offering or a new product. An electric toothbrush or a video-camera telephone are examples.

- Finally, a *discontinuous innovation* does involve the development of a new product and requires the establishment of new behaviour patterns – the development of computers, for example.

Communicability

If the attributes of the new product can be communicated easily and conveniently to the target segment, there is likely to be rapid diffusion – if the benefits/qualities of the product are obvious to potential customers then the uptake is going to be much faster.

Divisibility

If a new product offering can be available for trial without a major commitment, diffusion is likely to be rapid – divisibility implies that customers can sample the product offering (such as on a week's free trial) before returning it with no financial obligation.

Market-related characteristics

Three elements are important here.

Perception of needs

If the consumer can perceive his or her needs clearly, then the product will be diffused quickly because it can quickly be determined if the new product matches their needs. Many consumers may wonder to what extent they need their own computer system in the home, as the need for a total system is still not abundantly clear.

Consumer innovativeness

Diffusion will become easier if consumers, through their own cultural values, are more prone to try new products or services. Diffusion tends to be more rapid in Western societies than in Eastern cultures.

Purchasing ability

Even if many of the characteristics favourable to diffusion are present, the diffusion process will be slow if the majority of the consumers are unable to afford the new product offering.

There are strategic implications of the adoption and diffusion processes. If the diffusion process is taking longer than the firm expects it may be necessary to make product changes to achieve rapid diffusion, such as simplifying the product or adding additional features to enhance the benefits. The role of promotion is critical in increasing the rate of diffusion – the message can be one of testing the new product offering for a limited period with no obligation.

Product deletion

Product deletion occurs when a firm drops the product from production because it does not satisfy a sufficiently large market segment and therefore reduces the firm's profits and affects its ability to achieve its organisational objectives. Many firms find it difficult to delete a product. This may be partly due to objections from both management and employees, perhaps as a result of loyalty to the product, and partly due to the argument that it is necessary to have a 'loss leader' to have a diverse product mix. Volkswagen stopped the production of its Beetle model in Europe with reluctance, as did Austin Rover the model TR7 sports car.

In general, the methods of deletion are that:

- the product may be gradually phased out, making no attempt to change the marketing programme
- the product can be dropped immediately, especially when heavy losses are being incurred
- for technologically or functionally obsolete products such as models of computers, it is usual to let them die a natural death as customers buy up the remaining stock over a period of time.

The point is that a firm needs to develop strategy of planned obsolescence.

GLOBAL PRODUCT-LINE MANAGEMENT

A firm's product line is a group of closely related products that function similarly, are marketed through the same type of outlets or are sold to the same customer groups; a product mix is a set of all the product lines and items that a firm offers. The width of the product mix is the number of different product lines carried; the length is the total number of items in the product mix; the depth is the number of variants offered for each product. Consistency is the degree of relationship among product lines in terms of some given criteria (*see* Fig. 13.5).

In general, a firm's international product line is unlikely to be similar to its domestic line and will be smaller than the home market. This could be due to financial restrictions on the part of the firm – it may be testing the market first; or it has acquired local products in the foreign market; there are differences in consumer needs and tastes; government regulation affects the choice of products sold in the market, etc. The firm's international growth strategy also affects product line decisions. If the firm has expanded by internal growth, it is likely that a more homogeneous and narrower product line will be established. On the other hand, if

Fig 13.5 PRODUCT-MIX WIDTH AND PRODUCT-LINE DEPTH, SELECTED PROCTOR & GAMBLE PRODUCTS

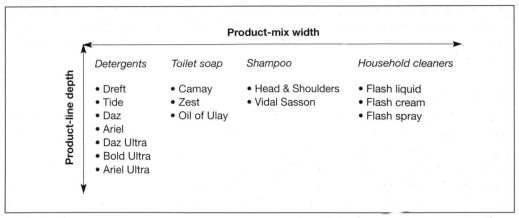

Source: Adapted from Dibb, S., Simkin, L., Pride, W.M. and Ferrell, C.C., *Marketing: Concepts and Strategies*, European edition (London: Houghton Mifflin, 1991), 215,

growth is attained by acquisition, then the firm will have increased its portfolio and may even drop some lines.

When a firm adds products to its lines in the international context, it needs to consider how this will optimise its global profits rather than just profits in a particular national market. On the other hand, it may add a product which may not be profitable for a national market, because it needs to evaluate the overall costs and benefits of its global programme.

Firms drop products for many reasons – poor profits, higher earnings potential from alternative products, lack of capacity to carry the product and so on. Whatever the reasons, the international manager needs to be aware that dropping a line in one market could result in increased overheads in other national markets. The firm could also drop the product domestically but add it to international markets, where it will be at the growth stage of the life cycle. The firm's foreign product line should not be too narrow, otherwise the few products have to bear a disproportionate burden of the entry cost (high marketing and management costs). There are many questions that the firm needs to pose:

● In which foreign markets should additions to the product line take place?

● Should new products be acquired or developed and are they congruent with the current product lines?

● How will adding to the product line affect the firm's performance?

Adding and dropping products needs to be considered carefully, for the decision must be consistent with the firm's overall global strategy. If the firm is going for uniformity in its international product lines, adding and dropping lines on a market-by-market basis could lead to product-line fragmentation, and this may conflict with the firm's overall global policy. The task is made no easier because markets do differ from each other, and change occurs in different directions and at differing rates. The firm needs to remain vigilant in order to maintain an adaptable and flexible product line.

SUMMARY

An ethnocentric approach views the foreign market as an extension of its domestic market. A polycentric firm views each national market as being different and unique, and develops individual marketing strategies for each market. A geocentric approach views markets which have similar characteristics, and does not perceive them as 'foreign markets' but global markets. A regiocentric approach views its main market as a sub-global group of markets – i.e. a cluster of markets. Product policy will be oriented towards a group of markets such as the EU, and developing pan-European product strategies.

One of the fundamental questions facing firms in global markets is the extent to which they should standardise or adapt their products. The factors encouraging standardisation are economies of scale in manufacturing, reduction in R&D costs, marketing economies, global consistency and serving global customers wherever they may be. Factors encouraging product modification include different consumer tastes and preferences, different levels of socio-economic development, host government influences in terms of mandatory regulations on product standards, tax regime and local content rule. There are different use conditions, and corporate history also influences adaptation strategies.

The main criteria are the nature of the product, market conditions, the business environment, market development, the infrastructure of the market and the results of a cost-benefit analysis. These must be considered before a firm can decide whether adaptation or standardisation is the most appropriate method of product design. Keegan's model is a useful heuristic device for a firm contemplating product adaptation or standardisation in its overseas markets.

Branding policy is a critical decision area in global marketing. The firm needs to decide whether it will have local, global or private branding strategies. A major concern for marketers is how to protect against brand piracy.

The attributes affected by international product strategies are global packaging, warranties and service. They all serve the function of promoting and enhancing the basic product benefits in the international market place.

New product development has six stages – product idea generation, screening, business evaluation, prototype, market testing and commercialisation.

Selecting product lines for the global market is fraught with difficulties. There are many determinants, such as government influences, level of economic development, firm's method of growth and type of entry mode chosen.

REVIEW QUESTIONS

1 Distinguish between ethnocentric, polycentric and geocentric approaches to product development.

2 What is the difference between a world product and a standardised product?

3 What are the advantages of product standardisation world-wide?

4 What factors encourage product modification?

5 Explain the alternative product–promotions strategies available to a product manager.

6   What are some of the approaches to brand strategies in global markets?

7   What type of products are amenable to one world-wide brand?

8   What are the problems with counterfeit products? How can a firm deal with these problems?

9   Briefly describe the promotional and protective aspects of packaging in global markets.

10 What factors influence new product development?

11 What are the key factors affecting a firm's international product mix?

DISCUSSION QUESTIONS

1   Discuss the impact of international product strategy on the other elements of the marketing mix.

2   Is there a distinction between a product and a brand?

3   'Standardisation is an elusive concept.' Discuss this statement.

4   Is the geocentric approach to product development the strategy of the future?

5   Discuss the notion that as consumers seek global brands the task of protecting brands from counterfeits becomes all the more difficult.

6   Is 'Sony' a good name to use for an international brand? What is the basis for your evaluation?

7   Critically evaluate the major determinants of a firm's product line in global markets.

8   Is it really so important for a firm to market test before it introduces a new product in the global market?

Case study

MADE IN AMERICA

It has long been a refrain among US executives bent on expanding into markets across the Pacific: 'Let's pass up Japan's tough markets and go for booming China and Southeast Asia'. Yet when President Bill Clinton presses the flesh with US business leaders during his mini-summit with Japanese Prime Minister Tomiichi Murayama on 20 November, he won't be hearing the 'Japan Bypass' song as much as he may hear a new tune titled 'Cracking Japan'.

American companies are making intriguing inroads into Japan's high-tech, auto, consumer goods, and retailing markets. Sure, a turbo-charged yen that's up 26 per cent versus the dollar since 1993 is one reason, because it makes US products so attractively priced. Yet subtle changes in buying habits, cracks in a fortress-like distribution system, and smarter marketing could set the stage for sustained growth in US imports. 'In the last two years, more changes in Japan [retailing] have happened than in the last 40,' says Takao Kondo, President of Budweiser Japan Co.

Shattered myth

Taken together, these trends explain why Japan's trade surplus with the USA declined 14 per cent to $23bn for the six-month period ended in September – the first year-on-year drop since 1991. True, the fall off owes much to the re-import of Japanese autos from US transplant facilities, and some of Japan's export momentum has merely shifted to offshore manufacturing centres. None of the US gains mean that all the barriers have suddenly vanished. Still, sales of such US products as autos and personal computers are expected to continue to increase. The Detroit auto makers are getting more serious about selling in Japan. At the recent Tokyo auto show, Ford Motor Company unveiled a right-hand version of its Taurus wagon and sedans that will hit the showrooms in 1996. Chrysler Corporation did the same with its compact Neon, which Chairman Robert J. Eaton hopes will shatter the myth 'that US companies aren't making a big enough effort to meet the needs of Japanese consumers'.

Some of the biggest gains are now being scored in Japan's long-coddled high-tech sector. Motorola Inc. has grabbed about 14 per cent of Japan's recently deregulated and now booming cellular-phone market. And US personal computer makers, led by Compaq, Apple and IBM, have grabbed 30 per cent of Japan's $9bn PC market by pricing their products 20–40 per cent below those of key rival, NEC Corporation. US computer makers will also get a big boost from Microsoft Corporation with its November 23 launch of English and Japanese versions of 'Windows 95' in Japan. Microsoft will peddle 'Windows 95' not only in traditional computer retail chains but even through Japan's convenience giant Lawson's, which has 5400 outlets. 'We would be disappointed if we don't sell 4 million copies a year,' says a spokeswomen. The ferment in Japan's notorious multitiered distribution system explains many of the US gains. The growing clout of Japanese discounters, for example, is offering US companies a unique shot at bypassing the nation's price-gouging wholesalers. Packard Bell Electronics Inc. is doubling its original 1995 sales target to 120 000 personal computers, thanks to its tie-up with discounter Daiei Inc.

Why now? The relatively new trend among Japanese consumers to demand value for their money also offers an opening for US retailers. Gap Inc. recently opened a 776m^2 store in the heart of Tokyo's ritzy Ginza district, betting that consumers will flock to its array of value-priced casual wear. Similarly, Campbell's Soup Company is taking aim at Ajinomoto Co.'s dominion of Japan's $500m soup market with the roll-out of four imported products in September. Why now? The drive for convenience so powerful in the US is sweeping into Japan.

No one is arguing that the long-term competitive battle is over, or even that the Americans will be able to wipe out their trade deficit with Japan, still expected to run to about $47bn this year. But the Japanese are seeing more goods stamped 'made in the USA'. If those gains prove sustainable, US companies that have resorted to bypassing Japan will certainly come to regret it.

Source: Brenner, B. and Updine, E.H., 'Made in America isn't the kiss of death anymore', *International Business Week* (13 November 1995).

Questions

1 *What is the importance of 'country of origin' in international product marketing?*

2 *What can the firm do with respect to standards to bolster its foreign market position?*

3 *Is adaptation of the firm's products the most desirable policy when a firm wishes to enter a foreign market?*

4 *How do companies use their brands as a key weapon to enter international markets?*

FURTHER READING

Vernon-Wortzel, H. and Wortzel, L.H., *Global Strategic Management*, 2nd edition (New York: Wiley, 1991). This book has an excellent set of articles on the standardisation versus adaptation debate.

NOTES AND REFERENCES

1 Kotler, P., Armstrong, G., Saunders, J. and Wong, Y., *Principles of Marketing*, European edition (Hemel Hempstead: Prentice-Hall, 1996).

2 Ibid.

3 Keegan,W.J., *Global Marketing Management*, 5th edition (Engelwood Cliffs: Prentice-Hall, 1995).

4 Levitt, T., 'The globalization of markets', *Harvard Business Review* (May–June 1983), 92.

5 Majaro, S., *International Marketing*, 7th edition (London: Routledge, 1993).

6 Gamble, A. and Payne, A. (eds), *Regionalism and World Order* (London: Macmillan, 1996); Garnaut, R. and Drysdale, P. (eds), *Asia-Pacific Regionalism: Readings in International Economic Relations* (New York: HarperCollins, 1994).

7 Levitt, op. cit.

8 Ibid.

9 Sorensen, R.Z. and Wiechman, U.E., 'How multinationals view marketing standardization', *Harvard Business Review* (May–June 1975); Douglas, S.P. and Wind, Y., 'The myth of globalization', *Columbia Journal of World Business* (1987), 19–20.

10 Quelch, J.A. and Hoff, R.J., 'Customizing global marketing', *Harvard Business Review* (May–June 1986).

11 Jain, S.C., *International Marketing Management* (Boston, MA: PWS-Kent, 1990), 422.

12 Thorelli, H.B. and Johnasson, J.K., 'International product positioning', *Journal of International Business Studies* (Autumn 1985), 57–76.

13 Walters, P.G.P. and Toyne, B., 'Product modification and standardisation in international markets – strategic options and facilitating policies', *Columbia Journal of World Business* (Winter 1989).

14 Levitt, op. cit.

15 Terpstra, V. and Sarathy, R., *International Marketing*, 6th edition (Orlando, FL: The Dryden Press, 1994), 267.

16 Toyne, B. and Walters, P.G.P., *Global Marketing Management*, 2nd edition (Boston, MA: Allyn & Bacon, 1993), 433.

17 Keegan, op. cit., 480.

18 Ibid.

19 Toy, S., Templeman, J. and Browder, S., 'A stronger tailwind for Airbus?', *International Business Week* (18 March 1996).

20 Jain, op. cit.

21 Keegan, op. cit.

22 Morris, B., 'The brand's the thing', *Fortune* (4 March 1996), 28–38.

23 Dahringer, L.D. and Mühlbacher, H., *International Marketing* (Reading, MA: Addison-Wesley, 1991).

24 Jain, op. cit.

14

Global service strategies

INTRODUCTION

A major component of world trade has been the increasing contribution of the service sector, and all types of services are being marketed globally, from financial services to tourism products. The focus of this chapter is to highlight the global marketing implications of services and explore the opportunities and problems that may arise as a consequence of the increased trade in the service sector. The issues that will be tackled in this chapter are outlined in the objectives below.

Objectives

This chapter will examine:

- the growth of services
- the nature and characteristics of services
- the major types of services
- the challenges facing service marketers
- the trends in the global marketing of services
- the impact of services on the marketing mix
- the strategies used in service marketing
- the internationlaisation of non-business marketing
- global person and place marketing.

In many of the advanced economies such as the USA, the UK and the other European Union (EU) countries, services have taken on a role of increasing importance, accounting for over 60 per cent of the gross national income over the last 20 years.[1] It is even higher in the USA where the service sector accounts for 69 per cent of gross national income and employs around 79 per cent of the US workforce. Of the 10 fastest-growing companies in the USA in 1994, six were service companies.[2] In general, the higher a country's *per capita* income the larger its service sector is likely to be. Even in low-income countries, services account for about one-third of the gross domestic product.[3] Globally, the service sector is growing rapidly and accounts for between 25 per cent and 30 per cent of world trade. While tangible goods such as shampoos and cars and intangible services such as travel and legal advice are both designed to satisfy consumer wants and needs, their marketing involves significant differences. In addition, the international marketing of services should be considered quite separately from that of industrial or consumer goods for a number of reasons:

1 the role of the service sector is expected to increase substantially in many national economies; it is estimated that over 50 per cent of multinational corporations in the next millennium will be service corporations;

2 the growth sectors in the world economy are expected to be in the service industries, especially tourism, telecommunications, transportation, financial services, computer systems and education;

3 the barriers to trade for services are quite distinct and different from those for product goods.

Box 14.1 **LLOYD'S OF LONDON**

Lloyd's, the London-based insurance market, was granted a licence to sell non-life insurance policies in Japan, which is well known for its very highly protected internal market. Although Lloyd's have been able to offer its business of reinsurance in Japan, this will be the first time that it will be able to compete directly against Japanese non-life companies. Lloyd's will focus on selling marine, fire and other non-life policies from April 1997. This agreement closely follows the December 1996 accord between Japan and the USA to phase out restrictions on foreign and Japanese companies' freedom to sell insurance policies. The deregulation of the Japanese industry is the latest example of how global competition is impacting on the domestic economies of many nations.

Source: Dawkins, W., 'Tokyo gives Lloyd's a licence to sell', *Financial Times* (10 January 1997).

Services are thus becoming a major component of international business and, as Box 14.1 illustrates, the internationalisation of services is unlikely to be threatened by protectionist policies. This chapter will examine the trends in service markets, the special nature of services, the types of services, the global marketing of services, challenges confronting the global service marketers and the impact of services on the global marketing mix strategies.

TRENDS IN SERVICE MARKETS

Rising economic prosperity, affluence, women in employment in the high-income countries and innovations in technology have led to changing life-styles and growth in all types of consumer services (*see* Fig. 14.1). It is anticipated that new forms of services will emerge as consumer demands increase, life-styles change and the rise in living standards continues. There are a number of factors[4] which help to explain the internationalisation of services and the growth of service organisations.

Fig 14.1 GROWTH IN SERVICE BUSINESSES

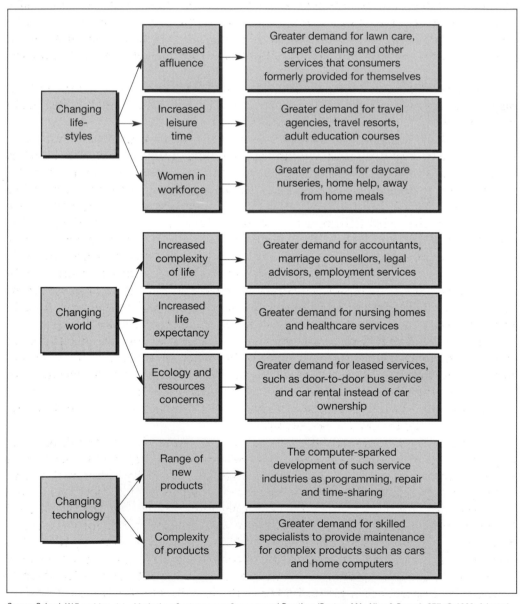

Source: Schoel, W.F. and Ivy, J.J., *Marketing: Contemporary Concepts and Practices* (Boston, MA: Allyn & Bacon), 277; © 1982. Adapted by permission of Prentice-Hall, Inc.

First, the globalisation of the world economy has led many manufacturing firms to pursue global strategies, which has resulted in the demand for knowledge and information on the trends, competitive environment and regulatory laws of specific foreign markets. This has led to the growth of service firms providing this type of information resource.

Second, although standardisation may be the ideal strategy, firms invariably need to adapt their products to suit the local environment. This has necessitated the need for engineering and design services, and in many instances after-sales service facilities. Finally, the cross-border movements of products is not a smooth flow. Firms have to overcome obstacles resulting from different customs, regulations, language, etc. Service firms have emerged whose role is to remove these obstacles – for example, freighting companies are used to deal with the various custom rules and procedures (*see* Chapter 12). It could thus be said that manufacturing firms which globalise their operations will incur additional costs which stem primarily from service requirements.

As services become increasingly important in national economies, they are likely to play an increasingly important global role, and service companies will undoubtedly look beyond their national borders for new markets.

The role of multinational corporations in offering services as their primary product line to gain a competitive advantage has also contributed to the importance of services in the global economy.[5] For example, many global companies that specialise in the provision of highly technical services need to invest in training (the service element) to stay ahead in the field. We can safely say that both privatisation and deregulation have contributed to the global transformation of the service sector. In the UK, the privatisation of British Telecom (BT) and subsequent deregulation of the industry has not only made the UK industry relatively more competitive, but has also influenced some EU countries into partial deregulation of their telecommunications industries, as in Germany. As a result of the partial deregulation moves, some of the European markets are now becoming more competitive and prices have been reduced, resulting in increased demand and a subsequent rise in the volume of global services trade.

Firms are also finding that as they expand internationally, they are able to benefit from the 'experience curve' (*see* Chapter 12). Insurance companies with a wealth of financial product development experience can adapt their products to new markets. For example, the US company American International Group Inc. is selling insurance policies directly to Chinese citizens in the People's Republic of China, and finding that consumers are responding favourably.

Education services are becoming more global in scope as well. Constraints on funding have forced many UK universities to look to overseas markets to boost their income flow – education is being seen as a global product by these institutions. Although this perspective has been prevalent in US universities for many years, it has only been taken seriously in the UK and European universities recently, as witnessed by the many advertisements for European-run MBA courses in *The Economist* magazine. Another major change has been the advancement in technology which has resulted in increased service trade. The use of computer systems has not only enabled companies to expand rapidly in the international market but has enabled them to manage their operations logistically. For example, DHL and Federal Express have utilised computers to their great advantage to provide an excellent delivery system to customers. The technological innovations in rapid data transmission have also allowed financial institutions to expand their service delivery world-wide.

Box 14.2

THE FIGHT FOR AIRLINE MARKET SHARE[6]

The competition is expected to become fierce as the European airline industry prepares for deregulation. In April 1997, the EU will end restrictions that prevent airlines from flying domestic routes outside their home countries. The fight for market share is already intensifying; for example, Debonair, a newcomer to the industry, charges between $80 and $146 for the London to Copenhagen route each way before tax. British Airways charges $287–$683 for a return trip while SAS charges $254–$683 for the same route. The larger operators are already positioning themselves for runs at neighbouring air space when the restrictions are lifted. Lufthansa plans to add a Bordeaux leg to its current Munich–Marseilles flight. BA is ahead in the game, for it has nine franchise arrangements that cover local British operators in deals that feed BA flights from South Africa. Even BA cannot relax, however, for low-cost operators are always carving out some niche market. One of BA's rivals is Virgin Express, which recently persuaded the Belgian airline Sabena to lease its loss-making Brussels–London routes, from which Virgin can then funnel passengers from Heathrow to Brussels and on to Virgin's seven other European destinations. Although prices are falling, it still has a long way to go to match the cut-throat environment of the USA.

NATURE AND CHARACTERISTICS OF SERVICES

Kotler *et al.*[7] define a *service* as: 'an activity or benefit that one party can offer another that is essentially intangible and does not result in the ownership of anything. Its production may or may not be tied to a physical product.' Similarly Stanton and Futrell[8] define services as:

> Those separately identifiable, essentially intangible activities that provide want satisfaction, and that are not necessarily tied to the sale of a product or another service. To produce a service may or may not require the use of tangible goods. However, when such use is required, there is no transfer of the title (permanent ownership) of these intangible goods.

Services range from those in the private sector such as travel, hotels, finance, telecommunications, transport, entertainment, estate agents, etc. to those in the government sector such as education, medicine, legal services, the police and many others. Examples of services in the non-profit sector would include charity organisations and religious institutions.

The linkage between services and products can be complex and convoluted; in general, most products are accompanied by services whilst services tend to have support products. It would be therefore difficult to find services which are now marketed without the involvement of some product. Some television firms may rent TV sets and apply the rental payments toward their eventual purchase; this provides both a service (rental) and a good (the television set, when the title is ultimately transferred to the customer). To take another example, an optician may provide eyecare examinations (service) and also sell contact lenses or spectacles (goods). It is this product–service mix which sometimes makes it difficult to define services clearly, for they are both varied and complex. Figure 14.2 illustrates how the service and product elements can vary considerably; products that are mainly intangible are classed as 'services'. The global service marketer needs to ascertain where the particular product offering is in the range dominant tangible to dominant intangible, for this will affect how the product is to be positioned. Although products and services interact, different customer groups will perceive this product–service combination in different ways. In some cases, services also compete with products. A customer can either buy a car (product) or lease it from a rental firm (service). Services do have several distinctive characteristics when compared to products, and it is these differences that will affect the type of

Fig 14.2 TANGIBLE AND INTANGIBLE PRODUCTS: PRODUCTS THAT ARE MOSTLY INTANGIBLE ARE CLASSED AS SERVICES

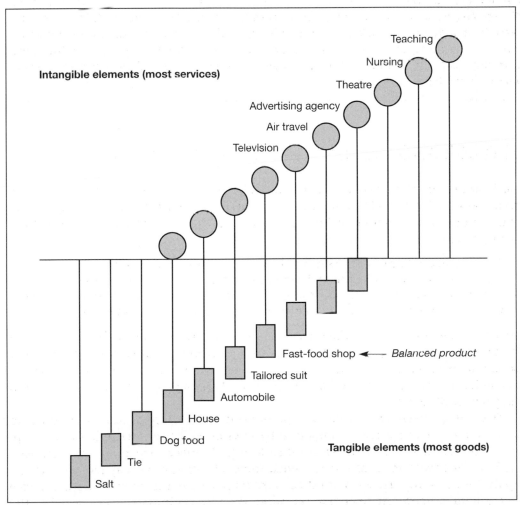

Source: Shostack, G.L., 'How to design a service', *European Journal of Marketing*, 16(1) (1982), 52.

marketing strategies a service firm will pursue compared to those used in product marketing.[9] According to Rushton and Carson,[10] the major difference between services and goods is that goods are produced whilst services are activities that are performed and not things. The distinguishing characteristics of services include intangibility, perishability, heterogeneity, inseparability and non-ownership.[11]

Intangibility

Services do not have tangible features – they cannot be tasted, heard, touched, seen or smelt before they are purchased. People going on holiday cannot sample the delights of the destination but only the promise of a good location and ambience, just as people going to a dentist cannot see the results before the purchase. This creates doubt in consumers' minds about the service they wish to purchase. Consequently, they look for quality of service before making up their minds, and will tend to look for signs to indicate this quality, such as the price, the promotional material, the place and the people working in the industries. This characteristic of services means that the organisations' promotional campaign must be effective and persuasive, concentrating on the *benefits* to be derived from the service rather than the actual service and advertising the tangible benefits of their intangible offers. For example, an insurance company will need to promote such benefits of its service as peace of mind and a quick and efficient payments system after claims are made. In the UK, the Legal and General Insurance company emphasises these benefits in its promotions.

Inseparability

Services are normally sold, produced and consumed at the same time, unlike physical products which are manufactured, stored, sold later and consumed separately. This *inseparability* of production and consumption can be illustrated in the case of a surgeon performing an operation. The surgeon is the person who provides the service and is therefore part of the service. However, the patient is also present as the service is provided, and both the provider and the patient can affect the outcome of the service. Inseparability means that a seller's service cannot be sold to a large market and that the service cannot be separated from the personality of the seller. The seller's reputation is frequently a key factor in the buying decision – if a particular rock group has to withdraw from a concert and is replaced by another group, then it will not be the same service.

It is, however, possible for a service to be sold by a person who represents the seller. In the case of a travel agent or insurance agent, they will promote the service that will be sold by the company producing it. Given the inseparability of the provision of the service from the seller, the marketing implications are that the firm producing the service needs to establish high quality and reliable training programmes for staff in these service industries.

Given that services cannot be exported like a product, this raises a few difficult questions for the internationalisation process. In addition, given that the customer must be present for the service to take place, this means that the service must be performed in the market itself. Is it possible to perform a service at a distance? This is possible through direct investment or franchising – many successful international service providers such as McDonald's, Avis car rentals, etc. have franchised their operations. Even banks such as Barclays Bank, Midland and Shanghai Bank, and Citibank offer automated teller machines (ATMs) to conduct banking business abroad. Involvement with the foreign customer in international markets requires greater cultural sensitivity and understanding of belief systems and preferences. This will assist the firm in delivering the service in an acceptable fashion.

Heterogeneity

The quality of a service may be variable whether it is provided by a service industry or by an individual seller. It is impossible to maintain a standardised output as each unit of service will vary from other units. A restaurant does not give the same quality of service each time we visit the establishment, nor will the quality of a particular provider's service be consistent – this will depend on the provider's mood, attitudes or other factors on the particular day. For example, your doctor's service will vary as will that offered by your favourite football team each week. Every tour of China will be different from any other such tour. It is therefore difficult to assess the quality in advance of buying the service. So service organisations need a programme to establish and maintain a high level of quality control and must aim for a consistency of quality service. This will be assisted by an effective human resource policy of staff selection, training and motivation as in the hotel, banking, retailing and airline industries. The implications for global marketing is that the service organisation can attempt to standardise the offering, although this may be difficult given that the personnel involved must use a high degree of personal judgement. It also raises questions of whether a standardised offering will satisfy customers in the various markets. Firms can standardise in a number of ways:

1 develop a standardised service package – e.g. packaged holidays;

2 give intensive training for personnel and make elements of the service offering as specific as possible, thereby reducing variation, such as McDonald's have for each specific job;

3 'customising' the service; a firm could tailor the needs for specific segments of customers. For example, banks offer specific services for expatriate customers on a global basis or travel agents might plan a unique travel itinerary for each traveller.

Perishability

In general, services are *perishable* and they cannot be produced and stored for periods of peak demand. Unsold cinema seats, unoccupied seats on airlines and empty hotel rooms all represent lost business that cannot be recovered. However, there are some types of service which can be said to be 'stored'. Life insurance services are purchased but are held by the insurance company (the seller) until they are required by the beneficiary (the buyer) at a later date.

A major feature associated with service industries is fluctuating demand, with variability across the seasons or across the hours of the day. Many summer holiday resorts are idle during the winter seasons, and public transport provisions such as underground trains in London have fluctuating demands during the day, with the peak periods occurring during the morning and evening rush hours. If demand was consistent then the perishability of services would not present such a problem.

The combined effect of perishability and fluctuating demand is that service firms have to maintain an operational capacity which can meet peak demands, but also may lie idle some of the time and therefore incur extra costs for the firm. Service firms can develop strategies to smooth out these fluctuations:

1 creative pricing strategies can be used to encourage off-peak demand – for example, low fares on the underground during non-peak times, low prices for afternoon cinema showings, low-cost weekend hotel packages and low telephone tariffs during the evenings and weekends;

2 alternative uses for idle equipment capacity during the off-peak seasons can be introduced – some universities offer their student halls of residence to tourists during the summer vacation months, for example.

In an international context, it is more difficult to smooth out fluctuating demand and supply adequately the service required in all markets. Thus some form of service 'inventory' may be necessary to meet demand requirements. One method is to cut the number of offerings at reduced prices and increase these if demand does not materialise – for example, the number of cheap fares on most transport systems such as airlines. In practice, it is very likely that a service provider will have excess demand in some international markets and idle capacity in others.

Ownership

According to Morden,[12] a fifth characteristic of services is non-ownership, and this has implications for marketing strategies. Purchasing a service allows the buyer only to have access to or use of that facility and not ownership and control, as in the use of a physical product. Examples are a hired dinner jacket, a rented television, or a rented car as opposed to your own. This lack of ownership in services may make them less desirable than owning the physical product, and consumers' perception of the value of the service may be considerably reduced. Service industries attempt to overcome this problem by informing the buyers of, say, leased televisions, photocopier machines and other industrial equipment, that leasing is good value as there will be constant maintenance and, perhaps after a certain period, a replacement with new and more up-to-date items.

Box 14.3   **OPENING OF TELECOMS MARKET**   **FT**

The British government opened the UK telecoms market yesterday to foreign companies. This means that new entrants and international carriers will be able to build and operate networks rather than rely on leasing lines from BT and Cable & Wireless. Some analysts believe that this liberalisation move could cost the domestic telecom companies loss of international revenue and market share amounting to £1bn. This move is an attempt to attract £5bn of investment and establish the UK as a regional communications hub. In addition, it will send a signal to the USA that the UK market is open to foreign operations

▶ **Box 14.3 continued**

and that the proposed $20bn+ merger between BT and MCI communications of the USA should be permitted, and that the USA should allow UK telecom operators to have the same access to the US market.

Source: Denton, N., 'Opening of UK telecoms market may attract £5bn', *Financial Times* (20 December 1996).

CLASSIFICATION OF SERVICES

Services can be classified in a number of ways. Dibb *et al.*[13] use a five-category scheme:

1 market type;
2 degree of labour involvement;
3 degree of customer contact;
4 skill levels of the provider;
5 aims of the service provider.

With respect to (1), the distinction refers to whether the customers are consumers or industrial buyers, and the implications of this division are somewhat similar to those for products. When the same service (telephone, gas or electricity) is sold to both consumer and industrial buyers, the service provider often has marketing groups for each customer segment. Consumer services may also be classified as convenience, shopping and speciality services. Dry cleaning, shoe repairs and similar personal services are normally purchased on a convenience basis, whereas car repairs and insurance are typically shopping services, usually involving some effort in comparing price and quality. Speciality services usually include professional services – financial, legal and medical.

The second method of classification is based on whether the service relies extensively on human labour or on equipment. For example, services such as education, medicine and hairdressing would be in the former category, while car repairs, public transport, etc. would be in the latter.

The third method is based on the level of customer contact, which can be subdivided into high- and low-contact services. High-contact services involve the client's presence for production to take place. The provider of services in a high-contact situation would need to be much more aware of the client's needs, the facilities must display high levels of maintenance and hygiene, and the actual process will be equally as important as the outcome. Examples would include dental check-ups, restaurants and hair salons. Low-contact services include activities such as repair shops, dry cleaners, etc., where the services are directed towards things, and the buyers of the service are not normally required to be present.

The fourth method of classifying services is by the degree of skill of the service provider. Professional services tend to be more complex and complicated, as in the case of solicitors, accountants and doctors, whereas non-professional services such as plumbers and catering are less complex and are self-regulated by trade associations.

The fifth way of classifying services is determined by the service provider's objectives – that is, whether a service is for profit or non-profit and whether it operates in the private or public sector. For example, a state school will have a different marketing programme from a private (profit-making) school in the UK.

CHALLENGES TO GLOBAL SERVICE MARKETING

As mentioned earlier, the global growth of services can be attributed to the changing nature of industrial economies, rising standards of living and changing life-styles rather than to marketing activities in the service industries. The lack of a marketing orientation in service industries in the past has perhaps been due to the difficult challenges facing service providers because of the unique characteristics of services (*see* Table 14.1), and also the perception that they were creators and not marketers of their services. This has now changed quite considerably, and many successful service organisations such as in the airline industries, banks and hotel chains have adopted highly sophisticated marketing strategies and techniques. The task of developing a marketing strategy in a service industry is challenging given the characteristics of services described earlier in the chapter. As in product marketing, the service organisation will need to establish its marketing goals, analyse its target markets, design and implement its marketing mix strategies and finally evaluate its programme. This section will briefly look at some of the elements of the service marketing strategy and the challenges.

Buyer behaviour

In general, there are many similarities between buyer behaviour for products and services, but there are some important differences which may be grouped into three categories – attitudes, needs and motives and purchase behaviour. At a basic level, the personal element involved in services is the key to the consumer's decision.[14] Rightly or wrongly, service marketers are sometimes perceived as being more personal, friendly and co-operative than goods marketers. It is important to understand why buyers behave in this way, and with a closer and better understanding it is possible to identify marketing opportunities. A brief review of the three differences mentioned above will provide a platform for the identification of these possibilities.

Table 14.1 UNIQUE FEATURES OF SERVICES AND THEIR MARKETING IMPLICATIONS

Unique service features	Resulting marketing problems
Intangibility	Services cannot be protected through patents Services cannot be readily displayed or communicated Prices are difficult to set
Inseparability	The consumer is involved in production Other consumers are involved in production Centralised mass production of services difficult
Heterogeneity	Standardisation and quality control are difficult to achieve
Perishability	Services cannot be inventoried

Source: Zeitham, V.A., Parasuraman, A. and Berry, L.L., 'Problems and strategies in services marketing', *Journal of Marketing* (Spring 1985), 35.

Consumer attitudes directly influence buying decisions. This is especially important to understand in service marketing because of the intangible nature of services. This intangibility tends to make buyers rely on subjective impressions of the service and its seller, and since services are perceived as being more personal than goods, consumers are more likely to be dissatisfied with their service purchases. This has enormous implications for global companies such as the Hilton and Hyatt hotel chains or international airlines like Lufthansa, British Airways and Singapore Airlines. Dissatisfaction with the personal elements of a service, such as an unfriendly waitress or an impolite air stewardess, are often the seed for a negative attitude toward the entire service. Hence the current vogue for customer care programmes and the attempt at the standardisation of customer services by international companies.

A comparison of needs and buying motives for goods and services suggests that similarities predominate. Essentially the same type of needs are satisfied whether the person buys the materials for a DIY home repair task or hires a firm to undertake the job. Although service needs have increased in importance, they can often be satisfied with new or modified goods as well as with services. For example, fast-food restaurants satisfy the consumer's desire for quick and convenient meals, but the same need can be fulfilled with microwave ovens and the development of better-tasting microwavable food products.

One need that service marketers should be able to satisfy better than their counterparts in the goods industries is the consumer's desire for personal attention. By appealing to this need the hairstylist, banker or insurance agent provides a form of satisfaction that the seller of goods cannot easily match. The desire for personal attention is often a dominant need satisfied by a service.

Differences between goods and services are most noticeable in the area of purchase behaviour. Selection decisions for tangible goods are normally more concerned with the operation of whether to purchase, whilst with services important attributes in the decision are the proper timing and selection of a service. This suggests several distinctions between purchase behaviour for goods and services: the degree of purchase planning may differ, and the buyer may be more personally involved in a service purchase.

Consumers are more influenced by friends, family members, neighbours and salespeople when buying services than when buying goods. The intangibility of services makes it difficult for buyers to judge quality and value and to inspect or sample the service prior to its purchase. Service buyers consequently depend more on the experience of others. This suggests two implications for service marketing. First, greater emphasis must be placed on developing professional relationships between service suppliers and their customers. Second, promotional efforts must be aimed at word-of-mouth promotion.

Environmental influences on services

In many respects, the economic, social–cultural, political–legal, technological and competitive forces exert the same types of pressure on service firms as they do on the producers of goods; however, certain environmental features have a greater impact on the marketing of services. What follows is a brief look at some of the environmental impact on services.

Economic environment

In the economic environment technological advances, population shifts and changes in consumer needs have contributed to increased spending on consumer services. The evolution of science and technology has altered productivity trends, and higher productivity in the manufacturing industries has helped to bring about a shift of workers to service industries.

Technological advances have also helped to create a higher standard of living for the average person, who currently spends a larger portion of his or her increased discretionary income on services. But the role of technology has also aided in circumventing barriers to trade, especially in its role in designing and delivering services. The use of advanced computer and telecommunications technology has allowed investment banks and other financial houses to transact across borders and transfer funds without much hindrance. This technology also allows intellectual property rights (services) to be transferred to another national market even if that firm is prevented from operating in the market. A firm can license another company in a foreign market to utilise the technology without having actually to be there. These two examples illustrate how technology can overcome trade barriers.

Population changes, particularly increased urbanisation, have widened the demand for personal and public services. In Japan, the demographic shift towards an older population by the year 2005 has resulted in new service demands such as better health care, pension products, convenience products, etc., and has also led to greater spending on consumer services. As a result, the prices of many services have risen rapidly. In contrast, the excess capacity in many goods industries has held the prices of their tangible outputs in check.[15]

Trade barriers tend to be more restrictive in the marketing of services than for goods, due mainly to the cultural links between a nation and the services it offers. Barriers to trade in services include both tariff and non-tariff elements (see Table 14.2).

Even more marked is the growth of consumer expenditure on business services. Companies in this field range from suppliers of temporary help to highly specialised marketing consulting services. Two reasons exist for this rapid growth of business services. First, business service firms frequently are able to perform such functions less expensively than the purchasing company can by itself. Enterprises can perform maintenance, cleaning and protection services for office buildings and industrial plants. Second, many companies who require, say, marketing research often require outside specialists.

Social–cultural environment

The social–cultural environment has a significant impact on the marketing of services. The increased use of counsellors and consultants has affected many aspects of modern personal, family and working lives. A few years ago, some of these services were not available, let alone influential; now there are even leisure consultants to advise consumers on what to do with their spare time. A variety of social–cultural trends are relevant to the increased marketing of services. For example, there is evidence that European consumers' tastes are shifting to a preference for services as status symbols. Travel, culture, health and beauty, and higher education have partially replaced durable goods as status symbols in many consumers' minds. Other European trends include a growing emphasis on security, which has widened the market for insurance

Table 14.2 BARRIERS TO INTERNATIONAL MARKETING OF SERVICES

Type	Example	Impact
Tariff	Tax on imported advertising	Discrimination against foreign agencies
	Tax on service contracts	Prices of international service providers higher than domestic providers' prices
	Higher fees for university students from outside the country	Decrease in foreign-student enrolment
Non-tariff Bilateral and multilateral country agreements	GATT multilateral lowering of barriers US–Korean insurance	Increased international market potential and competition Lowering of barriers to entry for US companies
Buy-national policies	Purchase US government of training services only from US companies	Discrimination against foreign suppliers
Prohibitions on employment of foreigners	Priority given to Canadian citizens for jobs in Canada	May prevent suppliers from going to buyers
Distance	International business education	Economies of bringing supplier to buyer, buyer to supplier or both moving to a third location
Direct government competition	Indonesian monopoly on telecommunications	Must market services to government
Scarce factors of production	Lack of trained medical workers in Biafra	Limits production of services
Restrictions on service buyers or sellers	Limited number of tourists allowed to visit North Korea	Limits growth of the restricted industry

Source: Dahringer, L.D. and Mühlbacher, H., 'Global marketing of services', Chapter 13 in *International Marketing* (Reading, MA: Addison-Wesley, 1991).

and investment services, and a greater concern for health, which has led to an increased demand for health clubs and medical services. Globally, the cultural dimensions affect services in a more pronounced manner than do goods. The inseparability characteristic of services means that firms may need to adapt their 'offerings' to suit local tastes and preferences – Kentucky Fried Chicken had to adapt its products in China to suit local palates. Business negotiations are very much subject to local norms and value systems. Language is a major cultural influence, and could be construed as a non-tariff barrier (NTB), especially in consulting services.[16]

Political–legal environment

The political–legal environment also influences service marketing. Service businesses are often more closely regulated than most other forms of private enterprise, with many firms being subject to government regulations in addition to the usual taxes, legislation and restrictions on promotion and price discrimination. Examples are easy to find, with the privatised water, gas, electricity and telecommunications companies all being subject to varying degrees of control. Service marketers must recognise the impact of such regulation on their competitive strategies. Four influences stand out:

- regulation generally influences the range and type of competition
- regulation reduces the marketer's array of options and introduces certain rigidities into the marketing process
- as the decisions of the regulatory agencies are binding, part of the marketing decision-making process must be aimed at understanding and predicting those agencies' actions[17]
- pressure groups may be established to lobby, and hence change or modify, the directions being taken by the regulatory bodies.

Technological environment

With respect to the technological environment, a large part of economic growth has historically resulted from increases in productivity coming from technological developments. The problem now, though, is how are increases in productivity to be accomplished in a service-dominated economy? This is a problem found throughout the developed world. Levitt[18] proposes that the solution to this is for services to assume a manufacturing attitude, where instead of expecting service workers to improve results by the greater exertion of energy, management must see what kinds of organisational structure, incentives, technology and skills can improve overall productivity. Here, Levitt cites McDonald's fast-food company as a good example of how a service can be industrialised, with everything being organised so that as little as possible can go wrong. Hamburgers are in colour-coded wrappers, a scoop has been devised to provide a uniform measure of french fries, and so on.

Competitive environment

The competitive environment for services represents a paradox: for many service industries, competition comes not from other services but from goods manufacturers or from government services. Internal competition is almost non-existent in some service industries. Price competition often is limited in such areas as communications and the legal and medical services. Many important service providers – such as hospitals, educational institutions, religious and welfare agencies – are non-profit organisations. Many service industries are difficult to enter – many require a major financial investment or special education or training, and many are restricted by government or regulatory body guidelines.

Direct competition between goods and services is inevitable because competing goods and services often provide the same basic satisfaction so that consumers can satisfy their service requirements by substituting goods. Competition has increased as manufacturers, recognising consumers' changing needs, have built services and added convenience into their products. Self-cleaning ovens and frost-free refrigerators have reduced the need for domestic employees, and video-cassette recorders compete with cinemas and other forms of entertainment. Consumers therefore have a choice between goods and services that perform the same general functions.

COMPETITIVE STRATEGIES FOR SERVICE MARKETING

Many companies have been successful in a diverse international market place with a variety of products from entertainment to fast foods. Firms can achieve success in the global market place by the following particular strategic moves:[19]

1 *customisation*: given that services are heterogeneous, companies can exploit this characteristic by customising their services. For example, some computer companies have excellent after-sales service; tour operators offer specialised package holidays like backpacking or cycling tours;

2 *uniqueness*: the more unique a service offering is, the greater the potential for global success, as it will attract international customers. The pyramids in Egypt or the Victoria Falls in Zimbabwe both attract vast numbers of international visitors. Entertainment artists such as Luciano Pavarotti or Oasis are unique products which cannot be duplicated;

3 *superior quality*: many firms can attain and sustain their competitive advantage by offering high-quality services at competitive prices. There are many examples of firms entering foreign markets and gaining market share at the expense of local producers. The Japanese car manufacturers competed on superior quality to gain extensive market share in both the USA and Europe. US franchising firms such as McDonald's, Hertz Rental Cars, Blockbuster Video rentals and Hilton Hotels all have excellent quality service as part of their offering;

4 *superior management system*: this is a key strategic asset for firms wishing to succeed globally, for good management systems ensure effective control and consistent quality. This enables a firm to transfer a standardised and high-quality management system to international markets. One of the most effective entry strategies for service firms is franchising, and this mode of entry involves a very well-structured and efficient management system which gives the company a competitive edge.

MARKETING MIX FOR SERVICE FIRMS

Although Kotler and Levy[20] wrote a classic article on marketing as a generic activity applicable for all types of organisations in 1969, it is only recently in the UK that this broadened concept of marketing has been accepted by many business and non-business organisations. The marketing concept is equally applicable to both the goods and service sectors, and the development of the marketing mix for service organisations follows a similar approach as for goods, but with adaptations where necessary. Indeed, it could be argued that because of the service characteristics, the marketing mix becomes part of the service, playing a critical role in shaping the total product. We will now examine the unique challenges of which a service firm needs to be aware in order to implement an effective marketing strategy.

Product

Like product planning, the service manager needs to make decisions about:

- the service to be offered
- the length and breadth of the service mix
- any augmentation to the service product, such as guarantees, payment methods or branding.

One of the problems for consumers is to understand what the service offerings are, and to evaluate alternatives. This stems from the fact that services are intangible and cannot be defined in physical terms. The intangible nature of services means that many marketing strategies used with tangible goods are of little or no use. Packaging and labelling decisions are very limited – in fact, service marketers are rarely able to use packages as promotional tools. The use of sampling as a means of introducing a new service to the market is also limited. Marketers of such services as squash clubs and satellite television frequently offer trial periods without charge or at greatly reduced rates to move potential customers through the stages of the adoption process and convert them to regular patrons.

Another aspect of the product offering is that the buyer invariably equates the service with the provider. The air stewardess or the lawyer becomes the 'service' an airline or solicitor's office provides. Services are perceived in terms of service personnel because of the absence of any tangible product attributes. This means that customers' perceptions of the organisation and its products will be based on the attitudes and behaviour of its personnel. The implications for the service organisation is that their staff have a critical role in generating good customer value and customer service. This underlies the importance for the organisation to have an effective selection, training, motivation and reward programme.

Another aspect of the service offering that the firm can provide to gain a competitive edge is the quality of its service. Given the intangibility of services, it is quite difficult to define 'quality' in an objective sense. Many consumers determine quality by comparing the perceived service of an organisation with the service they expect. If the consumer's actual experience exceeds the actual expected service then it is likely the service provider will receive repeat business.[21] The implications for managers of service industries with respect to quality control is that they need to commit themselves to quality as an organisational objective, to monitor and control service performance and finally to ensure good employee relations in the firm, as satisfied employees will result in good customer relations.

Given the perishability of services and the fluctuating demand, service managers can alter their 'service mix' by extending or contracting it as a way to meet changing consumer demand or to reduce seasonal fluctuations. For example, some firms work jointly with companies in related services. A car rental company may have arrangements with hotels and airlines whereby customers arriving at a particular airport will have a car and perhaps a hotel reserved for them. Another example of service firms extending their product mix are insurance companies who now offer a comprehensive package and life policies. Finally, augmenting the service 'product' is much more difficult to achieve; for example, an attempt to brand a service would encounter difficulties because of the problems in maintaining a consistent quality as mentioned earlier. However, this does not prevent service firms from using physical evidence to associate with the nature of the service – the use of in-house credit cards or membership cards such as those of the UK's Automobile Association (AA) represent the service to consumers.

Pricing of services

Price determination strategies in service industries do not substantially differ from those in goods industries. In developing a pricing strategy the service marketer must consider the demand for the service, the production, marketing and administrative costs, and the influence of competition. Many of the pricing strategies discussed for products can be applied equally to services. Variable pricing is used to overcome the problems associated with the perishable nature of services – airlines offer discounted fares on many highly competitive international routes, and car rental firms offer lower rates if their car services are rented for a week instead of a few days.

In general, the role of pricing in services is much more significant than in the case of tangible goods, because customers will perceive price as an indicator of quality given that other indicators are not available and they are unable to make comparisons between services. In the international context, this is critical as the service providers may not be based in the overseas markets and therefore price-setting in service industries can play a vital role in determining the firm's competitive edge.

There are, however, difficulties in setting prices within services. With tangible products the costs of production (fixed and variable costs) are more clear-cut than with services, where it is quite difficult to determine the minimum cost of a service provision. Indeed, price negotiation is an important part of many professional service transactions (car repairs, medical insurance, etc.). Specialised business services such as equipment rental, market research and maintenance services are priced through direct negotiation. While price competition is prevalent in some sectors such as banking, hotels and the travel industry, it may be limited in other services, especially the utilities (gas, water, etc.), whose prices are closely regulated and monitored by government agencies. With respect to hotels and travel products in some emerging markets such as China and Zimbabwe, there is differential pricing whereby tourists to those markets are charged premium prices relative to the local customers. This has resulted in tourists being very unhappy with the dual-pricing structures as they do not see an economic justification and indeed perceive it as an exploitative strategy.

Distribution of services

Service channels in general are simpler and more direct than those for products – this is largely due to the intangibility of services. The service marketer is less concerned with storage, transportation and stock control and typically employs shorter channels for distribution. However, this is not to say that all service providers are free from physical distribution problems. For example, firms renting out equipment (video cassettes, cars, etc.) do have to deal with stock problems, while if airlines have surplus seats (stock) this may affect their profitable operations.

Most services are generally produced and consumed simultaneously, and no intermediary is used, especially when the service cannot be separated from the provider (for example, in medicine and entertainment). The advantage of direct contact with the consumer is that the service providers can obtain immediate and detailed feedback, as well as the opportunity to personalise their services to suit the particular target market. The drawback of a direct service is that since the service is not separated from the provider at a point in time, it limits the seller's market in that the seller cannot be in two geographical places at the same time. However, with the advent of the video recorder, it is possible to have pre-recorded videos which can be 'consumed' by customers who are separated from the service provider by both time and space – pre-recorded videos of Madonna's music and educational videos as used by the Open University in the UK are examples.

Marketing intermediaries (middlemen) used by service firms are usually agents or brokers. For example, in the travel industry, retail agents often sell holiday packages developed by travel brokers, and these packages generally combine travel, hotel and restaurant services. Furthermore, the convenient location of the service provider to the consumer is important though not always possible. This need not be a handicap, for some service providers have extended their 'distribution' system in a number of ingenious ways. The banks, for example, have installed 24-hour ATMs in most cities across the globe for consumers to withdraw funds, obtain bank statements, etc. Some banks have even installed these machines in supermarkets. In this sense the 'machine intermediaries' offer convenience of location and are open 24 hours a day. Technological advances have thus overcome the perishability problem by allowing firms to open up new distribution options for global services. In addition, it has made world-wide linkages possible by letting service providers (such as credit card firms like Visa, Mastercard and American Express) offer services regardless of location.

Promoting services

The marketing strategy for services includes a promotional mix consisting of the most appropriate blends of personal and non-personal selling to inform or persuade the individual or business firms that represent the service provider's target market.

A frequently used promotional strategy is to make the service 'tangible' by linking it to concrete images. Hotels stress their physical features, emphasising elegance and cleanliness, and thereby providing clues to the service quality. The insurance and banking industries use logos or symbols to help consumers to differentiate and understand their services. For example, the UK insurance company Swinton emphasises its availability and ease of contact, while Legal and General's umbrella logo is symbolic of its power and dynamism. Other service marketers make their offerings seem more 'tangible' by personalising them through advertising which features well-known personalities and celebrities. In global markets, the same themes are used but the characters are localised to suit local cultural customs and tastes, although in some instances global promotional material is used (such as that used by British Airways in the USA and parts of the Far Eastern market).

A second strategy is to attempt to create a favourable image for the service or service provider. The most commonly used themes by service organisations are efficiency, status and friendliness. Singapore Airlines has a very successful campaign based on these themes.

A third strategy shows the tangible benefits of purchasing an intangible service. A local bank may show a retired small-business owner relaxing in the sun thanks to a retirement fund account established years ago. These and many similar themes help buyers relate to the benefits of the particular service that they would otherwise be unable to visualise.

The desires of many service buyers for a personal relationship with the service provider increases the importance of personal selling. Life insurance marketing provides a good illustration of the key role of the sales representative. Because insurance is a confusing and complex subject for the average buyer, the salesperson must be a professional financial advisor and develop a close, personal relationship with the client. Insurance companies and other service firms must develop a well trained, highly motivated salesforce for providing the high-quality, personalised service that customers require.

Given that services are intangible, their sales promotion is difficult. Possibilities for sampling, demonstration and physical display are limited and service firms typically do not use premiums or contests. In this case, publicity becomes an important medium for many services, especially for entertainment and sports events. Television and radio reports, newspaper articles and magazine features inform the public of these events, and stimulate interest. Contributions to charitable causes, employee services to non-profit organisations, sponsorship of public events and similar activities are also publicised to influence the public's opinion of the service firm.[22] In general, service marketers rely more on publicity campaigns than in the goods sector.

One final point to make is that the service organisation must adopt 'internal marketing'. This means that the service organisation must manage its service personnel who come into contact with customers, as well as other supporting staff, to be effective and to work as a team. This requires careful selection, training and development, good remuneration systems and a careful monitoring system. This process will ensure an efficient delivery system as well as maintaining quality standard, given that consumers tend to equate the efficiency and friendliness of employees with the quality of the service benefits.

GLOBALISATION OF NON-BUSINESS MARKETING

A substantial part of many national economies are made up of non-business organisations (NBOs), whose primary objective is something other than returning a profit to its owners. Non-business marketing covers marketing activities undertaken by individuals and organisations to attain goals other than a profit, a return on investment or other purely business objectives. It is possible to categorise non-business marketing into two types.

Non-profit organisation marketing

Non-profit organisation marketing is where marketing concepts and techniques are applied to numerous organisations, including the church, museums, charities, public libraries, schools, colleges, universities, hospitals, trade unions and political parties.

Social marketing

Social marketing is essentially a strategy for changing behaviour and involves the utilisation of marketing techniques. It is defined by Kotler and Roberto[23] as 'the design, implementation and control of programmes aimed at increasing the acceptability of a social idea or practice in one or more groups of target adoptions'. Examples of social marketing would include campaigns to encourage energy conservation practices such as recycling wastes like plastics and tin cans, and campaigning for human rights.

By definition, many NBOs do have international publics, as some of their causes transcend national interest. For example, the victims of famine in Africa and other parts of the globe have a world-wide audience; and many national universities attract international students, some even focusing on them as a target group. Many USA and UK universities have begun to set up 'mini' campuses in overseas markets – Boston University has many campuses in Europe and the UK, the University of Chicago has recently set up in Spain. Therefore, it is not surprising that many NBO promotions are really targeted at an international audience. A brief analysis will now follow, examining the differences in the development and implementation of marketing programmes between non-business and business organisations.

Differences between non-business and business marketing

There are very important differences between these two sectors that tend to limit the NBOs' marketing activities in various ways. A brief examination of these differences is given below.

Negative attitudes towards marketing

In general, NBOs tend to have a negative attitude towards marketing. They do not perceive their operations as a 'business' which requires the adoption of management techniques such as financial controls, marketing and human resource management. Many of these NBOs have only recently begun to accept and implement some of these business techniques. Most, such as trade unions, seem to be quite resistant to adopting marketing strategies, as seen in research conducted by Chee and Brown.[24] Marketing is perhaps seen as unethical, unprofessional and demeaning. Yet many of these organisations are practising 'marketing' in some form or another – whether they do it well or not is a separate issue. Trade unions develop 'products' (union services), price them (membership fees) and promote them (leaflets through branch officers). There appears to be some movement by the UK's trade unions in recent times to embrace 'marketing' strategies in their promotional campaigns, somewhat similar to the US trade unions, although they may not go as far to be 'business unions' like their US counterparts.

Church institutions advertise in newspapers and magazines (they prefer to call it information notices) and engage in personal selling (missionary work), though the church would not perceive itself to be engaged in marketing practices. On the other hand, although some NBOs believe themselves to be engaged in marketing activities, they tend to have a product rather than a market orientation – i.e. to select the products or services which they think their customers want, as in the healthcare industry or universities. However, many NBOs in the UK are beginning to adopt a more positive attitude towards marketing, albeit slowly. The trend to use marketing tools to publicise their aims and objectives has been used quite openly by NBOs in the USA – religious institutions have TV channels devoted to signing up new members.

Customers

Another major difference between business and non-business marketing is the type of groups that these organisations have to deal with. Business organisations have targeted their marketing activities to one major group, their customers. But NBOs can be said to have two major groups to target. The first is the *resource providers* who contribute finance, raw materials and labour inputs; thus one of the tasks of the NBOs is to attract resources. The second is its *customers* so that a hospital will target its patients, and a church its parishioners. There is a third possible group that some NBOs will need to pay attention to – its *public*, the groups which have an interest or impact on the organisation's activities. The significance of this difference is that NBOs will need to develop at least two distinct marketing strategies – one to the donor groups, another to its clients, and possibly a third to its public. In the present climate of higher education in the UK, a university will need to 'market' its activities to appeal to the government agency to obtain extra funding, whilst also marketing its reputation, courses and environment to potential students. The university will also need to deal with the media, and the local authorities, and the local community as well as its own staff members. An international group like Greenpeace has multiple groups to whom to target their promotional material in different national markets. Here again there is a need to differentiate themes and messages to suit local market characteristics. Promoting their material to European and US groups is one thing, but to target groups in the rainforest areas like Brazil or the Philippines would require a stronger and perhaps even a different strategy – many of the inhabitants in the emerging markets would have different perceptions regarding 'environmentalism'.

Controversial products

Another way in which NBOs differ from business organisations is that the NBOs' products can be controversial – groups lobbying against abortion such as LIFE (the anti-abortion charity) or for nuclear disarmament like the CND (Campaign for Nuclear Disarmament) movement, for example. Whether these are appropriate goals is another matter – the role of marketing is not to question the goals but to provide the necessary tools and concepts for the organisation to attain its objectives.

Perceptions and behaviour

Following on from the above point, a further major difference is that the objectives of NBOs are very different from those of profit-based organisations. Many NBOs tend to promote ideas as well as social practices with the ultimate aim of changing perceptions and behaviour. Charities such as Oxfam (UK) or Christian Aid (UK) have a number of objectives, from informing the global public of their existence and the services they provide, to raising funds for their overseas programmes in the emerging countries and raising awareness of the plight of disadvantaged groups in the poorer nations of the world. The objective of ASH (the anti-smoking group) is to dissuade the public from smoking; it may have considerable difficulty in getting its message across in China where smoking is considered a 'normal' social activity. NBOs also lack the discipline of measuring their performance against profitability. They may attempt to maximise their return from a specific service, with less exact goals such as service levels as the usual substitute for an overall evaluation. The net result is that is often difficult to set marketing objectives that are aligned specifically with overall organisation goals.

Organisation structure

Non-profit organisations often also have multiple organisation structures. A hospital might have an administrative structure, a professional organisation consisting of medical personnel and a volunteer organisation. This can lead to disagreements and confusion over the goals of the organisation.

However, these differences should not detract from the main issue, which is that whatever the complexity and the level of difficulty encountered in the two sectors, they should focus their attention on the satisfaction of the needs and wants of consumers, however defined.

DEVELOPING A MARKETING STRATEGY FOR NON-BUSINESS ORGANISATIONS

The techniques for planning and implementing a marketing strategy for NBOs are essentially similar to those for business organisations – to identify and analyse the target market and develop a marketing mix for the targeted segments.

Target market analysis

NBOs can be said to have two or possibly three target groups (*see* above) – the first being the *resource contributors* (or donor markets), the second its *client market* or direct consumers of the product, and the third the *general public* or indirect consumers. The donor markets for the UK university educational institutions comprise both government and private industry, their client market are the students, while the general public would include past students, parents, local industry and the university's board of governors. Segmentation techniques and analysis would be equally applicable to NBOs in which they are required to identify the characteristics of the donors, clients and public.

Product planning

NBOs will need to decide:

- what products they are offering to which target groups and in which overseas markets
- the type of product mix for each overseas market
- whether they need to have strategies such as branding for the product attributes.

The *product offering* to the client market could be a service, a course, an idea, a place or a person. This may sound an easy task, but it can be quite difficult to define precisely. What products do international organisations like Amnesty International or the Red Cross offer? The product offering in general is more difficult to define than is the case for profit-based business organisations. However, the product offering to the donor market is fraught with even more difficulties. Individuals and organisations may donate their financial resources and time to the NBO, but what benefits are they receiving in return? In the case of Oxfam, the returns may be intangible and therefore require special marketing efforts.

The *product-mix strategies* are also applicable in non-business marketing. NBOs can expand their product lines – in addition to religious services, churches can provide counselling services, social activities and even educational programmes. Universities can extend their range of courses to include night schools, distance-learning packages and even special intensive courses for a few weeks.

NBOs have begun to develop *product attributes*, such as branding strategies, in recent years. The Red Cross's famous cross and Amnesty International's trade mark of a candle surrounded by barbed wire are logos easily remembered by the public internationally. There is a danger with so-called branding symbols of some NBOs in some markets. Given the highly sensitive nature of their 'product offerings', both Amnesty International and the Red Cross can encounter 'resistance' from potential target markets either from governments who may block the distribution channels for their 'products' or consumers in the target markets who may not 'purchase' them for fear of reprisal from the authorities. In such cases, 'covert marketing' may perhaps be undertaken in the form of personal selling strategies rather than broad advertising.

Channels of distribution

Many NBOs tend to have simple and short channels of distribution, partly because the production and consumption of their products is simultaneous: in effect, no intermediary is used. If intermediaries are used, they tend to be agencies – for example, a political party or charity may employ an external fund-raising organisation. On the other hand, some NBOs become retailers themselves, selling products that are related to the organisation's core objectives. Greenpeace sells literature, posters, badges, etc. and Oxfam sells produce from the developing world and recycles the profits back to developing countries, all through its own offices.

In terms of physical distribution, NBOs need to be effectively located to serve both the donor and client markets. In terms of the client market, many organisations have set up systems that are accessible. The Open University has set up offices throughout the UK and abroad, and health organisations provide mobile X-ray units in certain parts of the country. In terms of the donor market, donations must be facilitated – for example, by the provision of different methods of payment such as credit card, cheque, etc. The distribution system must be set up to reach both sets of markets if the organisation is to function effectively and to achieve its aims.

Pricing strategies

There is a difference between pricing strategies for an NBO and for a business organisation, given that profit is not a major consideration for an NBO and that clients in many cases do not pay a charge – or, if they do, it does not reflect the real financial costs to the organisation. The Salvation Army, Church Army or the Samaritan organisation does not charge a price for their services to their clients, as their aim is to help those who cannot afford to pay.

However, we ought to introduce here the concept of *opportunity cost*, which is the cost of an alternative forgone. In this context, a person going to the Salvation Army or Church Army for help incurs a non-monetary cost in the form of travel and waiting time. Someone going to a rehabilitation centre which provides 'free' services pays a price in the form of the active participation that is required.

For other NBOs, financial considerations are becoming an integral part of their marketing strategies. For example, some museums and zoos are charging admission prices. Although these prices may not cover the full operating costs, the rest is being made up from contributions. These NBOs still need to address the issues of pricing strategies as for the profit-based organisations. The problem is that many NBOs are not aware of the costs of providing these services to their clients and thus it is difficult to calculate the pricing structures. However, some organisations do have a uniform price strategy (e.g. a university, which in general charges the same tuition fees for the majority of its courses).

Finally, there is the question of how to price the donor market. In this case, it can be said that NBOs do not set the price. It is in fact set by the donors, who will know how much they are going to contribute to the NBO – although some charities such as Save the Children Fund or Action Aid do suggest donations of £5, £10, £25 or £50.

Promotions

Promotion is the aspect of the marketing mix with which many NBOs are familiar. Direct mail, advertising and publicity are the primary methods of communication with their donor and client markets. Advertising has been used extensively to reach donor markets, particularly in the mass media of newspapers and journals. Oxfam, Population Concern, Save the Children Fund, Shelter and many other NBOs have relied on this method. Direct mail has also been used quite extensively to target particular groups to raise funds by a variety of organisations such as Amnesty International, Greenpeace, etc. Many other NBOs have also used advertising to reach their client markets – the British Army and the police have employed newspapers to increase recruitment to these forces. Higher education institutions have started to advertise heavily in specialist journals and newspapers to increase enrolments. Some environmental groups have staged world-wide concerts featuring famous artists to raise funds for the campaign to save the Brazilian rainforest as well as to publicise the cause.

Personal selling is also used, although it may not be perceived as such. Personal selling is employed by universities through its admissions officers, by Salvation Army volunteers who collect donations in city centres, etc. There is room for improvement in this area of promotion, as indeed in other areas as well. NBOs need to develop management training to run effective organisational, promotional and marketing strategies.

Control and evaluation

Controls are generally applied to ascertain whether the organisation has achieved its objectives as set out in the strategic plan, and to take action if they are not being achieved. However, measuring NBO performance is at present very difficult because there are few, if any, quantitative measures available, unlike for a business organisation whose performance can be measured against market share, profits, sales revenue, etc. How does one measure the performance of the Samaritans, Scope (the Spastics Society), Greenpeace and so on in an effective way? There may be proxy indicators but other 'factors' may have contributed to affect their outcome. Other NBOs, such as museums, may evaluate their performance by funds raised and the number of visitors per week or month. The anti-smoking lobby may measure its success by the decline in lung cancer deaths, but this decline may be due to other extraneous factors. These are challenging questions facing future NBO marketers, and ones that need to be tackled.

PERSON MARKETING

According to Kotler et al.,[25] *person marketing* refers to activities designed to create, maintain or change attitudes or behaviour towards particular people. Person marketing is practised by both people and organisations – the campaigns for political candidates and promotions for celebrities, for example. In political marketing, candidates target two markets: they attempt to gain the recognition and preference of voters and the financial support of donors. Increasing numbers of campaign managers are using computerised market research to identify voters and donors and then design a promotional strategy to reach these markets. Other promotional efforts include political rallies, fund-raising dinners and publicity, though these latter activities are more prevalent in the USA.

Sports personalities also use marketing to promote their image and their careers, with examples ranging from Tim Henman (UK tennis player), Paul Gascoigne (UK footballer), Steffi Graf (German tennis player), Jurgen Klinsmann (German footballer) to Aranxa Sanchez-Vicario (Spanish tennis player). Person marketing is not simply confined to sports but also applies to business leaders. In the UK, the former chairman of ICI Sir John Harvey-Jones is now a well-known 'celebrity', and his presence generates interest and attention. In the USA, the property tycoon Donald Trump has very effective personal marketing machinery. Through careful marketing and public appearances, celebrities such as these have become very successful in their careers, endorsing products and appearing in various commercials for well-known companies.

The process of person marketing is somewhat similar to product marketing. It involves research, the identification of target markets and segments, product planning (in this case, the person's image and relating it to the needs of the target market) and, finally, the promotion and delivery of the person, hopefully creating a celebrity.

PLACE MARKETING

Place marketing involves activities undertaken to create, maintain, or change attitudes or behaviour towards particular places.[26] Cities, counties and countries publicise their tourist attractions to potential visitors. Many communities launch marketing campaigns aimed at attracting new businesses to a particular area to stimulate economic growth. This type of business site marketing includes local campaigns to rent sites for use as offices, warehouses, factories, etc. to fairly large projects such as the development of industrial parks and huge office complexes such as the Canary Wharf project in London's Docklands.

At the national level, there are regional development agencies that try to sell to companies the advantages of moving to particular locations. The Welsh Development Agency and Scottish Development Agency have undertaken numerous campaigns to attract both national and international companies to locate their plants in those regions. In late 1996, the Welsh Development Agency announced that the South Korean conglomerate LG would be investing in a new plant in Wales (*see* Box 10.2). Even EU companies are attracted to some UK sites, such as Siemens of Germany which has built a plant in the North-East of England. Cities have also marketed themselves as locations for business or conference centres. Hanover in Germany is now marketed as the centre for international trade fairs, London is promoted as an international business and financial centre and Seville in Spain used the opportunity of Expo '92 to present itself as a city of great potential and a centre of culture. One of the most obvious examples of place marketing occurs in the battle to host the Olympic Games. Beijing, the capital of China, tried unsuccessfully to host the 2000 Olympics, which were finally won by Sydney, Australia. Certain nations have also embarked on marketing campaigns to present themselves as good locations for investment – Greece, Turkey and Singapore are examples.

One aspect of place marketing which needs to be mentioned is tourist marketing. This involves attracting tourists to certain destinations, whether they are resorts, cities or countries. In the UK, some regions such as Northumbria and Somerset offer holiday parks for caravan-based holidays,[27] while other firms market cottage holiday homes along the Devon coastline, emphasising its unspoilt and spectacular beaches. In a similar vein in France, the province of the Dordogne is marketed as a place of unparalleled scenic beauty and an unspoilt environment. On a national level, the tourist boards of various countries also market their attractions. The UK is normally marketed abroad as a country full of history and charm, whilst Austria tends to present itself as a picturesque country with the beauty of the Alps and medieval castles, as well as being the place where Mozart was born and wrote his music.

SUMMARY

Services are essentially intangible activities that provide satisfaction. Most products are accompanied by services whilst services tend to have support products. Services are the growth sectors in many developed economies; they have the following characteristics: intangibility, inseparability, heterogeneity, perishability and non-ownership.

Services can be classified in a number of ways, which may be helpful to marketing managers in developing their marketing mix. They can be classified into market types, the degree of labour involved in the production, the degree of customer contact, the provider's skill level and the aims of the service provider.

The characteristics of services present unique challenges to the global service marketer. In terms of the product offering, the intangibility of the product makes it difficult for the consumer to evaluate the service. International marketers, therefore, need to 'tangibilise' their offering in terms, say, of the physical environment in which the service takes place (such as the decor and ambience of a restaurant, and the staff service offered). This means that an organisation's selection, training, motivation and monitoring programmes have a critical role to play.

The role of pricing in services lies in indicating the quality of the service and, therefore, its competitive edge. A variable pricing strategy can be used to overcome fluctuations in demand because of the perishable nature of services.

Given the simultaneous production and consumption of services, service channels of distribution are generally more direct and simpler than those for tangible products. In addition, because of their intangibility, the marketer of global services is less concerned with storage and transportation and thus channels tend to be shorter.

Promoting services globally involves a mix consisting of the most appropriate blends of personal and non-personal selling. Given the intangibility of services, the aim of a global promotional strategy is to link the service with concrete images – e.g. the physical features of a hotel, emphasising its elegance and cleanliness. Personal contact with customers is an important element in international promotional campaigns. Personal selling has a key role because of the necessity to interact with customers, and publicity is an equally important medium, particularly in the entertainment and sports industries. A promotional strategy to increase word-of-mouth advertising is also important. Finally, 'internal promotion' within the organisation is critical to ensure that all staff understand and appreciate their role in conveying a high-quality service to consumers.

International non-profit marketing involves activities undertaken by individuals and organisations to achieve goals other than profit. Many international NBOs include educational, health, charitable, political and religious institutions. NBOs face three possible target groups: the donor groups, the clients and the public. The organisation will therefore need to develop one or more marketing strategies to attract the donor and the client markets.

The marketing concepts and techniques used in the business world are equally applicable to the non-business sector; however, the implementation of these strategies different. In terms of its product offering, the NBO will need to determine its business and which groups it wishes to target. Naturally, it will need to consider the product offering to both its donor and client markets. The NBO will also engage in product-mix strategies as well as product differentiation. The distribution channel strategy will involve establishing channels to the client market as well as to the donor group. In general, these channels are direct and simple, given that NBOs are involved with communicating ideas and service provision. In terms of pricing, strategies are different from those of business given the difficulty of quantifying the true cost of the service. In promotion, many NBOs have utilised the vast array of promotional tools available, ranging from personal selling and advertising to publicity. In terms of implementation, NBOs need to develop accurate and feasible performance indicators in order to control their marketing activities and to take remedial action when required.

'Person marketing' refers to efforts to cultivate the attention and preferences towards a person, whereas 'place marketing' involves activities to attract customers to a particular place, be it a business site or tourist site.

REVIEW QUESTIONS

1 Define a service.

2 Discuss the major characteristics of services.

3 What is good customer service, and why is it an important feature in the marketing mix?

4 Discuss the major reasons for the growth of global services.

5 What is the role of pricing in services marketing?

6 How would a service manager deal with the perishability problem in services?

7 Distinguish between business and non-business organisations (NBOs)?

8 What is the difference between a donor market and a client market?

9 What are the client markets for (a) a university, (b) a Buddhist organisation, and (c) the police force?

10 What benefits do donor markets receive from gifts to Amnesty International, the Conservative Party and the Oxfam charity organisation?

11 Why is physical evidence an important element in the service marketing mix?

DISCUSSION QUESTIONS

1 Relate the service characteristics of a night out in a restaurant.

2 What are some of the international marketing implications of service perishability?

3 Discuss some of the ways a firm can expand its services internationally.

4 Explain how the global sale of services differs from the sale of products.

5 Discuss some of the barriers to global trade in services. How can firms overcome them?

6 Discuss the effects of cultural factors on the global marketing of services.

7 Identify the key success factors in services that could lead to their success in global marketing.

8 What is the product offering of a

 ● trade union
 ● sports celebrity
 ● pro-abortion organisation?

MARKETING INVESTMENT BANK SERVICES[28]

The 126-year-old Frankfurt bank has hardly changed much during this period. However, Deutsche Bank (DB) is attempting a revolution in its major core businesses under the leadership of Chairman Hilmar Kopper to forge a new identity as a global contender in the highly competitive investment banking industry. His vision is to to be a major global player, to retain DB's position as the number one investment bank in Germany, as well as becoming a top European investment bank. According to Kopper, this is a radical and inevitable strategy for DB, given the changing world economy which is affecting both the German economy and its companies. The $471bn asset bank has built its businesses on a cosy relationship with German companies in which it often held shares. However, this banking culture is in its death throes as the Wall Street and London investment banks are muscling in on many of the European privatisation and merger deals.

To counter this, DB under Kopper is entering global investment banking and has already merged the bank's world wide investment activities into Deutsche Bank Morgan Grenfell (DMG) based in London. To achieve its global objectives, DMG has undertaken a series of actions on many fronts. Some of the actions and strategies undertaken include the following. In Germany, the bank is cutting costs, while in Asia, it is pitting new talent against the US, Japanese and British banks which had former colonial ties. In the USA, it is attempting to break into the market, without much success at present, and may emulate Japanese counterparts who spent billions in the 1980s in their attempt to enter the US banking market, with marginal success.

DMG is the least efficient of the Big Three banks in Germany with costs running at about 70 per cent of net income. Return on capital is about nine per cent compared with the US banks' average of 20 per cent. The financial position is not being helped by the bank's policy of hiring new talent using very high compensation packages in their attempt to become number one in Europe and a global contender. This hiring policy is in fact causing criticism from other investment banks, who argue that it is driving up costs for the entire industry. Competitors are claiming that the bank is 'buying' deals by underpricing its services. The bank concedes that it sacrifices margins to capture a major privatisation deal. The bank continues to spend billions in its transformation process – in the two years to the end of 1996, Kopper spent an estimated $730m (about half of 1995's $1.4bn consolidated net profit) to hire staff and install state-of-the-art trading rooms in Europe and Asia. The problem is that the hiring costs are swallowing up the savings made by the domestic cutbacks. The bank has shed 20 per cent of the 52 600 employees it had at the end of 1992 and over half of its 18 regional branches will close. However, there is still a real danger that the bank may become dangerously unprofitable.

In addition, the bank took a 5.2 per cent stake in Germany's fifth largest bank, the Munich-based Bayerische Vereinsbank. The rationale is that it will give DMG a voice in the consolidation of Germany's banking industry. DMG has plunged into life insurance alone and rejected a partnership with the German insurance giant Allianz. Deutscher Herold is now Germany's fifth largest insurer with nearly $2.5bn in premium income compared to Allianz's $8.6bn.

To add to DMG's woes, Europe is over-banked with 9500 different banks in the EU, with 40 per cent of them in Germany alone. Margins are slipping and both corporate and small-sized companies are exploiting the competition to shave a few basis points off loan interest charges. There is also a danger that Kopper has built an entity that is outside the bank's control. DMG's asset management subsidiary in the UK was investigated by British regulators after some irregular management of funds. This situation was quickly defused by the bank with swift actions in order to safeguard its $270bn asset management business. There were other losses for the bank such as the Metallgesellschaft metal and trading company which posted losses of $1.3bn from oil futures and other instruments it hid from DMG.

However, in spite of the difficulties mentioned above, the bank has come some way to achieving some of its goals. It was involved in Deutsche Telecom's partial $10bn privatisation package, advised the French Treasury on France Telecom's sell-off to the private sector and advised French retailer Auchan in its $3.7bn hostile take-over of Docks de France, the country's biggest buy-out. In Asia, it bankrolled two oil refineries in Thailand, the $3bn North-South highway in Malaysia and was involved with several telecom projects in the region.

Questions

1 *What are the key success factors in the global investment banking industry?*

2 *Evaluate the feasibility and suitability of DMG's global service strategy?*

FURTHER READING

Lovelock, C.H., *Services Marketing* (Englewood Cliffs, NJ: Prentice-Hall, 1991).

NOTES AND REFERENCES

1 McDonald, M.H.B. and Leppard, J.W., *How to Sell a Service* (London: Heinemann, 1987).

2 Czinkota, M.R. and Ronkainen, I.A. *Global Marketing* (Orlando: The Dryden Press, 1996); Teitelbaum, R.S., 'America's 100 fastest-growing companies', *Fortune* (17 April 1995), 75–100.

3 Zeithaml, V.A., Parasuraman, A. and Berry, L.L., 'Problems and strategies in services marketing', *Journal of Marketing* (Spring 1985).

4 Bradley, F., *International Marketing Strategy*, 2nd edition (Hemel Hempstead: Prentice-Hall, 1995).

5 Boddewyn, J.J., Halbrich, M.B. and Perry, A.C., 'Service multinationals: conceptualisation, measurement and theory', *Journal of International Business Studies* (Fall 1986), 41–57.

6 Reed, S. *et al.*, 'Airlines are fastening their seat belts', *International Business Week* (25 November 1996).

7 Kotler, P., Armstrong, G., Saunders, J. and Wong, V., *Principles of Marketing*, European edition (Hemel Hempstead: Prentice-Hall, 1996).

8 Stanton, W.J. and Futrell, C., *Fundamentals of Marketing*, 8th edition (New York: McGraw-Hill, 1987)

9 McDonald and Leppard, op. cit.

10 Rushton, A.M. and Carson, D. J., 'The marketing of services: managing the intangibles', *European Journal of Marketing*, 19(3) (1985), 22.

11 Terpstra,V. and Sarathy, R., *International Marketing*, 6th edition (Orlando, FL: The Dryden Press, 1994); Lovelock, C. and Quelch, J., 'Consumer promotions in service marketing', *Business Horizons* (May–June 1983).

12 Morden, A.R., *Elements of Marketing*, 2nd edition (London: DP Publications, 1990).

13 Dibb, S., Simkin, L., Pride, W.M. and Ferrell, O.C., *Marketing* (Boston: Houghton Mifflin), Chapter 22.; Valikangas, L. and Lehtinen, U., 'Strategic types of services and international marketing', *International Journal of Service Industry Management*, 5(2) (1994).

14 Feldman, S. and Spencer, M., 'The effect of personal influences in the selection of consumer services in marketing and economic development' (1967).

15 Gutfeld, R., 'The prices of services, unlike those of goods, keep rising strongly', *The Wall Street Journal* (11 September 1986).

16 Dahringer, L.D. and Mühlbacher, H., *International Marketing* (Reading, MA: Addison-Wesley, 1991).

17 Cook, B., 'Analysing markets for services', *Handbook of Modern Marketing* (London: McGraw-Hill, 1970).

18 Levitt, T., 'Industrialization of services', *Harvard Business Review* (September–October 1976).

19 McLaughlin, C.P. and Fitzsimmons, J.A., 'Strategies for globalising service operations', *International Journal of Service Industry Management*, 7(4) (1996).

20 Kotler, P. and Levy, S.J., 'Broadening the concept of marketing', *Journal of Marketing*, 33(1) (1969).

21 Bitner, M.J., Booms, B.H. and Tetreault, M.S., 'The service encounter: diagnosing favourable and unfavourable incidents', *Journal of Marketing* (January 1990), 71–84.

22 Ibid.

23 Kotler, P., and Roberto, E.L., *Social Marketing* (Macmillan, 1989), 24.

24 Chee, H. and Brown, R., *Marketing in the Non-Profit Sector: Trade Unions* (Bradford: Horton Publishers, 1990).

25 Kotler, P. *et al. Principles of Marketing*, 7th edition (Prentice-Hall, 1996).

26 Ibid.

27 Middleton, V.T.C., *Marketing in Travel and Tourism* (London: Heinemann, 1988).

28 Templeman, J., Lindorff, D., Reed, S. and Warner, J., 'Deutsche Bank's big gamble', *International Business Week* (14 October 1996).

15

Global channel strategies

INTRODUCTION

All products need competent distribution; even superior products may not be accepted by the market if they are not made available at the right time and place. The distribution process adds *utility* to a product or service. *Place* utility is created by making available the product–service in a location that is convenient to the consumer. *Time* utility is created when the good–service is available at a time that meets the customer's need. *Ownership* utility occurs when the customer takes possession of the product. Finally, *information* utility occurs when it is made available to customers, questions can be answered and applications knowledge provided. These utilities are a major source of competitive advantage for any firm and distribution strategy is thus critical for success in global marketing. To formulate distribution strategies is one of the most challenging and difficult tasks facing the marketer, as market channels in the world are the result of culture and tradition, and are one of the most highly differentiated aspects of many foreign country's marketing systems. A global distribution system must be adapted to the foreign market's established practices and based on customer needs rather than on the organisational need to streamline the distribution system. This chapter will cover the key strategic issues in the design, selection and management of distribution channels and the physical aspects of distribution (international logistics).

Objectives

This chapter will examine:

- the strategic importance of distribution strategy
- how channels of distribution can contribute to a firm's competitive advantage and the impact of globalisation on distribution structure and strategy
- the structure of distribution channels
- the factors affecting channel design
- the issues in managing distribution channels
- the selection, motivation and evaluation of intermediaries
- some of the major reasons for the development of 'grey markets'
- and analyse the Japanese distribution system
- the elements of global logistics – transportation, warehousing, inventory control, etc.

Distribution channels are organised networks that link the producer to the final end user. The channels may be groups of individuals or firms whose functions add utility to a good or service; these in turn, constitute the firm's source of competitive advantage. Distribution channel decisions are strategically important to a firm because:

1 the channel is the firm's major link with its customers;

2 the choice of channels will influence the rest of the marketing mix decisions in the short run – the pricing strategies adopted will need to reflect the margins allowed to an intermediary, for example;

3 channels take time to build and may not be easily changed or modified; they therefore involve the firm in a long-term commitment which could be costly to change;

4 the way the distribution system is structured will impact on which market segments can be reached and hence the type of marketing strategies that can be adopted and implemented by the company; the type of distribution system adopted will also influence the firm's ability to develop new markets;

5 the distribution system is an integral part of the firm's marketing programme, the means by which a firm can achieve its goals in the foreign market. However, problems can arise from conflicting objectives – for example, the firm may wish to maximise market share in the initial stages, whereas the intermediary may wish to maximise profits in the short run;

6 having control over the logistical and marketing operations does ensure some degree of success for a firm in the overseas market, but having an intermediary also implies some loss of control of the firm's marketing activities, so the firm needs to be very clear about the specific tasks that it expects the channel to perform.

Box 15.1 illustrates the importance of distribution strategy and how an innovative approach can gain competitive advantage for a firm.

Box 15.1

DAEWOO MOTOR[1]

Daewoo Motor of Korea is close to making a final decision on a site for a £700m car factory in the UK. This is expected to create more than 5000 jobs and eventually have an annual output of 100 000 cars. Although Daewoo has invested extensively in car and van plants in Poland, it was always part of their strategy to have a factory in the EU. In fact, the company has assembled an infrastructure in the UK to support the move into the production of cars. To precede the arrival of volume car assembly, the company will make massive investments in design, development, marketing and sales. The car industry has already been shaken by Daewoo's distribution strategy. It has broken away from the traditional sales through dealers to developing its own retail network; this attempt to establish a 'dealerless system' and the consequent lower-priced cars may yet give the company the competitive advantage it seeks in the UK market.

STRUCTURE OF INTERNATIONAL DISTRIBUTION SYSTEMS

The distribution decision is made more complex by the fact that the firm operates in highly differentiated distribution systems in overseas markets, with psychic and physical distance and lack of familiarity with the unique legal, socio-cultural, political and economic environment. The marketer needs to understand the structure of the distribution systems before he can develop an effective distribution strategy. No general strategy can be adopted – each product and every market must be considered on its own merits. But there are general principles guiding the design for an effective channel system, and these will be examined later in the chapter.

In general, firms use one or a combination of distribution systems.

Operating through independent intermediaries

Firms that uses intermediaries to establish contact with the final user are said to have independent distribution systems. These types of firms do not need to manage the distribution task in the overseas markets because they have selected entry methods which do not require them to take the responsibility for and management of the distribution networks. This applies to firms who have selected indirect and direct methods of entry. Indirect methods involve home-country channel members such as export houses, export management companies and export agents. Direct methods entail the use of foreign-channel members such as import intermediaries, local wholesalers and retailers. These distribution specialists serve different functions and provide different services, and as they are close to the end user they do affect the company they service. The implications of using these specialists will be discussed later, but for both categories of channel members, firms normally accept the distribution network offered. This situation could equally apply to other entry methods such as licensing or strategic alliances (Fig. 15.1 illustrates the different types of channel structures). The different methods by which companies enter foreign markets and the trade-offs that the firm has to make between control, costs and commitment were discussed at length in Chapter 11.

Integrated distribution system

This is when a company uses its own sales team to generate sales and deliver the products or services. For firms which have manufacturing or marketing operations in the foreign market, the responsibility for distribution to the final consumer lies with them. They will need to implement their strategic decisions with respect to channel design, management and distribution logistics. If a firm wishes to have an integrated distribution system, the following conditions should be present:

- the product is highly differentiated
- the product is very specialised and requires application knowledge
- a high level of service is required.

Complex and specialised products such as technical medical products or highly specialised software products which require a high level of service after a sale are suitable for an integrated system. The major advantages are that:

Fig 15.1 INTERNATIONAL CHANNEL CONFIGURATIONS, CONSUMER AND INDUSTRIAL PRODUCTS AND SERVICES

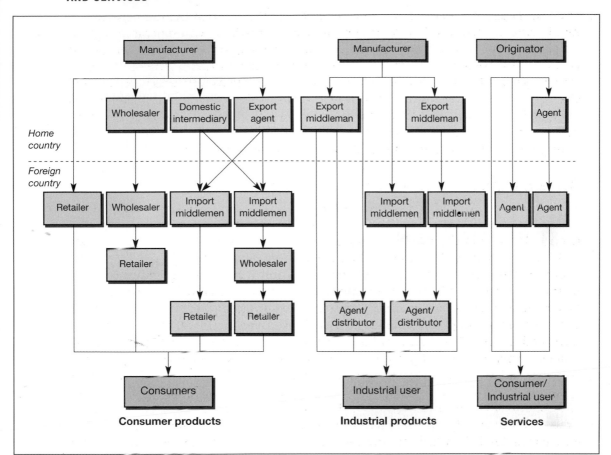

1 it enables the company to exert corporate control and motivate the channel members who are company employees;

2 it provides the opportunity for the firm to become familiar with the unique characteristics of the new market, and respond appropriately to what the customers require in terms of product features, delivery times, service levels, etc.;

3 it avoids some of the problems associated with the use of independent distributors, such as having only a part share of their time because they work for other principals, the agent's customer base being the wrong one for your company's image, the need to sever agency contracts with unsatisfactory distributors and the accompanying compensation package, etc.

The major drawbacks of an integrated system are:

1 high costs, due to large overheads from establishing a sales organisation and the recruitment and training of sales staff;

2 lack of familiarity with the language, local business practices and customs, socio-cultural and legal differences between the domestic and overseas markets;

3 intense competition if the firm is competing in a mature product category, and the key success factors in that stage of the product life cycle will be price and low cost;

4 legal and political impediments to establishing an overseas distribution network;

5 difficulties in accessing the right business networks, which is particularly important in some markets such as the Asia Pacific region.

Making the appropriate decision between an integrated or independent distribution system thus requires the marketer to appreciate the advantages and disadvantages of each option, and how they might contribute to the goals and objectives of the company's distribution strategy. As most companies do not wish, or are not able, to manage and control the distribution function totally, the design of channel relationships and strategy becomes critical.

IMPACT OF GLOBALISATION ON THE DISTRIBUTION FUNCTION

Given the long-term nature of distribution decisions, it becomes important for marketers to be aware of future developments. Distribution channels are not static structures, but evolve continuously in response to changes in the economic, political and legal environment. The following trends are worth noting.

Internationalisation of distribution formats

Formats such as supermarkets, discount centres, department stores and hypermarkets are being developed in both mature and emerging economies. Discount stores[2] are being developed in the UK and European markets and in the Asia Pacific region:

- Price/Costco, the giant US warehouse club company, has had branches in the UK since November 1993
- Kwik Save, a grocery discount store, is opening up in Scotland
- the French retail company, Carrefour, has opened Europe Discount in the UK
- discount stores are the fastest growing market segment in Japan.

Development of large-scale retailers

The trend in mature economies is the development of larger-scale retailers, meaning fewer and larger supermarkets:

1 Tesco, a large supermarket chain in the UK, opened larger out-of-town stores, and smaller city-centre stores (less than 10 000 sq. ft) were closed in 1989;[3]

2 the number of superstores increased by 33 per cent in Holland between 1982 and 1992.[4]

Perhaps the most spectacular example of the trend towards retail concentration and larger stores has been the international success of IKEA, the Scandinavian furniture retailer, with their 200 000+ sq. ft stores. The company has been extremely successful not only in Europe but in the giant US market as well. Europe's retail culture and landscape will be changed by these events and this may perhaps signal the beginning of the end of high prices and limited selection in European retail outlets.

This trend towards larger-scale outlets can be attributed to a number of factors:[5]

- the availability of refrigerators and freezers
- the development of transportation capacity, with the increase in car ownership
- the rise in two-income families with the consequent reduction in shopping time, but an increase in cash availability.

All these factors have contributed to the establishment of 'one-stop shopping' in large supermarkets and in out-of-town locations.

The intermediaries are globalising themselves

Some of the larger intermediaries are crossing borders in both developed and developing markets. They are acquiring local distribution companies or entering into joint ventures or strategic alliances with them. The trend towards the internationalisation of retailers can be attributed mainly to poor market opportunities in the retailer's home market, hence the push towards global markets. What has facilitated development of global retailers has been improved telecommunications, improved and new financing opportunities as a result of the development of global capital markets, and the lowering of entry barriers such as the formation of the Single European Market that motivated retailers to expand abroad.

Many firms from the UK, Europe, the USA and Japan have exploited these opportunities and internationalised their operations:

- UK companies such as Marks and Spencer have established outlets in France, Germany and Hong Kong. The Body Shop, the natural healthcare company, has grown rapidly internationally through franchising. Laura Ashley, the clothing chain, and Habitat, the kitchen and furniture chain, have both managed to establish successful retail shops globally

- European retailers such as Benetton, the Italian clothing chain, IKEA as mentioned before, Aldi, the German retail food chain and Escom, the German computer manufacturer and distributor, have also enjoyed a large degree of success in world markets

- US firms have been dominant in internationalising their distribution systems, with highly successful international retailers such as Pizza Hut, McDonald's, Kentucky Fried Chicken, Avis, Hertz, Tandy, etc.

Information technology

Perhaps the most significant factor that is currently having an enormous impact on the distribution system is the utilisation of technology. The use of electronic point-of-sale (EPOS) technology has accelerated supermarket checkout movements, reduced errors, improved inventory control and provided market feedback on consumer purchases and a more accurate assessment of which of the company's product portfolios are profitable.[6] The utilisation of appropriate technology will certainly be one of the key success factors in channel distribution strategies.

Direct marketing

Direct marketing is a marketing approach that involves direct access to the potential customer, and this industry is growing rapidly around the globe. (Direct marketing will be discussed at length in Chapter 17.) The main instruments of direct marketing are:

1 *telemarketing*, which involves selling by telephone; to use this approach pre-supposes that an efficient telephone service is available with a database of telephone numbers;

2 *direct mail*, which involves sending brochures, catalogues and other relevant information by post to the customers, with the goods shipped to them; this type of mail order is expected to grow substantially in the future;

3 *door-to-door sales*, which employs part-time salespersons and the use of door-to-door selling techniques; US firms such as Amway, Mary Kay cosmetics and NU Skin have met with considerable success in the overseas markets they have entered, particularly Japan and some of the Asia Pacific countries such as Taiwan.

In the EU countries, direct marketing expenditure accounts for only about one-third of all marketing expenditures compared to two-thirds for the USA. Total sales in the then 12 EU countries in 1995 was about a third of the US sales volume.[7] In spite of these figures, it is anticipated that future growth in the EU will be buoyant, although much will depend on the relaxation of regulations. The largest mail order market in the EU is Germany, followed closely by France and the UK. In the UK, direct mail is fairly well established, but telemarketing is increasingly rapidly, especially in the financial services sector.[8] Factors which will impact on the future growth of direct marketing include:

● improved telecommunications and postal services

● the presence of affluent consumers

● the increased use and acceptance of cashless payments, i.e. credit cards

● reduced time for shopping

● consumer life-style changes.

A company must be aware of the environmental and global trends that could impact on the future state of distribution systems if they are to remain competitive in world markets. There is a greater strategic focus now on direct distribution from manufacturing to the point of consumption and greater utilisation of centralised warehousing and distribution centres and on developing non-traditional distribution systems.[9]

FORMULATION AND MANAGEMENT OF A DISTRIBUTION STRATEGY

Formulating a global distribution strategy is fraught with complications as a result of the enormous variety of social, political and economic environments, different distribution cultures and country channel arrangements, etc. Establishing a distribution strategy involves making several key decisions (*see* Fig. 15.2).

Distribution density

This refers to the level of coverage or exposure for a product or service in the market. To market a product–service effectively requires an adequate coverage of the market:

- *intensive distribution* or mass distribution normally covers convenience goods such as food, washing powders, etc.
- *selective (or limited) distribution* is targeted at a particular segment of the market – shopping goods such as clothing, furniture, etc. where consumers visit one or two outlets
- *exclusive distribution* is for speciality goods. Consumers tend to be brand-loyal and will seek out the desired product.

The major determinant of distribution density is the consumer's shopping behaviour, but this differs widely among countries. In high-income countries, expensive cosmetics are sold in department stores or chemist shops, whereas in less developed economies the same products are likely to be sold in exclusive outlets.

Channel length

This is the distance between the producers and the final customer – i.e. this is determined by the number of levels, or different types of intermediaries. Longer channels, those with several intermediaries, tend to be associated with convenience goods and mass distribution. Japan has longer channels for convenience goods because of the

Fig 15.2 INTERNATIONAL DISTRIBUTION AND STRATEGY DECISIONS

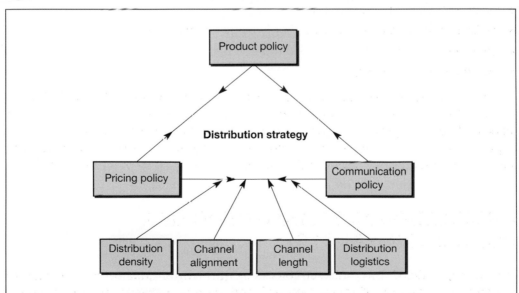

historical development of their distribution system. One implication is that prices do increase considerably for the final consumer.

Channel alignment

This refers to the ability of chosen channel members to achieve a co-ordinated and unified approach – i.e. it is the attempt to co-ordinate the actions of channel members into a unified approach for maximum efficiency. This can be achieved by the strongest channel member taking the leadership role. For example, in Japan the wholesalers rather than the manufacturers or retailers dominate the situation. But in many less developed countries with a limited distribution network independent distributors are very powerful because they have been given exclusive rights.

Distribution logistics

This is mainly concerned with the physical flow of the goods – i.e. warehousing, transportation, inventory control and order processing. This is discussed later in the chapter under Global logistics.

These four distribution decision areas:

● are interrelated

● need to be consistent with the product, promotional and pricing strategies

● cannot be approached independently.

CHANNEL DESIGN

After establishing a distribution strategy, the company will need to select appropriate channel members to support the overall distribution strategy. Thus channel design (which refers to the length and width of the channel) is a crucial decision in that a poor decision will affect the company's success. In addition, the channels selected and the type of intermediaries used will influence a firm's management and control of its distribution system. A number of factors influence the selection of channel members and the methods of selection are sometimes referred to as the 'Cs' method, first mentioned by Cateora[10] and subsequently elaborated on by Czinkota and Ronkainen,[11] who use an 11-Cs checklist. Other writers such as Usunier[12] adopt a 9-Cs method (see Table 15.1). These 'C' factors are important determinants for the management and the development of the channels, as well as the ability of the firm to change existing structures if required. This text will also adopt the 'Cs' method approach, incorporating the different authorities on this matter.

Company objectives

The company's overall objectives, competitive position and strategic marketing objectives will determine its channel design.

Thus its channel strategy must be consistent with its global marketing programme. The company can:

Table 15.1 THE 'C' METHODS OF CHANNEL SELECTION

Cateora	Czinkota and Ronkainen	Usunier
Cost	Cost	Cost
Capital	Capital	Capital
Control	Control	Control
Coverage	Coverage	Coverage
Character	Character	Character
Continuity	Continuity	Continuity
	+	+
	Customer characteristics*	Customer characteristics*
	Culture*	Culture*
	Competition*	Competition*
	Company objectives	
	Communication	

*Denotes external factors.

Source: Phillips, C., Doole, I. and Lowe, R., *International Marketing Strategy* (London: International Thomson Publishing, 1994), 389.

1 appoint independent intermediaries to promote its products and services;

2 establish an integrated distribution system to further the company's goals and objectives.

However, the relationship between the company's objectives and type of distribution channel design is not static and will vary according to the circumstances. When a company's operations expand in a market, this can have an impact on the channel design. Czinkota and Ronkainen[13] cite the example of Xerox, which produced copiers that accounted for 95 per cent of sales and sold through the firm's own direct sales force. It set a goal of having non-copier sales account for 50 per cent of the world-wide business in the 1990s. The company decided to change its distribution structure in France by the establishment of a wholly-owned and run chain of retail sales out-lets. Furthermore, it replaced its direct salesforce in small towns and rural areas with independent exclusive distributors.

The process of ensuring a strategic fit between the company's objectives and suitable global distribution channels is complex and difficult. Channel design is not only affected by the company goals but also by other factors, and these will now be discussed.

Box 15.2   COCA-COLA   **FT**

Coca-Cola has ended its collaboration with Pripps Ringnes, its local partners in Sweden and Norway, after 50 years. Coca-Cola is to build its own production facilities in the two countries as part of its independent strategy. Pripps Ringnes was formed in 1995 by the merger of Pripps of Sweden and Ringnes of Norway, and is controlled by Orkla of Norway. Coca-Cola's arrangement with Pripps and Ringnes goes back 42 years and 58 years respectively.

According to the managing director, Mr Bergqvist, the break with Coca-Cola was due to differences over the ownership of the production and distribution operations in Sweden

> ▶ **Box 15.2 continued**
>
> and Norway. The Norwagian company wanted to remain independent whilst Coca-Cola wanted part-ownership. It also appears that Coca-Cola were uncomfortable with Pripps Ringnes's dominance in the domestic market. The Norwegian company had 65 per cent of the carbonated drinks sector in Sweden, and had a leading position in beer and mineral water in both markets and is No. 2 in soft drinks. The Norwegian company expects extensive restructuring, and had relied on the US group's products for Skr2.7bn ($407m) or 35 per cent of its turnover. It is expected to receive a severance settlement from Coca-Cola of Skr1.1bn, and Pripps Ringnes was to continue to produce and distribute Coca-Cola products until March 1997.
>
> *Source*: McIvor, G., 'Coca-Cola severs links with Nordic suppliers', *Financial Times* (21 June 1996).

Capital

Capital costs refer to the financial requisites for developing a channel system. These include costs of inventory, accounts receivable, costs of goods in transit, preferential loans, the need for training, etc. All these cost items will have implications for the type of intermediary that is chosen. For example, an importer will often pay for the goods before they are sold to the final user, whereas, an import agent does not get paid until the goods reach the final customer. Choosing the importer will offset some of the capital costs incurred in setting up the channel system. On the other hand, establishing a direct sales channel will incur a significant investment. The type of channel and the basis of the channel relationships will therefore be determined by the firm's financial strength.

Cost

Channel costs can be divided into initial, maintenance and logistical costs.

Initial costs

These include costs of setting up channels, travelling costs to meet channel members, executive time involved, costs of negotiating the agreement, etc.

Maintenance costs

These refer to the costs incurred in maintaining a channel once it is established – the costs of the company's salesforce, margins of the intermediaries, travel expenses, communication and advertising, for example. However, advertising costs can be shared with the intermediary in the local market if a co-operative arrangement exists. Maintenance costs will vary depending on a number of factors such as the following.

1 The life cycle of the relationship with the channel member.

2 The life cycle of the product being sold in the local market.

3 The relative power of the producers and intermediaries. In the UK retail market, the giant supermarkets such as Sainsbury, Tesco and Asda hold considerable retail power and are now demanding that producers deliver to their centralised distribution centres. The effect has been to reduce manufacturer's power which had resided in their networks of distribution depots that delivered direct to the supermarkets.

The retailers are also implementing just-in-time (JIT) strategies to reduce their inventory costs, so that producers are being asked not only to deliver more frequently and in smaller mixed loads, but also to reduce their delivery time.[14] The hypermarkets in France have similiar retailer power, such as expecting the manufacturers to be responsible for the layout of the counter displays and/or help in sales promotion, etc.[15]

4 Sometimes producers protect their channel intermediaries against adverse market conditions and thus incur further costs. For example, producers may extend financial aid to intermediaries in difficult market conditions, and though in the short term a high cost is incurred it will pay dividends in the long run in terms of the good producer–manufacturer relationship.

Logistical costs

These refer to transportation, customs administration costs, storage costs and the costs of bulk breaking into smaller units.

Coverage

This refers to the coverage of the market in terms of the number of areas in which the producer's products are represented and the quality of that coverage. In major cities coverage is usually quite easy, however, it is also important for the firm to cover smaller towns and sparsely populated areas. The number of areas that a firm wishes to cover will depend on:

1 the dispersion of demand – concentrated markets will also tend to have concentrated competition as demand attracts suppliers;

2 the time period since the product was introduced to the market.

Coverage can take a number of forms:

1 *intensive*: distributing through the largest number of different types of intermediaries such as agents and wholesalers; it usually involves developing longer channels;

2 *selective*: choosing a number of intermediaries for each section to be covered; as with intensive coverage, longer channels are involved;

3 *exclusive*: involves only one area in a market and direct sales are normally involved.

If the global marketer wants to determine a distributor's or agent's coverage, they will need to examine the following aspects:[16]

1 sales office location, as this will indicate the focus of the intermediary's efforts;

2 salesperson's home base, as they tend to have good penetration of their immediate area;

3 past sales in particular geographic locations, as this is indicative of the intermediary's success in specific geographic areas.

Continuity

Of the four marketing mix decisions that a firm makes, channel design decisions are of a long-term nature and require substantial investment. The continuity of functions provided by the channel member is thus an important criterion for the firm to consider. It is imperative that the channel does not turn out to be unusable for a variety of reasons, due perhaps to competitors, environmental factors, unpredictable events or any other reasons.

For example, in some markets the intermediary may be a small family firm, and if one member opts out of the arrangement it could mean the closure of the company, or it may face financial difficulties or bankruptcy. Or a local intermediary may be dependent on government policy for imports and may be affected by sudden policy changes such as the imposition of exchange controls or the introduction of legal prohibitions on the sale of a product. This may act as a disincentive to the intermediary to commit themselves solely to one supplier.

The onus for retaining continuity rests with the global marketer because many foreign intermediaries tend to have a short-term perspective on the channel relationship. Czinkota and Ronkainen[17] cite the example of Japanese wholesalers who expect the manufacturers to follow up the initial success with continuous product improvement. If not, it is likely that the wholesalers will turn to local suppliers who may have comparable but lower-priced products. If the global marketer can show visible market commitment to the local market this is likely to ensure continuity. This can take many forms such as having a sales subsidiary or even a listing on the local stock exchange.

Character of the product

Channel design and strategy will be affected by the nature of the product attributes in the following ways:

1 perishable goods or those with a short shelf life will entail using shorter channels in order to reach the consumer quickly;

2 products requiring after-sales servicing (i.e. technical products) may result in the firm using direct sales or a trained agent in the market – a short channel;

3 non-perishable products such as soaps, batteries, etc. are likely to use long channels;

4 products with a high unit value are commonly sold by the company's salesforce – i.e. use a short channel; such high unit-price products are normally associated with complex products or those requiring product features to be explained in some detail, e.g. computers;

5 bulky products such as beer and soft drinks require the minimisation of distance and the number of times the products change hands between channel itermediaries before they reach the point of consumption; hence a short channel is best for these types of products.

Whatever the type of channel that is selected, it must be consistent with the overall product positioning strategy in the market, although fluctuations in the market environment may necessitate some changes. For example, a continuous recession may force the company to reposition its product from a very exclusive item to one of semi-luxury, and the corresponding change in distribution channels from upmarket store to general department store.

Product lines also affect the selection of channel members. Broader product lines are likely to result in appointing distributors who tend to stock a broad base of goods. On the other hand, agents will probably be used for narrower product lines because the agent will add the producer's goods to those from other companies.

Communication

Distribution channels require intensive and extensive communication for their smooth functioning. Good communication is an important factor in channel design and it will:

1 ensure that the channel member's activities conform to the company's global strategy;

2 effectively market the firm's products;

3 resolve any conflict situations that may arise.

There are various types of distances between the global marketer and potential distribution partner that may cause problems, and the global marketer must consider all these dimensions when selecting potential channel members. The shorter the distance between the potential channel member and the manufacturer, the better the candidate for the manufacturer. There are five aspects of distance to consider:

1 *geographic distance* – the physical distance separating the two partners, e.g. London to Tokyo or Paris to Sydney;

2 *cultural distance* – the differences in values, norms and behaviour between the two parties, e.g. Germans and Swiss business executives exhibit low-context communications behaviour, while Japanese and Singaporians display high-context communication patterns;

3 *social distance* – this refers to the degree of familiarity with each partner's operating methods, e.g. July is generally a holiday month in Norway in which little business activity is carried out, while in Islamic nations the Ramadan period of fasting is generally a quiet period when serious business is not conducted;

4 *temporal distance* – this measures the length of time between the placement of an order and the actual delivery of the product. The transportation and telecommunications revolution has reduced the length of time between an order placement and delivery – it is now possible to mail order a product from the USA and have delivery to the UK in a few days;

5 *technological distance* – this refers to the dimensions of compatibility, competitiveness, product experience and quality of product lines carried by the potential intermediary and the differences in process technologies between the two parties, e.g. exports from Zimbabwe are perceived as inferior to exports from the USA.

Effective communication can be achieved in the following ways:

1 personal communication – telephone calls, visits, faxes, visits by the manufacturer are important in reinforcing personal bonds between the parties;

2 exchange of personnel – these again increase the bonds between the distribution partners;

3 impersonal communication – corporate magazines or newsletters;

4 international and regional meetings – a useful forum for the exchange of information on strategic issues and marketing policies, and very useful for exchanging experiences.

The need for good communications between distribution partners is not lost on Japanese companies such as Honda, who spend up to 50 per cent of their working time talking and visiting distributors, agents and dealers. Given that the international distribution system is subject to a lot of interference, the global marketer must design a distribution system that ensures good information flow.

Control

Channel control is crucially important for global companies who want to establish global brands, a quality image and a consistent service. Ideally, the manufacturer would like maximum control which can occur only if it creates its own distribution network. The company needs to consider the trade-off between the degree of control and the level of resources commitment – more control implies higher costs of involvement:[18]

- different types of channel configuration will entail different degrees of control by the producer; the use of intermediaries will lead to the loss of some degree of control. If the relationship between the producer and intermediary is fairly loose, then the producer's ability to exert control is somewhat diminished

- the establishment of a manufacturer's sales office and the use of its own direct sales force means that control over price, promotion and outlets will not be relinquished by the manufacturer. However, it is most likely that in the early stages of market entry, the producer will use an intermediary to capitalise on their expert knowledge of the local market and business networks. However, as the producer gains experience and market sales increase, they will establish a sales office in the local market

- longer channels make it more difficult for the manufacturer to have any degree of control

- product or service type also determines the degree of control that can be exercised. With high-tech and industrial products control is easier as the intermediary is dependent on the producer

- an integrated distribution network will be used where a high level of service is required[19] – important for a product which requires long training for both seller and consumer.

Thus the price of more control for the manufacturer is higher costs; in addition, the exercise of control is more commonly a major source of conflict between distribution partners than any of the multitude of activities in the distribution relationship.

Customer characteristics

Given that channels create utility for customers, it is not surprising that customer characteristic is an important influence on channel design. It is probably the first criterion to consider in evaluating which channel represents the optimum for the firm in the overseas market. The global marketer needs to consider customer:

- numbers
- shopping habits
- reaction to different selling techniques
- income
- geographical distribution.

Needs of the above will naturally vary for different countries and consequently require different channel systems, and an appropriate channel implementation will give the manufacturer the competitive advantage. The distribution decision is affected by the customers' purchasing habits. Supermarkets will not be an ideal channel in India because many consumers cannot afford refrigerators or cars. Danone yoghurt is sold and distributed differently in Europe, the USA and Asia,[20] utilising self-service discount stores with spacious food areas in France and Germany, but using street markets or shopping malls in Hong Kong because consumers tend to purchase their food once a day.

Regardless of the stage of economic development, markets with a large number of customers will require multiple channel intermediaries. The converse situation also applies – as the number of consumers decreases, so does the need for intermediaries.

Customer characteristics may also force producers to focus on specific geographical segments. The French beer, Kronenbourg, entered the US market initially in the centre of New York and then extended to the metropolitan areas. Within five years, this beer was available nationally. The company catered to New York City's preference for imported products.

Culture

Of all the elements of the marketing mix, distribution is perhaps the most deeply rooted in culture, as it relates to relationships and everyday life.[21] When the global

---

Box 15.3   ESCOM

Escom, the German computer manufacturer and retailer, will close 65 of its High Street stores in the UK as part of its restructuring programme to reduce its losses. The company will still retain 170 stores in the UK which it had originally acquired from Rumbelows in 1995 as part of its European expansion strategy. The company specialises in cut-price multi-media PCs targeted at the home market. However, the PC market has slowed in Germany and the company has faced intense competition from Compaq, IBM and Dell. It is expected to face full-year net losses of DM125m ($81.5m) attributed to falling PC sales, price cuts and write-downs. Analysts have suggested that the company over-reached itself in the UK and other European markets as a result of its aggressive expansion plans.

Source: Taylor, P., 'Computer maker to close 65 stores', *Financial Times* (2 July 1996).

marketer designs a distribution channel they need to analyse in depth the distribution culture of the local market. Understanding the distribution culture entails an extensive analysis of the:

- existing distribution *structures* to gain entry
- *functions* performed by the intermediaries
- the *relationships* between channel members
- local *legislation* affecting intermediaries.

Complementary skills

In deciding which type of channel member to select, the global marketer will be influenced by the potential channel member's possession of complementary skills or expertise that could enhance its rapid entry into the market. Jeannet and Hennessey[22] cite the example of Compaq when it entered the global PC market. Compaq decided to sell through a network of capable authorised dealers to penetrate the market as they had strong sales and execution expertise, whilst the company focused on developing its products, marketing and technical expertise. This type of synergistic activity can increase the total output of the distribution system.

Competition

Gaining access to distribution channels poses a formidable challenge to the global marketer as it is critical to the implementation of the firm's marketing strategy. It is often the case that the most obvious channel distributor already has a relationship with your competitor and thus limiting access to the system. The assessment of the competition is an important criterion for global marketers in determining the company's channel design and strategy. Channel competition can occur in a number of ways:

1 through competitor products placed side by side in supermarket shelves;
2 through competitors (domestic and foreign) either blocking access or making it extremely difficult for other producers to enter the distribution system, especially if that distribution system is one that is commonly accepted by both consumers and traders. Czinkota and Ronkainen[23] cite the case of US suppliers of soda ash (used in steel, glass and chemical products) who were unable to gain entry into the Japanese market in spite of a price advantage. The main cause for this difficulty was the Japan Soda Industry Association's cartel control over the industry. It set the level of imports, specified which Japanese trading company was to work with which US supplier and purchased cheap US imports to sell to the intermediaries at higher prices. The Japanese Association gained in two respects: first, it received the profits and, second, it kept control of the market. The US producers tried to sell directly to the small and unaffiliated Japanese distributors, but this was unsuccessful as they were not prepared to risk cutting themselves off from their main Japanese suppliers. This is not a surprising reaction as relationships between manufacturers and intermediaries in Japan are of a long-standing nature and such allegiances do not change quickly, in spite of a better product or service.

A 'locked-up' channel is when a newcomer to the market cannot persuade any channel member to take on their products or service, in spite of sound economic and marketing reasons.

Other reasons why a channel may be locked-up are:

1 some intermediaries such as wholesalers do not have the flexibility to add or drop a product line, partly because they have an exclusive agreement with the supplier or because they may not want to risk upsetting a producer with whom they do a substantial volume of business;

2 channel ownership by local competitors is another reason for blocked access. In Japan, for example, most of the wholesalers of household electrical appliances are owned by the major manufacturers;

3 some intermediaries like retailers may select only products and brands for which there is a demand, and therefore avoid any real 'selling' of the producer's products. It will also be consistent for them to switch suppliers when the opportunity suits them. This practice of 'cherry-picking' can be detrimental to producers wishing to break into a market with new products, but is rational for the intermediaries as they are in the business to maximise their own profits.

It may therefore be necessary for the global company to improvise and use a totally different approach from its competitors in the market. This may entail more resource commitment and risks than the company had originally anticipated, such as engaging in a joint venture or forming a marketing strategic alliance to overcome the barriers. However, it is not always possible to manipulate these obstacles – for example, alcohol in Sweden must be distributed through the state-owned monopoly outlets. Finding alternative approaches to distribution entry is discussed later on in the chapter.

Box 15.4   **WALL'S**

Wall's relationship with its exclusive ice-cream wholesale distributors is being investigated by the UK's Office of Fair Trading (OFT). This follows complaints from its main competitors namely Mars, Nestlé, Lyons Maid and some wholesalers and distributors. Competitors allege that exclusivity agreements with many distributors and retailers have helped Wall's maintain nearly 70 per cent market share of the £250m a year market for impulse ice-cream (wrapped products bought for immediate consumption). It has been said that Wall's awards exclusive territories to wholesalers but demands that they sell only its products. However, Lyons Maid and Mars have developed successful ice-cream products, and the wholesalers and retailers now want to stock other products apart from Wall's range. The investigation could force Wall's owners, Unilever, to weaken Wall's ties with the wholesale trade.

Source: Oram, R., 'OFT probes Wall's distribution', *Financial Times* (12 January 1996).

Channel power

We have briefly discussed above how some competitors can block distribution channels by having either well established product lines or exclusive contracts with current channel members. The global distributor needs to be aware of the influence of 'power' structures in the distribution systems when designing their channel systems. There are two major dimensions of channel power.

1 Intermediaries can form a cartel and thus gain the ability to control the activities within the channel. Trade associations have been able to close the distribution system or successfully restrict channel alternatives of new entrants, for example, in some European beer markets.

2 The second aspect concerns the distribution of power between producers and intermediaries.This type of power relationship affects the global marketer's capacity to control the implementation of its channel strategies. The power relationship will vary between different countries and from one product market to another. The seven largest retail agents for supermarkets in France control over 80 per cent of the market, for example.[24] They thus have enormous power over the producers' strategic plans. Such retailers may expect incentives from producers before they agree to carry their products, and it may be necessary for the global marketer faced with such odds when entering a lucrative market to devise innovative entry strategies.

Accessing distribution channels

As discussed under Competition and channel power above, newcomers to a market may face barriers to entry to the distribution system. Access to the channels may be blocked because of competitor or government actions, as discussed. The global marketer faced with these kinds of obstacles can find ways to overcome them by developing innovative approaches to entry, as follows.

Acquisitions

The foreign producer can buy equity in an intermediary. For example, in Japan it is possible to do this via the banks who have joint ownership with large intermediary groups. A 10 per cent share is sufficient to enable the foreign producer to become part of the distribution network. It can, conversely, acquire a company in the local market to gain instant access to the distribution channels. The main criteria in choosing a company in this context would be its good relationship with the intermediaries or its own well established distribution channel. For example, Nestlé, the giant Swiss multinational company, pursued an acquisition strategy in 1988 and bought the UK confectionery manufacturer Rowntree Mackintosh. Not only did the company acquire a well-established distribution network but it also acquired some world brands. This is in itself a major advantage, since shelf space is scarce in supermarkets and consumers now focus on one or two major brands in the market which have become highly valued commodities in acquisitions. The Ford Motor Corporation acquired a 35 per cent stake in a Japanese national distributor, Autorama in 1989, to expand its sales in Japan.

Set up a new distribution venture

A producer can set up a direct distribution organisation to gain a share of the market. This is not only an expensive operation but requires patience and time to achieve the necessary objectives. However, once the producer gains market share of the intended target segment, it can relinquish the direct distribution network and persuade independent intermediaries to take on its now attractive products, which may be more cost-effective in the long run. A European truck manufacturer, IVECO, jointly owned by Fiat of Italy and Klockner–Humboldt–Deutz of Germany entered the US market by setting up its own distribution network. In 1990, Toys 'Я' Us opened its own retail outlet in Japan. An alternative to setting up one's own direct distribution system is to use a current distributor's own sales force.[25] The distributor may assign a sales representative to the manufacturer's products and the producer then agrees to subsidise the cost of this representative. The advantage of this approach for the producer is to hold costs down, as selling is done within the distributor's existing sales team and physical distribution network. The incentive for the distributor to get involved in such a co-operative arrangement is twofold. The new product can be a profitable addition to their product portfolio, and they obtain a 'free' sales person.

Original equipment manufacturer (OEM)

An OEM agreement occurs when an international producer supplies products to a local firm, who in turn sells the products under the local firm's established brand name. In this way, the international manufacturer gains access to the local firm's distribution network, while the local firm has an opportunity to widen its product range. There are numerous examples of OEM arrangements and Japanese companies have been very prominent in this respect. Matsushita sold its video recorders through OEM arrangements with major US companies like General Electric, RCA, etc. In recent times both Korean and Taiwanese companies like Acer have had OEM arrangements with European companies. However, there are drawbacks to OEM arrangements. As the international manufacturer's own label is not on the product, it will not get the exposure to local consumers and hence no brand identity in the market. The manufacturer will forgo control and independent channel decision making, although it does gain in volume turnover and saving expenditure on forming its own network which is why it presumably had an OEM tie-up in the first place. Finally, the manufacturer's fortunes in the market will depend on the efforts and performance of the local firm. This may be detrimental, as happened when the Japanese car manufacturer Mitsubishi had an OEM arrangement to supply compact cars to the USA's Chrysler Corporation. Chrysler had a weak run from 1983 to 1985 and no doubt Mitsubishi would have preferred to sell its cars direct to the USA.[26]

'Piggybacking' (joint marketing)

This occurs when a firm enters into a collaborative arrangement with a major manufacturer in a similar field, i.e. when one producer (the 'carrier') uses their established overseas distribution network to market the goods of another producer (the 'rider') alongside their own. The carrier can act as an agent by selling the rider's products on a commission basis; or they can act as a merchant and buy the products outright to re-sell them. This arrangement is extremely useful for firms who have difficulty in getting intermediaries to pioneer new products for them; in addition, the firm retains marketing control, especially over pricing and product positioning. 'Piggybacking' was used extensively by small high-tech electronics and biotechnology companies in the UK in the 1980s. In Japan, Sony is a carrier for a number of European and US firms. There are some drawbacks to this type of collaboration, such as the rider's products taking second priority to the carrier's product line. A detailed analysis of this mode of entry is given in Chapter 11.

Joint ventures

These are projects in which two or more parties invest and form a new legal entity especially in production activities, as discussed in Chapter 11. In the context of distribution joint ventures, an international manufacturer with no market access will form a venture with a local firm which has access to the distribution network. Many foreign firms have had to form joint ventures with Japanese partners in a similar but not competitive field to enter the Japanese market. The classic example is Kodak's joint venture with Nagase Sangyo, an Osaka trading company specialising in chemicals, to compete against its main rival Fuji in Japan.[27]

Franchising

Discussed extensively in Chapter 11, this is another alternative distribution entry strategy to rapidly enter and overcome traditional channel obstacles. Companies have successfully exploited franchising as a method of market entry in the global sphere. Although US companies such as McDonald's, Hertz, 7-Up, etc. dominate this field of activity, European companies have proved immensely successful with franchising such as Benetton of Italy and The Body Shop of the UK.

Other alternatives

Mail order and electronic marketing are among the alternatives to traditional channels.

Channel management

The previous sections examined how the global marketer must assess different factors in designing its channel configuration, and be aware of any changes in the character of the market place that may impact on the distribution network.

Channel management is concerned with reaching the company's intended target market segments. Managing direct distribution (i.e. when the firm sells direct to the retailer or final end user) is probably the easiest to manage. The company is relatively in control of the channel and has flexibility to respond to changing market conditions.

However, when the firm needs to deal with independent intermediaries, the firm's task becomes one of co-operation rather then control – i.e. it needs to maintain cordial relationships and minimise conflicts with its intermediaries. Conflict can arise from interpretation of duties, invoicing errors, etc.; this is critical because the company's success in the market depends on how well independent intermediaries do their job. This process is all the more arduous as the firm's competitive position and market conditions will vary from country to country, and the relationship has to be managed for a long period. The major responsibility of the global marketer is therefore to help the intermediaries to do their job and to make the relationship continually rewarding to them and to the firm. We now turn to some of the major issues that need to be addressed, such as intermediary selection, performance evaluation and control, so that the firm can achieve an integrated and responsive distribution network.

SELECTION OF INTERMEDIARIES

Once the channel design has been determined the international marketer needs to know what type of intermediary is required, and to find reliable intermediaries.

The global marketer faces two choices when determining the type of intermediaries.

1 What type of relationship should the manufacturer have – an agent or distributor? *Agents* generally operate on a commission basis, do not normally take title to the goods or carry stock, and take no responsibility for credit risks. There are many different types of agent, each with specific characteristics. *Distributors* are customers who have been given exclusive or preferential rights to purchase and re-sell a specific range of products from a supplier organisation. Distributors are, in effect, wholesalers whose remuneration comes from the difference between the purchase and resale price. In addition, they offer manufacturers a comprehensive marketing service.

2 What type of market entry should the global marketer select – direct exporting, indirect exporting or integrated distribution? *Indirect exporting* means that the firm sells to an intermediary within the domestic market, who in turn re-sells the goods to a customer abroad. *Direct exporting* occurs when the firm sells to a customer abroad, who may be the final user of the product or service or to an agent or distributor. *Integrated distribution* occurs when the firm invests abroad, such as in a sales office or distribution hub, to sell its products. Details and the implications of the different types of intermediaries have already been examined at length in Chapter 11, and will not be discussed further here.

As in a marriage, choosing the right intermediary will be a major factor in the success of the relationship. The global marketer in attempting to identify suitable candidates can be guided by a criteria list as illustrated in Table 15.2. The actual criteria used will

Table 15.2 SELECTED CRITERIA FOR CHOOSING AN INTERNATIONAL DISTRIBUTOR

Characteristics	Weight	Rating
Goals and strategies		
Size of the firm		
Financial strength		
Reputation		
Trading areas covered		
Compatibility		
Experience		
Sales organisations		
Physical facilities		
Willingness to carry inventories		
After-sales service capability		
Use of promotion		
Sales performance		
Relations with local government		
Communication		
Overall attitude		

Source: Root, F.R., 'Foreign market entry strategies', *American Management Association* (New York, 1983), 74–5.

vary by the type of product sold, and by industry. Obviously the list will be weighted according to the exporter's own determinants of a successful intermediary. The weights assigned each criterion and the ratings given to potential channel partici- pants depend on the company's distribution objectives and the nature of its business in given markets. It should be said that not all potential intermediaries in a particular market will match the firm's specifications equally well, and thus the firm may not be able to create the optimal channel arrangement it desires. It may be the case that the company would like supermarkets as intermediaries, for example, but these may not exist in some emerging economies. The criteria should help the global marketer avoid serious mistakes in selection, though it must be said that it is not uncommon for firms to select intermediaries without sufficient care. In addition, the global marketer should employ the following set of key criteria to assess the suitability of potential channel members.

Financial strength

The prospective intermediary must be financially sound and this involves both credit standing and cash flow position (this can be checked through credit rating services and references). This should indicate whether the distributor is performing its tasks adequately – i.e. making money, an ability to support its own operations without out- side financial assistance and the strength and will to take the risks involved.

Sales performance

The distributor's current sales record is a good indicator of potential sales volumes with respect to the global marketer's product line. To some extent, it also indicates the ability and quality of the management and sales teams.

Geographic and customer coverage

The market coverage is critical to assess for the global marketer, and should include the type of territory covered, the type of segments and how well they are served. Does the salesforce makes visits to customers and clients, and what type of personnel they visit – i.e. only purchasing agents or operational personnel as well? The latter is an extremely important aspect of customer service in a very competitive global market.

Product lines and product compatibility

It may be the case that both parties are interested if their products are complemen- tary, especially in industrial markets where the end users are looking for complete product or service systems. Another aspect to consider is whether there is a 'quality match' for products. This is important for promotional reasons, especially if the global marketer wants to have a high-quality positioning strategy, so it needs to ensure that the distributor is reputable. The global marketer also needs to consider how many product lines the intermediary is handling, as this is indicative of the amount of effort that may be put into your products. Its not unnatural that a distributor will tend to be active with products that are highly profitable, without too much selling involved.

Good connections

In many markets today business is conducted on a personal basis and is a key success factor. For intermediaries to be effective they should be well connected in both government and private circles and are regarded as respectable business persons. Trading in the Asia Pacific markets requires good connections to get a foothold in the system. To trade in China, businessmen accept the notion of 'Guanxi' ('connections') if they want to succeed in business in that market.

Facilities and equipment

The number and quality of the intermediaries' physical facilities should be adequate and properly located. The reputation of the global firm in the local market will depend on the provision of such facilities.

Professionalism

Both the distributor and the firm must conduct themselves professionally and adhere to proper ethical behaviour. The firm can enquire about the distributor's reputation by getting in touch with customers, suppliers, the local business community, etc. In addition, the firm needs to treat the distributor as an independent entity; this means that future strategies need to be discussed in conjunction with the intermediary in all aspects of the business from credit facilities, delivery schedules, warranty, technical and marketing support to after sales service, etc. What the expectations are from both sides should be clearly articulated.

The distributor's attitude is also important to gauge, especially with respect to commitment and co-operation with the manufacturer. If the potential channel member appears willing to engage in joint market planing, this is should be a good indication of a positive and supportive attitude. Before final contractual arrangements are made, it is an absolute necessity to visit a prospective channel member. This will give the firm an opportunity to assess the potential distributor's facilities and see their customers and other interested parties.

MOTIVATION

An important aspect of global distribution management is to keep the channel participants motivated, but this process is made more difficult because:

- of geographic and cultural distance
- channel members are not owned by the firm
- intermediaries are there to achieve their own goals which may not match the manufacturer's objectives for that specific country
- intermediaries will maximise their own profits from their choice of products and services, which may be from different companies.

There are many different ways of motivating intermediaries.

The monetary package

A powerful inducement is to offer higher than average gross margins, as the intermediary is there to make money by handling the firm's product. Other ways of motivating distribution partners include larger commissions, more advantageous credit terms, contributions towards promotional costs, etc. Other non-monetary rewards can contribute to superior performance as well as giving recognition and encouragement. These can include visits to the country of the producers, perhaps combined with a tourist itinerary.

Effective communication links

Building effective channels of communication between the manufacturer and the intermediary is critical for developing a long-term relationship. It creates a sense of being part of an organisation and distributor loyalty. This can be achieved by in-house newsletters, magazines, conferences, personal visits to headquarters, discussions of various policy objectives between the two parties, provision of on-line communications systems with intermediaries which can provide real-time information and reduced transaction time, conference calling facilities, which will help distributors and customers solve problems and spot opportunities, etc. All these will help generate a strong corporate 'culture' or 'spirit' among the many distributors. Rosson and Ford[28] found that distributor performance was at an optimum when there was a high degree of contact and decisions were made jointly between the producer and the intermediary. Periodic visits to intermediaries can have positive effects on motivation, for face-to-face contact will strengthen the personal relationship between the producer and distributor. Furthermore, the company can use such visits to resolve any problems that may have arisen and it also sends a clear signal to the distributors that their performance is important to the firm.

Marketing support

Strong promotional support and extensive advertising on a national level by the producer, or co-operative advertising with the intermediary, all make the distributor's job easier. In addition, participation in national or regional trade fairs and a regular supply of product and promotional material will all contribute to strengthened motivation and increased sales, and perhaps ensure that more attention is devoted to the manufacturer's product lines.

Training programme

This involves the training of intermediary staff in product knowledge, product know-how, sales, etc. which should contribute to an effective operation. Caterpillar found that its dealer training programme increased revenues by over 100 per cent for its dealers and thus gave it a competitive edge against its main Japanese rival, Komatsu.[29] Some firms even provide sales personnel to assist retailers, as in some Japanese department stores.

EVALUATION OF PERFORMANCE AND CONTROL

One of the major tasks of channel management is the regular evaluation and measurement of the performance of channel participants. Naturally, realistic and achievable performance standards should be set. These should include a number of areas such as sales volume per product or product line within a time period, market share, inventory level, number of accounts per sales territory, price targets, introduction of new products, etc. Evaluation should be seen as a diagnostic exercise to highlight weaknesses rather than as a punitive measure.

To ensure an effective implementation of the company's marketing strategy, some form of control over channel members will need to be exercised. To control the activities of intermediaries and avoid conflict, the firm must ensure that its corporate objectives are clearly communicated to its channel members. A firm can attempt to control through a number of ways:

1 to articulate clearly the specific responsibilities of each channel member and also have clear performance objectives as outlined above;

2 to have regular meetings and a report programme;

3 to award exclusive dealerships and prohibit the intermediary from carrying competitor products. This can be an effective method of control, as the dealer becomes dependent on the company. The producer's leverage is the product's patent and brand name, whilst the dealer's leverage is expertise and knowledge of that market. The British company producing the Filofax diaries had an exclusive dealer arrangement with a Japanese company, Apex Inc., in 1984, and this proved to be a profitable arrangement.[30]

The evaluation of performance and control against some agreed criteria needs to be interpreted with caution, as changing environmental conditions can prevent some objectives being achieved. However, if unsatisfactory performance is established, then this can result in the termination of the contract, but it can be a costly and complicated procedure in many parts of the world. Terminating an agreement in Belgium can be an extremely costly affair: intermediaries need three months' notice, can be entitled to compensation for expenses in developing the business, plus the value of any goodwill, and compensation payments to discharged employees. It is essential, therefore, that the original contracts should follow the standardised format acceptable within the country concerned (including any special points peculiar to that particular legal system) and be drawn up by a native lawyer in the host country. The standardised contract format is usually available through the home/host country Chamber of Trade and Industry.

However, it must be said that in spite of all the control mechanisms that can be put in place, manufacturers using independent distributors will have great difficulty in controlling them; it is difficult for a manufacturer to make sales forecasts, sales targets, etc. when it is unlikely to have access to the distributor's book or other records. The producer should use motivational methods rather than depending on control mechanisms to optimise intermediary performance.

'GREY' MARKETS

Many authorised channel members are facing a growing phenomenon known as the *'grey' market* or *parallel importation* which can be defined as follows:

> A grey market generally consists of those unauthorised distributors and dealers that circumvent authorised channel arrangements by buying a company's products in low-price markets and selling them in high-price markets at lower prices than those offered by authorised channel members.[31]

'Grey' market activities are not perceived as illegal by governments but are of great concern to multinational companies as they affect the company's distribution strategies and impact negatively on authorised channel members revenues. Products traded on the grey market range from consumer items such as watches, cameras and cars, to capital goods such as spare parts for aircrafts and mechanical diggers. The value of the 'grey' market in the USA has been recently estimated to be around $8–$10bn at retail.[32] Figure 15.3 shows the flow of a 'grey' market such as Seiko watches through authorised and unauthorised dealers.

Fig 15.3 'GREY' MARKET CHANNELS FOR SEIKO WATCHES

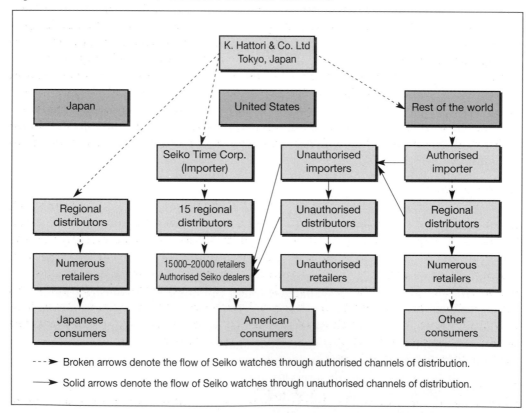

---► Broken arrows denote the flow of Seiko watches through authorised channels of distribution.

——► Solid arrows denote the flow of Seiko watches through unauthorised channels of distribution.

Source: Kaikati, J., 'Parallel importation: a growing conflict in international channels of distribution', Symposium on Export–Import Interrelationships, Georgetown University (14–15 November 1985).

Conditions for the 'grey' market

There are a number of factors which account for the rapid rise of the 'grey' market.

Existence of standardised products

In recent years global companies have adopted standardised product strategies to attain competitive advantages in global markets. These standardised products are then sold in different markets or to different customers at different prices. If products are priced higher in one country, for example, in France, the 'grey' marketer will purchase those goods in Asia Pacific or the USA, and then re-sell them at a discount to the French market at anywhere between 10 and 50 per cent below the list price, depending on the value of the product. In 1996, compact discs (CDs) sold for an average price of £10.00 per CD in the UK market, while for an average of $10 in the USA. Whatever the reasons for the anomaly in price structures, this large price differential is bound to attract 'grey' market activities. 'Grey' markets respond to market differences and anomalies more swiftly than the multinational firms.

Exchange rate fluctuations

Foreign currency fluctuations are another major source for 'grey' market activities. When companies implement their global pricing strategies, it is done with particular exchange rates. But every time exchange rates fluctuate, prices are not necessarily changed, as this would be impractical and very disruptive. Price differentials then occur, and when the differences between selected currencies are large enough this presents an opportunity for 'grey' marketers. One of the most celebrated cases concerns Caterpillar excavators and loaders in 1984–5.[33] During the period in question, the value of the US dollar was strong against other currencies; Caterpillar products built in Belgium, Japan and Scotland were imported into the USA and sold at prices 15 per cent lower than for the same equipment built in US plants. The converse situation occurred in 1987–8 when the Japanese yen was strong, and a 'grey' market developed in Japan for re-imported Japanese products such as cameras, television sets and cordless phones.[34]

Surplus products

If a distributor in one market is faced with an excess supply of a particular product, they may wish to dispose of this surplus to an international intermediary for less than the average margin to recoup some of their investments. An added incentive for the distributor to get rid of the stock is that, if they re-export the stock, they may obtain rebates on import duties and value added taxes, as is the case with EU countries. On the other hand, product shortages may also cause 'grey' markets to emerge; but in this situation it is more than likely that the 'grey' market goods will cost more than those that are obtainable from authorised dealers. In 1988, US computer manufacturers obtained their supply of DRAMs from unauthorised dealers in order to avert a shutdown of their production lines.[35]

Pricing strategies

'Grey' markets can also develop because there are price differences for the same product in different markets, not due to exchange rate fluctuations but deliberately established by the manufacturer as part of its global distribution and pricing strategy.

The price of the same model of camera is higher in the UK than in either Hong Kong or Singapore, and an independent UK dealer can obtain the camera at a lower price from a Singaporean distributor than the authorised UK camera intermediary.

Customer service requirements

To remain competitive, some manufacturers have increased their costs by having distributors maintain inventory parts to satisfy customer requirements, having store personnel trained in product knowledge and allocating store space for product demonstrations. All these activities will add value by developing brand preference and repeat business. These augmented product services will enhance the value of the product in question, and 'grey' marketers will become free riders on these services. IBM is one company that has such service commitments.[36]

The 'grey' market debate

Naturally there are proponents and opponents of 'grey' activities. Opponents of 'grey' marketing argue that:

1 the presence of 'grey' markets will encourage 'free riders' – i.e. taking advantage of manufacturer's trade mark and branding promotional investments;

2 consumers will suffer from parallel imports because they do not provide the normal guarantees or warranty-related services;

3 the owners of branded products and trade marks will suffer from loss of revenues; this could deter future investment in product development and the manufacturer will not reap the benefits of their marketing and promotional investments and ultimately, the consumer will suffer from the lack of product innovation;

4 the continued existence of 'grey' markets will eventually impact negatively on manufacturer–distributor relations.

On the other hand, the proponents of 'grey' activities argue that the very existence of 'grey' markets indicates that some manufacturers are overpricing in some markets; furthermore, these activities constitute 'free trade'. Consumers and those discount distributors who have found a niche segment will benefit. Argos is a UK discount store which sells some branded products at prices less than those charged by the authorised channel members. However, Argos is now finding it increasingly difficult to obtain supplies from the manufacturers of branded products, who do not wish to deal with them.

Response to 'grey' markets

It is expensive and time-consuming to track down 'grey' marketers; in fact, some of these activities are carried out by authorised dealers in the channel system, who subsequently lose the dealer franchise. Global manufacturers and authorised dealers have a number of options to deal with this problem.

Legal response

One option for manufacturers and distributors is to prosecute 'grey' marketers, although this option is long and drawn out, not to mention expensive. Only a few companies have been successful to date – for example, Seiko won an injunction against a New York department store.[37] Some court rulings have resulted in decisions in favour of the manufacturers, but leaving certain doors open for 'grey' activities to continue. In 1983, the US International Trade Commission recommended a ban on importing Duracell alkaline batteries from Belgium into the USA, but this was overturned by President Reagan on the grounds of free trade. Seeking legal means is thus fraught with difficulties and unsatisfactory results.

Ignore the problem

This may appear as an irresponsible and feeble strategy. However, there are sound reasons for this approach. As shown above, taking 'grey' marketers to court is difficult, costly and unsatisfactory, and customers may switch brands if they are unable to purchase the manufacturer's products at the discounted price. Some manufacturers and dealers also hope that external factors such as fluctuating exchange rates will minimise differential prices and therefore remove the problem.

Adapt the manufacturer's marketing strategies

Producers can modify their marketing mix strategies to counter this problem. With respect to the *pricing strategy*, the producer can:

1 change the price charged to authorised distributors to minimise the price differences;

2 restructure their discount schemes to deter dealers overstocking to get lower prices, because they may then sell unsold inventory on the 'grey' market and still obtain a margin;

3 have a standardised policy in all major markets, this would entail selling at the lowest price possible regardless of market size and location, and it also implies choosing a very efficient distribution system to implement this strategy;

4 offer price incentives to consumers – the Swedish camera company, Hasselblad, offered rebates to customers who purchased legally imported and serial numbered cameras and parts.[38]

With respect to its *product strategy*, the producer can manufacture different versions of the product for specific markets, and perhaps offer different names and warranties. Minolta and Olympus, for example, produce identical cameras specifically for the US market. This strategy is feasible only if the market is large enough to attain marketing and production economies. Finally, with respect to the *distribution strategy*, a manufacturer can threaten to disenfranchise dealers who are found to deal in the 'grey' market.

JAPANESE DISTRIBUTION CHANNELS

The purpose of focusing on the Japanese distribution channel is to illustrate how each country has its own unique distribution system which has evolved over many years, i.e. is country-specific. Japan is a major economic power today, and succeeding in that market is imperative for many companies if they are to remain globally competitive. Global marketers need to be aware that they cannot enforce their ideas of what,

Fig 15.4 CHANNELS FOR SOAP IN JAPAN

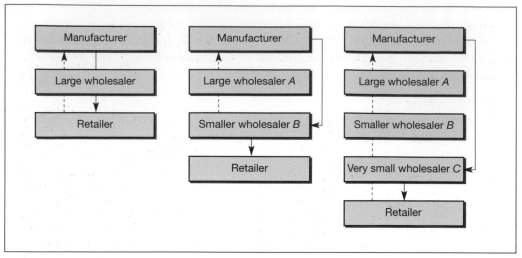

Source: Czinkota, M.R., 'Distribution of consumer products in Japan: an overview', *International Marketing Review*, 2 (1985), 39–51.

constitutes an optimum system in other markets, and must make efforts to 'fit' into the country's established patterns of operations.

The Japanese system has been described as complex, outmoded, inefficient and cumbersome, but what is clear is that, their distribution system is highly fragmented, encompassing numerous retail firms and different layers of wholesalers (many are small organisations and employ fewer than four people). Their distribution system would appear to be a confused and at times illogical structure, but Keegan[39] prefers to describe it as a highly developed structure which has evolved over time to satisfy the needs of the Japanese consumer.

The myriad of channel members differ more in number than in function when compared to their European and US counterparts. Figure 15.4 shows a variety of distribution alternatives for a simple consumer item like soap, and how it may move through three wholesalers before it reaches the retail outlet. Figure 15.5 shows how Japan has traditionally been segregated by product type and the subsequent development of many specialised marketing channels. Meat stores conduct about 80 per cent of their business in meat items, for example, and this generally applies to other specialist products as well; this specialisation occurs at both the wholesale and retail level. In spite of Japan's immense economic achievement, the distribution system has retained its antique structure.

Description of the system

What follows is a brief description of some of the most salient points of the Japanese system.

Personal relationships

The Japanese distribution network places great emphasis on the development of strong personal relationships with users to ensure both stable supply and prices over a

Fig 15.5 FLOWCHARTS OF SELECTED DISTRIBUTION CHANNELS IN JAPAN

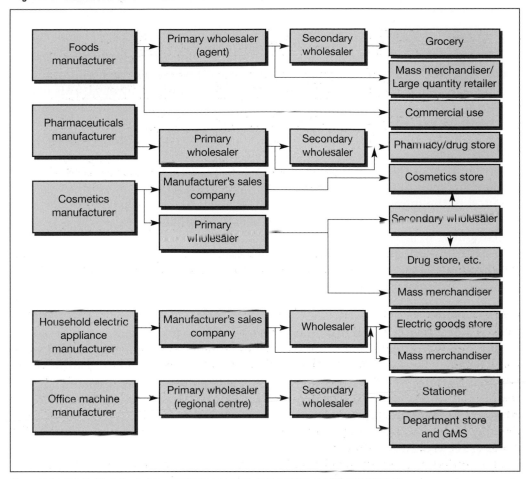

Source: Kobayashi, K., 'Marketing in Japan: distribution channels', *Tradepai International* (Winter 1980), 23.

long period, as opposed to the product satisfaction and price competitiveness in the European and the US systems. This strong relationship of service, loyalty and commitment to consumers is passed on to the whole distribution structure through the retailers to wholesalers and to producers.[40] This type of distribution channelling structure which vertically links the different intermediaries is known as a *Keiretsu*.

Credit and payment
Firms in the distribution arrangement operate with limited equity capital and much debt, which explains in part why the system has endured. Producers supply goods to wholesalers in return for promissory notes for up to six months. This type of deferred payment is known as *Tegatas*, and it allows wholesalers to manage on small amounts of capital. Credit is liberally extended throughout the distribution system, much as in France and Italy. The implication of this structure is that financial responsibility is a collective issue and not just an individual one, and thus, failure by one person will

have a chain reaction effect on the system. We can see here how the financial arrangements complement the distribution system.

Sale or return
The Japanese have an extremely liberal regime regarding the right to return unsold goods. Retailers take back goods from customers, and wholesalers are willing to take back unsold goods, even when they are not defective, from the retailers. This reflects the strong links of the distribution system to give the best service to the consumer and the close ties among many Japanese companies.

Delivery
High frequency of deliveries is very much part of the system. Wholesalers sell to retailers in small quantities at regular intervals; this is due to the limited financial resources of the intermediaries, the competition and a tradition of close personal contact amongst the intermediaries who trade with each other.[41] This system also serves the customers well. Many Japanese homes are small and lack storage space, and consequently they shop several times a week. The Japanese consumer also demands a very high level of service – such as availability of credit and free home delivery, long opening hours, right to return non-defective goods, etc.

Cultural values
The *Keiretsu* system is very much influenced by deeply ingrained cultural values in the society. The vertical structure of the *Keiretsu* reflects the importance of vertical structures in Japanese society. The emphasis on strong personal relationships in the distribution system also reflects the wider societal values of close dependency and high expectations: hence the frequent contact between producers and wholesalers to retailers which fosters close human relationships.

Criticism of the Japanese distribution system

Three main criticisms have been made by foreign companies:[42]

1 the channel members are in collusion with the public authorities to protect local businesses;

2 the *itten itchoai* system requires retailers to order only from specific wholesalers, who in turn are prohibited from selling to other retailers; in addition, the granting of exclusive dealerships in specific areas has the effect of restricting competition;

3 the system is costly, complex, inefficient and detrimental to the consumer; its continued existence is due to the Japanese desire to exclude foreign competition.

It could be argued that the system is not intentionally a barrier to entry but has simply evolved out of the historical and cultural situation. Keegan[43] goes as far as to suggest that foreign firms make two basic mistakes when dealing with the Japanese distribution system:

1 having an ethnocentric approach to the situation (i.e that distribution problems can be solved by cutting out the middleman and going direct to the customer, as done in the West); it is precisely because of the fragmented nature of the Japanese system that such an approach is not cost-effective;

2 using the trading companies (*Sogo Shosha*) to enter the market; the major problem is that this is an 'arm's-length' approach and the trading company may not really have an interest in furthering the expansion of the foreign firm's product lines except in low volumes to a small segment of the market.

Dealing with the Japanese distribution system

Successful entry in Japan requires acceptance of the market place and extensive market research into competitor products and customer needs as well as a well developed strategic marketing plan. It is not an insurmountable barrier as Ohmae[44] illustrated with the example of a US pharmaceutical company, Shaklee, which employed door-to-door techniques to sell vitamins and nutritive pills. Another US company, William Sonoma, by-passed the *Keiretsu* system by employing catalogue sales and having a limited number of their own retail outlets.[45]

Shimaguchi and Rosenberg[46] suggest a series of steps in order to enter the Japanese distribution system successfully.

1 Find a *Japanese partner*: this is a key success factor, for the partner will be able to guide you through the myriad and complex system. The partner will be an import agent ranging from a small agent to a *Sogo Shosha* (large trading company). A word of caution regarding the choice of trading companies: it is best that they do not represent a competitor's products, or be related to a *zaibatsu* (large conglomerate) which will tend to have competing lines. Furthermore, the foreign firm needs to decide on whether it wishes to ally with a firm in the same industry or a non-related sector. *Prima facie*, the former sector would seem to be the natural choice. However, in the long run, any product development from the joint venture could form the basis for a future competitor.[47]

2 Seek a *competitive positioning strategy*: the firm should offer its products as being unique and foreign, better quality or with price advantages, or all of them.

3 Identify *alternative distribution channels*: Philips marketed its coffee makers and shavers through large retail outlets, such as department stores, and small outlets.

4 Have a *long-term perspective*: firms should expect a long payback period and should therefore be patient.

5 Develop *empathy* and adopt the Japanese management philosophy and outlook, i.e. spend time and resources establishing a network of personal relationships in distribution and build trust and loyalty.

GLOBAL LOGISTICS MANAGEMENT

Logistics management, also called physical distribution management, is about planning, implementing and controlling the physical flows of material and final goods from the point of origin to the point of use to meet customer needs at a profit.[48] In much of the literature, physical distribution is used synonymously with logistics, but we should note that there is a subtle distinction between the two. The former involves the movement of the finished product from the factory floor to the final user at the lowest possible cost. Logistics, on the other hand, is more market oriented – i.e. it takes the customer as its starting point and works backward to the producer.

The major components of physical distribution are management and transportation modes, warehousing, inventory control and order processing. The task of co-ordinating all these activities in the global market place is complex because there are many factors which could impact on the flow of materials and products. However, the area of physical distribution has become a potential source of competitive advantage for firms in the global market place. Management has become concerned about the total cost of physical distribution, which accounts for up to 35 per cent of a company's expenditure. As it is such a high-cost activity, it is believed that substantial savings can be made in this area and, if successful, it can yield higher margins or translate into lower prices. Physical distribution is often perceived as a cost item and is considered to be the last frontier for cost economies. If this area of management is effectively restructured, it can save the firm time, costs, and increase its reliability. Given the potential for using this area as a means of gaining competitive advantages, there is now increased management attention in the logistics area (*see* Box 15.5).

The principal objective of the physical distribution system is to provide dependable and efficient movement of materials and goods from the supplier to the end user. Before this process is implemented the firm has first to decide the service levels it wishes to achieve:

● minimise reaction time between the time of the order and the actual order shipment

● maximise the number of orders received

● minimise the damage in transit

● minimise the difference between promised and actual delivery.

However, no logistical system can maximise customer service and minimise distribution costs at the same time. If the firm wanted to maximise customer service objectives as mentioned above, this would mean that the firm would need to keep large stocks, have multiple warehouses and use transport modes that would have premium rates, all raising distribution costs. Thus physical distribution involves trade-offs and the implication of this is that management decisions must be made from a systems perspective.

We can define global logistics as the design and management of a system that controls the flow of materials and products into and out of global companies. An overview of the logistics function is illustrated in Fig. 15.6. It encompasses the entire range of processes, in particular the relationship of the firm with its suppliers and customers. This systems approach enables the firm to see the linkages between the different functional operations concerned with both material and product movements. The implications of such a systems approach means the firm should be able to implement strategic operations to improve its logistical effectiveness and efficiency. These tools include: JIT delivery, resulting in low stock levels; early supplier involvement (ESI), which improves the movement of products; and electronic data interchange (EDI) for better order processing.[49]

Fig 15.6 THE LOGISTICS FUNCTION

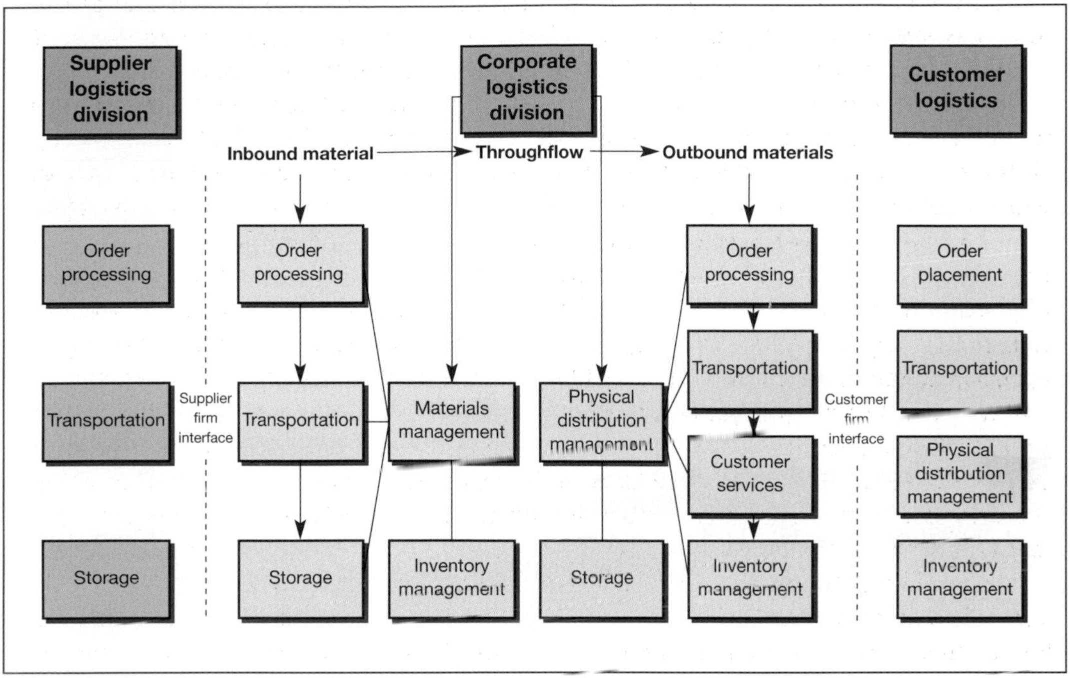

Source: Czinkota, M.R. and Ronkainen, I.A., *Global Marketing* (Orlando: The Dryden Press, 1996), 476.

The development of logistic management has resulted in the utilisation of three major conceptual tools:

1 *systems concept*: the implications of this paradigm are that material flow activities are not isolated but complex and extensive processes that are interacting with each other. The end result of this approach is that the firm can maximise benefits only if it collaborates and co-ordinates its various operations;

2 *trade-off concept*: this realises that linkages and interactions exist in the logistics system; tinkering with one part of the system will therefore impact on another area – for example, improving the quality of service will also increase costs, reducing inventories may result in lower costs for customers but could increase the cost of emergency deliveries.

3 *total cost concept (TCC)*: TCC is a useful measure which a firm employs when it wishes to optimise its physical distribution activities – if the firm has a set of logistical objectives it will design a system which will minimise the costs in order to achieve its objectives. The total distribution cost approach includes all those distribution-related costs and the cost of lost sales which may result from poor service performance and is expressed as follows:

$$D = T + W + I + P + O + S$$

D = total distribution cost of the system
T = transportation cost
W = warehouse cost

I = stock or inventory costs
P = packaging cost
O = order processing and documentation
S = total cost of lost sales due to not meeting service standards set.

Box 15.5   HAYS

The business services company, Hays, is hoping to acquire rival Christian Salvesen in a deal which is worth more than £1bn. The warehouse and distribution of goods industry grew rapidly in the 1980s, after companies such as the former National Freight Corporation pioneered the provision of third-party distribution and warehousing of goods. Due to increased competition in recent years, profits have declined considerably in this sector. Should this move succeed it would herald the first moves towards the consolidation of the European logistics industry. The announcement prompted shares in Salvesen to rise 60p to 349p, giving it a capitalisation of £1.01bn, whilst shares in Hays fell 26p to 414p, valuing it at £1.8bn. Shares in other firms in the industry rose on hopes that consolidation would lead to improvement in rates. Shares rose 15p to 217p in the Transport Development Group and shares in Tibbett and Britten rose 25p to 615p.

Source: Dyer, G., 'Hays seeks £1bn agreed deal with Salvesen', *Financial Times* (26 July 1996).

GLOBAL TRANSPORTATION

This deals primarily with the mode of transportation, which usually makes up between 10 and 20 per cent of the retail costs of imported goods. Controlling transportation routes is a key success factor for a firm involved in freighting goods (*see* Box 15.6). A major determinant of the availability of transportation is the level of economic development, so that in some markets air freight may be more developed than rail transportation. The transportation decision is affected by a number of factors:

- nature of the product
- frequency of the shipment
- distance to the location
- size and value of the shipment
- availability of transportation
- cost of different transportation alternatives.

Box 15.6   BR

British Rail (BR) was accused by freight operators of trying to stifle competition on routes between the UK and Europe. The suggestion is that BR is attempting to snatch all the available 'paths' (slots in the timetable) between London and the Channel Tunnel. Railtrack, the owners of the track and signalling, is understood to have reached an

> **Box 15.6 continued**

agreement with Railfreight Distribution (RFD), the BR subsidiary which operates trains through the tunnel, to acquire all 35 daily 'paths' in the timetable.

Passenger trains and freight operators must bid for 'paths' and pay Railtrack access charges, depending on the time of day and on the type of train. Current 'paths' were decided with BR in a deal completed in 1994. The Rail Freight Group, which represents freight operators, is concerned that if the regulators approve the new RFD deal it would effectively shut out the routes for the next three years for its members and private companies operating freight terminals. In effect, selling all the available train paths to one operator, the RFD, will give it a monopoly over shipments through the Channel Tunnel. This would contravene EU regulations, and the European Commission has told both the French and UK railways to give up 25 per cent of their share of tunnel capacity to rival operators. The regulators office said they were still considering the BR and RFD agreement.

Source: Batchelor, C., 'Freight groups accuse BR of stifling access to Europe', *Financial Times* (23 February 1996).

GLOBAL INVENTORY CONTROL

In general, global inventory levels exceed domestic levels to guard against contingencies in the logistical system. Two major decisions are involved in inventory management:

- frequency of order in a given time period
- the amount to order.

There is an inverse relationship between costs and the inventory decision. As inventory constitutes tied-up capital, attempts should be made to reduce it to the minimum required.

Global warehousing

Goods and materials need to be stored. How these products are stored is sometimes called the *materials handling arrangement*. Warehousing decisions centre on:

- where the firm's customers are geographically located
- the pattern of existing and future demand
- the customer service level required – i.e. how quickly a customer's order should be filled.

Some general observations can be made about warehousing facilities:

- if products need to be delivered quickly, then storage facilities will be required near to the customer
- for high-value products, e.g. computers, the location of the warehouse will be of minimal importance as these lightweight products can be air freighted.

Order processing

Order cycles can be shortened by rapid processing of orders, and the role of communications technology is critical in reducing the time factor. Not many countries have efficient and reliable communication systems, so possessing an efficient international order processing system would give a firm a competitive advantage.

Managing the global logistical system

The main objective of logistical management is to meet customer service levels at the lowest cost. All the different logistical aspects need to be co-ordinated, and this is the key to effective management of the system – i.e. utilising the systems – trade-off and total distribution costs approach. Firms therefore need to look carefully both at savings opportunities and the additional costs which may be incurred when making adjustments in parts of the logistical system.

SUMMARY

A global distribution strategy is important to the firm, for the choice of channels will ultimately influence the other marketing mix decisions. It also involves the firm in long-term commitments which it may find difficult to change, and there will be some loss of control. Finally there is the probability of conflict between the firm and intermediary as different objectives are pursued by each party.

There are different types of channel structures in the global market, from independent to integrated distribution systems. Globalisation is also having a major impact on the design and function of distribution systems. Major trends in distribution are the internationalisation of the distribution format and of retailing, the impact of technology and the innovation of alternative distribution methods such as direct marketing.

The global marketer also needs to make decisions on distribution density, channel length, channel alignment and logistics. In selecting the various alternative channels available, the firm's final choice will be determined by channel costs, coverage, control, continuity, communication, product characteristics, company objectives, competition, distribution culture, customer characteristics and complementarity.

Once the distribution system has been designed, the global marketer needs to select appropriate and reliable intermediaries, evaluate their performance, motivate them to deliver results and control their activities to ensure that they implement the company's marketing strategy.

The existence of grey markets is causing concern to global firms utilising standardised product and global branding strategies. Responses to this growing problem are to ignore it, seek legal avenues of redress and adapt the company's marketing mix strategies.

The Japanese distribution system offers major challenges to foreign firms because of its unique and idiosyncratic nature. To succeed in Japan, a firm will need to find a Japanese partner, seek a unique competitive positioning strategy, seek alternative distribution channels, have a long-term perspective and cultivate Japanese business values such as relationship-building, trust and loyalty.

Global logistics or physical distribution is concerned with the design and management of a system that controls the flow of materials and products into and out of a company. Physical distribution involves international transportation, warehousing, inventory control and order processing. To obtain optimum distribution performance all the different logistical elements need to be co-ordinated effectively and to be considered as a system. The main objective of logistical management is to meet customer levels at the lowest cost and improve the logistical system, thereby gaining a competitive advantage for the firm.

REVIEW QUESTIONS

1 What are the key elements of a distribution strategy?

2 What is the difference between intensive, exclusive and selective distribution?

3 What is distribution density?

4 What are the advantages and disadvantages of using an integrated distribution system?

5 What criteria should a global marketer adopt in channel selection?

6 What are the major elements in managing global channel relationships?

7 What are the main causes of channel conflict?

8 What actions can a company take to motivate channel members to perform effectively?

9 What is global logistics?

10 Explain the meaning of the 'total cost concept' (TCC).

11 Explain the meaning of transit time in global logistics.

DISCUSSION QUESTIONS

1 Why is international distribution more difficult than domestic distribution?

2 What is the relationship between channel costs and control?

3 How do channel intermediaries create utility for buyers?

4 To what extent is it true that the more developed an economy is, the shorter its channels of distribution?

5 How do the characteristics of the final consumer affect the evaluation of global channel options?

6 Examine the distinguishing characteristics of Japanese distribution channels.

7 What are the implications for the global marketer of current distribution trends in world markets?

8 How can a company attain or sustain its competitive advantage by innovating in the channel of distribution?

9 How does global logistics differ from logistics in domestic marketing?

10 Discuss the various ways that a firm can minimise its global marketing costs by paying more attention to its logistics.

Case study

GEHE AND LLOYDS

Gehe is still mulling over a bid for Lloyds Chemists. As Mr Dieter Kämmerer sits in his Stuttgart office contemplating whether or not to bid for Lloyds Chemists, the UK retailer already subject to a £528m offer from UniChem, one thought is uppermost in his mind. The chief executive of Gehe, Europe's largest pharmaceuticals wholesaler, ventured into the UK market last May when he bought AAH for £400m, and he had no cause to complain. 'We've had an excellent experience with our acquisition,' he said. 'Our estimates turned out to be correct. In fact, in terms of AAH's core business, the results have been better than expected.' There is some reason, then, to suppose that Lloyds would be a sensible further UK acquisition. AAH's activities are mainly in the wholesale business but it also has a network of pharmacies. At Lloyds, the balance is tipped the other way, suggesting that the two are 'rather complementary', as the 59-year-old Mr Kämmerer puts it. Gehe and Lloyds are still in talks after the German company requested confidential financial information earlier this week. But Mr Kämmerer is not letting slip any further information. He says Gehe has until 14 February to make a bid. Analysts suspect it would have been in the range of 450–500p a share to knock out the 408p friendly bid tabled by UniChem, the UK's leading pharmaceuticals wholesaler. Apart from offering more, a possible bid by Gehe would seem to have a further advantage for Mr Allen Lloyd, the group's founder. 'The UniChem bid is cash and shares,' one analyst pointed out, 'while Gehe would offer just cash. A straight cash bid would clearly have its attractions.'

Another reason why Mr Kämmerer is not likely to balk at reaching into Gehe's pockets to buy Lloyds is that he has considerable practice at making acquisitions. A series of aggressive purchases in France, the UK and elsewhere in Europe caused Gehe's sales to leap from DM3.79bn (£1.7bn) in 1990 to an estimated DM18.8bn in 1995. Net profits have kept up the pace, rising from DM59m in 1990 to DM140m in 1994. The German press estimated that Gehe would report net profits of DM180m in 1995, but Mr Kämmerer permits himself only a slight aside: 'If that's the case then they have underestimated us.' Financing the Lloyds purchase would not be a problem either, Mr Kämmerer says. The acquisition of AAH in 1995 was financed by a DM640m rights issue, but he says there are further funds available that could finance the Lloyds purchase. 'We can do this out of existing lines and, if necessary, we could do some additional financing which might include a tight issue,' he says, 'but I don't see any need for that at the moment. 'On top of that, analysts point out that Franz Haniel et Cie, the discrete but powerful family-owned transportation and service group which holds a 50.2 per cent in Gehe, has just raised funds through the disposal of a shipping unit. But while the odds seem to be on the side of Mr Kämmerer – a former IBM manager who came to Gehe in 1980 – joining the fray, his mind is not made up. 'If you are pursuing a long-term strategy as we are, you watch the markets and everything that's going on out there,' he says. 'Having made our appraisals we could say – given the sum of money that is to be spent – is this really what we want? Perhaps we would be better off spending the money in other regions.'

Source: Lindemann, M., 'Poised for fresh foray into the UK?', *Financial Times* (2 February 1996).

Questions

1 *Gehe's attempt to buy Lloyds Chemists is indicative of the internationalisation of retailing. What factors have contributed to this trend?*

2 *Discuss some of the major advantages for manufacturers and the implications for consumers of the trend towards international retailing.*

3 *What are the implications for channel management of international retailing?*

FURTHER READING

Christopher, M., *Logistics: The Strategic Issues* (New York: Chapman and Hall, 1992).

Ricks, D.A., *Blunders in International Business* (Oxford: Blackwell, 1993).

NOTES AND REFERENCES

1   Lorenz, A. and Ramesh, R., 'Daewoo set to build UK car plant', *Sunday Times* (Business Section) (16 June 1996).

2   Jeannet, J.-P. and Hennessey, J.D., *Global Marketing Strategies,* 3rd edition (Boston: Houghton Mifflin, 1995), 417.

3   Bidlake, S. 'High street revival in store', *Marketing* (26 October 1989), 19.

4   Rohwedder, C., 'Europe's smaller shops face finis', *The Wall Street Journal* (12 May 1993).

5   Jeannet and Hennessey, op. cit.

6   Ford, R., 'Managing retail service businesses for the 1990s: marketing aspects', *European Management Journal* (March 1990).

7   Jeannet and Hennessey, op. cit.

8   Hughes, M., 'Crossing the border into a brave new financial world', *The Guardian* (Money Section) (15 June 1996).

9   Bradley, F., *International Marketing Strategy*, 2nd edition (Hemel Hempstead: Prentice-Hall, 1995), 545.

10 Cateora, P.R., *International Marketing*, 7th edition (Homewood, IL: Irwin, 1993).

11 Czinkota, M.R. and Ronkainen, I.A., *International Marketing*, 2nd edition (The Dryden Press, 1990).

12 Usunier, J., *International Marketing* (Hemel Hempstead: Prentice-Hall, 1993).

13 Czinkota, M.R. and Ronkainen, I.A., *Global Marketing* (Orlando: The Dryden Press, 1996), 451.

14 Ibid.

15 Usunier, op. cit.

16 Jeannet and Hennessey, op. cit.

17 Czinkota and Ronkainen, op. cit.

18 Anderson, E. and Gatignon, H., 'Modes of foreign entry: a transaction cost analysis and proposition', *Journal of International Business Studies,* 17 (1986), 1–26.

19 Anderson, E. and Coughlan, A.T., 'International market entry and expansion via independent or integrated channels of distribution', *Journal of Marketing,* 51 (1987), 71–82.

20 Dahringer, L.D. and Mühlbacher, H., *International Marketing* (Reading, MA: Addison-Wesley, 1991).

21 Usunier, op. cit.

22 Jeannet and Hennessey, op. cit.

23 Czinkota and Ronkainen, op. cit.

24 Dahringer and Mühlbacher, op. cit.

25 Keegan, W.J., *Global Marketing Management*, 5th edition (Englewood Cliffs: Prentice-Hall, 1995).

26 Jeannet and Hennessey, op. cit.

27 'The revenge of the big yellow', *The Economist* (10 November 1990), 103.

28 Rosson, P.J. and Ford, I.D., 'Manufacturer–distributor relations and export performance', *Journal of International Business Studies* (Fall 1982), 52–72.

29 Cavusgil, S.T., 'The importance of distributor training at Caterpillar', *Industrial Marketing Management*, 19 (1990), 1–9.

30 Jeannet and Hennessey, op. cit.

31 Toyne, B. and Walters, P.G.P., *Global Marketing Management: A Strategic Perspective*, 2nd edition (Boston: Allyn & Bacon, 1993).

32 Czinkota and Ronkainen, op. cit.

33 Cespedes, F.V., Corey, E.R. and Rangan, V.K, 'Gray markets: causes and cures', *Harvard Business Review* (July–August 1988), 75–82.

34 Toyne and Walters, op. cit.

35 Czinkota and Ronkainen, op. cit.

36 Cespedes *et al.*, op. cit.

37 Blumstein, M., 'Seiko wins order to get Alexander's to change its ads', *New York Times* (August 1982), 24.

38 Balso, A., 'Score one for the grey market', *Forbes* (February 1985), 74; Jervey, G., 'Grey markets hit camera, watch sales', *Advertising Age*, 3 (15 August 1983), 62.

39 Keegan, op. cit.

40 Shimaguchi, M. and Rosenberg, L.R., 'Demystifying Japanese distribution', *Columbia Journal of World Business* (Spring 1979), 38–41; Czinkota, M.R., 'Distribution of consumer products in Japan: an overview', *International Marketing Review*, 2 (1985), 39–51.

41 Shimaguchi, M., *Marketing Channels in Japan* (Ann Arbor: 1978).

42 Usunier, op. cit.

43 Keegan, op. cit.

44 Ohmae, K., *Triad Power* (London: Collins, 1985).

45 Montgomery, D.B., 'Understanding the Japanese as customers, competitors and collaborators', *Japan and the World Economy*, 3(1) (1991), 39–60.

46 Shimaguchi and Rosenberg, op. cit.

47 Czinkota, M.R. and Woronoff, J., *Unlocking Japan's Markets* (Chicago: Probus Publishing, 1991).

48 Kotler, P., *Marketing Management: Analysis, Planning, Implementation,* 7th edition (Englewood Cliffs: Prentice-Hall, 1991).

49 Czinkota and Ronkainen, op. cit.

16

Global pricing strategies

Global pricing is generally more critical and complex than domestic pricing. It is critical because it affects the firm's ability to stay in the market, and it is complex because of the diversity of markets, with their different political and legal systems, consumer characteristics, etc. Price is an integral part of a product, for we cannot discuss product without considering price. Price is important as it affects demand for a product by communicating the attractiveness of the offer to the potential buyer, and it also generally affects the larger economy because of its effect on inflation. Price is also an integral part of the other aspects of the marketing mix, namely the product, promotion and place, and it is not more important than the other '3 Ps'.

It is assumed that the reader is familiar with the extensive literature on domestic pricing, this chapter will therefore focus on those aspects that are relevant to global pricing. In particular, an examination of the following is undertaken: the main determinants of foreign market pricing; export pricing; and some of the major managerial issues in pricing – such as price escalation, dumping, transfer pricing, foreign exchange risk management, and terms of payments.

Objectives

This chapter will examine:

- the major influences on the pricing decision
- the different global pricing strategies
- and compare export and domestic pricing
- the problems and impact of price escalation
- the impact of dumping practices
- and attempt to understand the role and problems of transfer pricing in international markets
- the role of the terms of trade in exporting
- the different methods of payment
- how a firm manages its foreign exchange risk.

THE NATURE OF PRICING

Price is an integral part of the marketing mix and it is also one of the strategies in the mix which can be changed quickly without huge cost implications. It could be argued that price is the only element in the mix which generates revenue whilst the others are cost-generating. This characteristic of price makes it a very important strategic marketing instrument; the danger is that firms may resort to price as a quick fix to their problems, instead of examining or making changes to the other elements of the marketing mix. Thus price should not be treated in isolation and should be integrated with the other mix elements. Box 16.1 illustrates the role of pricing in maintaining the firm's competitiveness in the global market and how companies can and are affected by their competitors' pricing policies.

What is perhaps critical to appreciate for marketing managers is the relationship between the price being charged and the perceived value of the product. Consumers will see price as being too high if the value is not there – for example, UK-made cars were perceived to be highly priced. On the other hand, a low price will not be helpful to a product that lacks value, such as the Amstrad computers in the UK market. The price of a product can therefore only be 'high' or 'low' in relation to its value and other features, so that a firm needs to set its price lower than the perceived value or exactly reflect the perceived value of the product. If there is added value to a product consumers will not mind paying a high price – i.e. 'they get what they pay for'.

The management of global pricing policies is more complex than in the domestic market; in particular, marketing managers need to determine the best way to price products which may be produced in one country and then marketed to another; or how pricing decisions in one country can impact on the firm's operations in other markets. In addition, pricing decisions have to be made for different types of buyers or purchasers. What type of prices should be set for consumers or industrial users, distributors or import agents, partners in a joint venture or even one's own subsidiaries abroad? This last type of buyer is a major managerial issue and is discussed under Transfer pricing later in the chapter. The firm also needs to determine the differential between export prices and domestic prices. Pricing decisions need to be made about

Box 16.1	MICROCHIP PRICES	

A sudden drop in 'spot' prices for computer memory chips has affected the share prices of semiconductor manufacturers. Samsung Electronics of South Korea, the world's biggest producer of DRAMs saw its share price fall sharply. DRAMs chips are data storage devices used in all types of computers. Spot prices have fallen by about $1 over the past two weeks to about $3.75 per chip in the USA and even lower in the Asia Pacific. Taiwanese chip makers have accused Korean companies of reducing prices to bolster earnings through higher sales volume and to maintain market share. US manufacturers are keeping a close watch on prices to see if import prices fall below the manufacturing costs of the foreign competitors. If so, they will be filing a trades complaint to possible charges of 'dumping' perhaps.

Source: Kehoe, L. and Burton, J., 'Electronics shares hit by Asian microchip price war', *Financial Times* (10 May 1996).

whether the price of a particular good in one overseas market should be higher, lower or even the same as in other foreign markets or as in the domestic market. This aspect is discussed separately under Export pricing.

DETERMINANTS OF INTERNATIONAL PRICING

The main determinants of a firm's prices in the international market place are indicated in Fig. 16.1 – they are divided into three major sub-groups of company internal factors, market factors and environmental factors. Companies operating in the global market need to consider all these, and in some markets some factors will be more relevant than others. Pricing decisions for specific markets also need to be integrated with the company's overall corporate global strategy. This section will review some of the pricing factors and their influence on pricing in global markets.

Fig 16.1 FACTORS AFFECTING GLOBAL PRICING DECISIONS

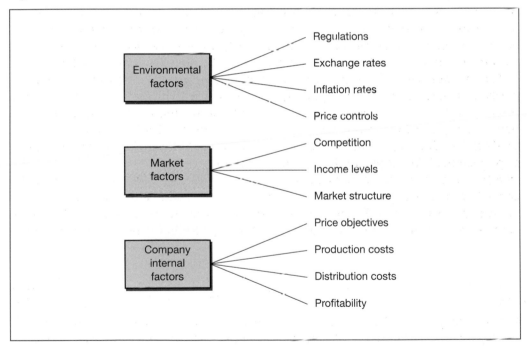

Company internal factors

Corporate and marketing objectives

A firm's objectives will vary from country to country, and it will adjust them as often as necessary to suit the prevailing market conditions. The firm's pricing objectives should be closely aligned to its marketing objectives, which in turn, are based on the overall corporate strategy. When setting price objectives, the firm needs to consider whether:

1 there should be global objectives or specific country objectives;

2 the parent organisation or the subsidiaries should determine the pricing objectives

The objectives of the company's pricing strategy are directly related to the various factors, as illustrated in Fig. 16.1. A brief synopsis of some of the most common pricing objectives in global marketing now follows.

1 *Return on investment (ROI)*: prices are set to achieve a predetermined level of return on the capital outlay in the short term.

2 *Market skimming*: the firm enters the market with a high price targeted at a segment that is willing to pay a premium price for the product. This pricing strategy:

   (a) assumes that the firm has a competitive advantage and a relative degree of security because of its new technology or know-how, and the new product is difficult to imitate easily;

   (b) is used in the introductory phase of the product life cycle when no or very few competitors exist, and the production capacity is limited;

   (c) has a major aim to recover high R&D costs; maximise revenue on a small volume of output and establish the customer's perception of high product value; this latter aim would also reinforce the product's positioning in the market place.

Many electronic products, from microwave ovens to mobile telephones, when they first come on to the market tend to have price-skimming strategies before the prices are gradually lowered. The reaction of competitors will greatly affect the success of this pricing strategy.

3 *Market penetration*: this is a much more aggressive approach and a highly competitive weapon. Prices are set at a deliberately low level to rapidly increase sales and gain market share and keep competitors at a distance. With this policy, the product is sometimes sold at a loss for a short period of time. Japanese and South Korean firms have used this strategy very effectively to gain leadership in certain sectors, especially cars and electronic goods. Samsung, the South Korean conglomerate, was selling microwave ovens in the USA at around $300 whilst most models retailed around $350-$400.[1] The main assumption of this approach is that lower prices will increase sales, and this may not always be so.

4 *Market stabilisation:* prices are set in such a way that the likelihood of the market leader retaliating is minimised. The *status quo* is maintained and market stability is ensured.

5 *Early cash recovery*: when a firm has liquidity problems, a pricing strategy will be adopted that generates high volumes of sales and leads to a high cash flow. This normally occurs when the products are in the mature or declining stages of the product life cycle or the market simply does not have a future. This strategy involves giving special offers and discounts to consumers who pay promptly.

6 *Prevent new entrants*: a low price is set in order to prevent others from entering the market because of low returns and the danger of becoming involved in a price war. One of the drawbacks for the firm employing this approach is that it may not have the income to make the requisite investment to compete in the future.

7 *Pricing to reflect product differentiation*: for firms with a broad product range who wish to segment the market on the basis of price, this approach can distinguish the different products. Such price differences are not necessarily linked to the cost of production, and they are also designed to create perceptions of the product's value and indirectly to increase the firm's profits.

Costs

The cost structure of a firm is a major factor in price determination, largely due to the simplicity of assessing price on the basis of cost, and it also sets the price floor for the long term. The costs incurred would include the following: procurement, production, logistical and marketing and distribution costs. In addition to these normal domestic costs, the firm must take into account the export-related costs which will influence the final overseas price – these include additional transportation, freight and insurance costs, storage costs, local taxes, VAT, overseas communication and promotional costs, foreign exchange risk costs if dealing with foreign currencies, costs of modifying the product if required, etc. We have also to add the intermediary costs, which depend on the channel length, intermediary margins and logistical costs. The combined effect of the overt and hidden costs will result in the final price of the product being excessively over the domestic price. This is known as 'price escalation'.

Full cost pricing

The crucial question is not whether costs are considered but rather what kind of costs should be considered and to what extent. It may be argued that *full cost* should be used in product pricing for the international markets – i.e. all costs (fixed costs, R&D and domestic costs, e.g. advertising costs, etc.) should be paid for by the overseas customer. This approach means that the firm begins with a domestic price and then adds on the various overseas costs such as insurance, customs duties, etc. This method is very ethnocentric and, although simple, can lead to very high prices for the end user abroad and perhaps render the product uncompetitive.

Marginal cost pricing

On the other hand, we can use the *marginal cost pricing* approach which is more incremental in nature. This method of assessment assumes that some costs such as administrative and advertising costs and R&D costs are already accounted for in the home market, and should therefore not be included in the overseas price. The overseas floor price would be based on the actual production costs and the international marketing costs. Arguments in favour of this method are:

● that the domestic market gains in its fixed costs because they are now spread over a larger production volume, i.e. achieving economies of scale;[2] in addition, the firm also gains from the experience effect. Abell and Hammond[3] showed that it provides the firm with the opportunity to reduce costs and increase profits

● it is sensitive to local conditions, and subsidiaries can set their own prices; for example, Japanese companies have been practising this pricing strategy to penetrate the global markets and maintain their market share.[4]

The case against this position is that:

- in the long run a firm must not only be price-competitive but also cost-competitive
- the overseas subsidiaries may not take into account the full costs borne by the parent organisation
- as trade barriers continue to fall in most of the developed economies, arbitrage will eliminate any price differential that may exist between markets.

Environmental factors

Exchange rate

The environmental factors are the external and uncontrollable variables in the foreign markets. One major variable is the fluctuation in the *exchange rate* (discussed later in the chapter). To avoid any foreign exchange risks, the firm would choose its own currency but they may lose the sale. To receive payment in the importer's currency may incur potential losses. It is sufficient to mention here that an appreciation or depreciation in the relative value of a currency can affect the firm's pricing structure and profitability.

Inflation

The rate of *inflation* is another major variable which could affect the cost and pricing of the product. Countries with an inflationary environment will require the firm to constantly adjust its prices and the firm's product may turn out to be more expensive. In certain countries with hyperinflation, such as Brazil where inflation rates were averaging 2000 per cent annually in the 1980s, the selling firm should price its products in a third currency like the US dollar and then translate the price into the local currency on a daily basis. An inflationary situation will normally benefit sellers but it is accompanied by the following factors:

- costs may rise faster than the inflation rate
- in markets with high inflation rates price controls are normally implemented, thereby preventing the firm from raising its prices in the market
- economies with hyperinflation tend to enforce strict foreign exchange controls and the firm will thus not be able to remit its profits.

Hence, pricing in inflationary environments is not easy, particularly when price controls are instituted.

Price control

Government *price control* regulations can also affect the firm's pricing strategy. Many governments tend to have price controls on specific products related to health, education, food and other essential items. Price controls are defended on political and economic grounds. Firms exporting to these markets will have to abide by the price guidelines and operate as if in a regulated industry. In some cases, the returns on investment may not be acceptable and some multinationals may even stop investment and perhaps even cease production.[5] In some less developed economies there are more government restrictions on prices – Cadbury-Schweppes ceased production in Kenya in 1982 because of poor returns on investment. The UK pharmaceutical company Glaxo stopped further investments in Pakistan because of rigid price curbs. Even some European countries such as France have regulations which forbid price rises to combat inflation.

Market factors (demand conditions)

Customer demand

One of the critical factors in foreign market pricing is *customer demand* which, in turn, is a function of many factors among which price is just one. The relationship between price and demand is expressed in the concept of the elasticity of demand, which measures how responsive demand will be to a change in price. Marketers will need to understand the price elasticity of demand to determine the firm's price levels. The other considerations affecting demand include consumers' ability to buy, the place of the product in the customers' life-style – i.e. a status symbol or everyday use product – non-price competition, prices of substitute products, etc. All these factors are interdependent and they also will vary from market to market, so that, having the same price in two distinct markets is likely to result in different volumes being demanded. The nature of the demand will determine the *price ceiling* for the firm. The market can be stratified in that the firm needs to make a judgement about level of demand at several price levels in each foreign market. However, to estimate demand requires the availability of information, this can prove to be difficult and very costly in many markets in both developing and under-developed economies. A firm moving from a UK information-saturated market to an East European one which is just beginning to develop consumer awareness would have difficulty obtaining information, as well as finding that consumers in those markets are not used to obtaining information to make comparisons between different products.

Intermediaries

For the global marketer, a further consideration when setting prices is to consider the intermediaries as well as the consumers. The producer and intermediary have to co-operate if the pricing strategy is to succeed. If the manufacturer wishes to pursue a penetration pricing policy, then it must ensure that the intermediaries' margins are satisfactory and competitive. What has complicated the producers' decision in the last decade is the growing power of the retail intermediaries, demanding competitive prices and thus putting a squeeze on the manufacturer's margins. The UK retailing giant Marks & Spencer demands low-cost and high-quality products from its suppliers.[6]

Competitors

The pressure of *competitors* can also affect international pricing. The firm must price its product more competitively if there are other sellers in the market. In the markets of Kenya and Zimbabwe, where there are import controls and few competitors, medium-priced cars and luxury models such as the BMW and Mercedes-Benz are exorbitantly expensive, yet the same cars are relatively cheaper in the EU countries where there is more competition with other car producers from countries such as Japan and Sweden.

Market structure

The type of market structure or nature of competition (i.e. oligopoly or monopoly) can influence the firm's pricing strategy. A firm entering an oligopoly market where only a few sellers dominate the industry will be under pressure to keep its prices in line with the existing firms. On the other hand, a sole supplier of a product has a virtual monopoly in a given market and will thus have greater pricing flexibility. The utilities and telecommunications industries in many economies are either still under government control, or if deregulated still enjoy considerable monopoly power in the market. British Telecommunications (BT), for example, can still charge high tariffs with no real threat of competition in spite of the existence of Mercury, the second major carrier in the UK. In a more competitive market structure where there is ease of entry and many sellers, it is much more difficult to raise prices. However, for most branded products firms still have some discretion over price, though it will be limited to some extent by what the competitors charge.

Box 16.2   TARIFF CUTTING

Countries which reduce their import tariffs tend to gain bigger and longer-lasting economic benefits than is recognised. A study by the Australian government has also shown that industrialised countries' economic performance since 1970 have been determined more by the speed of tariff cuts than by tackling domestic reforms. The Economic Planning Advisory Commission (EPAC) found that for every one per cent point fall in the industrialised countries' tariffs, on average it raised their total productivity by more than three per cent and GDP by two per cent. Finland is given as an example of a country which previously had very high tariffs, and when tariffs were reduced its growth rate exceeded the average for industrialised economies in the 1970s and 1980s. France is another country whose economy grew substantially from cutting its tariffs.

Source: de Jonquieres, G., 'Benefit of tariff reduction not fully recognised', *Financial Times* (9 April 1996).

PRICING STRATEGIES

Global price setting

The firm's international pricing policy should reflect its corporate objectives, philosophy, development costs and the industry's cost and payment structure. In addition, it should also consider the external and environmental factors, as already discussed. According to Keegan,[7] there are a number of steps to establish a base price:

- the price elasticity of demand needs to be established
- the fixed and variable costs on projected sales need to be estimated, and any adaptation costs have to be taken into account
- costs associated with the international marketing of the products – i.e. promotion, distribution and intermediary costs – have to be identified
- select a price range which offers the highest contribution margin.

The final base price is established only after components of the marketing mix are considered and they do have a major impact on the final price of the product. There are problems in attempting to follow the steps suggested here, due to difficulties in obtaining information about the market and its consumers and in estimating the demand for a product. In China, for example, information is not readily available and consumers may be suspicious of information-gathering by market researchers because of a 'closed society mentality' from before the economic reforms in the 1980s. Many firms therefore rely on experience and intuition, and extrapolate potential demand for the intended market from markets which are judged to be similar.

At this stage, it is interesting to compare the European and US methods of price-setting with the Japanese.[8]

Figure 16.2 illustrates the Japanese process of price-setting. The Japanese initiate the process with market research and by developing the product characteristics. Most US

Fig 16.2 PRICE-SETTING, THE JAPANESE WAY

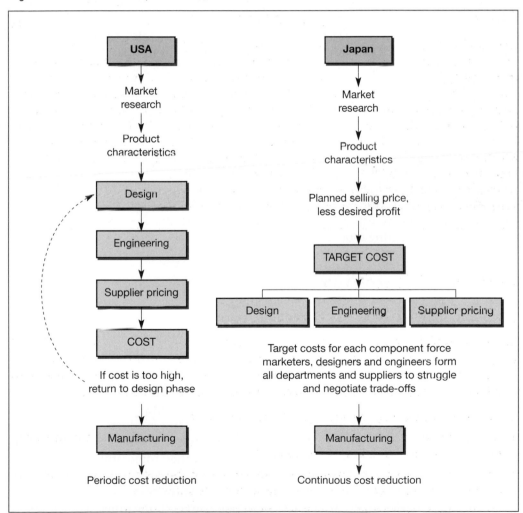

Source: Robert, M., *Strategy Pure and Simple: How Winning CEOs Outthink Their Competition* (New York: McGraw-Hill, 1993). Reproduced with permission.

and European companies follow a similar pattern, but they diverge from the Japanese at the next stage. The Japanese calculate the target cost figure by taking the anticipated selling price and deducting the desired level of profit. Only once this is done are the engineering, design and supplier pricing required to meet the target cost addressed. There will be a round of negotiations to develop trade-offs between the different divisions in the value chain. On agreement, manufacturing begins with a continuous reduction process taking place. European and US producers tend to determine costs only after the engineering, supplier and design factors have been discussed. If costs are considered too high, the process goes back to the drawing board or design stage. Robinson[9] and Keegan[10] have identified a number of approaches to pricing in global markets:

1 standard world price/extension/ethnocentric pricing;

2 adaptation/polycentric/market-differentiated pricing;

3 invention or geocentric pricing.

Standardised pricing

This means that the firm charges the same price for a product in every foreign market in which it operates. This implies that the firm has taken into account mandatory considerations such as taxes, regulatory requirements, variations in foreign exchange rates, etc. The buyer is expected to absorb the transport costs and import duties. The advantages to the company is that it is a low-risk strategy, it is simple, appears equitable and removes any possibilities for arbitrage. The conditions for this type of pricing are when the firm's competitive position does not vary frequently from one market to another and it enjoys a monopolistic position in the market. The major drawback of this approach is that it does not respond to local market and competitive conditions. This type of pricing is not customer orientated and the products may end up underpriced or overpriced depending on the local factors. Hence the firm may not maximise its returns in each local market. It also implies that the firm is not utilising its pricing as a marketing tool to achieve its objectives.

Adaptation/polycentric market-differentiated pricing

This means that the price for the firm's products will vary according to local market needs and competitive conditions. Subsidiaries will be free to set prices to suit local conditions but this does not extend to transfer pricing in the organisation. Furthermore, no attempt is made to co-ordinate prices from one market to the next. This approach assumes that the firm is not a price-taker. However, there are a number of disadvantages with this method.

1 If there are significant price differences among different foreign markets, this will create opportunities for arbitrage and 'grey market' activities. This danger of *parallel imports* means that firms will take advantage of buying products in lower-priced markets and selling them in higher-priced markets. If a video-cassette recorder (VCR) is sold for £400 in the UK and £600 in France, then some firms will buy VCRs in the UK and sell them in France for a profit. 'Grey markets' can develop because buyers in one market are informed immediately about prices in other markets, and unauthorised dealers import the goods from one market to the other. 'Grey markets' exist in the EU for products such as cars and perfumes (*see* Chapter 15).

2 Giving the subsidiaries the power to determine prices may mean that headquarters will lack control to monitor or implement any directive from the centre. Furthermore, the centre's invaluable experience and expertise in pricing strategy will not be utilised at the local level.

3 Local managers may not benefit from headquarters' experience in other local markets when they make their decision.

Overall, it could be said that not enough attention will be given to the interests of the firm as a whole to aid the company in achieving its strategic objectives.

Invention/geocentric pricing

This approach attempts to take the best of both approaches discussed above. The firm does not fix a single world price, nor will it allow its subsidiaries complete freedom to set prices. The implications of this method are that the firm's foreign pricing decisions should not be made just by the local subsidiaries but under strong headquarters direction and oversight – i.e. local pricing strategies should be integrated into the corporate-wide pricing strategies. This would eliminate sub-optimal policies and yet the firm can still respond to local market needs.

GLOBAL PRICING ISSUES

Price escalation

Price escalation occurs when there is an increase in the product's price as transportation, local taxes, customs duties, distributor margins, export documentation charges, insurance, etc. are added to the factory price. Figure 16.3 illustrates how price escalation occurs, when a product can end up costing 65 per cent more than the domestic price. Many companies do not appear to be aware of rapid price escalation and are more concerned with the final price of the product to the importer. Price escalation can prevent a firm entering a market. However, there a number of options open to management to counter this.

1 The producer can accept a cut in their export margins.

2 The firm can reduce the channel length if possible, by circumventing some channel members and selling direct to the large wholesalers. In some markets, such as Japan, this is most unlikely to occur given the complex nature of the distribution system, where channel members have influence in the system should they be overlooked.

3 The firm can persuade the intermediaries to accept a lower margin. This is possible only if the intermediaries are dependent on the firm for much of their business.

4 The firm can reduce the cost of the product by adapting it to a cheaper version or making a smaller model of the product and also enjoying lower duties on it.

5 The firm can reduce its costs of production in a number of ways. It can try and find savings in the manufacturing process by having production and procurement economies. Or it can consider manufacturing abroad by licensing, joint ventures or setting up its own facilities. If the market is considered large enough this can prove to be profitable in the long run.

Fig 16.3 PRICE ESCALATION

	Domestic channel	Export channel	
	£	£	£
Firm's net price	40.00[a]	40.00[b]	40.00[c]
Insurance and shipping costs		4.00	4.00
Landed cost		44.00	44.00
Tariff (20% on landed cost)		8.80	8.80
Importer's cost			52.80
Importer's margin (25% on cost)			13.20
Wholesaler's cost	40.00	52.80	66.00
Wholesaler's margin (33⅓% on cost)	13.33	17.60	22.00
Retailer's cost	53.33	70.40	88.00
Retailer's margin (50% on cost)	26.66	35.20	44.00
Retail price	80.00	105.60	132.00
Price escalation		32%	65%

Notes:
[a] Firm to wholesaler to retailer.
[b] Firm to foreign wholesaler to retailer.
[c] Firm to foreign importer to wholesaler to retailer.

The international product life cycle

Global marketers can be aided in their pricing decisions by studying the international product life-cycle model (IPLC).[11] The main assumption of the model is that as the product moves through the IPLC, the firm's flexibility to adjust prices declines. The main stages are as follows.

Introductory and growth stages
The product is new to the export markets, there are few competitors, demand is inelastic and the normal pricing strategy is a high price (skimming).

Maturity stage
This is the mass market stage (i.e. standardisation phase). The product's competitive advantage is being eroded. There are more competitors in the market, there is downward pressure on price and there is a decline in output and exports. Firms will move production to low-cost countries and cost reduction becomes imperative. Firm is a price-taker and price becomes an important marketing and competitive tool.

To avoid being a price-taker, the firm needs to continuously innovate, generate new products, reposition their products, etc. so as to enter the early phase of the IPLC again, and thus influence and determine the pricing decisions.

Dumping

This is the practice of setting export prices at a level lower than in the domestic market. Imported products are sold at very competitive prices which could prove detrimental to the local firms producing a similar good. Boeing has accused Airbus Industrie, the European aircraft consortium, of dumping because it was selling comparable models some $10–$20m below the actual cost. Airbus Industrie is said to be able to do this because various governments are subsiding the consortium.

Dumping is a form of price discrimination and, if employed as a business strategy, the setting of differential prices is done with certain objectives in mind. In the context of international business, if the aim is to destroy the domestic industry, then host governments are concerned, and hence have passed anti-dumping laws. Dumping is considered illegal in many countries, but it is very difficult to prove that it has occurred. Low prices may be due to higher productivity and/or a more efficient firm. Austin Rover, the UK car manufacturer, sold its models to EU markets in the 1980s at a price which was below the UK domestic market. Was this dumping?

Several types of dumping[12] can be identified, as follows.

Predatory dumping

This involves selling the product at a considerable loss to gain access to the market and thus drive out the competitors. When this occurs the firm can charge higher prices, as it now has a monopoly position in the market – i.e. the firm that dumps its goods will earn lower profits in the short run but gain very high profits in the long run. Many Japanese companies (electronic manufacturers and steelmakers) have been accused of this practice in both Europe and the USA. However, after prolonged litigation not many of the cases have been proved.

Persistent dumping

This occurs when a firm consistently sells at lower prices in one market than in others and it is a permanent type of policy. A firm undertakes this kind of pricing policy because of different market conditions. If the foreign market has a very elastic demand curve then the firm is likely to differentiate prices. Many Japanese electronics companies charge higher prices in the home market than in the EU or the US markets. They are able to do this because of limited competition in the home market and also in order to maintain or gain market share abroad.

Sporadic dumping

This occurs when a firm wants to get rid of unsold stocks. One way is to sell at a lower price in the home market. However, this could result in a price war which could threaten its competitive position. The alternative is to cut its losses and dump the excess in markets abroad where they are not usually exported to.

Unintentional dumping

This occurs because of the existence of time lags between the date of the sales agreement and the arrival of the goods. It may be the case that exchange rate fluctuations cause the final price of the good to be below the price prevailing in the manufacturer's home market.

Reverse dumping

This occurs when the price of the good is much lower in the manufacturer's home market; this situation can arise when the overseas market's demand curve is fairly inelastic.

Is dumping really such a bad practice? The main types of dumping discussed involve charging lower prices in foreign markets than in home markets. They undoubtedly benefit the foreign consumers more than the local consumers. Furthermore, it could be argued that it encourages competition. The existence of cheap imported goods will result in some winners and losers, and if we accept the economic principles underlying free trade then overall the gains outweigh the losses. Anti-dumping voices want protection against what they see as *unfair* competition, and for the national economic security of the country. There is no doubt that dumping is a widespread practice, and it could be argued that in spite of this, the host governments should still allow some harmful dumping to occur to gain the benefits of free trade. There are other methods firms can legally use to overcome dumping legislation:

1 the firm can base its strategy on non-price competition, such as the creative use of credit facilities to consumers and distributors – this is tantamount to a price reduction, and it circumvents the dumping laws;

2 another strategy is to differentiate the home product from the exported item, by having different brand names for comparable models. This, in effect, removes the basis for any price comparison and thus avoid charges of dumping;

3 another method is to move the location of production to the host market – the advantage of this move is that the manufacturer's home prices do not have to be lowered. Furthermore, the manufacturer could minimise higher costs by outsourcing their supplies and components to remain competitive in the host market.

Firms in the host market can meet the import challenge by evaluating their competitive position and that of foreign competitors. They could also consider the following measures:

1 focus on a particular segment where their leverage is strongest rather than attempting to compete across a wide spectrum of goods;

2 reconfigure their value-added activities so as to attain the competitive edge;

3 if fundamental cost differences cannot be eliminated, consider changing the product; this could take the form of value-added additions to the product which must really add value in the market, and the competitors must not be able to imitate these differences easily and quickly if the firm is to maintain its competitive advantage.

TRANSFER PRICING

This refers to a multinational firm's pricing of goods and services between its headquarters and subsidiaries. Initially, with domestic operations the transfer pricing system was developed with the aim of:

- motivating divisional management to achieve goals
- providing flexibility to enable divisional management to achieve their goals
- furthering corporate goals.

Transfer pricing arises whenever a business is divided into separate units, each of which has their own management structure and organisational objectives. Transfer pricing can create problems because it is not determined in the market place through the interaction of willing buyers and sellers; and this can result in a situation where foreign transfer prices are set at a level that does not reflect a fair value. For example, if the transfer pricing is set too low, then the 'seller' suffers depressed profits while the 'buyer' achieves substantial profits. If it is set too high the 'seller' gains only at the expense of the 'buyer', even though corporate profits are not affected in aggregate (*see* Fig. 16.4). Given that a business is broken up into several units, each with its own objectives and managerial responsibilities, arbitrary transfer pricing will have the effect of preventing one unit achieving realistic objectives, while making it easier for another. Arbitrary transfer pricing will also have a net effect on the whole organisation, in that the effectiveness of the organisation as a whole may be undermined. Transfer pricing must therefore reflect the individual needs and aspirations of each of the units or divisions involved.

In the international context, the transfer pricing process is complicated by an environment which has fluctuating exchange rates, different economic, political and social parameters, varying degrees of government regulations and tax regimes, etc. Given the context in which multinational corporations operate, we will examine some of the main reasons why transfer pricing manipulation occurs and how it is used strategically by companies in the global market place.

Fig 16.4 EFFECTS OF TRANSFER PRICING

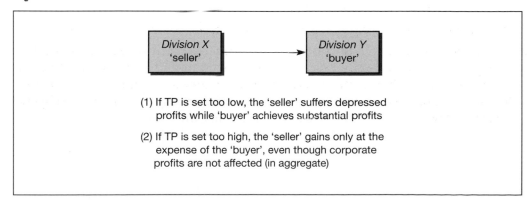

Minimise global tax liabilities

Given that countries have different levels of taxation, a multinational company (MNC) will attempt to maximise profits in low-tax economies. This achieved by setting high transfer prices for goods and services sold from countries with lower corporation tax to another subsidiary of the firm in a high-tax location. Conversely, branches operating in countries with high corporation tax will set low transfer prices to subsidiaries in low-tax countries.

Avoid home and host government regulations

Governments can place barriers on the inter-country movement of dividends, interest and capital. If a foreign government places restrictions on the repatriation of dividends, interests or royalties, a MNC can manipulate transfer pricing to shift funds out. Funds can be moved out of one country (Kenya) to another (the UK) by setting high transfer prices for goods and services supplied to a Kenyan subsidiary, and by setting low transfer prices for goods and services sourced from the Kenyan subsidiary. The alternative is to position funds in the UK by setting low transfer prices for goods and services supplied to a UK-based subsidiary, and by setting high transfer prices for the goods and services from that subsidiary. A MNC can overcome restrictions placed by home governments on overseas investment by similar manipulations. The company will provide financing to its subsidiaries by setting a low transfer price for goods and services sent to the subsidiary, and overpaying the subsidiary for any goods received, for example.

Minimise risk of uncertanty

A MNC can move profits or assets out of a country that has frequent devaluations or chronic balance of payments difficulties. Thus the firm can manipulate transfer pricing to remove funds from a country where the currency is expected to devalue.

Reduce tariff duties (*ad valorem*)

This involves quoting low transfer prices to countries with high tariffs. This has the effect of lowering the value of the goods and services, and thus this lowers the tariff payment.

Avoid sharing profits

The firm may want to accumulate profits in a wholly-owned subsidiary rather than one that is minority-owned, such as a joint venture.

Whatever the motives for manipulating the transfer pricing mechanism, the global marketing manager's aim is ultimately to ensure that the company is competitive in the global market place, exploits foreign market opportunities and achieves an effective distribution of goods and services.

SETTING INTERNATIONAL TRANSFER PRICES

There are alternative approaches to transfer pricing, which will vary with the product sold, the nature of the company and the markets concerned.

Transfer at manufacturing cost

The transfer price is set at the level of the production cost. This means that the subsidiary will contribute to corporate profits by generating sales, while the manufacturing operations in the home market are evaluated on efficiency rather than profitability criteria and they generate economies of production. This method ensures that duties are kept to a minimum and it assumes that lower costs will enhance subsidiary profitability and the entire company gain overall.

'Arm's-length' transfer pricing

This refers to the price that would have been achieved by unrelated parties in a similar transaction – i.e. the subsidiary is charged as any buyer outside the company. This method does assume that it is possible to identify what the arm's-length price is if there are no external buyers. Difficulties can arise if the subsidiary is allowed to purchase from elsewhere and the external source is cheaper and of better quality than the home company's.

Cost-plus approach

The transfer price is arrived at by adding a profit mark-up at every stage of movement through the corporate system. This approach may result in a price that is unrelated to the competitive or demand conditions in the global market. The formula used varies, but it is a method which can minimise company time spent on the problem and it does motivate the home and subsidiary units.

Market-based transfer price

This price is achieved from the price required to be competitive in the global market place. The problem with this approach is defining what constitutes 'cost'. Given that costs decline with the volume of production, the company needs to establish how it should price its goods – on current or planned volume levels.

Regardless of which method is used, MNCs must be prepared to justify how these prices have been set. Furthermore, they need to be aware that laws are not contravened and avoid some of the transfer price manipulations discussed earlier on. A number of factors have been found to have a major impact on transfer price setting:[13]

- market conditions in overseas markets
- competition in the overseas market
- achieving a reasonable profit level for subsidiaries
- home country income taxes
- economic conditions in the overseas market
- overseas import restrictions and tariff duties

- overseas market price controls
- foreign country taxation
- overseas market exchange controls.

MANAGEMENT OF FOREIGN EXCHANGE RISK

This section will examine risk management and the services that are offered by financial institutions to companies wishing to counter these risks. The choice facing the exporter is:

- use the 'home' currency
- use the buyer's currency
- use a 'third-party' currency such as the international reserve currencies – the US dollar, Swiss franc or deutschmark.

The outcome is based on a combination of factors:

- the buyer's preference
- exchange rates and their stability
- freedom of exchange (lack of exchange control or otherwise)
- the availability of currencies in the importer's country
- government policies.

Further considerations are whether the exporter needs a particular currency to pay for imported supplies, and the likelihood of gaining an advantage over competitors by pricing in the local currency. It cannot be stated which currency is best in all circumstances, but it should be noted that if necessary price can be used to a certain extent to compensate for potential exchange rate losses.

Forward exchange markets

An exporter can protect against loss caused by fluctuating currencies during the sale contract period by taking out a forward exchange contract. The differences between spot and forward rates and, therefore, between spot and forward markets are as follows.

Spot rate

A *spot rate* currency is the rate of exchange which is used for currency dealing without any advance arrangement for the purchase or sale having been made. The spot rate is quoted for immediate delivery of the currency to the buyer two working days later. The spot rate is the all-important rate, with quotations for delivery or settlement on dates other than the spot date being calculated in relation to that rate.

For example, a UK exporter receiving payment from a French buyer for 200 000 French francs, with the bank buying at 10.50 francs to the pound (£), would give £19 047.62 to the exporter (i.e. 200 000/10.50=£19 047.62). The fact that 200 000 francs were owed to the exporter would have been known for some time as it was likely that a period of credit had been granted to the buyer, so the exporter will expect to be able to exchange the foreign currency proceeds in order to cover costs and make a profit. However, an adverse exchange rate movement could threaten these profits and losses could be substantial.

Forward exchange contract

The foreign exchange risk can be overcome by means of a *forward exchange contract*, whereby the exporter arranges for a bank to sell or buy a quantity of foreign currency at a future date, with the rate of exchange determined 'now'. The trader will know in advance how much foreign currency is to be received, and so protection can be gained from adverse movements of exchange rates.

A forward exchange contract is a firm and binding contract between a bank and its customer for the purchase (or sale) of a specified quantity of a stated foreign currency. The contract also states the rate of exchange. If this is fixed at the time of the contract, it is known as a 'fixed contract'. If a time between two dates for the payment or purchase of the currency is specified it is referred to as an 'option contract'. A forward contract will provide cover against exchange risks for a period of up to five years ahead or even longer, but typically the rates are quoted for one month, two months, three months, six months or 12 months.

In addition to the two types of contract it is necessary to realise that the forward rate varies from the spot rate, with the forward rate for selling the foreign currency being quoted at a premium (i.e. it exchanges for more domestic currency than the spot rate), or at a discount (if it exchanges for less). The difference between spot and forward rates is determined by market forces, of which the most important is the difference in the prevailing interest rates being paid by banks for fixed deposits in the two currencies concerned.

To reduce the complexity it is necessary to remember that a premium is subtracted from the spot rate, whilst a discount is added to the spot rate. Forward rates are, therefore, quoted as adjustments to the spot rate. Table 16.1 shows the differences between the spot and forward buying and selling figures when the spot rate for the Italian lira against sterling is 2100–2110 and the three months' forward rate is 2150–2160. When buying or selling, the lira is worth less three months from now than the spot market price: the reverse would be true if the forward rate was lower than the spot price. Unlike the rates used in the previous examples, the rates quoted here reflect the rate at which a bank is willing to purchase lira, being the higher rate, whilst the lower rate will be that at which it will sell lira for sterling – so banks *sell low and buy high* in order

Table 16.1 DIFFERENCES IN SPOT AND FORWARD RATES: £ AND LIRA

	Bank sells 1m lire at	Bank buys 1m lire at
Spot rate £1 = 2100 – 2110 lire	£476.19	£473.93
3 month's £1 = 2150 – 2160 lire forward rate	£465.12	£462.96

to cover their costs and to make a profit on foreign exchange transactions. If the forward rate is higher, the quoted currency will be cheaper than the spot rate.

Therefore, it needs to be remembered that if the forward rate is more expensive than the spot rate, it is quoted as a premium on the spot rate, meaning that the forward rate will be lower by the amount of the premium. If, on the other hand, the forward rate is cheaper than the spot rate, it is quoted as a discount on that rate, with forward rates being higher than the spot rates by the amount of the discount. The longer the period of the forward contract the larger the premium or discount will be, so the contracts typically quoted for 1–12 months will all have different rates quoted, much as one would expect interest rates to vary, the longer the period of the loan.

There are alternative and additional ways of coping with exposure in foreign currency. The following methods are not in order of importance but are intended only as a guide to what is possible.

Matching

This refers to the ability of the company to match expenses against receipts in that currency. This obviates the need to cover against exposure as there is no worry concerning the strengthening or weakening of that currency *vis-à-vis* any other. The development of foreign currency accounts in the UK since 1979 has helped in this respect.

Straightforward as this approach sounds, it to must be looked at rather more carefully, as within any organisation there will be plenty of occasions when payments occur before receipts. It may be advisable to look at these alternatives as a portfolio of devices that will help in sorting out the financial side of exporting.

Borrowing

With this method, money is borrowed in the foreign currency in which payments will be received. These payments can then be used to repay the loan, and can be seen as an alternative to a forward contract. For example, US$100 000 may be borrowed in the knowledge that this amount will eventually be received from the payments for exports, the dollars being converted at the spot rate, thereby avoiding the exchange risk. The technical issues involved in this method have been glossed over, but it must be said that this approach is not necessarily any cheaper in the long run than the use of forward contracts.

Currency options

This method can easily be confused with a forward exchange option, but unlike the latter, a currency option can be purchased by an exporter giving the right to buy or sell an amount of foreign currency at a future date, usually after three months. The Bank of England defines the currency option as

> a contract offering the purchaser the right but not the obligation to buy [a call option] or sell [a put option] a given quantity of a specified financial instrument at a predetermined price [the strike price] either before or at a fixed future date.

The growth in this market has meant that the currency option is, according to the Bank of England, a complement to the larger, established spot and forward markets.

The purpose of a currency option is to help reduce exposure, particularly in certain situations when a forward contract may be inappropriate. In a situation where there is uncertainty about foreign exchange receipts, or when a company wishes to produce a price list for its goods in a foreign currency, it would be rather pointless to fix a forward contract as the firm would not know if it had won any export orders.

Currency options, then, are another way of hedging which puts a limit on the losses that can be incurred on the spot market, but they do not eliminate all the potential profits from movements in the exchange rates that a forward contract would prevent. Despite their increased use, currency options are hindered by the high costs involved in taking them out, five per cent of the total amount covered, which has to be paid in advance.

Financial futures

Futures in a foreign currency are contracts to buy or sell a quantity of a foreign currency at a future date. This may again seem similar to forward contracts, but they differ in that they can be reversed, and that they are for a fixed amount of currency being traded on the London International Financial Futures Exchange (LIFFE) market in London.

The alternatives reviewed here give a flavour of the methods used to reduce foreign exchange exposure; none of them are without their advantages and drawbacks. Each of the options should be weighed carefully before deciding on the appropriate course of action.

EXPORT PRICE QUOTATIONS (TERMS OF TRADE OR SALE)

The atmosphere in which overseas trade is carried on is charged with potential conflict and beset with potential problems, such as:

- bottlenecks at ports/airports
- dislocations due to accidents, which add costs to the undertaking
- bad weather
- strikes
- currency fluctuations, which can vary the actual payment received.

Thus, for the above reasons, it is necessary to proceed cautiously and to spell out quite clearly in the export price quotation:

- the terms to be used, and wherever possible to build in safeguard clauses
- the responsibilities and duties of the buyer and seller.

Trade terms are critical in all international transactions because they can be legally binding, and a number of decisions have to be made concerning who pays what, and who is responsible for:

1 the cost of freight;
2 the cost of insuring the goods whilst in transit;
3 other costs (export licence/export tax).

The buyer and seller have to agree on these decisions when the export contract of sale is signed. The way export prices are quoted are known as *trade terms* or *sales terms* such as FOB, CIF, DDP, etc. There are two systems of definition used by firms in international trade. One is INCOTERMS 1990 (International trade terms) which was developed by the International Chamber of Commerce. The other is the Revised American Foreign Trade Definitions (1941). The trade terms are shorthand expressions, each symbolised by a recognised three-letter code, and they set out the rights and obligations of the parties concerned with the transit of goods. They are also very useful and effective as a marketing tool.

In general, trade terms have no legal status unless there is legislation providing for them or the courts accept them. If the buyers and sellers accept the trade terms in the sales contract, then the trade terms are legally binding on the parties to the sale. The use of INCOTERMS 1990 is voluntary in Europe, and in practice the courts and arbitration panels tend to accept them even if they are not explicitly stated. It is beyond the scope of this chapter to describe in detail each trade term, so only a brief description of the main terms will be attempted here.

Trade terms

Ex works (EXW)

The seller's main responsibility is to make the goods available at his factory. The buyer bears the costs and the risks from that point on and the entire transit to the destination. Ex works represents the minimum obligation for the seller and the maximum obligation for the buyer.

Free carrier (FRC)

The seller is responsible for delivering the goods to a carrier – usually a multimodal transport operator – at a named point. This could be the railway station, seller's premises or the road haulier's premises. The risks of damage or loss passes to the buyer at that time.

Free alongside ship (FAS)

When the goods are placed alongside the ship on the quayside, the seller's obligations ceases. All the costs and risks, or loss and damage passes to the buyer at that moment. In some instances, the buyer has the responsibility to clear the goods for export.

Free on board (FOB)

This term generally means on board a transportation carrier at a named point. There is a range of FOB terms and virtually all specify a named point in the country of exportation. The comparable Incoterm is FCA (Free carrier) and in used for air, ship or rail transportation. The seller's responsibility extends to the port of departure when the goods are loaded on board the ship. Once the goods pass the ship's rail the buyer bears the costs, risks or loss.

Cost and freight (CFR)

The seller bears the costs and the freight or (C&F) to the port of destination. The buyer then bears the risk as the goods cross the ship's rail in the port of shipment.

Cost, insurance and freight (CIF)

The seller is in a similar position as in CFR, but they also have to provide marine insurance during the carriage. The buyer bears the risk as the goods cross the ship's rail, and the insurance policy then covers the buyer's risk.

Freight or carriage paid (FCP)

The seller pays carriage to the named destination. The buyer bears the risk when the goods are delivered to the first carrier (whatever mode of transport is used).

Ex ship (EXS)

The seller is responsible for all the costs and risks of bringing the goods to the port of destination. The buyer then bears the responsibilities from there onwards.

Ex quay (duty paid or duty for buyers account) (EXQ)

The seller bears all the costs and risks until the goods are at the destination quay. This may include customs' duties on entry. The buyer bears the risks and responsibilities after they take delivery from the quay.

Delivered at frontier (DAF)

The seller bears all the risks and costs until the merchandise arrives at the named frontier. The goods are cleared through the import frontier by the buyer, who then bears the costs and risks including paying the duty if required.

Delivered duty paid (DDP)

The seller delivers the goods to the buyer at the country of destination, and includes import duties if required. DDP can be delivered exclusive of taxes. This term of sale represents the maximum commitment for the seller, and the minimum for the buyer.

However, conflict may arise between buyer and seller as each of the parties tries to limit their obligations as much as possible. The *seller* will try to negotiate an ex works contract, whilst the *buyer* will try to convince the seller to deliver the goods duty paid to the buyer's premises – i.e. DDP. But a buyer or seller cannot easily make a better contract by merely shifting costs and responsibilities to a contracting party. Which choice of trade terms to use will depend on a number of factors.

Market situation: In a highly competitive market situation, a seller may offer prices to a buyer that are comparable to the prices offered in the buyer's domestic market such as Ex Quay or DDP. As a minimum, the seller should arrange and pay for transportation (C&F, CIF, FCP). It is worth noting that any additional costs and risks accepted by the seller are always reflected in the price.

Control of transport and insurance: Firms who export large and regular volumes of goods will be in a strong bargaining position to obtain better terms from their carriers and insurers than the occasional buyer. Under these circumstances, the seller should not limit their obligation to ex works, FAS or FOB but accept C&F or CIF terms.

Political and social factors: If normal conditions of trade exist between countries with well-organised container ports, peaceful labour conditions, no risk of congestion in the ports, strikes or interruptions of trade, then the exporter should choose a term in which responsibilities extend to the arrival of goods at the destination, such as ex ship, ex quay or DDP. However, the exporter may think that such risks are difficult to estimate and therefore difficult to include in the calculation of the price. The firm may prefer the buyer to assume the risks and thus choose FAS, FOB, C&F or CIF.

Governmental involvement: Some governments may lay down guidelines or even instruct parties in their country to buy and sell on certain trade terms. Therefore, it is likely that they will encourage firms to *sell* on CIF terms and *buy* on FOB terms. There are a number of reasons for this:

1 trade terms constitute an important tool for directing the flow of goods to national carriers and the domestic insurance market;

2 they also save foreign currency for the nation – the seller who undertakes to pay for carriage and insurance will include these costs in the final price, and the country thus obtains more foreign reserves.

Use of exceptional clauses

A trade term which extends the seller's obligation to deliver in the buyer's country can mean extra costs and risks. But the risk of loss or damage is generally covered by cargo insurance. However, it is with unforeseen events such as labour disruptions, wars, sudden imposition of duties, government intervention, etc. that the risk of costs increases and puts a heavy burden on the affected party. In general, such risks can be shared between the parties under the contract of sale terms. General conditions of trade always contain 'relief clauses' – these attempt to alleviate the seller's burdens to deliver. Depending on how it is included and worded in the contract, they can provide very good protection for the exporter; the exporter can then afford to extend their obligations and select a trade term that extends their responsibilities.

The judicious use of trade terms can thus be a very powerful weapon for the firm's marketing strategy. We will demonstrate the effects of using different trade terms on the final price. The example concerns a shipment of cloth from the UK to Milan by sea. The exporter wished to receive a basic price of $3.00 a metre and the enquiry was for 3000 metres. The exporter could look forward to receiving a total of $9000.00 at their factory. The costs at all stages of delivery to Milan were as in Fig. 16.5.

1 If 'ex works' was quoted, the price would be $9000.00 because there would have been no additional costs to add. But the exporter needs to specify 'Packing at cost' since export packing is seldom included in the cost. If this is the case, then the price would be $9300.

2 If FAS was quoted, the exporter would need to add the cost of taking the goods by rail to the port. The price would be $9750.00.

3 If FOB was quoted, then port charges would be added including any documentation. The price would now be $9810.00.

Fig 16.5 THE EFFECT OF TRADE TERMS ON PRICE

Price of the cloth, unpacked at works	9 000.00
Packing costs	300.00
Transport to docks by rail	450.00
Port dues and loading charges	60.00
Frieght by sea to Genoa	875.00
Landing charges at Genoa	90.00
Duty payable on 3000 metres of cloth	1 200.00
Transport from Genoa to Milan	150.00
Insurance, all risks to Milan	100.00
Total	12 225.00

4 With a CIF quotation, freight and insurance would be included to the nearest port – in this case, Genoa. While this has been shown as $100.00 this was right through to Milan, so it may be necessary to add only $80.00, the CIF price would then be $10 765.00.

5 With DDP, all the following would have to be added – landing charges at Genoa, the duty payable on the cloth, the full insurance and the freight from Genoa to Milan. The final price delivered to the customer's warehouse in Milan would be $12 225.00.

EXPORT RISKS

There might be a large time lag between the placing of an order and the receipt of the goods, as well as the necessary delay in the transportation of the goods and the complexity of export documentation, so an exporter might have to extend credit to the purchaser. Indeed, a firm that depends very heavily upon exports will have a large amount of working capital tied up in such arrangements. This will necessitate the help of banks in providing for working capital assistance.

Further considerations to take into account are control over debtors and debt collection, and the need to chase payments on bad debts, which are a particular problem in some areas of the world. This unreliability of some buyers can come from two sources: either the buyer refuses to accept the goods or refuses to pay for them. In both cases, the exporter is left with having to decide what to do in such circumstances, all of which involves more time and money.

Currency of quotation

International trade and exporting is undertaken by invoicing the buyer in one of the following:

- the currency of the buyer's country
- the currency of the exporter's country
- the currency of a third country
- a currency unit such as the European Currency Unit (ECU).

The ECU is as yet little used in the business sector, although it is used quite extensively within government bodies. For the present, references to foreign exchange will be kept to the first three possibilities. A brief review of the advantages or otherwise of using the ECU is given later in the chapter.

The main problem for both importers and exporters is the foreign exchange risk in invoicing or being invoiced in another currency. The following example shows how a UK exporter runs the risk of reduction in profits on sales to the USA.

Suppose a UK exporter sells goods to a US importer for £20 000, with the exchange rate standing at £1=$1.50. The US importer who is not being invoiced in US dollars expects to pay $30 000 for the goods. If by the time payment is due the exchange rate has changed to £1=$1.60 then the US importer would expect to pay $32 000 for the goods, thereby losing $2000. On the other hand, if the exchange rate had fallen to £1=$1.40 then the importer would have to pay only $28 000 to buy £20 000 and hence settle the debt. The foreign exchange risk has been completely borne by the importer.

Using the same example, but changing the currency to be used for invoicing purposes to sterling, then the exchange risk would be borne by the exporter – a $30 000 invoice would be turned back into £20 000 at the exchange rate of £1=$1.50. However, with the increase in the rate to $1.60, $30 000 buys only £18 750 (a loss of £1250 on the deal), but with a fall to $1.40, $30 000 buys £21 429 (a gain of £1429).

Box 16.3   **AIWA**

The Japanese audio manufacturer, Aiwa, a subsidiary of Sony Corporation, suffered a 12 per cent decline in recurring profits before tax and extraordinary items in the 12 months to end-March 1996. The company blamed the strong yen and tough price competition for its current state. This is in spite of the fact that Aiwa moved to overseas low-cost production centres, but the low-cost benefits were wiped out by competition and the resulting discounts of its products.

Source: Terazono, E., 'Strong yen shares blame for decline of Aiwa', *Financial Times* (15 May 1996).

The acceptance of the degree of risk depends to a large extent on the currency for invoicing purposes, with neither party wishing to accept the risk unless they are prepared to gamble on the rate moving in such a way that they can profit from it. This requires great nerve, backed up by good forecasting of the foreign exchange markets.

However, if the company is able to match receipts and payments, as can be achieved by a company which receives US dollars in receipt for goods and then matches this to an invoice to be paid in US dollars for goods supplied, then there is no currency risk to take into account. Most small and medium-sized enterprises, for example, are not likely to be in this situation, and must therefore seek ways of reducing the foreign exchange risk.

Financial laws, customs and government regulations

Of vital importance to the exporter is the need to appreciate and understand the laws and customs of the country so that a successful marketing strategy can be devised. In the case of finance for international trade it is important to study the ways in which trade is conducted in different countries. The advent of both formal and informal trading blocs should help to produce some uniformity of procedures such as rules for collections and custom and practice for documentary credits.

Government regulations vary from country to country. Amongst the most common forms of regulations are export and import licensing, trade exchanges, import quotas and health and safety regulations. Of interest here are the exchange control regulations that need to be understood so that an assessment can be made by the exporter of whether payment for goods supplied are likely to be forthcoming.

Exchange restrictions come in various guises which can, for instance, affect the ability of a firm or individual to hold accounts in a foreign currency, and which may impact on the ability to import goods and to pay for them in any currency, to borrow foreign currency or yet again to buy and sell foreign currency on the spot and forward markets. Even a country with a liberal attitude towards its foreign exchange markets might reintroduce selective restrictions if it wished to reduce or stop trade with that country.

It is clear that many firms would be dissuaded from exporting because of these additional hurdles, but as with most hurdles there are ways of overcoming them. The first step is to acknowledge their existence so they may be incorporated into the planning system, and then to seek help from organisations which offer specialised services. Banks are an obvious source of assistance when looking for help with foreign exchange issues and when seeking to raise finance for international trade.

Many of the following sections describe a very complex subject without giving the usual examples of how particular companies deal with the issues raised. The reasons behind this are that, first, attention to specific detail on the actual methods on offer is vital if the reader is to understand how they work and, second, it should be appreciated that companies would not wish to divulge their methods of operation in, for example, the provision of credit terms to an overseas customer.

EXPORT PAYMENT METHODS

Methods of payment vary in so far as they reflect the degree of risk to be accepted by the exporter, and the following summary should be regarded in that light.

Payment in advance (cash with order)

This is the best possible method of payment for the exporter. However, this form of payment is extremely rare in exporting since it means that an overseas buyer is extending credit to the exporter when the opposite is the normal method of trading. In addition, the risk here is transferred to the buyer, as after payment has been received the seller might then fail to export the goods at all, or might despatch the goods but they do not arrive at their destination either in the condition expected or in the specification required.

Further considerations are that exchange controls must allow for a total payment in advance, and that there is no likelihood of a sudden import–export ban on goods. When Iraq invaded Kuwait in 1990, the UN agreed to a set of trade sanctions against Iraq – this could not have been foreseen by exporters to that country.

Despite the rarity of full payment in advance, it should be remembered that it is quite common for a cash deposit to be made in advance, which is then backed up by another method of payment.

Open account

At the other extreme from cash with order comes the open account, with the goods and accompanying documents being sent direct to the buyer who has agreed to pay within a certain period after the invoice date, usually not more than 180 days. In the meantime the buyer can dispose of the goods as and when necessary, which is normal practice when goods are purchased on credit. This method is becoming increasingly popular in the EU. It is less risky where the buyer and seller have a long-standing business relationship and there are few government restrictions.

Bill of exchange

A bill of exchange is defined as

> an unconditional order in writing addressed by one person to another, signed by the person giving it, requiring the person to whom it is addressed to pay on demand, or at a fixed or determinable future time, a sum certain in money to, or to the order of, a specified person or to bearer.

In more straightforward terms, it means that an exporter prepares a bill of exchange which in drawn on an overseas buyer (or even on a third party) for the sum agreed as settlement. These bills can be drawn either in sterling or in a foreign currency and may be one of two types: a *sight draft* is made payable at sight, i.e. on demand; a *term draft* is when the buyer is receiving a period of credit, with the buyer signifying an agreement to pay on the due date by writing an acceptance across the face of the bill.

The advantages of payment by means of a bill of exchange are that it provides a convenient method of collecting payments, and that it ensures greater control over the goods by the exporter, as until the bill is paid or accepted by the buyer, the bank will not normally release the shipping documents, so the buyer is unable to take delivery of the goods.

An exporter can pass a bill of exchange to a bank in the UK, from where the bill is forwarded to the UK bank's overseas branch or to a correspondent bank in the buyer's country. This bank, known as the *collecting bank*, presents the bill to the drawee for immediate payment if it is a sight draft, or for acceptance if it is a term draft. This is known as a *clean bill collection* because there are no shipping documents, but it is more likely that bills will be used in a *documentary collection* method of payment. In this case, the exporter sends the bill to the buyer through the banking system as described above, together with the shipping documents. The bank then releases the documents on payment or acceptance of the bill by the buyer.

Promissory notes

Promissory notes are rather like an IOU. They are similar to bills of exchange in that they are subject to the same rules, but instead of being drawn up by the person expecting to be paid, they are made by the person owing the money in favour of the beneficiary.

Documentary credits

Between advance payments and open account in terms of risk come documentary credits which, when transmitted through a bank usually in the exporter's country, become the means by which the exporter obtains payment. Dudley[14] defines the documentary letter of credit as being

> a written undertaking given by a bank on behalf of the buyer, to pay the seller an amount within a specific time, provided the seller presents documents strictly in accordance with the terms laid down in the letter of credit.

The exporter is provided with a very small risk of non-payment as long as the condition of the credit is met together with the advice and assistance of the banking system and a set of international rules governing the credit system. Likewise the importer is also provided with advantages as there will be a check to see whether the exporter has complied with the conditions, i.e. the issuing bank checks the documents. The buyer can also insist on goods being received by putting a time limit on the letter of credit, and also receives the advice of the issuing bank. It should also be noted that the cost of issuing the letter of credit is usually shouldered by the buyer, and that these buyers account for 20 per cent of UK exports. Letters of credit are split into two types – revocable and irrevocable.

Revocable letter of credit
A revocable letter of credit is rare because it means that the terms of the credit can be cancelled or amended by the overseas buyer without prior notice. Despite this risk, there are situations where a revocable credit might be useful, such as when goods are shipped by an exporter over time and payment is required for each separate batch. If the buyer is unhappy with the goods in the first shipment, the letter of credit can be cancelled.

Irrevocable letter of credit
An irrevocable letter of credit, as the name would suggest, gives more security to the exporter, since it can be amended or cancelled only with the agreement of all parties to the credit – i.e. the buyer, issuing bank, advising–confirming bank and exporter. However, there is still a degree of risk to the exporter which should be borne in mind. UK banks advise and/or confirm letters of credit, and if advised without confirmation

Fig 16.6 THE SEQUENCE OF EVENTS WHEN AN IRREVOCABLE UNCONFIRMED DOCUMENTARY CREDIT IS USED IN INTERNATIONAL TRADE

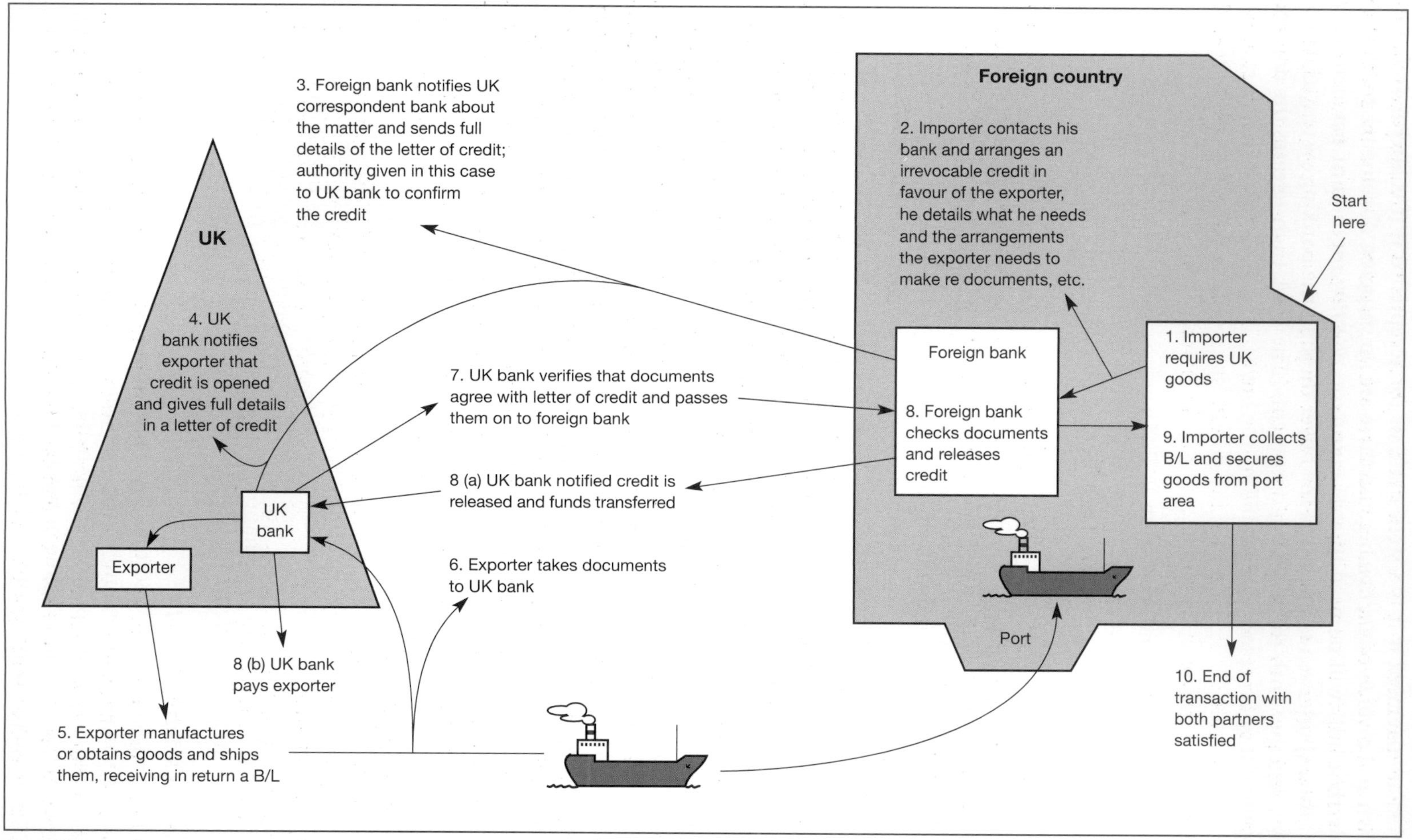

Foreign country

Start here

1. Importer requires UK goods

9. Importer collects B/L and secures goods from port area

10. End of transaction with both partners satisfied

2. Importer contacts his bank and arranges an irrevocable credit in favour of the exporter, he details what he needs and the arrangements the exporter needs to make re documents, etc.

Foreign bank

8. Foreign bank checks documents and releases credit

Port

3. Foreign bank notifies UK correspondent bank about the matter and sends full details of the letter of credit; authority given in this case to UK bank to confirm the credit

7. UK bank verifies that documents agree with letter of credit and passes them on to foreign bank

8 (a) UK bank notified credit is released and funds transferred

6. Exporter takes documents to UK bank

UK

4. UK bank notifies exporter that credit is opened and gives full details in a letter of credit

UK bank

8 (b) UK bank pays exporter

Exporter

5. Exporter manufactures or obtains goods and ships them, receiving in return a B/L

Source: Watson, I.., *Finance of International Trade* (London: Institute of Bankers, 1986).

then no undertaking to pay the exporter is given by the bank. The exporter will have to rely on the value of the issuing guarantee which could be affected by political risks or even the credit standing of the overseas bank. Any doubts arising from the issuing bank's standing can be reduced only by looking for a confirmation, which is to all intents and purposes an additional guarantee by a bank in the exporter's own country. With a confirmed irrevocable letter of credit the supplier is virtually assured of payment provided that the terms and conditions of the credit are properly met. The progress of an irrevocable letter of credit is illustrated in Fig. 16.6.

METHODS OF SETTLEMENT

This section covers the ways in which payment is actually made. Unlike the review of the methods of payment in the previous section, the following summary does not consider the degree of security for the exporter, but focuses on the way in which the overseas buyer will settle the debt.

Payment by cheque

If the overseas buyer draws a cheque in favour of the exporter the buyer will post the cheque to the UK exporter, who then presents the cheque to its bank. The UK bank will send the cheque to the buyer's bank which will then pay the amount of the cheque and debit its customer's (i.e. the buyer's) account. The bank in the UK will pay the exporter after deducting collection charges. Further considerations are mainly to do with the currency used for settlement, so that if the buyer writes a cheque for an amount in sterling, arrangements will have to be made with the buyer's bank to have the account debited with an appropriate amount of the local currency. If, on the other hand, the cheque is written in the buyer's currency, then the UK exporter may have a foreign currency bank account in that currency with a bank in the UK. Arrangements can be made to have this account credited with the cheque payment. Various types of bank accounts are now provided by the major banks to suit the business client who receives regular payments in foreign currency. If this is a one-off or infrequent occurrence a foreign currency bank account may not have been opened, in which case the exporter will have to arrange with the UK bank to have the sterling account credited with an appropriate amount.

The difficulty for the exporter is the length of time taken for the money to be credited to the account. This is a serious inconvenience which, together with the collection charges levied by the bank for providing this service, plus the risk of the cheque being lost in the post or the fact that it might 'bounce', are reasons for reconsidering this rather simple method of payment.

Bills of exchange

The bill of exchange can be used as a negotiating tool. For example, an exporter may hold a bill of exchange which does not mature for another 60 days. However, the exporter requires immediate payment which they can obtain from a bank against the security of the bill. A bill of exchange can therefore be used as a method of obtaining finance as well as settling accounts.

Banker's draft

This is defined as a cheque drawn by a bank on one of its own bank accounts. A banker's draft might be issued by an overseas bank in favour of the exporter which, if expressed in sterling, is usually drawn on a bank in the UK, and if expressed in a foreign currency is usually drawn on itself or another overseas bank.

Sterling drafts drawn on a UK bank can be paid in for the credit of the exporter's account and cleared in the normal way. It is often possible for the exporter to make arrangements with the UK bank for foreign currency drafts to be negotiated (i.e. purchased) or for sterling funds to be credited to the exporter's account.

Bankers' drafts are fairly commonly used, but they are a slow method of payment and the drawbacks are therefore similar to the use of cheques. Unlike cheques, however, they have the advantage for the exporter that direct notification of payment is received.

Box 16.4   NCM CREDIT INSURANCE

NCM Credit Insurance, the UK's biggest short-term export insurer, carried out a survey on conditions for UK exporters to continental Europe. They found that many UK companies had experienced a rise in overdue payments from customers in the EU. The amount of overdue payments rose five per cent in the 2nd quarter of the year compared with the same quarter of 1995; but in the 1st quarter of 1996 it was one per cent lower than the 1st quarter of 1995. The survey also showed that many countries in the EU were experiencing problems as they made attempts to meet the Maastricht convergence criteria for European monetary union. The survey covering export activity among NCM's 6000 customers showed that the value of payments not paid on time in Germany rose 17 per cent in the year to June; payment delays by customers in Spain rose 20 per cent compared with a year earlier and in Holland by 41 per cent for the same period. Companies exporting to France and Italy faced no changes. One in five UK companies suffered losses as a consequence of non-payments, and the low-growth phase is expected to continue as the EU economies strive to achieve the conditions set for economic and monetary union.

Source: Bowley, G., 'Exporters suffer from continental late payments', *Financial Times* (10 July 1996).

Mail transfer, Telegraphic transfer and SWIFT

Mail transfer

Mail transfer or MT is a payment order made in writing, sent by an overseas bank to a UK bank which can be authenticated as having been authorised by an official of the sending bank, and which instructs the overseas bank to pay a certain sum of money to a specified beneficiary. As with bankers' drafts, the UK bank will have an account in the name of the instructing bank and it is this account which will be debited with the amount paid to the beneficiary whose account will be credited by the UK bank. The difference between the banker's draft and MT is that the letter is sent by the bank itself to another bank, and not by the bank's customer to the overseas supplier.

Telegraphic transfer

Telegraphic transfer (or TT) is the same as MT, except that instructions are sent by cable or telex, which costs more to the customer but has the advantage that it speeds up the payment. Additional advantages of this system over MT are that there is no likelihood of instructions being delayed or lost, but it does have the drawback of lack of authentication by signature, only by a code word.

SWIFT (Society for World-wide Inter-bank Financial Telecommunications)

This is a co-operative group of member banks which has established a computerised network in order to improve the administrative efficiency of the banks and to speed up payment transfers between the member banks. Most banks in Western Europe and North America are members of SWIFT, so the use of MT or TT should decline. SWIFT has its own comparable methods of payment using the computer systems of the member banks.

SUMMARY

Global pricing is influenced by the firm's international strategy, the marketing policies that flow from it and conditions in specific markets. Three major categories of factors impact on the firm's pricing decisions – company internal factors, competitive factors and environmental factors.

There are a number of important differences between domestic and international pricing. Management have to tackle the pricing problems and opportunities arising from transfer pricing, price escalation, foreign exchange fluctuations, the international product life cycle, dumping practices and the use of trade terms to gain competitive advantage.

Price standardisation is difficult to maintain because of various constraints such as different inflation rates, exchange rate fluctuations, etc. Price adaptation is more customer oriented but it can lead to 'grey' markets.

Choosing the appropriate method of payment can reduce risks for the exporter and at the same time can provide conditions conducive to trade, such as negotiating credit terms with the buyer or taking out a forward exchange contract to minimise currency fluctuations.

REVIEW QUESTIONS

1 Outline the main pricing objectives of a global marketing strategy.

2 What are the major environmental factors affecting the pricing decision?

3 What is price escalation and what are its main causes?

4 What are some of the ways in which export prices can be quoted?

5 Explain how the inflation rate and the exchange rate can affect the way you price a product.

6 What is 'dumping'?

7 Under what conditions can a firm engage in differential pricing in the global market?

8 Compare the different methods of payment used in international trade.

9 What is transfer pricing?

DISCUSSION QUESTIONS

1 What factors might favour a differentiated pricing strategy in global markets?

2 What pricing strategies would you recommend to a firm with global ambitions?

3 Why is price escalation a problem? Suggest ways to deal with this problem.

4 Is dumping beneficial to the consumers of the importing country? Who gains from this process?

5 How is the international product life cycle relevant for international pricing strategies?

6 Discuss the notion that there are few benefits to be gained by implementing a standardised pricing policy in world markets.

7 Why are host governments wary of multinational corporations' transfer pricing policies? What would be the ideal approach for establishing an export transfer price?

8 Discuss the use of terms of trade as a competitive tool.

9 Discuss the importance of payment terms when making international sales.

Case study

EUROPE'S SOFTWARE COMPANIES[15]

When IBM in 1972 refused proposals from five computer programmers to develop an order-entry program they had already designed for a customer, the five formed their own company, SAP, to exploit the technology used to develop the program.

The Walldorf-based German company is now a market leader in software applications for business computer networks. The company's recent software product, R/S, can combine companies' accounting, payroll and inventories, etc. on personal computer networks.

SAP is making inroads into the US market and increased its net profits by 15 per cent in 1993 to DM146m on sales that were up 33 per cent to DM1.1bn.

However, SAP is going against the European trend. According to International Data, a Massachusetts-based market research firm, Europe buys almost as much software as the USA but produces only a fifth as much.

In Europe's own market too, European purchasers represent only a third of sales; the USA supplies the region's demand, amounting to 60 per cent. Europe has a trade deficit in packaged software of $18bn per annum. However, things are not improving – out of 30 profitable firms in Europe, 19 are US-owned. According to London consultancy Input, there were only nine in 1989. Excluding SAP there were only seven European firms selling in excess of $100m worth of software and related products a year.

The German company, Software AG, has a $380m turnover selling high-end database tools, while the UK's ACT Group does equally well in financial software. The other five companies selling software to large companies are Groupe IBSI of France and the UK's McDonnell Douglas Information Systems, Misys, Micro Focus and JBA International.

Cap Gemini and Debis are two examples of European software firms specialising in customer programming, computer services and consulting for more limited regional markets. Although dominant in Germany, Debis has not made an impact elsewhere. Cap Gemini lost money in its attempt to become a global company. These two firms are hoping to increase sales of stand-alone software with a focus on obtaining contracts with corporate clients.

Why can't Europe's firms compete more widely?

Despite good technology Europe is fragmented in terms of culture, currency, language and legal systems. This means that the region does not have the economies of scale that US companies have at home. Germany is Europe's largest market with 11m PCs as opposed to the US domestic market of 57m. The USA has an equally large number of mainframes, workstations and network servers. A new US software company thus has a headstart.

European software firms are hampered by having to provide manuals, menus and help services in dozens of languages as each country has its own technical rules, cultural preferences and distributors.

The US software company, Intuit, recently bought by Microsoft, had to adapt the Quicken personal-finance program to cater for a non-cheque-writing culture. Moreover, Europe has no Silicon Valley – a deep pervasive computer culture – where people talk about computers all the time. Europe publishes far fewer computer science articles, according to the Institute for Scientifc Information in Philadelphia.

The EU, through various schemes, has attempted to develop its own Silicon Valley by pumping money into software research. National programmes also back companies with grants, capital and contracts. However, there may be some misjudgement as to what to back.

Finding sufficient amounts of capital in Europe is difficult. The US venture capital companies are providers of capital for new firms. They provided over 200 software companies with $630m in 1993. US investors injected twice as much venture capital, buy-outs and other investments as Europeans into markets of equivalent size ($10bn as opposed to $4.4bn), according to Venure Economies, a Boston Consultancy firm. Seven per cent of Europe's funding went to computer-related projects compared with 24 per cent of the USA's.

This might be due to European investors being less sure of seeing an early reward. The NASDAQ stock market in the USA is the route by which small companies quickly go public, winning funds for their backers. Europe has no equivilent so European venture capital goes to established companies that have begun to bring in money. The USA provided 14 per cent of their money for start-ups in 1993 compared with Europe's three per cent.

New European software companies spend their early years searching for capital. The small UK company Recognition Systems, producing specialised data analysis tools, survived on one or two grants and its founders' credit cards. France's Business Objects and TechGnosis used consultancy earnings to develop stand-alone products. When these companies were ready to launch into the US market they had powerful allies to help market their product – Business Objects had AT&T and Oracle and TechGnosis had Digital Equipment and IBM.

SAP has done much the same. Its first sale, a contract to supply accounting and purchasing software worth DM1m, was to a German subsidiary of UK chemical giant ICI. This contract with ICI introduced SAP to other European countries, and the company acquired early experience in writing programmes in several languages.

The offices of an ICI subsidiary in Toronto was SAP's first North American home. Customers such as the chemical company, DuPont, and oil company, Mobil, exported SAP products to their headquarters and to other foreign projects.

Looking to America

Why not become a US company if US companies are what the market expects? The UK trade journal *Computer Business Review* maintained in 1994 that nearly 20 per cent of Europe's top 50 software companies had moved their corporate headquarters to the USA. Insignia Solutions and Synon, for example, sport US management and headquarters in Silicon Valley; both began as British firms and still have a UK presence.

Founded in France with what it calls 'core team', Neuron Data is now incorporated as a Silicon Valley producer of programming tools. Other companies also plan to become American.

The USA is likely to remain a main producer of software. US companies which set the pace in PC software are doing the same in multimedia software. In niche markets, such as educational software, where cultural know-how counts for more than technical acrobatics, there is a need for European firms such as SAP. However, the next Microsoft-type of success story will be in the USA if Europe continues to be divided linguistically and culturally.

Questions

1 *What do you perceive to be the major cost factors confronting software producers in the European market?*

2 *Discuss some of the factors in the European market which will impact on the pricing strategies of software companies.*

FURTHER READING

Abdallah, W., *International Transfer Pricing Policy* (Westport, CN: Quorum Books, 1989).

'Counter-trade', *The Banker* (May 1989).

NOTES AND REFERENCES

1 Henkoff, R., 'This cat is acting like a tiger', *Fortune* (19 December 1988), 69–76.

2 Buzzell, R.D. and Gale, B.T., *The PIMS Principle: Linking Strategy to Performance* (New York: The Free Press, 1987).

3 Abell, D.F. and Hammond, J.S., *Strategic Market Planning: Problems and Analytical Approaches* (Hemel Hempstead: Prentice-Hall, 1979).

4 Onkvisit, S. and Shaw, J., *International Marketing: Analysis and Strategy* (New York: St Martin's Press, 1993).

5 Frank, V.H., 'Living with price control abroad', *Harvard Business Review* (March–April 1984), 137–42.

6 Treadgold, A.D., 'The developing internationalisation of retailing', *International Journal of Retail and Distribution Management*, 18 (1990), 4–11.

7 Keegan, W.J., *Global Marketing Management*, 5th edition (Englewood Cliffs, NJ: Prentice-Hall, 1995).

8   Robert, M., *Strategy Pure and Simple: How Winning CEOs Outthink Their Competition* (New York: McGraw-Hill, 1993).

9   Robinson, R.D., *International Business Management* (Orlando, FL: The Dryden Press, 1978).

10 Keegan, op. cit.

11 Giddy, I., 'The demise of the product life cycle model in international business theory', *Colombia Journal of World Business* (Spring 1978).

12 Onkvisit and Shaw, op. cit.

13 Burns, J.O., 'Transfer pricing decisions in US MNCs', *Journal of International Business Studies* (Fall 1980), 23–9.

14 Dudley, J., *Exporting* (London: Pitman Publishing/NatWest Small Business Bookshelf, 1989).

15 'Europe's software débâcle', *The Economist* (12 November 1994), 101–2.

Global promotional strategies

INTRODUCTION

Promotion means communicating with the customer and the goal of the promotional mix is to create awareness, interest, desire and action on the part of the international consumer – i.e. it seeks to influence the buying behaviour of potential and current customers. In international markets it is often quite difficult to achieve a co-ordinated strategy with the rest of the marketing mix because of the variability in the availability, quality and scheduling of the promotional tools, which will affect the firm's degree of success. This chapter will examine the major strategic issues that affect global promotion and discuss the major elements of the promotional mix.

Objectives

This chapter will examine:

- the global promotional mix
- the communication process when multicountries are involved
- the major limitations to global communications and promotion
- advertising's global role
- the globalisation versus localisation arguments
- media issues and discuss the criteria for agency selection
- how media diversity affects the options available to a global marketer
- the different types of personal and industrial selling activities and types of salesforce
- the issues in managing the global salesforce
- the objectives and major types of sales promotion techniques and the factors determining their choice
- the competitive and complementary nature of sales promotion
- the role of global public relations and its effectiveness for firms in overseas markets.

The function of promotion in international markets is similar to that in domestic operations – i.e. the firm communicates with its various audiences so as to inform, persuade and stimulate a response from the appropriate market segment in its attempt to achieve certain corporate goals. However, the global aspect is more concerned with the co-ordination of the firm's various national marketing programmes in order to develop an integrated strategy.

The aim of this chapter is to examine the various elements of promotion in global marketing and to point out the different environmental conditions under which the global marketer is operating and subsequent constraints imposed on the firm's strategic choices. The communications effort will be subject to cultural differences in various markets, language barriers, different advertising laws, the availability of promotional tools, etc. The issues and problems in co-ordinating and integrating the firm's global promotional strategies are then discussed.

The company involved in global marketing is confronted with a number of important strategic decisions:

- How will the environmental constraints affect the promotional campaign?
- Should a 'pull' or 'push' strategy be the focus of a particular campaign?
- To what extent should the promotional programme be localised or standardised to take account of market differences?
- What should be the content and nature of the promotional message, given the differences in the targeted buyers cultural and economic attributes, availability of media, regulations governing promotion, etc.?

According to Toyne and Walters[1] promotional strategy is

the blending of the advertising, publicity, personal selling and sales promotion activities of a company to achieve a particular response from one or more of the markets it intends to serve. These four elements of the promotion mix are used to enhance the company's image *vis-à-vis* its competitors and/or to inform, educate, and influence the attitudes and buying behaviour of the individuals, companies, institutions, and/or government agencies that make up a targeted market.

Box 17.1 | **BRANDING IN A GLOBAL WORLD[2]**

The increasing globalisation process will mean a shrinking world, which means the global brand promotion is becoming increasingly important for the overall success of the product. Research by Interbrand, a brand consultants, has shown that consumers are prepared to pay a considerable premium for Superbrands, and many would not accept an own-label version for free. One cannot underestimate the power of Superbrands in the globalised world economy. Coca-Cola has always been a dominant force in world branding and occupied the number one position for many years. In fact, Coca-Cola and Coke are two of the most recognised trade marks in the world. Coca-Cola was recently knocked off the top spot by McDonald's in a review by Interbrand, although rival research firms indicated that Coke was still standing firm as the best brand. Interbrand's review in a book called *The World's Greatest Brands* was scored against four criteria: brand weight – dominance over the market; brand length – the extension a brand can achieve outside its category, such as Virgin has demonstrated; brand breath – how wide a brand appeal is to consumers; and

▶ **Box 17.1 continued**

brand depth – such as ethics and loyalty. Other top brands have also lost ground in recent findings; for example, IBM has lost ground to Microsoft, while Kellogg has dropped from second place to 16th.

THE PROMOTION MIX

There are a number of activities which constitute the promotion mix – advertising, personal selling, sales promotion and public relations. These four elements exist in various combinations in any business setting in any global market and under any competitive conditions. These components are not mutually exclusive, and it is difficult sometimes to determine which of the four is being utilised in a particular campaign. For example, in a trade fair, newspapers are used by firms to advertise the event and this could constitute advertising; on the other hand, company representatives at the fair use personal selling to obtain sales. Furthermore, it is quite common for firms to offer free gifts and price discounts during the display and these constitute sales promotion tools. In general, in many markets it is usual to find that personal selling is used extensively in industrial products, and the marketing of consumer goods relies more on advertising and sales promotion. In addition to the communications mix, the rest of the marketing mix must be integrated with the promotional tools to achieve a clear, cohesive and forceful message. For example, Georgio Armani is very careful in its selection of frontshop locations to convey exclusivity, quality and style; an incorrect location would be inconsistent and in conflict with the high prices charged, the product quality and promotional communications. Table 17.1 illustrates the communications mix tools.

THE MARKET COMMUNICATION PROCESS

The communication process consists of a source, encoding, message, decoding and destination – i.e. effective communication involves a sender, a receiver and a message but marketing promotions provide the communication channel. The *sender encodes* a message. 'Encoding' is a step that transforms the idea or information into a form that can be transmitted, e.g. spoken or written words. The message is then transmitted through a *channel* and the *receiver decodes* the message. For the receiver to understand the coded message, it must consist of information that the receiver can relate to and be encoded with relevant images and words common to the receiver's experience. The receiver must not only be informed by the message but must be persuaded to accept and act upon the information as suggested. Promotional messages must therefore be coded in such a way that the receiver reacts favourably. The targeted market segment provides the feedback to the source. It is difficult to predict how effective the communication process has been because of interference ('noise') affecting any one of the five stages. Many factors which are external to the firm can interfere with the communication process. Figure 17.1 on p. 522 illustrates some of the attributes for effective

Table 17.1 TYPICAL MARKETING–COMMUNICATIONS MIX TOOLS

Advertising	Personal selling	Public relations	Sales promotions
Newspapers	Sales presentations	Annual reports	Rebates and price discounts
Magazines	Sales meetings	Corporate image	'Bundled' deals
Journals	Telemarketing	House magazines	Samples, coupons, premium and gifts
Directories		Press relations	Competitions
Radio		Public relations	Direct mail-direct marketing-database marketing
Television		Events	
Cinema		Lobbying	Salesforce incentive schemes
Posters		Crisis management	Trade fairs and exhibitions Sponsorship
Transport			
Other associated costs: photography, typesetting and cinema production			

Source: Phillips, C., Doole, I. and Lowe, R., *International Marketing Strategy* (London: International Thomson Publishing, 1994), 341.

communication – i.e. to make sure that the message is as intended, the sender needs to select an appropriate medium and use cues and symbols that are familiar to the receiver. When the sender of the message is in one culture, such as The Body Shop in the UK, and the receiver is in another, such as in Japan, it may be the case that the message encoded in the British culture may not 'work' in the oriental culture. There are many factors which affect the channel through which a message is conveyed. Figure 17.1 illustrates some of those factors which may act as barriers to effective communication. Differences in some of these socio-cultural and economic factors, especially between the home and overseas countries, can lead to differences in product perceptions and purchase behaviour. Thus the international environment presents a set of unique problems which can act as barriers to global communications.

LIMITATIONS ON GLOBAL PROMOTIONS

Marketers often approach promotion from an ethnocentric perspective – i.e. what works at home will work elsewhere. This approach will not necessarily work in all markets as the target markets will differ in their characteristics and buyer behaviour.

Fig 17.1 ELEMENTS OF THE GLOBAL COMMUNICATION PROCESS

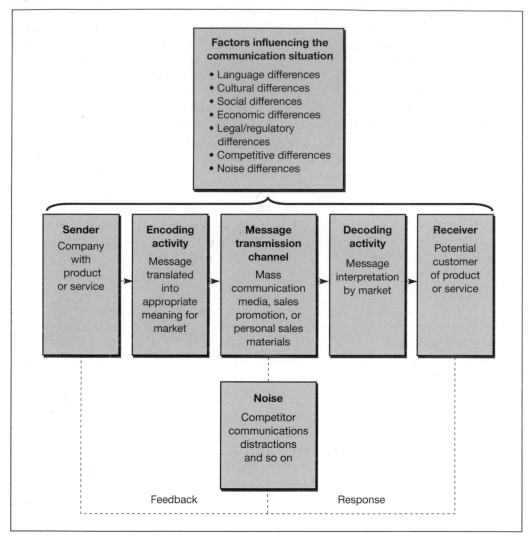

Source: Toyne, B. and Walters, P.G.P., *Global Marketing Management: A Strategic Perspective*, 2nd edition (Boston, MA: Allyn & Bacon), 542. ©1993. Reprinted by permission of Prentice-Hall, Inc.

Cultural barriers

The elements of the cultural environment include religion, aesthetics, education, social organisation, etc. (*see* Chapter 6). It has a major influence in the communication process, and it affects people's values, attitudes, perceptions and interpretations of signals and symbols, their preferences for products and patterns of purchasing behaviour. The global marketer needs to be culturally sensitive, to know the 'rules of the game' in order to be successful. These factors need to be considered when the message and media plans are being prepared. Most of the problems of global promotion stem from a failure to interpret the local culture. Global marketers have subtly changed their focus recently. Instead of focusing on cultural differences only and then adapting their strategies to suit the particular overseas market, they are now concentrating on cultural similarities in different markets. This approach increases opportunities and enables the firm to attain global products and brands through standardising its marketing strategies.

Symbols represent feelings, ideas and other aspects of a culture; advertising and packaging are two areas where symbols can have an impact on a firm's promotional activities. The use of colour in advertising must be sensitive to cultural norms – in many Asian countries the colour white is associated with mourning, hence an advertisement for a detergent in markets in the West where whiteness is emphasised would need to be altered for promotional activities in some Asian markets. The colour red stands for good luck and life in the People's Republic of China and purple represents quality; these colours are ideal for packaging purposes in that market.[3]

A country's values and norms also affects promotion in a number of ways. Many European countries have strong individualistic and achievement oriented cultures. A firm structuring its reward system for a salesforce must take this into account where individual achievement is highly valued. In contrast, Japan has a very group oriented and collectivist culture. A firm operating in that culture needs to be aware that reward for achievement is shared by an individual's group team and not by the particular individual who may have been largely responsible for the success.

Language barriers

When the firm operates in different cultures and languages, it is more than likely that the firm has to translate and even change its sales promotion materials, slogans, brand name, etc. An advertising campaign based in one language may be totally ineffective and inappropriate in another. The global marketer has to make strategic decisions in the following areas:

- There are many languages in the world and the marketer has to decide which language to select to optimise its advertising campaign in the various markets. In Belgium, Canada and Switzerland two or more languages are spoken and the firm needs to establish which of these languages will be most appropriate.

- There is always the danger that the language subtleties will be lost, and translations of advertisements tend to suffer from inaccuracies. There is also the risk of using outdated slang and making costly translation errors. For example, 'Body by Fisher' was translated into Flemish as 'Corpse by Fisher'; and in Latin America 'Avoid Embarrassment – Use Parker Pens' was translated as 'Avoid Pregnancy – Use Parker Pens'.[4] Therefore, a firm that needs to translate, must not only ensure accuracy but also convey the nuances of meaning.

Stages of economic development

The effectiveness of the communication process is also affected by the stages of economic development and the prevailing economic conditions.

Literacy levels
Countries with low literacy rates will require a different promotional strategy, in that more visual rather than written or oral media will be used, such as posters, cinemas, billboards or the radio. Television will certainly not be a major medium in these markets.

Agency availability
A lack of advertising agencies can also hamper an effective promotional campaign. Countries like China have only a few agencies when compared to population size,

whereas the UK has more than 500. The quality of agencies is an important variable in determining the success of the campaign.

Media availability

This can affect the firm's ability to reach the target market with the message. There are two aspects to this. The first refers to a poor communications infrastructure – a medium such as television which is heavily used in the UK and Europe may not be available as a cost-effective medium in some foreign markets (in India, for example, the ownership of television sets is approximately one set per 200 persons whereas in the UK and Europe it is almost one for every two persons). The second aspect refers to state regulations in terms of advertising time available – France, for example, has restrictions in terms of the number of minutes advertising allowed per day.

Social factors

The attitude towards advertising and promotion by both consumers and the business community has a major influence on the effectiveness of the communication process. Attitudes affect the type of media to be used, the level of advertising expenditure and the interpretation of the promotional message. Norwegian and German consumers tend to interpret messages literally when compared to the Spanish or Italian buyers.[5] Only 40 per cent of French consumers and under 50 per cent of the Danish buyers felt advertising was beneficial and helpful compared to 80 per cent of Norwegians.[6]

Competition

A major influence on the promotional process is the competitive situation. The global firm will compete against the communication strategies of both national and international competitors. Naturally, the type, size and promotional strategies used by competitors will vary from one national market to another. The global marketer will thus adapt their promotional strategy and the timing of their efforts in response to competitors. The presence of the global firm will provoke different reactions – some will follow the global firm's course of action, while others will retaliate. For example, if France Telecom were to enter the European markets aggressively, it would expect a similar response, as was the case when Procter & Gamble entered Western Europe and provoked the local companies to intensify their advertising campaigns.

Legal and regulatory factors

The selection of media and promotional content in terms of comparative statements, use of superlatives, type of products that can be promoted and use of samples in promotional material are influenced by both government regulations and the advertising industry's code of conduct.

- Strict codes of conduct can affect the advertising campaign and rewrites may be required. For example, superlatives are forbidden in advertising messages in Germany, weight reduction products are not allowed in Finland and advertising messages may not be directed at children in Sweden. There are also restrictions on the types of products which may be advertised (*see* Table 17.2).

- Government taxation can influence the effectiveness of a promotional campaign. Tax laws can affect the cost of promotion and the choice of media. France has

Table 17.2 COMPARISON OF EUROPEAN ADVERTISING REGULATIONS

	Tobacco	Alcohol	Pharmaceuticals	Miscellaneous
Austria	Banned on TV	Subject to a large number of regulations	Advertising for prescription drugs is forbidden by law	Ads showing brutality or degradation to women are banned, advertising for video-cassettes is banned
Belgium	Not allowed	Restricted in general	Prohibited in general	A variety of restrictions apply to food advertising; cosmetics and sanitary products advertising is permitted under certain conditions; adverts with a political or religious content are forbidden; ads for sweets must show a health warning
Denmark	Banned	Restrictions and voluntary restraints in some cases	Forbidden for non-prescription pharmaceutical drugs	Very strict restrictions exist for products aimed at children and young people
Finland	Banned	Banned	Restricted for non-prescription drugs	Advertising is not permitted for certain slimming products and products of an 'intimate' nature
France	Banned	Banned, especially for drinks with a high alcohol content	Prior approval is required from government authority	
Germany	Forbidden	No restrictions so far	Banned	Advertising for war toys and games of chance is forbidden; restricted advertising when aimed at children and young people
Republic of Ireland	Cigarette ads are banned; pipe tobacco and cigar ads permitted but regulated	Liquor ads are banned, but wine and beer ads are permitted but regulated	Prohibited in general	Forbidden for pregnancy tests, contraceptives and betting
Italy	Banned in all media	Restricted	Restricted	
Netherlands	Voluntary restrictions	Voluntary restrictions	Voluntary restraint and subject to screening by experts	Sweet ads on TV must display toothbrush symbol
Portugal	Banned	Strict restrictions	Authorisation required in advance	Car ads must contain costs of taxes and insurance, as well as figures on fuel consumption
Switzerland	Banned	Banned	Banned	Ads with religious or political content are forbidden; advertising which compares brands and services of different competitors is allowed if comparisons made are true
UK	Pipe tobacco and cigar ads are permitted but strictly regulated	Voluntary restraints	Ads for certain products or treatment are banned; restrictions on others	Ads with pornographic content or anything offensive to public taste are forbidden; restrictions on ads for political or religious organisations

Source: STERN: The Media Scene in Europe, 3 (1991).

proposed a tax on TV and radio advertising which would increase the cost of this medium; this could act as a disincentive to the firm, given that a global promotional campaign is already generally more expensive than in the home market on a *per capita* basis.

The above factors all influence the effectiveness of the communication process, and impact on the development of a variety of promotional campaigns in national markets.

GLOBAL ADVERTISING

Advertising is a key tool in global communications. Although advertising principles do not vary from country to country, the objectives and methods employed will differ in the different markets. There are three major measurements for determining the importance of promotional activity in a particular market:

1 total advertising expenditure, which gives a good indication of the level of competition in that market;

2 advertising expenditure by industry;

3 advertising expenditure by media, which indicates the importance of different types of media in a national market.[7]

Global advertising is an important communications medium and it is the most visible and controversial promotional element in the communication mix because of its extensive use and one-directional method of communication. It is also a relatively cost-effective method and it can effectively position the product which then becomes difficult to dislodge. A successful advertising campaign can be utilised as an asset which can then be transferred to different markets. To emphasise its importance, it is estimated that by the year 2000 the global advertising expenditure will reach a staggering figure of $650bn.[8]

The rapid development of the global market is causing shifts in the role of advertising. In the USA, the EU and Japan, advertising is one of the most important elements of the promotional mix, especially for consumer products. For most other products, personal selling is the next most important promotional tool. In general, the appropriate role of advertising within the promotional mix will vary among national markets. Even if advertising is strategically the best format for some markets, firms will not adopt it, if the media is not available or advertising facilities are not adequately developed.

The global marketer has a number of important decisions to make to ensure the development of appropriate campaigns in each national market:

● whether to standardise or localise the campaign

● selecting the advertising message

● selecting the agencies

● selecting the media

● determining the budget and evaluating the effectiveness of advertising

● organisation of the advertising strategy.

Standardisation versus localisation of advertising

An important decision area for global marketers is whether an advertising campaign developed in the domestic market can be transferred to foreign markets with only minor modifications. Complete standardisation of all aspects of a campaign over several foreign markets is rarely attainable. Standardisation implies a common message, creative idea, media and strategy. Standardising global advertising can lead to a number of advantages for the firm.

1 *Reduction of advertising costs* from three sources: first, production costs will be reduced in terms of artwork, printing, etc.; second, the advertising concept can be transferred to other markets with only minor modifications; third, economies of scale will be attained by centralising the advertising campaigns in the head office, as opposed to having different local offices. Esso's 'Tiger in your tank' campaign, Coca-Cola, Sony, McDonald's, etc. are all advertised universally with virtually the same advertising approach.

2 It is easier to project a *consistent product image*.

3 It ensures that the *corporate-wide objectives* will be consistent and maintained in most overseas markets.

However, standardised advertising may encounter obstacles.

1 *Language obstacles*: it will be difficult to standardise slogans or explanations because of translation difficulties. For example, General Motors' brand name for one of its models was the Vauxhall 'Nova' – this does not work well in Spanish-speaking markets because the brand name sounds like 'no go'.

2 *Perception problems*: although the product need may be universal, this does not mean that the message appeal can be global, because consumers in different markets perceive products differently. Kentucky Fried Chicken, for example, is viewed as an ordinary meal in the UK and USA but in Japan it is looked on as a special meal for special occasions. The message will therefore need to be changed to suit local tastes and life-styles.

3 *Multiple objectives*: advertising objectives may have to be different in various markets because environmental factors, such as the level of education, *per capita* income, etc. are different. For example, the German car manufacturer Volkswagen promotes its VW Golf in the UK in the medium- to high-price range, as a car for the upwardly mobile consumer segment, yet advertises it in Germany merely as an ordinary efficient vehicle.

4 *Legislative obstacles*: many governments maintain tight regulations on message content, language, sexism and product types that can be advertised (*see* Table 17.2 on p. 525). Strict regulations are found and enforced in industrialised economies rather than in developing economies where the advertising industry is as yet not highly developed.

5 *Literacy levels*: if the market has a high level of illiteracy then the advertising message and type of media need to be adapted for this market.

6 *Lack of media choice*: this also acts as a constraint on standardising the advertising campaign. Extensive magazine advertising, as in the UK and Europe, may not be possible in other markets. Television advertising is also highly restricted in many countries.

7 *Different market segments for the same product*: an advertising strategy may have to be modified because the firm wishes to reach a different consumer segment in other markets. For example, bicycles in the UK are promoted as recreational products whereas in many developing nations they are promoted as an important means of transportation.

Although there are many obstacles to standardising advertising, it is probable that a modularised approach will be adopted. Pepsi-Cola used this approach by using a core commercial featuring Tina Turner and added local rock stars to the main footage where appropriate to suit the particular market in question.[9]

Firms adopting a high degree of standardisation base their strategy on two assumptions – first, that the different national markets are similar in product function and conditions of use. Second, that the different targeted market segments will respond in a similar way to the global promotional campaign. On the other hand, firms adopting a customised advertising strategy base their approach on the assumption that consumers in national markets have different product perceptions and preferences.

Media selection

Global media selection is more difficult than in the domestic market and there is much variation between and among national markets in the kind of media that are being used. The criteria for selecting the appropriate media are:

- the target audience
- media availability
- media coverage
- media effectiveness
- media costs.

Media availability

The media required may not be available or available only on a limited basis; commercial television, for example, is still not widely available in the Scandinavian countries. Access may also be restricted – the time available per day may be limited or the type of products that can be promoted may also be limited by law in many countries, as illustrated in Table 17.2. On the other hand, there may be too great a media choice and this can also create some problems. For example, to advertise nationally in India could involve advertising in over 200 daily newspapers.

Media coverage

A problem with international advertising is generating adequate reach and frequency. Attaining this may require a combination of different media. Advertising high-quality healthcare products solely on television would not be adequate to reach all the required target market. The firm will need to combine television advertising with other media such as magazines, radio and newspapers. However, using a wide variety of media also spreads the budget thinly, which then affects the degree of frequency. The alternative to this is for the marketer to introduce the product over a smaller target market in one or two countries in order to attain the required reach and frequency.

Media effectiveness

Another problem confronting the global marketer is the measurement of how effective the media campaign has been. The relative lack of data will make it difficult to verify the effectiveness of the campaign. In some markets, reliable data is not available, or is even non-existent; some media, like newspapers, are extremely difficult to monitor. The process is further complicated by the 'spillover effect', whereby there is advertising exposure in more than one market. For example, an Austrian household may also see advertisements designed for the German market. This makes it even more difficult to obtain accurate data, and the advent of satellite television will simply compound this problem.

Media costs

Global advertising incurs higher costs than in the domestic market for the following reasons:

1 translation costs are incurred;

2 rewriting advertisements to be culturally acceptable is a further cost;

3 there may be a higher percentage of wasted circulation due to the fragmented nature of media in some foreign markets;

4 inefficient production runs may be incurred because of the need to produce different material on a smaller scale for each market. For examle, the Parker Pen Company sells the same product in all markets but the advertising differs considerably in each: in Germany, the advertisement headline is 'This is how you write with precision', whereas in the USA the theme of the message is based on image and status.[10]

Agency selection

The global marketer needs to consider the following points when selecting an advertising agency for its global promotional campaign:

● market coverage – the markets that the agency deals with should be those that coincide with the firm's

● the provision of good-quality service

● international cohesion – a firm that requires a fairly standardised international campaign will need to seek out an agency which provides a good international approach

● the firm will need to be spending a considerable amount on advertising to attract or interest international agencies.

GLOBAL PERSONAL SELLING

Personal selling occurs when a customer or prospective purchaser is met in person by a representative of the firm for the purpose of making sales. On a per contact basis it is the most expensive of all the promotional tools, but personal selling is very effective and flexible. It is a very effective tool when the market is concentrated and the products are of a high unit value and not frequently purchased. These type of

| Box 17.2 | DAEWOO CARS LTD[11] |

The Daewoo story is already a marketing legend. Daewoo Cars Ltd is the UK subsidiary of the South Korean Daewoo Group – the world's 30th-biggest industrial corporation. The UK business was established in May 1994, and it had the objective to bring a range of Daewoo cars to the UK market in spring 1995 and capture one per cent of the UK market by 1997. It faced a few challenges – the company and its cars were an unknown quantity and there was no service structure. Daewoo's promotional strategy took the motor industry by storm in October 1994, stating that it would take control of its distribution chain and deal directly with customers and therefore discard the dealers in the system. Its unique selling proposition was to be the most customer-focused brand in the motor industry. In addition, it had a partnership with Halfords to provide an instant national service network. With just two models and a fledgling retail network, Daewoo sold 13 169 cars in nine months in 1995. By the end of 1996 it had achieved its one per cent target market share with 35 000 cars.

products require demonstrations and products will be fitted to the customer's individual needs. It is flexible in that any customer objections or requests can be dealt with on the spot. In many East Asian cultures, personal contact is important to selling and businessmen tend to discuss business only with persons who come highly recommended by a mutual acquaintance.

Global personal selling is used mainly in industrial markets for selling technical goods such as industrial machinery, computers, industrial plants, etc. or business services. It is rarely used for consumer goods or services – if so, it is used for cars and durable consumer goods and personal financial services. Personal selling tends to be more important in international than in domestic markets; in many cases, subsidiaries are more involved with personal selling than headquarters, whose involvement is limited to a varying degree.

The factors which determine the degree to which a company is involved in personal selling in a national market are its local marketing objectives, the level of its market presence and extent of the local distribution network.

Personal selling versus advertising

Personal selling is the next major communications tool after advertising. Although it shares with advertising the common aim of creating sales, it differs from it in a number of respects:

1 advertising is a one-way communication process whereas personal selling is a two-way communication process with instant feedback;

2 advertising suffers relatively more 'noise' than personal selling;

3 advertising relies on non-personal medium of conduct and sales presentation compared to the face-to-face contact in personal selling;

4 compared to advertising, personal selling takes a larger share of the promotional budget; this may be due to cheap abundant labour, especially in emerging economies, thus making it easy to hire a large salesforce; another reason can be

attributed to limited media availability and advertising restrictions that reduce the amount of advertising the firm can undertake in a particular market;

5 advertising can control the message more than personal selling because the sales-force will respond appropriately in the situation, and this may differ from the firm's pre-prepared message and format;

6 personal selling is much more persuasive than advertising because the salesperson can adapt the sales pitch to fit in with the customer's personality and product needs, while advertising has a simple pre-set message targeted to a larger audience and with very limited customer contact.

Types of personal selling

There are several types of personal selling:

1 *creative selling*: this involves persuading a new buyer to take a trial order; this type of selling is quite difficult in foreign markets because the seller lacks the intimate and diverse knowledge of the buyer's environment – for example, the role of religion is quite important in business negotiations and practices in Middle Eastern countries;

2 *missionary selling*: this involves a manufacturer's sales representative working closely with an intermediary – for example, the salesperson works with the foreign agent to provide information to end-users or even sets up training packages for the distributor's salesforce;

3 *technical selling*: this is a type of consultancy pitch, in that the technical knowledge of the firm's products are emphasised – a computer salesperson might advise clients on improving inventory control while still encouraging them to purchase the hardware; this type of selling is used extensively in the industrial marketing of heavy machinery, chemicals, etc.;

4 *trade selling*: this involves the salesperson assisting the intermediaries in foreign sales promotion, which in turn increases the volume of sales to the intermediary.

Salesforce personnel

Sales personnel may be:

1 *nationals*: these are personnel who are based in the home country – for example, a UK citizen who sells pharmaceutical products for Hoffman La Roche, the Swiss-based company, in the UK; the advantages of using nationals are:
   (a) they have a better market knowledge and understanding of the social-cultural environment;
   (b) they cost the firm less compared to other types of sales personnel;

2 *expatriates*: these are employed by a firm in a country other than their own – for example, a British citizen who works for the British company ICI in Denmark; they are usually employed when there is rapid market growth in the country concerned;

3 *cosmopolitan personnel*: these are usually employed at management level and tend to be from one country employed by a firm based in another and working in a third – for example, a UK engineer who works for a French company in Spain.

Salesforce management

A firm that enters a foreign market generally relies on a distributor or import house. This intermediary will normally have an established salesforce team and the global firm does not need to develop its own team. However, if the firm wants to be intensively involved in a particular market it needs to establish and manage a salesforce team. The choice of a local salesforce will be influenced by:

● cost factors
● the type of business activities undertaken
● the extent of control required over the sales personnel.

The success of a global promotional strategy depends on the management of the firm's salesforce. The salesforce must be carefully recruited, trained and motivated for global customers.

Recruitment and selection

Global companies have encountered difficulties when recruiting qualified sales personnel in certain local markets, for a number of reasons:

1 the shortage of qualified sales personnel with the requisite characteristics; this problem is more acute in emerging economies;

2 the image of selling varies in different markets. In Europe, selling has a fairly low status and companies have problems recruiting high-calibre staff, and the global firm will need to spend more time to find the best talent. In contrast, some markets, such as the USA, accord sales personnel a relatively high status, and they have career paths that can eventually lead to middle and senior management positions. Firms tend to have little difficulty in recruiting talented personnel in these markets.

The personal characteristics and skills necessary and important for success will vary with the social and business environment that the person has to operate in. However, there are a number of criteria when selecting host-country sales personnel, such as linguistic skills, maturity, motivation and adaptability. Language ability has in the past been the major criterion, given the importance of communications, but it is debatable whether this criterion is a good indicator of the person's potential in the long term. In addition, given the diversity of tasks in different markets, the notion of an 'ideal type' salesperson for one type of industry, let alone across all markets, is questionable. Job descriptions are bound to vary globally and a particular sales job will also be a function of other factors such as the company's marketing strategy, distribution channels and product line. To compound the problem, the salesperson will also be operating under different environmental conditions of religion, race, etc. These are natural segmenting variables which should also be reflected in the makeup of the salesforce to avoid group conflict. In a predominantly Muslim market it is unlikely that a firm would send a Hindu or Protestant representative; other examples of potential group conflict are German versus French, and Irish versus English. In cases where recruitment is extremely difficult, the global firm can facilitate its rapid entry into a local market by acquisition or joint venture to utilise the local salesforce capabilities. In the pharmaceutical industry, Merck acquired Banyu Pharmaceutical in Japan as a way to acquire a large salesforce.

There are also costs to the employees who are based in a foreign country. These are mainly personal such as family ties, children's education, adaptation to foreign cultures, pressures on family relationships as a result of living abroad and possibly 'missed' career opportunities at home.

Training

Some of the shortcomings encountered in recruitment and selection can be compensated for by training and salesforce management. Many international firms are beginning to realise the importance of training their workforce to compete effectively in global markets. The importance of training human resources as a critical factor in attaining and sustaining competitive advantages has been well understood by many Japanese companies, which have extensive and varied programmes.[12] The Japanese computer company, Nippon Electronic Corporation (NEC), has extensive training programmes ranging from learning languages, negotiating skills to familiarisation with business cultures.[13]

The type of training programme will be a function of the job demands, new product applications and the salesforce's previous training. The training programme is normally done at either local or regional level and the global marketers' input is providing creative ideas, training manuals and materials, holding forums and meetings for subsidiary sales personnel to exchange ideas and experiences. When the firm is global or the firm has high tech products, training takes place at the international level – large companies like IBM have a European training and development centre. It is not unusual to find a global firm training the sales staff of distributors, but the training here would be of a very specialised nature.

Motivation and remuneration

Successful salesforce management depends on motivating salespeople. Many Western global firms have great difficulty in retaining and motivating salespeople in various national markets.

Motivating sales personnel is more challenging in foreign markets than in the domestic market, because the status of selling will vary in different markets and the willingness of the salesperson to engage in conversation with strangers will also vary in different cultures. These two factors can act as a major hindrance to motivation. Cultural differences influence and impact on the level of motivation in the salesforce, so motivation must be constructed to meet local needs. The nature of the rewards will also vary according to different cultures. In the USA, economic rewards are powerful motivators, while Europeans tend to be motivated more by non-economic rewards, and collective achievement is highly valued in Japan.[14]

Work by Harpaz[15] on the labour force in seven countries indicated that the major work objectives were good wages and interesting work. These work goals appear to be consistent globally among different age groups and between genders.

The challenge for the global marketer is thus to assess the mix of monetary and non-monetary rewards appropriate for each particular market. In addition to a bonus or commission for meeting projected targets, a firm could offer a strong incentive by awarding top performers with a vacation or foreign trips. Apart from visiting the firm's international headquarters the trip also offers the winner an opportunity to visit many tourist attractions. For example, Caterpillar offers working vacations to its top sales personnel, and this appears to be a more effective motivation scheme than a straight monetary remuneration.

In emerging markets where both material and service goods are in such short supply, as in the Eastern European economies, a prime motivating scheme was to have the salesperson train in the global company's headquarters for a short period. This gives the sales representative not only an opportunity to go shopping but also visit some tourist sites. In markets where selling has a low status, a global company can overcome this by giving financial rewards, titles, offer training and publicising the achievements of its top performers.

In recent years, direct selling companies such as Amyway and NU Skin have grown exponentially. These companies bypass the normal distribution chain of retailers and wholesalers and distribute through their network of salespeople or distributors. To achieve such growth rates, these companies have compensation packages that motivate their distributors. It is not uncommon to have commissions ranging up to 30–40 per cent. This is in addition to bonuses rewarded for reaching target sales and recruiting new distributors.[16] The corporate culture of these direct selling companies is also a major incentive for the salesforce – for example, many distributors are attracted by the independence, potential earnings and sense of achievement which is implicit in the direct selling culture.

Control and evaluation

The company needs to know whether it is managing its salesforce efficiently. When companies pay on a commission basis, then close monitoring of the salesforce is essential to ensure that the company's strategies are being implemented satisfactorily and its targets met. The following are good control techniques and indicators of saleforce efficiency in a particular overseas market – the use of quotas, average sales-call time per contact, average revenue per sales call, percentage of orders per 100 sales' calls, reporting arrangements, the establishment of itineraries and sales territories, etc.

Although the company may have markets in distant markets, it still needs to evaluate saleforce performance for a number of reasons:

1 how the saleforce performs in a foreign market will establish the company's success level. The company can assist the local management with ideas and application of evaluation techniques. In this way, the local managers will be getting good saleforce performance;

2 evaluation enables the company to make international comparisons amongst its portfolio of markets. There are various criteria that the company can employ in making these comparisons, such as salesforce cost as a percentage of total sales, average revenue per sales call, etc. This type of information can then be used to assist weaker markets to improve their performance.

Telemarketing

The rapid changes in telecommunications and information technologies have had an impact on global personal selling. It is not always necessary now to have face-to-face contact with customers, this can be done over the telephone. Telephone selling has been available for many years, but it is only recently that it has been utilised extensively. This is due to improved quality as a result of advances in telecommunications technology, lower running costs and increased availability of telephones for private households, especially in the developed economies. All these factors have contributed to growth of this method of selling, now known as *telemarketing*. The telemarketing approach involves cold calling by sales representatives, telephone market surveys, follow-ups to customer requests for information as a result of print advertisements and calls which are designed to develop a customer database. This mode of selling is also being promoted by the establishment of an 0800 telephone system facility. This tends to be a free service number paid for by many companies in Europe and the USA. It makes telephone communication easy through the use of a simple coded number. It gives the potential buyer easy access to the seller where they can make enquiries and service calls. The added advantage is that the caller does not pay for the call except for some overseas markets, even then local rates apply. In addition, this facility streamlines communications, reduces costs of servicing a market through fewer visits to the territory, develops closer buyer and seller relations because of the inexpensive call rates, and when the office is not manned this facility can be transferred to a different number. When the British Airways 0800 office is not manned in the UK, especially late at night, the calls to the UK office are transferred to a British Airways office in New York. Such a facility makes customer contact efficient, effective and controllable. It increases the speed of customer response to an advertisement and thus improves customer service. It is cost-effective as it removes the middleman and it provides a valuable market database and sales leads without incurring expensive risks. In general, the majority of international telemarketing campaigns are currently focused on business-to-business contacts because many companies have the facilities of a combined telephone/fax/telex which makes it easier and more reliable to conduct this mode of promotion. There are, however, problems with telemarketing with respect to individual privacy. Certain EU countries such as Germany have strict privacy laws, which prohibit cold calls to protect the privacy of consumers; on the other hand, the UK, the Netherlands, France and Italy do not restrict outbound telemarketing.

Industrial selling

Selling consumer goods or services is quite distinct from selling industrial equipment or business services. For the latter market, particular promotional procedures are necessary if an industrial products firm wants to succeed in the global market. These are selling through a consortium and the use of international trade fairs.

Consortium selling

A consortium is a group of companies that works together as a unit in order to achieve a common objective. In this context, the consortium would operate as a group seller and would tend to be engaged in bidding for larger tenders. Sometimes a nominee will be used to preserve anonymity during the negotiations. A consortium:

1 enables the individual firms to bid for large tenders because the combined capacity of the individual units makes it feasible;

2 helps individual companies to share the risks, especially of very large projects;

3 gives the individual firms a competitive edge, as the group can offer a 'turnkey solution' to the prospective client ('turnkey operation' is a solution which the

buyer attains; it can be a plant or system and can be commenced at the turn of a key, i.e. all the building and testing is carried out by the contractor(s), who hand over a fully functioning plant to the owner);

4 means that the customer has to deal with only one supplier and this simplifies the process considerably.

Consortia undertakings range from railway modernisation, power generators to hospital and irrigation projects. Given that many of the consortium projects will vary in nature, the consortium is usually set up for only the one project, and when completed it is dissolved. Some of the firms may come together again for another project, perhaps with new member firms, but it is unlikely that the second project will be so similar to the first that the consortium can function as an unchanged unit. Given the nature of consortium projects, it is not surprising that negotiations between member firms of the consortium are difficult and complex. Furthermore, consortium operations are highly technical and bid document preparations are time-consuming and expensive. Consortium selling appeals to firms who have customers requiring a 'turnkey solution' or for firms that sell industrial equipment which represents only a small proportion of a larger project.

International trade fairs

International trade fairs involve producers, distributors and other sellers displaying their products or services to current and prospective customers, suppliers and the media. There are more than 8000 trade shows globally, creating over $25bn of business.[17] Trade fairs are generally associated with industrial goods although some consumer goods are represented as well. In the UK, almost a quarter of most manufacturing companies' promotional budget is spent on trade fairs. Most fairs are held annually, for example, the Hanover Fair in Germany, the Milan fair in Italy and the Guangzhou Trade Fair in China. There are also specialist fairs for cars, medical equipment, chemicals, etc. which tend to be held annually world-wide, although some are not held every year. An example of a specialist trade fair is the Aerospace show in Paris or Farnborough in the UK.

International trade fairs are effectively 'temporary offices' for companies in the market place, and they offer ideal opportunities for firms to introduce new products and make personal contact with potential customers. They are also an excellent method for promoting a firm's products at a modest cost to an audience of visitors at the fair, an audience that is very receptive as they normally come with a firm intention to place orders. International trade fairs offer a number of other benefits to a firm:

1 they provide customers with the opportunity to study new products, and to see them being demonstrated;

2 they are a cost-effective method of promoting the company's products to a large group of potential buyers. It saves much time and effort, as they provide direct contact with potential buyers, especially useful for new companies that want to enter a market but have no contacts, or for a small exporter fresh to the market;

3 they are an important source of market intelligence: the company can obtain feedback and evaluate the effectiveness of its promotional strategy, and can compare the competitor's products and buyer reaction to them;

4 it is a useful forum to solicit and find potential intermediaries, contact government officials and decision makers and continue to cultivate business contacts;

5 trade fairs are also used by companies to boost the morale of employees and intermediaries.

However, there are also some compelling reasons for firms not to participate in trade fairs:

1 they are a costly exercise – costs related to the design and construction of the company stand, rental costs of furniture and space, transportation and labour costs, etc. The company could reduce its costs by exhibiting at government-sponsored fairs or export development offices;

2 companies need to determine which fairs are the most appropriate for their products and what products to specifically display, given the enormous number of trade fairs each year. There is the additional problem of co-ordinating and planning the exhibition with the company's agents or distributors.

Standardisation versus adaptation

The standardisation of personal selling in the firm's various markets would be difficult to achieve. The style and quality of personal selling will vary enormously, not only from one company to another but also from product to product and from one target group to another. There are many reasons why a customised personal selling strategy is preferable, as the following examples illustrate.

Meetings

Given that the distribution members are located within a particular market, we can expect that selling styles will differ in each market. In Europe, it is common to have a sales discussion over a game of golf, over lunch and even after business hours meetings over dinner or in a nightclub. This mixture of business and social functions is expected by many clients in the European markets; whereas in the USA, business meetings tend to be scheduled for breakfast or lunch. In Japan, it is not unusual for sales personnel to call on employees in the workplace with the explicit agreement of the employers.

Negotiation strategy

The saleforce's negotiation strategy will need to be adapted to suit the client's cultural system – i.e. an understanding of the client's culture and not using stereotyping notions to identify the client's negotiation characteristics. In a negotiation simulation exercise,[18] it was found that negotiations between the Chinese led to better results when competitive strategies were used, whereas negotiations between Americans tended to use problem-solving tactics which quite frequently influenced outcomes.

Personal selling tactics

A company may also need to modify its personal selling tactics to suit each market. In some Asian markets, personal networking is critical for success. The Avon company tapped into this trait by visiting the homes of only friends and relatives rather than employing its usual door-to-door selling adopted in the US market.

In spite of the strong arguments against standardisation, some companies have adopted a fairly standardised approach. For example, Eastman Kodak has standardised its operations on a regional basis in European markets.[19] Each European market will have one person in charge of the whole copier–duplicator programme. Each market will have its own team of service, sales and customer-service representatives; the sales representatives are involved in customer analysis, deciding the right type of equipment and installation and taking overall charge of that account. However, each team is expected to respond to any customer in the European markets within hours.

Push versus pull strategy

Managing a balance in the promotional mix is usually based on the effectiveness and costs of the different promotional components. One of the most common promotional mix decisions the global marketer has to make is how to balance the advertising and personal selling strategies in specific markets. This is sometimes referred to as the *pull* versus *push* strategy choice. In a domestic or single country environment, the *push* strategy emphasises personal selling in the promotional mix. The objective is to put pressure on the members of the distribution channels to stock and display the company's products, in spite of the fact that it is a very expensive promotional tool. Push strategies are generally used by firms selling to the government sector or selling industrial or complex technological products. The *pull* strategy relies more on the use of advertising directed at the end user of the product or service; in this instance, the pressure is put on the distribution channel members to stock the product as a result of the pressure of consumer demand. This type of strategy is generally used for consumer-type products and where a large segment of the market is being targeted.

Pull strategies tend to be used in the following situations.

1 If the channel length in a particular market is long, this involves more costs and effort to 'push' the products through the system. To overcome the channel inertia inherent in long distribution chains, the firm is likely to use the pull strategy. Many overseas markets, such as Japan, are likely to have convoluted and long channels, and it is not surprising that many companies adopt pull strategies in that market.

2 Related to the channel system, another important factor is whether the company can utilise its distribution leverage with the channel members. In some markets shelf space is limited and there can be an intensive struggle to get the company's products on, especially when competing against other brands. In these circumstances, it may be prudent to adopt a pull strategy and hope that consumer demand will impel the retailer to carry the firm's products.

3 Product complexity also influences the choice of strategy. With less complex products a firm tends to employ a pull strategy, whereas sophisticated and technologically complex products usually require the firm to assist customers, and a push strategy is used.

4 The size of the target market will also affect the type of strategy used. If the firm's product is widely consumed then a pull strategy would be instituted.

5 Consumer shopping behaviour is another variable affecting the choice of strategy. If self-service is the dominant mode of buying behaviour, then a pull strategy would be most appropriate.

One major assumption of the adoption of the pull strategy in any market is the accessibility to the media, i.e. the existence of an infrastructure of electronic media such as radio, TV, newsprint, etc. In addition, 'access' also refers to whether there are restrictions on the type of media used, product to be advertised and restrictions on target groups (e.g. children) and time availability (hours of advertising allowed per day on a TV channel) (*see* Table 17.2 on p. 525). European markets tend to be more restrictive than the USA. If the access is limited to some degree in one form or another, the firm may be better off using the direct salesforce to complement the limited pull strategy in any particular market. The *push* strategy is normally used in the following conditions:

1 the decision is determined by the channel length; a short channel is conducive to this type of strategy;

2 when a product needs to be explained to consumers because of its complexity; in some emerging markets where consumers may lack the necessary knowledge to understand the product, greater efforts will be required by the saleforce team.

GLOBAL PUBLIC RELATIONS

Public relations (PR) is concerned with images – i.e. the activity of public relations is to build good relations and improve understanding between a company and all with whom it comes into contact, both within and outside the organisation. The 'public' is any group that has an actual or potential impact on the company's activities. There are of course different types of public (*see* Fig. 17.2) and it is the major objective of public relations to present a favourable impression to one or more of them. Some have argued that organisations are ill-prepared to defend a company's reputation

Fig 17.2 AN ORGANISATION AND ITS PUBLICS

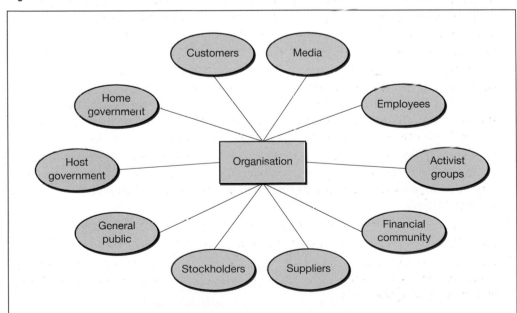

when required. According to Fombrun,[20] company reputation is everything because it creates economic value and when this reputation is threatened it can wreck a company's brand and stock value. He believes that good company reputation is a precious corporate asset and embodies the company's uniqueness and hence is a critical competitive strategic tool. He refers to this asset as 'reputational capital', and its full value is realised only when its lost. PR is used to promote not only organisations but also products, places, people, ideas, activities and nations.

PR today is a broader concept and can include publicity activities as well. When compared to advertising, the general public is likely to believe publicity because it is 'free' and is not directly influenced by the firm. This positive aspect of publicity makes it an invaluable asset. Although it is 'free', this characteristic of publicity is often viewed by companies as a promotional component that is not possible to manage, because the company does not control what is said about the organisation or its products, nor how and where it is said. As the company does not control the publicity communications, it cannot rely on this tool alone. Publicity can be very positive for the firm – for example, German cars in general have a positive image with UK consumers as a result of feature articles in magazines, press releases, etc. However, global publicity can result in an equally negative image which is beyond the control of the company. In 1990, the Perrier mineral water company in France had much negative publicity after traces of benzene were found in their bottled water. The company's handling of the situation did not help matters – in the early stages, the firm did not answer many queries and this gave the impression of arrogance. The firm also appeared evasive at times when it did issue some kind of response. World-wide sales slumped dramatically and the company has yet to recover its previous sales targets.

Internal PR is especially important in multinational companies to create a cohesive and appropriate corporate culture. The use of staff newsletters, videotapes, training manuals, audio material, etc. all help to create and reinforce a sense of corporate identity. Externally, the company would also like to establish its global identity and increase sales and other corporate objectives.

The objectives of a PR campaign will therefore include some or all of the following.

1 To promote an *awareness of the existence of the company*.

2 To *anticipate and counter criticism of the company*, and to *minimise damage* to the corporate image. These can be based on:
   (a) *product issues* – the famous and now classic case of Nestlé's dubious and imprecise promotional methods with respect to infant's milk powder in Africa, which resulted in a high level of infant deaths. There was a boycott of Nestlé's products and the company's image was adversely affected for a considerable length of time;
   (b) *corporate conduct* – for example, the UK ferry company P&O employed a PR firm to explain away its mismanagement of its striking workers in the early 1990s. Other examples include the fraudulent activities of some of the members of the board of directors of Guinness breweries in the UK; the role of Union Carbide in the Bhopal disaster in India, in which they were accused of not responding quickly and appropriately; and, most recently, many famous global companies such as Levi Strauss & Co, Marks & Spencer, etc. have been accused of using child labour to produce their products in countries such as India, Puerto Rico and Honduras;

(c) criticisms may also be levelled at companies based on the *markets* they deal with. For example, many firms have been accused of trading with the former apartheid regime in South Africa or with the Iraqi government.

3 To *overcome prejudice against the use of the company's product*. A public relations campaign will attempt to counter negative perceptions or to convey positive images. For example, British Nuclear Fuels spent considerable resources to promote the public acceptance of nuclear power as a clean source of energy. Thus, in a sense, PR can be seen as a form of corporate diplomacy when it attempts to convey constructive images to the various publics, so that both parties benefit.

4 To promote and establish a *brand image in a foreign market*.

5 To increase a company's *sphere of influence* and achieve a high profile.

Responding to criticisms and influencing the public positively can reap enormous advantages. For example, if the financial public has a favourable image of the company, it could improve its borrowing facilities. Although PR is not marketing, it could therefore be said that achieving good relations with the publics is essential to marketing success for the company. Firms can obtain help with public relations from a number of sources. Many multinational companies such as British Petroleum and Toyota have their own PR departments, whereas other firms can employ specialist PR consultants or the PR departments of the big advertising agencies. The larger PR firms do offer a 'full service' and this integrated package includes amongst other things media relations, speech writing, obtaining publicity and media training on how to be interviewed on television, radio and answering questions.

The types of public relations tools and techniques that can be employed include the following:

1 as well as being a useful marketing tool, sponsorship is also a very effective vehicle to gain public relations exposure, especially for firms that want to enter foreign markets in which they are not yet well known. Sponsorship of the arts and sports is a growing industry in Europe – the UK company Allied Lyons sponsored the Royal Shakespeare Company and Germany's Becks beer used arts sponsorship to launch itself in the UK market. Coke sponsored the London Marathon, and many Japanese companies such as Sharp and Sony have used their logos on UK football teams' shirts;

2 lobbying government, politicians, opinion leaders and pressure groups;

3 news releases – to find or create favourable news about the company;

4 stage special events, such as visits by well-known celebrities, competitions, publicity stunts, firework displays, grand openings, hot-air balloon releases, etc. These are all designed to reach and interest the target groups. Richard Branson of the UK's Virgin company embarked on several hot-air ballooning events;

5 audio-visual presentations, include video and audio cassettes, films and slides are all very essential communication tools;

6 printed reports, company newsletters, brochures and other publications can be utilised to reach and influence the target market;

7 the use of corporate identity materials which are distinctive and attractive would help the public to identify and immediately recognise the company and is closely allied to the above point – the use of business cards, logos, stationary, uniforms, etc.

8 embarking on community projects is an effective method to increase public recognition of the company, as well as to gain goodwill from the public. This can take many forms such as raising funds for the handicapped such as Mencap in the UK, or simply donating to charitable causes;

9 the company could also increase its profile and influence by giving talks to trade associations, schools, etc. Speech is an essential tool in PR, and some companies such as the Stock Exchange and Lloyds of London have a panel of speakers just for this purpose.

The major strategic decisions that have to be made in public relations are similar as for the other promotional tools – i.e. the management needs to determine the PR objectives, selecting the PR message and vehicle, implementing the plan and evaluating the results of the PR effort. PR results are difficult to measure, as the impact is indirect because this activity is used in conjunction with other promotional tools. The crude measures involve media exposure such as 5000 column inches of news and pictorials, x minutes of air time, etc. Although not very satisfying, it does at least give an indication of the cost of the time and space that was purchased. However, the sales and profit figures give the best measure, if they are obtainable.

Although PR is not marketing it is important to effective marketing, in that PR activities complement other promotional tools. It achieves this by establishing a credible environment in which the promotional tools can be used more effectively; hence it is sometimes seen as below-the-line promotion.

UK whiskey, for example, commands a premium in many foreign markets because of the positive image that is cultivated by the industry. Any promotional activities in the overseas markets will be undertaken within this context. It is precisely because of this role of PR that its function is described as *megamarketing* or the fifth 'P' of marketing.[21] What this means is that in today's competitive business climate a firm needs to influence the external environment (public opinion and any public who have power) through PR activities. This broader concept of PR is an attempt to ensure that the market is receptive to the company and its products. Thus marketing in the global market entails not just the management of the 'four Ps' but also PR. The methods for achieving this are varied and many.[22]

1 Use of *corporate advertising*. If the company wants the market to be aware of its existence and products, one method is to take out full-page advertisements in prominent national newspapers and journals such as *The Wall Street Journal*, *Financial Times*, *Der Spiegel*, *Le Monde*, *The Economist*, etc. Hitachi did precisely this in the US market in the 1980s; the Union Bank of Switzerland and Nokia, the Finnish telecommunications group, have both taken out full-page advertisements just prior to major launches into various markets. Even Japanese and US companies advertised in China before the products were available.

2 Let the *company CEOs* be the major communicators and public persona – Bill Gates of Microsoft, J. O'Reilly of Heinz Inc., and Akio Morita, former CEO for Sony, are all examples.

3 Use *government support and initiatives* to support the firm's export and marketing strategies in international markets. It is not uncommon for heads of state to aid the export efforts of companies – Mrs Thatcher's visits to the Middle East markets in the 1980s certainly facilitated the trade agreements for the UK arms industry; when President Bush visited the Far East in the early 1990s, there was much effort to expedite trade agreements.

4 Enhance the company's *government negotiation and lobbying* skills. Many Japanese firms faced much resentment and hostility in the early phase of their export expansion. Learning from their experience, many firms now appreciate that they need to manage the external political/public environment too. A number of key success factors are to develop lobbying and negotiation skills and invest heavily in philanthropic activities in the arts, education and so on.

GLOBAL SALES PROMOTIONS

'Sales promotion' is a term that has sometimes been used to describe all those activities that do not fall directly under personal selling, public relations and advertising. Sales promotions are short- to medium-term activities that can add value to the sale. These various activities are supposed to stimulate interest and provide the motivation to purchase the goods and services Sales promotion is targeted not only at the consumer level but also at the middlemen in order to gain their support. It is also used in industrial selling. For example, some pharmaceutical firms in the USA[23] sponsor trips for their wholesalers, or doctors are given gifts.

Sales promotion techniques are varied and numerous, ranging from coupons, samples and contests to trading stamps. Sales promotion can be effective in many markets, but the techniques employed need to be accepted culturally, legally and psychologically, as illustrated in Table 17.3. In Puerto Rico, there was resistance to using company coupons,[24] as the word *coupon* was associated with food stamps or government handouts by the Hispanic residents. Any sales promotion techniques need to be adapted to suit the cultural meanings and symbols of the market.

Table 17.3 INTERNATIONAL VIEW OF SELECTED SALES PROMOTION METHODS

Coupons	Require literacy and some sophistication on part of retailers and consumers Require well-developed backward channels to handle redemption For new product introductions, usually require well-developed print media Social status perceptions affect effectiveness
Contests and sweepstakes	Cross-national use complex due to differing legal requirements Prize choice should vary to match target-market tastes Likely to be less effective where mass media coverage is poor Require some sophistication on part of retailers
Price-offs	Likely to be ineffective in environments where prices are subject to bargaining Require some sophistication on part of retailers Subject to trade misuse
Stamps	Ineffective where target market is not amendable to delayed gratification Unfeasible in unstable economic conditions (for both manufacturer and target market) Handling and redemption both require fairly stable and sophisticated channels
In, on, and near packs	Do not require literacy Do not require extensive mass media support Do require secure distribution channels and some control over channel members May require packaging adaptation depending on level of channel development

Source: Dahringer, L.D. and Mühlbacher, H., *International Marketing* (Reading, MA: Addison-Wesley, 1991), 500.

Sales promotion techniques

Companies operating internationally employ a variety of sales promotion techniques. We can distinguish three categories of techniques, as illustrated in Table 17.4.[25]

1 *Price-reducing techniques*: under this category the price of products are reduced in one form or another. This can be in the form of promotional discounts, use of coupons and trade allowances.

2 *Add to value or perceived value*: this technique involves giving free samples, coupons attached to a product or close to it, bonus packs and premiums; all these add value for the customer. For example, some UK magazines and newspapers 'give away' hundreds or thousands of pounds of gifts when readers enter contests or subscriptions to a magazine. Some supermarkets give a free sample when a large item has been purchased, such as getting a free toothbrush with a large tube of toothpaste.

3 *Provision of information*: techniques that provide information include displays, exhibitions, trade shows, product demonstrations and special events. These techniques are particularly important for technical products. They are normally used in conjunction with other sales promotion techniques.

Sales promotional objectives

The major objective of any type of sales promotion technique is to stimulate and enhance sales, as illustrated in Table 17.4. Sales promotional techniques targeted at consumers have the objective of enticing them to a trial purchase. The rationale for this is that the customers' risk perception will be considerably reduced when they have had an opportunity to try a product or service. Free samples over the cheese counter or a free one-day training session given to potential participants by a training/consulting organisation are all very effective sales promotional techniques. Some techniques are designed to persuade trial users to become regular buyers or repeat purchasers of the product or service. Purchasing three items of soap for the price of two, or the frequent flyer programmes operated by most European airlines such as Swissair, British Airways and Scandanavian Airlines, are examples; with these programmes, customers earn air miles for their flights and can redeem them for free travel. Sales promotion techniques can also be used strategically by the company to develop their distribution system, especially in highly competitive markets. Distributors can be influenced to increase their orders by giving them trade allowances, samples and the use of competitions. The company can also aid the distributors by providing information to the target customers through trade shows and exhibitions.

Factors determining the choice of sales promotion techniques

There are a number of factors which affect the type of sales techniques to employ. Some of these factors are culture-bound, which the global marketer needs to be especially aware of, and others transcend any cultural barriers and have to be considered regardless of the market that the firm is operating in.

Values/norms

As mentioned above, the type of sales promotion technique must blend in or be consistent with the cultural values or norms of the target market. This is all the more urgent with the opening up of the European Union (EU), with the consequent free

Table 17.4 SALES PROMOTION TECHNIQUES

Technique	Objective	Target	Key issues
Reduce price			
Coupons	Encourage trial or repeat purchase	Consumers	Channel capacity
Trade allowances	Build distribution; increase orders	Intermediaries	Legal constraints; channel power
Price-offs	Encourage repeat purchase	Consumers	Pricing laws
Add to value or perceived value			
Samples	Encourage trial purchase; build distribution; increase orders	Consumers; intermediaries; staff	High cost
In, on, and near packs	Increase perception of value	Consumers	Space limitations; service norms; impact on price
Self-liquidating premiums	Encourage trial or repeat purchase; extend image; reinforce advertising	Consumers	Relate to product
Continuity premiums	Reward users; encourage repeat purchase	Consumers	Channel capacity; value of premium
Bonus packs	Increase perception of value; convert trier into user	Consumers	Space limitations; service norms
Contests and sweepstakes	Encourage trial purchase; draw attention to other promotional messages	Consumers; intermediaries; staff	High cost; lack of mass trial; legal constraints
Provide information			
Displays	Draw attention to product; provide information	Intermediaries; consumers	Must combine with other techniques
Special events	Draw attention to product; provide information	Intermediaries; staff	High cost
Trade shows and exhibitions	Create presence in target's mind	Intermediaries; staff	High cost; usually for industrial or durable goods
Product demonstrations	Allow consumers to evaluate product without risk; build distribution	Consumers; intermediaries	High cost

movement of goods and services. It is only natural and logical for companies to want to build a pan-European sales promotion strategy with the expected economies on logistics and premium purchasing. However, one of the major constraints for companies wishing to work on a pan-European basis will be the cultural factor. In particular, a target market's acceptance of the sales promotion techniques will be critical and it has been said that the sales promotion industry in the UK is perhaps a bit more developed and sophisticated than its European partners.[26] There are many instances of 'cultural conflict' in the literature; for example, in the UK, there is a cultural acceptance of on-pack price reductions but this is not so in Italy, which requires permission from the Finance Ministry first.

Cost factor

Global marketers not only need to assess the total cost of the sales promotion campaign but also need to estimate roughly what contribution the outlay of the promotional effort will make towards increasing sales. The global marketer has to estimate which is the most economical method of sales promotion, and yet one that achieves the desired results. Using coupons in a campaign, for example, will turn out to be less expensive than giving out free samples; however, this may not be the most appropriate strategy if the objective is to encourage consumers to have a trial run of the product. In the case of some products such as food or drink, only the use of samples can communicate the product benefits.

Channel members' affinity

Channel members such as retailers and wholesalers must be willing and able to accommodate the logistical requirements of a sales promotion campaign. Channel members must be willing to provide storage and shelf space for bonus packs that are to be used in the sales promotion campaign. Point-of-purchase displays and coupons need to be accepted by the channel members, the latter method requiring much effort and time to process them which could prove unpopular with retailers, as happened in Northern Europe.

Channel power

The role of power in the channel system has a bearing on the types of sales-promotion techniques to be used. If the retailers have a high degree of channel power they may extract considerable trade allowances with the manufacturers. Marks & Spencer and Tesco stores in the UK, Albert Heijn in Holland and Carréfour in France all wield enormous power over their suppliers. Conversely, if the manufacturer has a high degree of power then the retailers are unlikely to obtain many trade concessions.

Legal restrictions

The use of some sales-promotion techniques is forbidden by legal restrictions in many national markets, and it is not surprising that many sales promotional activities are relatively under-utilised, due largely to legal rather than to psychological barriers. Compared to the USA, the EU countries not only have a larger number but also a more diverse range of restrictions. This diversity of legal barriers makes it very unlikely that the EU will be able to standardise its promotional regulations in the foreseeable future. For example, 'money-off next purchase' is not permitted in Germany but is legal in Spain; 'discounts on the next purchase' is valid in Belgium but illegal in Denmark. The global marketer needs to consult the local authorities in each specific market to ascertain the particular legal characteristics before embarking on a promotional campaign. Table 17.5 (overleaf) provides a brief summary of the legality of 20 different sales promotion techniques across some of the EU countries.

The rationale of various EU governments to restrict or ban some sales promotional methods is that:

1 special offers such as free gifts, money-off vouchers, etc. that accompany a sale improperly influence consumers, as the real value of the product/service is often hidden;

2 sales promotion campaigns disrupt and distort consumers abilities to make rational buying decisions by stimulating impulse buying behaviour; as well as hampering them from meaningfully comparing prices of similar goods;

3 large companies have the resources to implement an effective sales promotion campaign at the expense of the smaller companies; the effect is that larger firms enjoy an inequitas position in the market-place, and consumers will not have the opportunity to compare products on the basis of quality and value for money.

Some of the most widely used promotional techniques will be discussed below to illustrate how they might be affected by local regulations.

Use of premiums and gifts

There are practically no legal restrictions on the use of premiums in the UK, whereas most EU countries tend to have limits on the value of the premium given. In France, it is forbidden to offer premiums that are conditional on the purchase of another good, and the value of the premium must not exceed seven per cent of the product's price if it is below FF500. The Scandinavian countries, Belgium and Germany all have very strict laws with respect to promotion, as they wish to protect the consumers from being misled about the true value of the product/service. In general, all free premiums are illegal in Germany, but if a realistic price is charged then premiums are permitted if their value is very small or they represent a product accessory. In the Netherlands, premiums must not exceed four per cent of the value of the product, and there must be a connection with it. In Italy, the Finance Ministry decides which products can be promoted this way and it also establishes the maximum value of the premiums. 'With purchase or in-pack' premiums are illegal in Belgium; they are allowed only if the premium is an accessory to the main product or is not generally available, or the premium is of low value. Many non-EU countries such as Venezuela and Argentina also have very strict laws; these countries almost prohibit the use of merchandise premiums. Japan does not allow the value of the premiums to exceed 10 per cent of the value of the product that is to be purchased.

'Reduced prices' and discounts

Laws against price discrimination may prevent the use of price reductions in many sales promotion campaigns in the EU. The UK, France and the Netherlands allow on-pack price reductions. Germany allows 'price reductions', but the authorities must be notified in advance if the company is going to have a sale. Generally, these sales tend to be limited to occasions such as a winter or summer sale, the end of a product line or a company anniversary. This is unlike the USA, where sales of all types for all occasions are permitted. Furthermore, any quantity discounts should lie within the industry's percentage range, and discounts for payment on delivery should not exceed a certain percentage. In Belgium, multiple purchase schemes are allowed but the price

Table 17.5 WHICH COUNTRIES ALLOW WHICH PROMOTION?

	UK	Irish Republic	Spain	Germany	France	Denmark	Belgium	Netherlands	Portugal	Italy	Greece	Luxembourg
On-pack price reductions	●	●	●	●	●	●	●	●	●	●	●	●
Banded offers	●	●	●	?	●	●	?	●	●	●	●	?
In-pack premiums	●	●	●	?	?	?	?	?	●	●	●	?
Multi-purchase offers	●	●	●	?	●	?	?	●	●	●	●	?
Extra product	●	●	●	?	●	●	●	●	●	●	●	●
Free product	●	●	●	●	●	●	●	●	●	●	●	●
Reusable/alternative use pack	●	●	●	●	●	●	●	●	●	●	●	●
Free mail-ins	●	●	●	?	●	●	?	?	●	●	●	?
With-purchase premiums	●	●	●	○	●	○	?	●	●	●	●	○
Cross-product offers	●	●	●	○	●	?	○	●	●	●	●	●
Collector devices	●	●	●	○	●	?	?	●	●	●	●	?
Competitions	●	●	●	?	●	?	●	●	●	●	●	●
Self-liquidating premiums	●	●	●	●	●	●	?	?	●	●	●	?
Free draws	●	●	●	○	●	○	○	○	●	●	●	○
Share-outs	●	●	●	○	?	○	?	?	●	?	●	○
Sweepstake/lottery	?	?	●	○	?	○	○	○	●	?	●	○
Money-off vouchers	●	●	●	○	●	?	○	●	●	?	●	○
Money-off next purchase	●	●	●	○	●	○	●	●	●	?	●	●
Cash backs	●	●	●	?	●	●	●	●	●	○	●	●
In-store demos	●	●	●	●	●	●	●	●	●	●	●	●

Key: ● Permitted ○ Not permitted ? May be permitted

Source: Norgan, S., Marketing Managment: A European Perspective (Wokingham: Addison-Wesley, 1994), 337. Reprinted with permission.

> **Box 17.3** BT AND OFTEL
>
> British Telecommunications (BT) clashed with the telecommunications watchdog OFTEL, after they banned a joint promotion between BT and British Sky Broadcasting (BSkyB). The promotion rewarded members of BT's Friends and Family discount scheme with up to £39.60 of free calls if they were also subscribers to BSkyB, the satellite television company. BT paid for the television advertising and BSkyB paid BT for the free calls. In addition, BT paid for some advertising costs of the special offer under which members of the Friends and Family scheme qualified for discounts on their telephone bills and BSkyB fees. OFTEL's argument was that BT's promotion was discriminatory in that it targeted and offered continuing benefits to only those who became and remained BT and BSkyB customers. In addition, OFTEL said that BT had breached its licence by offering preference to certain customers over others. The costs to BSkyB of making the payments to BT in respect of calls were offset by the costs of the publicity paid for by BT. In effect, the cost of providing the free calls was funded in whole or part by BT.
>
> *Source*: Cane, A., 'OFTEL bans BT venture with BSkyB', *Financial Times* (23 October 1996).

may not exceed over a third of the combined price. In addition, the product that is promoted should be available separately at the normal price. Discounts in Scandinavia are generally restricted and Austria prohibits cash discounts that discriminate between different groups of customers.

Samples

Germany limits the size of the sample pack, and restricts door-to-door free samples which have a limited population coverage. If the product has been on the market for some time, then samples are completely banned. Alcoholic beer samples are banned in the USA.

Sweepstakes and competitions

Sweepstakes are not encouraged in the EU because they are perceived by the authorities as a scheme which can deliberately mislead the public, because the stake is not free but is embodied in the higher price paid for the promoted product. In addition, sweepstakes encourage gambling and promote an undesirable morality. In the UK, the laws relating to competitions are that if a purchase is not required then chance must determine the winner. But if a purchase is a mandatory requirement, then the use of skills should decide the winner. In contrast, games won by chance in the Netherlands are illegal, but competitions that require the exercise of skills are permitted, but the prizes should not exceed a certain value, currently around 2500 guilders. In Belgium, irrespective of whether a product or service is purchased, the competition must involve a large degree of skill. France has similar competition laws as the UK and Italy allows competitions, but they are subject to tax. In Germany, competition is allowed if the purpose is to draw attention to the product, but there must be no order form to accompany the competition details, otherwise it is illegal.

INTERNATIONAL DIRECT MARKETING

Direct marketing involves direct access to the customer, and the major tools of this approach are telemarketing (discussed earlier), direct mail, door-to-door selling, catalogues, electronic media (home shopping and cable television) and 'off-the-page' selling via cut-outs in magazines and newspapers.

Direct marketing has become an important medium of selling over the last decade especially in the developed economies of the EU and the USA. The EU countries which have had rapid growth include the UK, Belgium, France and the Scandinavian countries. In spite of its growth, direct marketing expenditure in the EU constitutes only about a quarter of all marketing expenditures compared to two-thirds in the USA. Future growth in the EU will depend on the extent of government regulation on promotions, which are tightly controlled. Germany has one of the most restrictive regulations, whereas the UK and the Netherlands have a more liberal approach. Direct marketing has also grown rapidly in some Asia Pacific countries, such as Singapore and Hong Kong.

Growth of direct marketing

A number of factors has contributed to the rapid growth and development of international direct marketing:

1 the costs of traditional forms of promotion such as advertising and sales promotion have escalated to such a point that companies are searching for alternative methods;

2 the rapid developments in information technology in areas such as databases and desktop publishing have facilitated the production of high-quality in-house direct marketing materials, especially for small and medium-sized companies;

3 developments in mail technology have reduced the costs of distributing direct marketing materials;

4 the development of database technology has not only facilitated the development of lists of prospective customers, but has also made it available to companies;

5 the development and the immense growth of the Internet or 'information superhighway' has increased the availability of interactive facilities, whereby customers can order directly from the system;

6 the extensive use of direct marketing by companies has also accelerated its development. There are many benefits associated with using direct marketing which companies find attractive – the outcomes are measurable; names and addresses of consumers are stored in a database which can be used for future direct marketing campaigns or even sold to other firms; consumer profiles can be built from information based on the company's sales files, customers' residential neighbourhood, socio–demographic characteristics, etc.; and direct marketing is both a convenient and an effective marketing tool.

Direct mail

Direct mail can be a very cost-effective method for reaching global consumers, as it can be targeted to a specific niche group. Not only is direct marketing very flexible in the format, type and amount of information conveyed, but it can also send very personalised messages to the target audience. The type of information can be very selective and can vary from special discounts to availability of credit packages. The company can include a variety of response mechanisms including an international freephone 0800 number so customers can call back for further information. Virgin UK and the financial services company Direct Line, for example, have freefone numbers in their direct mail materials.

Another advantage of direct mail is that a firm can gain first-mover advantages in a market, as the competitors will not be initially aware when a campaign is launched. There are virtually no restrictions in terms of media space, airtime or copy deadlines to meet. A direct mailshot can thus be varied in terms of content, size, geographical coverage and timing.

In terms of the global market, direct mail offers companies an excellent opportunity to enter foreign markets in a cost-efficient way. A recent example of a firm using this medium to enter overseas markets is Citibank of the USA, which embarked on a direct mail campaign in the UK in late 1996. Direct mail also offers the firm a high degree of control as well as enabling it to experiment by varying the approach used in different global markets. Indeed, direct mail has achieved the fastest growth in business-to-business advertising – over half of all Spanish companies, two-thirds of Danish companies and over three-quarters of German companies have used direct mail for business-to-business advertising. However, there are certain preconditions for direct mail to be effective, in whatever market the company may operate:

- the target group must be easily identified and defined narrowly
- an efficient and economical global postal system must be in place
- there must be an efficient and effective collection system for the shipped goods
- the materials or catalogue will naturally require to be translated into the respective foreign languages
- the effectiveness of direct mail depends on the availability and quality of the mailing lists, and the accuracy of mailing lists is extremely important; obtaining precise lists, however, may not always be an easy task, but the presence of list brokers, especially in many of the developed markets, does alleviate some of the difficulties of atttaining reliable lists
- customers will be wary of ordering and sending money to foreign firms which are unknown to them; it is therefore not only necessary, but also essential, to establish a local address in the market if a firm wishes to achieve a fairly high degree of success.

Catalogues/electronic media

The use of catalogues was perhaps the first major form of direct marketing in the UK. This method involved advertising an organisations range of household/personal products through a mailing or in magazines, and those interested would send off for a catalogue that could be ordered directly from the home. Alternatively, orders could be placed with agents, the latter being rewarded with payment of commission or given discounts on their own purchases. This incentive scheme is also an attempt by the supplier organisations to encourage consumers to become potential agents for the company.

The advantages of this type of direct mailing for the company are that:

- it bypasses the traditional use of retailers, thereby retaining control and attaining higher margins
- it positions the product as an exclusive product, as it is only obtainable from this route
- the company develops a customer database, and it has control and access to it, which would not have been the case had retail intermediaries been used.

However, there are certain disadvantages associated with this mode of promotion:

- higher administrative costs due to the need to check customers' credit references, given that payment are by cheque or credit instalments
- higher incidence of bad debts
- it will miss a segment of the market who will buy only if they can see and feel the merchandise.

It could be argued that an extension of the principle of catalogue promotion is electronic media. This is the use of media where an offer is transmitted electronically and the response may be made through the same medium. Under this definition, we include facsimile, television (e.g. cable) and a computer terminal. Advertising using this medium is already extensive on the Internet for a variety of goods and services, such as the buying and selling of shares and home shopping. Some supermarkets in the UK are conducting tests to evaluate the viability of using such a medium. The advantages of such a mode of promotion, especially in a globalised consumer market, are:

- accessibility to world consumers at an incredibly low cost for the firm
- huge savings on time
- virtually a 'paperless' ordering system, reducing the paperchase of the traditional systems
- almost immediate response
- the electronic command will be flowing simultaneously through the sales, inventory control and payments sections, thus creating a faster and more reliable system.

Perhaps one of the major disadvantages of electronic mail is the potential abuse of consumers, especially when firms bombard customers with unsolicited advertising material.

SUMMARY

Global communication involves the transmission of information from a source to a receiver, and in a business context this communication occurs through promotion. The communication encodes an idea, image or information into the words, pictures or symbols that constitute the message. Effective communication means that the message received is that intended by the sending firm. Of all the marketing mix, promotion is most vulnerable to misinterpretation and misuse, which are major obstacles to effective communication and promotional messages in a global market. Communication and advertising is particularly challenging, as the firm's strategic choices are constrained and modified by a number of factors – the promotional effort will be subject to different legal requirements, cultural and language barriers, the availability of media, the level of literacy in the target market and the cost of the promotional effort. These are the major types of limitations that international marketers will encounter in their global promotional campaigns. The effective implementation of the promotional programme is crucial to a firm's marketing success in the global market place. An international marketer therefore needs to use the promotional tools within the opportunities and constraints posed by the environment and communication channels.

One of the major decisions that an international marketer needs to make is to determine whether the advertising campaign should be standardised or localised, given that there are advantages to be gained from both strategies. The firm also needs to make a decision on the selection of media. This is a difficult task in international markets because the firm needs to examine media coverage, media availability, and cost and effectiveness if a campaign is to be successful. Another major decision area for consideration is agency selection. Before a decision can be made, the firm will need to consider factors such as the agency's coverage, financial expenditure and quality of service.

Personal selling involves direct communication between a seller and a buyer; there are different types of personal selling such as creative, missionary, technical and trade selling. A salesforce may be direct or indirect and salesforce personnel may be nationals, expatriates or cosmopolitan. The management of the salesforce team is critical to a firm's success in the foreign markets – the salesforce must be carefully recruited, trained and motivated.

Global public relations is the management of the images that a company wishes to project to its many publics, given that the organisation's image is a valuable strategic asset in the competitive market place. Public relations (PR) is an important and sensitive task for global marketers. The ability to control this type of publicity is often more difficult in international markets as internal factors cannot be influenced by a company.

Sales promotion can be divided into three broad categories – those that add value to the product, those that provide information and finally those that reduce price in some form. There are a number of factors that affect the types of sales promotion techniques to utilise – these are channel power, costs, cultural values, regulatory constraints and channel capacity.

Direct marketing involves direct access to the customer via telemarketing, direct mail, door-to-door selling, catalogues, electronic media (home shopping and cable television) and 'off-the-page' selling through cut-outs in magazines and newspapers. Direct marketing grew significantly in the 1980s and is increasingly being used by companies. The factors that have contributed to companies utilising this mode of promotion are that it can be targeted precisely at the desired market segment, the results are measurable, customer databases can be developed that can be used repeatedly, promotional messages can be personalised and there is greater marketing flexibility when employing this method of promotion.

REVIEW QUESTIONS

1 Identify the major environmental factors that act as barriers to effective international promotion.

2 What are the advantages of standardised advertising?

3 What are the decision criteria in selecting media?

4 What is the difference between creative selling and technical selling?

5 What are the three main categories of sales promotion?

6 What factors influence the choice of sales promotional techniques?

7 List the major factors that have contributed to the growth of direct marketing.

DISCUSSION QUESTIONS

1 Are there major differences between domestic and global promotion?

2 Why is public relations (PR) considered more important in the international than in the domestic sphere?

3 Of the three aspects of sales management (recruitment, training and motivation) is any one more critical than the others for improving performance?

4 What is the difference between publicity and advertising?

5 Why is it that personal selling plays a proportionately larger promotional role in international markets than in the domestic market?

6 Do you agree or disagree that the promotional problems faced by global marketers are rapidly disappearing?

Case study

COMPETITION IN EUROPEAN TELEVISION[27]

A battle is looming for Europe's television consumers, fuelled by the ambitions of European media companies and aided by technological developments such as digital compression. This will bring a huge choice in the number of channels on the air. Hollywood studios hope to muscle in on the European scene, too, which will create a clash of interests. The difference between existing broadcasters and the new breed of competitors is that the latter expect viewers to pay.

To date, the five European companies that have announced subscription-financed digital television channels are Kirch of Germany, CLT of Luxembourg, Nethold of Holland, Canal Plus of France and BSkyB of Britain.

Most competition will be between France and Germany especially when CLT launches 20 channels in both countries in the spring. Arch-rival Kirch will introduce sports, film and special-interest channels in Germany. Canal Plus is to launch a digital version of the current analogue pay service.

More channels can now be slotted into frequency spectrums and distributed by satellite relatively cheaply. However, there are steep costs to be met by customers, who will not only have to pay for subscriptions but also pay for digital decoders before they can receive the new channels.

The Hollywood studios are hoping for a bidding war between European companies for the rights to their films. Kirch and RTL of Germany, for example, have already won the rights to various Steven Spielberg films.

The studios have to decide how they will charge digital channels. For instance, where a film might be shown hourly should an overall fee, a fee charged for each transmission, or a flexible revenue sharing system be charged for near-video-on-demand (NVOD)? The deal Hollywood agrees will affect new channels and create a conflict of interest for studios. This will occur if studio bosses sell to the channel offering the highest price because the media companies that own most of the studios also have their own channels. These are Disney Channel which is part of BSkyB's package in Britain, and MTV, the music channel owned by Viacom which also owns Paramount studios. The companies may want to retain the film and music rights for their own TV channels. Besides this they will want their channels to be part of the digital 'bouquets' put together by the very companies which have purchased those rights for their own channels.

There is a precedent for the sorts of squabbles that lie ahead. Lyonnaise des Eaux, a French conglomerate, is one of the few European NVOD services that has made agreements with studios. Multivision, launched in early 1994, was prevented from showing major films before they had received a showing on France's pay-television giant, Canal Plus.

The other European commercial NVOD venture, Holland's TeleSelect backed by American Graff Pay per View, has only non-exclusive rights to films. It seems from Multivsion's experience most of the takings from NVOD will not go to the TV channels but to the owners of the film rights. Viewers pay FF29 to Multivision which keeps only FF6. FF14 is claimed by film rights holders and FF9 to the cable distributor.

Increasing competition will mean the large US media groups will want to avoid lengthy commitment to long-term deals. In 1993, when Time Warner was poised to launch a children's network in Germany, it found that Leo Kirch controlled the German rights to most of the Warner cartoon library for the forseeable future. In contrast, the Multivision and TeleSelect deals with Hollywood are on a three-month basis.

A few media barons, such as Silvio Berlusconi and Leo Kirch, control a large portion of the rights but with the impact of NVOD and shorter licensing periods these middlemen could find themselves redundant in the future.

Questions

1 *Explain how the possible advent of mass cable television in Europe will affect a company's promotional strategies.*

2 *Are there any particular promotional mix strategies that will play a proportionately larger promotional role in cable television?*

FURTHER READING

Black, S., *Introduction to Public Relations* (London: Modino Press/Pitman Publishing, 1993).

Czinkota, M.R. and Woronoff, J., *Unlocking Japan's Markets* (Chicago: Probus Publishing, 1991).

Jung, R.L., 'Selection and training procedures of US, European and Japanese multi-nationals', *California Management Review* (Autumn 1982), 15.

Norgan, S., *Marketing Management: A European Perspective* (Wokingham: Addison-Wesley, 1994).

Usunier, J., *International Marketing* (Hemel Hempstead: Prentice-Hall, 1993).

NOTES AND REFERENCES

1 Toyne, B. and Walters, P.G.P., *Global Marketing Management: A Strategic Perspective*, 2nd edition (Boston: Allyn & Bacon, 1993).

2 'Battle of the brands rage', *Marketing Business* (December–January 1996/97).

3 Darlin, D., 'Japanese ads take earthiness to levels out of this world', *The Wall Street Journal* (30 August 1988).

4 Ricks, D.A., *Blunders in International Business* (Oxford: Blackwell, 1993).

5 Rijkens, R. and Miracle, G.E., *European Regulation of Advertising* (Amsterdam: North Holland, 1986).

6 Toyne and Walters, op. cit.

7 Ibid.

8 Boddewyn, J.J., 'Barriers to advertising', *International Advertiser* (May–June 1989).

9 'Advertising: Tina Turner helping Pepsi's global effort', *New York Times* (19 March 1986).

10 Cote, K., 'Parker Pen finds black ink', *Advertising Age* (13 July 1987), 49.

11 Simms, J., 'A driving force', *Marketing Business* (February 1997), 20.

12 Jung, R.L., 'Selection and training procedures of US, European and Japanese multinationals', *California Management Review* (Autumn 1982).

13 Dahringer, L.D. and Mühlbacher, H., *International Marketing* (Reading, MA: Addison-Wesley, 1991).

14 Ibid.

15 Harpaz, I., 'The importance of work goals: an international perspective', *Journal of International Business Studies*, 21(1) (1990), 75–93.

16 Scott, G.G., *Success in Multi-Level Marketing* (Englewood Cliffs, NJ: Prentice-Hall, 1991).

17 Garrett, E.M., 'Trade shows', *World Trade* (December 1993), 88–9.

18 Graham, J.L. *et al.*, 'Buyer-seller negotiations around the Pacific Rim: differences in fundamental exchange processes', *Journal of Consumer Research*, 15 (1988), 48–54.

19 Lawton, J.A., 'Kodak penetrates the European copier market with customised marketing strategy and product changes', *Marketing News* (3 August 1984), 6.

20 Fombrun, C.J., *Reputation – Realising the Value from the Corporate Image* (Cambridge, MA: Harvard Business School Press, 1996).

21 Terpstra, V. and Sarathy, R., *International Marketing*, 6th edition (Orlando, FL: The Dryden Press, 1994).

22 Ibid.

23 Onkvisit, S. and Shaw, J., *International Marketing: Analysis and Strategy* (New York: St Martin's Press, 1993).

24 Hernandez, S.A., 'An exploratory study of coupon use in Puerto Rico: cultural vs institutional barriers to coupon use', *Journal of Advertising Research*, 28 (1988), 42.

25 Dahringer and Mühlbacher, op.cit.

26 Lyons, J., 'German suppliers are jealous of us in the UK', *Promotions and Incentives* (January 1989).

27 'Let a hundred channels bloom, but mind the thorns', *The Economist* (25 November 1995), 109–10.

18

Negotiation strategies

INTRODUCTION

Marketing in international markets requires negotiating skills. These skills are required when seeking to enter a market via an agent or distributor, setting up sales functions, establishing a joint venture or a production facility, as well as seeking to sell. Further situations where negotiation plays a role are when mergers and acquisitions are part of the strategy to gain market share and scale economies. If a marketing strategy is to be implemented, negotiation is a vital part of the equation. Failure to appreciate how this is carried out will put undue strain on progress or even severely jeopardise it. While action can be taken, for example by making sure that negotiation skills are represented in the marketing team, the need to understand how different societies and cultures influence this process also has to be recognised. What might be normal practice in decisions between buyers and sellers in the UK cannot be expected to be so in China, the USA or France. If firms are to be successful on an international scale then they have to learn and act upon the differences that exist.

Objectives

This chapter will examine:

- the anatomy of negotiations
- the negotiating approach to marketing
- selling–buying and negotiation strategies
- cross-cultural approach to business negotiations.

THE ANATOMY OF NEGOTIATIONS

Box 18.1 summarises the problems that North Americans (Americans and Canadians) have faced when negotiating with Chinese and Japanese officials and companies.

Box 18.1   CULTURAL HURDLES FOR NORTH AMERICAN NEGOTIATORS[1]

Two experiences

In the early 1980s, American motor executives set foot in China for the first time to negotiate a joint venture to assemble cars. According to one account, they experienced a setting made for ritual, not one for close personal ties. What they expected to be difficult turned out to be extremely easy; and what they considered trivial produced astonishing actions from the Chinese.

American negotiators from General Motors had similar experiences with Japanese officers from Toyota.

Hurdles perceived by North Americans

Some of the hurdles that American negotiators have perceived with Chinese and Japanese negotiators are noted below.

Chinese

Chinese negotiators are vague about their role or position and responsibilities. They seem manipulative with feelings of friendship, obligation, guilt and dependence – i.e. they try to shame Americans into certain kinds of concessions. Other hurdles are that the Chinese will not take risks, seem evasive and use delaying tactics, feign ignorance to gain more information, negotiate concurrently with one's competitors, and sign contracts without feeling bound by them. Their negotiators in the average session also outnumber Americans.

Japanese

Japanese negotiators are perceived as constantly pressing for information from their American counterparts, but do not reciprocate; are very slow to make concessions (give too little, too late); and conceal their top man. They are also perceived to be inscrutable communicators who use oblique ways.

In sum, Americans feel that both Chinese and Japanese are 'tough' negotiators, and that it is difficult to negotiate with them. They probe for information without offering it themselves. They also push for concessions without reciprocating as much or as often as Americans are accustomed to.

Contrasting negotiation profiles

Some aspects of the negotiation process that vary by culture are highlighted by the examples below.

Basic concept of negotiation

Definitions of what 'negotiation' means differ from culture to culture. What is negotiation? What do people do in negotiation? Japanese rely on generating solutions from the

▶

> **Box 18.1 continued**

information available while Americans use an exchange model (proposal–counter-proposal). Japanese also emphasise relationships as well as substantive goals during negotiations.

Selection of negotiators

Another factor that varies across different cultures is the basis on which negotiators are selected. Different bases include status, ability and experience.

Communication complexity

How much do people rely on verbal or non-verbal signals to communicate their messages? The more people rely on non-verbal signals, the higher the complexity. For instance, there is lower complexity for Canada and the USA versus higher complexity, or more reliance on non-verbal signals, for China and Japan.

The examples given above indicate that hurdles emerge because the cultures differ. There are two gaps that explain these hurdles: one is an information and knowledge gap. Even if Americans know about these cultural differences, they do not use the knowledge effectively, or they act on bad advice.

There are several points to consider with respect to the cultural aspects of negotiation. First, culture is not the only factor nor perhaps even the greatest influence on negotiation outcomes. Second, there are several potential traps in discussions about cultural differences – for example, stereotyping (i.e. assuming that any one individual is going to reflect the group average or the group norm), and perceiving a culture as static when in fact it contains dynamic elements. Third, every negotiator is a product of at least one culture – culture influences behaviour and the negotiation process. To be able to negotiate, negotiators must select strategies that fulfil some culturally-relevant criteria. One is co-participation: both sides must recognise the other side's behaviour as part of the same negotiation process. The other is responsiveness. What you, as negotiator, should do in some aspect is be responsive to what the other side is doing. There should be mutual movement – both sides must move from their original positions over the duration of the negotiation.

Box 18.1 raises a number of questions:

1 What is negotiation?

2 How much do people rely on verbal or non-verbal signals to communicate their messages?

3 How high are the hurdles to effective communication if the cultures differ widely?

Negotiating is in fact an everyday occurrence for all people, although many would not recognise it as such. At work, home and at leisure the ability to be able to deal with conflict of interests is one that comes naturally to the majority of the population. At work, as part of a marketing team and working in the familiar environment of the domestic market place, the formal skills required to successfully conclude a business deal can be learned. When working in this familiar, but nevertheless sometimes stressful environment, the participants know the rules, and the non-verbal messages can be interpreted fairly quickly and easily.

In business, many agreements are the subject of negotiation, being based on legal foundations and accepted business practice. If the human, legal and business issues are brought together then the process of agreement is complex enough. Change the context, in this case moving to an international dimension, and the situation becomes more difficult to deal with. The Japanese lay great stress on *Ningensei* or humanity.[2] UK negotiation often fails to communicate this, preferring to work on the hard facts of profits, costs and return on investment and emphasising the need to have quick decisions – fairly common practice in the home market. However, in failing to emphasise *Ningensei* by developing goodwill the negotiations can be put in jeopardy.

It is not only in the international arena that there is an increasing emphasis on joint ventures and corporate alliances, as organisations realise that they cannot undertake every activity. Reaching new customers, innovating, restraining costs and gaining access to additional resources and knowledge are all areas where alliances need to be sought.[3] These alliances–partnerships can and do involve foreign partners, as seen in the European defence industries, where high costs and increasingly sophisticated technology have made partnerships essential. What is true of defence firms is also the case in many other industries.

Box 18.2 reviews some of the issues about partnerships and the skills needed to make them effective.

Box 18.2   ### WHY PARTNERSHIPS MAY NOT LAST[4]

Partnerships need not be created to last indefinitely. Indeed, many successful ventures are intended to be limited-duration pairings that enable the partners to develop some specific capability or resource. Once that goal has been reached, the need for continued partnership disappears. Many partnerships, however, come to an end much earlier than their creators had intended, without attaining their full objectives. Researchers and management experts who have studied and written about organisational partnerships agree on one thing: they are highly fragile organisational forms. Conflicts between partners – over varying levels of strategic and financial commitment to the venture, varying goals and expectations from it, or lack of consensus about its goals – can break a partnership. According to Rosabeth Moss Kanter of the Harvard Business School, partnerships face 11 potential 'deal-busters':

1 *strategic shifts*: partners move in different directions, priorities change, and therefore partner terms and arrangements that worked at one point become less satisfactory;

2 *uneven levels of commitment*: some partners care about the alliance more than others do;

3 *imbalance in information and resources*: some partners are richer than others, have larger and more expert staffs, can afford and know more and therefore gain more power over the partnership, but risk alienating the less powerful;

4 *benefit imbalance*: because of how partners derive revenue from the venture, some stand to gain more than others if decisions move in certain directions;

5 *premature trust and the absence of institutional safeguards*: things are brought to the partnership, such as proprietary knowledge, before it is determined how to protect those items;

▶

▶ **Box 18.2 continued**

6 *conflicting loyalties*: partners also have other ties and relationships (sometimes of greater value) which compete for their time and attention;

7 *under-management*: more time is spent on striking the deal than managing it, or senior people then leave it to less powerful junior people to be involved in the venture, or responsibility is shared too broadly (decisions by consensus), so there are no clear tie-breakers or direction-setters;

8 *hedging on resource allocation*: the venture is starved by inadequate funding or insufficient rewards for participants;

9 *lack of a common framework*: partners can't work across divergent structures, processes, procedures and styles, but those very differences make it difficult to set common standards for operation matters;

10 *internal politics*: partners don't recognise and deal constructively with conflicts;

11 *competition*: perhaps the ugliest form of corporate divorce occurs when one partner, having learned much from the other, severs the tie and moves into direct competition with it; the experience of Schwinn Bicycles has often been cited in this regard – after entering joint manufacturing agreements with sources in Japan and China, the company saw its priceless marketing and production knowledge co-opted: those one-time partners have taken over the market, leaving Schwinn in their wake.

Again, it is also possible for strategic partnerships to end simply because they have fulfilled their goals. The alliance formed by Hewlett-Packard, for example, to launch its Kittyhawk product, was not useful beyond that event. As more is understood about the functioning of partnerships, and they are formed with more precise and measurable goals, this happy form of dissolution is bound to become more common than the alternative.

Keys to ongoing success

Most observers agree that the success of a strategic partnership has more to do with what happens after the deal is done than with the design and structure of the deal up front. This is because conflicts or implementation problems that arise after the partnership is up and running are often not given the same level or intensity of attention as at its launch. This is hardly surprising, given that partnerships demand a constant supply of what is any organisation's scarcest resource: management attention.

Again and again, it is shown that good decision making depends on having the right people involved at the right level in the venture. Often, researchers and advisors call for heavy senior management involvement throughout the lifetime of the partnership, but that is rarely realistic. Instead, the emphasis must be on involving those second-tier managers with the information, expertise, or authority required to formulate and take effective action. Top management's involvement can therefore be focused on the evaluation of the partnership, and on the ongoing investment justified by its current and potential benefits.

That investment, again, must be understood from the beginning to be greater than what would be required in a merely transactional relationship. At the very least, management must authorise some form of special training or education to make people aware of the partnership's goals and how they translate into individual actions. A dangerous tendency in strategic partnerships is for one or both parties to try to appropriate the strength of the other. As well as defying the spirit of the partnership, this can have dangerous

> **Box 18.2 continued**
>
> consequences for the would-be usurper: by taking its eye off the ball with regard to its real strengths, it may quickly lose its competitive edge.
>
> Attention to communication, commitment, and competence allows managers to deal with the tensions that inevitably arise over such issues as resource allocation, strategic direction, and activities' scope. Institutionalising the structures and behaviours that support the ongoing management of the partnership is crucial to partnership success because there are many potential sources of misunderstanding, mismanagement, and misalignment between partners.

Partnerships and working relationships are an integral part of business practice and will affect many businesses, whatever their size and location. Negotiation lies at the heart of this development, as does the ability to implement agreements or basically to make things work.

Relational marketing

As firms move towards partnerships and enter new (foreign) markets, the issue of relationships comes to the fore. This appears to raise the profile of relationship marketing, which is an area where many businesses are seeking to develop what they regard as a new expertise. This would be a mistake given that relational marketing has been the norm in many cultures for a long time. The point here is to look at the exchange needs of a given market. In Western countries relationship marketing at the tactical level involves loyalty schemes, also supported by the development of databases of customer information that can be used to assist with the creation of further exchange possibilities. Moving to the strategic level, this form of marketing looks at retaining customers through legal, economic, and technological time bonds.[5] Lastly, the aim of many companies is to use relationship marketing as the driving philosophy, which looks to build partnerships that last over time with customers.

For relationship marketing to work, it has to depend on the delivery of a quality product that customers really value. Key words occur again and again – exchange, quality, value and, by implication, trust – all areas where there can be difficulties for the organisation as it seeks to move its concept of relational marketing to foreign markets. So, for example, the use of tactics such as loyalty schemes in a culture that places a high emphasis on emotional elements is likely to fail.

> **Box 18.3**   ECONOMIC DEVELOPMENT[6]
>
> When economies are at the early stages of development, they are made up of businesses using small-scale production approaches and usually focusing on local markets. Relationships between buyer and seller are a normal part of everyday business and are, therefore, easy to achieve. As business is built on a relationship, the supplier can judge the creditworthiness of a potential buyer and assert the quality of a product, while the buyer can measure the quality of a product at first hand.
>
> Mass production depends on economies of scale and through this to the use of price advantages in the market to gain customers, and to compete against smaller and less

▶

> ▶ **Box 18.3 continued**

efficient suppliers. Here, the direct knowledge of the buyer by the supplier and the supplier by the buyer becomes more difficult. The change from small, local production, to large national units is a move from relational-dominant to transaction-dominant exchange.

In a transaction-dominant situation, other clues and guides have to be used to judge a product. Branding and advertising are the most obvious ways in which this takes place. In addition, word of mouth and looking at others' experiences of a product become useful sources of information on which to help base a judgement.

The transaction-dominant position is now itself under threat, as customers become critical and suspicious of advertising and brands. Developing alongside this is the increasing sophistication of customers in developed economies, with a need to experiment, switch brands and generally seek to try out alternatives. Retailers have taken advantage of this to develop own-brands and the relationship that can be built with their customers via this means. Changes in technologies, production and customer information open up the possibilities of gaining production economies, with a one-to-one relationship with customers.

Box 18.3 looks at the changes that have taken place in developed economies, showing that relational approaches are nothing new, only the way they are enacted and the methods used. In the three areas noted, the role of exchange means different things over time. The major element that contracting parties provide for each other is the capacity to exchange. In relational-dependent exchanges, there is no necessary prior knowledge of the parties, but that the exchange will have some influence on future exchanges, whilst in transactional exchanges the last condition is not met. The emphasis of social elements in exchange is important for relational marketing, as various other factors and considerations will play key roles.

Cultures where the social aspects of exchange are an important part of that exchange can lead those who trade solely on economic benefits to find business conditions difficult. To understand the social and economic issues tied up in cultures that place an emphasis on both is to understand the motivation of players in the market place.

Lastly, exchange takes place within a system governed by rules, regulations and norms. Exporters can fail in foreign markets because they do not understand both formal rules and regulations and the unwritten rules of behaviour that are depended upon by those who operate in a relational culture.

As shown in examples throughout this chapter, Far Eastern cultures operate on trust, which is built up over a long period, where getting to know business partners helps to lay the foundation for future business. An exporter who expects to set up a commercial relationship based on signing a contract and emphasising the need for efficiency, speed and profitability will fail in such situations.

Marketing exchanges

The issues raised by relational marketing in different countries has raised the profile of exchange and trust. Marketing exchanges are not just between buyer and seller as individuals, but also between organisations and firms, while the exchange process itself is supported by many players whose role is to facilitate the exchange.

Marketing is about the exchange process, so understanding how this operates in different cultural climates becomes a critical factor in successful marketing management. Exchange has two areas of interest – the products of the exchange (e.g. the products involved) and the process of exchange. To understand the exchange process means understanding these issues, with the challenge being with the need to appreciate the components of a marketing relationship.

Communication between two parties is at the core of buying and selling. To be effective at selling is in a real sense to be effective at communication. Communication has other attributes, as it also aids understanding, enhances co-operation and as we have seen builds trust. Further communication in the future becomes a possibility if relationships have been built on good foundations.

Taking the general theory of communication, it has to be a two-way process, with a sender and receiver of a message, who in turn becomes a sender, and so on. As seen in the simple communication diagram (Fig. 18.1), the sender encodes a message, chooses the medium for its transmission, which when received is decoded by the receiver. However, noise and distortion, as with electrically transmitted messages, can lead to problems for the decoder. This simple version can be enhanced by looking at issues of non-verbal communication, written and oral issues such as stress, loudness and so on. All of these help in the exchange process, if it is handled carefully and knowledgeably, to gain new understanding, seek solutions and understand each of the participants' needs.

Distortion is a major factor in all communications, which affects either the encoder–sender, the decoder–receiver, or both. Noise is the way that distractions come into play to reduce the effectiveness of the message. In international markets, these problems can arise from unfamiliarity with behaviour, gestures, use of symbols that can lead to conflicting interpretations and a move away from the original meaning. Further distortion of communication occurs when assumptions are made by the participants in, for example, a buying–selling situation, when expectations about the behaviour of one of the participants leads to problems – it might be assumed, for example, that the seller knows what the buyer wants, but this may be based on a false premise.

Fig 18.1 THE COMMUNICATION MODEL

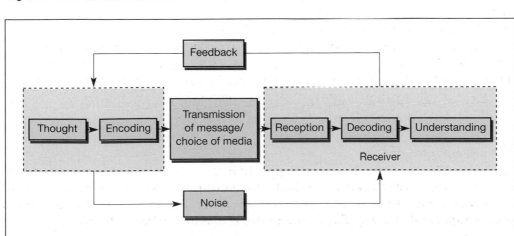

Communication becomes more difficult when the assumption is that both sides, in using the same business vocabulary, can reach a mutual understanding. In emerging economies, such as Eastern Europe and Russia, the use of terms such as 'accountants', 'costs', 'managers' etc. does not mean the same as in the UK, for instance. Although there has been a move towards the Western model, with titles fitting more closely the jobs people do, there is still room for doubt if the role of managers in Russia has the same connotation as it does in Western Europe.[7] This situation alludes to the influence of culture over communication, which covers the range from non-verbal and written communication to the set of shared cultural, religious and moral premises on which individuals in nations build their abilities to get on.

Barriers clearly exist when cultures meet, as they do at the personal level when business negotiations are carried out. Failing to pick up cues or by responding in ways that are unexpected, or even offensive, can lead to difficulties. As business and marketing activities require communication to take place in many circumstances, at many levels throughout the organisation and with various organisations, this element can be crucial.

THE NEGOTIATION APPROACH TO MARKETING

The anatomy of negotiations reveals the hidden or less clearly visible issues relevant to the negotiation process. It is necessary to look at negotiation techniques before moving to a synthesis of anatomy and techniques in the section on cross-cultural considerations in marketing negotiations.

Negotiations involve two levels – one is the rational decision-making level, the other, as we have seen, is at the psychological and social level. Psychological and social elements are affected by culture – negotiations can be as much to do with the psychological as with the rational. Leaving aside cross-cultural issues, this section is a resumé of the issues raised by negotiation.

When there is a failure to reach an optimal resolution psychological factors that effect negotiations will include such factors as attitudes and expectations about the participants, perception and misperceptions, the need to avoid conflict, the need to win, and so on.

Boxes 18.4 and 18.5 look at some of the techniques and considerations involved in negotiation. Although the overview cannot do justice to the substantial studies on the issue, the two boxes do at least raise a number of issues that can be summarised under a 'best-practice' banner. They impinge on buyer–seller (marketing) situations insofar as they identify what issues will arise both in preparations for negotiations and during discussions and after the event. However, taking this general advice too far can mislead and be counter-productive. It is useful to look at both the buying and selling process a little more carefully to provide a focus for when negotiations need to be planned and executed.

Box 18.4 PLANNING FOR THE NEGOTIATION[8]

Before the negotiation begins it is helpful to plan. Know whether you are in a win-win or win-lose situation. Be sure of your goals, positions and underlying interests. Try to figure out the best resolution you can expect, what is a fair and reasonable deal and what is a minimally acceptable deal. What information do you have, and what do you need? What are your competitive advantages and disadvantages? What are the other's advantages and disadvantages? Give some thought to your strategy.

It is very important to be clear on what is important to you. Be clear about your real goals and real issues and try to figure out the other person's real goals and issues. Too many negotiations fail because people are so worried about being taken advantage of that they forget their own needs. People who lose track of their own goals will break off negotiations even if they have achieved their needs because they become more concerned with whether the other side 'won'.

It is helpful to have a min-max strategy. Have a 'walk-away' position. When entering a negotiation or conflict resolution, make sure you have already thought about answers to these questions:

1 What is the minimum I can accept to resolve the conflict?

2 What is the maximum I can ask for without appearing outrageous?

3 What is the maximum I can give away?

4 What is the least I can offer without appearing outrageous?

5 What answers is the other person likely to have to these questions?

It is important to know your competitive advantage – your strongest points. Also you need to know the advantages to the other's argument. Similarly, know your weaknesses and the other's weaknesses.

In most conflict resolution or negotiation situations, you will have a continuing relationship with the other person, so it is important to leave the situation with both sides feeling they have 'won'. It is very important that the other person doesn't feel that he or she has 'lost'. When the other person loses, the results are often lack of commitment to the agreement or even worse, retaliation. The most common failure is the failure of negotiating parties to recognise (or search for) the integrative potential in a negotiating problem; beneath hardened positions are often common or shared interests.

Separate people from the problem

Address problems, not personalities: avoid the tendency to attack your opponent personally; if the other person feels threatened, they will defend their self-esteem and make attacking the real problem more difficult; separate the people issues from the problem. Maintain a rational, goal-oriented frame of mind: if your opponent attacks you personally, don't let them hook you into an emotional reaction; let the other blow off steam without taking it personally; try to understand the problem behind the aggression.

Emphasise win-win solutions

Even in what appears to be win-lose situations, there are often win-win solutions; look for an integrative solution; create additional alternatives, such as low-cost concessions that might have high value to the other person; frame options in terms of the other person's interests; look for alternatives that allow your opponent to declare victory.

▶

▶ **Box 18.4 continued**

Find underlying interests

A key to success is finding the 'integrative' issues – often they can be found in underlying interests.

We are used to identifying our own interests, but a critical element in negotiation is to come to an understanding of the other person's underlying interests and underlying needs. With probing and exchanging information we can find the commonalties between us and minimise the differences that seem to be evident. Understanding these interests is the key to 'integrative bargaining'. The biggest source of failure in negotiation is the failure to see the 'integrative' element of most negotiations. Too often, we think a situation is win-lose when it is actually a win-win situation. This mistaken view causes us to often use the wrong strategy. Consider a situation where you boss rates you lower on a performance appraisal than you think you deserve. We often tend to see this as win-lose-either he/she gives in or I give in. There is probably a much higher chance of a successful negotiation if you can turn this to a win-win negotiation.

A key part in finding common interests is problem identification. It is important to define the problem in a way that is mutually acceptable to both sides. This involves depersonalising the problem so as not to raise the defensiveness of the other person. The student negotiating a problem with a professor is likely to be more effective by defining the problem as 'I need to understand this material better' or 'I don't understand this' rather than 'You're not teaching the material very well.'

Use an objective standard

Try to have the result based on some objective standard. Make your negotiated decision based on principles and results, not emotions or pressure; try to find objective criteria that both parties can use to evaluate alternatives; don't succumb to emotional pressure, assertiveness, or stubbornness.

Try to understand the other person: know his/her situation

Often we tend to focus on our needs, our goals and our positions. To successfully resolve conflict, it is important to focus also on the other person. We need to figure out what the other's goals, needs and positions are as well as their underlying interests. We need to think about the personality of the other person, how far we can push, how open or concealed we should make our positions.

Acquire as much information about the other's interests and goals: what are the real needs versus wants; what constituencies must he or she appease? What is his or her strategy? Be prepared to frame solutions in terms of his or her interests.

An important part of this is to recognise that people place very different values on issues than ourselves. A clean room may be much more important to you than it is to your roommate. We must understand how the other person sees reality, not just how we see it.

If through pressure, deception or sheer aggressiveness, we push people to the point where they see themselves as likely to lose; this creates problems. The opponent will retaliate and fight back; losers often lose commitment to their bargain. Also negotiators get reputations that can backfire. Remember that settlements which are most satisfactory and durable are the ones that address the needs of both parties.

Box 18.5   NEGOTIATION AS A SEQUENCE OF EVENTS[9]

There is a tendency to think about conflict or the negotiating situation as an isolated incident. It is probably more useful to think about conflict as a process, or a complex series of events over time, involving both external factors and internal social and psychological factors. Conflict episodes are typically affected by preceding factors and in turn produce results and outcomes that affect the conflict dynamics.

A negotiation usually involves a number of steps including the exchange of proposals and counter-proposals. In good-faith negotiation, both sides are expected to make offers and concessions. Your goal here is not only to try to solve the problem, but to gain information – information that will enable you to get a clearer notion of what the true issues might be and how your 'opponent' sees reality. Through offers and counter-offers there should be a goal of a lot of information exchange that might yield a common definition of the problem.

Such an approach suggests that the importance of perception–conflict is in the eye of the beholder. Thus, situations which to an outside observer should produce conflict may not if the parties either ignore or choose to ignore the conflict situation. Conversely, people can perceive a conflict situation when in reality there is none.

Next, once aware of the conflict, both parties experience emotional reactions to it and think about it in various ways. These emotions and thoughts are crucial to the course of the developing conflict. A negotiation can be greatly affected if people react in anger, perhaps resulting from past conflict.

Then based on the thoughts and emotions that arise in the process of conflict resolution, we formulate specific intentions about the strategies we will use in the negotiation. These may be quite general (e.g. plan to use a co-operative approach) or quite specific (e.g. use a specific negotiating tactic).

Finally, these intentions are translated into behaviour. These behaviours in turn elicit some response from the other person, and the process recycles.

This approach suggests we pay particular attention to five generalisations:

1 conflict is an ongoing process that occurs against a backdrop of continuing relationships and events;

2 such conflict involves the thoughts, perceptions, memories and emotions of the people involved; these must be considered;

3 negotiations are like a chess match: have a strategy; anticipate how the other will respond; know how strong your position is; know how important the issue is; know how important it will be to stick to a hardened position;

4 begin with a positive approach: try to establish rapport and mutual trust before starting – try for a small concession early;

5 pay little attention to initial offers: these are points of departure; they tend to be extreme and idealistic; focus on the other person's interests and your own goals and principles, while you generate other possibilities.

The intangibles: other elements that affect negotiation

Intangibles are often the key factors in many negotiations. Some of these intangibles are:

▶

> **Box 18.5 continued**

1 personalities: be conscious of aspects of your personality such as your own needs and interpersonal style as well as the other person's personality; these factors will play a key role and understanding yourself will be an important factor;

2 your own personality and style: how much you trust the person; how you are free with your emotions; how much you want to conceal or reveal;

3 physical space: sometimes where the negotiation takes place can be important – check if you are negotiating in a space you are uncomfortable in while another is comfortable;

4 past interaction: if there is a history of conflict resolution with this person, think about how this history might affect the upcoming negotiation;

5 time pressure: think about whether time pressure will affect the negotiation and whether you need to try to change this variable;

6 subjective utilities: be aware that people place very different values on elements of a negotiation (for example, in negotiating for a job, you may place a high value on location and relatively lower on salary; it is important to be aware of your subjective utilities and try to ascertain the other person's subjective utilities); it is difficult to know in advance or even during the negotiation what a particular outcome will mean to the other party – finding out what is 'valued' is one of the key parts of negotiation.

Understand the context for the conflict:

1 What are the important personal and organisational consequences of the conflict? What are possible future consequences?

2 What behaviour patterns characterise the conflict?

3 What are the substantive issues? Are the issues biased by each side's perceptions and feelings?

4 What are the underlying or background factors that have led to the situation and the related feelings, perceptions and behaviours?

SELLING–BUYING NEGOTIATING STRATEGIES

Selling

Bradley[10] identifies five stages to the selling process:

1 the seller identifies possible problems in the customer firm; here, the seller seeks to identify the issues that need resolving in an encounter with the buyer;

2 gaining the buyer's attention – this is the key stage, as without this the next stages won't take place; many distractions and problems emerge here, with a lack of time, other influences/distractions that can all lead to a less than successful sales effort;

3 collecting data and information on the customer to help diagnose the requirements of the customer; here, also, there is a need to determine the buyer's main buying impulse – why they require the product;

4 selling programmes are prepared that will identify the need of the buyer and how the seller's product and support services will meet this need;

5 having convinced the buyer, and motivated them to see the product offered as the best one for their requirements, the final stage consists in clearing the sale – here, there is a need to employ techniques to influence the buyer to come to a decision; agreements are drawn up that can be periodically revisited to note when changes have occurred in the buyer's circumstances that need the seller to make adjustments.

Buying

Five steps can also be identified here:

1 the buyer identifies a need, which can either be derived from internal stimulus, such as a need for further supplies, or triggered by a salesperson;

2 there is a change in company circumstances, such as a move into a new market, development of a new product, or investment in production facilities; buying in these circumstances is very time-consuming and less routine than a repeat purchase order;

3 the identification of a new need will involve people from both inside and outside the organisation; when a new situation arises the number of those involved in buying (and selling) will be higher than for a repeat purchase order;

4 buyers develop criteria for the evaluation of information against which to judge the buying decision; the seller needs to know what these are, so that they can be added to the shortlist and from there move to the 'capture' of the order;

5 the final stage involves reviewing the competing offers to look at price, quality, service and so on.

Although this approach has kept the buying and selling process separate, it is clear from this summary that in many areas they merge. In cases and examples used throughout the book, 'best-practice' selling companies are those that seek to move to an intimate understanding of the needs of their customers so that the best, if not the optimal solution, can be provided.

Taking the factors so far covered to review the buying–selling relationship, negotiators need to be aware of the needs and requirements of both sides of the discussion. A review of the exchange issues, along with the building of trust and the requirement, if possible, to create a win-win situation suggest that preparation and a need to understand both the rational and psychological issues of the buying and selling negotiation process are vital requirements for success in every market a firm operates in.

Cross-cultural issues, as has been shown, provide a problem for companies and their staff who may not be aware that this can compromise what may have been very successful strategies of negotiation in their home market. Creating a win-win situation can become more difficult if exchange relationships also involve the building of trust, with the business transaction occurring at a later stage. Emphasising the profit, cost and quality aspect of a product can lead to a lost sale if it has not been able to take account of the relational foundation for business.

CROSS-CULTURAL APPROACH TO BUSINESS NEGOTIATIONS

Much of the preceding analysis has looked at the issues bound up with negotiations and buying and selling. The examples used showed the need to be aware of cultural and hence, communication, issues that play a part in negotiations and which need to be understood in order to create favourable conditions for business to take place. The unexpected is still possible, but if it occurs in a context that has created a positive framework for action then the outcome can still be beneficial for both sides. Box 18.6 outlines the differences Western managers will find in China, compared to operating in their own home markets, an issue already examined in Box 18.1 (p. 559). Put the differences in culture and communication alongside new and perhaps surprising business structures, then negotiations can be prone to misunderstandings and the possibility of breakdown. The role of the People's Liberation Army (PLA), which has been partly privatised in order to marry defence and industry, means that Western companies may be negotiating with them directly. In 1996, the PLA was estimated to control 50 000 factories and had absorbed £600m[11] from various joint venture partners and investors. The enterprises covered included private medical care, hotels, Baskin-Robbins ice-cream franchise and telecoms. Norinco (China North Industries Corporation) trades in technology and manufactured products, but also is involved in publishing, finance, travel, as well as firearms and explosives. Negotiators from PLA-backed industries know modern management techniques, have good connections with government and have considerable influence. Knowing the culture, communication and industry structure would help to allay possible problems, but not ones that involve the intelligence agencies of the USA and Western Europe, investigating some of the activities of PLA companies keen to be involved in the export of armaments.

Box 18.6   **WORKING WITH THE CHINESE[12]**

Western managers discover differences between a Chinese partner's approach and their own in terms of culture, business goals, incentive and motivation. In addition, the Chinese negotiating partner may have limited or no decision-making power, since approval of the project may rest with another authority.

Western managers also discover that they are going into an environment that is difficult for business investment. It is necessary to do some 'pioneering', which is to carve out a favourable micro environment to make the project succeed.

Cultural constraints

There are cultural differences that impinge on doing business in China.

Profit may be perceived as Western exploitation
Many Chinese still perceive that it is immoral for a foreign businessman to make money in China. During negotiations, the Chinese will want to know the Western partner's actual cost of manufacturing or cost of operation in order to reduce this share to the least possible amount. Upon achieving that goal they will feel that they've done a good job for their country morally and for their side of the enterprise.

▶

▶ **Box 18.6 continued**

Group identity

The distinction made between someone 'in the group' and someone 'outside the group' often determines how a Chinese individual behaves in their relationships with others. Different codes of conduct may apply to relationships within their immediate group consisting of family, friends and work unit or company and relationships with 'outsiders' including foreigners as well as other Chinese.

Attitude towards success and failure

The Chinese manager's inexperience in international business and/or lack of knowledge of technology and business professionalism may lead to feelings of insecurity and vulnerability.

The Chinese manager will try to compensate for those feelings of inadequacy by 'encircling and disarming' the Westerner in order to reduce their perceived unfair advantage. This is the 'CEO Syndrome', where the foreigner receives special treatment and is made to believe that he belongs to the 'in-group'. He is met at the airport, taken to a luxurious hotel, wined and dined and informed that he is receiving preferential treatment because he is a special friend of China. In the course of this 'treatment' he is likely to agree to all sorts of grandiose schemes. And because he is convinced that he has a special relationship with the Chinese, it is unlikely that he will pay attention to anyone who tells him about problems in China. Upon his return to corporate headquarters he will assign some manager to China to implement those plans. When that happens, the Western company is already operating at a disadvantage because it may be impossible for the manager to implement what the senior executive has promised.

Perceptual barriers that originate with Western managers may put them at a disadvantage

The Westerner may overcompensate for fear of committing a cultural blunder by not saying anything. While it is good to have an awareness of Chinese social norms, it is better to be direct. The Chinese are capable of discerning whether the foreigner is acting in good faith and whether they are a person of goodwill.

An understanding of cultural differences goes a long way in eliminating these barriers to effective communication. The key to successful negotiation lies in recognising that beneath these cultural constraints both sides have the same fundamental needs and interests.

Basics of negotiating

It is important to be very firm on principle, including business ethics, issues related to profitability and corporate policy during negotiations. This provides some guarantee of the business venture's success and helps the Chinese to understand contemporary business methods. In terms of negotiating style, courtesy, respect and patience should be the rule at all times.

Tips for a successful project

Finding the right Chinese partner in the right location is the key to a successful joint project. It is ideal to find someone who is motivated by a genuine desire to accomplish something for his country or for future generations. This powerful motive exists in the minds of Chinese entrepreneurs, managers and progressive reformers who approve these projects, and should not be underestimated.

Establish a clear understanding with that Chinese partner about the nature of partnerships. Each participant must work in their own interests, but at the same time consider their partner's legitimate interests and avoid putting them in an untenable position.

▶

> ▶ **Box 18.6 continued**

It is important to submit one's proposal to the actual approval authority as quickly as possible. Typically, one meets with negotiators and managers who are not the final decision makers. Determine the network of approval agencies and authorities that is appropriate for your project. Then contact the key person in each of those agencies and cultivate their understanding and acceptance of your project.

Send in the appropriate people. Professionalism is important, knowledge of technology is good but what is more important is someone who understands people and has good interpersonal skills.

Start small with something practical, and learn how to do business successfully in China before tackling larger projects.

Where cultures differ, as they do between the UK and China for example, communication, understanding and assumptions can lead to difficulties in bringing the two sides together and creating the type of win-win situation that is an example of good practice (*see* Boxes 18.4 and 18.5).

In the introduction to the Marketing environment, the requirement to understand, character, motives, attitudes and life-style as prerequisites to the use of business marketing information was seen as essential. In a similar way, the negotiation process depends for success upon just such a combination. In multiethnic countries such as the UK and elsewhere, business is often undertaken with those from varying cultural backgrounds, whilst country experts exist to provide insights into the way a country and its people operates. 'Experts' exist on the doorstep of many companies; the problem is often a failure to recognise the potential for the exploitation of this. Marketers in the UK have been accused of overlooking the needs (and potential) of ethnic populations that exist within the UK. As a result, the potential of these markets has not been realised. The *Building Business Bridges* report published in 1996[13] showed that the ethnic population had a spending power of £10bn, but a survey suggested that many were offended and/or felt excluded by the marketing strategies of many companies.

Failure to appreciate and understand ethnic groups in the 'home' market, can translate to a similar attitude when seeking to do business in foreign markets. In the UK because 80 per cent of ethnic consumers are under 25, there will be a doubling of the ethnic population within 50 years (going from 5.5 per cent in 1997 to 11 per cent in 2047). (In terms of the working population, a much higher proportion will come from the ethnic groups.) What is true for the UK is also true of other countries such as France, with different solutions being proposed as to how to incorporate, integrate or build understanding of the different populations. This example points to the importance of cultural communications in all markets, rather than this being a problem peculiar to international marketing.

Certain factors impact on negotiations in changing cultural circumstances.

Content of communication

The content of communication can be 'interpreted' only with knowledge of the role of the participants – power, status and ability to influence decisions, physical environment and the actual focus of attention (the subject for discussion negotiation). High-context cultures depend more on the role of participants rather than the communication itself. In low context cultures the emphasis is on the words.[14] France is seen as an example of a high-context culture, whereas Germany is low-context.

Cognitive structures

Cognitive structures are thought to differ between East and West. In the West people, think things out in a logical way, depending on abstract expressions of reality to understand the world. Eastern cultures tend to be more intuitive and use the senses more, emphasising the particular rather than universals, being sensitive to relationships and the importance of harmony and balance. There is also an emphasis on not losing face or showing ignorance.

Integration orientation against distribution orientation

With a distribution orientation, the view is that there is a division of a fixed cake, that leads to the possibility of a win-lose position as there is seen to be little need to boost interdependence. Contrast this with a distribution orientation, where the assumption is accepted that the size of the cake can be increased if co-operation can be established. Negotiators in this situation also seek to understand the nature of the other party's business and their needs and requirements. In this circumstance a win-win solution can emerge.

The nature of negotiations is such that there should be a combination of the two orientations. However, the increased emphasis on relational marketing (and the importance of this approach in many developing economies) means that there is a higher dependency on a distribution orientation, which can be enhanced when both sides have high aspirations and there is an ability to see the future – i.e. both sides strive to see new solutions jointly developed and where common ground can be established.

Problems still remain with an integrated attitude, as indeed they do with all negotiations on whatever basis they are conducted. If the cake can be enlarged, how will it then be distributed? Can integrative approaches be anything other than drawn out when dealing with a company from another culture, with the resulting increase in costs?

Time

A culture which holds a cyclical and thereby an integrative concept of time will lean towards the concept of negotiation as one round of a recurrent relational process. Cultures that hold a linear view will look at time as a sequence. For the Japanese, the need to understand their past is seen as vital for understanding them as negotiation partners, whilst for Americans time is a resource which should not be wasted. The Japanese therefore hold a cyclical view, whilst the Americans hold a sequential view. Does this matter in negotiations? If they are to succeed, then the Japanese require time for creating a rapport and building up personal as well as cultural understanding. Americans find this frustrating and a waste of time – failure could then spring from this issue.[15] In reality, cultures borrow from each other in many areas, and it is the same with the concept of time. So on project planning, the approach of Western countries may be used because of its success, but can lead to misunderstandings if the Western business partner believes that scheduling is taking place according to a sequential model.

Oral and written agreements

Many cultures are relationship rather than outcome orientated, with the Chinese concerned with a general statement rather than a formal contract. In many respects, therefore, the differences boil down to the building of trust and understanding that many cultures value, against the outcome approach that tends to put less emphasis on the need to build on these and instead values the use of written agreements (i.e. business relationships tend to be impersonal).

These areas suggest differences, but there has been some movement towards the use of similar understanding via international agreements, such as the GATT rounds. It is also interesting to note that what is suggested about Eastern and Western cultures has a great deal of similarity to the current debate in the UK, the USA and elsewhere about the different perspectives that men and women may bring to the role of manager.[16]

Table 18.1 summarises the influence of culture on (business) negotiations, identifying four major ways in which differences can be identified. Summarising the differences again takes the issue back to relationship building and the emphasis in some cultures on specified outcomes such as a contract.

NATIONAL NEGOTIATION STYLES

Producing an archetype of negotiation styles for different countries is a simplified way of explaining the basis from which negotiations will typically commence. Each country has a different perception of others, with the Italians viewing the French in a different way to the British or the Canadians.

To include these additional features would be to complicate the picture unnecessarily. There are many examples throughout the book of such shorthand descriptions of various countries.

This section looks at the British style of negotiation, comparing it to that in the Middle East, an approach that holds a mirror up to a Western approach and introduces the Arab and Islamic context.[17]

British

The British style of negotiation has been characterised in the following way:

1 a soft-sell approach is essential, as an air of confidence and restraint is important for negotiators (sellers), who must avoid being too 'pushy';

2 the British are less motivated by money and have a need to make sure that decisions are agreed by senior managers, a factor that slows down decision making;

3 the role of negotiator or purchaser has a strong influence on negotiations, which complies with the British requiring a soft-sell approach, where the seller must be careful not to overstep the line and then be seen as too aggressive and insistent;

Table 18.1 IMPACT OF CULTURAL DIFFERENCES ON INTERNATIONAL MARKETING NEGOTIATIONS

Behavioural predispositions of the parties	
Concept of self with others	Impact on credibility in the awareness and exploration phases
Interpersonal orientation	Individualism versus collectivism/relationship versus deal orientation
In-group orientation	Similarity/limited good concept
Power orientation	Power distance/roles in negotiation teams/negotiators' leeway
Willingness to take risks	Uncertainty avoidance/degree of self-reliance of negotiators
Underlying concept of negotiation/negotiation strategies	
Distributive strategy	Related to in-group orientation/power distance/individualism/strong past orientation
Integrative strategy	Related to problem-solving approach and future orientation
Role of the negotiator	Buyer and seller's respective positions of strength
Strategic time frame	Continuous versus discontinuous/temporal orientations
Negotiation process	
Agenda setting/scheduling the negotiation process	Linear-separable time/economicity of time/mono-chronism/negotiating globally versus negotiating clauses
Existence of a common rationality between the partners	Ideologism verusus pragmatism/intellectual styles/wishful thinking
Communication	Communication styles/degree of formality and informality
Negotiation tactics	Type and frequency of tactics/mix of business with affectivity
Outcome orientations	
Partnership as outcome	Making a new in-group – marriage
Deal/contract as outcome	Rules between the parties/legal systems
Profit as outcome	Accounting profit orientation (economicity)
Winning over the party	Distributive orientation
Time line of negotiation	Continuous versus discontinuous/there is no real time line to negotiation

Source: Usunier, J., *International Marketing: A Cultural Approach* (Hemel Hempstead: Prentice-Hall, 1993).

4 the British are more contextual in communication that the Americans, often being indirect, which places an emphasis on the need to interpret their negotiating position;

5 English-language issues are taken very seriously, with pride being taken in the style of writing and correct use of language.

Arab–Islamic

The difference here is that the previous style referred to a nation, i.e. the UK, whilst this looks at a number of countries which share a faith and general Islamic culture. Not all of these countries (e.g. Iran) are Arab, and they have substantial non-Islamic groups residing in them:

1 the role of intermediaries is important, particularly when reducing the cultural differences that divide Westerners and Arabs;

2 the traditions and historical and cultural influences of the countries should be acknowledged and respected;

3 emotion and demonstrativeness linked with pragmatism are apparent; relationships and friendships are very important, which leads to loyalty;

4 Islamic values on important financial issues, such as interest rates and profits, are subject to Koranic law, which is integrated differently across the Islamic countries, but which is nevertheless still taken seriously; alternative ways may have to be found to finance a project to meet these laws.

Box 18.7

ENGINEERING A GLOBAL CULTURE[18]

New strategies were needed at UK-based international engineering group APV to make it more globally effective. The company, with markets in 42 countries across North and South America, Europe, the Middle East, Africa, Asia and Australasia, realised it needed to change its own corporate culture and improve its global operations.

The company, which is involved in process engineering, component manufacture and distribution primarily for the food and drinks industry, has three divisions.

Aware that much more could be achieved across APV by different ways of working, including networking across the company, the company set out to change from a more traditional structure to a matrix structure, with operational and industry managers working with each other for the first time.

On a world-wide front, APV had been dealing abroad as a 'local' company. A global approach was needed, not least in dealing with cutomers who are, themselves, becoming globalised.

Lindley Training, based in the Peak District and Yorkshire, began a partnership with APV about a year ago and started the relationship by bringing together 25 senior managers from seven countries who had not worked together before to look at underlying issues and develop strategies.

A collaborative framework was achieved by team- and trust-building exercises, using a mixture of techniques such as psychometrics, futures thinking and scenario planning. Other meetings have since taken place with follow-up work in some countries.

Lindley Training acts as catalyst and helps the company think through policy and strategy, using skills and knowledge managers already have, to decide where to go.

APV now prepares its managers before they go abroad which helps them get up to speed more quickly.

SUMMARY

Two styles showing influences over behaviour may be recognised – formalised (for example, Koranic law) or a set of shared preferences (that in the UK case means preference for the soft-sell approach). Here though, changes must be recognised, influences traced and trends identified. In the UK, Thatcherism, privatisation and the rise of the self-employed sector, along with borrowings from US business practice, have all influenced negotiation style but, certain values and ways of behaviour maintain themselves or change only slowly.

For the marketer, there is a need to prepare well in advance for all negotiations, but particularly those with businesses and individuals from other cultural backgrounds. Taking time to build relationships helps the marketer to appreciate their perspectives on time, written agreements and preferences for certain styles of communication. A degree of caution is essential when seeking to interpret the prevailing situation and the assumption that each side understands the other.

All negotiations, whatever the basis on which they are conducted, will present challenges and produce questions to be addressed. International marketing negotiations will often depend for their success on a willingness to take the long-term view when looking at building a successful partnership, as a buyer, seller or investment partner (see Box 18.7) with business drawn from a non-'Anglo-Saxon' or Western nation background.

The building of trust and relationships is a new business issue for many Western companies. Although not new in concept, it is new in the way it manifests itself as part of a need to build marketing relationships. The increasing importance of intellectual capital[19] and the requirement of firms such as General Electric and Kodak to exploit this potential may create more favourable conditions for the development of relationships with foreign parties of whatever sort. However, there will always be cultural differences that will need the skills and awareness of informed marketing managers.

REVIEW QUESTIONS

1 List the areas in domestic markets where negotiations will take place in order to facilitate business.

2 Identify any additional areas of negotiation that international marketing will involve.

3 What is relational marketing as applied to international business? How does this differ, if at all, from relationship marketing?

4 Show how buyer–seller situations can converge to form an effective business relationship.

5 List the factors (e.g. time) that can lead to differences between the negotiating parties, although they may be assumed to be universally accepted.

DISCUSSION QUESTIONS

1 What is the problem associated with using what amounts to 'national stereotypes'?

2 If in the UK ethnic groups are overlooked or misunderstood, what chance does British business have of creating favourable conditions with foreign businesspeople?

3 Will the increasing importance of women as managers in the UK and USA help to create favourable conditions for relational marketing?

4 Is it possible to teach marketing managers good international negotiating techniques, without first changing corporate culture?

5 Is Western business able to take the long-term view of building relationships, if the emphasis is on short-term profitability?

Case study

RETAIL BUYING IN JAPAN[20]

The USA has had a trade imbalance with Japan for some time, with attention being focused on the tariff barriers that Japan has erected as a significant restriction on US trade. However, non-tariff barriers (NTBs), particularly those associated with establishing business relations with the Japanese, have also been cited, particularly when looking at business negotiations, as a lack of cultural understanding has caused many business ventures to founder.

Research by Alpeert *et al.* (1997) focused on relationship marketing, an approach that fits in with Asian cultural norms and which the Japanese respond to in a positive way. Five factors in Japanese retail buying were identified by the researchers that significantly affected US sellers:

1 entry order of supplier's brand;

2 loyalty or commitment to established suppliers;

3 interaction style between supplier and buyer;

4 size of the supplier;

5 supplier's country of origin.

Each of these is reviewed below.

Entry order

The pioneer brand – i.e. the first one into the market – has a strong advantage in the Japanese situation. Shelf space is limited as shops are smaller; when a new category is successful, the product is continually improved (*Kaizen*); the Japanese market is more homogenous than the US, so that a pioneer brand is quickly established at the national level, leaving few opportunities for follower brands. Preference is therefore given by Japanese buyers for pioneer over follower brands.

The difficulty lies in establishing a pioneer brand, as Japanese firms manufacture most products, so the majority of foreign brands have to be considered as followers.

Commitment and loyalty to established suppliers

Mutually beneficial relationships are preferred by the Japanese, but take time to develop. Existing partners are therefore preferred to new ones, thereby reducing the reliance on legal contracts. Few foreign firms have been in Japan long enough to establish long-term relationships.

Proven partners are considered more valuable than unknown (foreign) ones. A long-term orientation is an effective indication of the closeness of the relationship.

Interaction style between supplier and buyer

This can be seen by reference to principled as compared to caring approaches:

1 *principled*: this refers to the guidance offered by company rules and procedures; these take precedence over the satisfaction of the buyer;
2 *caring*: this means putting the buyer's satisfaction first (over company operation procedures).

The difference can be explained by seeing that the caring supplier can always be counted on for help, whilst the principled supplier might not be. This could lead to exploitation of the seller by the buyer, but in Japan the buyers seek to restrain themselves from making unreasonable demands.

Although changes are occurring in Japanese retailing that reflect many of the changes taking place in Western countries, there is still a preference for caring over principled approaches.

Size of the supplier

Japanese consumers tend to prefer large suppliers, particularly as they trust a corporate name rather than an individual brand. The other reason is that long-term relationships need to be based on the stability of the supplier, with size acting as an indicator of how likely this is going to be. Smaller suppliers may not have the resources to support the costs of developing a long-term relationship, for example.

Supplier's country of origin

Goods from some countries are deemed to be of lower quality than the Japanese alternative. This is a contentious area, but there is evidence to show that goods from the USA are perceived as being of lower quality than goods from Japan or Europe. Japanese buyers feel more comfortable with Japanese suppliers as the 'intercultural distance' is smaller.

Implications

If the findings by Alpeert *et al.* are a good indication of the challenges faced by US (or European) companies, then ways need to be found to overcome them. Some suggestions are summarised below:

1 pioneer products are of critical importance in gaining entry to the market, but these must contain major unique features;
2 smaller suppliers without a pioneer product would expect to encounter greater difficulty in gaining entry; one option is to take advantage of the private-label boom in Japan, and when the dollar is weak, to provide low-cost supplies;
3 reciprocal loyalty can be developed only by staying with a supplier, however low the short-term benefits seem to be;
4 suppliers should learn and adapt to cultural norms, particularly when developing a caring style.

Not all of these factors are of equal importance, with country of origin, for example, having a greater impact than some of the others. Developments taking place in Japan have been noted in other parts of this book, and reveal a complex and changing situation.

Questions

1 *Japan is the world's second largest economy, with many Western countries finding it difficult to break into the market. How much justification is there to assert that non-tariff barriers (NTBs) are the major reason for a lack of success in penetrating this market?*

2 *Is it relevant to talk about an 'Asian' style of negotiation, that applies to countries like China and Japan?*

3 *What possible changes in strategy might a Western seller have to consider if they wished seriously to target the Japanese market?*

4 *How far will the emphasis on relationship marketing in Western economies be useful in developing buyer–supplier links in Japan?*

FURTHER READING

Campbell, N.C.G., Graham, J.L., Jolibert, A. and Meissner, H.G., 'Marketing negotiations in France, Germany, the United Kingdom, and the United States', *Journal of Marketing*, 52 (1988), 49–62.

Cunningham, M.T. and Homse, E., 'An interaction approach to marketing strategy', in Hakansson, H. (ed.), *International Marketing and Purchasing of Industrial Goods: An interaction approach* (Chichester: John Wiley, 1982), 358–69.

Dwyer, F.R., Schurr, P.H. and Oh, S., 'Developing buyer–seller relationships', *Journal of Marketing*, 51 (1987), 11–27.

Fisher, G., *International Negotiation* (Chicago: Intercultural Press, 1980).

Hall, E.T., 'The silent language of overseas business', *Harvard Business Review* (May–June 1960), 81–98.

Hutton, J., *The World of the International Manager* (Oxford: Philip Allan, 1988).

McCall, J.B. and Warrington, M.B., *Marketing by Agreement* (Chichester: John Wiley, 1989).

NOTES AND REFERENCES

1 Weiss, S., 'Negotiations with the Pacific Rim: cross cultural challenges and strategies' (Simon Fraser University, February 1992).

2 Usunier, J., *International Marketing: A Cultural Approach* (Hemel Hempstead: Prentice-Hall, 1993).

3 'Strategic partnerships', Ernst & Young, *Business Monitor* (1 May 1996), 498.

4 Ibid.

5 Palmer, A.J., 'Relationship marketing: local implementation of a universal concept', *International Business Review*, 4(4) (1995).

6 Ibid.

7 Galenko, V., Strakhora, O. and Kuzmin, S., 'Russian enterprise management and the economic crisis', Proceedings of the Second Annual Conference on Central and Eastern Europe, The Business School, Buckinghamshire College (June 1996).

8 Wertheim, E., 'Negotiations and resolving conflicts: an overview (Northeastern University, 1995).

9 Ibid.

10 Bradley, F., *International Marketing Strategy*, 2nd edition (Prentice-Hall, 1995), 582.

11 Sheridan, M., 'Chinese army winning trade war', *Sunday Times* (9 March 1997).

12 Rittenberg, S., 'Negotiations and building effective working relationships with people in China' (Simon Fraser University, March 1991).

13 Dwerk, R., 'Losing the race', *Marketing Business* (March 1997).

14 Hall, E.T., 'The silent language of overseas business', *Harvard Business Review* (May–June 1960).

15 Usunier, op. cit.

16 Grant, L., 'The age of optimism', *The Guardian* (27 May 1997).

17 Usunier, op. cit.

18 'Engineering a global culture', *Personnel Today* (27 February 1997).

19 Stewart, T., 'Brain power: who owns it, how they profit from it', *Fortune* (17 March 1997).

20 Alpeert, F., Kamins, M., Sukano, T., Onzo, N. and Graham, J., 'Retail buyer decision-making in Japan: what US sellers need to know', *International Business Review*, 6(2) (1997).

PART 5

The implementation of global marketing strategies

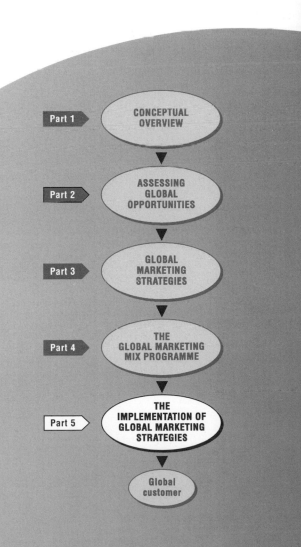

Part 5 consists of three chapters and the focus is on putting the strategies into practice.

Chapter 19 Organising the global marketing effort

This chapter provides a careful assessment of the types of structures that firms can utilise to accommodate their global strategy orientation.

Chapter 20 Controlling global marketing

In this chapter the problems and solutions to managing global marketing planning and control issues are examined.

Chapter 21 The future of global marketing

This chapter looks at the challenges facing global marketers in the light of repaid change, intense global competition and external forces beyond the control of any firm. The formulation and implementation of marketing strategies by any company must take into account the above points and yet be adaptable to the changing situation if they are to be successful in the next millennium.

19

Organising the global marketing effort

INTRODUCTION

The UK company Rank, the owner of the Hard Rock Café chain, looked towards the possibility of setting up a joint venture with Rhino Records (a subsidiary of Time Warner). The aim was to capitalise on 25 years of business of the Hard Rock Café company, which opened in London in 1971, by releasing a compilation CD of music from that era.

The move by Rank came after it had acquired full control of the company in 1996, and to lever more mileage from the brand. Under this arrangement merchandise, typically T-shirts and other memorabilia, would be complemented by CDs and a 2000-seat auditorium in Ranks Universal City joint venture theme park in Florida, sited next to a new Hard Rock Café. Concerts would themselves be beamed to other cafés around the globe and the music recorded for release on yet more CDs and tapes.

To pursue this strategy, Rank had to look at the rest of its businesses which would conflict with it, by competing for cash and other resources, and which could harm the potential success of the venture. The chief executive, in realising the potential conflict started to pull the company out of what were regarded as peripheral areas and to rationalise what was regarded as a complex management structure and to build on the core business of leisure and entertainment.[1]

Rank's example is by no means unique and reveals that to pursue a successful corporate strategy it is important to consider its effects on the organisation itself, looking at the structure, systems and procedures and the core competences of the business. To be successful in the pursuit of an objective like Rank's requires taking into account the internal as well as the external environmental issues that impose on strategy. Companies who work on the assumption that structures and management systems will take care of themselves may well find difficulties in persuading others of their ability to deliver on stated objectives, a factor that could raise questions for those who are to finance the move into new areas, especially where competition is keen and success more difficult to predict.

This chapter focuses on the organisation, looking first at its ability to accommodate corporate strategy and second on the global marketing effect.

Objectives

This chapter will examine:

- organisation design
- types of international organisation structure
- the importance of life-cycle issues for international organisations.

ORGANISATION DESIGN

Strategy is implemented through the organisation; the organisation is designed to deliver strategy in the most efficient and effective way possible. Efficiency and effectiveness are not easy aims to meet, but nevertheless they must be prime concerns in realising corporate and marketing strategy. In the context of the international firm, this must be to create competitive advantage across its chosen markets.

It is worth reviewing the general issues concerning organisational design before proceeding to a review of the structures that are adapted to suit the needs of the market. Structure serves a purpose, the aim is to co-ordinate the activities of employees so that they can work in an effective way to achieve corporate objectives. In addition, the structure and co-ordinating mechanisms must be designed so that they motivate employees, increasing the likelihood that customer needs and requirements can be met, that responses to change in the market can be anticipated and acknowledged and to promote constant improvements in product and service quality. This is the challenge of organisational structure. Without recognising this challenge and responding to it positively, managers may unwittingly be undermining strategy, even before it has had a chance to prove itself in the market place.

The building blocks of organisational structure are differentiation and integration, both of which help to influence the behaviour of people who are assigned to departments or sections. Differentiation is concerned with the splitting up of the tasks of the organisation and assigning these to a group of people so that they can create value by becoming efficient at carrying out their tasks. Vertical and horizontal differentiation can be found in organisations. *Vertical differentiation* occurs at different levels in the organisation and the problem is how much delegated authority should be given to these groups and their managers. Despite the move to the delayering of organisations to make them leaner and fitter to meet the challenge of what is seen to be a fast-changing market place, the problem still remains of how many levels should there be and how much authority they should have.

The organisational structures reviewed later in this chapter have to be reviewed as answers to the differentiation problem.

Horizontal differentiation is when people are divided into departments or functions, that cover areas such as finance, marketing, R&D, and so on. The issue here is the requirement to serve the market in the most appropriate way, and to help create value. Finance departments are to be found in the majority of organisations, to give the relevant tax and regulatory authorities the financial information they require. However, the need to supply financial data to managers and other groups of workers is just as important, particularly if they are expected to run their operations efficiently and to respond to market opportunities. This requires the organisation to consider how integration can take place across and within the groups that have been created.

Integration is vital for the organisation to achieve if it is to pursue its goals. The problem with organisational charts and diagrams is that they suggest that linkages are made across hierarchical and horizontal divisions, an assumption that can lead to complacency.

Good organisational design is required to ensure that bureaucratic costs – i.e. the costs of running the organisation – are kept to a minimum, while ensuring that the value creation of each area of the organisation is enhanced, both of which provide their distinctive contribution to the pursuit of excellence in the market place.

Structure and strategy

The key question is whether structure is determined by strategy, or vice versa. Various writers have plumped for 'structure follows strategy', while others have asserted that the reverse is in fact the case.[2] Burglemann[3] has argued that the two interact with each other. What is certain is that the pursuit of a strategy, such as that associated with the Rank organisation outlined in the Introduction to this chapter, reveals the need to amend or adapt the structure to accommodate the goals of the new strategy. The case of Hyundai, seen in Box 19.1, can be used to suggest that the restructuring taking place is resulting in new competition emerging, in this case from other parts of the demerged Hyundai *Chaebol*, that will itself necessitate committing the newly independent mini-Hyundais to a rethinking of their direction.

Box 19.1

HYUNDAI[4]

Mr Chung Ju-Yang, the founder of Hyundai, decided to transfer his stock of the majority of the 45 companies to his sons and nephews; this resulted in the setting up of a decentralised framework, made up of smaller companies.

The restructuring is influential in many ways, most notably as an example to other *Chaebol* (conglomerates) in South Korea. Despite the success of the South Korean economy and its *Chaebols*, they are often criticised for being inefficient and unable to respond quickly enough to rising competition from many quarters. Government experts have also supported the move away from the highly diversified pattern that many have adopted since the 1950s, to a concentration on fewer areas where they possess global competitive advantage.

In Hyundai's case, the move by the founder is the first step towards the achievement of this aim, with the decentralised group of companies focusing on a few strategically important industries that pursue profitable opportunities rather than maintaining profitable operations, as happened in the past.

One of the new 'mini-Hyundais', the company known as Hyundai Precision and Industry – which oversees amongst other areas production of railway engines, sports vehicles, military equipment and wishes to move into steel production and aerospace – is chaired by Mr Chung Mong-Koo. Other parts of the *Chaebol*, such as Hyundai Motors, will be under the control of other members of the family. Formal breaking up of the

▶

> **Box 19.1 continued**

group will happen only slowly, as cross-holdings will mean that interests will be maintained, despite government limits placed on them in an attempt to break the hold of the country's *Chaebol*.

The introduction of mini-groups will introduce more competition, as different groups will be competing in similar markets, with Hyundai Motors competing with Hyundai Precision in sports vehicles, such as the four-wheel drive market.

Sharplin[5] argues that the more relevant question is to ask whether strategists should be constrained by the organisational structure or if this too should be included in their thinking. The answer that Sharplin prefers is that through the modification of structure, strategists can change patterns of behaviour within the organisation, and it is this change which is more significant than looking at instances of behaviour.

Centralisation or decentralisation?

Is centralisation or decentralisation of authority to be preferred? Decentralisation is where middle and lower level managers are provided with authority to take on more responsibility, the argument here being that these managers are better placed to respond to 'local' pressure for quick responses to dynamic situations. Many organisations have followed the basic premise that faster-changing market situations require decentralisation. However, decentralisation pursued as a 'good thing' in its own right overlooks the merits that centralisation brings with it. For example, central control can ensure that processes that can be significant in providing common levels of services for customers, collecting data on customers and so on, are looked at.

Johnson and Scholes[6] look at examples of centralisation found in organisations drawn from both the private and public sectors. Here the centre is a master-planner, developing central plans with prescribed roles for divisions and departments. These parts of the organisation deliver their specific aspects of the plan, with the annual budget being used as a key controlling mechanism, capital allocated to support strategic objectives, an imposed infrastructure and central services. The advantages of a centralised approach are that it can enable tight control over costs and lead to a co-ordinated approach. Here, though, there are dangers where low-level managers can see their role as solely tactical, requiring them to focus on budgeting issues, and putting forward cases that can provide more money for aspects of their work. Involvement of these managers and their teams is limited in the strategic sense, overlooking the contribution that this group can make to the organisation – they possess knowledge, skills, and their own networks of contacts that can be an important source of intelligence on the needs and requirements of the market.

Decentralisation is not the same as total independence for a division. Most of decentralisation has been concerned with a move from a rigid control system towards what Johnson and Scholes[7] refer to as the 'strategic shaper', which finds the centre concerned with overall strategy, plus policies on such things as personnel, market coverage, environmental care, and so on.

The central role as strategic shaper is based on the agreement of business or operational plans produced by divisions within the framework laid down by the organisation. Performance is assessed against the plan, with the annual budget being an important consideration. Control in this instance is agreeing the division of responsibilities for strategy between the centre and the divisions.

Managers can face particular challenges with the 'strategic shaper' approach, starting with the need to move from tight controls towards the acceptance of a new role in deciding on their own business plan objectives, looking at their ability to offer both external services to customers and internal services to other divisions. In universities and colleges, for instance, new programmes can be developed within a Faculty Plan (external service to customers), whilst the faculty can offer services to other faculties by helping to create new programmes to service their external clients. A Business and Management School, for example, can offer its services to support Art Management degrees offered by the Faculty of Art.

The role for managers is, therefore, very different with this approach, and as is the case with all structural and organisation issues there are drawbacks. Regarding competition, the development of alternative systems can, if allowed to build up, become a threat to overall strategy and planning. Decentralisation following this approach is not a substitute for retaining control.

Box 19.2 considers other issues relevant to the problems of structure, integration and differentiation. Business environments and their impact on these issues is reviewed, showing that a common approach – i.e. one that all organisations should follow – is not the answer; rather structures should be those that tend to suit the environment and can be adapted as circumstances change. This contingency approach has its drawbacks: it may suggest that the organisation is always looking for the 'right fit' between itself and its (perceived) environment.

Box 19.2   BUSINESS ENVIRONMENT AND STRUCTURAL CONSIDERATIONS[8]

The business environment can be divided into four main types:

1 Simple;
2 Complex;
3 Stable;
4 Unstable.

In the first of these, companies will be faced with few uncertainties and pressures for change, while in the second there are more variables to be found, leading to greater uncertainty. This can come from the number of markets in which an organisation operates, either due to its diversification strategy or because of the number of international markets it chooses to operate within. The third situation occurs when a market is facing few pressures to change, allowing the firm to predict with some certainty market situations that facilitate planning and strategic considerations. The challenge of working in this environment is change that can come from an unexpected quarter.

Lastly, unstable environments are characterised by the frequency of change, which gives rise to uncertainty. Past events and trends cannot, in an environment such as this, be used as a guide to future development.

In these four situations the need to develop a structure that can accommodate these challenges should be considered. From the point of view of operating in the international market place, complex and unstable environments will be of interest.

▶ **Box 19.2 continued**

To meet the challenge of unstable environments, many companies attempt to build structures that promote horizontal rather than top-down communication; likewise job definitions will tend to be less formalised and that promotes a more fluid organisation, sometimes referred to as 'organic' rather than 'mechanistic' in nature. (This is a reference to the polar extremes as exemplified by Burns and Stalker (1961), who saw that organisations would move between these points, adopting structures, systems and processes that suited the business environment.)

A relatively simple approach that looks to push all organisations towards the organic approach, overlooks the robustness of some mechanistic views, such as specialisation, clear hierarchies and vertical communication, plus the various external environmental circumstances that may favour this type of structure – co-ordination and control rather than more fluid organistic approaches.

An alternative way to look at the structure and strategy and external environmental issues is via Mintzberg's (1995) building blocks, made up of the operating core, strategic apex, middle line, technostructure, support staff and ideology (*see* Fig. 19.1):

1 the operating core is made up of staff who are engaged in the productive work of the organisation;

2 the strategic apex is made up of senior managers, whose job it is to direct the organisation in line with its mission;

3 the middle line is the middle-management level, and focuses on administration and supervision of work following the guidance provided by the strategic apex;

4 the technostructure is the staff who provide the technical side not directly allied to the operating core – work that is carried out by finance staff, etc. who provide technical support;

5 the support staff provide services to support the core, such as catering;

6 the ideology links all the elements together, representing the values which help to form a common bond.

Organisations can choose to develop a configuration to support strategy which is dependent on the environment, work and complexity of the task (*see* Table 19.1 on p. 594).

A number of configurations have been identified by Mintzberg.

Machine bureaucracy

Machine bureaucracy is built on the importance of the technostructure or the need to regulate activities, leading to an emphasis on bureaucratic procedures that are appropriate when the environment is either simple or static.

Professional bureaucracy

In this, the importance of the operating core has been increased, and is often found where there is a high degree of professionalism required to join the core, in hospitals and universities, for example. The corresponding role of the technostructure is reduced, and any move by this group to exert influence will tend to be reduced. Core operatives are used to working on their own initiative with the problem being for the organisation to respond quickly to a changing environment.

▶

▶ **Box 19.2 continued**

Fig 19.1 THE 'PULLS' ON AN ORGANISATION

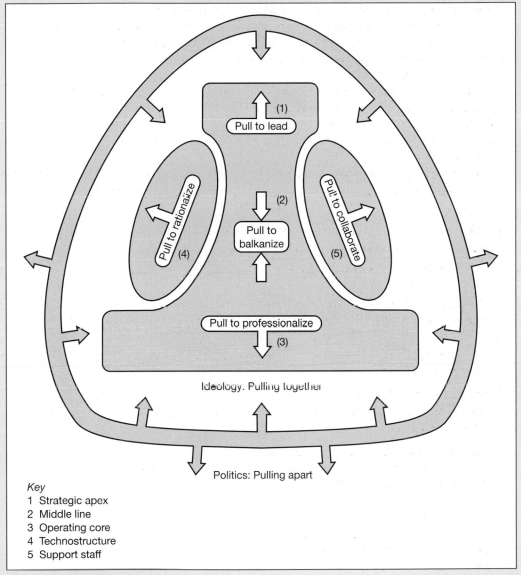

Key
1 Strategic apex
2 Middle line
3 Operating core
4 Technostructure
5 Support staff

Source: Mintzberg, H., 'The structuring of organizations' in Mintzberg, H., Quinn, B.J. and Ghoshal, S. (eds), *The Strategy Process* (Englewood Cliffs: Prentice-Hall, 1995).

Divisionalised form

This form reveals the importance of the middle managers, and provides power and influence for this group, creating what is often referred to as 'robber baron' mentality, or autonomous areas. This form has been seen as a threat to firms as they seek to set out new strategies to move into more dynamic and complex environments.

▶ Box 19.2 continued

Table 19.1 ORGANISATIONAL CONFIGURATIONS

Configuration	Prime co-ordinating mechanism	Key part of organisation	Type of decentralisation
Machine Organisation	Standardisation of work processes	Technostructure	Limited horizontal decentralisation
Professional organisation	Standardisation of skills	Operating core	Horizontal decentralisation
Diversified organisation	Standardisation of outputs	Middle line	Limited vertical decentralisation

Source: Mintzberg, H., 'The structuring of organizations' in Mintzberg, H., Quinn, B.J. and Ghoshal, S. (eds), *The Strategy Process* (Englewood Cliffs: Prentice-Hall, 1995).

This configuration has been under review, and has resulted in restructuring to reduce the number of middle managers, whilst focusing on the need to enhance the responsibilities of the operation core, along with quality assurance approaches that build up the influence of the technostructure.

Adhocracy

This is the most complex of the configurations, with a move away from formalised systems and procedures. It depends more on project teams to get work done and is best suited to complex and dynamic situations which require quick responses to market needs. This work identifies the pull and tensions prevalent in organisations, and the challenges they will face in meeting change.

Mintzberg's work on organisational configurations provides a way to understand the various pulls which exist within the pure types reviewed. Co-ordination will take place using the following methods:

1 mutual adjustment that occurs between people in the operating core;

2 direct supervision, where work is supervised by the strategic apex;

3 standardisation of work processes through systems that define how work should be organised;

4 standardisation of outputs, often through product/service specifications;

5 standardisation of skills, particularly important where professional activities take place;

6 standardisation of norms, where the employees adhere to the same core beliefs.

Using the configurations defined in Box 19.2 and the co-ordination approaches, it is possible to see how strategy–structure issues can be resolved. Table 19.1 shows Mintzberg's organisational configuration, identifying both situational factors and design parameters. This suggests that a machine bureaucracy structure is appropriate for large companies in very simple but static situations.

A match at one moment will not mean that this is going to help when, for example, the environment changes, producing a mismatch. When change comes many organisations find difficulty in adjusting to the new circumstances. It should be recalled that change can come from situations outside of the organisation's control, so that a fall in barriers to entry can introduce new competitors; but equally a shift can be of the firm's own making, as when it alters its strategy and moves into new markets – does it then seek to alter its structure?

Organisations in making decisions to move in a certain direction will also, for quite complex reasons, decide not to move in another. Sometimes this can be because the new direction would challenge existing methods of working, so a firm with low-cost competitiveness may ignore high-value-added market segments. Mintzberg's organisational configuration can, when applied to a firm, be used to challenge its current ways of operating, as they may be too limited.

TYPES OF INTERNATIONAL ORGANISATION STRUCTURES

If organisation design is so important for strategy (and strategy so important for design), then it is a useful starting point to consider how structures can be put together, and how once set up they can be adapted to suit new circumstances, particularly as regards international activity.

The main types of organisation division can now be summarised.

By function

This is found in organisations in the public and private sectors, and activities can be grouped together according to the principles of specialisation, or the need to use the same resources. Each organisation has to decide how this should be done, but work is typically organised round the firm's value-creation activities. In manufacturing firms, this is done by tasks (R&D, production, marketing, and so on) and elements (i.e. the application of shared expertise serving a number of operational areas, including personnel and management accounting.

By production/service

This occurs when specialists are separated by product, with R&D, production, marketing, etc. supporting a product or service. Unlike the situation just outlined, where central control can be maintained, this structure has the danger that the divisions will start pulling against each other; it also tends to duplicate activities that may well be less than cost-efficient. Divisionalised structures are often justified in large highly diversified organisations.

By location

The geographical solution is justified when an area requires separate treatment, particularly as regards the needs of customers. Difficulties faced here are to define the geographic boundaries, to make them, for example, large enough to satisfy the investment, but to set up a co-ordination mechanism, whereby corporate benefits may be obtained.

Although there are other methods of dividing up work, such as by type of customer, these three structures tend to be found in many organisations. Pure forms of these are rarely found, but a combination can be seen in most companies. There can, for example, be activities based on functions, while in other parts of the organisation a structure based on location can be identified. Senior management has to decide how to co-ordinate activities in these situations and must understand that some evaluation of the structure is to be expected as those operating within them come to understand their roles more fully and adapt to them over time, thereby changing the structure – an issue raised in Box 19.2.

Box 19.3 takes the basic designs one stage further by looking at the need to co-ordinate activity as the firm moves into the international market place, identifying five underlying reasons for this move and the challenge in co-ordinating the activity that results. Box 19.4 provides a summary of the main points, by means of straightforward questions, leading to five possible archetypes that can be adopted. These are then explained in more detail, with the option left to senior management to choose the structure which will best achieve corporate objectives with the most efficient operation. However, as has already been argued, organisational diagrams do not and are not intended to show the challenges that managers must be aware of in adopting a particular design. Each and every structure has to be soberly appraised for its ability to deliver.

Box 19.3

CO-ORDINATION[9]

Organisations need to co-ordinate their activity to achieve corporate objectives. This is a challenge for businesses operating within their home territory that becomes more pronounced with moves into international areas. St John and Young (1995) point to three functions in particular, that are vital for business success – marketing, manufacturing and product development. If these functions have conflicting interpretations of needs and requirements they may fail to co-ordinate their activities.

To overcome this possibility, a number of responses are possible, dependent upon the precise strategy followed by the company. Each function can have a different set of priorities and may have as a result a view on priorities that may counter those in the other two functions. It may make sense for the marketer to follow a differentiation strategy, whilst for production, standardisation (with its affect on scale economies) may be more important. Product development mainly focuses on changes in product design, while overlooking or ignoring improvements in processes valued by the customer. Overcoming these problems requires a form of co-ordination and control approach that can maintain progress and efficiency. St John and Young categorise the approaches under two general headings:

1 formal–bureaucratic, with the emphasis on rules, policies, procedures and planning processes which govern action and behaviour;

2 informal–culture mechanisms, with the use of team committees that can influence decisions and activities.

▶

> ▶ **Box 19.3 continued**

As the operating environment affecting the company becomes more complex, as happens with many types of international activity, then greater efforts have to be made to effect co-ordination.

Five international strategies can be identified, all of which require a reconsideration of the co-ordination effort, affected as they are by market and product scope, demand patterns and competitive issues.

Value enhancing

This approach focuses on the export of goods from the home base; there are no changes (or only a few) to the product. It often means that export sales and foreign market development issues are located in a staff department within the company. Manufacturing operations are not greatly affected by this approach.

Conflicts that do exist often focus on market information and operating issues, not on the more significant ground of strategic choice. The environment, therefore, is stable compared to other international strategies and co-operation can be promoted through formal means such as adapted systems and procedures.

Resource acquisition

This strategy looks at the ownership of foreign-based production facilities or raw materials. This will not on its own cause difficulties, but in circumstances where demand patterns are changing with the need for rapid response, the foreign-based production facilities may not be able to respond as quickly as necessary, or are found to be inappropriate. This will produce tensions between marketing and production. Conflicts here are linked to fundamental issues of strategy and market positioning. In these circumstances, formal strategic planning will be used to clarify priorities and gain effective co-ordination between the three functions. This could produce changes in sourcing policy, with new supply opportunities identified as circumstances change.

Multidomestic

As noted in previous chapters, this strategy recognises that each national business has a unique requirement concerning products and service levels, so that each country or region is seen as independent. In these circumstances, the three functions are replicated, supporting the business effort in specific areas.

The problem of international co-ordination is that it has to happen within a function, with marketing in one country co-ordinating with marketing in another to facilitate the transfer of marketing knowledge. Production will also find co-ordinating as important in seeking economies of scale, whilst product development will require information on technical and related areas.

Global strategies

With this particular strategy, products become standardised, with production reduced to a few locations to help achieve economies of scale, and strategy being determined for the whole organisation. The focus for strategy is on low costs, with an increasing preference for high quality. Clearly a global strategy will require more co-ordination between production, marketing and product development as markets become integrated and material and goods flow across national borders.

▶

▶ **Box 19.3 continued**

In these circumstances, the issue of logistics and time for delivery, plus the still crucial need to consider cultural differences, can drive a wedge between production and marketing. However, by pursuing a global strategy the flows of materials and goods, despite the complexity, are predictable and therefore manageable, so that the issue of how far cultural issues should be acknowledged can be reviewed. Changes to suit local cultural demands do not change the basic product offering. Co-ordination comes from both formal and informal approaches. Using MIS and IT, procedures and policies can help to reach economies of scale and standardisation. Cross-functional teams are often formed, bringing together the three functions to help review existing product and market developments and seek to develop new products.

Transnational

Some industries have to exist in a space somewhere between the multidomestic and global approach. This is known as a 'transnational strategy', found, for example, in telecommunications. Raw materials and components can be sourced from the global market place, whilst products can be developed to serve national markets. This is an environment that is less stable, requiring constant adaptations that impact on production economies.

Co-ordination here comes not from within a group but between groups, as they demand access to scarce resources. So product–market teams to serve national markets will co-operate to produce a product solution for that particular situation; this requires bidding for resources that others are also targeting, which can engender a climate of suspicion and a failure to share information and build co-operation.

Co-ordination in transnational companies can take place using the following approaches:

1 market and technical reviews undertaken by senior managers;

2 using staff managers to promote liaison and integration to pull groups/teams together;

3 frequent policy reviews;

4 formal strategic planning processes that aim to ensure that co-ordination takes place at the product and market levels;

5 laid-down operating systems and procedures;

6 development of career paths that allow managers to transfer across product and market groups, and therefore between nations;

7 emphasis on the socialisation process, to encourage a common understanding of what the organisation is trying to achieve.

Box 19.4   STRUCTURES[10]

Jauch and Glueck make the point that effective strategic management comes about only when the strategy and the organisational structure match. The question, 'Do we have the right organisation for our strategy?', is something that all chief executives ask. This question can be broken down into four basic parts, the first two of which concern themselves with the division of responsibilities amongst the labour force, whilst the remaining two focus on co-ordination and control:

▶ Box 19.4 continued

- What tasks are required to put the strategies into operation?
- To whom should these tasks be assigned?
- How interdependent are these tasks?
- How can the organisation be sure that the tasks assigned will be performed?

There are no 'right answers', and therefore 'right structures', for all organisations, but successful firms are those that tend to have organisational structures that fit their specific needs in terms of their corporate objectives, strategies, corporate culture, etc.

There are many ways in which an international firm can be organised. These can be reduced to five organisational structure archetypes:

- international division structure
- geographic structure
- functional structure
- product-based structure
- matrix structure.

International division organisation

This type of structure is depicted in Fig. 19.2 (overleaf). The firm's activities are separated into domestic and international divisions, with a major objective being to develop the firm's international business interests.

This structure is most suited for firms which:

- wish to develop international business and greater international expertise
- do not have adequately trained executives to manage an international organisation.

However, there are drawbacks to this structure which will be revealed as the firm expands, bringing problems of co-ordination as the business becomes too diverse. In addition, as the domestic and international spheres develop, conflict may emerge in the areas of product development and R&D.

Geographic structure

This type of structure (*see* Fig. 19.3 on p. 601) overcomes some of the problems of the international division structure, in that:

- domestic and foreign activities are integrated
- markets are separated into geographic regions
- corporate headquarters have responsibility for international planning.

The advantages of this type of structure are that:

- there is a clear demonstration of authority
- the co-ordination of different functional areas of management is enhanced
- resources can be pooled.

▶

599

▶ **Box 19.4 continued**

Fig 19.2 INTERNATIONAL DIVISION STRUCTURE

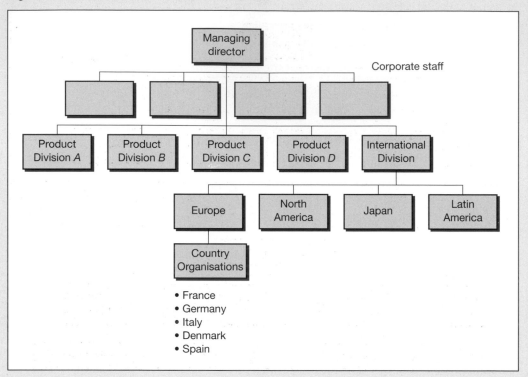

The disadvantages of this type of structure are that:

● to work efficiently, the structure depends on a small group of highly effective managers

● there is the likelihood that certain product lines will be ignored as there is no overall responsibility for a specific product.

Functional structure

Companies can be organised by function. To do this on an international scale, the senior managers for such functions as finance, marketing, production, etc. take on responsibility for all functions whatever the country of operation.

Figure 19.4 shows this type of organisation, often best suited for narrow or homogeneous product lines. In this situation, the organisation structure can be kept simple, co-ordinated by the senior manager for that function, but with support from subordinates, and will have responsibility for a region or country.

This form is to be found in companies working in their home markets only, but is less common in international markets where there are few regional variations and little need to extend the narrow product lines.

Product-based structure

Under the product-based structure (*see* Fig. 19.5) the major focus is on product lines. The firm is divided along product lines and each division becomes a cost centre, with the

▶ **Box 19.4 continued**

Fig 19.3 GEOGRAPHIC STRUCTURE

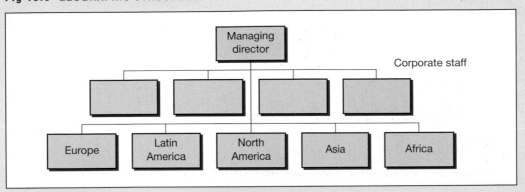

Fig 19.4 SIMPLE FUNCTIONAL STRUCTURE

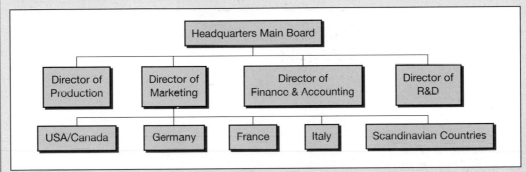

Fig 19.5 PRODUCT-BASED STRUCTURE

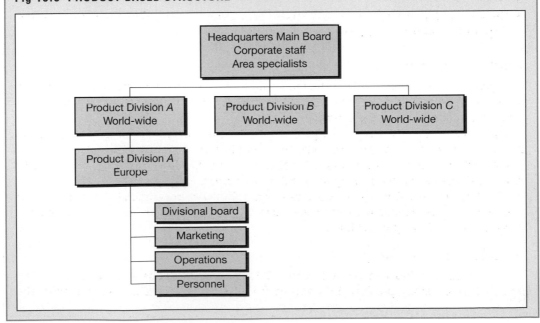

▶ **Box 19.4 continued**

divisional head responsible for profit margins. A key feature is the decentralisation of the structure which allows local managers greater freedom in their decision making.

The structure suits firms which have:

- a diversified product line
- a wide variety of final customers
- production sites in many locations.

Major advantages of this structure are:

- decentralisation
- a highly motivated group of divisional heads
- product development and elimination can be achieved relatively easily, without affecting the rest of the firm's operations in a major way.

The disadvantages of this structure are:

- co-ordination problems can arise
- certain product areas, particularly minor ones, may be overlooked
- when division heads move up the corporate ladder, there is a danger that they may bias policies in favour of their former product areas.

Matrix organisation

The matrix structure's unique features (*see* Fig. 19.6) are its dual chain of command and flexibility. Matrix structures are most often suited to organisations which have limited resources and need to be responsive to changing environmental conditions.

The strength of this structure is that it can respond to different political and economic environments because it incorporates the elements of product-based and geographic management. The product manager will have world-wide responsibility for Product X, while the geographic managers will be responsible for all product lines including Product X in the market. Both managers will overlap and this is a good basis from which to make major decisions. Another feature of matrix structures is the duality that exists – in dual budgeting, dual personnel evaluation systems, etc. This can be seen as positive in that the outcome will be interdependence of opinion and contributions.

The major disadvantages of this structure are:

- the possibility of a power struggle as a result of the dual command structure
- according to Jain (1990), these structures tend to collapse in times of crisis
- communication becomes more complicated
- uncertainty exists in determining who decides what in certain circumstances.

Which organisational form is best? Empirical work suggests that the structures adopted by firms tend to reflect their management outlook, experience, history, and even that firms can adapt the three basic types to produce hybrid models. The main point to bear in mind, however, is that the best organisational structure is the one which fits the organisation's environment and internal characteristics (the SWOT approach!) and that to remain effective strategic management implies changing the structure as the strategy changes, e.g.

▶

▶ **Box 19.4 continued**

Fig 19.6 MATRIX STRUCTURE

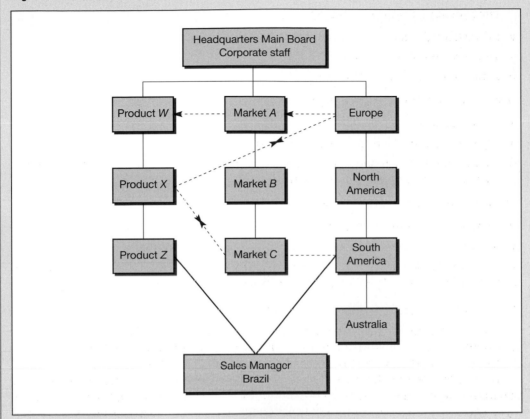

moving from indirect to direct export, or if the organisation experiences problems with its existing structure.

Many companies have found that no structure is ideal when dealing with the challenges of the international market place. Companies have now started to look at processes, rather than structures, which can develop new perspectives and attitudes that can assist with the demands of global integration and the need to meet local needs and wants.

By looking at processes, companies have focused on three issues:

1 developing a clear corporate vision;

2 developing managers and employers so that they understand and share the corporate vision and work towards the achievement of corporate goals;

3 integrating activities so that people feel part of the corporate team.

Essentially, organisations following this approach are evolutionary. Chandler and others have shown that many firms have moved from function to product to matrix structures, so it can be argued that this is evolutionary in nature. The difference is that the focus on processes is intended to be evolutionary. Three of the main types have been identified by Quinn.

> ▶ **Box 19.4 continued**
>
> **Starburst**
>
> This organisation is developed to promote innovation, which it seeks to do by splitting off new products into separate divisions and set targets for growth. Johnson & Johnson operate in a similar way to this, and promote entrepreneurial activity by a new division.
>
> **Cluster**
>
> Here the emphasis is on the development of cluster (teams) which carry out specific tasks. Clusters are fairly permanent teams for key activities. When the need arises to solve other problems, then a new small cluster will be developed. Volvo have used such an approach, but it requires a highly motivated group of people to see it through.
>
> **Network**
>
> These organisations are very flat, with communication between individuals and groups being high. The points of these organisations, which Quinn refers to as 'modes', contain the accumulated knowledge of the organisation and can work without formal authority interventions.
>
> Organisations that are serviced-based, such as consulting firms and others based on knowledge, depend on such an approach.
>
> Due to the increasing importance for future growth, the network organisation has become of greater importance.
>
> The three types mentioned above can be incorporated into the organisation's thinking whatever the type of industry; by this, we mean that by focusing on the process, these three designs are ways to stimulate innovation, entrepreneurial activity and speed up communication and decision making.
>
> Many companies would do well to consider these issues alongside both structure and strategy in their pursuit of market opportunities. If they pursue them, then senior management conceptualisation of the challenge facing them will change as well.

The need to realise that organisational forms will bring challenges puts the onus on managers to find new, novel or even well-tried and tested ways to overcome them. Instead, therefore, of seeing organisational designs throwing up problems that have to be controlled or even negated, successful companies seek to find where opportunities exist to benefit from such circumstances.

St John and Young[11] use the example of IBM which had a multidomestic approach (a structure based on location) that had resulted in delegation of product decisions; this was a benefit to Japan, that had new products developed for it, but the company was not reaping the benefits in other markets. The solution was to see how products developed in one area could be transferred to others, thereby gaining the benefits of co-ordination and communication. Any alternative approach could have resulted in a centralisation of decision making and the loss of local initiative and innovation and a new product opportunity.

LIFE CYCLE OF INTERNATIONAL ORGANISATIONS

Organisations evolve over time due to the changes that come about as a result of their increasing involvement in international activity. Starting out as an exporter with sales accounting for a small part of the company's turnover, the company changes its structure to suit the new situation. With the success of this approach, expansion then takes place, with an increasing amount of turnover taken up by this activity.

The higher the level of involvement in international business, the more likely it is that the different groups of customers will need to be catered for in more complex environments. Organisations will therefore need to adapt to meet these challenges, which can be described by reference to the international organisation life cycle, a cycle that shows the stages of development an organisation goes through as it becomes more involved. Quite clearly, it is not the case that all organisations move through every stage, and at the same rate. The purpose of the life cycle is to provide a framework that helps to see how an organisation focuses on its tasks and deals with the issues of responsibility and co-ordination.

The life cycle has five stages.

Exporting

Either opportunities in the domestic market become scarce (the market is saturated or a recession has caused difficulties), or an opportunity is seen or invitation given to export. From these first stages, that emerge from necessity or opportunities, an export department is created that is a function of the company following the formal policies and procedures of the firm.

Sales office

If the move into foreign markets is a success and potential demand is seen to offer further possibilities for growth, then a sales office will be set up in a market or markets that have already begun to be important in sales terms for the company. This will reinforce both local market contacts and further assist with research into new market opportunities. This operation will be under head office control.

Regional market centres

These centres act as co-ordinators, particularly with regards to marketing where they ensure that corporate objectives are adhered to. Despite their name, these centres may not be organised just on geographic lines, but by product group or other variations. Here the emphasis is on both decentralisation and centralisation.

Matrix

As noted earlier, the matrix organisation is a complex arrangement that requires a great deal of sophistication to enable it to work, particularly as it can accommodate a national and product approach. Despite its ability to cater for the needs of the market, many organisations have been unprepared for the consequences of such an approach, requiring as it does an emphasis on participation, a shared corporate vision and effective communication. In a sense the matrix approach depends on integration, rather than on specialisation by either product or country.

Strategic business units

A strategic business unit (SBU) is based on a group of employees that manage a product or group of products which serve a clearly defined market, by which is meant that both customers and competitors are clearly identified. The SBU can be a free-standing unit, similar to a product-focused structure, or it can be the way a business plan is effectively carried out. Either way, an SBU can be used to focus on international needs and requirements that are seen to be more effective responses to global integration.

The life-cycle concept shows the organisation developing towards a fully integrated approach – i.e. from export through to SBUs – requiring changes to the structure and operations of the organisation, so from central control at the sales office stage to a fully integrated approach for the development of global opportunities. Significant adaptations have been noted by Majaro, the major ones being reviewed in Box 19.5.

Box 19.5

INTERNATIONAL BUSINESS STRUCTURES[13]

When an international business reaches a certain size and complexity there develops what Majaro has described as either a 'macropyramid', 'umbrella' or 'interglomerate' structure. These structures are based on the three levels of strategic, management and operational requirements needed by all organisations.

Macropyramid

This is found in multinational companies who have developed a highly centralised approach based on a high-profile role for the company's headquarters. The strategic business units have some autonomy, but are largely dependent on the strategy laid down by HQ. In marketing, therefore, plans and the marketing mix are all set down by the centre who work on the basis that markets are largely the same wherever they are located. Marks & Spencer is an example of such a company, as is McDonald's. In such situations managers will lack autonomy, but then move to HQ to develop their career.

Umbrella

Here, the company has taken a view that planning should be decentralised, providing autonomy for foreign business units. The role of HQ is to set corporate objectives, leaving the business units to develop their own plan in response to the guidance that has been laid down. From the marketing point of view, the marketing mix can be adapted to suit local market circumstances, with the development of separate strategies. This can pose problems for any centralised functions, such as R&D, with tensions rising between the periphery and centre.

Interglomerate

Here, SBUs can be large businesses in their own right, so in such circumstances the centre is concerned more with financial performance than with influencing strategic plans. Businesses can be purchased or sold according to their (financial) performance. From a marketing point of view, there is an acceptance that the main focus is on financial returns, with corporate planning and marketing being the responsibility of the business unit.

These structures develop and evolve over time, a form that is not found appropriate to the business as it develops can evolve into a new structure to suit new circumstances. All structures, however, involve a trade-off, between autonomy and central control across international markets.

DEVELOPMENTS IN ORGANISATIONAL DESIGN

Businesses realise the importance of being responsive, but the challenge lies in knowing what this means. Many internationally known companies in the clothing and pharmaceutical industries, for instance,[12] produce a chain of services and integrate these in ways appropriate to the needs of their customers. Glaxo–Wellcome gains a high proportion of its competitive advantage from its service activities.

If this is true in clothing and pharmaceutical activities it is true also in other manufacturing-based industries, where due to automation the major value-added set of activities stems from quality, style and presentation as well as pre- and after-sales care. This development has permitted companies to reduce their need to manufacture internally, but instead to focus effort on research, development, supply relationships, and so on. The outsourcing that has taken place has created the possibility to achieve economies of scale by exploiting opportunities for outsourcing on a global scale. The result for European firms is shown in Box 19.6.

Box 19.6

EUROPEAN BUSINESS PRACTICE[14]

Daimler–Benz is Germany's largest conglomerate, which is 24 per cent owned by Deutsche Bank, a bank that also has holdings in other companies, such as Metallgesellschaft, a commodity trader. The mainland European approach to business has blurred ownership through a system of cross-holdings, thereby encouraging long-term relationships to be built up with suppliers and managers of capital – a system admired elsewhere as it had helped to produce the economic miracle of the rebuilding of the post-war German economy. Allied to the complex system of ownership was the power given to various stakeholders – in particular, worker representation on works committees has spread throughout the EU as part of the Social Chapter of the Maastricht Treaty.

For the European system to function at all, trust has to exist between those who supply capital and those who manage it. In countries such as France, Italy and Germany, banks have seats on the board and are prepared to take a long-term view. In France and Italy, an elite group of managers has been trained, usually at a university, who are educated in the accepted practices of building up these long-term relationships and perspectives.

Despite the good performance of many European economies in the years after the Second World War, in the 1980s and 1990s the performance of businesses has been declining. Profit margins and net profit have been lower among European firms than US, whilst the return on equity of German businesses in 1994 was half that found in US ones. One explanation for this poor comparative performance is that German business generated a third less output from each unit of capital than US firms.

The European approach is under challenge from the system preferred by economies such as the US, where relationships do not depend on 'trust' in the European sense, but on public guarantees of good behaviour. The arm's-length relationship promotes the shorter-term thinking of US firms that looks at shareholder returns and hostile take-overs to promote shareholder value, a feature that was abhorrent to Europeans as it sought to undermine social cohesion.

The advent of global markets in finance has produced a challenge for Europe. Not only have product life cycles decreased, the need for innovation has risen and markets have

▶

> **Box 19.6 continued**

started to overlap, but global financial markets have reduced costs – a threat to the link between national banks and national companies. This has encouraged firms like Daimler to raise finance in the markets of London and New York. Allied to this development has been the move to privatised nationalised industries and the Single European Market (SEM) that has reduced barriers to take-overs and mergers. In France, foreign ownership of shares rose 25 per cent in 1994.

Changes of this type are affecting the way business is carried out, a fact recognised by the EU particularly as regards unemployment and job creation. Many European firms now set themselves profit targets – an indication that shareholder rights are being promoted. Restructuring is a result of this approach, with firms looking to focus on core business, with companies like Volvo (vehicles and construction) and Paribas (investment bank) selling off their peripheral interests.

Corporate governance has become a key issue in many countries such as the Netherlands, as a reaction to bribery scandals, but also as the old linkages between suppliers and managers of capital become more distant.

The move to the US approach is only partial, but it has had an influence on the way managers think and the way strategy is set and marketing plans are implemented.

This situation raises real questions for strategy, structure and operations, which Quinn, Doorley and Paquette[15] summarise as asking, activity by activity: 'Are we really competitive with the world's best here?' The answer may be to outsource in such a way that non-strategic activities can be taken over by others, thereby concentrating on the core (strategic) activity. An upshot of this is that organisations become flatter, with all that this means for reviewing internal issues related to co-ordination, specialisation and other structural matters. It is not easy for many companies to shed the past, by moving away from full control over all their activities; neither is it easy to determine what exactly the strategically important activity ought to be.

It was seen earlier in the chapter that the importance of activities, rather than the end product itself, can be a more effective way of looking at the purpose of the organisation and therefore of its design. Customers can be more influenced by levels of service – covering time, reliability, cover for breakages and recompense for late delivery – than about the physical product, which may be matched by other competitors. This has given rise to a new possibility: that market share, which requires pricing and other short-term tactical manoeuvres, should perhaps be seen alongside market activity that can build up effective experience that itself can generate future opportunities and competitive advantage.

If services are the way to create high profitability and competitive advantage, then new and perhaps more radical forms emerge, that cover the core activity, and permit the company to co-ordinate a changing network of the best production and service supplies on a global basis.

Looking at the new and still emerging industries of biotechnology, nanotechnology and information technology (and related industries), the stress will be on the management of intellectual or knowledge-based systems, which in itself creates a challenge for managers in controlling and organising activities.

| Box 19.7 | THE IMPORTANCE OF THE SUPPLY CHAIN[16] |

Some companies have understood the benefits of integrating the supply chain with technology and people in reaching their stated goal. Many have found that cost savings of up to five per cent in logistics and 15 per cent in the cost of purchased goods have enabled them to see an overall reduction of up to 20 per cent in costs. The benefit has been that customer service as well as cost savings have provided the platform for building a dominant market position. Despite the success of some companies, many European businesses have still to take steps in realising the importance of the supply chain.

Ernst & Young, in a survey carried out in 1995 on manufacturing companies, found that 60 per cent of managers believed that there were no external barriers to change. However, 65 per cent identified significant internal barriers, a feature that has been found in other surveys which were noted in earlier chapters of this book.

Internal obstacles were to do with employee attitudes to change in working practices and their other responsibilities. The outcome has been that many companies have taken little action on this issue.

The main barriers identified by the Ernst & Young survey in the development of a strategic approach to this issue were a general failure to identify best practice, the integrity of MIS was suspect, producing problems in the identification of costs, etc., and lastly experience in implementing change programmes whilst maintaining customer service levels.

If a business-wide approach was to be adopted (the key to success) then six areas emerged as being of critical importance:

1 customer service;
2 produce range;
3 infrastructure;
4 planning and operations management;
5 information management;
6 supporting organisation structures.

Taking the last of these, successful companies recognise that effective organisational structures should no longer be based on vertical functions, but rather on horizontal processes that cut through functional areas of responsibility. An effective supply chain – a key feature in looking at marketing effectiveness and building competitive advantages – includes a number of organisational and management challenges:

1 creating customer-focused cross-functional teams;
2 ensuring that individuals and teams have clear roles and responsibilities, and are measured against business objectives;
3 empowering teams and individuals to make operational decisions;
4 creating a corporate culture that emphasises the importance of responsibility and accountability;
5 developing training and education programmes that encourage a multiskilled workforce and which raises awareness of the supply chain and customer service, whatever the country of operation;
6 creating a culture that seeks centrally to improve both internal and external customer service.

Bartlett and Ghoshal[17] argue that strategic thinking has outdistanced organisational capabilities, which has often resulted in companies developing more complex organisational forms to complement more complex strategic approaches that were themselves influenced or fashioned by more complex market and environmental situations. The matrix structure was one such solution and, as already noted, was a way to seek integration for the global market. In many instances, though, this type of structure is subject to stresses and strains, with dual reporting, unclear responsibilities, overlapping responsibilities, loss of accountability and the confusion that many customers experienced in dealing with a matrix structure; this led companies to question their worth, with many moving back to the older well-tried approaches.

However, moving back to the well known, will not deal with the chaotic environment that many commentators see as the main challenge for years to come.[18] In essence, the strategic plan formulated at the highest management level has had to give way (to some extent at least), to personal relationships that work not in a formal but an informal way through multidirectional communication channels and personal contacts.

Top managers have, according to Bartlett and Ghoshal, to build the most viable and flexible strategic process and thereby focus on the management and development of people, an issue that is often a block on change, as followed up in Box 19.7. If attention is paid just to strategy and structure, and organisational physiology is ignored, then the firm is left with the bare skeleton but not the vital systems – which, taking the physiology analogy a bit further, would include nerves, blood supply and other vital systems that permit the body to live and develop. Companies that focus on organisational psychology first, rather than on changing the structure to effect change, are helping to build an organisation that can look at communication and decision processes, backed up where necessary by changes to the structure. It is this that can support a matrix approach, rather than the use of such a structure, to bring forward changes in thinking, building new relationships and changing attitudes and behaviour which are by their very nature long-term.

The common characteristics of those companies which have transformed their organisational psychology can be summarised as:

1 development and communication of a clear corporate vision;

2 development of human resource tools to broaden perspectives and to identify with corporate goals;

3 integration of activities into the corporate agenda.

It is worth quoting in full the summary provided by Bartlett and Ghoshal on the challenge that many companies still face:

Since the end of World War II, corporate strategy has survived several generations of painful transformation and has grown appropriately agile and athletic. Unfortunately, organisational development has not kept pace and managerial attitudes lag even further behind. As a result, incorporating new common design strategies ... [seems] impossible to implement, for the simple reason that no one can effectively implement third generation strategies through second generation organisations run by first generation managers.

Today, the most successful companies are those where top executives recognise the need to manage the new environmental and competitive demand by focusing less on the quest for an ideal structure and more on developing the abilities, behaviour and performance of individual managers.

Box 19.8	ORGANISATIONAL TRANSITION[19]

Six key dimensions essential for building a successful organisation have been identified by Flamholtz (1995):

1 identification and definition of a viable market niche;

2 development of product and/or services suitable for the chosen niche;

3 acquisition and the subsequent development of resources needed to operate the firm successfully;

4 development of operational systems for day-to-day activities;

5 development of management systems required for the long-run functioning of the firm;

6 development of an organisational culture that will guide and inspire the organisation.

According to Flamholtz, these six tasks constitute a pyramid of organisational development, or a series of stages that have to be undertaken in an integrated way to develop a successful firm.

What this means for managers is that they are provided with the challenge of ensuring that these issues are given due weight and consideration and can be seen as influencing and being influenced by each other. Organisations should consider themselves in competition at each level, rather than at the product–market stage. So competition for resources to develop effective operational and management systems are equally important in supporting and sustaining product–market effort.

The top four levels of the pyramid constitute the organisation's infrastructure; however, problems can occur when the infrastructure is not commensurate with the organisation's size, which can happen as they develop. Seven stages of growth have also been identified by Flamholtz.

1 *New venture* – The major issues here are to identify markets and the development of suitable products for them. This stage will be from when sales are zero to when they reach $1m, and during this time the firm will place emphasis on all the tasks identified by the pyramid, but with the emphasis placed squarely on product and markets in order to survive this critical stage.

2 *Expansion* – This presents a new range of challenges, as resources need to be increased to meet demand, so new personnel are taken on, functions created, capital equipment purchased and even new premises sought. The operational systems that are used to function will at the new venture stage come under pressure. Pressure is seen at all levels, and many firms find this stage difficult to negotiate, and may even fail with good order books but problems of cash flow which put the company out of business.

3 *Professionalisation* – To survive at Stage 2, the organisation needs to change from one that is essentially entrepreneurial to one that needs to plan, control and define functional and individual responsibilities. Many employees will note the shift, particularly at managerial level, when they become 'managers' rather than a typical manager-operative. The challenge here is to develop management systems.

4 *Consolidation* – Once through Stage 3, the firm has to turn its attention to corporate culture, as due to the growth of the organisation it is no longer possible to transmit the culture on a personal, day-to-day contact basis. New staff need to be socialised, not by contact with those who were employed at Stage 1, but by a more formal process.

> **Box 19.8 continued**

5 *Diversification* – At this stage, extra growth is often a major consideration, so new products and markets will be sought out. This often occurs at sales of $250m, and requires the reintroduction of innovation and entrepreneurialism. This may require creating new divisions that eventually become new ventures, thereby returning to Stage 1. Those employees who joined at Stages 3 and 4 never possessed or needed have the entrepreneurial spirit, so the challenge is to create the conditions for this to happen.

6 *Integration* – Diversified firms are more complex, operating in many markets. Managers now have the challenge of integrating separate units/divisions into a cohesive corporate group, but at the same time allowing space and scope for development. This requires a focus on culture, management and operational systems and resources.

7 *Decline/Revitalisation* – All organisations will reach a stage of (relative) decline. The problem here is to revitalise, which can be done via new markets that can help re-establish a vibrant presence. Stage 7 means that all areas need to be considered – in essence, this is a return to Stage 1.

Organisations may fail at any of these stages, associated either with success (growth) or failure (decline and ageing). In an international context, the organisation may see itself moving through these seven stages, but at Stage 2 exporting can be used to facilitate further growth, whilst at Stages 3, 4 and 5 overseas sales offices, production facilities or the move via foreign direct investment could be proceeded with. Stage 5, diversification, can then include foreign markets. Although making the picture more complex, the move into these new markets in no way invalidates the issue of looking at the infrastructure of the firm and its ability to cope with new challenges.

Devising new organisational infrastructure may then be more important than the structure itself, and this fits with the experience of companies and scholars, where the need to look at organisational configuration and the new skills of managers and employees are key matters to go alongside product–market strategy, rather than being considered as a secondary issue.

SUMMARY

Throughout this chapter, it is stated that to be effective in international markets companies must consider the need to build and develop competitive advantage, which can be achieved via offering effective products to customers and ensuring that the organisation is so structured that it can achieve this. If this means outsourcing, restructuring and making certain that structure follows strategy, then this is to the good. However, by constantly focusing on external group needs many firms have overlooked the importance of making sure that employees are best placed to contribute to corporate strategy. It may be, therefore, that as many of the those quoted here have argued, time and attention must be given to the human resources of the company, as it is from here that key marketing advantages – especially with the increasing emphasis on service and knowledge-based industries – will be derived in the international market place.

REVIEW QUESTIONS

1 What are the principal issues to be considered in organisational design?

2 Outline the main organisational structure types that are used by international organisations.

3 What are the advantages and drawbacks associated with each organisational structure type?

4 Identify the stages found in the life cycle of international organisations.

5 Summarise the main problems associated with the links between strategy and structure.

DISCUSSION QUESTIONS

1 Why have companies often focused on structural issues rather than organisational development concerns?

2 Is the matrix structure inappropriate for most organisations?

3 Is it more important in the international market place to get the issues of centralisation and decentralisation right, than in a domestic company?

4 Network organisations, flatter organisations and outsourcing are all claimed to be new ways to solve the problem of building an effective organisation. Is this true; what problems are associated with each?

5 In what way is the organisational design issue of concern to the international marketing manager?

Case study

MARKETING ACROSS EUROPE[20]

Introduction

Companies that trade across borders have to address the issue of how they organise their marketing effort to reflect the realities of the European Union. Rethinking marketing strategy to deal with a unified, but diverse single market poses organisational challenges. The following examples show how two companies are facing up to this challenge.

MapInfo

This company was founded in the USA in 1986, specialising in desktop mapping software, a system that enables companies to visualise geographically and analyse data about their business market.

The company has a UK-based European head office, working through fully-owned subsidiaries both in the UK and Germany. Other markets are covered by third parties.

The target market for MapInfo is large organisations across vertical markets that can be found in all EU countries. The main objective is to create an awareness of the company, that incorporates the broadcasting of the mission, product and company sales strategy. One problem is that desktop mapping is an immature market and there is a need to educate the target market, meaning that PR plays an important part in the marketing mix.

Company strategy is to centralise the messages and positioning and to localise delivery. The European managing director works on the basis that communications will always need to be tailored to each country, as well as dealing with the problems of separate currencies that will still exist with the creation of a single European currency covering the first wave of countries to sign up to the Euro.

In the UK, France and Germany, the view is that they are large enough to be treated separately, while the Scandinavian countries, as well as Benelux, are used to being treated as single markets. Italy and Spain are given separate representation when they generate enough revenue to justify their own sales office.

MapInfo has three centralised functions – marketing, technical services and finance. As the larger markets grow, the local subsidiary will be given greater autonomy in finance, for example, but marketing will always be centralised, thereby saving effort and helping to keep costs under control. Marketing knowledge is still important at the local level, as each market will have different ways in which communication, for example, will operate.

Visa

Visa is the most widely used credit-debit card in the world. It is governed by regional boards throughout the world, consisting of the member banks. Global policy decisions are taken by an international board.

Visa UK was formed in 1992; prior to this date, the UK was part of the Europe, Middle East and African board. Visa UK reports to the UK board and to the Central Visa European marketing division. International marketing is the responsibility of a team who look at product development and any issue related to cross-border activity. This is a vital issue as Visa is used across borders, so uniformity and consistency are important. Visa right from the outset has always had to take a European and global view.

There are differences across Europe in the way the company has developed. The UK has traditionally been a credit-card market, following the US model, while France perceives Visa as a debit card, where money is debited from the account at the end of the month.

The company tries to maintain consistencies across markets, but has to take account of national differences on how cards are used. This allows a pan-European campaign aimed at business travellers, while still recognising the need to cater for the differences between personal users. TV ads are developed with assistance of the marketing representatives from the banks, agreeing objectives and the brief and how the campaign will be rolled out country by country.

In the UK, with business growing strongly, there has been an increase in marketing activities. However, any development takes place within the framework of products and services available internationally. Clearly defined responsibilities help to get the best out of the central–local splits in the company, with the emphasis on the teams involved working well together.

Questions

1 *What factors have influenced MapInfo and Visa in their decisions to centralise?*

2 *How influential are marketing issues in determining structure?*

3 *How has strategy influenced the standard issues faced by both companies?*

4 *In what way have process issues influenced structural decisions?*

FURTHER READING

Bartlett, C.A. and Ghoshal, S., *Managing Across Borders: The Transnational Solution* (Boston: Harvard Business School Press, 1989).

'Managing today's international company', *Business International* (1990).

Jain, S.C., *International Marketing Management*, 3rd edition (Boston: PWS-Kent, 1990).

Tully, S., 'The modular corporation', *Fortune* (8 February 1993), 106–14.

NOTES AND REFERENCES

1 'Hard Rock Café tunes into music through Rhino deal', *Sunday Times* (15 December 1996).

2 Sharplin, A., *Strategic Management* (New York: McGraw-Hill, 1985).

3 Burglemann, R.A., 'A model of the interaction of strategic behaviour, corporate context and the concept of strategy', *Academy of Management Review*, 8(1) (January 1983), 61–70.

4 'Hyundai to accelerate decentralisation', *Financial Times* (2 January 1997).

5 Sharplin, op. cit.

6 Johnson, G. and Scholes, K., *Exploring Corporate Strategy*, 3rd edition (Englewood Cliffs: Prentice-Hall, 1993), 358.

7 Ibid.

8 Burns, T. and Stalker, G.M., *The Management of Innovation* (London: Tavistock Publications, 1961); Mintzberg, H., 'The structuring of organizations', in Mintzberg, H., Quinn, B.J. and Ghoshal, S. (eds), *The Strategy Process* (Prentice-Hall, 1995).

9 St John, C.H. and Young, S.T., 'Functional coordination within the global firm', *International Business Review*, 4(3) (1995).

10 Jauch, R.L. and Glueck, W.F., *Business and Policy Strategy Management*, 5th edition (McGraw-Hill, 1988); Morten, M.S., 'Emerging organisational forms: work and organisation in the 21st century', *European Management Journal* 13(4) (December 1995): Reviews the work of A.D. Chandler and J.B. Quinn.

11 St John and Young, op. cit.

12 Mintzberg, op. cit.

13 Majaro, S., *International Marketing* (London: Routledge, 1991).

14 'Le Défi Américain, again', *The Economist* (12 October 1996).

15 Quinn, J.B., Doorley, T.I. and Paquette, P.C., 'The intellectual holding company: structuring around core activities', in Mintzberg, H., Quinn, B.J. and Ghoshal, S. (eds), *The Strategy Process* (Englewood Cliffs: Prentice-Hall, 1995), 346.

16 Ellermore, S., 'Distribution and logistics: transferring the supply chain', The Internet Global Services Co Ltd (November 1995).

17 Bartlett, C.A. and Ghoshal, S., 'Matrix management: not a structure, a frame of mind' in Mintzberg, H., Quinn, B.J. and Ghoshal, S. (eds), *The Strategy Process* (Englewood Cliffs: Prentice-Hall, 1995), 381.

18 Nilson, T.H., *Chaos Marketing* (New York: McGraw-Hill, 1995).

19 Flamholtz, E., 'Managing organisational transitions: implications for corporate HRM', *European Management Journal*, 13(1) (1995), 139–51; Judge, W.Q., Stahl, J.R. and Stahl, M.J., 'Middle manager effort in strategy implementation: a multinational perspective', *International Business Review*, 4(1) (1995).

20 Mayur, L., 'Breaking down the barriers', *Marketing Business* (June 1995).

20

Controlling global marketing

INTRODUCTION

Organisations are concerned with channelling human efforts towards attainment of organisational objectives.[1] The organisation has to integrate efforts and direct them towards the attainment of organisational goals, so all organisations will have to influence or control the behaviour of people if they are to achieve this.

In Chapter 19, the issues related to organisational design were seen as organisational control issues that influenced implementation control. To gain control over the behaviour of employees a combination of techniques must be utilised – the use of budgets, rules, job descriptions, appraisals and other performance indicators. Together, these form part of the organisation control system.

Marketing managers have an interest in strategy, marketing objectives, market research or the tactical issues associated with the marketing effort, but they also need to understand systems and procedures that exert control over the implementation of strategy, which are just as important to understand as any other facet of the marketer's job.

This chapter will focus on issues that can raise the relevance, and therefore the importance, of control systems.

Objectives

This chapter will examine:

- operational control in global marketing
- measuring and evaluating performance
- control and global management.

OPERATIONAL CONTROL IN GLOBAL MARKETING

PepsiCo, the US soft drink and snack group, announced in early 1997 that it was to sell off its fast-food business and concentrate on its soft drinks business.[2] The reason for the move, after 19 years of involvement in fast food, was a setback that the company had experienced in its competition with Coca-Cola and poor performance by the quick-food outlets of Pizza Hut, Taco Bell and Kentucky Fried Chicken.

The rationale behind the change was summarised by the company's chairman and chief executive, who pointed out that soft drinks and fast food had different dynamics and that the company believed that the businesses would thrive if they were split and had two separate and distinct managements and corporate structures.

PepsiCo is not the only company to have looked at the benefits of splitting itself in two (or more) parts and seeing these new companies move away from each other. Thorn–EMI split itself in two in 1996, with EMI, the music business, and Thorn electrical goods and retail going their separate ways. Distinct organisational structures and management can then, it is argued, focus on the area they know best, and adopt plans and strategies that can take the 'new' company forward.

These examples have been cited to show that planning can often entail the unexpected, the unusual, or the innovative response to a challenging market place. In many reviews of planning it is often implicit that the marketing objectives and strategy assume that the company will stay as it is, which is often counter-productive to the marketer, as limitation of both money and resources may often be the result of belonging to a conglomerate.

Changes in organisations can also occur when they restructure or rationalise operations to help them become more efficient in the delivery of a product or service. The changes at GEC (see Box 20.1) provide an example of this.

GEC, which is in the *Financial Times*'s survey of the world's 'Top 500' companies was ranked 172nd by market capitalisation ($17bn),[3] but was keen to move away from what was regarded as an out-of-date structure and management organisation, with the subsidiaries reporting directly to the managing director, to one where autonomy was considered a priority, mainly to improve flexibility and to develop more robust responses to changing market circumstances. In PepsiCo and GEC, changing circumstances have led to the need to look again at structural issues; by implication, this will have a significant impact on the implementation and control approaches that will result.

Box 20.1
GEC RESTRUCTURING[4]

The UK's GEC announced that from 1 April 1997 it has to restructure the £10bn a year engineering and electronics firm into five divisions. The new divisions will supervise the day-to-day management of the company's subsidiaries, with considerable autonomy over investment decisions.

Market analysts, in responding to the move, supported the changes, arguing that a modern management structure was being put in place that could be supported by the shareholders.

The managing director also embarked on a strategic review of GEC's businesses. The three main US businesses – medical equipment manufacturing, Picker International; Gilbarco, makers of petrol pumps; and Videojet, the printer manufacturer, will be organised into a separate division.

An industrial group will be set up, which will control a portfolio of manufacturing businesses including Avery & Berkel the weighing machine makers. The three other divisions will comprise: GEC Macon in defence; GEC Alsthom the joint venture electrical maker; and GPT making telephone equipment.

In effect, successful firms will survive and prosper when they respond positively to the complex and dynamic environment that is found in international markets. The firm has to manage the many relationships that are required for successful operation. Implementing international marketing strategy requires the development of networks (as shown in the review of good export practice in Chapter 12) that facilitate this process. Managers will need to assess the effectiveness of marketing performance, which can be undertaken by means of marketing audits, a typical example of which is shown in Box 20.2. Adapting this to the international market place is a straightforward activity; what is not so easy is the interpretation of the data emanating from such an exercise, and this method can also not appraise the value of the informal networks that are a necessary part of international marketing. Managers have to be aware of the limitations of such approaches and interpret the findings with a fair degree of caution.

Box 20.2

MARKETING AUDIT[5]

Senior management has the responsibility to ensure that the company is pursuing optimal policies as regards its corporate and its marketing strategy. Control needs to be applied to both, with a marketing audit being a comprehensive examination of a company's marketing environment, objectives, strategies and activities. This is undertaken to determine any problem areas and any new plan of action.

In summary, the audit covers the following.

1 The marketing environment;

   (a) what are the organisation's major markets, and what is the segmentation of these markets; what are the future prospects of each market segment?

   (b) who are the customers; what is known about customer needs, intentions and behaviour?

   (c) who are the competitors, and what is their standing in the market?

   (d) have there been any significant developments in the broader environment (for example, economic, or political changes, population or social changes etc.)?

2 Marketing objectives, strategies and plans:

   (a) what are the organisation's marketing objectives and how do they relate to overall objectives? Are they reasonable?

   (b) are enough (or too many) resources being committed to marketing to enable the objectives to be achieved; is the division of costs between products, areas, etc. satisfactory?

   (c) is the share of expenditure between direct selling, advertising, distribution, etc. an optimal one?

   (d) what are the procedures for formulating marketing plans and management control of these plans; are they satisfactory?

   (e) is the marketing organisation (and its personnel) operating efficiently?

3 Marketing activities – organisation, systems and productivity:

   (a) a review of sales price levels should be made (for example, supply and demand, customer attitudes, the use of temporary price reductions, etc.);

> ▶ **Box 20.2 continued**
>
> (b) a review of the state of each individual product (i.e. its market 'health') should be made, and of the product mix as a whole;
>
> (c) a critical analysis of the distribution system should be made, with a view to finding improvements;
>
> (d) the size and organisation of the personal salesforce should be studied, with a view to deciding whether efficiency should be improved (and how this could be done);
>
> (e) a review of the effectiveness of advertising and sales promotion activities should be carried out.

MANAGEMENT CONTROL AND STRATEGY

Budgets are used as an expression of a strategy in financial terminology, but they provide a financial measure rather than a measure of strategic success. Strategic control and financial controls taken together provide key data. Strategic control looks at targets for market share, product quality, timetables for action plans and targets for cost relative to competitors' costs. Strategic targets are necessary to link strategic plans and operating budgets. However, many companies pursue profit as the key goal, which places a high value on budgeting control and short-term profit, an approach that can often hide problems inherent in the strategy.

Strategic control is subject to uncertainty as there are few systems that can produce the required performance measures. Budgeting control can do this, but has the drawback shown above, of short-term, profit-related control. Strategic control can require trade-offs between current financial performance and competitive position over the longer term. Goold and Quinn[6] identified two ways – formal and informal – in which strategic control and review can be exercised.

Formal systems

This begins with a strategy review, with 'milestones' of strategic objectives of both a quantitative and qualitative type being developed. These include: market share, quality measures, innovation, customer satisfaction, and so on. Milestones are moves towards long-term goals. Target achievement levels, which are reasonably precise and which incorporate strategies – for example, competitive benchmarks, can be set relative to the competitor.

Formal monitoring of the strategic process then takes place.

Informal systems

Many organisations fail to adopt a formal system, for several reasons:

1 any one objective has the potential to unbalance the business, so that the pursuit of market share affects profitability objectives – i.e. it appears to downgrade them;

2 informal approaches provide the flexibility that can lead to innovation;

3 communication systems should be open and many formal systems appear to close them down; a narrow focus on a particular objective could act as a blinker for managers who fail to grasp wider changes and movements.

Is there, then, a compromise position between formal and informal systems? Goold and Quinn suggest guidelines for this that focus on different circumstances. A few examples are given below.

1 In the fast-changing fashion goods industry, firms have to respond quickly. In such rapidly changing circumstances, a system of low formality will be more appropriate, as new circumstances arise and responses must be made. (Note that low formality still implies some formal systems.)

2 A high-risk strategy, such as developing a new product, would require control systems that incorporate performance criteria so that problems can be identified and acted upon. Companies with high-risk strategies could find that the survival of the business could be put in question if these fail.

3 Competitive advantage – those businesses with only a few sources of competitive advantage, such as quality, can use formal control methods that focus on these vital areas.

The approach used by Goold and Quinn shows how difficult it is to adopt a universal approach to control and review of strategy. What applies to corporate strategy also applies to international marketing, with a mixture of formal and informal approaches being required. A failure to think through the control and implementation aspect can result in production inefficiency, inappropriate and costly organisational design, marketing costs higher than necessary and the cost of entering a new (foreign) market being seriously underestimated – a failure to realise the extra costs associated with transportation, staff training, insurance, exchange cost, service levels, and so on.

Control frameworks provide the opportunity, however exercised, to make sure that the strategy remains on track and that lessons can be learned.

MEASURING AND EVALUATING PERFORMANCE

Companies involved in international markets have to rely on both financial and non-financial measures in the pursuit of their chosen strategy. Both are required as without non-financial approaches, marketing-relevant issues, such as customer satisfaction, can be overlooked, whilst financial controls via budgets can lead to improved co-ordination, performance and profitability.

Control systems can be viewed in another way, by output and behaviour. Output focuses on the use of balance sheets, profit and loss accounts, and sales information. These approaches produce information at regular times during the year, with foreign-based parts of the organisation filing information for head office review. Behaviour controls comprise policies, mission and vision, and are generally summarised as the 'corporate culture'. These focus on the socialisation process and the importance of social interaction; Box 20.3 summaries some of the issues found by companies that operate in a number of locations.

Functional areas will be the subject of different control mechanisms, allowing for the fact that each of them is under different influences and constraints. In the case of marketing, which compared to finance allows for behavioural issues, leading companies to use control approaches that can respond to the needs of the function.

Box 20.3   OPERATIONS STRATEGY[7]

Multinational organisations have four types of strategic operations decisions to make:

1 Where should their operations facilities be located?

2 How should their operations network be managed across national boundaries?

3 Should operations in different countries be allowed to develop their own way of doing business?

4 Should an operating practice which has been successful in one part of the world be transferred to another?

Questions such as these were raised under the organisational design challenge with examples of various companies used to show how they had responded. Looking at the four questions from an operational point of view, certain issues can be highlighted that influence the implementation of strategy as well as control issues.

Location
Different configurations of operations will be appropriate for different organisations. Four configuration strategies can be identified.

Home-country configuration
This is the simplest approach, with the location of production in the company's home base and exporting goods to foreign markets. Direct control is retained over operations, and there are often other reasons for this approach such as those locational benefits identified by Porter in the *Competitive Advantage of Nations*, where companies gain a number of benefits from their home country.

Regional configuration
The company's markets can be divided up into regions, such as Europe, North America, and so on. This division will often bring forward the need to make each area as self-sufficient as is consistent with the parent's international strategy. From the marketing point of view, this makes sense if there is a degree of homogeneity between the markets in a particular region, but other considerations also pay a significant role, such as a region needing to possess the full range of operating capabilities to make and distribute the products. Industrial markets that require a quick delivery and after-sales service often benefit from this closer relationship between regional organisation and customers.

Global co-ordinating configuration
As seen in Chapter 19 on organisational design, the approach here is to develop global co-ordination with operations focusing on a narrow set of activities and products, and then distributing them to customers around the world. Production can be located in countries where production costs are low for those products that require a high labour content, for example. Co-ordination of production, distribution and marketing will then be organised by the head office of the company.

Combined regional and global configuration
Regional structures are simple to set up, while global approaches have the advantage of using the best locations. To take advantage of both, companies might give their regions a fair amount of autonomy, while looking for the possibility of moving goods between regions. Conflict over this approach is the biggest challenge, with a balance requiring to be struck between autonomy and efficiency.

▶

> **Box 20.3 continued**

When the configuration has been determined, the need to manage across national–political boundaries becomes paramount – in fact, this should be considered in line with the configuration issue. The problem is how a company can exploit the advantages of geographically dispersed sites, while seeking to get them to work together.

Multinationals have the ability to compare the performance of plants in different parts of the world, which helps them achieve both a global and multicultural perspective. This was the case with Nissan's factory in the UK that bid for, in 1997, and won the contract to build a new car, rather than one of the Japanese factories. Ford, on the other hand, rejected their UK Halewood plant as a location for the production of the new Escort range. Similarities between companies in looking for the best location for production hide marked differences in the way they manage the whole process, with Nissan looking to develop local (UK) managers, whilst Ford move executives from one location to another at regular intervals.

Regionalisation will produce differences in practice, as cultural backgrounds, economic realities, history etc, see the development of differing operating practices. This then creates tension between the benefits that can accrue from regionalisation and the need to improve corporate values.

Lastly, the transference of operations practices is a major consideration. Operations practices which have been successfully used in one region can be transferred to other regions, but will they work? An obvious example is the Japanese just-in-time (JIT) system which has been transferred to many of that country's companies operating in the UK. The JIT approach is used in Nissan's UK factory, but took time to move its way through the supply chain, and there are a lot of car component manufacturers in the UK who still fall behind in their ability to work with this system. Organisations who have attempted to use JIT in other industries have found the transition very difficult, as it requires changing work practices and decades of operating systems.

Likewise, the transfer of practices developed in Germany, France and elsewhere, via the Maastricht Treaty's Social Chapter, is proving contentious in the UK.

The transfer of operations practice often has to adapt to new circumstances. In the UK, JIT was readily understood from the technical viewpoint, but the consensus approach that it also depended on for its success in Japan has had to recognise the more confrontational management culture that is found in 'Anglo-Saxon' economies. The industry structure as well as the cultural environment is often very different, as for example in the UK where specialist and highly technical design-and-build operations in the car industry make it a world leader where JIT is not a major consideration.

Long-term transference of operations approaches – i.e. the successful implementation of a new system – often requires them to be adaptive, thereby creating a new highly original approach.

Czinkota and Ronkainen[8] point to the fact that US-based MNCs tend to place a high value on quantitative data. The benefits of this lie in being able to compare the foreign-based units against internal benchmarks. However, this centralised approach fails to adjust to or account for the different pressures that these operations face. Inflation, tax, regulatory regime, exchange rate changes can all have an impact on performance. The periods when data is collected can have an additional influence. Internal data can be collected on a monthly, bi-monthly or quarterly basis, whereas environmental data, that can perhaps reveal disturbances in the business environment and hence impacts on the organisation, is not likely to be reviewed as frequently. This can lead to decisions being taken without due care and consideration, and lead to the failure properly to assess prospects.

Three other factors can affect control.[9]

Communication systems

This focuses on the degree to which organisations use available systems (such as e-mail) to the full, or whether they depend on more tried and tested, and therefore more traditional methods. A survey by US firms operating in Europe found that European firms generally tended to rely on the latter rather than the former, a factor that influenced US firms in their location decisions. The reason for the relative lack of use of electronic communication was explained by the more rigid labour market controls found in EU countries compared, say, to the UK.

Another aspect of communication is the distance between the head office and the overseas division. The greater the distance, the more likely it is that time, expense and errors will rise, a feature that might promote the use of electronic communications systems that operate in real time.

Data

Economic, industrial and consumer information is a necessary part of control. In countries where this data is readily available and dependable, such as the UK, marketing planning and control can work on the basis of accurate external data. Where this is not readily available, as is the case in many of the emerging markets, there are problems. How, for example, is it possible to estimate market share, and to know when this has been achieved, without accurate data? In 1996, Russian economic data showed that the country's GDP had fallen by six per cent, at the same time as the *Financial Times* was including Russian firms in its '500 index' of the world's leading companies and the prospects for the economy were thought to be improving.[10] The interpretation of the data by economists revealed that it had underestimated GDP output figures by not accounting for the burgeoning service sector; some companies had also reported lower output to avoid taxation.

Environment

As outlined above, the diversity of environments will influence the development of the marketing plan and its implementation. The needs of the local situation will, therefore, on occasions differ from corporate goals, and this has to be taken into account.

Management

As seen in Box 20.4, the management approach will differ from one country or location to another. If a centralised system is used, communications will need to be developed to support such an approach. If a decentralised system is preferred then day-to-day communication becomes less important, but clear goals must be set to enable the operating unit to decide how best to achieve them.

Box 20.4

CONTROL SYSTEMS[11]

Market controls cover stock market price, return on investment (ROI) and transfer pricing. Stock market price fluctuations act on managers insofar as they provide an indication of the market's view of company and therefore management performance. ROI performs the function of evaluating the company against others and initiating action if the company is under-performing. Another use of ROI is inside the organisation itself, where divisions can be compared in their ability to earn a ROI predetermined in the corporate plan.

Transfer pricing is the method of setting a price whereby one part of the organisation transfers goods to another. Most commonly used in multinational companies, the transfer price can either be set by using a market-based method (i.e. the price charged will be determined by the prices charged by a competitor), or a cost-based method (which sets prices relative to a full-cost method) can also be used. Both approaches have drawbacks: the cost-based method has to determine the amount to go to the supplying division, while the market-based approach, in using competitors' prices, may be over-compensating the supplying division, which could be more efficient.

For market controls to work, there has to be a means of comparison available for them to be effective instruments.

Output control involves the organisation setting targets for divisions, functions and even individuals. These are of three types – divisional targets, functional targets and individual targets.

Divisional

Standards here can be for sales, growth market share and productivity. Managers then work to organise matters so that they can meet targets. The aim is to raise standards over time, and this might mean that co-operation is required to achieve this. So one division working with another might achieve better economies of scale, efficiency gains and even flexibility.

Functional

These, as the name suggests, set goals for functions of the organisation, such as sales or marketing. Sales targets are an example here, with a periodic review to check progress and/or take corrective action. The importance of functional activities has been recognised by such approaches as Porter's value-chain analysis, where the efficiency and constantly improving standards of a function can provide a key competitive advantage.

Individual

These can be set where it is straightforward to monitor and evaluate the individual's contribution. In areas where team working has been encouraged or where the task is complex, setting individual targets becomes impossible and the targets then move to the team, division or functional levels.

Output targets, as with market control, have problems. These kind of targets can place an emphasis on short-term issues that eat away at the long-term strategy of the organisation. Relationship marketing and sales targets, for example, do not sit happily alongside each other, with the former looking to build a relationship over time that encourages repeat purchases whilst the latter looks at monthly sales.

ESTABLISHING A CONTROL SYSTEM

Jeannet and Hennessey[12] identify a good control system as being made up of three elements:

1 the establishment of standards;

2 the measurement of performance against standards;

3 the analysis and correlation of deviations from the standards.

Each of these elements is simple to understand and conceptualise, but their use in practice creates tensions and problems. It has already been noted in the formal and informal control approaches suggested by Goold and Quinn above that recognition has to be given to the need to combine them if effective control is to be exerted.

The dilemma here is that without the three elements control may be impossible; but overdue reliance on them creates the illusion of control that can lead to problems. Corporate strategy can be harmed by ineffective or defective control systems.

Standards

Performance standards are chosen to help evaluate performance. Hill and Jones[13] identify four standards:

1 efficiency targets;

2 human resource targets;

3 internal functions targets;

4 environmental targets.

Efficiency targets focus on areas such as productivity, profit, quality, costs, and so on. Human resource targets look at job turnover, absenteeism, moral and job satisfaction, in order to set acceptable levels for the organisation. Internal function targets, which cover areas such as creativity, decision making and communication, are more difficult areas to deal with, but highlight the importance of these issues for the company. Lastly, environmental targets focus less on the physical environment, although this can form a key part of areas under consideration, and more on the business environment – the ability to manage networks of stakeholders and influence regulatory and law makers.

As seen in the previous chapters all of these issues are important for the international marketer to appreciate; all firms must be able to understand and deal with these facets of business activity.

Performance against standards

Measurement of performance against standards can occur at various levels in the organisation, from the corporate down to the individual level.

Using standards does not come without problems. One obvious difficulty is knowing which standards to use. An emphasis placed on particular standards, such as cost performance, might clash with those for environmental issues that pick up changes in the business environment that might provide a more balanced view. Managers may judge themselves successful in their cost performance but find that the product is rejected in the market place.

Implied in the problem of choice of standards is the issue of compatibility. As with corporate objectives, tensions can exist between standards that can cause problems for the organisation. Driving down costs can often be achieved by reducing labour costs and increasing workloads. This can then increase pressure and raise absenteeism, which in its turn hits productivity. Seeing the connections between performance standards is a necessary part of appraisal of corporate performance.

Performance standards can, like corporate objectives, also be seen as having a trade-off over time – i.e. short-term issues such as cost control against long-term improvements that come from R&D, training and capital investment. Other issues apply to the choice of standards, but it is necessary to see that a combination of standards can provide an appropriate response to control that balances short- and long-run issues.

Analysis of performance

The reason for setting standards and reviewing performance is to see how far the objectives of the organisation are being met. Performance has to be evaluated to seek to understand why a variance has occurred, and to take corrective action. Reasons for underperformance against standards can be many and various, the thing being an ability to appraise a situation, reach conclusions and take effective action. In firms that have operations spread over many countries, this process is complicated by the issues of distance, communication and culture. The last of these may produce differences that are unexpected, forcing companies to spend money training their managers and gaining their acceptance of the control mechanisms they wish to adopt. Above-average performance can be rewarded, whilst consistently below-average performance can be penalised. The key is to provide managers and their staff with the tools to undertake analysis, support their actions in dealing with deviations, and endeavour to build continuous improvements in operations.

Analysing performance can be undertaken in such a way that it focuses on short-term solutions, which can detract from future long-term growth and profitability. Short-term cost and income problems and their allied solutions can lead to the eradication of a variance at the expense of long-term market growth – as, for example, in cutting out a product that has long-term potential due to short-term cost problems.

Control is exercised in ways that budgets and plans hint at but fail to make explicit. Stacey,[14] summarising the work of Hofstede, focuses on the way in which control is exerted, this being defined in terms of:

1 degree of ambiguity in the objectives;

2 measurability of the performance to be controlled;

3 extent to which the outcome of actions are known; and

4 extent to which the activity being controlled is repetitive.

Six forms of control can be identified, being used according to the combination of the four circumstances:

1 *routine control* – used where there is little ambiguity in objectives; performance can be accurately assessed, outcomes of actions are known and the activity is repetitive;

2 *expert control* – used if the activity is not repetitive, but the conditions outlined in (1) still apply; there is then the possibility of expert intervention;

3 *trial and error* – used where the outcome of actions is uncertain, making predictions difficult; neither routine nor expert control will be possible, with the need to discover effects of intervention through trial and error – a possibility that exists when actions are repetitive;

4 *intuitive control* – used if objectives are unambiguous and performance is measurable, but actions are not repetitive and outcomes known – where actions are not repetitive there is only one chance to take an action and trial and error control won't work; managers in these circumstances have to rely on intuition;

5 *judgemental control* – used when objectives are clear, but everything else is not; judgmental control then becomes essential;

6 *political control* – the use of power, negotiation, persuasion and manipulation in circumstances where little is clear and in effect every situation is unique.

How do these six types of control and the four circumstances relate to international marketing? When moving from a domestic base into a new (international) market, the activities and actions required will be many and various. Controlling the '4 Ps' can be grouped into one or more of the familiar ways of setting objectives and measuring performance and exerting control. International marketing managers' work goes beyond the work of the marketing function, i.e. the '4 Ps', incorporating strategic considerations and other less measurable activities. The emphasis placed on organisations continuously adapting to change also produces situations where objectives conflict, and outcomes are unknown features that are found in the more complex situation of international global markets where control is a more challenging issue than many firms and their managers expect.

CONTROL AND GLOBAL MANAGEMENT

With many organisations moving to either increased involvement in global markets or entering them for the first time, the major challenge for companies is to develop, utilise and retain managers who are able to work in new and challenging environments.

In Chapter 6 on planning, the philosophy of managers towards international markets and working with colleagues drawn from varying cultural backgrounds was seen as imperative in being successful. Having an open 'style' of management, being prepared to experiment, to listen, to understand were all considered to be key qualities required of such managers. Likewise, in looking at organisation, planning processes and control, similar understanding and appreciation is of paramount importance. Problems exist here:

1 companies often fail to realise the unique stresses and strains of such appointments or that the unique skills developed can help achieve marketing objectives;

2 postings to foreign countries may not carry much weight in terms of career development;

3 training and management development programmes are inadequate to prepare personnel for such posts;

4 basic marketing mistakes can be made due to a lack of stress on international management development.

Each of these will be explored further, but it can often be assumed that globalisation and increased communication links via the Internet, faster transport links, and so on, can obviate the need to think through the use of personnel in foreign markets. Cultural differences remain which can, and do, provide challenges for a manager brought up in one system (national and corporate cultures of, say, the UK) to adjust to another. Planning, control and motivation of staff can be seen in different ways, with new questions being asked and solutions sought. Boxes 20.5 and 20.6 provide a summary of these planning and control issues, and the differences that can be found between the US, European and Japanese approaches to management.

Box 20.5

EUROPEAN MANAGERS[15]

Research carried out into European management in 1994 aimed to see if there was common ground in the way managers across the EU countries carried out their jobs. The conclusions drawn from this research was that whilst there was no common European model, there were many similarities, except when it came to the UK, where practice was closer to the US approach. Two models of management style can be summarised:

The American model

1 Emphasis on shareholders' profits;

2 strong competition, that is expected to lead to customer satisfaction;

3 individualism through personal achievement and professional mobility;

4 functionalism and professionalism;

5 emphasis on product orientation rather than customer orientation.

The European model

1 People orientated and internal negotiation important, particularly with unions;

2 management of cultural diversity;

3 management between extremes and between long- and short-term;

4 emphasis on stakeholders rather than shareholders;

5 adaptation to customer needs;

6 integration of individual into the firm;

7 little distinction between personal and professional life.

The example used in Chapter 19 on the convergence due to the existence of global markets does not invalidate the models outlined here. Convergence has been noted by CEOs who took part in the survey, with each model bringing a benefit – the Japanese model emphasises customer orientation, the US profits and the European people orientation and the management of cultural diversity. Convergence would not of itself suggest a fusing of the three, and if this occurred it would not help to iron out the tensions inherent in such a model.

The European model, with its emphasis on managing cultural diversity, requires the ability to manage complexity, which itself places an emphasis on communication, negotiation and implementation skills. Investment in these areas by both trainers and organisations (businesses) would enhance the marketing effort.

Box 20.6

STRUCTURES, PLANNING AND CONTROL[16]

Chapter 19 looked at the issue of structures and their relationship to strategy, which itself has to adapt to new demands and conditions found in the market place. One issue that was emphasised was the implication of operating flatter structures in order to reduce costs, increase efficiency and effectiveness. Sometimes referred to as 'downsizing', this form of restructuring has an impact on the way managers and other personnel work, which also raises issues to do with planning and control. Figures 20.1 and 20.2 show the shift that takes place, from the traditional plan–organise–control approach to that which involves leaders and teams.

Fig 20.1 TRADITIONAL ORGANISATIONS

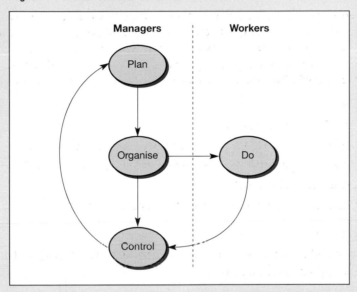

The most notable shift is where teams take over some responsibility for planning and control, requiring all workers to be directly familiar with the processes and issues involved, plus the requirement to continually improve performance – this emphasis on teams and implied ways of operating is not to suggest that all the older structural forms are obsolete, as in many circumstances they serve the business well, as shown in Chapter 19. What is accepted as the basic premise of 'world-class organisation' is that new ways of thinking and competing are required, with past success being no guarantee of it continuing into the future.

For these changes to work, teams need information, ability to make decisions and power to carry them out, and both organisational structures and control mechanisms have to change to accommodate this. Ideally, functional barriers have to be reduced as teamwork across the organisation is necessary to provide a viable product to the customer. Managers change their role to that of leader. Traditionally, the manager planned and budgeted and made decisions which were then investigated and action taken. In the 'world-class organisation', the manager has turned into a leader, which means that they seek to make changes, bring teams together to solve problems, locate resources to carry these out and trust the team to get on with the job in the way they think best. This does

▶

▶ **Box 20.6 continued**

Fig 20.2 WORLD-CLASS ORGANISATIONS

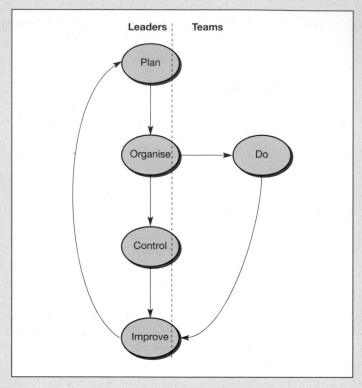

not imply a lack of control, the abolition of budgets and reporting procedures: it means that responsibility for them is taken on by teams, shared with leaders and then reported to senior management.

As noted elsewhere, good (marketing) managers recognise the shortcomings of all the systems and structures that they operate within. The 'world-class organisation' is not without its own stresses and strains that have to be recognised and managed. In the move from the 'traditional' approach to a team-based one problems will emerge. Some of the more serious ones are listed below.

Stress

As the organisation changes from a stable predictable set of relationships to one where change is a constant feature, many will find that they are unable to adjust – the workers to team membership; the managers to leaders. Many will leave. Downsizing has been criticised because of the zeal with which some companies have cut their workforce, leaving additional work for those who remain.

Complex problems

If teams are to solve problems and these teams comprise of those with less training and knowledge, then investment in them becomes essential. Training and development is, however, an area where cutbacks are often made – a fact that produces problems for managers and teams alike.

> ▶ **Box 20.6 continued**

Retention of staff

Changes can produce a loss of goodwill, with workers seeking to leave, either for other companies or by early retirement, or by taking redundancy. Retention and replacement of lost personnel can become a major problem, as expertise is lost and is difficult to replace.

Core competencies

To gain competitive advantage it is necessary to build core competencies that the organisation uses to innovate and build a successful presence in the market place. Moving from a stable structure and control system to a new situation can jeopardise the investment required.

Recognising the potential strains, does not mean staying with the known. Moving to a 'world-class organisation' requires involving teams in planning and control and the realisation that they are part of the marketing effort.

If national or regional models of management present alternative approaches and solutions, then so too do the strategies pursued by companies. Hollingshead and Leat[17] apply a set of typologies to review the approaches adopted by multinational enterprises (MNEs) – these are familiar from the strategies and structures that are open to MNEs, namely ethnocentric, polycentric or geocentric. All are reviewed here from the point of view of management approaches.

Ethnocentric MNEs work on the premise that what works in the country of origin can be extended to new operations located on foreign territory, so recruitment and selection, remuneration and training and development are all heavily influenced from the centre. Local labour will be recruited, but staffing procedures and remuneration will all be controlled from head office. Cultural diversity and its management is not given a high priority.

Polycentric firms work on the assumption that local managers and workers are better placed to deal with the needs and requirements of the local market, promoting decentralisation. Recruitment, remuneration and training therefore focus on the needs of the local operation, but again little in the way of managing in a complex environment and dealing with cultural diversity is required.

Geocentric firms, combining both local and international (global) approaches, operate in a complex structure in a complex environment. Corporate objectives take precedence, with the organisation required to respond to both local and also global ones. An integrated approach to management recruitment will be pursued, needing both a high level of cultural awareness and the pursuit of global objectives by managers (and workers); training and development will place a strong emphasis on language training and on managing in a culturally diverse environment.

Geocentric firms can be the most successful, as it is best placed to gain benefits of global and local goals.

Planning and control

In practice, the division between planning and control is not clear cut. If planning is defined as a formal statement of what is intended at some future point, it is built on expectations (and information) available to the 'planner' at a moment in time. As the plan is implemented, unexpected (i.e. unplanned) events will happen, producing a movement away from the plan. Control is, therefore, the means by which the organisation copes with these changes, either by action to bring operations back on line, or if required to amend the plan itself in the light of new circumstances. Planning and control issues overlap, without there being a clear demarcation between them.

In organisations that are flatter and based on less hierarchical relationships, how is control (and planning) facilitated? Marscham et al[18] point to a move in some MNCs towards greater decentralisation, with the shift facilitated by the development and use of networks of personal relationships. Networks are aimed at benefits gained from horizontal communications and the accompanying breakdown in internal barriers. Here, though, there are difficulties. Will the organisation be able to exert control, and how will they (or should they) contain activities? As important is the acceptance by middle managers of such approaches, where any degree of resistance to management's move towards empowerment will reduce the effectiveness of the initiative. Other researchers[19] concur with the observation that MNCs and others need to control, to check if corporate objectives are being achieved, as well as to create the environment to facilitate innovation and new forms of working.

Stacey points to the problems of seeking to adopt loose–tight control in an organisation that has developed a flexible structure. Advocating a clear hierarchy and short-term control, he points to the problem of moving too quickly in the direction of increasing participation; dysfunctional behaviour and problems with control will result. Attempting to replace hierarchies with groups will cause problems; far better to have a clear hierarchy (structure) and management information and control systems. In these circumstances, managers will not be tempted to do what they like, as to achieve anything they will have to build support, obtain 'permission' to proceed and by so doing gain resources to carry out their tasks. Planning and control can therefore be obtained in an organisation that wishes to see more participation in strategy via interpretation of strategic goals at various levels. None of this is a substitute for planning and control – merely it works differently, depends more on informal (political and cultural) control methods, and requires a change in the way senior managers understand their role.

The issue of empowerment can be seen as threatening in many cultures, where there may be a preference for hierarchies and formal decision-making approaches. As already noted, what works in the context of the USA or UK may fail in a European or emerging market context, or require adaptation.

Managers can feel threatened by the use of personal networks and horizontal communication that is beyond their immediate control. Kane Elevators' Northern European Area[20] wanted to adopt a prescriptive reporting approach, insisting that personnel in sales subsidiaries communicate with two engineering resource centres through a specified contact. The benefits of informal communication and the gains expected from empowerment were reduced. Using technology to monitor communication might allow more control, but that could fly against the public pronouncement that they were seeking to encourage initiative and risk-taking.

Organisational structures and control, and the moves to create new (and evolutionary) forms present challenges and problems, both issues are reviewed in Boxes 20.7 and 20.8. The overall need is to promote competitive advantage, that understands customer needs and requirements, and structure and control approaches that can move and adapt to achieve this. As this occurs, new challenges are encountered that need to be addressed, rather than moving back to traditional methods that are inappropriate in a global context.

Box 20.7 INTERNATIONAL MARKETING PLANNING AND DECISION MAKING[21]

Thorelli and Becker identify five international marketing decisions that need to be made and planned for:

1 the commitment decision, which looks to commit the firm to market opportunities abroad;
2 the country-selection decision, which identifies those countries that offer the best target markets;
3 the mode of entry and operations, identifying the best (most effective) way of entering the target markets;
4 the marketing mix, focusing on the mix of marketing instruments which will be most effective in the chosen market;
5 the marketing organisation decision, which looks at the most effective response to co-ordination, control and flexibility.

These decisions cannot be taken in isolation from each other – the marketing mix is influenced by the mode of entry as well as the country selected. General planning approaches such as those shown in Fig. 20.3 can be combined with the international marketing planning matrix (Table 20.1), with each cell of the matrix representing a step in the planning process.

Some of the steps (cells) may already be seen as redundant – for example, the commitment decision may already have been made to start the process off. However, a review of each of the cells can reveal how they are interconnected, feeding through to the lower (tactical) levels of marketing budgets.

Table 20.1 THE PLANNING MATRIX

International decisions	Marketing planning variables					
	Diagnosis of situation	SWOT analysis	Objectives	Sales vol. costs/profit forecasts	Marketing programme	Marketing budgets
A Commitment decision						
B Country selection						
C Mode of entry						
D Marketing strategy						
E Marketing organisation						

Source: Thorelli, H.B. and Becker, H., *International Marketing Strategy*, 3rd edition (Oxford: Butterworth-Heinemann, 1990).

▶

▶ **Box 20.7 continued**

Fig 20.3 CYCLE OF MARKETING PLANNING

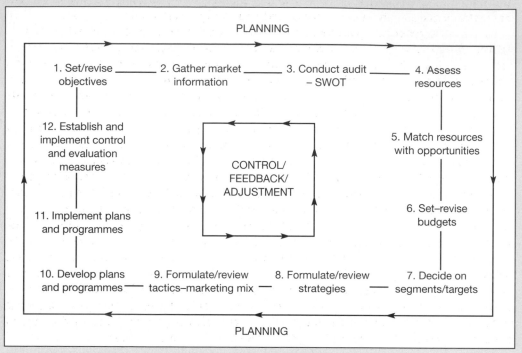

Source: Hutchings, A., *Marketing: A Resource Book* (London: Pitman Publishing, 1995).

Checklists for each decision are a means of illustrating the issues raised; it is not necessary to take a step-by-step approach to the checklist, seeing only that there is an interconnectedness between the issues, and with the realisation that these approaches are not a substitute for judgement on the part of senior managers.

For firms new to international marketing, or for those seeking to review operations, the matrix and checklist approaches are a means of structuring the approach. The realisation that flexibility and change are required in international markets would suggest that the end result is seen as a process of review that enhances understanding but is not a substitute for decision making. The checklist on international markets organisation is reviewed here as it focuses on organisations, planning and control.

<table><tr><td>Box 20.8</td><td>TARGET COSTS[22]</td></tr></table>

Target costing has made its mark in industries in which products require a good deal of production assembly – cars, cameras, and bulldozers, for example. However, the discipline target costing offers has uses outside the assembly environment.

In processing companies, where the characteristics of the process – time, temperature, and pressure – determine the performance of the product, the focus of target costing shifts from the product to the process. A steel company would tend to focus on the costs

> **Box 20.8 continued**

associated with routes and processing time; a paper mill, on those associated with speed and breakage. The key issues – understanding market needs, ensuring satisfactory financial performance at a given price, not exceeding the target cost – remain.

Similarly, target costing can be applied to services, for which the focus is the service–delivery system. As in process-intensive manufacturing, process is inextricable from product – think of the issues that are important to the delivery of health care and fast-food functions. Where services and process-intensive manufacturing diverge is in their flexibility. It is enormously expensive to convert a paper machine so that it can produce a grade or weight that was not considered in its initial design. Service–delivery systems, however, are a different matter. In people-intensive, customer-responsive service–delivery system, it is not only possible to add new services, it can be hard not to – menus are easy to extend; room services can easily be added; consulting firms or law firms can always enter a new area of practice. Where is the discipline that ensures that these extensions are profitable?

Because a single service–delivery system may be used to deliver a wide range of services, determining the profitability of individual services becomes an exercise in the arbitrary allocation of costs. In services, particularly those in which waiting time is critical, it is the systemic effects of individual new services – for instance, the extent to which they make the process more complex – that determine whether their revenues and value to customers offset their costs. Target costing can still facilitate a discussion of the appropriateness of a new service, but only if it focuses on the systemic impact of the service extension and questions whether this impact aligns with company strategy and profitability goals. In service industries as in other industries, target costing can help organisations resist the urge to create new market offerings simply because they have the ability to do so.

SUMMARY

This chapter has focused on issues related to control, looking at the importance of implementation of strategic plans. With the focus on formal and informal control systems and the variety of approaches required to implement and operate them, marketing managers need to be expert in the majority of such approaches.

The awareness of standards, performance against standards and the accompanying analysis are similarly vital elements in using the organisation's resources in the most cost-effective way. The use of standards can present problems in itself, as it may depend on quantitative data in circumstances that make the capture, use and interpretation of such information difficult, and in some cases impossible. In these situations, additional approaches to control may be required. As international marketing managers face a variety of situations, their awareness of, and ability to use, these alternative techniques are essential.

Working in foreign countries introduces managers to alternative approaches that were summarised in the models of management seen in the USA and Europe. Although Asian and Islamic approaches can also be seen as offering alternative management models, these main models are the most influential, and can be seen to be converging to some extent.

Management development by companies to prepare their managers for working in different environments is vital if they are to prosper and survive, particularly when opting for a geocentric approach that attempts to gain the benefit of global approaches allied to local responses, which put managers into unfamiliar environments that require skills in dealing with complex and changing circumstances.

REVIEW QUESTIONS

1 Describe the differences that exist between formal and informal control systems.

2 List the factors that affect control systems.

3 What are the key ingredients that go to make up a good performance system?

4 What factors can make the interpretation of performance difficult?

5 Identify the possible differences in the assessment of performance that might exist between a manager brought up within the European model, as compared to a UK manager.

DISCUSSION QUESTIONS

1 Why are implementation and control stages often overlooked in the strategic planning framework?

2 Do we really need managers who are aware of all the control issues raised by Hofstede?

3 If most MNCs follow a polycentric or ethnocentric approach, why is so much stress laid on managing diversity?

4 Do new methods of manufacture and use of information technology present a challenge for the traditional methods of control?

5 'Managing the international marketing effort of the company requires awareness of both specific control methods (i.e. the '4 Ps') and generic strategic control mechanisms.' Discuss this statement.

Case study

RETHINKING PEPSICO'S STRATEGY[23]

In early 1997 PepsiCo announced that it was to sell off its $11bn-a-year fast-food business comprising Pizza Hut, Taco Bell and Kentucky Fried Chicken, the idea being to sharpen the company's focus. What was to remain was the beverage business with over $10bn sales and the snack-food business with $8bn sales.

The refocusing was brought about by the poor performance of the company compared to its main rival Coca-Cola. Although PepsiCo enjoys higher sales in the US market it has fallen behind in the faster-growing overseas market, with nearly $4bn sales compared to Coca-Cola's $13bn; moreover, its profit margin of 4.6 per cent was well below that of Coca-Cola, who achieved 25.5 per cent.

In the 1970s PepsiCo moved into the purchase of fast-food outlets, as it felt that long-term growth and profit would come from these businesses rather than from beverages and snacks – a strategy that made sense insofar as many economies (particularly the Soviet-style economies) were 'closed', and developing economies offered few prospects for growth. When the company did try to enter markets, it met with little success – it sought to enter the French market with Friters, which failed as the French customers preferred other foods. Since the 1970s and early 1980s, the fast-food outlets have met with fierce competition from the likes of McDonald's, whilst attempts to take market share from Coca-Cola in their strongest markets failed.

The fast-food restaurant business has also had to face the capital costs of starting up in emerging markets such as China and Eastern Europe and the developing economies of countries such as India. Although the company is the world's largest restaurant owner with over 28 000 outlets, it underperformed compared to companies like McDonald's when it came to profitability.

In other markets, the company experienced difficulties in its beverage business. In Brazil, it took a $400m charge when its largest foreign bottling company almost went bankrupt. In Venezuela its bottling partner went over to Coca-Cola.

A major difference between PepsiCo and Coca-Cola comes with bottling. Coca-Cola has spun off its bottling operation to its 44 per cent-owned subsidiary Coca-Cola Enterprises (CCE). The company relies on CCE and seven other independent bottlers to distribute and sell its products world-wide. PepsiCo owns and operates most of its bottling operations in many countries, which incurs high expenses. PepsiCo has 480 000 employees compared to Coca-Cola who have 32 000.

The snacks business Frito-Lay, which includes Doritos, Cheetos and Friters, provides 44 per cent of PepsiCo's profit. Sales growth ran at 30 per cent a year making this the star of the company's operations. International potential is large, with foreign customers consuming 2lb of snacks per year, compared to the average American who eats 17.5lb. Persuading foreign customers to switch to one of the Frito-Lay products is one solution; the other is to increase total consumption. In the UK, for example, the Doritos brand had been built up to a $60m business in the 18 months to December 1996.

A benefit of the spin-off will be the ability to pass on some of the $8bn debt to the restaurant company, providing PepsiCo with resources for an acquisition. However, an alternative to acquisition is to improve profits in the international beverage business by concentrating on growth markets such as India, China and Eastern Europe.

Analysts estimated at the time of the announced split that by focusing on soft drinks and the snacks business a 10–15 per cent long-term growth rate in earnings per share was possible, thereby putting the company alongside its old rival Coca-Cola.

New markets open up with the new strategy, particularly ones that due to the involvement of the company in fast-food restaurants were once closed to it. McDonald's, which refuses to sell Pepsi-Cola, could be encouraged to take the product as it is not now seen as a competitor.

Questions

1 In selling off the restaurants, PepsiCo is sacrificing opportunities for growth in this sector to focus on its core business. How can this be justified?

2 What control issues are raised by the case study?

3 Coca-Cola is both more successful and more profitable than PepsiCo; is it too late for PepsiCo to compete with its rival?

4 A perfectly logical strategy adopted in the late 1970s has become a questionable one in the late 1990s. What does this say about the company's strategic planning process?

FURTHER READING

Bonoma, T.V., 'Making your marketing strategy work', *Harvard Business Review* (March–April 1984), 69–76.

Greenley, G.E., *Strategic Management* (Englewood Cliffs: Prentice Hall, 1989).

Kotler, P., *Marketing Management*, 7th edition (Englewood Cliffs: Prentice Hall, 1994).

Pfeffer, J. and Salancik, G.R., *The External Control of Organisations* (New York: Harper and Row, 1978).

Shapiro, A.C., 'Evaluation and control of foreign operations' in Vernon-Wortzel, H. and Wortzel, L.C. (eds), *Strategic Management of Multinational Corporations: The Essentials* (New York: Wiley, 1985), 225–39.

NOTES AND REFERENCES

1 Flamholtz, E., 'Effective organisational control: a framework, applications and implications', *European Management Journal*, 14(6) (December 1996).

2 Tomkins, R., 'PepsiCo to spin off its fast food business, *Financial Times* (23 January 1997).

3 FT500, *Financial Times* (24 January 1997).

4 Ibid.

5 *Marketing Planning and Control*, BPP Study Text (London: BPP, 1991).

6 Goold, M. and Quinn, J.J., *Strategic Control: Milestones for Long-term Performance* (London: Hutchinson, 1990).

7 Slack, N., Chambers, S., Harland, C., Harrison, A. and Johnston, R., *Operations Management* (London: Pitman Publishing, 1995).

8 Czinkota, M.R. and Ronkainen, I.A., *International Marketing*, 3rd edition (Orlando: The Dryden Press, 1993).

9 Jeannet, J.P. and Hennessey, H.D., *Global Marketing Strategies*, 2nd edition (Boston: Houghton Mifflin, 1992).

10 FT500, op. cit.

11 Hill, C.W.L. and Jones, G.R., *Strategic Management: An Integrated Approach* (Boston: Houghton Mifflin, 1992).

12 Jeannet and Henessey, op.cit.

13 Hill and Jones, op. cit.

14 Stacey, R.D., *Strategic Management and Organisational Dynamics* (London: Pitman Publishing, 1993).

15 'Dealing with diversity: management education in Europe', *Selections* 11(1) (1994); 'International models of management development', *Selections* 11(1) (1994).

16 Tersine, R., Harvey, M. and Buckley, M., 'Shifting organisational paradigms: transitional management', *European Management Journal*, 18(1) (February 1997).

17 Hollinshead, G. and Leat, M., *Human Resource Management: An International and Corporate Perspective* (London: Pitman Publishing, 1995).

18 Marscham, R., Welch, D. and Welch, L., 'Control in less-hierarchical multinationals: the role of personal networks and informal communication', *International Business Review*, 5(2) (1996).

19 Stacey, op. cit.

20 Marscham, Welch and Welch, op. cit.

21 Thorelli, H.B. and Becker, H., 'Stratetic planning in international marketing' in Thorelli, H.B. and Cavusgil, S.T. (eds), *International Marketing Strategy*, 3rd edition (Oxford: Butterworth-Heinemann, 1990), 557–68; Hutchings, A., *Marketing: A Resource Book* (London: Pitman Publishing, 1995), 278.

22 Cooper, R.C. and Chew, W.B., 'Control tomorrow's costs through today's designs', *Harvard Business Review* (January–February 1996), 93.

23 'Shake-up to put sparkle into Pepsi', *Sunday Times* (26 January 1997).

21

The future of global marketing

INTRODUCTION

The need to understand current trends and to appreciate what they mean for the organisation has been a major theme throughout this book. Each part has identified changes that currently require a response.

Part 1 gave an overview of globalisation, the opening up of markets and the challenges that this brings. Part 2, in reviewing planning and strategy, asked how far formal planning approaches were suitable for a world that was changing fast and where competitive advantage could be quickly eroded. The global market environment highlights the many changes, challenges and opportunities that the international marketing manager will have to grapple with in entering a market. The complex nature of the marketing environment is one of the biggest single challenges facing marketers, not just for those wishing to enter or expand business in chosen markets, but also for those in domestic markets where, due to the fall of trade barriers and changes in public procurement regulations, what were once heavily protected markets have become open for competition – a trend exacerbated by the advent of firms using the Internet for marketing. Changes of this magnitude require all organisations in both the public and private sectors to meet a significant challenge.

Parts 2 and 3 provided an in-depth review of the research and information systems that can shed light on marketing issues, from environmental changes to consumer behaviour. The availability of secondary research data to a wider variety of clients, via on-line services, which was previously expensive and inaccessible was noted – a move that has seen prices fall as competition from suppliers increases. The need for public sector organisations as well as 'not-for-profit' groups to access this material means that marketing-led approaches are now appropriate to solve problems of fund-raising, recruitment and message promotion for organisations that had traditionally fought shy of using commercial approaches.

Part 3 and Part 4 dealt in detail with the strategies available and the marketing mix options that companies can adopt to build successful international organisations. Here again, new developments were noted that provide choice and opportunities for aware organisations. Taking one example, that of counter-trade from Chapter 12, the use of the Internet to inform companies of a government's counter-trade policy reveals the evolution of a form of business (counter-trade) to meet an environmental change (the Internet).

Lastly, Part 5 focused on the organisational form, planning processes and control methods from the viewpoint that broader changes in the market have to be met by changes in strategy and the organisation itself. New ways of working are of significance to the company and the marketer, as they vary the profile of marketing by an insistence on customer needs and requirements being met by all parts of the organisation. In a real sense marketing, has become a generic rather than functional activity in which every individual must be competent.

This summary is an important forerunner of the issues raised in this chapter. The need has been identified to keep abreast of changes in the business environment and equally to be proactive – i.e. to see a trend or change that will affect business over the next 10–20 years, and to respond to it. This is often seen as nothing more than gazing at tea-leaves – who could have foreseen in 1980 that by the end of the decade the Soviet Union-dominated, centrally-planned economies would have re-emerged as democracies (to a greater or lesser extent) and would have adopted many market-led solutions to their economic problems? How could the likes of Microsoft have foreseen the increasing importance of the Internet, or a company such as Shell correctly identified the rising influence of consumers' environmental concerns when it sought to sink an obsolete oil platform in the North Sea? It is doubtful that any one could have foreseen the swiftness of the changes in Eastern Europe, but there had been evidence for some time that other global developments – such as the rising importance of Asian economies – were imminent. The point is to see the whole picture as well as individual elements, so that global changes can be seen as presenting challenges to all nation-states whether centrally-planned or market-led. The outcome was not certain for individual countries, but the global pressure for change was building.

In the Shell and Microsoft examples, environmental concerns and technological changes have been topics in the mass media for some time; again, specific events will present unexpected challenges for companies to which they need to respond.

One clear challenge is that of natural environmental change. Global warming, with its implied influence on climate, will change the nature of demand in those countries it affects. This, however, is a superficial response. There could be movements to head off the problem by reduction in emissions which could cause changes in the way products are made or even in the types of products required. Pressure is now placed on companies to produce products in ways that do the least harm to the environment. None of these developments can be ignored by the marketer; at the marketing strategy level they impact on the '4 Ps' by, for example, influencing packaging, means of delivery to the market, and so on. From a global prospective and different countries have differing priorities and, are at various stages of development in their policies on environmental issues, whilst the regulating agencies such as the WTO grapple with the implications of environmental protection for free trade. Such environmental issues have to be given a high priority, as global changes will be a major consideration in the coming years.

To look at the future of global marketing is to focus attention on the potential of such issues to determine the macro and micro environment for the foreseeable future. General headings have been used under which a number of issues and themes will be reviewed that will interest organisations and their global marketing managers over the next decade.

641

Objectives

This chapter will examine:

- the evolution of global competition
- global customers
- gaining competitive advantage in global markets
- ethical issues
- the future of marketing (a summary).

THE EVOLUTION OF GLOBAL COMPETITION

Box 21.1 picks up on an issue that has been raised elsewhere in this book, namely that 'globalisation' as understood by the WTO, the World Bank, the IMF and others has to be seen against the background of regionalisation. In this sense, 'regionalisation' means the establishment of various types of trading blocs, to which virtually all the existing nations belong. Although agreed by the WTO, and supported by others as a way of establishing the benefits of commercial trade within a specified area, they beg as many questions as they answer. Do they, for example, follow rules and procedures laid down by international bodies such as the WTO? If they do, what is the point of creating them in the first place? On the other hand, if they establish their own procedures, how will this match up with the WTO and could they create new barriers to trade? Regional trading blocs, in trying to serve two masters – i.e. the interests of the region and of the WTO – may simply lead to inertia. *The Economist* article in Box 21.1 certainly sees such a danger, particularly when it comes to liberalising trade where there are strong vested interests.

Another difficulty seen in the expansion of regional trading areas is how far they should move towards integration to create a truly integrated market place. Many of the EU member states have grave doubts, not just about the single currency but also about the possibility of the creation of a super-state. Although seen by supporters of the EU as a far-fetched notion, the super-state has undermined support for further integration, making it more difficult to proceed.

Box 21.1   SPOILING WORLD TRADE

By the sorry standards of much of this century, world trade looks in rude health. In the 1930s, protectionism helped poison the world economy. After the Second World War, tariffs and other trade barriers fell too slowly. However, over the past decade, many of the restrictions that have stifled international commerce have been relaxed – thanks in large part to the lengthy Uruguay Round of GATT talks, completed in 1993. Since 1990 world trade has grown by six per cent a year, compared with less than four per cent a year in the 1980s. As if to confirm the importance that governments now attach to the subject, there is now a World Trade Organisation (WTO), with 126 members, to police the new regime

▶

▶ Box 21.1 continued

and to take the cause of free trade further into areas, such as agriculture, services and investment, where there are still far too many restrictions.

When the feasible is the enemy of the good

Thanks to the recent explosion of regional trade arrangements, whose members agree to liberalise trade among themselves, the WTO is just one cook among many stirring the free-trade broth. Only a handful of the WTO's members are not already part of some other local club. The EU has 15 members and could soon have more. Some Americans are already looking for ways to meld together the North American Free Trade Agreement (NAFTA), which was formed with Mexico and Canada, with Mercosur, a customs union formed by four South American countries. Free trade areas (FTAs) are planned in both Southeast Asia and South Asia. And the 19-strong Asia Pacific Economic Co-operation (APEC) forum has a grand plan for 'free trade in the Pacific' by 2020.

Most governments and many free traders believe that regional FTAs are a step in the right direction. Their defence is usually a mixture of economic principle, practical diplomacy and visionary politics. First, they ask, how it can be possible for countries to agree to scrap tariffs among themselves and not make trade freer. Then they argue that it is often easier to make a deal in a small group than in the unwieldy WTO. And, finally, trade agreements, they say, are politically valuable: if countries are tied by commerce, they are less likely to start shooting at each other.

The first of these arguments, plausible as it seems, is simply false. Regional 'FTAs' need not make trade freer. By liberalising trade only with their neighbours, countries are by definition discriminating against those not lucky enough to be in the local club. Some goods will be imported from other members of the FTA at the expense of producers elsewhere; and members will begin to specialise in industries in which they lack comparative advantage.

The EU has a bloated farming industry while many producers in poorer countries suffer from not being able to serve its markets; and NAFTA has complicated 'rules of origin' requirements, stipulating how much of a car needs to be made in Mexico to qualify as 'NAFTAN', and so enter the US tariff-free. It is always better to liberalise without discrimination than to open up only to neighbours; sometimes, selective opening is worse than doing nothing at all.

The argument that, despite this danger, regional trade areas (RTAs) represent a speedier, more practical way to proceed than does the WTO, is also open to question. True, the Uruguay Round lasted more than seven years, and even now governments are struggling to finish off some outstanding negotiations, but slow progress bedevils regional arrangements, too. Despite much talk about expansion, the membership of NAFTA is stuck at three; APEC is moving at a glacial pace. Similarly, although the local clubs sometimes broach subjects long before the WTO (for instance, NAFTA has a treaty on foreign direct investment (FDI)), they can also introduce possible bugbears (NAFTA also contains worrying agreements on standards for labour and environmental protection).

The emergence of the WTO has raised the hurdle: the architects of regional agreements know they will have to defend their plans against the charge of setting back liberal trade, and adjust their plans accordingly. That is fine, but it raises a question: would it not be simpler, after all, to make these deals at the WTO?

That leaves the last 'political' argument – that bodies such as APEC and Mercosur have brought old enemies together.

▶

> ▶ **Box 21.1 continued**

If governments paid more attention to the threat of regionalism, that would be an excellent start. One excuse for their not doing so is that the WTO's own system for policing regional trade agreements is a mess. At present, each new FTA or customs union is appraised by a committee, open to all members and with extremely vague terms of reference. Unsurprisingly, only six of the 70-odd committees formed since the GATT began have ever reached a firm conclusion. It would be much better if agreements were examined by a smaller team of independent scrutineers with a precise mandate to assess the effect on world trade – and, in particular, the way that the new agreement treats outsiders.

It can be hard to say whether any FTA is so restrictive that its costs outweigh its benefits – though Mercosur, by some calculations, fails the test, and the case for the new ASEAN agreement also looks weak. Most agreements are a mixture of good and bad. The long-term challenge for the ministers who met in Singapore in December 1996 was thus twofold: to change the worst details in their own regional deals; and, even more important, to press ahead with multilateral trade liberalisation in the WTO. Governments have a chance to make this new institution the strong catalyst for liberal trade which they have long said they wanted.

Source: 'Spoiling world trade', © *The Economist*, London (7 December 1996).

A second view of regionalisation is that produced by regional trading blocs themselves. Again using the EU as an example, the concept of 'subsidiarity', whereby decisions should be taken at the lowest possible level, has reinforced the importance of regional government. A concept familiar to the Germans, but not the British, it has meant that political and economic structures have had to be adapted to cope with the demands of this approach.

Regionalisation can therefore be seen as the importance of the grouping of nations as well as regions within these nation-states. It is here that the earlier references to the demise of the nation-state can be seen to be focused. (Equally, the power to evolve and adapt that nation-states possess still shows its importance in many areas of its personal, business and cultural life. Regionalisation can be seen as altering the dynamics of this structure, rather than heralding its demise.) For the marketer, globalisation can be seen as offering opportunities for the creation of global brands with all that entails for production, distribution, promotion, and so on. Regionalisation, on the other hand, presents a new challenge (opportunity) in that regional governments, such as the Länder in Germany, can have a large influence on location, subsidies and other aids to companies wishing to locate in a specific area.

Regional trading areas, with new and evolving regulatory regimes can, like the EU, require marketers and companies to know how to influence (lobby) the relevant authorities to set a favourable climate for business and marketing. Here, though, there are problems of perception. 'Marketing' for a UK or US executive can mean a certain way of undertaking business that can be alien to a marketer from an Asian or mainland European background. It can lead to misunderstanding and misperceptions of what should be incorporated in rules and regulations, and just how far marketers should go in the pursuit of business when there are no guidelines. Marketers have to be aware of just how much this can influence how a trading area wishes to proceed on issues such as promotion, distribution, take-overs, and so on.

Box 21.2 presents the argument that globalisation, as promoted in the majority of research and in the financial press, can lead companies to expect a 'domino effect' – i.e. that globalisation is an irreversible force before which all will fall. (The term 'domino effect' was first put forward to explain the influence of Communism, with countries falling 'like dominoes' as it moved across the globe.) Globalisation is not, however, like a domino effect, and many companies are taking the trouble to understand the countervailing forces to it. This can be done by bringing in country experts (those who have a cultural, historical and sociological–anthropological understanding of a country or area), and those who have a different perception of the issues. By these means, companies can appreciate the instability of many situations – as, for example, the long-standing dispute between the Czech Republic and Germany over the 'German'-populated parts of the Republic.

Box 21.2   EMERGING PARADIGMS[1]

The traditional view of planning has been very dependent on a mechanistic view of the business environment. A new view, based on the biology of emergent forms, attempts to replace systems and functions with a more dynamic view of interrelationships, which looks at evolving connections that form higher-order, open-ended patterns that take the form of a self-organising systems. This approach knows that the future cannot be anticipated from an external perspective, which frees strategic thinking from its requirement to know the future.

The challenge for companies in the late 1990s and the early twenty-first century is to define the boundaries and shapes of the puzzle. Traditionally, the requirement was to collect evidence and fit these pieces together to understand not just where we are now, but where we are going. There are numerous examples of how this has failed to work, with extrapolations, Delphi and other methods failing to pick up a trend, with disastrous results. Barnett argues that it is who is asking what kind of question that becomes important. So if a cash-rich food company executive sees the puzzle as acquiring companies producing trendy food products, this is different from redefining what 'food' might mean in the future and seeking acquisitions outside traditional food companies.

A major car manufacturer can reap the benefits of the global economy, providing it with the opportunities to gain economies of scale and to establish a global strategy to gain these benefits. But is globalisation inevitable? Does it have drawbacks, what are its costs and what are the possibilities that it could be threatened? Using conventional approaches, one might conclude that in the car industry the move towards globalisation is inevitable and accelerating, and that all companies have to be ready with a suitable (strategic) response. A company seeking to deal with this hired those with alternative views, ranging from anthropologists through to country specialists, particularly regarding Southeast Asia and Eastern Europe. They brought forward convincing concerns about regional conflicts and resource conflicts – e.g. over water. Environmental concerns and cultural understanding of intellectual capital were also included, showing that a crude use of globalisation analysis pointed the way to an integrated world that might not happen. The upshot was that globalisation was pursued as a strategy, but by using 'design for disassembly' (DFD), a concept used by BMW which meant that production, distribution and marketing systems could be broken down into regional or local systems if so required, a more strategic approach, given the issue of counterveiling forces, was adopted.

▶

> ▶ **Box 21.2 continued**

Traditional thinking was challenged by this approach:

1 there is uncertainty about the trend of globalisation;

2 discontinuaties may affect global control;

3 there is a need to think smaller as well as bigger;

4 there is a need to take into account the importance of culture and religion as major influences on regionalisation and globalisation.

Strategic planning is the only method available to think ahead. Barnett wishes to approach strategy by starting from epistemology – i.e. that one's position–perspective fundamentally shapes the questions asked, the scope of the queries, the appropriate data and the answers accepted. Barnett's 'dialogics' help to break down a mindset that could be detrimental to a company if the prevailing view is not challenged.

Imperceptible forces – ones that are difficult to quantify or difficult to incorporate – can have major consequences, and they need to be recognised and discussed. Business boundaries can be changed as rules change, as with the concept of business that the Internet is producing.

Lastly, learning from mistakes in an environment that is unstable is more important than trying to get things right. Strategic planning in these circumstances then involves more people, both inside and outside the organisation.

Box 21.2 gives us another perspective on regionalisation, and one that takes seriously the importance of religion and culture to an area that can produce some unexpected upheavals, best seen in the conflict in the former Republic of Yugoslavia. Other, less extreme differences exist in Spain and Belgium, and can upset the assumption that these countries possess a people who adhere to one dominant culture. The solution, as reviewed in Box 21.2, is for companies to see the opportunities that are created as well as the need to act in a flexible way at the local level – an example of thinking globally, but with the ability to act locally in both a marketing and an operational sense.

Regionalisation will influence global competition, despite the Internet and the ability to transport goods and people more quickly around the globe. It is possible for globalisation to be halted by these pressures, as it was by two world wars earlier in the twentieth century.

GLOBAL CUSTOMERS

Complex environmental forces are shaping the marketing environment, many of which can point in opposite directions to those suggested by the simple application of globalisation. Regionalisation is one amongst many of the trends picked up by the use of PEST analysis, plus the more focused five-forces model. The marketing manager faces challenges in understanding and interpreting this complex situation, with response depending on the organisation's involvement in foreign markets.

Changes in the environment force firms and marketers to adapt strategies to new circumstances, as well as seeking to understand new markets and customers. Box 21.3 looks at the emergence of China as a major market for all kinds of products including alcoholic beverages. Three companies are preparing to look at their response to this change. In fact, there are challenges on a number of fronts. From the point of view of Tsing Tao, the leading Chinese brand of beer, which is popular in many Chinese restaurants abroad, the challenge is that it controls only two per cent of the domestic market. Building market share as new foreign companies enter the market will be a major issue for the firm's marketers. Likewise, the foreign firms have to decide where in such a vast country they should direct their business.

Box 21.3

CHINA'S ALCOHOLIC BEVERAGES MARKET[2]

The commercial production of alcoholic beverages in China grew by two-thirds between 1991 and 1995. For producers of beer, spirits and wine hoping to win the loyalty of China's 1.2bn consumers, the reality of the market place is sobering. China is a crowded playing field, with more than 800 local breweries and tens of thousands of regional distillers; its under-developed infrastructure makes setting up a nation-wide sales and distribution network impossible, with customer tastes varying widely from province to province.

A few beverage makers have developed strategies that have a good chance of paying off. Three companies that seem to be doing things right – one in beer, the second in spirits and the third in wine – can be used as examples.

Beer is China's fastest-growing alcoholic beverage. Demand has grown at an annual 20 per cent for the past 10 years, yet *per capita* consumption is 12 litres (3.1 gallons) a year, about an eighth of that in the USA. Tsing Tao, China's leading brand, controls only two per cent of the market.

New Zealand brewer Lion Nathan came to China in 1995 determined to learn from predecessors' mistakes. Rather than launch a costly nation-wide marketing and distribution blitz, as Fosters and Anheuser–Busch had done, Lion Nathan focused on the Yangtze Delta region, one of the three most prosperous regions in China. It met with 50 brewers before settling on a joint venture partner, Taihushui Brewery, in Wuxi, which controlled 70 per cent of its local market. Lion Nathan took its time introducing its own brands, concentrating at first on improving the quality of Taihushui's local brand and doubling its production capacity. In 1996, Wuxi Lion Nathan Taihushui Brewery, as the 80/20 joint venture is known, made operating profits of US$1.6m, double 1995's earnings.

About a third of all alcoholic beverages produced in China are varieties of *baijiu*, a traditional white liquor made from the grain sorghum, and ranging in quality from raw to refined. With more disposable income, consumers are upgrading to better brands. Anhui Gujing Distillery, China's fifth-largest *baijiu* producer, has not only raised prices across the board but has also gradually shifted its production to the more expensive blends. As a result, Anhui Gujing's profits have grown 22 per cent annually over the past three years, compared with an industry rate of just six per cent. Its stock market valuation has more than trebled since being listed on the Shenzhen Stock Exchange in 1993.

The government, concerned about the strain on grain supplies caused by *baijiu* production, is promoting wine as a healthier alternative. The Hong Kong business elite is making wine fashionable as well. In the province's classier hotels and restaurants, wine is replacing cognac as the drink of choice, and the habit is steadily trickling down to the wealthy Guangdong Province. Four Seas Mercantile Holdings, a Hong Kong snack-food and beverage distribution company, seems to be in the right spot to profit; it has the exclusive licence to distribute the wines of the USA's largest winery E. & J. Gallo, in both Hong Kong and China. Four Seas says that orders jumped from an average of 40 000 bottles a month early in 1993 to 312 000 bottles a month in late 1993.

Taking the market and breaking it down by types of alcoholic beverage produces a better understanding of the dynamics of the market place. From the change in customer drinking habits, moving up to more expensive (branded) drinks, to the existence of small local producers of drink such as *baijiu*, the dynamics of the market are changing. Marketers have to be aware of these dynamics, and respond according to their resource position and degree of commitment to the market. Global customers may often mean access to previously closed markets such as China. Global customers, as with those who show similar tastes and preferences regardless of the country of residence, are often seen as a desirable group to pursue. In either case, the necessity to think through the implications forces companies to consider the production, distribution and retailing issues of this approach.

The rate of change in the market place means that customer tastes and preferences can quickly change, making this an area of great uncertainty. Using the example of China in Box 21.3, the change in customer preference (at least for the rich minority) means that their taste for branded lines increases. The changes can come about through cyclical change. An example of this is the pop music industry in the UK,[3] which accounted for £2.6bn in earnings in 1996, more than the utilities-based industries of the country. Part of the explanation for the rise in sales, and the popularity of British pop music, was a downturn in other markets, both in economic activity and invention and innovation from pop artists. The downturn created an opportunity which was then exploited by the industry as new talent came on the scene. If new talent emerges elsewhere a similar change in fortune could seriously hinder the export-earning potential of the industry.

This example reveals the importance of appreciating the dynamics of the industry, how customer preferences work and the need to see the interconnections and opportunities that go with the market. Technological changes, such as satellite television, can assist with this, but it also has to be recognised that technology can increase local interest as well as fostering the possibility of global influence. Digital broadcasting for both radio and TV presents opportunities for more local provision as well as catering for specialised tastes across the globe. In this sense, 'global' and 'local' go together.

GAINING COMPETITIVE ADVANTAGE IN GLOBAL MARKETS

Box 21.4

THE WORLD OF MARKETING[4]

Increased globalisation and competition have added to capacity at an unprecedented rate that has seen a concomitant increase in competition. In the majority of industries there is overcapacity, leading to the situation where supply will lead demand for many years to come. This situation has huge implications for companies, where the ability to raise prices has been greatly reduced and a period of low inflation is expected to be the norm. Pricing will have to be set at correct levels in the competitive environment that is expected to prevail.

▶ Box 21.4 continued

Increased competition requires companies to be more innovative with both their products and the way they are delivered to the market place. This has resulted in competition being based on intellectual capabilities, rather than natural resources or economies of scale. One example where this is most noticeable is in the new industries based on telecommunication, computers and software. With specialisation and integration of technology into everyday life, we are seeing new industries emerge and new challenges in managing the interdisciplinary approaches that are required.

With the use of technology and telecommunications in business, companies have been able to downsize, and workers now compete with each other for business, whether they are based in India or Australia. The intellectual capabilities of workers count for more than wage rates.

There are several other significant changes and developments.

1 Customers in developed markets are more sophisticated, with more choices open to them. This presents the marketer with a challenge: how to differentiate a product. This is more difficult given that companies can imitate a product very quickly, leading to the paradoxical position that innovation is essential, but its advantages can be eroded very quickly – i.e. competitive advantage is only short-lived.

2 Marketers should:
   (a) create customer value;
   (b) differentiate product;
   (c) obtain, usually through price, part of the customer value for shareholders;
       each of these is more difficult in the competitive global environment.

3 Marketers have to cope with a blurring of the line between elements of the distribution channel, or even its abolition by direct marketing relationships. New possibilities open up when service stations offer a supermarket range of grocery goods. Food products can be found in a variety of outlets, where previously they were purchased only in a narrow range of shops.

4 Downsizing, delayering and the use of IT provide opportunities both for large companies and SMEs. SMEs can specialise and respond more quickly to market conditions than their larger counterparts, a feature that is welcomed in foreign markets as well as domestic ones.

5 Functions have to work together to meet the challenge of globalisation and the increasing importance of the customer, whose needs have to be met by every part of the organisation.

6 Marketing has been traditionally encapsulated in the '4 Ps'. However, in the competitive global environment a better way of appreciating the role of marketing is to see it as made up of three activities:
   (a) seek customers;
   (b) keep customers;
   (c) manage the marketing function.

7 Successful market-orientated companies share the following characteristics:
   (a) information on all important buying influences pervade every corporate function;
   (b) strategic and tactical decisions are made interfunctionally and interdivisionally;
   (c) decisions are executed as flawlessly as possible.

▶

> ▶ **Box 21.4 continued**
>
> 8 Companies not only need to consider marketing issues, but also need to look at management processes, particularly finance and human resources. Finance is itself undergoing change and can be seen as being of importance because it presents new opportunities. Sainsbury's is linking with a retail bank to offer financial services for its customers, for example. Human resource management also involves marketing insofar as it needs to recruit and retain those who thrive on the demands of working together to meet the global challenge and to derive personal benefit and satisfaction from so doing.

Box 21.4 provides an overview of the main changes facing marketing. Although, this can be interpreted as one expert's view on the main trends, it picks up on many of the issues raised throughout this book. It points to a need for companies and their personnel to realise the challenge, both direct and indirect, of globalisation. Even if globalisation is not a 'one-way street' beset by forces that can turn it in unexpected directions, its influence is such that companies have to appreciate that it presents a challenge. Public and private sector organisations require strategies to survive and prosper that have at their heart a marketing perspective.

Competitive advantage is going to become a vital part of the organisation's armoury, but at the same time it will come under attack more quickly as companies innovate and gain information on each other's performance and product via on-line information sources. A study by the DTI and the CBI in the UK,[5] supports the view expressed in Box 21.4. In this study into the best practice found in UK companies, four areas were isolated that helped companies succeed:

1 winning companies are led by visionary enthusiastic champions of change;
2 winning companies unlock the potential of their people;
3 winning companies know their customers;
4 winning companies constantly introduce new differentiated products and services.

These four are not in order of importance, and take time to implement based on the knowledge and experience of those involved throughout the organisation.

The characteristics of winning companies as noted by the CBI/DTI study can be identified by taking two of the areas noted above.

Knowing their customers

1 Know and anticipate the future needs of all customers;
2 have a realistic understanding of competitors and how to beat them in competition for their customers;
3 focus on the customers and cultivate an active partnership towards total customer satisfaction.

Continuously introduce differentiated products and services

1 Have a 'product and services after next' philosophy;
2 exploit new technology and legislate to devise new product innovation;

3 customise the product and service;

4 radically improve speed to market;

5 adopt multifunctional teams to drive innovations forward.

All of the views and studies so far quoted have derived from the USA and the UK. Are these changes happening elsewhere? Can the influence of globalisation be seen to affect companies in Japan, Korea and other fast-growing economies in similar ways, or will it have less influence?

In Japan's case, the economy is seen as being overregulated and as a consequence hampered in its adjustments to globalisation. Many Japanese companies have surplus workers, particularly having located operations overseas where, in many economies this would mean laying off or firing workers. In Japan, the law currently forbids this when the parent company is making a reasonable profit. One of the proposals being considered is for the creation of a holding company which would hold the assets, whilst the profits were left to accrue to the individual parts of, for example, Matsushita's operations. Loss makers could be identified and action taken. Estimates suggest that by changes such as this unemployment in Japan would double from the 3.3 per cent level seen in 1996.[6] Globalisation and the adjustment to it will see major problems of structural unemployment in countries that have traditionally had full employment levels.

Other Pacific Rim countries will see the same pressures mount. South Korea[7] and other 'Tiger' economies will, it is forecast, experience a slowdown in growth, which will be caused by structural problems. Overcapacity in such industries as electronics, steel and petrochemicals plus productivity slowdowns and a lack of technological innovation will produce pressure to change the 'guaranteed job for life', as seen in South Korea. Developing countries such as the 'Tiger' economies will need to address the protectionist and regulated nature of their system in order to adjust to the new circumstances.

How will this affect marketers? Marketing is set to influence corporate strategy in more decisive ways, and it is also an important feature of everybody's perception of their role. In essence, all personnel have to be aware of their role in attracting and retaining customers. As economies restructure, new opportunities and threats will emerge that require further innovation and an emphasis on quality in all markets; this will depend for its achievement on the understanding by all workers of their part in the process.

Changes of this nature will produce unexpected challenges for companies, as the familiar becomes unfamiliar with a (re)thinking of what this means for business. For example, UK exporters to the Republic of Ireland, where the growth and success of the Irish economy has presented business opportunities, have found that their preconceptions and prejudices can hold them back when undertaking business there. This example shows how far the ability to learn quickly about new and/or changing circumstances has become a key advantage in international marketing.

An example taken from Nigeria in Box 21.5 suggests that business activity can take various forms. Officially, the bulk of trade is carried out by government agencies or by multinational corporations. But, as in the case of India, official statistics overlook the importance of the services of intermediaries and traders, providing a more robust picture of economic activity. Marketers looking at Nigeria and India and focusing on official statistics could, therefore, miss the considerable potential of both countries. The way business and trade is carried out varies from the Western model, presenting a challenge in understanding how it operates.

Box 21.5

SMALL COMPANIES IN NIGERIA[8]

Tackling adversity with diversity

According to official statistics in Nigeria, most trade is carried out by governments or multi-national companies. There appears to be little contribution from indigenous entrepreneurs, reinforcing a commonly held belief that Africa does not have enough entrepreneurs who are able to move beyond survival into significant wealth accumulation.

This is linked to the difficulties indigenous entrepreneurs face in acquiring the necessary management and entrepreneurship skills to succeed in the formal sector, coupled with a tendency for bribery and corruption to cream off any added value.

The study indeed confirms that the two significant constraints on cross-border trade are foreign exchange-related problems (the non-exchangeability of the Naira through official channels) and the harassment of traders.

Yet these very problems have been turned into entrepreneurial opportunities. There is a huge informal, or parallel, economy, transporting large volumes of goods from which successful traders can make considerable amounts of money. In addition, an 'alternative' financial system has been created, based not on government sales of restricted foreign currency but on the activities of several thousand currency traders who really determine the Naira's exchange rate.

For most traders, constant harassment is a way of life. At border crossings there may be a dozen checkpoints (one army, one customs, the rest police), each of which imposes searches.

There are several ways of evading harassment. Traders can simply pay up to lubricate the speed of transfer; they can use bush paths (but this risks robbery); goods can be concealed, mainly to avoid extortion rather than smuggling to avoid duties.

But the most common method is to use specialist intermediaries, independent carriers called *kelebes* who operate from 'stations' close to the border posts. The *kelebes* carry the trader's bags or other containers while the trader casually walks across the border. Once over, a fee is paid to the *kelebe* (and any helpers they have sub-contracted).

A great deal of trust is needed in these transactions since the *kelebe* could easily make off with the goods, especially if the trader were detained. The reliance on trust is even more pronounced in the case of large-scale goods transported by lorry. Here the specialist intermediaries are drivers who undertake to take the goods across the border, using bribery to join armed convoys, for example.

These are complicated procedures: the detailed mechanics of cross-border trade take years to learn and there is a system of apprenticeship as effective as any in the formal sector.

The rewards can be substantial and successful traders have moved into a wide range of activities from car and computer imports to cotton processing on farms bought from trading profits and conglomerate businesses with assets of millions of Naira.

Entrepreneurial lessons

While there are many petty traders who simply establish well-tried routines and never innovate, the study identified others who were constantly looking for new profitable products – and 'pluriactivity' is again a feature.

The most successful entrepreneurs tend not to operate themselves but to sub-contract the risk to others. This 'brokerage' role is a crucial aspect of entrepreneurship. Trust in relationships is paramount to the informal system. Because there is a disregard of written rules (the official system) this does not mean that well-observed rules do not exist.

> ▶ **Box 21.5 continued**

Profit is extracted by several intermediaries at 'boundary exchanges' and the complexities of the trade require much learning-by-doing. Infrastructure chaos is paradoxically beneficial to traders, because it keeps the multinationals out.

The official view may pessimistically be that harassment of traders adds costs to products, which are inevitably passed on to poor consumers. Loss of revenue to government leads to higher taxes and more external borrowing from neo-colonial institutions. Bribery and corruption impoverish the traders, decreasing motivation and wealth accumulation.

There is a different picture. The system would appear to produce entrepreneurial opportunities for far more people than would otherwise benefit from 'official' trading. Traders benefit by being able to reduce competition from less knowledgeable competitors because it takes so long to learn the system. An army of intermediaries also makes a living out of the system who would not have any utility under a more regulated one.

In conclusion, these two examples show that entrepreneurship appears to thrive wherever one looks for it. It may not take familiar Western forms, but the essentials of value extraction are always there, limited only by the ingenuity of the informal entrepreneurs themselves.

Pacific Rim 'Tiger' economies, a European 'Tiger' economy, Ireland, and the developing country of Nigeria all show opportunities for business. Each situation will require scrutiny if the marketing potential is to be assessed. Firms looking for future business opportunities are required to adjust to new and novel situations, rather than working on the assumption that what works in existing markets will work in new markets, or even that the marketing strategy will continue to work effectively as countries and markets change.

ETHICAL ISSUES

Privatisation, and the rising importance of markets rather than government agencies as providers of goods and services, presents political problems. How will governments answer for private companies' actions, in particular those that make decisions based on profit, rather than the needs of the citizens? In the UK, water companies and rail companies are regulated, but are free to make decisions on how they go about their business. Job cuts, mergers, dividend payments, and management remuneration are all areas where problems can arise, in so far as the public perception may be of managers benefiting themselves at the expense of the citizen. Increasing privatisation, with the introduction of competition in previously regulated areas, places the emphasis on companies to show that they are behaving in a responsible way. This is often via a code of conduct, and as seen earlier in the book is often influenced by pressure groups and stakeholders.

From a selfish point of view companies in, for example, the gas supply industry in the UK, who issue a code of conduct that sees them behaving responsibly and with ethical parameters, can be said to make marketing and business sense, given that they face open competition for the first time. A code covering the behaviour of sales personnel, level and quality of service, behaviour of other (non-sales) staff and commitment to environmental protection can all be seen to bias customers towards the company. A number of issues arise from this which will become more significant over time:

1 customers expect companies to behave in ethical ways;

2 ethical investment funds monitor the performance of companies – how they deal with equal opportunities, the environment, recycling, and so on;

3 governments in many countries monitor performance against ethical criteria;

4 information on total company performance – i.e. covering financial and non-financial performance – is readily available via the news media and the Internet;

5 continued restructuring and privatisation in many countries will create further calls for ethical statements and codes of conduct from the privatised organisations;

6 organisations such as Greenpeace and Friends of the Earth operate across political boundaries and can focus attention on a company's failure to act with ethical responsibility.

All these developments have been highlighted by examples throughout this book and are emphasised in Boxes 21.6 and 21.7. As a company's performance comes to be increasingly judged by non-financial criteria (even if financial performance is still the key performance indicator), marketers have to make sure that these issues are treated with as much concern as the '4 Ps', – or, to put it another way, that the '4 Ps' embody good practice. In Box 21.4 the marketing emphasis upon attracting and retaining customers was noted. To do this means monitoring environmental concerns, animal welfare, behaviour of managers and other forms of behaviour of interest to the customer (and a variety of stakeholders and pressure groups).

Box 21.6

ETHICAL POSITIONING[9]

When Shell took the decision in 1995 to dump its redundant oil platform, the Brent Spar, in the North Sea, it felt the full consumer wrath within a few weeks; such was the outrage that the company had to back down. The irony of this situation was that the company thought of itself as the champion of corporate responsibility, aware that business had to take account of its impact on the environment and society, which Shell summarises in its 'Statement of General Business Principles'.

Weight was given to scientific experts, without recognising that another constituency – the general public – had also to be taken into account. Ignoring their views proved very damaging to Shell's reputation, despite the fact that the original decision to dump was eventually supported by environmental groups. The company found that it could no longer determine its corporate responsibility without reference to other groups who wished to exert their influence.

'Ethics', in the broadest sense of the word, is rising to the top of the corporate agenda. Many companies are increasingly seizing the chance to take an ethical stand on particular issues, so that where once ethical positions were the preserve of niche players such as The Body Shop or Tradecraft, they are being embraced by 'mainstream' organisations such as the UK's Co-operative Bank and Sainsbury's food retailing organisation.

What are the reasons for this increase in importance? In the USA, Federal fines can be levied if a corporation is found to be acting in ways detrimental to the well-being of a

▶

▶ **Box 21.6 continued**

particular group. Lucas (now Lucas Varity) was fined $106m for keeping false records of gear boxes, while Daiwa Bank received fines of $340m for concealing loses of $1bn. However, under Federal sentencing guidelines, penalties can be reduced if a company can show that it has an ethical policy in place that will pursue wrongdoing.

A further reason for the rising importance of ethical issues is that in the UK, for example, companies have a vested interest in protecting their corporate reputation, so that despite decentralisation managers must be aware that certain of their actions can damage the brand, an issue directly related to marketing. Marketing cannot be entirely divorced from this issue – British Telecom has argued that if the company's customers feel that the company is in tune with them, then they will do business. But are ethical approaches merely defensive, designed to prevent the brand or company being tarnished in the eyes of customers, or can they be a more integral and positive part of marketing? Both approaches can be seen, depending on the product on offer. The Body Shop, Ben & Jerry's (US ice-cream manufacturers), and the Co-operative Bank all use the ethical approach as a key element in their marketing. For businesses, such as alcoholic drinks and car companies, however, this is not an option. The incorporation of ethical issues into company policy is nonetheless a way of meeting the demands of existing law and of proposed changes to the legislative and regulatory environment.

Many companies have policies on the protection of the physical environment and equal opportunities, while some have codes of conduct involving customers, suppliers and the local community. The Institute of Business Ethics in the UK estimates that over 60 per cent of all large companies have a policy on all or most of these issues.

Although many of these policy statements are for internal use, they can involve consultation with the company's stakeholders – as, for example, The Body Shop undertakes in its Ethical Audit. How far this can be undertaken across countries that can have different priorities and differing considerations and values remains to be seen. Another problem is the need to balance the needs of stakeholders against those of shareholders.

Box 21.7

LIMITS TO CORPORATE RESPONSIBILITIES[10]

Friedman (1962)[11] argues that:

> there is one and only one social responsibility of business – to use its resources and engage in activities designed to increase its profits so long as it stays within the rules of the game, which is to say, engages in open and free competition, without deception or fraud.

He identifies six problems in a company having social responsibility:

1 spending someone else's money – the cost of social actions are involuntarily borne by shareholders, customers and others;

2 competing claims – some actions can involve the deliberate sacrifice of profits or create muddy decision making;

3 competitive disadvantage – social actions have a price;

4 competence – firms may not know what their social responsibilities are, or if they have the skills to deal with them;

> **Box 21.7 continued**

5 fairness – do we want corporations who will often be 'playing God' in this situation;

6 legitimacy – the government should have a social responsibility role.

Each of these points raises particular problems, particularly as many still accept the classical model of competition put forward by Friedman. Ethicists identify three levels of duties of responsible people (and managers):

1 avoid causing harm;

2 prevent harm;

3 do good.

Negative duties are stronger than positive duties, and four criteria have been identified that can be helpful to the organisation in knowing when to act:

1 critical need;

2 proximity;

3 capability;

4 last resort.

Because of the danger of assuming that someone else will act when others are present, or because one is trying to find out who is the 'last resort', or because of the possibility of 'pluralistic ignorance' (not acting because no one else is and the situation seems less serious), no one may act at all! The criterion of 'last resort' is less helpful than the others, with the remaining three criteria being better guides to taking action.

What is of concern in one country is not necessarily of interest in another, but the existence of global communications systems means that behaviour in one country where, say, environmental controls are lax can soon be reported and can hit a company's business. Marketing and ethical issues can thus be seen as both being influenced by globalisation.

The increased use of global communication systems, along with privatisation and deregulation, will increase the importance of how a company behaves in whatever market it is involved with. A failure to recognise this influence could be very damaging in the short and long term.

| Box 21.8 | INTERNET COMMERCE[12] |

The World Wide Web is becoming a good place to shop for bargains. Customers are already able to get life insurance, airline tickets, cars, computers, books and other items.

With recent developments it will in many cases be easier and more convenient to shop this way. By the end of the decade, on-line retail sales are predicted to grow by 10 times their present level, while business-to-business transactions are expected to grow by 10 times that level.

> **Box 15.1 continued**

Forrester Research in Cambridge, Massachusetts, predicts that on-line shopping will grow from $518m in 1996 to $6.6bn in 2000. When business-to-business selling on the Web is factored in, it is expected that between 1995 and 2000 Web sales will increase from $1bn to $117bn. This forecast is based on the assumption that the number of Web 'surfers' will grow during the period, from 16m in 1996 to 163m – and that the capacity of the Internet will rise to accommodate the growth.

The appeal for Web commerce will be facilitating corporate buying and selling where companies can post their supply requirements at a Website where anyone can bid on them. General Electric was one of the first to do this through its Web-based Trading Process Network, which accounted from about $1bn of its purchases during its first 12 months of operation.

Browsing through company Websites can also help to assess the suitability of prospective companies, that, for example, exporters may wish to trade with. Equally, small and medium-sized enterprises on a tight budget can search for information on new markets, reach (potential) customers, and start negotiations that can lead to a sale or the establishment of a partnership.

Other factors can be seen to be of interest here. SMEs, in gaining access to the Internet at a relatively low investment, can compete with larger companies as long as they can support themselves with an effective logistical system and can use niche market approaches. SMEs can gain advantages over larger companies, as one of their claimed major strengths is flexibility and adaptability. The marketing opportunities of the Internet, assuming it maintains its promise, bring competition to large companies from smaller ones. Another advantage for SMEs is the international nature of the Internet, that will promote goods, effect communication and payments across the globe in new and quicker ways. International marketing opportunities therefore open themselves to the majority of companies who are prepared to see them.

Good marketing practice still needs to be learned. The Internet cannot overcome the fact that competing in a global and competitive market place requires knowledge and understanding, not just by a company's marketers but also by all the managers and operating personnel. Failing to appreciate this, seeing only the opportunities as new forms of marketing, will continue to place the ill-prepared company at a competitive disadvantage.

SUMMARY

Some of the general trends concerning the future of marketing have been mentioned in this chapter. Each one requires a response if companies are to adapt to changing circumstances whether in their home or foreign markets. The involvement of more companies in the international arena is expected through the increased use of the Internet (Box 21.8 looks at the development of the Internet, and what this may mean for business). Despite difficulties such as security of electronic cash transactions and widespread ignorance of the usefulness of Internet trading, many organisations are now promoting themselves through this medium or at a more advanced level are actively trading, either because of the speed of response to customer requests and/or due to broadening of the market.

REVIEW QUESTIONS

1 What are regional trading areas (blocs)?

2 Outline the countervailing forces to globalisation.

3 Why are previously successful countries like Japan finding the challenge of globalisation as difficult to deal with as other countries?

4 Summarise the main changes in marketing that globalisation has brought.

5 Review the importance of ethical issues in marketing.

6 In what ways is the use of niche marketing techniques linked to the use of the Internet by SMEs?

DISCUSSION QUESTIONS

1 Why are many countries worried by the increasing importance of the Internet?

2 How far are SMEs prepared for the challenge of the Internet and international marketing opportunities?

3 Why has privatisation increased the importance of corporate behaviour?

4 Why are marketing and corporate structures and systems so closely linked together when looking to create competitive advantage?

5 As marketing becomes a 'generic' management skill, does it have a future as both a separate corporate function and an academic discipline?

Case study

MULTIBUSINESS COMPANIES[13]

In the USA companies breaking themselves up has become the corporate fad. Company demergers have become more important in US corporate life than leveraged layouts were in the 1980s.

Many multibusiness companies (MBCs), which cover business in a variety of areas, have found that the disparate activities are worth less as part of one business than if they were sold off. This is due to frictions between business units who have to vie for funds and personnel, which leads to reduced performance. It is estimated by research carried out by Sadter, Campbell and Koch (1996) that between 10 per cent and 40 per cent of value is destroyed when an MBC is formed. Companies such as ICI moved along the break-up route with its decision in early 1997 to sell off its Tioxide business and other examples are provided in Table 21.1. It is not just in the Anglo-Saxon economies of the USA and UK that this process can be seen. Sandex of Switzerland is selling off its chemical business, whilst Chargeurs, in film and textiles, is splitting itself in two, an example followed by Thorn–EMI which separated the rental and music side of the business in 1995.

The total market value of stock market companies in the USA and UK stood at $10trn in early 1997; at least half of these companies could gain from being broken up. According to researchers break-up adds 20 per cent to the company's stock market value, with the possibility that up to $1trn in extra value could be realised.

Table 21.1 COMPANY DEMERGERS

Year	Company	Spin-offs
1990	Courtaulds	Textiles
	Racal	Vodafone cellular phones
	BAT	Argos catalogue retailer
	Wiggins Teape	Appleton paper
1993	ICI	Zeneca pharmaceuticals
1994	ECC	CAMAS construction materials
1995	Hanson	US Industries
	Thorn–EMI	Thorn rentals
1996	Hanson	Hanson Industries
		The Energy Group
		Millennnium Chemicals
		Imperial Tobacco
	British Gas	British Gas Energy
		Transco pipeline
	Lonrho	Hotel business
	P & O	Bovis Homes
1997	ICI	Tioxide

Source: Observer (16 February 1997).

Break-ups are a way of revolutionising the business. Instead of moving for conglomerate status, demergers allow management buy-outs or buy-ins that focus attention on what might have been an overlooked part of the business. A study by J.P. Morgan in 1995 showed that an average spin-off company performed 25 per cent better than the market during the first 18 months after break-up.

If a company sells off a business on the assumption that a new empire can be built, it has not learnt the lesson of demerger practice. However, are all companies seen as targets for demergers, and are there ways by which a company can organise itself to spread the benefits of its name (brand) across differing businesses, without these forming part of a MBC?

Virgin has its name on operations in 22 countries on six continents. The Virgin trade mark can be found on computers, cola, vodka, video games, travel firms, cinemas, condoms and airlines. In 1996 revenues of $3.2bn were generated from this activity. Is this an MBC that has failed to achieve growth and should it therefore be demerged?

Many of the Virgin companies are private companies where Richard Branson only partly owns the concerns; other investors take on the risk by investing in the businesses, benefiting from the Virgin brand. The problem with this approach is that the brand could be spread over too many products without the direct control of a formal structure. Richard Branson controls scores of companies through a network of holding companies. He likes to keep the businesses small, so that when a business reaches 60 or 70 personnel he will think up a new idea, then promote the deputy manager and others to be bosses in a new business.

The Virgin Group is constantly being reshuffled, with business shifted among the holding companies. Public records show that the Virgin name is sometimes used by others for a fee, also revealing that some companies that use the Virgin name are totally divorced from Virgin enterprises. So Virgin Interactive Entertainments, makers of video games, is 100 per cent owned by Spelling Entertainment – a subsidiary of the US corporation Viacom.

In 1995, 116 MGM Cinemas were purchased with a US partner, 90 were sold off; retaining only those which could be turned into multiplexes. In May of that year a Singapore business-man purchased an 11 per cent stake in Virgin Cinemas Group, with a holding company being formed that will own 40 per cent of Virgin Cinemas, which in turn is controlled 72 per cent by Virgin and 28 per cent by the Singapore businessman. By organising in this way capital-raising, risk-sharing and rationalisation are all possible. Virgin Retail is only 25 per cent owned by Virgin with the majority owned by W.H. Smith.

These other companies, such as W.H. Smith, are content to earn profits on the reputation of the Virgin brand. Companies have been sold off (such as Virgin Music to EMI in 1992) to fund the airline business, where it has been competing against British Airways on the profitable Atlantic routes, plus the setting up of Virgin Express, providing cheap flights to Europe. The Virgin Atlantic airline is directly controlled by Richard Branson. The move from a cash-generating business in music to one where there is a need to continue the investment (airline) is where as a fund manager it would not be correct to say that this has been a move justified in the short term.

Brand investment in the Virgin brand, holding companies, new ventures and direct management of risky businesses that require building up are the way in which the business has sought to keep its entrepreneurial drive and its ability to cash in when a business requires extra investment: a solution has been evolved that will help to retain a dynamic that keeps it from the need to demerge itself from underperforming businesses which have to be forcibly sold off due to the pressure of shareholders and others.

The trend to demerge can bring with it new solutions to the setting up and running of companies that the Virgin Group has found to be its answer to the challenge.

Questions

1 *What pressures are companies under to sell off and demerger non-core businesses?*

2 *If a company sells one business and then from the proceeds buys another, has this solved the problem of a multibusiness company (MBC)?*

3 *How effective is the Virgin Group's answer to the MBC dilemma?*

4 *Can branding be successful across various products, services and countries?*

5 *Does the supposed demise of MBCs create greater or fewer opportunities for SMEs?*

6 *Is the push to sell off non-core businesses visible in non-'Anglo-Saxon' economies?*

FURTHER READING

Further reading is a matter of accessing sources appropriate to the organisation and, as shown throughout this book, the press, journals and research papers are all valid sources of information from which insights and perceptions can be gained and trends identified.

NOTES AND REFERENCES

1 Barnett, S., 'Style and strategy: new metaphors, new insight', *European Management Journal*, 14(4) (1996), 347–55.

2 Prochmiak, A., 'Quenching China's thirst', *Fortune* (3 March 1996), 121.

3 Sinclair, D., 'Land of pop and glory', *The Times* (19 February 1997).

4 Shapiro, B.P., 'Tectonic changes in the world of marketing', in Duffy, P.P. (ed.), *Relevance of a Decade* (Boston: Harvard Business School Press, 1994).

5 'The winning business: the factors that spell success', Confederation of British Industry (1997).

6 Valery, N., 'Japan loosens up', *The World in 1997*, *The Economist* (1996).

7 Bastin, J., 'Asian angst', *The World in 1997*, *The Economist* (1996).

8 Scott, M., Fadahunsi, A. and Kodithuwakkus, 'Tackling adversity with diversity', *Mastering Enterprise*, *7*, *Financial Times* (March 1997).

9 Garrett, A., 'Do the right thing', *Marketing Business* (July/August 1996).

10 Smith, N.C. and Quelch, J.A., 'Pharmaceutical marketing practices in the third world' in Buzzell, R.D., Quelch, J.A. and Bartlett, C.A. (eds), *Global Marketing Management: Cases and Readings*, 3rd edition (Reading, MA: Addison-Wesley, 1994).

11 Friedman, M., *Capitalism and Freedom* (Chicago: University of Chicago Press, 1962).

12 Styp, D., 'The birth of digital commerce', *Fortune* (9 December 1996); 'Wearing the export Web', *Overseas Trade Supplement* (September 1997).

13 Laurance, B., 'Multi-armed monsters set to dismember', *Observer* (16 February 1997); Fox, N. and Obins, R., 'Virgin unveiled', *Sunday Times* (13 October 1996).

PART 6

Cases in global marketing

Part 6 of the text contains three cases which provide an opportunity for readers to apply the concepts developed in the book. The choice of cases reflects the diverse challenges that confront the global marketer, ranging from assessment of the global environment to planning and control of international operations; they also illustrate the complex task of formulating and implementing a global marketing strategy.

1 **Häagen-Dazs ice cream – the making of a global brand**

2 **The BMW acquisition of the Rover Group**

3 **Exel Logistics – internationalising a distribution brand**

CASE STUDY 1

Häagen-Dazs ice cream – the making of a global brand

'We like to do things differently from everyone else.'
Simon Esberger, Marketing Director, Häagen-Dazs

In 1989, Grand Met decided to launch Häagen-Dazs in Europe with the objective of building the biggest ice-cream brand in the world. In order to appreciate what a challenge this was for the management of Häagen-Dazs, it is instructive to recall the situation of the ice cream in Europe in the late 1980s and early 1990s.

The European ice-cream market was dominated by big multinational companies. Unilever, the Anglo-Dutch conglomerate, was the biggest ice cream manufacturer world-wide, with a 40 per cent share valued at £6bn annually. It was followed by Mars, Inc. of the USA, and Nestlé of Switzerland. Mars had recently become an important competitor in the ice-cream market after very successfully extending its chocolate countlines into the market at a premium price. Some of these multinational companies offered a wide product range, from economy to standard and luxury ice cream. The strength of these multinationals was obscured by the fact that many of them operated under different local names in each European country. For example, the Zug-based company Effem, which even today has a quasi-monopoly of the Swiss market for confectionery ice cream, was a subsidiary of Mars. France's Glace-Findus was a subsidiary of Nestlé, which operated there under the brand name Gervais, but under the name Camy in Spain and Portugal, and Frisco in Switzerland. Unilever owned Bird's Eye Wall's in the UK, Langnese-Iglo in Germany, Iglo-Ola in Denmark and Sagit in Italy. One additional source of strength of these companies was their stranglehold on freezer space at the retail level.

To the competition in every country market in Europe must be added many independent and semi-independent local companies. Schöller, for example, was a traditional £800m brand in Germany which, through a joint venture agreement, marketed the premium ice cream of Mövenpick. In the premium ice-cream segment, Mövenpick had a 55 per cent share in Switzerland. In the UK alone, there were over 1000 commercial ice-cream manufacturers, according to the Ice-Cream Association, a British-based industry group. If the market shares of these local players are taken together with those of the multinationals, it can be seen that the markets were highly concentrated. For example, in Italy, 90 per cent of the ice-cream market was dominated by Sagit (which commanded a 35 per cent share), Italgel-SMe and the

Sammontana and Samson groups. In France, Glace-Findus, Cogesal (a subsidiary of Unilever) and Ortiz-Miko together had a 55 per cent market share. In the UK, Wall's had about a 44 per cent market share, followed by Lyons Maid with just less than 10 per cent.

The fastest-growing competitors in Europe were the private labels. In the UK, with a traditionally strong presence of retailer brands, private-label share had grown by 24 per cent, to reach almost 30 per cent of the total ice cream market in 1991. In the take-home sector, private labels had slightly over 46 per cent. Although private labels were less significant in Germany and in France, they were still important and their market shares continued to grow rapidly. Much of the private-label business was in economy or standard ice cream, although some retailers with strong quality images had recently introduced upmarket premium ice creams, including the UK Marks & Spencer store chain and Safeway.

The development of a global or Eurobrand was hampered by the fact that ice-cream consumption patterns varied significantly across Europe. In terms of volume, the highest European *per capita* consumption was found in Sweden (13.6 litres per person per year), followed by Norway (11.9 litres) and Finland (11 litres). Then there was France (6.5 litres), Germany (5.5 litres) and the UK (7.8 litres). These *per capita* consumption levels were significantly lower than in North America or Australia. Of the total size of the world ice-cream market, which was 3.25bn gallons in 1990, 45 per cent (1.463bn gallons) was consumed in the USA, and 22 per cent (0.72bn gallons) was eaten in Europe. In terms of taste, large differences could be found as well. Whereas, for example, 85 per cent of ice cream in the UK was non-dairy (generally considered to be of lower quality), this type of ice cream, called mellorine in the USA, hardly existed anywhere else in Europe, except in Portugal and Ireland. There were also large differences with regard to the place where ice cream was consumed. In France, the impulse sector accounted for 28 per cent, while the take-home sector accounted for 72 per cent. In Italy, the impulse sector accounted for 41 per cent, in the UK for 43 per cent, and in Germany for 62 per cent of the total ice-cream market in 1990.

The overall market for ice cream in Europe was nearly stagnant from 1985 onwards, growing by about 1–1.5 per cent a year. The year-on-year growth of the market had declined since 1989, both in absolute and in real terms. For a long time, the ice-cream sector had been considered a boring and low-growth category, highly seasonal, with most sales during the summer months. Consumers were mostly children. The establishment of a new brand was believed to require significant TV advertising support to gain national distribution and failures of new products were frequent. The average life of a brand was about three years. A good illustration of the difficulties of introducing and establishing a brand in Europe is provided by Unilever's attempt to establish Carte d'Or premium ice cream. This brand was originally developed for the French market, where it was successful. Quickly it was rolled out across Europe; in some countries, such as Germany and Belgium, it met with success, but not in others. Unilever's experience in the UK is revealing. First introduced in the mid-1980s, it was re-launched in 1990. By October 1992, Carte d'Or was launched for a third time, having failed in every previous attempt to establish a niche for itself in the upmarket. Another UK brand, Elite, which was a home-grown effort of the Unilever subsidiary Bird's Eye Wall's, was introduced in 1988, and then taken off the market in 1990. Alpine, another Unilever brand introduced in 1984, had also disappeared by 1990.

Remarkable results for Häagen-Dazs in Europe

In 1989, Grand Met took their turn on the European premium ice-cream market. Early sales increases, in spite of a modest market budget, were encouraging. In 1990, sales were $10m. And by September 1991, Häagen-Dazs's sales were reported to have reached $30m, nearly all in the UK, France and Germany. By 1992, its sales were reported to have more than tripled, to nearly $100m, making Häagen-Dazs the market leader of premium ice cream in Europe.

In the UK, the original launch country, Häagen-Dazs had taken a 19.5 per cent value share of the premium sector (or 28 per cent according to Häagen-Dazs), which represented one-eighth of the total ice-cream market in just two years, according to Warburg Industries. Häagen-Dazs had increased its share of this total market from 0.5 per cent in 1990 to 4.9 per cent in 1991 (Nielsen Frozen Food Service). During the same period, the UK ice-cream market took a dip from £753.9m to £762.8m. The introduction of Häagen-Dazs in the UK – helped by world-beating Mars countline extensions (Mars, Bounty, Galaxy, Milky Way and Snickers) into the ice-cream market in 1988 – had increased the profile of luxury ice-cream in the UK and Europe, making it the fastest-growing sector of the ice-cream market. Moreover, taking the USA as an example, the prospects for Häagen-Dazs looked good. In 1991, luxury ice creams had taken a 47.6 per cent share of the US market (as against around 16 per cent in the UK in 1991, up from five per cent in 1988), with standard and economy ice cream accounting for 38.1 per cent and 14.3 per cent, respectively. Thus Häagen-Dazs could expect many Europeans to upgrade into the luxury ice-cream market.

According to experts, the brand value of Häagen-Dazs had risen steeply, from $250m in 1988 to $782m in 1993. In 1993, Häagen-Dazs became the top-ranked ice cream among the world's most valuable brands.

The making of a global brand

It all began in 1988, when the British Grand Met acquired the assets of the venerable Pillsbury Co. of Minneapolis as part of a $5.6bn take-over. Back then, Häagen-Dazs was already the leading premium ice cream in the USA, with strong sales coming from Japan. The brand had been around in the USA since 1960, when Reuben Mattus, a Polish immigrant, set out to produce the best ice cream in the world. Reuben Mattus began selling ice cream from a horse-drawn wagon to stores in the Bronx before creating the Häagen-Dazs name. In relation to his business philosophy, he noted: 'When I came out with Häagen-Dazs, the quality of ice cream had deteriorated to the point where it was just sweet and cold. Ice cream had become cheaper and cheaper, so I just went the other way.' In 1982, Häagen-Dazs was sold for the first time in Canada, and in 1984 it started selling in Japan. The Häagen-Dazs brand was acquired in 1983 by the Pillsbury Company. In Europe, Häagen-Dazs was little known. There were some restaurants in Paris that had carried the brand since 1987, and in 1989, the upmarket department store Harrods of London began to sell it.

It was not until the middle of 1989, when Grand Met moved the world-wide head-quarters of Häagen-Dazs to the UK, to lead the European expansion, that the brand received its due attention in Europe. The newly formed subsidiary embarked on an ambitious global marketing plan, backed by a $50m campaign to expand European sales. The objective was to reach world-wide sales of $1bn by 1995 (from $400m in

1991) at margins most other manufacturers could only dream of. This corresponds to a world-wide market share of five per cent of the luxury ice-cream market. They currently have six per cent of the US market. In Europe alone, annual sales were expected to reach $300m by 1995, against $10m in 1990, trying to do in three years what took Häagen-Dazs 30 years in the USA. The plan called for a staged launch in the UK (first through regional distribution around London and the affluent South-East, followed by a national launch), then in France, Germany, Holland, Belgium, and Sweden in 1989, followed by the remaining EC and EFTA countries. By August 1991 it had rolled out in seven EC countries, and by the end of 1992 it was in all 12, as well as in Japan, Taiwan, and South Korea.

The conventional marketing practice and tradition of the European ice-cream business would have called for a marketing pull strategy, with heavy spending on TV advertising and significant heavy trade and consumer promotions to achieve trade sell-in. The chances of success for such a strategy seemed obvious at the time. Being one of five pillars of the food interest of $15bn Grand Met conglomerate – the others include Brossard (industrial pastry and cakes), Green Giant (tinned and frozen vegetables), Pillsbury (a broad line of dry grocery and refrigerated dough products), Erasco (cooked dishes) and spirits (J. & B., Baileys, Smirnoff) – Häagen-Dazs could have expected the parent company to shell out the required substantial marketing investments. Moreover, as part of Grand Met, Häagen-Dazs could have virtually assured sales through that company's leisure and restaurant establishments, which included the Burger King chain, Godfather's Pizza and Bennigan's Steak and Ale restaurants – more restaurant outlets world-wide than anyone save PepsiCo.

Instead, Häagen-Dazs opted for the unorthodox three-pronged marketing push, which had worked so well for them in Japan. The objectives were to increase awareness of the Häagen-Dazs brand and to have as many people as possible try the product, to generate significant word-of-mouth publicity. In the process, it radically changed the rules of the game in the European ice cream business. First, there was the opening of posh ice-cream parlours in upmarket areas with a heavy footfall in large and affluent European cities. These ice cream parlours were developed to become the shop window of the brand. Finished to the highest standards of store design, they are in essence cafés (not to be compared with the sterile take-out atmosphere of most end-of-corner ice-cream shops), with ample space for seating; some even feature terracotta floors. Tables are granite top with brass edging, and seating is upholstered in leather. The walls have been hand-marbled in muted 'earthy' colours below a brass dado rail. The natural materials used throughout convey a sense of 'quality'. All in all, these stores are significantly upgraded in comparison to the Häagen-Dazs stores in the USA.

By November 1990, Häagen-Dazs had 18 gilded ice-cream parlours in the UK, France and Germany. By the autumn of 1991, it had opened 30 ice-cream parlours at a cost of between $40m and $50m. And by the autumn of 1992, it had 53 outlets in Europe, for a total of 383 in the world. Some flagship stores (Leicester Square in London) count a million visitors a year. Its first parlour in the prestigious 16th arrondissement on Place Victor Hugo in Paris had become the second busiest outlet after Tokyo in only one year.

Second, there was the penetration of food-service accounts with quality hotels and restaurants. Key to this part of the marketing strategy was a sort of co-branding arrangement that stipulated sale of Häagen-Dazs only to accounts who branded the product on the menu, thereby ensuring not only more sales of Häagen-Dazs, but also increased awareness of the brand in the right places. The penetration of food-service accounts was assisted by clever promotions in which, for example, in return for proof of purchase of a 500 ml tub of ice cream, consumers received a voucher entitling them to a meal for two at reduced prices in participating restaurants. In one such promotion in the UK, 100 gourmet restaurants, including the dell'Ugo in London, signed up. This promotion encouraged restaurants that were not yet distributing Häagen-Dazs to become stockists.

Third, there was the targeting of retail accounts, which included a roll-out into supermarket chains, delicatessen, cinemas and convenience stores anywhere, from bakeries to video stores, and the like. Since the product needs careful handling, stores were chosen selectively. The major thrust was a retailer support package that combined tried and proven bestseller launches (i.e. new flavours tested in the Häagen-Dazs-owned ice-cream parlours) and heavy in-store sampling; a freezer support package offering retailers thousands of in-store branded glass-fronted chest freezers, which display products by flavour in a self-contained rack. The freezers are an essential part of Häagen-Dazs's marketing strategy since they separate Häagen-Dazs from other ice creams that have to be looked for deep down in the retailer's jammed freezer cabinet. Moreover, freezers in stores in continental Europe have traditionally been of poor quality, if they were available at all. Häagen-Dazs charged a small rental fee. By May 1992, Häagen-Dazs was in 4000 stores in Europe.

Notwithstanding this significant and unique marketing push, Häagen-Dazs's success in Europe was helped – if not largely determined – by its excellent product delivery, and the way it chose to build and communicate the Häagen-Dazs brand identity to its chosen target audience.

Product quality and brand identity

To gain an appreciation of Häagen-Dazs's superior product quality, it is important to understand the different types of ice cream available in Europe. A first distinction can be made between dairy ice cream and non-dairy ice cream. Dairy ice cream contains only dairy fats, at least 56 grams of milk fat per litre of finished ice cream (10 per cent dairy fat), of which half (28 grams) must be made with double cream. The overrun (a measure of the amount of air, which gives ice cream its light texture) must not exceed 100 per cent. Non-dairy ice cream contains vegetable fats or other superior non-dairy fats. Both American and Italian ice creams are dairy ice creams, although some of the Italian ice creams sold (in the UK, for example) contain non-dairy fat. American ice cream has a very high proportion of cream and low levels of added air, giving it a firmer, denser texture and a very creamy taste. Particulates are often added. Italian ice cream has a lighter, rather icy texture and is lower in fat concentration than American-style ice cream. In Europe, Italy is synonymous with ice cream and is distinguishable on a quality dimension. Economic and standard ice cream have a minimum level of fat (five per cent for economy and eight per cent for standard) and a minimum level of milk solids (7.5 per cent). They are based on milk plus non-dairy or vegetable fat, rather than on cream, and usually have a maximum permissible overrun. They usually contain artificial flavouring. Economy and standard ice cream tends to be sold in bulk packs at very low prices. Most of the ice cream in Europe is of this cheap type. Then, there is luxury ice cream. Premium luxury ice cream has to contain between 10 per cent and 143 per cent dairy fat, with an overrun of 80 per cent to 100 per cent, while super premium luxury ice cream has a dairy fat content of above 14 per cent (between 15 and 18 per cent) and an overrun below 45 per cent. Most luxury ice creams are made with natural ingredients; a few use eggs/egg yolk.

Like most ice creams in America, Häagen-Dazs has a very high dairy (butter) fat content (18 per cent), which comes from fresh double cream, and a very low air content (overrun is only 20 per cent). This is possible because Häagen-Dazs manufactures ice cream in a manner that minimises the formation of ice crystals during the freezing process. When Häagen-Dazs was first introduced in the European market, no ice cream had such a high dairy fat content with such a low air content. Only Häagen-Dazs used 100 per cent natural ingredients, no artificial colouring, preservatives, emulsifiers (a chemical way of achieving what homogenisation does mechanically) or stabilisers (they act as sponges to soak up excess water). Instead of using stabilisers, Häagen-Dazs uses fresh pasteurised egg yolk. In blind tests, Häagen-Dazs was clearly distinguishable from other brands. Some other brands had the same fat content, but none had such a low percentage of overrun. Most other brands had some form of artificial colouring or flavouring, preservatives, emulsifiers or stabilisers added. Some brands (e.g. Unilever's successful Gino Ginelli brand), had even been positioning in the premium market, even though the ice cream was based on non-dairy fats.

The superiority of the Häagen-Dazs ice cream can be measured. In 1990, the *Sunday Times* panel tasted the most widely available brands of luxury dairy chocolate ice creams and awarded each product a star rating up to a maximum of five. The panel was looking for an ice cream with plenty of body and a dense, smooth texture. Five stars went to Marks & Spencer (£2.50 for 500 ml), four stars went to Häagen-Dazs (£2.95 for 500 ml) and Wall's Carte d'Or (£2.49 for 750 ml), three stars to Loseley (£2.55 for 750 ml), and three stars to New England (£1.86 for 500 ml).

Another ice-cream testing session was arranged by the *Sunday Telegraph* as part of their coverage of 'National ice-cream week'. Vanilla (the most popular ice-cream flavour in the UK) and chocolate ice cream were evaluated on a scale from 1 to 10. The judges gave the following scores to the various ice creams (only the best, those with seven points or more, are listed in Table C1.1).

Table C1.1 ICE-CREAM SCORES

Brand/Vanilla	Price*	Score	Brand/Chocolate	Price*	Score
Häagen-Dazs	£3.29	9	Manx Ices' Lady Godiva	£5.25	9
New England Extreme	£2.99	8	Loseley Park	£2.69	8
Criterion Gold Medal	£1.80	7	Häagen-Dazs	£3.29	8
Manx Ices' Lady Isabella	£2.75	7	New England	£1.99	7
Dayvilles	£1.49	7			
Rocombe Farm	£3.15	7			

Note: * Prices refer to a 500ml tub.

One aspect of the brand is its physical quality, its objectively verifiable superiority over competitive brands. In blind tastings such as those described above, consumers are able to distinguish Häagen-Dazs from other brands. This is attributable to its higher fat content and lower overrun, which makes for a heavier, denser, richer and creamier ice cream. Another aspect of the brand is its perceived quality and preference. Perceived quality and preference for a certain ice cream brand is something in the eye (or, rather, taste-buds) of the beholder. Different people like different things, and have different tastes. The experts above may be able to distinguish Häagen-Dazs from the rest, but overall prefer Manx Ices' Lady Godiva or the private-label brand of Marks & Spencer.

As far as the ice-cream market is concerned, Häagen-Dazs is located in the upper end of the market of premium or super premium ice cream. Häagen-Dazs defines its brand identity as being a '100 per cent genuine, sensual, sophisticated adult treat'. The attribute '100 per cent genuine' is emphasised by its mythical Scandinavian heritage and its ersatz brand name, which sounds like something Danish, Swedish or Norwegian. Amongst Europeans, these countries call up images of nature, freshness, cleanliness, the high country, in much the same way as images of clear spring waters in the Rocky Mountains do for Americans. For its European launch, Häagen-Dazs undertook its first major package update in 30 years. The aim of the redesign was to achieve a more upmarket look, consistent with the product's positioning in Europe. Pictures of fruit were added to emphasise the quality and purity of its ingredients. The new tub gives visual clues regarding Häagen-Dazs's superior taste. The tub also carries a careline phone number. While these numbers are quite common in the USA (83 per cent of US packaging carries these numbers), only eight per cent of packaging in the UK (30 per cent in France and 15 per cent in Germany) features carelines.

To further underscore the premium positioning, the in-store freezers installed across Europe feature a prominent listing of the most affluent cities around the world: London, New York, Paris, Brussels. This adds a global association to Häagen-Dazs, something that evokes images of top fashion houses, the world of haute couture, and luxury life-styles. But most consistent with its premium quality positioning is Häagen-Dazs's bold stance on price. Throughout Europe, it charges a hefty premium. In the UK its price is 30–40 per cent higher than its immediate competitors, Loseley and New England. On the average, Häagen-Dazs is eight or nine times more expensive than the cheapest ice cream in the market. In Germany, a half a litre of Häagen-Dazs costs the same as a litre of local premium ice cream. At one point in time, the slogan of its German advertising campaign was: 'Everything gets more expensive, Häagen-Dazs stays expensive.'

The target market

Häagen-Dazs's marketing is focused on sophisticated and well-off couples, maybe married, maybe not, probably without children – able and willing to pay a premium. A company spokesperson described its consumers as follows:

> These people regard Häagen-Dazs as a very personal thing, definitely not to be shared with the family, as they would ordinary ice cream. They eat ours as a couple, or they serve it at a dinner party.

Häagen-Dazs is also targeting the global or European consumer, most likely to be the same whether they are living in London, Brussels, Paris, Berlin or Athens. Häagen-Dazs views ice cream not as a child's reward for good behaviour, but as a sophisticated adult treat; an indulgent experience to be enjoyed – an affordable luxury.

To communicate these values to the target market, Häagen-Dazs used media advertising, sponsorship deals and free publicity. The media campaign was first launched in the UK with a budget of $750 000, and then expanded throughout Europe. Total European ad budget for 1991 was $10m. A close-up look at the UK campaign gives an opportunity to find out how Häagen-Dazs communicates these values to consumers.

The marketing of Häagen-Dazs in the UK

The UK media campaign broke in Summer of 1991 and ran twice for three months. With the twin objectives of increasing awareness of the Häagen-Dazs brand name and positioning it as a sensual and sophisticated adult treat, management of Häagen-Dazs and its agency, Bartle Bogle Hegarty (BBH), decided to develop a high-profile, provocative campaign. Black and white photographs were shot by French star photographer Jean Loup Sieff, with pictures inspired by the sensual US movie, *Nine and a Half Weeks*, starring Mickey Rourke and Kim Basinger. The creative brief was to create a buzz about the product, and the campaign's theme became 'The Ultimate Experience in Personal Pleasure', with the ending on every copy: 'Häagen-Dazs – Dedicated to Pleasure'. The pictures were accompanied by a self-consciously serious text describing the product, not overselling it. At a time when most ice cream advertising (87.5 per cent) was on TV, including that of its immediate competitor, New England, Häagen-Dazs deliberately chose the press for its ads, so as to communicate more intimately with its target audience. Thus the media plan was important. Instead of blanket coverage in every newspaper and magazine, the agency chose the regular weekend issues (not the weekend review sections and Sunday supplements, which are usually highly optional reading) and women's magazines. These issues were also chosen because they are read at a very relaxed and leisurely time, just as one would enjoy Häagen-Dazs ice cream.

The impact of the campaign was unexpected. In a post-test ad impact measurement, 11 per cent of ice-cream eaters could recall the campaign. Within a few months, awareness had jumped to over 50 per cent. An econometric analysis showed a 59.7 per cent increase in sales (over £800 000) as a result of advertising – 78 per cent of this growth was from increased consumer demand, with the rest from more widespread distribution, as the trade recognised the success of the campaign. Within the launch area, brand share rose from 2.3 per cent in 1990 to 26.1 per cent in February 1992; its brand share was nearly twice that of its UK competitors, New England and Loseley, combined. At the end of 1991, BBH won the Media Week Advertising 'Campaign of the Year' award, due to its exemplary management of the advertising process, from the creative brief and development to the media planning and scheduling, the meticulous attention to audience duplication, and the like. In 1992, it won the Gold Award in the Marketing IPA Advertising Effectiveness Awards competition in the category of new consumer goods and services, as well as the 1992 Marketing Week/ITV Awards for Marketing competition, in which Häagen-Dazs was short-listed as the New Product of the Year. In March 1993, top accolades went to the Häagen-Dazs campaign in the 1993 newspaper advertising awards competition. Much more important than the hoo-ha surrounding the awards given to Häagen-Dazs for excellence in creative development and media strategy, was the landslide of free publicity that the ad campaign generated. Perhaps a little too suggestive in some people's opinion, experts believe that the campaign generated free publicity on TV and radio worth as much as the original advertising budget. The British Advertising Standards Authority (ASA) received 64 complaints about the campaign. But while this figure is certainly high, it does not compare to the thousands of complaints generated by the infamous Benetton posters within days of their appearance on billboards.

Next came the sponsorship of important events throughout the UK, in particular the arts, using the by-line: 'Dedicated to Pleasure, Dedicated to the Arts'. Each sponsorship deal was chosen to fit into Häagen-Dazs's brand concept and consumer target. In summer of 1991, it co-sponsored the Luciano Pavarotti concert in Hyde Park. With up to half a million attendees, Häagen-Dazs expected to sell 15 tonnes of ice cream from its impulse line. Then, there was the £15 000 sponsorship of the avant-garde Opera Factory's latest production of *Don Giovanni*. Slight changes had been made to the play's script to accommodate Häagen-Dazs. When Don called for the 'sorbet' to be brought in every night of the opera's performance at London's South Bank arts complex, a tub of Häagen-Dazs ice-cream was brought in, instead. As one can imagine, this change went against the feelings of some staunch art lovers, which again won a large amount of free publicity. Its third arts sponsorship deal was the *Guardian*'s Edinburgh Festival supplement. This supplement, widely regarded as the most comprehensive guide to the Festival, featured competitions offering Häagen-Dazs prizes as well as heavy brand advertising. The arts sponsorship programme was extended in 1993 to include further opportunities, such as the HA HA!, an outdoor sculpture exhibition at Killerton House, Devon, the reopening of the Fruitmarket Gallery in Edinburgh, and Video Positive 93 in Liverpool. Further sponsorship included social and sporting events at Henley and Ascot.

Ice-cream wars

The Häagen-Dazs assault on Europe caught local and multinational companies off guard. Over the years, these competitors had offered European consumers a lower quality ice-cream, and in the case of the UK a mediocre ice-cream. Häagen-Dazs's superior quality product changed all that. So did Mars's extension of its confectionery countlines into the ice-cream market. The entries of Häagen-Dazs and Mars created an exploding market for luxury dairy ice cream. No longer was ice cream a children's market of quality-insensitive consumers who accepted sickly ice-cream sticks and lollies as a treat during the summer months.

Competitors were quick to follow in the footsteps of Häagen-Dazs and Mars. New England, for example, an American-style premium ice cream that had been in the UK since 1973, was at that time considered the UK's foremost producer of super premium ice cream. In 1986, it went national. Sales grew rapidly to about $3m in 1988. It operated an ice-cream parlour in Harrods' food hall. With the entry of Häagen-Dazs, New England started to revamp its marketing approach. It refocused on the same ice-cream market – young, single adults with a high disposable income – and repositioned its product range as a 'sensual and indulgent experience'. In 1991, it went on TV for the first time with a commercial that played on the famous restaurant scene in *When Harry met Sally*, using the by-line: 'One taste, and you're away.' Because of its explicit sexual content, the ASA banned some of the ads throughout the UK. The campaign was later screened in cinemas, however. Next, New England merged with the ice-cream interests of Cricket St Thomas, a rival premium ice-cream manufacturer. The company further strengthened its brand portfolio in 1992, when it introduced the New England Ultimate ice cream, which contained 18 per cent butter fat, double cream and an overrun of 30 per cent. The Ultimate came in packs of 500 ml at a retail price of £2.99, just under the price level of Häagen-Dazs. Packs carried the words 'No artificial anything'. New England's market share had grown to 9.5 per cent (by value) against the 19.5 per cent of Häagen-Dazs in the UK premium ice-cream sector in 1992.

There were numerous other local brands that tried to give Häagen-Dazs a run for its money. These included Loseley, a British ice cream that had been sold in the UK for over 25 years. Then, there was Thornton, Dayville, Mackie's Traditional Luxury Dairy ice cream, Lyons Maid, and J.G. Quicke and Partners, with its Luxury Devonshire super premium ice cream. All of these local competitors had launched new products in the luxury ice-cream sector. Some of them attempted to take a share of the market by giving consumers a clear price advantage over Häagen-Dazs. The marketing strategies of these competitors bore remarkable similarities to the Häagen-Dazs strategy. Most used sampling and taste testing in supermarkets, or event sponsorship. Lyons Maid, for instance, after being taken over by Clarke Foods, improved its product range and re-launched in the spring of 1992 at the mid-price market. Clarke also introduced a super premium brand ice-cream in a 500 ml tub, with a price 65 per cent higher than in 1991 but still below that of Häagen-Dazs. The launch was backed by a £2m TV ad campaign (headline: From our family's obsession with ice cream), radio and other promotional spending of £1m, plus a sampling programme. The British consumer did not accept this new upmarket positioning of Lyons Maid and Clarke (about 60 per cent of its production goes to private label), and by September 1992 the company was in receivership. In November 1992, Nestlé swallowed the assets of Clarke Foods.

The multinationals had also been jolted by Häagen-Dazs. After failing to upgrade and to place several of its ice-cream brands, Unilever, through its Bird's Eye Wall's subsidiary, launched Too Good To Be True, an ice cream that promised all of the pleasure of premium ice cream but none of the guilt. Too Good To Be True was virtually fat-free and tried to capture market share from Häagen-Dazs. With the same objective, Heinz launched is Weight Watcher's ice-cream brand, also in 1992. In the autumn of 1992, Unilever further introduced a super premium ice cream without the Wall's name. And through a joint venture arrangement with Cadbury, its subsidiary Bird's Eye Wall's launched the Cadbury Cream. Reactions to Unilever's attempt to get its foot in the door of the UK premium ice-cream market were not all positive. Some retailers pointed out that the move was 'too little, too late' or 'too copycat'. Beyond new product launches and new flavours, the battle was fought through increased ad spending. In 1991 alone, spending grew by 42 per cent in Europe.

By the end of 1993, it was clear that Häagen-Dazs was the runaway leader of the ice cream wars. It had increased its market share despite the assault of local competitors, multinationals, and private labels, and Häagen-Dazs maintained a significant premium over any other manufacturer with any volume sales worth mentioning. Other strong contenders, such as Mars, had seen their market share falling in 1992, due to the significant inroads made by other multinationals, especially Unilever, with its Magnum premium ice cream on a stick. Unilever and its subsidiaries appeared to have difficulties breaking away from its economy and standard ice cream image. The company's strength was in the children sector.

The growth of private label had little impact on Häagen-Dazs. Safeway's World of Flavours and the Marks & Spencer product range, offering quality at a lower price level, have grown, but they have taken sales from different consumers, namely families with a closer eye on the balance between price and quality. Häagen-Dazs has established a sort of peaceful coexistence between its super premium brand and private labels.

Prepared by: Professor Erich A. Joachimsthaler, The International Graduate School of Management, University of Navarra, Spain.

The BMW acquisition of the Rover Group

Background

The 1978 licensing agreement between Rover and Honda had developed into a wide-ranging strategic alliance by the time British Aerospace (BAe) acquired the Rover Group from the UK government in 1988. BAe agreed under the terms of sale not to sell Rover until August 1993 at the earliest. Honda had the right to be informed of any intent to sell and offered first refusal over the balance of equity.

The car industry in the early 1990s

The recession in many parts of the world continued to be the dominant industry factor affecting both Rover and Honda during 1992 and 1993. Rover announced losses of £83m in February 1992, including a £45m write-off as a result of withdrawing from the US market. Honda's profits during 1992 fell by 32 per cent.

George Simpson, Managing Director of Rover, knew that although the company had gained immeasurably from its collaboration with Honda, there were still many problems to overcome if he was to create a business with sustainable profits. Although break-even was down from 530 000 to 450 000 units per year, sales were still running at fewer than 420 000. Simpson knew that international sales had to play an even greater role in the future.

A major restructuring of the business occurred early in 1992 and as a consequence the internal objectives regarding overseas sales were raised from 45–60 per cent of total turnover. Rover also signed Japanese-style agreements with its workforce which included a radical 'Jobs for life' guarantee.

The restructuring split the company into three new trading divisions:

- Rover Europe – Managing Director, Graham Morris
- Rover International – Managing Director, Chris Woodward
- Rover Marketing – Managing Director, Kevin Morley.

During this period, Rover continued to learn an enormous amount about quality and manufacturing techniques through the Honda alliance and was even training BAe staff in lean manufacturing techniques. Other Japanese car manufacturers were, however, setting up operations in the UK and Simpson felt that the restructuring and working agreements were necessary to compete with them on level terms.

The process begins

The first indication of what lay ahead came in March 1992. Volkswagen shocked the entire car industry by announcing that it would like to buy Rover in order to gain a foothold in certain markets. In reality, the company was impressed with the outcomes of the Rover–Honda agreement and extremely interested in an alliance with Honda. Ford also let it be known that it was interested in the possibility of acquiring Rover. BAe responded to these informal advances by simply restating that under its agreement with the British government, Rover could not be sold until at least August 1993.

By late 1992, however, speculation about Rover's future was rife. BAe Chairman John Cahill said that he had no intention of selling Rover, although earlier in the year, he had talked of a long-term strategy based around core businesses in aircraft and defence.

Volkswagen had bought both Seat and Skoda in the meantime, and was no longer thought to be in a financial position to bid. Fiat and Peugeot were also interested, although Jacques Calvet, Chairman of Peugeot, was known to display an almost legendary hostility towards Japanese companies.

Honda had purchased its 20 per cent stake in Rover only as a sign of good faith. As far as it was concerned, the relationship was a complete success and in fact had become the envy of the motor industry. It was based on trust, reciprocal need and mutual benefits. Honda's CEO Nobuhiko Kawamoto was convinced that there were important political factors ruling out any increased shareholding and Honda was, in any case, short of money.

Collaboration intensifies as competition increases

George Simpson continued to demonstrate his belief in collaborative deals by increasing Rover's stake in its joint venture with Lombard Finance and entering into talks with the Bulgarian government about a 49.9 per cent stake in a joint venture to assemble and sell Maestros when UK production ceased.

Honda was by now building its own manufacturing facility in Swindon and Rover had opened a new £200m factory at Cowley. The collaborative agreement with Honda had played a significant part in the planning process for the new facility, as the future of two companies became steadily more linked and interdependent.

In March 1993, BAe was forced to repay £110m to the UK government following the row over so-called sweeteners and state aid at the time of the original Rover purchase.

At around the same time, The Economist Intelligence Unit published a report which concluded that Rover was too small to survive as an independent manufacturer and had insufficient volume to service such a wide model range. The report also stated that by the year 2000 the car industry would be dominated by a group of only five global manufacturers:

● General Motors
● Ford
● Toyota
● Volkswagen
● Nissan.

In late 1993, the Rover 600 was jointly launched with the new Honda Accord. Engines and gearboxes were the same in both ranges, and most other components were also shared.

George Simpson restated Rover's joint strategy of co-operation with Honda and a continued move upmarket – 'Roverisation', as he called it. He estimated that Rover had saved around £150m in development costs on the 600 due to the alliance and that had further contributed to lower break-even volumes. Nobuhiko Kawamoto, however, was reported at around this time (somewhat significantly in the light of later developments) as saying it would be difficult for Honda to continue the sharing of technology and designs if Rover was sold to another manufacturer.

In June 1993, George Simpson explained in an interview why Honda would not increase its stake from the current level of 20 per cent. He repeated that the success of the alliance was based on mutual trust and the creation and nurturing of relationships which facilitated synergies; and that this would not necessarily be enhanced by a larger shareholding.

Simpson knew that Honda already considered Rover part of its 'empire' and did not therefore consider it necessary to use scarce resources to obtain full control. He felt the alliance would continue to expand along the value chain from process technology and product development into areas such as shared distribution.

Rover by mid-1993

The company had by this time successfully exploited the alliance to create a chic image combining British styling and Japanese reliability. Quality had improved to such an extent that Rover dealers complained they had insufficient work to carry out under warranty.

Rover's performance had even been instrumental in raising the share price of BAe. Unit volumes were up 20 per cent on the year before, sales of Rover cars in Japan were up 40 per cent for the same period, due to the penetration of middle and upper segments of the market and the break-even point was falling to around 400 000 units per year as cost savings continued to accrue from the alliance.

Sales of the Land Rover four-wheel drive range were running ahead of production capacity and so, perhaps inevitably, speculation about the Rover's future ownership arose in the press again during August. Rover's gains compared favourably with the reductions in volume being experienced by the other car manufacturers (see Table C2.1).

There was around this time talk of a management buyout (MBO), but with BAe maintaining an equity stake prior to eventual flotation. However, the dynamics of the car industry had moved on – VW were now thought to be in financial trouble and Ford were trying to digest Jaguar. The biggest question centred around whether BAe should sell Rover at all, particularly in the short term.

Rover was poised to widen its joint venture policy even further by entering a development project with Kia or Korea to produce a new V6 engine for top-of-the range models (this would also have the effect of slightly reducing Rover's dependency on Honda's engines).

BMW – the need for strategic change

BMW was less troubled than most European car companies by the recession of the early 1990s. It had not only avoided short-time working but remained in profit throughout the period.

Table C2.1 EUROPEAN CAR SALES, 1993

Manufacturer	Volume (000)	Change (%)	Market share (%)
Volkswagen	1886	–20.1	16.4
General Motors	1489	–11.8	13.0
Peugeot–Citroen	1405	–14.4	12.3
Japanese manufacturers[1]	1396	–12.8	12.2
Renault–Volvo	1373	–16.0	12.0
Ford	1316	–13.3	11.5
Fiat	1272	–20.6	11.1
BMW	371	–15.0	3.2
Rover	363	+ 9.7	3.2
Mercedes	334	–14.0	2.9

[1] Japanese category includes Nissan, Toyota, Mazda, Honda and Mitsubishi.

The company had monitored Rover's progress for a period of years as the two companies were of similar size in terms of unit volume and increasingly competed in certain market segments.

On 13 May 1993, Bernd Pischetsreider succeeded Dr Eberhard Kuenheim as Chairman of BMW, and his first task was to carry out a strategic audit of the whole business. The conclusion he reached was inescapable. Like Rover, BMW was too small to survive on its own as a manufacturer into the twenty-first century. The company needed to extend its range and achieve economies of scale in sourcing, production, distribution and R&D.

By a process of eliminating alternatives, it appeared that Rover was of potential interest in this regard. On direct instructions from Pischetsreider, BMW's R&D director visited all of Rover's facilities during September 1993 and drove every model in its entire range. Senior management of BMW then spent the period until Christmas digesting every piece of financial, marketing and strategic information available on Rover.

Rover had already been in discussions with BMW for some time about the possibility of using a BMW diesel engine in the new Range Rover, as Honda lacked diesel engine expertise. As this relationship and the investigations developed, Pischetsreider began to realise that with Rover they could 'offer a comprehensive range of cars in virtually every category'.

In fact, as BMW's senior management studied future market trends and the joint capabilities, they realised that the two companies were a perfect fit. The Rover brands, in particular Land Rover, had considerable value. Having observed the efforts of Mercedes to develop a four-wheel drive during the 1980s, Pischetsreider could see the synergies emanating from selling a range of off-road vehicles through BMW showrooms, with the added benefit of applying Land Rover's four-wheel drive expertise across the BMW car range. The development and brand promotional costs involved in achieving these objectives organically would almost certainly be more than Rover's market value.

The final phase

BMW made an informal approach to BAe in October 1993 about the possibility of acquiring the Rover Group. They also contacted Honda in order to gauge reaction, but received no response at all. Honda was concerned at the prospect of a third party having open access to joint secrets, and were anxious not to lose their grip on Rover. However, under the cross-shareholding agreement, Honda had to be formally told that Rover was potentially for sale and given first option to buy the remaining equity. Nobuhiko Kawamoto felt this afforded Honda a high degree of protection.

Privately, he was prepared to raise the stake to 40 per cent but could see little benefit in going further. He had his own problems as Honda was stuck half-way between mass-market volumes and being a niche manufacturer. Moreover, as pressure caused by the strong yen had seen its profits fall by 32 per cent Honda was financially in no real position to bid for the whole of Rover.

On 6 November 1993, the first press speculation linking BMW with Rover appeared. Comment centred around similarities in size and the complementarity of product range as well as the difficulties both would face in trying to stand alone. BAe responded by saying that Rover was now part of its core business and this, together with the announcement of George Simpson's departure to head Lucas Industries, seemed to indicate that no sale or flotation of Rover was imminent.

On 19 January 1994, however, at the first extraordinary meeting of the supervisory board in the history of the company, BMW made the decision to bid for Rover. The formal offer was made on 26 January and on the following day, after a meeting lasting five hours, the BAe board decided to accept the offer in principle. BMW would pay £800m and take on around £900m in net debt and off-balance-sheet finance.

Honda had raised its previous offer to £165m for a further 27.5 per cent of Rover. George Simpson was told by BAe management, however, to take the next flight to Tokyo and to inform Honda that this latest offer had been refused. He was to offer Honda the opportunity to increase its shareholding to 51 per cent. BAe would continue to hold 49 per cent as long as agreement was reached on a market flotation within five years. Honda refused to increase its offer and the meeting between Simpson and Kawamoto was described as 'extremely tense'.

The alliance – implications of the acquisition

John Towers, Managing Director of Rover Cars, did not find out about the bid until the day after the BAe board meeting. He was immediately concerned about the reaction of his Japanese partners and the possible implications for the company. By Saturday however, in a meeting with Tim Sainsbury MP, a minister at the Department of Trade and Industry, BMW reassured the UK government that their fears over job security, and the impact on Anglo-Japanese relations, were unfounded.

Following this meeting, and approval from the UK government, the deal was concluded 10 days after the formal offer. Honda was said to be 'surprised and humiliated' and threatened to sever all links with Rover, privately saying that it would never do business with BMW, their fiercest rival in the USA.

Honda immediately set up a taskforce to assess the benefits of continuing the alliance which, it was realised, would also allow a 'cooling-off' period. John Towers attempted to explain to Honda that in the end it was BAe's problems that had set the agenda, regardless of the relationship built up during the alliance.

Neither BAe nor Honda had wanted ownership of Rover, and so BMW had won. By this move, they were to become the largest 'specialist maker' of cars in the world, with a range of potential synergies with its new subsidiary – including range extension, economies of scale across the board, access to front-wheel and four-wheel drive technology, one of the best small-car engines in Europe and a selection of valuable (and in some cases under-developed brands).

Although shaken by the acquisition, the reaction of Honda's senior management underlined the cultural differences involved in the original alliance. BAe had clearly been discharging its obligations to its shareholders. Even so, the behaviour shown in breaking trust was absolutely inexplicable to the management team within Honda.

On 17 February, a delegation from BMW and Rover, including both MDs, flew into Tokyo for talks with Honda. BMW wanted Honda to swallow its pride and to work along with both companies. The only response was a statement from Nobuhiko Kawamoto which said: 'We will accelerate our policy of establishing independent and self-reliant operations in Europe.'

On existing relations with Rover he went on to say:

> We will continue those that are beneficial from a business standpoint such as mutual sourcing of parts and components – although our relationship with Rover Group will continue, the acquisition by BMW has caused a fundamental review of our European strategy.

On 17 February, the cross-shareholding was formally dissolved with a new payment from BMW to Honda of £116m.

Toshio Ishino, head of Honda UK, said the company would continue to honour its agreements to supply components to Rover, but hinted that there would be no further major collaborative projects. This conflicted with claims by John Towers that the alliance would continue beyond 2006.

Bernd Pischetsreider has made it clear that his intention is to transform Rover into an exclusive upmarket producer involving development of new models, and he also has implied that this leaves little scope for future collaboration with Honda.

He plans to turn Rover into a brand as strong and exclusive as BMW and at the same time double or even treble world sales. As part of this strategy, Pischetsreider realises that BMW's logistics technology has to be transferred to Rover in order to build cars to individual customer specification, as opposed to the Honda system of batch production of 30 identical cars.

The success of this extraordinary Honda–Rover alliance can perhaps be measured by the fact that BMW bought Rover partly for reasons linked to quality and engineering excellence. Rover will be transformed gradually – but totally – by its new parent, and it remains to be seen whether that process will leave any scope for a continuing relationship with Honda.

Prepared by: N. S. Potter, Birmingham Business School, University of Birmingham.

CASE STUDY 3

Exel Logistics – internationalising a distribution brand

In the four years from 1989 to 1993, Exel Logistics grew to be a market leader in distribution and supply chain services. It became the major operating division of National Freight Corporation (NFC) PLC and is a FTSE 100 company listed on the London and American stock exchanges. With a turnover of almost £600m in 1992, Exel Logistics were operating 3700 vehicles, 1.6m sq. metres of warehousing and almost a million cu. metres of cold storage capacity. Its companies employed over 14 600 staff and operated out of 220 distribution centres across the UK, mainland Europe and North America. Independent research carried out in 1991 confirmed that Exel Logistics was the UK market leader for contract distribution services, a goal reached well within the three-year target set at launch in 1989, when the company described itself as 'a successful business that has grown out of a previously unsuccessful state owned parent company'.

Exel Logistics must now decide how far it wants to go in becoming a truly global brand, and what strategies to pursue to achieve its aims.

Background and buy-out

NFC, Exel Logistics' parent company, had its origins in post-war Labour government policies aimed at nationalising transport in the UK. In 1979, the Conservative government began its privatisation programme with NFC. The sale was scheduled for 1981 with an anticipated capital price of £50m–£55m but, due to the recession, postponement was advised. However, an alternative plan was put forward by management and employees, who with the backing of multinational investors secured an employee buy-out. NFC was sold into private ownership for £53.5m in February 1982 – some would say it was the UK government's most successful privatisation.

Prior to 1982, NFC's financial performance was poor, but after the buy-out it quickly became very successful, partly because as it was the old road transport part of British Rail, it had property to sell or redevelop (stations and land close to the railways). The charismatic leadership of Sir Peter Thompson was another important advantage. He created the possibility and then the reality of broad employee ownership and went on to instil a unique employee participative company culture which was integral to the success of the company.

Post-1982, NFC experienced rapid growth and in preparation for its flotation on the Stock Exchange in 1989 was restructured into four divisions – Distribution, Transport, Home Services and Property and Travel. This enabled all previous elements of the distribution business to come together with NFC's Distribution Division under Robbie Burns (MD) and followed a decision to refocus the previously separate distribution functions based on a stronger single brand image worldwide.

In January 1989, the sales and marketing director and managing director were faced with the difficult task of reorganising, pruning and bringing marketing input to an assortment of companies, acquired after this restructuring. This mixed bag of 12 brands consisted of the seven companies they already had, those transferred on 1 January from NFC's Special Services Group and one overseas acquisition, Dauphin in North America. NFC's aim was to launch 'a new distribution company' on the back of the high profile Stock Exchange flotation in February 1989. After much research, it was decided that Exel Logistics would be the umbrella name for all NFC's distribution, warehousing and transport interests and would emphasise the importance of the strategic management of the whole supply chain, including:

- the transfer of information between interdependent but separate parties within it
- the flow and storage of raw materials, parts and finished inventory
- transfer to and from manufacturing plants
- finished goods storage
- delivery to customers, including home delivery if required.

Contracts with customers would include all or part of the above from the provision of warehousing – even design and building – through all operational aspects, to final delivery.

Changes in the UK distribution market

During the last decade the UK retail market place has undergone huge changes. Manufacturers' volumes and fleets have been decimated due to the reduction in numbers of smaller town-centre retail outlets and growth in size of the larger multiple, edge-of-town retailers. Other trends such as retailers centralising distribution operations and taking control of their own supply chains had the same effect – a fall in demand for shared-use distribution. This meant a radical rethink of distribution activities and many operators set up specific divisions to cope with growing and changing retail industry demands.

Until quite recently road haulage was perceived as a low-profile industry, but these changes imposed a higher status, with logistics moving from being an operational necessity to a strategic means by which companies could gain competitive advantage. It has become a key area in which manufacturers and retailers have to be good in order to drive down costs and improve service. The investment required for a company to run its own distribution operation is often enormous – fleets, warehouses, depots, maintenance and IT all tie up a high level of capital expenditure, and thus it has become no longer feasible for many companies to retain in-house operations.

One solution has been the increased use of third-party or outsourced distribution. This replaces customers' fleets and/or warehouses with a separate operational framework managed and owned by a third party, often providing a more efficient and cost-effective service than shippers were able to provide for themselves. Third-party distributors had to refine their marketing approach as the market place grew and became more demanding and ultimately they had to design and manage logistics solutions to meet customers' changing needs. The use of third-party distribution provides tailored, often dedicated, contractual solutions and can encompass transport, warehousing or other contract services, such as labelling and packaging. Operators must be flexible enough to keep fully abreast of new technology, support customers and apply strategic, tactical and operational reviews – in effect, continuously strengthening and managing the whole supply chain. Customers quickly realised that buying in this expertise allowed them to concentrate on their core businesses of manufacturing or retail selling, and increasingly expect their distribution networks to provide all or part of their supply chain management.

Structure of Exel Logistics (UK)

When Exel Logistics was launched, the constituent companies were being asked to change into something that did not exist, thus there was a certain amount of internal resistance.

They had to work on establishing group and team identities within the company and implemented a three-way organisational split.

1 Exel Logistics Grocery and Leisure – where the business focus was on serving the grocery, catering and drinks market sectors and the customers were mainly food and drink producers and retailers.

2 Exel Logistics Consumer and Industrial – customers ranged from consumer product retailers and manufacturers to a cross-section of industrial product manufacturers and distributors such as Vauxhall, BMW, Woolworths and Argos.

3 Exel Logistics Temperature Controlled Services (TCS) – this division worked closely with (and generated specialist business from) the food and grocery divisions within the company. It soon became market leader in the distribution of chilled and frozen food with a fleet of 500 vehicles, 27 depots and 2300 staff. With the expansion of the UK chill-food market they turned a number of existing cold storage facilities into chilled distribution centres for short-life products. This improved the financial performance of TCS and the division was back in profit by 1991.

These three business groups were in force until mid-1992 when, after further growth, they were reorganised and split into four management teams, the main change occurring with the amalgamation of Grocery and Leisure into Exel Logistics Grocery. With total revenue exceeding £300m per annum, retail and manufacturer grocery distribution was split between two internal management teams but with one external sales and marketing team. This new business unit now controlled all food distribution – retailers and manufacturers, ambient and temperature-controlled, including Exel Logistics Chillflow (dedicated to one client), and was felt to be consistent with market place requirements (*see* Fig. C3.1).

Exel Logistics Industrial now encompassed Exel Logistics Newsflow (distributing 70 per cent of UK national newspapers) and DMS (rebranded Exel Logistics Media Services), the UK's largest independent book distribution company with a £54m turnover. Operating alongside Newsflow it built on the base of newspaper distribution and worked towards market leadership in all print media distribution. To some extent Exel Logistics Industrial was a catch-all, with a series of sub-sectors and targeted

Fig C3.1 EXCEL LOGISTICS: STRUCTURE AFTER MID-1992

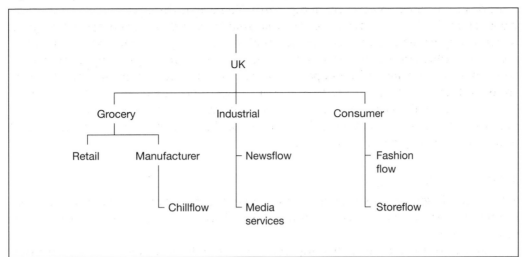

marketing, directed at ensuring that potential customers in those sub-sectors, such as electronics or automotive, were aware of Exel Logistics' presence.

Exel Logistics Consumer was the non-food retail division and included Fashionflow and Storeflow. Major contracts were with do-it-yourself outlets and department stores such as Comet, Woolworths, Superdrug, Boots, Bhs, Habitat, Marks & Spencer and Mothercare.

Marketing for the whole company however, was done as if there were still just three main sectors – Grocery, Industrial and Consumer – with all new business development effort contained within three sales teams.

Strategic directions for Exel Logistics

By 1990, NFC/Exel Logistics had reached a point where the options were either to seek greater penetration in the home market via new market segments or to look to expand overseas.

In the home market they could either:

1 seek to develop new market sectors – as Exel Logistics' new businesses were previously predominantly food- and retailer-based, they could try to open up new sectors where they were not strong (e.g. petrochemicals or pharmaceuticals); or

2 develop new services within the food sector – their existing strength lay with ambient and frozen food distribution (a static market) whilst the chill-food sector was growing.

This second option seemed to provide a potential opportunity. More and more outlets were selling fresh dairy produce, yoghurts and short-life products. By effectively altering the temperature control systems in existing cold stores, Exel Logistics could easily facilitate a move into this sector.

Background to the frozen food market

The easiest distribution area for market sector monitoring is the frozen market because cold-storage capacity is registered (Lloyd's Register) and can be easily measured. Three years ago extra market place capacity was added as Tesco and Asda (two large supermarket groups) built their own distribution composites (multi-temperature warehouses) which included chilled and frozen storage. They were thereby removing products which had previously been in other people's storage capacity and putting them into their own, thus adding to available capacity even though the frozen food market had stopped growing. Total frozen storage capacity had been approx. 200m cu. ft per annum, increased capacity in these new cold stores took it to 220m. At this time, manufacturer distribution was usually either direct to store or to distributor's stores. Recently, cold stores had been built or added to the market specifically to meet demand for EC intervention stocks. This boom time for the industry had increased capacity from 160m to 200m cu. ft, but after 1986 changes in the government's Common Agricultural Policy (CAP) meant that intervention stocks were being withdrawn from the beef and butter mountains and overall market demand for storage fell to around 180m cu. ft. With demand down by 10 per cent and capacity up by 10 per cent, the result was severe overcapacity in the market and fierce price competition. This was tackled by cold-storage providers moving to reduce storage rates to attract new business and to seek alternative types of contract, making it a very competitive sector.

In the past, NFC companies like Tempco Union and Alpine had profited by freezing and storing intervention stocks but because of external market place changes they had to suddenly shift and become more involved in stock movement – distribution rather than storage. Other major operators tried to stabilise the market by selling off their older, less efficient cold stores and moving over to the chill sector. This is an example of external market factors created by government (EC) legislative change and European policy changing a market place.

With an expanding chilled-food market in the UK, there were opportunities to build market share even though competitors already existed, e.g. Unigate (UCD) and Express Dairies–Coldstream were manufacturer-driven distribution systems and others like Northern Food Transport (NFT) were already strong in this sector. In the late 1980s companies like Christian Salvesen, Tempco Union and Alpine dealt with predominantly frozen produce and wanted to move into this high-value-added area (with chilled produce being perishable, time becomes a saleable commodity). Exel Logistics wanted a share of this growing market.

However, after examining the options, the company returned to their initial vision, of being a truly international company, the problem was – how to get there.

The move to North America

By the late 1980s, NFC recognised that they were still very dependent on domestic UK earnings and began to encourage all their companies to seek new business overseas. It was decided to expand via Exel Logistics in the USA first, partly because of the size and type of market but also as their only overseas acquisition so far was American (Dauphin in 1986). Expansion in the USA was a key element in the strategy to develop Exel Logistics' brand internationally. The aim was to become the US market leader in warehousing and logistics via services to global clients. In 1990, 25 per cent of NFC's profits were generated in the USA – the new target was to achieve a 40–50 per cent overseas contribution by 1995.

The market for the storage and distribution of goods in the USA was in essence very different from the UK market, and took two forms:

1 short-term provision of public warehousing on 30-day terms with no contracts, in effect a shared-user system;

2 less common, contract warehousing, a dedicated system with 1–5-year contracts.

The existing shared-user acquisition, Dauphin, was profitable and offered a convenient, high-margin service. This was opposite to that offered in the UK, where shared transport/storage was often a low-margin service. Dedicated warehousing in the USA was not widespread and was perceived as low-margin for low risk. This cultural difference is important – it was wrong to assume that the UK system would be interchangeable, the strategy needed to be different and adapted to local conditions.

Within the distribution industry, contract work provides greater security (linking customers into long-term contracts) and in the UK Exel Logistics and NFC had formed disciplines of tight financial management and risk control and as a result had developed real strengths in this area. By moving to the USA they sought to enhance the level of dedicated work but at the same time they continued to offer what the American market traditionally wanted – shared usage with five or six manufacturers' loads being delivered into individual wholesaler's or retailer's stores or regional distribution centres with the ability to buy transport in from local full-truck load (FTL) movers on overnight long-distance runs.

Exel Logistics had inherited NFC's first overseas acquisition – Dauphin Distribution Services. This was one of the largest warehousing and distribution businesses serving the food and grocery trades in the Mid-Atlantic region (clients included Procter & Gamble). The company had 3m sq. ft of warehousing at 12 locations with 600 employees. This family-owned company was seen as a natural partner for the employee-owned NFC. Its successful acquisition encouraged further expansion and thus there evolved a multiphased strategy for a conscious move to develop in the USA. Dauphin gave Exel Logistics a foothold in the US market place by delivering a range of consumer and manufacturers' products into one of the largest population centres (about 80m people on the North East Seaboard). Based 150 miles inland from New York, with relatively cheap labour and land costs, Dauphin's complex of large-scale warehouses was only an overnight trip from this highly populated area. They offered a consolidation service to manufacturers, with goods being stored, picked and moved from Dauphin's warehouses directly to New York. Manufacturers were able to buy transport movements at FTL prices even though they may not have had a full load to be dropped at each delivery destination, again effectively shared distribution – exactly what the UK market was moving away from.

Even though Exel Logistics did not ideally want to be acquisition-led it was decided that in order to expand geographically, acquisition was the strategy most likely to succeed in generating critical operating mass in a number of other regions. Thus it was first necessary to decide which other major population centres it was essential to be in and then determine which companies with at least 1m sq. ft of warehousing (preferably more) with several large clients were potential acquisitions. It was not always easy to get a match between what was available to acquire and what suited both the company culture and local market conditions.

In 1989, Distribution Centres Inc (DCI) based in Columbus, Ohio was bought. This second acquisition was closer to the UK formula of a dedicated contract business. It was an entrepreneur-led company which distributed medical and office supplies, pharmaceuticals and consumer products almost nation-wide and shared similar values with its new parent. There were 18 locations (some on the West Coast and in the south) 5m sq. ft of warehousing and 700 staff. DCI gave Exel Logistics the opportunity to expand its dedicated business in the US market and brought important key customers such as Du Pont, Lever and again Procter & Gamble. This acquisition provided an excellent complement to the operations of Dauphin and was a well-run company where, like many US companies, quality of service was important. Post-acquisition, transport was still being bought in and the main difference for customers was that whereas before they dealt with a family-owned company, they now had to deal with a British-owned company with a bias towards five-year dedicated contracts. Like Dauphin, DCI was a successful acquisition.

Exel Logistics pursued its geographical strategy and concentrated on five main centres – the North East; the Mid-West and Chicago; the South East and Atlanta; the South (Texas and Dallas); and the West Coast (San Fransisco and Los Angeles). With five primary regional targets and perhaps 12 sub-targets (Denver, St Louis and Kansas, etc.) it was becoming very clear where they needed to be and what they wanted to buy. With dominance in the grocery–consumer manufacturing sectors, they could now either begin to look at new sectors or diversify within logistics services and investigate what other products–services could be beneficial complements, such as, warehousing, road transport or trucking.

The next acquisition followed this line of thinking, a move into transport, with Minute Man Delivery Systems (1990). This Boston-based company undertook dedicated distribution across the USA, but mainly in the North East and was 90 per cent contract-backed. It had a turnover of $30m and gave Exel Logistics a different industrial client base with Toyota, Nissan and Chrysler.

This sector was felt to be attractive and facilitated a move into new areas with automotive and business service clients (Minute Man also provided a dedicated paper-moving service for, among others, several North East local banks); even so, Minute Man was a low-margin company.

In 1991, the fourth American acquisition was Universal Terminal Warehouse Company (UTW) a Texas-based local warehouse operation, mainly shared use, in Dallas, Houston and San Antonio. With five warehouses, 670 000 sq. ft of storage capacity and 150 staff, it distributed grocery, paper and health products as well as industrial and chemical products. It brought additional major client names to the international customer base like Philip Morris, Nestlé and Colgate. This acquisition continued the strategic plan to develop from an already well established and profitable base in the North East across the USA through the Southern States into the West.

In 1992, there were two more acquisitions. J.H. Coffman and Son Inc. was a distribution and warehousing company based in Los Angeles. It was acquired to extend coverage to the West Coast and the Mid-West and Chicago. It had over 40 years' experience in the healthcare, grocery and consumer product market with 375 000 sq. ft of warehousing and 40 staff.

In July, Trammell Crow Distribution Corporation (TCDC), based in Dallas, was bought. This contract warehousing business had 6m sq. ft of warehousing, 44 distribution centres, 600 employees and a turnover in 1991 of £27.6m. As well as warehousing, the company was also involved in value-added services, including the management of inter state transportation and packaging operations. With business divided between consumer and industrial sectors, it gave access to the petrochemical sector, with clients like Exxon and Shell.

James Watson, Chairman of NFC, commented:

> This is a further important step in becoming the acknowledged leader in the provision of logistics services in North America. It virtually completes our acquisition programme in the USA and sets the stage for a period of strong organic growth.

These acquisitions may have been driven by geography but they also facilitated entry to new market sectors. Exel Logistics now had a presence in four out of the five main regions, missing out in Atlanta (South East) – here, as no acquisition target matched the criteria, a greenfield operation was set up by building warehousing for a core client (Reckitt and Coleman) with extra capacity for use by others on a contract basis.

Apart from Dauphin, all other acquisitions – DCI, Minute Man, UTW, Coffman, TCDC – fell within a three-year period. Exel Logistics's North American headquarters was initially in Chicago, but regional offices soon opened in Harrisburg, Atlanta and Dallas and the headquarters subsequently moved to Columbus, Ohio.

In 1991, the resultant organisation from the US acquisitions were divided into three operational units.

Exel Logistics – Grocery Services Inc. (was Dauphin)

With its main focus on warehouse management for grocery, health and beauty products, it operated from three complexes in Pennsylvania with total storage capacity of 1 380 000 sq. ft. Major customers include some of the US top brand suppliers – General Mills, Nabisco, Procter & Gamble.

Exel Logistics – Dedicated Distribution (was Distribution Centres Inc.)

Also warehouse management, based in Columbus Ohio, with 18 locations on South, West and East coasts of the USA. They mostly dealt with non-food products and multinational customers – e.g. Lever Bros, Du Pont, Sharp Electronics.

Exel Logistics – Dedicated Delivery Systems (was Minute Man)

Provided a portfolio of products and services based on the physical transport side of the business, such as traffic management, vehicle supply and maintenance and out-of-hours delivery. There were 500 vehicles which served 43 states and customers included Nissan, Toyota and Chrysler.

These acquisitions created an organisation which probably became the leading logistics business in the USA, with a turnover in excess of £100m, 18.5m sq. ft of storage, over 3000 employees, and 600 vehicles working from 40 depots nation-wide. It provided a range of services to many market sectors and customers included several

'*Fortune* 500' companies. The process was strategically logical, it evolved through acquisition on a geographical basis; sometimes available companies were fitted into the strategy rather than being strategy-led, e.g. Minute Man was made to fit because it was available for sale; although it broadened their product offer, it was not ideal at that stage of their strategic development.

By the end of 1992, Exel Logistics' strategic acquisition programme in the USA was virtually complete with a presence in over 30 states. They were now able to offer warehousing and/or transport in each of their five major target regions. In addition, by following contacts with important existing US clients, Exel Logistics also developed initial small operations in Mexico and Canada.

The Single European Market

To meet increasing demand and customers' changing needs from the creation of the 1993 Single European Market (SEM), many distribution contractors felt they had to expand geographically and broaden their range of services along with, or preferably before, their customers. Operators targeted their efforts at market sectors they were best equipped to serve, which for Exel Logistics offered the prospect of exporting to the Continent the concept of dedicated distribution which they had developed so successfully in the UK retail sector. And there did appear to be a market opportunity. Whilst the UK grocery market was already contracting out 70 per cent of its distribution needs, in Germany and France the figure was only 15 per cent (*Director*, August 1990).

Whilst some manufacturers set up pan-European production and distribution facilities, retailers were more cautious. The UK's leading retailers were preoccupied with the battle for national market share and really only Marks & Spencer and Iceland took the bold step of opening stores under their own facia; in addition, Tesco and Woolworths began to expand outside their home markets. For UK retailers (in 1992–3), the scale of their European business remained a small percentage of their total trade, Sainsbury's for example had approximately 18 per cent of the UK grocery market but Europe-wide this dropped to three per cent. So while leading UK supermarkets were used to dominating the home market they were only small fish in the Euro-pond. However, expansion did continue, with the Burton Group in Spain and Germany, Boots in France and Texas Homecare in Spain.

The SEM also saw the beginning of expansion by European retailers into other member states – e.g. Aldi, Netto, Naf Naf into the UK, IKEA and Benetton across Europe. Developing retail operations within Europe meant extending communication lines, and (even more crucially) managing the whole supply chain.

Market place developments such as pan-European manufacturing and retailing concentration, product proliferation and technological developments should lead to less stockholding, more centralised warehousing, increased road transport and greater availability of products in Europe. In the future, consumers will demand greater choice and food freshness continent-wide; this should increase demand for sophisticated logistics skills, as pioneered by the leading UK companies. After the advent of the SEM, success in the domestic market will not necessarily ensure success in Europe; competition will come from both other national and international companies as well as independent operators from low-wage countries already used to operating in a more regulated environment.

Exel Logistics' strategy in mainland Europe

Food distribution entails the movement of large, physically bulky products with relatively low value when compared to, say, cars or computers and tends to have been operated on a local, national rather than a global or international basis. Food logistics was seen as 'the art of the possible' for Exel Logistics.

As outlined, having achieved UK market leadership by 1991, Exel Logistics faced several strategic options. Following successful moves in the USA, it was decided that the strategy would be parallel development in mainland Europe, concentrating on the food–grocery sector. This was mainly because other industrial sectors where they lacked strength were already international markets dominated by major international players – e.g. Shell, BASF, Ford. The food sector, however, was determined more by local tastes, local retailing and local markets.

The arrival of SEM acted as a stimulus for expansion and Exel Logistics' first step was to follow existing UK customers into new markets. They decided on a priority sequence of countries by looking at the geography, the economic stage of development, market prospects and where existing clients wanted to develop their business. The first opportunity arose with Marks & Spencer when Exel Logistics built a distribution centre for them at Evrey near Paris to serve their stores in France. This strategy was not enough on its own, but it did allow them to establish initial credibility in the country – a 'footprint in the sand'. Although this was initially a low-risk way to develop a pan-European operation, it soon became necessary to decide whether being credible to existing clients in new countries was enough (reactive expansion) or whether they should also begin to look both at other domestic companies wanting to expand overseas and at acquiring existing distribution businesses in new countries (proactive expansion).

Again, the route of growth by acquisition in specific geographical areas was chosen and in 1991 the brand was launched first in Spain, then Germany, France and Holland; and they aimed to be No. 1 in food manufacturing and retail distribution in Europe by 1995. They proceeded with the rapid acquisition of businesses, seeking small to medium-sized but strategically important grocery distribution and warehousing companies. These were often family-owned and required minimum investment on existing infrastructure since they were serving the needs of existing clients, although in new markets.

Overall, Exel Logistics' policy was to build on their successful development of dedicated distribution in the UK and to export it into mainland Europe, but where possible using experienced local management.

Spain

The first acquisition was Sadema (1990) – Spain's third largest transport and distribution company. Turnover was £6.3m, supplying chilled and ambient warehousing and distribution for leading Spanish food manufacturers from 15 locations. The business was owned by four manufacturers – in effect, clients with long-term contracts who had combined their operations. Sadema had national coverage, including the Balearic and Canary Islands with 13 owned and two franchised operations. With large distances between population centres, Spain had few major international distribution operators and in effect offered less competition than France or Germany. Exel Logistics saw easy market entry, in a growth area, with low risk.

Robbie Burns (Exel MD):

> We believe that a high quality logistics service based on the UK model will be increasingly demanded by major national and multinational companies now growing so rapidly in Spain to meet rising consumer expenditure.

The major competitor, a Unilever subsidiary called SAD, had recently been bought by Swiss-owned Danzas. Unilever were actively pursuing a policy of outsourcing and seemed to be choosing a different third-party operator in each country – Exel Logistics had already acquired some of their distribution interests in the UK with SDP and Alpine. In Germany, Unilever had sold its frozen food business to Salvesen, another UK competitor.

Exel Logistics had to decide what service to offer in the Spanish market. They wanted dedicated business using their existing expertise in warehouse management to gain secure profits but, as in the USA, there was some reluctance in the market to buy this service and Spain's physical size really required a network solution. However, since 1990 Exel Logistics have had some success in signing dedicated business with Marks & Spencer expanding into Spain; Digsa, a Spanish grocery retailer and Olympus. It was still difficult to get across the British concept of this method of distribution, which is about offering nation-wide delivery with economies of scale. Sadema was rebranded Exel Logistics–Iberica with its own corporate identity and image and became one of Spain's top three logistic companies. In 1992, successful expansion continued with a new contract with Oxford University Press and in 1993, Pirelli.

Germany

The first German acquisition was Hellweg Tiefkuhl (rebranded Exel Logistics – Deutschland) in June 1991. A frozen product distribution company with trans-shipment operations, it had the ability to service all of Germany, including the old East, from a single cold-storage centre near Dortmund in, at most, 48 hours. It was almost a parcels-style operation for frozen foods, a potential high added-value service. It fell within the buying criteria, a small family-owned, low-risk food business, operating profitably.

In the autumn of 1991, Exel Logistics bought from the liquidators a food products and catering distribution company called Restaurant Services. Rebranded Exel Logistics – Restaurant Services, it was to seek new business and operate contracts aimed at developing deliveries to the restaurant and catering market. However, difficult trading and adverse economic conditions subsequently slowed business growth in Germany.

The most recent acquisition in January 1993 was a company called Macke and Son, another small family business; it provided ambient food distribution for two clients aimed at the grocery market. With net assets of £2.1m the company operated from a 177 000 sq. ft site with 130 staff and 64 vehicles. It was rebranded Exel Logistics–Kloppenburg on 1 January 1993.

France

October 1991 saw Exel Logistics' first acquisition in France, BOS Finances. This chilled and frozen distribution family business was a market leader in the chilled sector. It operated in the north-west region under regional company names, STM, STB and Frimotrans, and covered about one-third of the country. Concentrating on chilled distribution for meat, cheese and fish produce, it offered a service based on speed and quality providing fast overnight transport. Clients include Carréfour and Intermarche. The network of 13 temperature-controlled locations gave Exel Logistics a sound geographical base, considering they already had the Fashionflow operation for Marks & Spencer near Paris. The new group continued to operate under the management of the Boucher family at the headquarters in Brittany, under the Exel Logistics – France brand name. The turnover was £17m with 500 staff, 200 vehicles and 14 000 cu. m of warehouse capacity.

In 1992 Sodiaal, a temperature-controlled warehousing and distribution company (also a producer of regional cheeses) was acquired. Based in the central French region of Clermont Ferrand, it brought 24 staff, 50 000 sq. ft of warehousing and 10 vehicles to the company.

Holland

In October 1991, Exel Logistics bought Food Express Intl BV, Holland's largest independent food warehousing and distribution company, which served the Benelux countries. With a turnover of £7.3m, 50 vehicles and 150 staff, it operated transport by owner drivers on a sub-contract basis. This was an ambient and chilled-food distribution operation for grocery products operating from two centres covering all of Holland, with Unilever as a major client. Rebranded as Exel Logistics – Nederland it was an important entry point into the Benelux countries. In 1992, Exel Logistics in Holland moved outside the food sector by gaining contracts with Apple Computers and Texas Instruments.

By the end of 1991, Exel Logistics had a capability over a large area of mainland Europe, with access to local markets and local expertise. They had therefore achieved their initial goal of entering priority geographical markets and had to decide on their next step. They could continue to build a presence in new countries like Austria and Portugal, proceed with further acquisitions in existing countries or slow down. The Board advocated a period of consolidation. They decided to concentrate on their existing acquisitions, build on their initial presence, grow their businesses organically and get and develop the right people.

Nothing new was bought until November 1992 when they acquired two more French regional distribution businesses, Transports Pujos and Transports Martin, in Toulouse and Nice. Like BOS, both were family-owned and provided specialist transport for long- and short-life chilled products for manufacturers, retailers and restaurants. When linked with BOS they gave five regional companies, but not quite national coverage for frozen and chilled foods.

Exel Logistics's strategy at the end of 1992 was still not complete, they did not have credibility in all countries over all grocery product temperature ranges, the existing businesses offered:

- Spain – ambient and chilled
- Germany – frozen and chilled only
- France – mainly chilled, some frozen
- Holland – mainly ambient.

Without networks at all temperature ranges, it would be impossible to link food networks between countries to become a true pan-European distributor. Even with this strategic gap, organic growth was beginning, new work was gained in both Spain and Holland. Where there was organic development, it tended to be in warehouse contracts rather than transportation which was often sub-contracted out to owner drivers.

Exel Logistics found that in mainland Europe most of the networked systems were not food oriented, but biased more towards industrial group haulage. The main pattern of movements were in a wide range of products without the hygiene, sanitation or temperature-controlled requirements of food. The food sector required technical expertise and was sensitive to legislative and temperature requirements. As for retailing, in the UK trends were dictated by what was happening in the move from town-centre to out-of-town shopping, leading to huge changes in supply chain management. By experiencing and learning from both, Exel Logistics developed strengths that they wanted to export overseas, but above all they have built on the need for flexibility.

The position at the end of 1992

Growth in the UK has continued and in 1991 the company received awards for implementing successful environmental policies from the Worshipful Company of Marketeers and trade magazine *Motor Transport*. The company's commitment to quality of customer service has been recognised through the application of the 'Quest for Excellence' quality campaign, culminating in 12 sites being awarded the international quality standard ISO 9002 in 1992.

NFC's target of reaching 50 per cent of its revenue from overseas business by 1995, appears to be on course. These overseas earnings are derived from all divisions, not just distribution. But with Exel Logistics currently earning 40 per cent of its income from overseas (and rising) whilst at the same time providing 47 per cent of NFC profits, this represents almost 20 per cent of overseas revenue for its parent company from Exel Logistics alone.

Exel Logistics has become one of the major supply-chain service providers in the UK, the USA and mainland Europe, with world-wide sales in 1992 of £600m and over 220 depots world-wide. Growth by acquisition alone will not be enough to ensure success, either in Europe or the USA. With an initial and fast-growing presence in Spain, France, Holland and Germany the company is now faced with yet more choices if it is to become a truly international brand.

Prepared by: Valerie Bence, Cranfield School of Management. The author acknowledges the assistance given by the Director of Sales and Marketing, Exel Logistics (1994).

INDEX

EPRG #12

BRUNEL UNIVERSITY LIBRARY

Bannerman Centre,
Uxbridge, Middlesex,
UB8 3PH

Renewals: www.brunel.ac.uk/renew
OR
01895 266141

LONG LOAN

WITHDRAWN

XB 2598074 2